A Companion to Eighteenth-Cent

CW01665277

WILEY BLACKWELL COMPANIONS TO HISTORY

This series provides sophisticated and authoritative overviews of the scholarship that has shaped our current understanding of the past. Defined by theme, period and/or region, each volume comprises between twenty-five and forty concise essays written by individual scholars within their area of specialization. The aim of each contribution is to synthesize the current state of scholarship from a variety of historical perspectives and to provide a statement on where the field is heading. The essays are written in a clear, provocative, and lively manner, designed for an international audience of scholars, students, and general readers.

WILEY BLACKWELL COMPANIONS TO EUROPEAN HISTORY

A Companion to Europe 1900–1945
Edited by Gordon Martel

A Companion to Eighteenth-Century Europe
Edited by Peter H. Wilson

A Companion to Nineteenth-Century Europe
Edited by Stefan Berger

A Companion to the Worlds of the Renaissance
Edited by Guido Ruggiero

A Companion to the Reformation World
Edited by R. Po-chia Hsia

A Companion to Europe Since 1945
Edited by Klaus Larres

A Companion to the Medieval World
Edited by Carol Lansing and Edward D. English

A Companion to the French Revolution
Edited by Peter McPhee

WILEY BLACKWELL COMPANIONS TO WORLD HISTORY

A Companion to Western Historical Thought
Edited by Lloyd Kramer and Sarah Maza

A Companion to Gender History
Edited by Teresa A. Meade and Merry E. Wiesner-Hanks

A Companion to the History of the Middle East
Edited by Youssef M. Choueiri

A Companion to Japanese History
Edited by William M. Tsutsui

A Companion to International History 1900–2001
Edited by Gordon Martel

A Companion to Latin American History
Edited by Thomas Holloway

A Companion to Russian History
Edited by Abbott Gleason

A Companion to World War I
Edited by John Horne

A Companion to Mexican History and Culture
Edited by William H. Beezley

A Companion to World History
Edited by Douglas Northrop

A Companion to Global Environmental History
Edited by J. R. McNeill and Erin Stewart Mauldin

A Companion to World War II
Edited by Thomas W. Zeiler, with Daniel M. DuBois

For further information on these and other titles in the series
please visit our website at

www.wiley.com

A COMPANION TO EIGHTEENTH-CENTURY EUROPE

Edited by

Peter H. Wilson

WILEY Blackwell

This paperback edition first published 2014
© 2014 John Wiley & Sons Ltd
Edition history: Blackwell Publishing Ltd (hardback, 2008)

Registered Office
John Wiley & Sons Ltd, The Atrium, Southern Gate, Chichester, West Sussex, PO19 8SQ, UK

Editorial Offices
350 Main Street, Malden, MA 02148-5020, USA
9600 Garsington Road, Oxford, OX4 2DQ, UK
The Atrium, Southern Gate, Chichester, West Sussex, PO19 8SQ, UK

For details of our global editorial offices, for customer services, and for information about how to apply for permission to reuse the copyright material in this book please see our website at www.wiley.com/wiley-blackwell.

The right of Peter H. Wilson to be identified as the author of the editorial material in this work has been asserted in accordance with the UK Copyright, Designs and Patents Act 1988.

All rights reserved. No part of this publication may be reproduced, stored in a retrieval system, or transmitted, in any form or by any means, electronic, mechanical, photocopying, recording or otherwise, except as permitted by the UK Copyright, Designs and Patents Act 1988, without the prior permission of the publisher.

Wiley also publishes its books in a variety of electronic formats. Some content that appears in print may not be available in electronic books.

Designations used by companies to distinguish their products are often claimed as trademarks. All brand names and product names used in this book are trade names, service marks, trademarks or registered trademarks of their respective owners. The publisher is not associated with any product or vendor mentioned in this book.

Limit of Liability/Disclaimer of Warranty: While the publisher and editor have used their best efforts in preparing this book, they make no representations or warranties with respect to the accuracy or completeness of the contents of this book and specifically disclaim any implied warranties of merchantability or fitness for a particular purpose. It is sold on the understanding that the publisher is not engaged in rendering professional services and neither the publisher nor the author shall be liable for damages arising herefrom. If professional advice or other expert assistance is required, the services of a competent professional should be sought.

Library of Congress Cataloging-in-Publication Data

A companion to eighteenth-century Europe / edited by Peter H. Wilson.
p. cm. — (Blackwell companions to history)
Includes bibliographical references and index.
ISBN 978-1-4051-3947-2 (hbk. : alk. paper) – ISBN 978-1-118-73002-7 1. Europe—History—1648–1789. 2. Europe—History—1789–1815. 3. Europe—Civilization—18th century.
I. Wilson, Peter H.
D286.C57 2008
940.2′53—dc22

2007049382

A catalogue record for this book is available from the British Library.

Cover image: Dutch school, eighteenth century, A study of Leevwarden in Holland with a herd of Friesian cattle in the foreground. Iona Antiques, London, UK / The Bridgeman Art Library.
Cover design by Richard Boxall Design Associates.

Set in 10 on 12 pt Galliard by Toppan Best-set Premedia Limited
Printed in Malaysia by Ho Printing (M) Sdn Bhd

1 2014

Contents

Illustrations

Maps

Figures

Notes on Contributors

Ronald G. Asch is Professor of Early Modern History at Freiburg University, having previously held positions at the German Historical Institute, London, and Münster and Osnabrück universities. His books include *Der Hof Karls I. Politik, Provinz und Patronage 1625–1640* (1993), *Nobilities in Transition: Courtiers and Rebels in Britain and Europe, c. 1550–1700* (2003), and *Jakob I (1567–1625). König von England und Schottland* (2005).

Mark Berry is a British Academy Postdoctoral Fellow (2004–7) and Fellow in History at Peterhouse, Cambridge. He has written widely on intellectual and cultural history from the late seventeenth century to the present day, with a special interest in the interaction between music, history, politics, and philosophy. His work on Wagner has been awarded the Prince Consort Prize and Seeley Medal. *Treacherous Bonds and Laughing Fire: Politics and Religion in Wagner's Ring* is published by Ashgate.

Michael Bregnsbo is an Associate Professor of History at the University of Southern Denmark at Odense. His research interests include early modern Danish and European history, especially state building, political history, church history, and the history of historical ideas, on which he has published several books and articles.

Clarissa Campbell Orr is Senior Lecturer in History at Anglia Ruskin University, Cambridge Campus. She has edited and contributed to *Queenship in Britain 1660–1837: Royal Patronage, Dynastic Politics and Court* (2002), and *Queenship in Europe 1650–1815* (2004), and written other articles on court studies, gender, and enlightenment in the eighteenth century, including the chapter "Dynastic Perspectives" in T. Riotte and B. Simms (eds.), *The Hanoverian Dimension to British History* (2007).

Markus Cerman is Associate Professor of Economic and Social History at the University of Vienna. He has published on European economic and social history from the late Middle Ages until the twentieth century including, together with J. Ehmer, T. Hareven, and R. Wall, *Family History Revisited* (2001), together with H. Zeitlhofer, *Soziale Strukturen in Böhmen* (2002), and, together with R. Luft, *Untertanen, Herrschaft und Staat in Böhmen und im Alten Reich* (2005).

Alan Forrest is Professor of History at the University of York, where he currently co-directs the Centre for Eighteenth-Century Studies. His recent publications include *Napoleon's Men: The Soldiers of the Revolution and Empire* (2002), *Paris, the Provinces and the French Revolution* (2004), and together with J. P. Bertaud and A.

Jourdan, *Napoléon, le monde et les Anglais* (2004).

Philippe Girard is Assistant Professor of World History at McNeese State University in Lake Charles, Louisiana. His works include *Clinton in Haiti: The 1994 U.S. Invasion of Haiti* (2004) and *Paradise Lost: Haiti's Tumultuous Journey from Pearl of the Caribbean to Third World Hot Spot* (2005). He is currently working on a history of the Haitian revolution.

Jan Glete is Professor of History at Stockholm University, Sweden. He has published several studies of Swedish economic history. His more recent books include *Navies and Nations: Warships, Navies and State Building in Europe and America, 1500–1860* (1993), *Warfare at Sea, 1500–1650: Maritime Conflicts and the Transformation of Europe* (2000), and *War and the State in Early Modern Europe: Spain, the Dutch Republic and Sweden as Fiscal-Military States, 1500–1660* (2002).

Molly Greene is Professor of History at Princeton University with a joint appointment in the Program in Hellenic Studies. Her interests include Ottoman history and the history of the Mediterranean basin, with a particular interest in the Hellenic world. Her publications include *A Shared World: Christians and Muslims in the Early Modern Mediterranean* (2000) and, as editor, *Minorities in the Ottoman Empire* (2005).

Gregory Hanlon is University Research Professor at Dalhousie University in Halifax, Nova Scotia. His books include *L'Univers des gens de bien: Culture et comportements des élites urbaines en Aquitaine au XVIIe siècle* (1989), *Confessions and Community in Seventeenth-Century France: Catholic and Protestant Co-existence in Aquitaine* (1993), *The Twilight of a Military Tradition: Italian Aristocrats and European Conflicts 1560–1800* (1998), *Early Modern Italy 1550–1800* (2000), and *Human Nature in Rural Tuscany: An Early Modern History* (2007).

Lindsey Hughes was Professor of Russian History and Director for Russia Studies at the School of Slavonic and East European Studies, University College London, until her death in 2007. Her major publications include *Russia in the Age of Peter the Great* (1998) and *Peter the Great: A Biography* (2002). She also edited the *Slavonic and East European Review*.

Beat Kümin is Associate Professor in Early Modern European History at the University of Warwick. His research interests focus on social centers in local communities. Publications include *The Shaping of a Community: The Rise and Reformation of the English Parish 1400–1560* (1996), the co-edited collection *The World of the Tavern: Public Houses in Early Modern Europe* (2002), and *Drinking Matters: Public Houses and Social Exchange in Early Modern Central Europe* (2007).

Beverly Lemire is a Professor and Henry Marshall Tory Chair at the University of Alberta, Canada. Co-editor of the journal *Textile History* since 2002, her publications include *Fashion's Favourite: The Cotton Trade and the Consumer in Britain 1660–1800* (1991), *Dress, Culture and Commerce: The English Clothing Trade before the Factory* (1997), and *The Business of Everyday Life: Gender, Practice and Social Politics in England 1600–1900* (2005). She also co-edited the interdisciplinary collection *Women and Credit: Researching the Past, Refiguring the Future* (2002).

Mary Lindemann is Professor of History at the University of Miami, Coral Gables, Florida. She is the author of four books: *Patriots and Paupers: Hamburg, 1712–1830* (1990), *Health and Healing in Eighteenth-Century Germany* (1996), *Medicine and Society in Early Modern Europe* (1999), and *Liaisons dangereuses: Sex, Law, and Diplomacy in the Age of Frederick the Great* (2006). She is currently writing a volume on political culture in three early modern cities: Amsterdam, Antwerp, and Hamburg.

David M. Luebke is Associate Professor of History at the University of Oregon. He is author of *His Majesty's Rebels: Communities, Factions and Rural Revolt in the Black Forest* (1997) and many articles on seventeenth-century political culture, including

"'Naïve Monarchism' and Marian Veneration in Early Modern Germany" (*Past & Present*, 1997) and "How to Become a Loyalist: Petitions, Self-Fashioning, and the Repression of Unrest" (*Central European History*, 2005).

Jerzy (George) Lukowski is Reader in Polish History at the University of Birmingham and is currently serving as Head of Department of Modern History. From 2003 to 2005 he was the beneficiary of a Research Readership from the British Academy. His books include *Liberty's Folly: The Polish-Lithuanian Commonwealth in the Eighteenth Century* (1991), *The Partitions of Poland: 1772, 1793, 1795* (1999), *The Eighteenth-Century European Nobility* (2003), and, with W. H. Zawadzki, *A Concise History of Poland* (2nd edn., 2006).

Thomas Munck is Reader in History at the University of Glasgow. His books include *The Peasantry and the Early Absolute Monarchy in Denmark, 1660–1708* (1979), *Seventeenth-Century Europe 1598–1700* (2nd edn., 2005), *Computing for Historians: An Introductory Guide* (1993), and *The Enlightenment: A Comparative Social History 1721–1794* (2000).

Ciro Paoletti is a librarian, a former infantry officer of the Italian army, and Director of the Association for Military and Historical Studies. His books on eighteenth-century warfare include *Tra i Borboni e gli Asburgo: le armate terrestri e navali italiane nelle guerre del primo Settecento (1701–1732)* (with V. Ilari and G. Boeri, 1996), *La corona di Lombardia, guerra ed eserciti nell'Italia del medio Settecento: 1733–1763* (with V. Ilari and G. Boeri, 1997), *Gli Italiani in armi: cinque secoli di storia militare nazionale 1495–2000* (2001), and *Il principe Eugenio di Savoia* (2002).

J. L. Price is Reader in History at the University of Hull. His publications include *Culture and Society in the Dutch Republic during the Seventeenth Century* (1974), *Holland and the Dutch Republic in the Seventeenth Century* (1994), *The Dutch Republic in the Seventeenth Century* (1998), and *Dutch Society 1588–1713* (2000).

Michael Rapport is Senior Lecturer in History at the University of Stirling and author of *Nationality and Citizenship in Revolutionary France: the Treatment of Foreigners, 1789–1799* (2000) and *Nineteenth Century Europe, 1789–1914* (2005). He is currently working on a history of the 1848 revolutions in Europe.

Torsten Riotte is a research fellow at the German Historical Institute, London. His Ph.D. thesis has been published in German translation as *Hannover in der britischen Politik (1792–1815)* (2005). He has co-edited, with Brendan Simms, *The Hanoverian Dimension in British History, 1714–1837* (2007) and is currently working on a study of George III and the Old Reich. His latest project is a study of the Hanoverian royal family and their experiences during the Austrian exile after 1866.

Michael Schaich is a research fellow at the German Historical Institute, London. He is the author of *Staat und Öffentlichkeit im Kurfürstentum Bayern in der Sprätaufklärung* (2001), co-editor, with Jörg Neuheiser, of *Political Rituals in Great Britain, 1700–2000* (2006), and has edited *Monarchy and Religion: The Transformation of Royal Culture in Eighteenth-Century Europe* (2007).

Marc Schalenberg is Assistant Professor at the University of Zurich, having worked previously at Humboldt University, Berlin. His publications include *Humboldt auf Reisen? Die Rezeption des "deutschen Universitätsmodells" in den französischen und britischen Reformdiskursen, 1810–1870* (2002), and a co-edited collection, *... immer im Forschen bleiben* (2004). He is currently working on a comparative history of German residence towns in the eighteenth and early nineteenth centuries.

Hamish Scott is Professor of International History at the University of St Andrews. A Fellow of the British Academy, he is the author of *The Rise of the Great Powers 1648–1815* (with D. McKay, 1983), *British Foreign Policy in the Age of the American Revolution* (1990), *The Emergence of the Eastern Powers 1756–1775* (2001), and *The Birth of a Great Power System 1740–1815* (2006).

His edited books include *Enlightened Absolutism: Reform and Reformers in Eighteenth-Century Europe* (1990), *The European Nobilities in the Seventeenth and Eighteenth Centuries* (2nd edn., 2 vols., 2007).

Deborah Simonton is Associate Professor of British History at the University of Southern Denmark having worked previously at the University of Aberdeen. She is the author of, among other books, *The Routledge History of Women in Modern Europe* (2006), editor of *A History of European Women's Work, 1700 to the Present* (1998), and has co-edited *Women and Higher Education, Past Present and Future* (1996), *Gendering Scottish History, an International Approach* (1999), and *Gender in Scottish History* (2006). She is currently writing *Women in European Culture and Society* for Routledge.

Christopher Storrs is Reader in Early Modern European History at the University of Dundee. His books include *War, Diplomacy and the Rise of Savoy, 1690–1720* (1999) and *The Resilience of the Spanish Monarchy 1665–1700* (2006).

Andrew C. Thompson is a College Lecturer and Official Fellow in History at Queens' College, Cambridge. He is the author of *Britain, Hanover and the Protestant Interest, 1688–1756* (2006) and is currently working on a biography of George II.

Joachim Whaley is a Fellow of Gonville and Caius College and Senior Lecturer in German at the University of Cambridge. He is the author of *Religious Toleration and Social Change in Hamburg 1529–1819* (1985; new edn. 2002) and of numerous articles on eighteenth-century German cultural and intellectual history.

Dennis Wheeler is Reader in Geography at the University of Sunderland. His principal research area is historical climatology, in which he uses naval and other documents from the past three centuries to reconstruct the climate of the time. He has also studied the influence of weather on naval battles in the age of sail and has published over a hundred papers. His books include *Regional Climates of the British Isles* (1997) and *Statistical Techniques in Geographical Analysis* (2004).

Peter H. Wilson is G. F. Grant Professor of History at the University of Hull, having worked previously at Sunderland and Newcastle universities. His books include *War, State and Society in Württemberg, 1677–1793* (1995), *German Armies: War and German Politics 1648–1806* (1998), *The Holy Roman Empire 1495–1806* (1999), *Absolutism in Central Europe* (2000), and *From Reich to Revolution: German History 1558–1806* (2004).

Acknowledgments

Any attempt to cover an entire century of European history inevitably involves a high degree of selection and compression. The present volume is very much a team effort, but its basic conception and structure are my own, and responsibility for whatever limitations they have imposed on the themes covered rests with me alone. I would like to thank all the contributors for the exemplary professionalism with which they delivered their texts within a tight schedule. Hamish Scott wrote his chapter during the tenure of a Major Research Fellowship, and wishes to record his thanks to the Leverhulme Trust. Finally, we are all indebted to Tessa Harvey, Gillian Kane, and their colleagues at Blackwell for their advice and support.

P.H.W.

Map 1 Eastern Europe showing the expansion of Russia

Map 2 The Partitions of Poland 1772–95

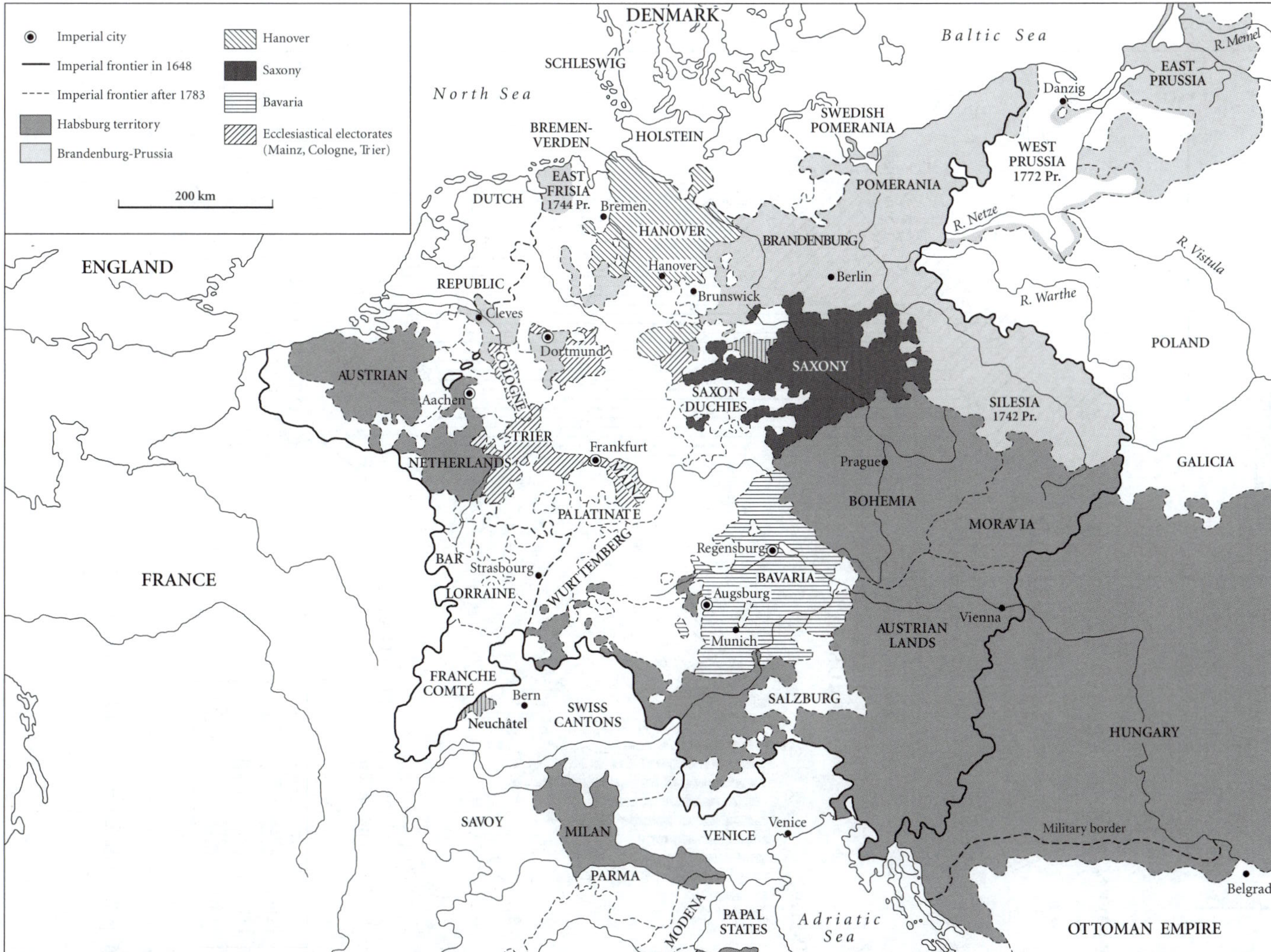

Map 3 Central Europe 1745

Map 4 Europe in 1763

Map 5 Italian states *c*.1690

Map 6 Italian states *c*.1790

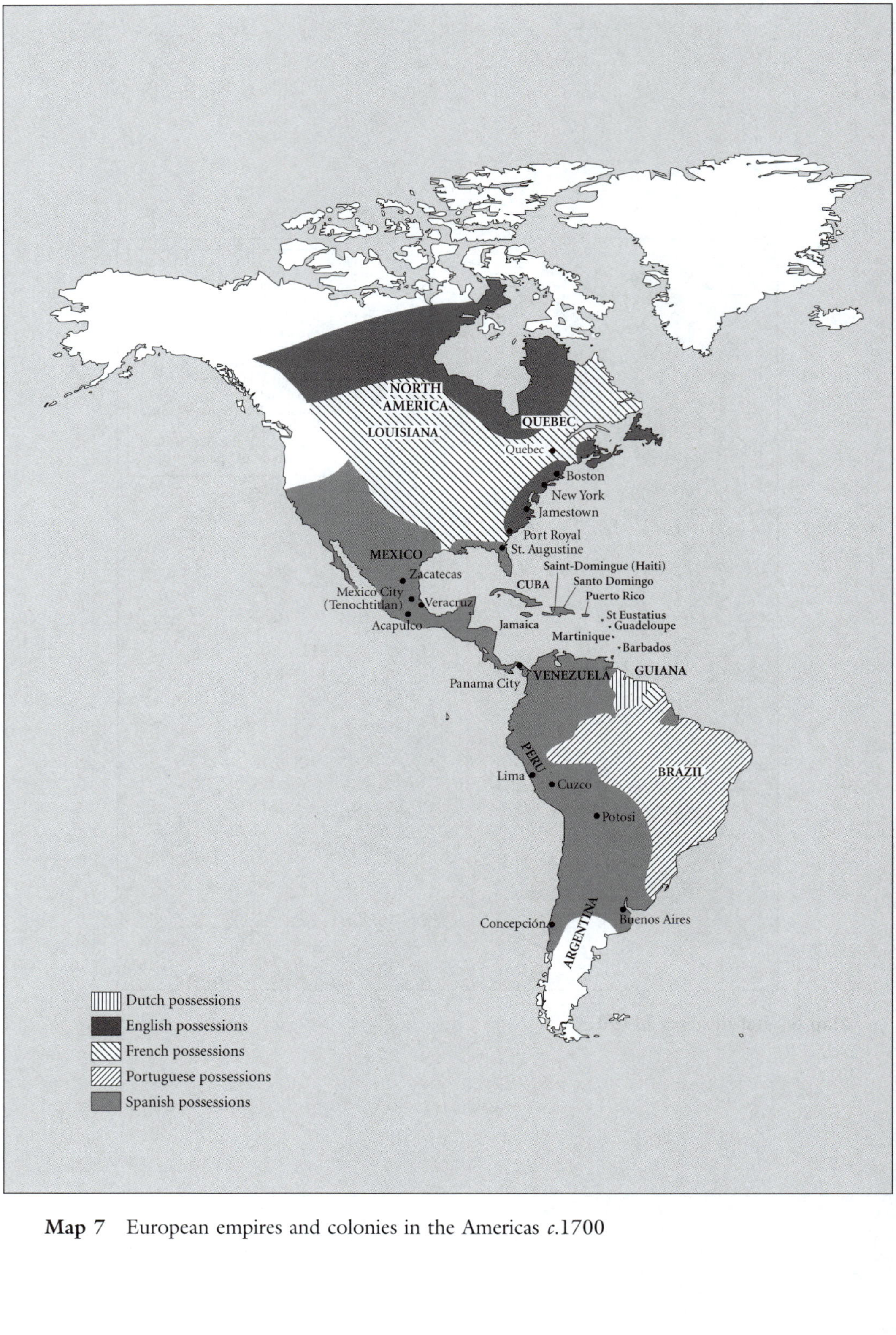

Map 7 European empires and colonies in the Americas *c.*1700

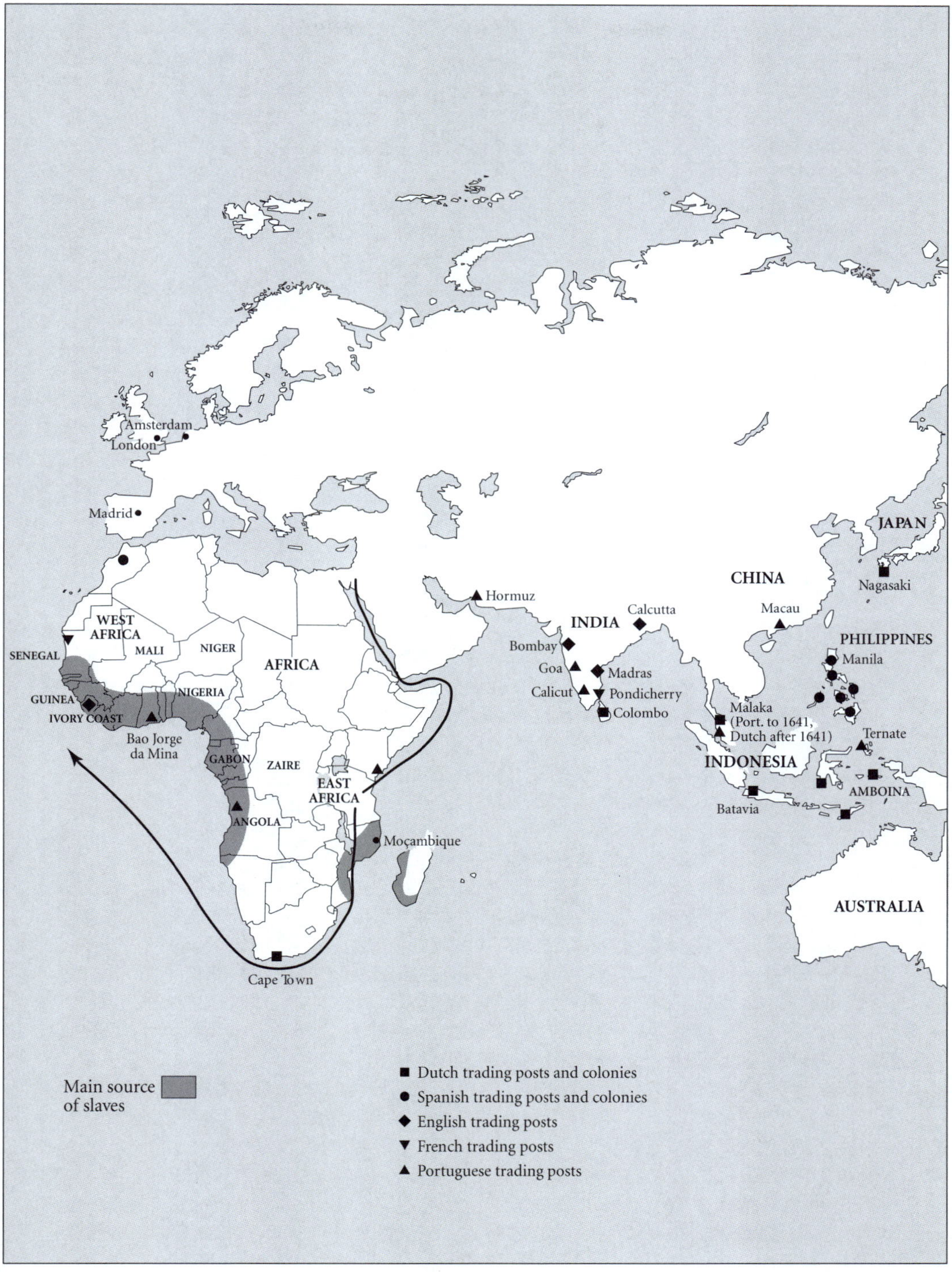

Map 8 European conquests in Southeast Asia

Introduction

PETER H. WILSON

For most modern geographers, Europe is no longer a continent, but the western tip of Afroeurasia, the world's largest land mass. There is some doubt whether historians should also still treat Europe as a distinct field. The current interest in world history questions older national and regional subdivisions as artificial constructs deriving largely from the nineteenth century, while so-called "micro-historians" encourage us to examine each community in detail and to explore individual experience. Yet eighteenth-century Europeans saw themselves as living in a distinct continent. Though influenced by physical geography, their concept of Europe was primarily cultural: a means to distinguish between themselves and other peoples. Like all such cultural constructs, definition depended on identifying boundaries often associated with the perceived character of communities rather than the physical locations they occupied. This was most problematic to the east where there was no agreed physical frontier, but even to the west, bordered by the oceans, many questioned whether the inhabitants of the British Isles or Iceland were fully fledged Europeans (Wolff, 1994).

Europeans were not unified by a single religion, despite the lingering legacy of the medieval ideal of Christendom. The eleventh-century schism between Western Catholicism and Eastern Orthodoxy left an indelible mark on the European consciousness, with many of the inhabitants in the Catholic west, north, and south no longer regarding the followers of the Orthodox faith to the east as part of a common civilization. Politics reinforced this division, as Russia, the primary Orthodox state, expanded eastwards into Siberia and central Asia from the sixteenth century, and only resumed a more western political orientation around 1700. The majority of the remaining Orthodox believers lived in the Balkans where they fell under the rule of the Islamic Ottoman empire between the late fifteenth and early sixteenth centuries. With possessions across North Africa and the Middle East, the Ottoman empire was a true world power that, until 1699, refused to entertain the possibility of permanent peace with any other civilization and was only gradually integrated into a common diplomatic order with European states during the eighteenth century. Yet Greece, that came to be regarded by the late eighteenth century as the cradle of European civilization, lay firmly under Ottoman rule from 1460 to 1829, apart from a brief

A Companion to Eighteenth-Century Europe, First Edition. Edited by Peter H. Wilson.
© 2014 John Wiley & Sons, Ltd. Published 2014 by John Wiley & Sons, Ltd.

period of Venetian control from 1699 to 1715. Meanwhile, the sixteenth-century Reformation shattered Catholic unity and produce a variety of competing strands of Protestantism. After a century and a half of strife, Protestants and Catholics largely abandoned attempts to align religious conformity with political authority by the later seventeenth century. As a result, most states contained either a Catholic or Protestant official majority, with dissenting minorities of varying size, faith, and legal status. Throughout, Jewish communities persisted, particularly in central and east-central Europe.

While they rarely matched religious boundaries precisely, political frontiers nonetheless became more distinct across the sixteenth and seventeenth centuries. These divisions were articulated in the language of sovereign states that gained acceptance during the seventeenth century, though it remained disputed whether such states should interact as equals, regardless of size, wealth, and form of government, or whether they should remain in some kind of hierarchical order. Seventeenth-century wars had largely resolved disputes over which states were fully sovereign, and how their governments were to be organized internally and what authority they should exercise over their own peoples. However, the eighteenth century still saw struggles over the size of individual states, with competing claims to certain provinces and even entire states leading to numerous "wars of succession," since rulers' legitimacy generally rested on dynastic inheritance. Such conflicts were also related to the continuing struggle over international status, with the century opening with the defeat, in the War of the Spanish Succession (1701–14), of French pretensions to occupy pole position in a hierarchical order. Subsequent conflicts saw the gradual integration of struggles for regional pre-eminence, for example over the control of the Baltic, into an overarching conception of a single system containing several major and more numerous minor powers. Prior to the re-emergence of French power after 1789, conflicts no longer centered on the pretension of one state to occupy a commanding position, but rather disputes over the relative "balance of power" between the components of this single system.

To these religious and political divisions can be added further differences in language, custom, social organization, and economic activity, separating not only sovereign states and communities of believers, but individual provinces, communities, and groups within these. The practicalities of distance in an age still reliant on horse and wind power for propulsion simply reinforced these distinctions. Nonetheless, it is clear that there existed a common sense of belonging, even if Europe's extent and the character of its inhabitants remained matters of dispute. The French philosopher Voltaire spoke of Europe as "a kind of republic divided into several states." Some conceived of this as a formal political order, such as the Abbé de St Pierre, who urged European sovereigns to agree a common court to arbitrate their differences as a means of guaranteeing perpetual peace. For most, however, Europe was a complex set of broadly common aspirations and beliefs, shared at least by intellectuals, those with formal education, and many of those wielding political, economic, and social power. These ideas instilled confidence, born of the conviction that Europeans possessed a unique capacity to overcome intractable problems, as well as a superior culture, inherited from ancient Greece and Rome that together were regarded as the well of human civilization. Such ideas did not go unchallenged during the eighteenth century as Europeans discovered more about the world beyond their shores.

Nonetheless, it is possible to detect a shift from faith that the Christian God would assist all who believed in him, to a conviction that Europeans already possessed innate qualities for success. This shift was related to the move away from the pessimism characterizing the previous hundred years, the "iron century" of hardship and conflict, and towards a more optimistic "age of reason." Structural changes clearly assisted this. There was a modest improvement in long-term weather conditions after a particularly unfavorable decade around 1690. European demography progressed from simple recovery from earlier seventeenth-century losses to steadily accelerating growth around 1730. Whereas Europe's population had grown by a modest 20 percent in the sixteenth century, and again in the seventeenth, it doubled between 1750 and 1850 and continued to increase rapidly thereafter. Crop yields that had remained largely static since the later Middle Ages, also experienced dramatic improvement, while other activities witnessed rising productivity. Many remained desperately poor, but the overall capacity to produce a surplus beyond immediate needs increased. Luxuries were no longer the preserve of a narrow governing elite, but became available to the growing and increasingly self-conscious and assertive "middle classes."

Confidence grew with awareness of gradually improving conditions, while the sense of achievement simply reinforced feelings of superiority over non-European peoples. Alongside this, however, was a growing sense, among some Europeans at least, that they were members of a common humanity to which they bore some responsibility for their actions. Self-confidence and a sense of destiny were paradoxically reinforced by the Britain's reluctant acceptance of the independence of its North American colonies in 1783: the first significant defeat of European imperialism in world history. While the Americans broke with Britain, they nonetheless established a state and society closely modeled on an idealized version of European civilization that appeared to confirm that European values and institutions would eventually encompass the entire globe.

If there are good reasons for us to treat Europe as a distinct field for historical research, how confident can we be in using the eighteenth century to demarcate our time frame? The division of history into discrete centuries flows naturally from our familiarity with chronological time and makes sense pedagogically by allowing us to subdivide the long human story into more manageable segments. We like our stories to have a beginning, middle, and end, as well as a plot and sense of direction. Do the dates 1700 and 1800 make sense in these terms? Historians writing before the present, self-consciously "postmodern" age were already well aware of these questions. Their studies offer the alternatives of a "short" eighteenth century, running from 1713 to the 1780s (Anderson, 1987; Black, 1999; Woloch, 1982), or a "long" one that, for British historians generally begins with the Glorious Revolution of 1688 and ends in the defeat of Napoleonic France in 1815. Those with a more "continental" perspective tend to stretch to dates back to 1648 and forward to 1789 or even 1815 (Treasure, 1985; Winks and Kaiser, 2004). This longer period is variously labeled the "age of absolutism" or the "old regime," as defined primarily according to the prevailing political philosophy and practice of strong monarchy, justifying its authority on claims to guarantee order and social stability after a period of upheaval and religious conflict over the previous century and a half.

The disagreement over dates not only reflects the differing significance attached to particular events, but also divergence over historical approach. Both the "long" and "short" eighteenth centuries were initially defined according to criteria developed by historians writing in the nineteenth century; in many ways the formative period of modern historical scholarship. Such writers gave preference to high politics, especially the wars and diplomacy that marked the "rise" or "decline" of Europe's great nation-states. They also emphasized intellectual trends, especially those associated with the language of liberal constitutionalism, personal liberty, and capitalist economics. While these factors no longer feature so prominently today, other historiographical developments question the appropriateness of using the eighteenth century as a distinct phase in Europe's past. The division of modern history into "early" and later stages tends either to subsume the eighteenth century within a longer early modern period beginning around 1450 (Cameron, 2001; Dewald, 2003; Wiesener-Hanks, 2006), or split it between these two modern epochs. The former option generally retains the French Revolution of 1789 as its end marker, but the latter pushes the start of later modernity back to around 1750. For example, the Consortium on the Revolutionary Era (until recently "Revolutionary Europe"), an influential US-based academic network, works within the rough parameters of 1750 to 1850 and interprets this as a period of fundamental transition. The same period has been identified by the German historian Reinhart Koselleck as the "saddle" (*Sattelzeit*) between modernity and pre-modernity (Brunner, Conze, and Koselleck, 1972–97: vol. 1, pp. xiv–xv). Such ideas have been hugely influential, not least because they chime with the interpretations advanced by social and cultural theorists working in the 1970s to 1990s. Many of these theorists are inherently hostile to the claims advanced by earlier writers for the "modernity" of the eighteenth century. This dispute over the meaning of modernity and the validity of the values ascribed to it has largely replaced the division marked by political ideology that colored much of twentieth-century historiography. These twenty-first-century differences, like those of the past, exist beyond the self-serving agendas of some participants because there are genuine problems of interpretation.

There are many good reasons for taking the 1750s as a more significant dividing point than either the 1700s or 1800s. Older scholarship already identified the mid-eighteenth century as marking a shift from a state primarily concerned with restoring order and promoting stability after earlier upheavals, to one that had greater confidence in its ability to reshape society along more efficient and productive lines. Traditionally, this has been labeled a move from the "classical absolutism" epitomized by Louis XIV in France (r. 1643–1715), to the "enlightened absolutism" exemplified by monarchs like Catherine II of Russia (r. 1762–96). Internationally, the mid-eighteenth century saw the emergence of Prussia as a fifth "great power" alongside Austria, France, Russia, and Britain, establishing a pattern that remained basically unchanged until the end of World War I. The 1750s witnessed a lasting shift in the global balance of European power as Britain triumphed over France in North America and India. Though Britain's position in the former was diminished by American independence in 1783, its gains in India continued throughout the later eighteenth century and sustained imperial predominance into the twentieth century. Rising agricultural productivity, particularly in Britain and the Netherlands, assisted the changes customarily labeled the Industrial Revolution that started to become more apparent in some areas around 1750. Social change likewise showed signs of accelerating, fuelled by demographic growth. The rapidity as well as the scale of these changes became manifest in more marked social differentiation, clearer divisions of labor, and the emergence of new occupations. Culturally, the mid-eighteenth century is perhaps less important for truly new ideas than for the wider dissemination of more secular ways of thinking, as well as the engagement of broader sections of the population in more freely ranging debates on human society. Nowhere is this more apparent than in the publication of the *Encyclopédie*, a 28-volume compendium of new knowledge edited by Denis Diderot and Jean d'Alembert between 1751 and 1772, to which over 150 people contributed. A further seven volumes were later added to what became a major best-selling publishing venture.

These debates over the significance of particular trends, and how best to study them, inform the contributions to this volume that is nonetheless based on a chronological division roughly from 1700 to 1800. While not suggesting that either year marks a dramatic turning point, there are valid reasons to frame the eighteenth century as a distinct period in Europe's history. Many developments certainly began much earlier, while others continued far beyond 1800, as the subsequent chapters make clear. However, when the perspective is widened beyond Europe to examine Europeans' impact on the world, the eighteenth century emerges more distinctly. Again, individual chapters will explore this in greater depth, but some important aspects can be noted here. Britain and Russia emerged around 1700 as countries with political, social, and economic systems of global importance. Both had been rather peripheral powers till that point, but were confirmed as major world powers by 1800. Perhaps more fundamentally, the eighteenth century saw the culmination of long-term trends that were to shape world history for the next 200 years and beyond. Europe now achieved a unique global position as a concentration of technological (especially maritime), economic, and military power, supported by sophisticated state infrastructures with the ability to project their influence well beyond their own frontiers. Individual elements of this unique mix were not unknown elsewhere, nor had Europeans achieved this combination unaided or without borrowing ideas and practices from other peoples. The different strands had their roots far in the past, while their development accelerated from the fifteenth century, but it was only in the eighteenth that they fully came together and made a more significant impact outside Europe. In doing so, they also transformed Europe, providing the basis for European global predominance (at least economic and military).

This fusion produced a set of institutions, best defined broadly as cultural practices and assumptions, both formal and informal. In short, they were a way of doing things, coordinating activities, setting priorities, and allocating resources. Individual elements were not unique, but their combination was distinctly European. Seen in a broader time frame, these institutions provide perhaps a better definition of modernity than either the French or Industrial revolutions that have traditionally served as markers. More importantly, these institutions, such as state structures and forms of education, were present across Europe and not merely in those countries engaged in overseas trade or conquest.

Some explanation of the structure and approach of the volume is required before proceeding further. Recent scholarship gives particular emphasis to certain approaches that have added greatly to our understanding of the eighteenth century.

One is the interest in the connections between Europe and other parts of the world that urges greater sensitivity towards the non-European elements in European history. Another has been the emergence of new forms of cultural history that move beyond the largely quantitative methods used before to study society and economy by utilizing previously under-used sources that shed light on individual experience and perception through an examination of aspects like "discourse," gender, identity, and non-elite cultural practices. Such approaches nonetheless need to be balanced with other perspectives, including those whose accepted status as "traditional" should not blind us to their continued utility. There is a danger that current fashions impose their own boundaries on the past – however unintended – thereby unduly diminishing the significance attached to other topics. One example is the current paradigm of the "Atlantic World" that preferences Europe's transatlantic links (especially with North America) over connections to other parts of the globe. This is undoubtedly related to the predominance of English-language work in published history, and the relatively generous research resources of British and US academic institutions compared to those elsewhere. The emphasis on shared cultural connections also unwittingly threatens to revive the older Cold War Atlantic paradigm that trumpeted common western European-American democratic values (Palmer, 1959).

Similarly, the new cultural history has concentrated so far primarily on developments associated with information exchange through the "public sphere," and the emergence of leisure and consumerism. Such topics were largely overlooked previously, but provide valuable insight into the lives of women as well as men, children as well as adults. They have also left rich seams of written and visual sources, and represent trends that not only spread geographically and socially after 1700, but helped to distinguish the eighteenth century from those that preceded it. These topics appeal to us also because they appear closer, and thus more accessible, to our own experience. However, with the exception of consumerism, only a fraction of those living in eighteenth-century Europe were affected directly by them. The new cultural history reinforces the tendency inherent in the Atlantic approach to reduce European history to that of the continent's north-western corner and to concentrate on the "swelling" urban middle classes engaged in commerce.

There is a need to look beyond the Atlantic seaboard and at the majority of Europeans for whom life was often very different. It is also important in this present age of closer political integration and means of rapid communication to remember that eighteenth-century Europe was divided into many different states and hundreds of thousands of communities varying considerably in size and internal stratification. This is a substantial volume, but even here it is impossible to do justice to the myriad of local distinctions. A measure of this can nevertheless be conveyed by presenting essays on individual countries and regions. This should not be misconstrued as a return to more distinctly nationalist perspectives, but as a reflection of Europe's fragmented character at a time when the local and particular loomed large in everyday experience. Concepts of "nation" and "nationalism" can be found in eighteenth-century discourse, but their grip on the popular imagination lay in the future, nor were they synonymous with later nineteenth-century definitions. As the contributions to this volume make clear, most European states were still "composite" or dynastic ones, patchworks of different regions bound together by complex webs of political, legal, economic, and religious ties rather than those of language and national sentiment.

The content of the more thematic chapters reflects trends in recent scholarship discussed above. If such topics as military and state institutions receive less space than they perhaps would have done in an equivalent book produced 20 years ago, they have not gone away. Instead, questions about the limits of state authority and the degree of its "modernity" by 1800 have been reinvigorated by research into the public sphere and other issues associated with the new cultural history and the "linguistic turn." Equally, new perspectives are being opened on economic change through the study of the cultures of consumption, as well as the methods and social relations of production. No attempt has been made to favor one approach above another. Instead, it has been left to individual contributors to offer their own evaluations of recent research from the conviction that historical knowledge is best advanced through a broad dialogue between those working in different fields. However, the focus remains firmly on Europe, and the decision to give more space to eastern, northern, and southern Europe has consequences for how other aspects can be tackled. There is still space for the debates on such matters as globalization, the Atlantic world, intellectual currents, middle-class sociability, and the culture of consumption, but these have not been allowed to dominate.

The volume builds on thematic coverage of society, economics, and culture, before moving towards a more chronological and national focus as it shifts to political and international issues. Part I starts by examining the environmental context of the sustained population growth that began during the eighteenth century. Subsequent chapters investigate key sections of society and areas of economic activity. The omission of a separate chapter on the "middle classes" is deliberate, since these are customarily given too much prominence for a time that was still primarily agrarian.

Part II opens with the current debate on the rise of a public sphere as this offers a good place to explore different areas of cultural and intellectual life. Discussion of such aspects as religion, medicine, and the Enlightenment provide the cultural dimension for the tangled web of national histories detailed in Part III. Here, each chapter highlights differences and similarities in the challenges faced by monarchs and governments, as well as how their responses can be related to wider shifts in state–society relations across the century. One of these chapters focuses explicitly on Britain's relations with the rest of Europe and so will form a bridge with the companion volume on eighteenth-century Britain that already contains excellent coverage of Britain's place in the wider world (Dickinson, 2002). The last two parts shift attention to political and international issues, without losing sight of their social, economic, and cultural contexts. The opening chapter of Part IV guides the reader through the major changes in Europe's political map and explains the emergence of what is commonly called the great power system. The next three chapters expand and deepen this by exploring Europe's external contours, both in terms of relations between its component parts and with other areas of the globe. The final part consolidates the volume by more detailed examination of key political developments introduced elsewhere, and by focusing on the French and other European revolutions commonly held to have brought the century to a close, both chronologically and in the sense of ending the "old regime."

Bibliography

Anderson, M. S., *Europe in the Eighteenth Century 1713–1783* (3rd edn., London, 1987).

Black, J., *Eighteenth-Century Europe* (2nd edn., Basingstoke, 1999).

Brunner, O., W. Conze, and R. Koselleck (eds.), *Geschichtliche Grundbegriffe* (8 vols., Stuttgart, 1972–97).

Cameron, E. (ed.), *Early Modern Europe* (Oxford, 2001).

Dewald, J. (ed.), *Europe 1450–1789: An Encyclopedia of the Early Modern World* (6 vols., New York, 2003).

Dickinson, H. T. (ed.), *A Companion to Eighteenth-Century Britain* (Oxford, 2002).

Doyle, W., *The Old European Order 1660–1800* (2nd edn., Oxford, 1992).

Palmer, R. R., *The Age of the Democratic Revolution: A Political History of Europe and America 1760–1800* (Princeton, 1959).

Treasure, G., *The Making of Modern Europe 1648–1780* (London, 1985).

Upton, A. F., *Europe 1600–1800* (London, 2000).

Wiesner-Hanks, M. E., *Early Modern Europe, 1450–1789* (Cambridge, 2006).

Winks, R. W. and T. E. Kaiser, *Europe from the Old Regime to the Age of Revolution 1648–1815* (Oxford, 2004).

Wolff, L., *Inventing "Eastern Europe": The Map of Civilisation in the Mind of the Enlightenment* (Stanford, 1994).

Woloch, I., *Eighteenth-Century Europe: Transition and Progress, 1715–1789* (New York, 1982).

Part I

People, Production, and Consumption

Chapter One

Eighteenth-Century History and the European Environment

Dennis Wheeler

Historical Climatology: Review and Development

Recent concerns about future global warming have prompted scientists to look to the past, and there is a growing understanding of how climate has changed over the centuries and recognition that such changes have had consequences for the societies that experienced them. The eighteenth century is of particular interest, because it was from that time that temperature, rainfall, and other instrument-based data began to be gathered following the invention a century earlier of the barometer and the thermometer, by Torricelli and Galileo respectively. For earlier periods reliance is placed on contemporary documents such as tax returns, farm and estate records, chronicles, letters, and diaries from which the climate record can be inferred. It is now acknowledged that the careful analysis of such items can provide an unexpectedly detailed picture of the climate and weather of the time. It is this recognition that has given rise to the discipline of "historical climatology." Some of the early research in this field was conducted by historians, exemplary amongst which is the work of members of the French Annales school such as Fernand Braudel and Emmanuel Le Roy Ladurie (1972). On the climatological side, endeavors began earlier, though with little immediate effect. The Swiss scientist Louis Dufour (1870) and his French contemporary Alfred Angot (1885) both recognized the climatological significance of documentary sources, as did Charles Brooks (1926) some years later in the UK. But it is the contributions of Professors Hubert Lamb (1982, 1988), Christian Pfister (1984), and Rudolf Brázdil (1996) that set "historical climatology" on its present path and Brázdil et al. (2005) have provided an overview of the current state of historical climatological studies in which they stress the developing interest in past responses to weather extremes and variations.

This concept of social vulnerability is an important one that has recently been accorded increased attention in the social sciences by writers such as Oliver-Smith (2004). Not all, however, agree on the role that the environment plays in social evolution, and Fogel has argued that famines are "related to an extremely inelastic demand for food inventories, rather than to natural calamities" (1992: 280). A

A Companion to Eighteenth-Century Europe, First Edition. Edited by Peter H. Wilson.
© 2014 John Wiley & Sons, Ltd. Published 2014 by John Wiley & Sons, Ltd.

century earlier, Durkheim (1882), in his desire to provide sociology with the methodological objectivity of the sciences, was of the firm opinion that social history was only explicable in terms of social factors.

Despite such reservations, Ingold (1992) proposed that environmental and human history are inseparable and that each is implicated in the evolutionary life of the other. Post (1990) has also offered some interesting reflections on the connections between mortality, disease, and subsistence crises in which he observed that the latter "were invariably preceded by natural calamity" (1990: 241). He recognizes the more direct connections to food supply and prices, but argues that such connections are anything but predictable, nor do they conform to any recognized pattern. For him, natural disasters exercise control over poorer elements of society through the medium of such issues as problems of sanitation, unemployment, and vagrancy, all of which would hasten the onset of epidemics and facilitate their spread. Pfister and Brázdil (2006) have, from the climatological side, offered similar views. Nevertheless, occasionally quantifiable relationships have been discovered. Parry and Carter (1985) found that the pre-industrial agricultural "frontier" of southern Scotland rose or fell by 140 m for every degree of temperature change. But it is Parry who best summarizes the problem: "The task of evaluating the impact of changes of climate on the path of economic history is an extraordinarily difficult one. It embraces two disciplines which have traditionally adopted very different paths of enquiry and which require from their disciples very different realms of expertise" (1981: 319).

Such areas of uncertainty and debate notwithstanding, there is an undeniable link between climate and the success or otherwise of agricultural systems and food supply. In the long term, climate sets limits to the nature and variety of crops that can be successfully cultivated. Across northern Europe, for example, wheat production is confined to the drier and warmer districts, its place being taken by barley where growing seasons are shorter, or by oats as the climate becomes cooler and wetter in northern and more western districts. These are, however, the broadly defined circumscriptions on agriculture set by long-term average conditions and might be described as first-order climatic controls. But climate is both variable and unpredictable, and year-by-year changes can lead to good or bad harvests with inevitable consequences for political and economic systems as food prices fluctuate to reflect provision and demand. These might be described as second-order controls, and they form the focus of this chapter. They are, as noted above, complex and have responses that are more sensitive and less predictable than those of first-order effects. Subsistence agricultural practices are, for the most part, more vulnerable than commercial systems where reserves can be stored or traded to offset periods of shortage, and while some eighteenth-century systems were benefiting from investment and from the so-called "agricultural revolution" in farming practices that began in England, others lagged behind. Fagan (2000) is highly critical of the conservatism and inefficiency of French agriculture in the eighteenth century, which left it anachronisitically sensitive to inclement weather. Elsewhere in Europe, Pfister and Brázdil observed in connection with case studies from central Europe that "A group's ability to anticipate, cope with, resist and recover from crises and disaster depends on a variety of social, economic, political and environmental processes" (2006: 115). More generally it is important to note that average crop yields – a product of first-order influences – are less important in the current context than the risk and frequency of failure in meeting the minimum demands, which depend upon the second-order controls.

The Climate of Eighteenth-Century Europe

There is general agreement concerning the climate of Europe during the eighteenth century. Not only were the thermometer and barometer much-improved instruments at this time, providing more reliable measures than those of their predecessors, but the age of Enlightenment had created an intellectual atmosphere in which data and observations were gathered, recorded and compared often within the context of organized networks, or through the agency of learned societies. Such endeavors began as early as the seventeenth century when the grand duke of Tuscany, Ferdinand II, established the Accademia del Cimento (Academy of Experiments) in his native Florence. In 1654 Ferdinand and Leopold de Medici established the first international network of observatories, the so-called Rete Medicea, that included not only Florence but also Bologna, Parma, Rome, Milan, Paris, and Warsaw (Camuffo, 2002). It ceased operating in 1667, but just 10 years later the Royal Society's first curator, Robert Hooke, devised a scheme for making standardized weather observations. Early in the eighteenth century Johann Kanold set up a network of corresponding observers (Brázdil et al, 2002) with quarterly reports being published from 1718 to 1726. In 1770 Karl Theodor, then Prince-Elector of the Palatinate, established an observational network through the Societas Meteorologica Palatina, the correspondents of which could be found as far afield as Stockholm and Rome, while in 1778 the Société Royale de Médecine was founded in Paris and organized its own network of observers (Kington, 1988a). The political uncertainties of the closing years of the century were to bring these enterprises to a regrettable conclusion. None of these notable endeavors should, however, diminish the contribution of those many observers across Europe who engaged in weather studies in a spirit of individual inquiry. Most notable in Britain, if only because his observations and writings have been made so accessible by the efforts of Kington (1988b), is Thomas Barker of Lyndon Hall, Rutland, whose daily record extends, remarkably, from 1733 to 1800. These instrumental observations provide a platform on which our knowledge of the climate of the century is based, but the even greater wealth of documentary records of floods, droughts, crop return, estate papers, and other documents provide yet further evidence. Deriving absolute temperatures and rainfalls from non-instrumental sources remains an area of debate, but climatologists have enjoyed much success in producing carefully scaled indices of these two important phenomena.

Drawing on such sources, objective and statistical substance is given to the study of past climates by the central England temperature series. This dataset of monthly temperatures starts in 1659 and continues to the present day, being brought up to date each month by the UK Met Office (<www.metoffice.gov.uk/research/hadley centre/CR_data/Daily/HadCET_act.txt>). It was developed by the late Professor Gordon Manley (1974), and while it represents conditions in England, it is also broadly representative of trends across most of western and central Europe. Figure 1 is based on this series and reveals only too clearly the problem of generalized statements made on such an inherently variable phenomenon as climate. The year-to-year changes are so marked that "running means" are used to smooth out

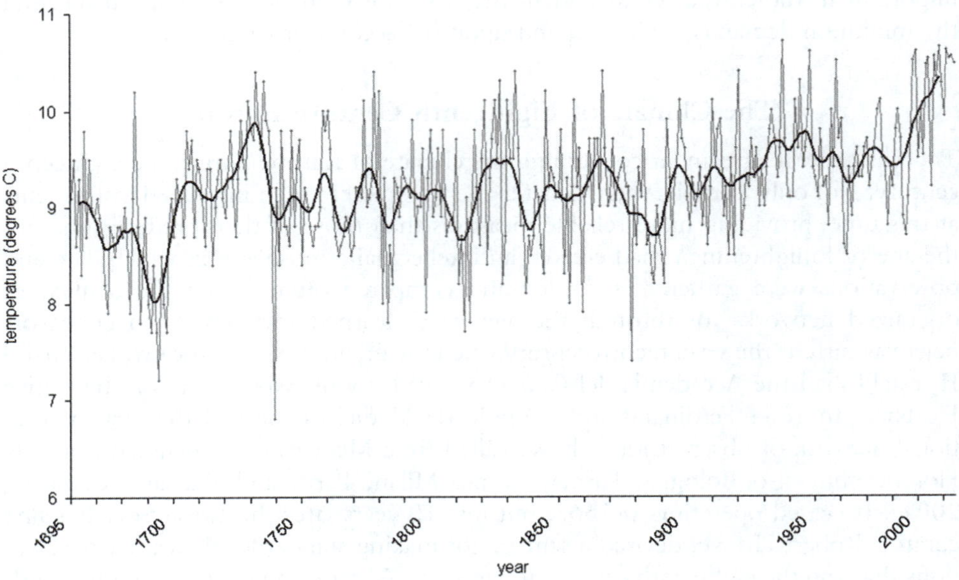

Figure 1 The central England temperature annual series, 1659–2005. The 12-year running mean (to identify the longer-term trends) is superimposed in bold

such variations and to reveal the underlying trends. Useful though such a summary is, it fails to convey any sense of the variations within the year. Temperatures are, however, one part of a wider climatological picture. Regionally based rainfall records begin only in 1766 with England and Wales series prepared by the Climatic Research Unit of the University of East Anglia (<www.cru.uea.ac.uk/cru/data/>). In contrast to temperatures, rainfall can vary greatly over short distances and it would be wrong to extend the climatological picture presented by the England and Wales data beyond that region. Snowfall, because of its often more dramatic consequences and episodic character, was often recorded and allows for long series to be constructed, and that of Manley (1969) takes the British record back over 300 years.

There is, however, no suggestion that the climate of the eighteenth century was in any way unique. It wasn't, and it should be seen within the longer-term changes taking place in the past millennium. The so-called "Little Ice Age," which prevailed from the fourteenth to the nineteenth centuries, is generally regarded as the coldest period of European history since the retreat of the great ice sheets some 10,000 years ago. Moreover, the closing decades of the seventeenth century had been the very coldest of the period, with well-documented reflections on the horrors that accompanied crop failure: famine, disease, and rising food prices. By comparison, the opening years of the eighteenth century, must have been seen as almost benign, as temperatures underwent a slow, if at times faltering, recovery.

The combination and timing of extremes of precipitation and of temperatures of the type experienced during the Little Ice Age were often critical. For many forms of production, cool and wet summers can be more damaging than cold winters. Dry springs can be harmful for germination of crops, while wet summers can create havoc

Figure 2 Merchant shipping frozen in the ice at Rotherhithe Stairs during the great frost of 1789. *City of London Libraries and Guildhall Art Gallery*

with the harvest. Such disruptions to the agricultural system have been described by Pfister and Brázdil (2006) as "Little Ice Age-Type Impacts" (LIATIMP) They single out long wet spells as being particularly detrimental, leading to a reduced flour content in grain and also leaving crops vulnerable to molds and attacks by the grain weevil (*Sitophilus granaries*). Such prolonged spells of wet weather can also be harmful outside the growing season, and when they occur in autumn they can deplete soils of nutrients, particularly soluble nitrogen. Cold springs can also create problems by delaying germination or destroying emergent crops with late frosts.

The data to hand provides a useful point of departure in any attempt to grasp the climatic character of the eighteenth century. The closing years of the seventeenth century were remarkable by any standards, and the conditions of the eighteenth represent a general improvement. But cold spells continued to occur, with occasionally alarming consequences partly as a result of their wholly unexpected nature bringing in their wake disruptions to life, the economy, and agriculture (figure 2). The 1730s were, for example, amongst the warmest until the recent years of "global warming," but the decade concluded with the coldest year in the central England series (1740). Other cold years followed, and major crises of mortality, food supply, and food prices occurred in the 1740s and 1770s. Both coincided with periods of poor weather. The mortality crisis of the 1740s saw death rates rise by 21 percent across Europe (Post,

1990), while the corresponding figure for the 1790s was 17 percent. The rates varied from region to region, but Post has presented a detailed analysis of these two critical periods and claims the 1740s mortality wave to have been "an outstanding fact of European population history" (1990: 245). In both cases the immediate cause of much of the mortality was disease. At a time when the average expenditure on food accounted for over 65 percent of the income of the laboring populations, such groups were always vulnerable to price increases and a consequent diminution of their dietary intake. The degree to which malnutrition gives rise to vulnerability to disease is another complicating factor but one for which there exists a prima facie case to answer.

This is not the arena in which to debate the possible causes of the Little Ice Age, other than to note that in this "pre-industrial" age control was exercised by factors in addition to the greenhouse gases that dominate public thinking in the early twenty-first century. Solar variation is an important element, and the quiescence of the sun during the Maunder Minimum between approximately 1645 and 1715, a time when sunspot activity seems to have all but ceased, is held to be a significant factor in the abiding and extreme coolness of that same period (Beckman and Mahony, 1998; Eddy, 1976). Also of importance were the volcanic eruptions of the period. The atmospheric dust veils created by such events could lead to global and regional cooling of the order of up to a degree, and cause serious local disruption, although the effects rarely extend beyond 24 months of the eruption. The 1780s were years of notable volcanic activity (Lamb, 1970) and of anomalous weather patterns. Significant eruptions occurred in Iceland in 1783 (Eldeyjar, Lakigígar, and Skapta Jökull), Hekla erupted in 1784, Vesuvius in 1785, 1787, and 1790, and Etna in 1787, to which can be added a number of equally large eruptions elsewhere in the world whose dust veils embraced the planet. The economy of Iceland suffered immediate consequences, but other areas were not spared, and ash falls in northern Scotland were sufficient to destroy crops, while further afield in Holland the sulfurous atmosphere also reduced crop yields. Stothers (1996) describes the spread of the dust cloud, citing evidence from such distant locations as Budapest, Rome, and the Middle East. The results were no less dramatic in central Europe and the winter of 1783/4 was the sixth coldest in the Prague record, followed in 1785 by the coldest spring on record in Europe. Dust was noted in Prague within weeks of the eruption on June 6, 1783. Such falls of acid aerosols, dust, and the concentrations of associated gases were widespread and were known as "dry fogs." These events may have had results other than those of reducing crop yields, and Witham and Oppenheimer (2005) have suggested that were two peaks of mortality, one in August and September of 1783, and the other in January and February of 1784, that might have accounted for over 19,000 deaths in Britain. Gratton et al. (2005) make similar claims for mortality peaks in France and the Low Countries.

The longer-term, climatic, results of such large volumes of dust being discharged into the atmosphere were also significant. Písek and Brázdil (2006) have presented evidence for summer cooling and winter warming in the two to three years following such eruptions, but the picture is by no means consistent. There is evidence also (Kington, 1988a) that the normal westerly circulation of the European mid-latitudes began to break down in this decade. The current average is over 90 westerly days per year, but in 1785 it fell to just 45. July 1783 was the warmest in the central England temperature series until the recent years of global warming, but there were also some very cold winters in 1784 and 1785. The spring of 1785 was exceptionally cold, prolonging an already severe winter. This was followed by drought, causing a forage crisis in French farms in particular. Rye and oat bread replaced wheat bread, which could be afforded only by the wealthiest in French society. At this time over half the income of a French peasant was spent on bread, and the economic strains imposed by the costs of the American War of Independence, which had concluded in September 1783, found the country ill prepared for such a series of agricultural failings.

Not long afterwards, the year 1788 was one of the driest on record with only 63 percent of normal rainfall. This picture of extreme weather was widespread across Europe and the winter of 1788/9 was again severe (figure 2), at a time when over 80 percent of the income of the poorest classes in France was spent on bread. As has been observed, "this is not to attribute the revolution which changed French society to the weather, but it can hardly be gainsaid that the weather intensified the pressures that released the explosion" (Lamb, 1982: 238). This is, however, an extreme case and the diversity of climate and of political and social consequences across Europe is so wide as to forbid helpful generalizations. For this reason, the following sections treat Europe in distinctive parts, each displaying different responses to similar, but by no means identical, climatological stimuli.

The British Isles: Adaptation and Evolution in a Maritime Setting

The term maritime will have one connotation amongst historians, another for climatologists. For the latter, it signifies a climate at once temperate yet often humid; one in which droughts occur but are neither regular nor frequent. Yet even within that definition lie shades of meteorological character that create the differences between the demands of Highland Scotland and the agricultural advantages offered by lowland England (Wheeler and Mayes, 1997). In all areas, however, the first three decades of the eighteenth century were a time of increasing warmth and recovery from the rigors of the closing decades of the previous century, particularly in Scotland, where the marginal character of much agrarian enterprise left it always vulnerable to even small shifts of climate. In the 1690s the harvest failed for seven years in a row, and at one stage it was reported that 20 percent of the population had been reduced to begging. Others removed to Ulster to escape the agricultural disaster of their homeland. Not without good reason these times were known in Scotland as "the ill years of King William's reign." How far such impositions weakened the Scottish economy and reduced its political will, perhaps paving the way for the Act of Union in 1707, can only speculated upon. As a measure of the abiding coolness of this period, travelers to Scotland often noted permanent snow on the Cairngorm summits. In 1771 Thomas Pennant recorded on a visit to the highlands that "many of them [were] topped with perpetual snow" (2000: 82). This intrepid traveler also noted that a local laird not far from Dingwall "holds the forest from the crown by a very whimsical tenure, that of delivering a snowball on any day of the year that is demanded . . . for snow lies in the chasms of Ben Wyvis in the form of a glaciere through the year" (2000: 108). This remarkable persistence of snow, perhaps ice also, suggests temperatures some 2 degrees Celsius lower than those that prevail today.

From this low point the agricultural sector began to grow during the first half of the eighteenth century. It has been suggested (Michaelowa, 2000) that the average rate of growth was 0.6 per cent between 1700 and 1760, slowing to 0.1 percent over the following 20 years. At the same time the numbers of livestock increased, as did their average weight (Deane and Cole, 1962), and the weight of livestock sold at Smithfield doubled during the century. Such developments must not be attributed exclusively the general climatic improvement of the times. In the same century agricultural practices were improved by the efforts of, amongst others, Lord Townshend and Thomas Coke. But these were not years of unremitting growth. There were setbacks when climate failed to provide the necessary warmth or moisture and Hoskins (1968) identified 1709, 1740, and 1759 as being particularly troublesome. The cold conditions of 1740 had immediate consequences. Livestock prices rose in response to the failure to provide fodder, while riots occurred as grain was being moved for export (Charlesworth, 1983). Yet even this catastrophe was partly offset by the diversification that had taken place in English agriculture. Had wheat been the overwhelmingly dominant cereal crop its loss in the ground over the winter of 1739/40 would have disastrous. Fortunately, barley and oats were also popular and were sown in the spring, thereby offsetting the loss of the winter wheat. It is interesting to note that France, with less ability to diversify, suffered more under an almost identical climatic regime.

The second half of the century revealed little tendency to marked or continued warmth, and it was rainfall that lent character to these 50 years. The decade 1751 to 1760 provided 10 wet summers with an overall average rainfall some 25 percent greater than that for the present day. The periods 1763–72 and 1775–84 also provided summers some 15 percent wetter than might today be anticipated. But it was only in marginal areas of Scotland and Ireland that crop failures were severe. That of 1783 was notable, and in Stirlingshire the unripened corn was buried beneath the winter's first snow on October 31, but this was a coolness aggravated by the great volcanic eruptions in Iceland noted above that cast their gloomy veil of dust over much of northwest Europe.

The problems of Scotland's climate were intensified by oceanic as well as atmospheric changes. The seventeenth and eighteenth centuries saw the southward extension of cold Arctic water to replace the warmer waters of tropical origin – the so-called North Atlantic Drift – more commonly associated with the seas around the north of the British Isles. The purely climatic consequence of this shift was to rob the region of much of the warmth otherwise derived from the Atlantic waters, with the result that the temperature contrast between southern England and Scotland was increased. This had the further consequence of creating a situation in which Atlantic depressions became stormier and more active. The "Great Storm" of December 1703, described by Defoe (1704) and more recently by Brayne (2002) and Wheeler (2003), was but one of a number of severe events; Lamb (1991) provides a detailed list of these occurrences. The storm of Christmas 1717 claimed 11,000 lives around the margins of the North Sea. Further severe storms punctuated the following decades, but the 1790s were remarkable for the number of extreme events: 1791 (with two), 1792 (with four), and 1795. Although they were episodic in character, the loss of life that they caused (an estimated 8,000 killed in the 1703 storm) and coastal flooding with damage to housing, farmland, and stock, had notable short-term consequences for those unlucky enough to experience them. The Great Storm of 1703 is estimated top have caused £2 million of damage in London alone. But they mark events and conditions that were short-lived and episodic in character; after this conditions returned to the climatic norms that had prevailed previously. It is, therefore, difficult to gauge their more enduring influence on the economy, although the lack of evidence suggests them to have been transitory in this respect. It should not be forgotten that these storms differ in degree, but not kind, from the hundred or more cyclonic systems that cross northwest Europe each year in what is one of the world's stormiest and most unsettled climatic regions.

Iceland and Scandinavia: The Challenge of Ice and Cold

It is perhaps not surprising that in a cool period, the northern latitudes should suffer to a marked degree. Yet the problems that beset communities in these outermost reaches of Europe were even greater than might be expected. It is fortunate that both Norway and Iceland are well documented in respect of agricultural activities in the eighteenth century. In Norway the *landskyld* (land rent) could not be charged without official assessment and the value was fixed as a proportion of the farm's yield. The documents relating to these assessments have survived and provide a vivid picture of decline and crisis in eighteenth-century Norway in the face of climatic and environmental change. Grove and Battagal (1980) have provided a study of the records from the Sunnfjord Figderi region of western Norway, the results of which apply equally to other areas. *matrikkel* (general tax) commissions of inquiry were held in 1667 and again in 1724, the results of which reveal that environmental decline has already set in across the region, but the 1740s seem to have been years of unprecedented catastrophe here as elsewhere in Europe, with 1743 being notably inclement and producing heavy rains and consequent landslides. Cattle and fodder crops were the key agrarian elements. Regrettably the hay production was not itemized, but the cattle population in this period fell by about 20 percent, although this decline varied from sub-region to sub-region. Remission of taxes (*avtak*) could be applied for on the basis of damage by floods, rockfalls, and advancing glaciers to farmland and buildings, although not on the basis of poor weather alone, and here the evidence of widespread problems is unambiguous and assessments of tax reductions of up to 50 percent were not unknown. The difficulties tended to be worse in the upland, more marginal, areas and less marked on the coast, but nowhere was immune to environmental threats. Whereas the loss of livestock might be attributed directly to climatic change and cooling, which reduced the growing season, lower fodder production led to reductions in the capacity for winter stall feeding. The cooling climate not only lowered the altitudinal limits on agriculture, it also, in a picture to be recreated in the mountainous areas of central Europe, encouraged glacier advance, landslides, rockfall and floods (over frozen ground). Matters were most serious in the period 1740–60, with floods being a common cause for seeking *avtak*. The crop failures of 1741, 1742, 1748, and 1773 seem to have been associated with mortality peaks, and while some deaths may have been the direct consequence of starvation many were the result of disease, such as typhus and dysentery, that found a vulnerable population at these times. Thereafter conditions seem to have stabilized, although at a lower level of agricultural activity than had prevailed a century before.

The corresponding situation in Iceland (Ogilvie, 1980) was similar, but exacerbated by the yet more marginal and vulnerable setting of this society. Not only is the island sensitive to modest changes of climate but the latter is cold enough to support the island's ice cap with the associated risks of flooding and of glacier advance that were familiar in Norway. The volcanic eruptions noted earlier add a final, equally unwelcome, aspect to the gamut of environmental risk in the form of lava, ash, and earth tremors. Moreover, Iceland's northern coast in particular lies beyond the immediate reach of the warm waters of the North Atlantic Drift, leaving the area subject to lower sea and coastal temperatures and to occasional freezing that rendered the all-important coastal trade and fishing all but impossible.

In common with Norway, the 1750s were among the worst years of the century. The combination of cool conditions with high precipitation encouraged ice cap accumulation and glacier advance. Farms were abandoned and sea ice persisted late into each year, reaching a climax in 1756 when the sheriff of Húnavatnssýsla, whose jurisdiction extended to northwest Iceland, observed: "The sea was covered by ice the whole summer and this has prevented all fishing and all delivery of foodstuffs from Copenhagen and also affected grass crops and it has not been possible to harvest the little which has been grown because of the continual fog, sleet and rainy weather" (B.S., 1756). Starvation was not uncommon and crime rates increased as families found themselves unable to meet their needs from the meager products of their agricultural activities. The economy was based on livestock and winter stall feeding, and the succession of poor and wet summers that marked the period led to the loss of livestock either by enforced slaughter or starvation as fodder supplies failed to meet the winter needs calculated (in modern day needs) as 3 cubic feet of fodder per sheep, 10 to 15 cubic meters per horse, and 35 to 40 cubic meters per cow.

Milder conditions in the 1770s were not, however, sustained and the 1780s were arguably (Ogilvie, 1992) the coldest of the century, a decade made worse by the eruption of the volcano Lakagígar (Laki) in 1783, which cast a dust and ash veil over the island that poisoned plant life and led to loss of animal and human life on a huge scale. It is estimated that 9,000 died of starvation in its aftermath. It was this same dust that destroyed the crops in northern Scotland that same year, while the temperature of the northern hemisphere was is estimated to have fallen by 1 degree Celsius.

Fishing was an important and traditional component of the economic system of Iceland, providing food not only for domestic consumption but also for export. The incursion of sea ice, most common along the north coast, but much less frequent to the south, limited the possibility of fishing. Such obvious difficulties obscure a more profound consequence of environmental changes at the time. While acknowledging the problem of manning the fishing boats after the smallpox outbreak of 1708–9, climatic conditions also played a significant role, with the southwards encroachment of cold Arctic waters lowering sea surface temperatures everywhere. The incursion of cold Arctic waters had a direct cooling effect on the climate, adversely affecting the cod (*Gadus spp.* – the principal catch for Iceland fisherman). Cod require sea temperatures in the order of 4 to 7 degrees Celsius in order to reproduce (Woodhead and Woodhead, 1959). As sea temperatures fell below this critical range, stocks moved southwards and out of easy reach of Iceland, thereby inflicting an additional blow to an already beleaguered agrarian system. Such evidence suggests that the northern seas as far south as the Faroes were dominated by Arctic water and were inhospitable to cod for much of the century and well into the following one. One official record from western Iceland in 1744 reports that "everywhere the cod catch was the worst that people could remember for many years . . . in most places most boats did not catch more than about 10 fish and in many places less" (cited in Grove, 1988).

Given this background, it is scarcely surprising that the population of Iceland should have fallen dramatically during the century. The 1703 census estimated the population to be 50,358. The smallpox epidemic that followed is thought to have reduced it by one-third, although the 1734 census gives a total of 43,377, suggesting a recovery from the earlier decline. This demographic trend continued through the more temperate years of the 1730s and 1740s, rising to 48,000 in 1755. The climatic deterioration of this decade was soon registered in mortality, however, and the 1759 estimate was 42,822. A recovery then took place, but the devastation of the 1780s saw the population plummet to 38,363 in 1786.

Western and Central Europe: Changing Climate in a Continental Setting

The general trend of climate in central Europe followed that for other parts of the continent. A steady recovery until 1740 from the devastation of the 1690s was followed by cold years of the early 1740s, the 1750s, and the 1780s. Yet the years of recovery were by no means without incident. In central Europe the 1720s and 1730s were marked by wet summers, while brief periods of recovery were observed in Switzerland in 1759–63 and again in 1778–84. Cold and wet conditions dominated between these spells, and the cool summers were of critical importance because the winter snows did not melt, thus allowing the alpine glaciers to advance into farm and grazing land. The period 1769–71 was particularly difficult, with the staples of wheat, milk, and potatoes being in short supply and famine setting in where the problem was most acute. Weather diaries from Bern and Zurich add some statistical substance to these observations. Between 1705 and 1714 snow covered the ground on only 42 days on average, but this rose to 111 days in the cold winters of 1730–1, 1769–70, and 1788–9. Such data suggest a mean temperature some 1.5 degrees Celsius lower than those that prevailed for much of the twentieth century. Springs tended to be cool, with winter extending well into March. The protracted snow cover allowed the parasite *Fusarium nivale* to flourish and attack cereal crops to devastating effect.

Meanwhile, for western Europe, and for France in particular, the work of Le Roy Ladurie (1972), using the dates of grape harvest, has offered a detailed picture of temperature fluctuations over the centuries from the mid-1300s onwards. This series is of particular value as grape harvest dates – at least until modern times, with new technologies – provided unusually high statistical correlations with summer temperatures. The grape harvest dates have also been shown to corroborate the instrumental record of Manley's central England temperature series. In common with other regions of Europe, the temperature fluctuations take the character of groups of warm or cool years and not, predominantly, of individual years. Ladurie identified 1711–13, 1739–52, and 1765–77 as times when springs and summers were cool. On the other hand, 1718–37, 1757–63 and 1778–83 were periods of relative warmth. Nevertheless, grape harvest dates reflect only the spring and summer (growing season conditions) and Ladurie fails to note, for example, the catastrophic winter of 1708–9, when it is estimated that 100,000 died in France alone. Nonetheless, even here the picture varied from region to region and was less severe in those areas with more diversified agricultural economies such as Brittany.

The early 1770s witnessed severe subsistence crises in central Europe as a series of cold and wet autumns and springs, beginning as early as the late 1760s, with late snows and cool summers, caused grain prices to rise dramatically. In the German states and Austria the price of cereals rose by 111 percent, raising the specter of famine, disease, and mortality. In Bohemia the cost of rye rose by a factor of 3 between 1769 and 1771, and of oats and barley by a factor of 4. This led to severe social dislocation as unemployment, begging, and crime all increased. Pfister and Brázdil (2006) estimate that Bohemia's population fell by 250,000 (10 percent of the total) and that it took 13 years for a full demographic recovery, forming a bleak a backdrop to the serf uprising of 1775. But, importantly, the same authors also draw attention to the less dramatic responses in the nearby districts of Bern, where social vulnerability was mitigated by measures such as poor relief and by a better system of market integration that allowed the export of grain in times of plenty, but its import when required by internal demand. The mercantilist policies of the Habsburg domains, that included the Czech lands, prevented such freedom of trade.

These data can be supplemented by the growing volume of instrumental observations gathered in France from the 1780s under the auspices of the Société Royale de Médecine that established one of the world's first organized networks of meteorological observatories (Kington, 1988a). With some justification, both from the point of view of data availability and of its historical timing, Ladurie could claim that the 15 years that preceded the French Revolution are amongst the most interesting periods for the historian of the vine and of climate. The years from 1778 to 1781 witnessed hot summers and excellent grape harvests, not only in France but also in the nearby Rhineland and German vineyards. The following year saw a marked decline when a cold and wet summer took its toll. The following year was no better, and in Champagne, for example, the yield was 60 percent below normal. A pattern was then set for poor summers with diminished productivity not only in grapes but across the full spectrum of agricultural activities. The year 1788 offered only a temporary respite for wine production but, and as a reminder of the complexity of connections between climate and agriculture, this was a poor year for wheat, the warmth coming too early for this crop. Then came the tragedy of 1789 when the winter and spring proved to be exceptionally cold, with matters scarcely improved by an indifferent and wet summer. How far the climatic events and consequent agricultural failures of these years contributed to the French Revolution is a question that may never be satisfactorily answered.

The Mediterranean World: Water-Limited Agrarian Systems

Climatic conditions in most of northern and western Europe are broadly similar in being mid-latitude and humid in character. The driving seasonal force is temperature variation. These considerations no longer prevail when the Alps or Pyrenees have been crossed and the Mediterranean region beckons. Here the rainfall, usually so plentiful to the north, is a commodity to be cherished and water supply a matter of greatest social and political importance.

With the exception of the mountainous areas of Italy and Spain and of the high Meseta of the latter, temperatures remain above the growing limits for most plants (5°C) throughout the year, and it is rainfall that marks the progress of the seasons. Summer is the dry season, while spring, winter, or autumn are the times of year when rain might be anticipated. The impression provided by the mean annual figures, many of which are comparable with those of northern European sites, are deceptive because they disguise the seasonal pattern and the huge losses to evaporation and transpiration that often leave less than 25 percent of the rainfall to meet local water demands, of which agriculture is commonly the most important. Many agrarian activities tend to be circumscribed by water availability, and from Roman, and more certainly Moorish, times, irrigation schemes of a complexity and sophistication not found elsewhere in western Europe have created some unique landscapes and administrative structures, including long-standing institutions such as famous Tribunal de las Aguas de la Vega de Valencia. This venerable foundation dates from at least the medieval period and governs water supply to the many irrigated holdings in the *huerta* that still exist around the city (Glick, 1970). Historical climatic studies have yet to exploit fully the documentary sources available in Spain and Italy, and elsewhere they have scarcely been examined in any detail; the study by Font Tullot (1988) of Spain's climatic history is uniquely comprehensive for the region. He points to some themes that Iberia shares with its northern neighbors: the cold winters of 1708–9 and 1716–17, with warming then characterizing the next three decades as Spain also began to recover from the most intense phase of the Little Ice Age. Cold conditions returned, as they did elsewhere, in the great winter of 1739–40, and in a description reminiscent of those who portrayed in words the famous frost fairs on the Thames, Rico Sinobas observed of the effect of great frost on the river Pisuerga in Valladolid: "throughout the river remained frozen to a great depth, people crossed it as if it were a field. They danced, took teas and played games" (1854: 25). Such cold conditions, which continued to plague the country for much of the century, brought heavy snows, exacerbated by Spain's mountainous character and generally elevated nature. The century overall was characterized by storms and frequent heavy rainfall. Barriendos Vallve and Martín-Vide (1998) found that the Mediterranean littoral was particularly subject to severe rainfall events between 1760 and 1800. In Andalusia, Rodrigo et al. (1999) have demonstrated again that it is rainfall, either through an abundance or through deficiency, that exercises the principal control over agriculture. They suggest that the poor harvests of 1750, 1751, and 1752 were the result of drought, while those of 1764, 1765, 1768, and 1770 were a consequence of floods and excessive rainfall. Summers were, as always, dry, but widespread droughts were less frequent than has been the case since, although that of the temporary warm phase of 1749–53 stands out. Local droughts occurred, and that of 1718–25 in Aragon was severe enough to all but destroy local agriculture. There were similar local problems in the Mediterranean coastal areas and Balearics in 1772–4, but the Kingdom of Naples escaped the worst consequences of the subsistence crisis that marked at that time the lands to the north of the Alps.

Severe weather doubtless caused problems, but the general availability of water did much to promote agriculture in the years following the uncertainties of the War of the Spanish Succession. It might also have provided an important basis for the developments brought about by the reforming Charles III (r. 1759–88). It was, however, generally recognized that Spain's agricultural system was backward in terms of capital, land tenure, and technology. This left it always vulnerable to the natural vicissitudes of climate to a degree unknown in other more developed agrarian economies. Charles III's reform moved some way to improving the situation (Vicens Vives, 1969), but Spain, and indeed other Mediterranean nations, continued to labor under this handicap of environmental vulnerability.

Conclusion

The political and cultural diversity that characterized Europe is matched by its environmental, geographic, and climatic divisions, and the foregoing case studies and examples warn against offering generalizations concerning the interactions between these physical factors and social systems. This is not, however, to deny that such connections exist. Then, as now, societies at all stages of social and economic development can find themselves vulnerable to the seemingly capricious, sometimes devastating, consequences of extreme weather and climate. As a measure of the continuity of the vulnerability of societies to natural disasters, the victims of famine, flood, and drought in eighteenth-century Europe would have identified with the residents of the more exposed districts of New Orleans in the aftermath of hurricane Katrina in 2005.

Bibliography

Angot, A., *Etude sur les Vendanges en France* (Paris, 1885).

B.S. (Bréf til Stiftamtmanns úr Húnavatnssýsla 1736–1792) (National Library, Reykjavík).

Barriendos Vallve, M. and M. Martín-Vide, "Secular climatic oscillations as indicated by catastrophic floods in the Spanish Mediterranean coastal area (14th–19th centuries)." *Climatic Change*, 38 (1998), 473–91.

Beckman, J. E. and T. J. Mahoney, "The Maunder Minimum and climate change: have historical records aided current research?," *Library and Information Services in Astronomy III, ASP Conference Series*, 153 (1998), 212–17.

Brayne, M., *The Greatest Storm: Britain's Night of Destruction, November 1703* (Stroud, 2002).

Brázdil, R., "Reconstructions of past climates from historical sources in the Czech lands," in P. Jones et al. (eds.), *Climatic Variations and Forcing Mechanisms of the Last 2000 years* (Berlin, 1996).

Brázdil, R., H. Valášek, and J. Macková, "Climate of the Czech lands during the 1780s in light of the daily weather records of Parson Karel Bernard Hein of Hodonice (southwestern Moravia): comparison of documentary and instrumental data," *Climatic Change*, 60 (2003), 297–327.

Brázdil, R., H. Valášek, Z. Sviták, and J. Macková, *History of Weather and Climate in the Czech Lands*, vol. 5 (Brno, 2002).

Brázdil, R., C. Pfister, H. Wanner, H. von Storch, and J. Luterbacher, "Historical climatology in Europe – the state of the art," *Climatic Change*, 70 (2005), 363–430.

Camuffo, D., "History of the long series of daily air temperature in Padova (1725–1998), in D. Camuffo and P. D. Jones (eds.), *Improved Understanding of Past Climatic Variability from Early Daily European Instrumental Sources* (Dordrecht, 2002).

Charlesworth, A., *An Atlas of Rural Protests in Britain 1548–1900* (London, 1983).
Deane, P. and W. A. Cole, *British Economic Growth 1688–1959* (Cambridge, 1962).
Defoe, D., *The Storm: or, a collection of the most Remarkable casualties and Disasters which happe'd in the late Dreadful Tempest by both Sea and Land* (London, 1704).
Dufour, M. L., "Problème de la variation de climat," *Bulletin de Société Vaudoise des Sciences naturelles*, 10 (1870), 359–556.
Durkheim, E., *The Rules of Sociological Method; and Selected Texts on Sociology and its Method* (1882; London, 2002).
Eddy, J., "The Maunder Minimum," *Science*, 192 (1976), 1189–1202.
Fagan, B., *The Little Ice Age: How Climate Made History 1300–1850* (New York, 2000).
Fogel, R. W., "Second thoughts on the European escape from hunger, famines, chronic malnutrition and mortality rates," in S. Osmani (ed.), *Nutrition and Poverty* (Oxford, 1992).
Font Tullot, I., *Historia del clima de España: cambios climaticos y sus causas* (Madrid, 1988).
Glaser, R., *Klimageschichte Mitteleuropas. 1000 Jahre Wetter, Klima, Katastrophen* (Darmstadt, 2001).
Glick, T. F., *Irrigation and Society in Medieval Valencia* (Cambridge, MA, 1970).
Gratton, J., R. Rabartin, S. Self, and T. Thordarson, "Volcanic air pollution and mortality in France 1783–1784," *Comptes rendus Geosciences*, 337 (2005), 641–51.
Grove, J., *The Little Ice Age* (London, 1988).
Grove, J. and A. Battagel, "Tax records as an index of Little Ice Age environmental and economic deterioration, from Sunnfjord Fogderi, western Norway 1667–1815," in C. D. Smith and M. Parry (eds.), *Consequences of Climatic Change* (Nottingham, 1980).
Hoskins, W. G., "Harvest fluctuations and English economic history," *Agricultural History*, 12 (1968), 28–46.
Ingold, T., "Culture and the perception of the environment," in D. Parkin and E. Croll (eds.), *Bush Base, Forest Farm: Culture, Environment and Development* (London, 1992).
Kington, J., *The Weather of the 1780s over Europe* (Cambridge, 1988a).
Kington, J., *The Weather Journals of a Rutland Squire* (Oakham, 1988b).
Lamb, H. H., "Volcanic dust in the atmosphere: with a chronology and assessment of its meteorological significance," *Phil. Trans. Royal Society of London*, series A, 266 (1970), 425–533.
Lamb, H. H., *Climate, History and the Modern World* (London, 1982).
Lamb, H. H., *Weather, Climate and Human Affairs* (London, 1988).
Lamb, H. H., *Historic Storms of the North Sea, British Isles and North West Europe* (Cambridge, 1991).
Le Roy Ladurie, E., *Times of Feast, Times of Famine: A History of Climate since the Year 1000* (London, 1972).
Manley, G., "Snowfall in Britain over the past 300 years," *Weather*, 24 (1969), 428–37.
Manley, G., "Central England temperatures: monthly means 1659 to 1973," *Quarterly Journal of the Royal Meteorological Society*, 100 (1974), 389–405.
Michaelowa, A., "The impact of short-term climate change on British and French agriculture and population in the first half of the 18th century," in P. D. Jones et al. (eds.) *History and Climate: Memories of the Future* (Dordrecht, 2000).
Ogilvie, A. E. J., "Climate and economy in eighteenth century Iceland," in C. D. Smith and M. Parry (eds.), *Consequences of Climatic Change* (Nottingham, 1980).
Ogilvie, A. E. J., "Documentary evidence for changes in the climate of Iceland. A.D. 1500 to 1800," in R. S. Bradley and P. D. Jones (eds.), *Climate Since A.D. 1500* (London, 1992).
Oliver-Smith, A., "Theorizing vulnerability in a globalized world: a political ecological perspective," in G. Bankoff, G. Frerks, and D. Hilhorst (eds.), *Mapping Vulnerability: Disasters, Developments and People* (London 2004).

Parry, M. L., "Climatic change and the agricultural frontier: a research strategy," in T. M. L. Wigley et al. (eds.), *Climate and History: Studies in Past Climates and their Impact on Man* (Cambridge, 1981).

Parry, M. L. and T. R. Carter, "The effects of climatic variation on agricultural risk," *Climatic Change*, 7 (1985), 95–110.

Pennant, T., *A Tour in Scotland 1769* (repr. Edinburgh, 2000).

Pfister, C., *Das Klima der Schweiz von 1525–1860 und seine Bedeutung in der Geschichte von Bevölkerung und Landwirtschaft* (2 vols., Bern, 1984).

Pfister, C., *Klimageschichte der Schweiz 1525–1860. Das Klima der Schweiz von 1525–1860 und seine Bedeutung in der Geschichte von Bevölkerung und Landwirtschaft* (Stuttgart, 1988).

Pfister, C. and R. Brázdil, "Social vulnerability to climate in the Little Ice Age: an example from central Europe in the early 1770s," *Climate of the Past*, 2 (2006), 115–29.

Písek, J. and R. Brázdil, "Responses of large volcanic eruptions in the instrumental and documentary climatic data over central Europe," *International Journal of Climatology*, 26 (2006), 439–59.

Post, J. D., "Nutritional status and mortality in eighteenth century Europe," in L. F. Newman (ed.) *Hunger in History* (Oxford, 1990).

Rico Sinobas, M., *Memoria sobre las causas meteorológicofisicas que producen las constants sequías de Murcia y Almeria* (Madrid, 1854).

Rodrigo, F. S., M. J. Esteban-Parra, D. Pozo-Vázquez, and Y. Castro-Díez, "A 500-year precipitation record in southern Spain," *International Journal of Climatology,* 19 (1999), 1233–53.

Stothers, R. B., "The great dry fog of 1783," *Climatic Change*, 32 (1996), 79–89.

Vicens Vives, J., *An Economic History of Spain* (Princeton, 1969).

Wheeler, D., "The Great Storm of November 1703: a new look at the seamen's records." *Weather*, 58 (2003), 419–27.

Wheeler, D. and J. Mayes, *Regional Climates of the British Isles* (London, 1997).

Witham, C. S. and C. Oppenheimer, "Mortality in England during the 1783–4 Laki Craters eruption," *Bulletin of Volcanology*, 67 (2005), 15–26.

Woodhead, P. M. J. and A. D. Woodhead, "The effects of low temperatures on the physiology and distribution of cod *Gadus morhua* L. in the Barents Sea," *Proceedings of the Zoological Society of London*, 133 (1959), 181–99.

CHAPTER TWO

Gender

DEBORAH SIMONTON

Introduction

> Women have generally quicker perception; men have juster sentiments . . . Women often speak to shine or to please men; men, to convince or confute. Women admire what is brilliant, men what is solid. (More, 1777: 9)

> The Sexes have now little other apparent Distinction, beyond that of Person and Dress: Their peculiar characteristic Manners are confounded and lost: The one sex having advanced into *Boldness*, as the other have sunk into *Effeminacy*. (Brown, 1757: 51)

This chapter asks questions about how eighteenth-century Europe fashioned ideas about what it meant to be male or female and how concepts of masculinity and femininity shaped the ways people understood and constructed their society. It reflects the emergence of gender as a key tool of analysis within history and the increasing tendency for historians to pay attention to the changing cultural meanings of masculinity and femininity in the histories they write. More and more topics previously seen as gender-neutral are being radically rethought with the understanding that not only did both men and women shape the past, but also that their relationships and the construction of gendered identities were central to how the past was fashioned and understood.

The intellectual currents of the eighteenth century were fundamental to disturbing, discussing, and articulating a range of conceptions of gender. Alongside shifts in ideas about masculinity and femininity, men's and women's lived experience demonstrated the ways that people understood and negotiated gender with respect to the economic, socio-political, and intimate contexts within which they operated. We should not be so sanguine as to expect that a single model of male and female existed, nor that a consensus about sexual difference emerged. Ideas about femininity, masculinity, and gendered relationships in eighteenth-century European society were constructed from a range of materials and understood on a number of levels. Thus, lived experience and custom merged with older ideas and with newer thought

A Companion to Eighteenth-Century Europe, First Edition. Edited by Peter H. Wilson.
© 2014 John Wiley & Sons, Ltd. Published 2014 by John Wiley & Sons, Ltd.

emerging from the Enlightenment to create multilayered views of what it meant to be male and female.

Gender and Historiography

Gender has become an important prism for articulating the past across diverse strands of historical inquiry. In particular, gender history owes a debt to women's history, but also to debates in literary theory and anthropology. Of course, women's history has its own long past, the early stages of which fell into the "women worthies" tradition, but also produced the seminal work of Alice Clark (1982), Ivy Pinchbeck (1930), and Léon Abensour (1923). From the late 1960s, the feminist movement, with its interest in recovering women's past, gave impetus to women's history. The feminist political context was a positive influence, questioning the creation and context of "sex-roles" and recognizing that gender itself was an unstable category. The thriving social history of the same era, particularly the French Annales school, was an important "bedfellow" where reclaiming history for the common people found resonance in restoring "ordinary" women to history. Thus this pioneer generation questioned narratives that denied women historical agency or dismissed their experience and activities as ahistorical.

A central concern was how women's subordinate status had developed, and how historical oppression appeared to derive from and be reproduced in institutionalized and personal domination of men, i.e. patriarchy. However, "the trouble with patriarchy" was that it seemed to imply fatalistic submission, allowing no room for women's agency and defiance. It did not reflect the "kaleidoscope of forms within which men and women have encountered one another" (Rowbotham, 1981). This concern led to developing a more historically grounded understanding of patriarchy and to recognition that patriarchy is the product of constructing gender, which ascribed social meaning to roles and prescribed patterns of sexual dominance and subordination (Alexander and Taylor, 1981). The emphasis on patriarchy, however, posed a different problem for masculinity. If men were perennially seen as oppressors, it became especially difficult to theorize a positive reading of masculinity and the construction of maleness (Segal, 2006). The idea of patriarchy as "father rule" was indispensable not only because men wielded power in the family but because it was important for their self-respect that they do so (Tosh, 1999: 3).

As women's history became more sophisticated, it became more sensitive to context, plurality, and nuance, and especially gained a greater recognition and appreciation of difference. It shifted away from "compensatory history" and concern with victimization to more fully explore female agency. It also turned to poststructuralist approaches, placing greater stress on relationships between representation and social reality. Drawing attention to meanings, symbols, and rituals, historians were more able to question categories like "woman," "man," and gender, and to challenge such apparently stable categories. Thus women's history issued a radical challenge to historians, "to write a history that credits women's and men's lives" and that began "to shake up many fundamental assumptions in the wider discipline concerning matters of causality, significance, the frames for historical periods, turning points, and markers as well as the biological basis of sex difference" (Quataert, 2007: x).

Indeed, from the outset, the issue of gender and constructed sex-roles was a central concern. As Natalie Davis wrote over 30 years ago in a seminal article, "we should be interested in the history of both men and women, that we should not be working only on the subjected sex any more than a historian of class can focus exclusively on peasants" (Davis, 1976: 88). A decided shift in the 1980s articulated gender as a lens into the past. Joan Scott's "Gender: a useful category of analysis" (Scott, 1986) marked the importance of this move, as did the launch of *Gender & History* in 1989.

Increasingly historians like Scott, Davis, Arlette Farge, Lynn Hunt, Bonnie Smith, Leonore Davidoff, and Jean Quataert showed that culturally mediated conceptions of gender established the frameworks in which society operated. Differences of class, nation, locality, age, sexuality, motivation, and access to power have a crucial impact on the ways that gender operates. Changing conceptions of sexual difference and ideals of masculinity and femininity informed the gendered nature of work, public life, and political activity. Instead of seeing sexual differences between men and women as the reflection of purely natural biological differences, they accepted the notion that these differences were socially constructed, and therefore varied with time, place, culture, class, and ethnicity. The process of de-essentializing maleness and femaleness by underlining and articulating their historical construction enabled historians to demonstrate that they were malleable, changeable, and historical (Downs, 2004). Gender was reformulated from a shorthand for "woman" to a comprehensive category of analysis that examined the social organization of sexual difference and the profound relationships of power (Scott, 1986, 1988).

One of the effects of the shift to gender history was to stimulate interest in men's history. As historians reconceptualized women as a socio-cultural group, "men also [became] visible as sexual beings" (Bock, 1989: 10). As feminism posed a challenge to male power, the need to rewrite men's stories also became pressing, since the cultural constructions of masculinity were not only couched in language that required rethinking but also no longer reflected men's lived experiences. Normative masculinity had become a "measuring stick" based on a dominant ideal of power and superiority, which was not only stereotypical but also was also not historicized nor culturally situated. Thus historians like John Tosh, Michael Roper, Philip Carter, Tim Hitchcock, and Robert Nye have challenged the model and developed sophisticated analyses of shifting perceptions of masculinity.

Women's history not only situates women in "society" but also comments on their relationships with men, while the converse is also true. Decoding masculinity furnishes insights into men's relationships with each other, as well as with women. Davis set the agenda: "Our goal is to discover the range in sex roles and in sexual symbolism in different societies and periods, to find out what meaning they had and how they functioned to maintain the social order or to promote change. . . . to explain why sex roles were sometimes tightly prescribed and sometimes fluid, sometimes markedly asymmetrical and sometimes more even" (Davis, 1976: 88).Thus, gender history challenges an approach where the discourse and the language are male and the narrative remains gender-blind.

Defining Gender

Definitions of gender in the eighteenth century were often ambivalent, drawing on a mixture of scientific thought and the Enlightenment but also inflected by established patterns of thinking which had at their base the ancient Judeo-Christian tradition that depicted women as evil and dangerous. While the socio-political issues raised by gender were of little interest to many, constructions of gender were central to the Enlightenment discourses. A fundamental contradiction rested on the dichotomy that, "the Enlightenment promised universal rights, and then redefined those rights in gendered terms" (Caine and Sluga, 2000: 3). At the same time gender itself was a disruptive influence on the Enlightenment "project," so that great energy was spent on trying to rationalize the concept of universal rights with sexual difference. Rewriting the Enlightenment over the last 40 years has brought issues of gender into the light, and indeed has exposed the conundrums posed by gender (Goodman, 1998; Outram, 1995; Rendall, 2005: ch. 9; Tomaselli, 1985). The lack of coherence in Enlightenment discourses is important to gender: views of women's and men's natures, rights, and positions did not achieve a consensus nor project an agreed formulation. Based on Nature and science, and laced with received religion, eighteenth-century authors argued that men and women were "naturally different" and that these differences not only shaped their characters, but also suited each sex to specific activities and roles in society. A central difficulty, however, was the very slippery character of the term Nature itself, and throughout Enlightenment discourses it achieved a multiplicity of meanings. The "problem" of Nature thus lay at the heart of multiple definitions of gender, and the appeal to Nature, which was translated into a liberating appeal for the rights of "man," was interpreted very differently for women.

In many respects the voice of the Enlightenment was male and the discourse was masculine. Authors wrote from the basis of the "rights of man," in theory a universal principle, but which clearly was about men and specifically men like themselves; Rousseau explained in *Discourse on Inequality*: "It is about man that I have to speak, and the question I shall be examining teaches me that I shall be speaking to men" (Crampe-Casnabet, 1978: 319–20). The pervasiveness of a masculine conception of the Enlightenment is apparent from the positive association of masculine virtues with the intellectual qualities to be striven for and which characterized superior minds of both sexes: strength, resilience, and potency. Mary Wollstonecraft saw her times as a battleground between the "narrow opinions of superstition" versus "the enlightened sentiments of masculine and improved philosophy" (Wollstonecraft, 1989: 6–7). The voice of the Enlightenment was not only male, but the way of thinking had a muscularity that was perceived as masculine.

The Enlightenment created a public realm for the discussion and transformation of opinions – a place where men could escape from their role as subjects and gain autonomy in the exercise and exchange of their own opinions and ideas (Habermas, 1989: 11). Many male writers were engaged in claiming autonomy and legitimate intellectual space, in opposition to the established practice of patronage and hired dependency (Outram, 1995). Thus in the political, legal, and economic spheres, men actively reconstructed their world in their own image. Business was reconstructed as a male space, the male position as paterfamilias was more overtly theorized, and in politics and the workplace men more often articulated their status and authority.

The construction of masculinity relied on a male nature that came to embrace a set of "virile" qualities such as creative energy, endurance, capacity for invention, a taste for the rational, and a speculative intelligence. Male strength, physically and metaphorically, was a central element of the gender dichotomy. This "new man" was sensitive, generous of feeling, chivalrous, and morally, physically tough. As David Hume described,

> A man is lord in his own family . . . As nature has given man the superiority above woman, by endowing him with greater strength both of mind and body; it is his part to alleviate that superiority, as much as possible, by the generosity of his behaviour, and by a studied deference and complaisance for all her inclinations and opinions. . . . the male sex, among a polite people, discover their authority in a more generous, though not a less evident manner; by civility, by respect, by complaisance, and, in a word, by gallantry. (Hume, 1987: i, xiv, 40)

Masculinity therefore owed much to a notion of honor, which encompassed courage and daring but also include compassion and loyalty. Bourgeois men came to share this vision of honor and to identify with the personal values and virtues associated with masculinity (Nye, 1993: 16–17). The Enlightenment ideal of Nature was crucial in linking mind and body so that outward appearance became a measure of inner worth, "Give his body constant exercise, make it strong and healthy, in order to make him good and wise . . . make a man of him in strength, and he will soon be a man in reason" (Rousseau, 1974). The association of mind and body also placed higher value on physical beauty, so that the male body was to be an example of virility, strength, and courage, expressed through bearing and appearance (Mosse, 1998: 23), and echoes the distaste expressed by John Brown about men who degenerated into "effeminacy." Achievement by merit became central to male self-identity, and a central tenet was the imperative to enhance family position. Thus marriage, acquisition, and inheritance strategies were fundamental to the ways that noble and bourgeois families strove to achieve status and honorability. Robert Forster (1980) has shown how the Depont family of La Rochelle moved in three generations from maritime merchants to *rentiers* and ennoblement. This rise was to be achieved by honorable practices, through self-denial, thrift, and self-discipline, so that "the claim to honor became . . . separable from the honorable behavior through which families strove for honorability" (Nye, 1993: 39).

Debate on the "natural woman" focused on female physical and mental capabilities and ultimately on her biological and social role as mother. Femininity was seen as primarily deriving logically from a unique and specific female nature, so that not only was she distinctive and different from man, but also she had her own "natural" roles and activities. Linking ideology with scientific discourses, women's "acknowledged delicacy and weakness of person" disqualified them from "heavy, robust activity" (Brown, 1765: 6). Thus a large body of literature designated the female as ideally suited for the domestic scene, and the domestic scene as their ideal world. Such writers not only set new limits to the powers and pursuits of women; they also added extremely durable theoretical justifications for existing legal, economic, social, and educational disabilities. On the one hand, the identification of women with an idealized domestic role defined the character of their activities; on the other, it appeared to enhance their image, sanctifying as virtues characteristics arising from their supposed weaknesses. Yet weakness, no matter how gloriously it was described, meant that women required not mates, but protectors. In assigning increasing importance to a refuge for women there was a strong current of sexual protection. Female timidity was ascribed as the basis for their modesty, which Brown called "an ingenuous fear of shame" (1765: 11). Paradoxically because women were "naturally" able to achieve a higher moral plane than men, they were often ascribed a special responsibility as arbiters of morality and virtue. This operated in two ways: in a private, domestic sense and in a more public, global sense. With growing emphasis on the importance of childhood in shaping adult character, mothers, or potential mothers, were charged with bringing up children according to Christian values and virtues. The emphasis on the proper moral education of children was also a reflection of the concern for posterity and the society as a whole. As the child is father to the man, so the woman was the mother of adult virtue.

During the century medical definitions of the gendered body influenced redefinition on male and female bodies so that "truths of biology" operated to replace "divinely ordained hierarchies or immemorial custom as the basis for the creation or distribution of power in relations between men and women." That is, the idea that the female body was the inverse of the male, and female organs of reproduction being seen as homologies of male equivalents, was gradually replaced by the view that male and female bodies were distinctly different (Laqueur, 1990: 193, 149–50). Importantly, biology and culture were seen as an entity, so that biological difference directly produced the social roles ascribed to each sex. Thus "[w]omen's capacity to bear and suckle children was taken to define their physical, psychological and social lives" (Jordanova, 1989: 29).

The *philosophes*' view of women is problematic, highly complicated, and not in the least uniform. Great controversy surrounded the new social role as wife and mother. Had the "natural law argument" initiated by Jaucourt in the *Encyclopédie* triumphed, potential existed to create a feminist agenda within Enlightenment thought. Instead, Rousseau, who stressed sexual difference and a female domestic role, exercised greater influence. Nevertheless, other writers held contradictory positions, so that Voltaire, Montesquieu, and Diderot did identify the discrepancy between laws that excluded women from positions in public life and the actual power women were capable of wielding. They argued for the common humanity of men and women, but retained a double standard of morality. While they justified women's familial role, all three depicted maternity as a temporary condition of her life (Outram, 1995). In the event, however, "woman" was not their central concern, so that voices like von Hippel, Condorcet, and Wollstonecraft remained isolated clarions. There were multiple readings of femininity, no one model informed female development, and prescription was not analogous to action.

The language of the Enlightenment thus expresses a tension in the concepts of male and female, and indeed, a great deal of effort focused on defining femininity in the eighteenth century. While many older, negative images of women receded, they were replaced by philosophical, medical, and scientific attempts to explain gendered social and cultural differences as "natural" and thus "right and inevitable" (Outram, 1995: 81). Ultimately the legacy of the Enlightenment for women is ambiguous. On the one hand, opening avenues of discourse, rethinking the origin and rights of "man," criticizing established and historical patterns of society and culture, and insisting on freedom made a significant contribution to shaping society and culture. At the same time, women's engagement with the process and the language used to define women and woman's place were far less liberating.

Clearly these newer formulations had their heart in the bourgeoisie. Much of educational theory and child-rearing practices also reflected middle-class concerns, and for many women the enhanced role as educator was a welcome addition to their self-identity. The core values were also transposed onto plebeian culture, where the implications were much less clear. We still have relatively little knowledge of the wider reception of these ideas, though tract literature and personal contact between the classes indicate a concern of the bourgeoisie for the values of the poorer in society. In the same way as social roles were gender-determined, so were assumptions about what skills and knowledge girls and boys needed. Education was as much about shaping gender as it was about reflecting it.

Gender difference was an important criterion in educational provision and the preferred location of learning. A wide range of influences, including custom and ideology, meant that home education was far more readily advocated for girls than boys, together with heavy criticism of boarding schools. Girls often expected to spend their life in the world of house and home, while their brothers could anticipate a life of work, politics, and public affairs; a contrast that was more pronounced in the middle and upper classes than amongst the laboring orders. Evidence suggests that such concerns were implemented in practice, with the home figuring more significantly for girls than boys, even where families could afford to send girls away (Hans, 1951; Simonton, 2005). Boys' ultimate aim was to earn well enough to support a family, hoping to gain a position with prospects. Girls, however, were expected to marry and contribute to household and family.

The malleability of children, explicit in Locke and Rousseau's writing, influenced the shape of education across Europe and across the classes, and became central to the belief that education should specifically create the social individual. Education was "the art of forming a man on rational principles, and yet making him capable of entering into the community and becoming a useful and good citizen" (Williams, quoted in Stewart and McCann, 1967: 39). Thus man would develop the self-discipline necessary to control his passions and to attain virtue: "The Great Business of all is *Vertue* and *Wisdom*. Teach him to get a Mastery over his Inclinations, and *submit* his *Appetite to Reason*" (Locke, 1909–14: §200). This "useful education" shifted curricular emphasis so that it aimed to equip children for gainful employment. Locke recommended subjects outside the classical regime favored in grammar schools, and newer schools for middle-class boys advertised that they would teach useful social virtues, such as sobriety, obedience, industry, thrift, benevolence, and compassion (Plumb, 1975: 69). An approach evolved that blended traditional views of society with a more scientific, practical, utilitarian view of the role of education and the person's place in society.

Simultaneously, "useful" education for the laboring orders became important. Middle-class fears that educating laborers' children would have dangerous consequences for the social and political order often resulted in prescriptive schooling to create obedient, well-behaved, deferential Christians. Thus Hannah More opened schools where her goal was "to form the lower class to habits of industry and virtue. . . . To make good members of society (and this can only be done by making good Christians) has been my aim" (quoted in Jones, 1952: 52). Educational tracts were vaguer about boys' expectations than those of girls. Injunctions about girls' schooling argue the central purposes were to mold good domestic servants, housewives, and mothers, but except for occasional references to apprenticeship, boys' occupations or expectations received little mention. Boys were, of course, expected to work and encouraged to improve their occupational prospects, but within their own social order, and without encroaching upon middle-class prerogatives. Ideology was formulated around a domestic and "non-working" image of woman so that the middle classes viewed only certain kinds of work as appropriate for laboring women. A study of English schools for the laboring orders points up the differences in provision of school places and curricula. On average there were about nine schools for "laboring" boys to every eight for girls, and schools consistently provided fewer places for girls than boys in the ratio of about two places for boys to one for each girl. Across the classes, boys were more likely to have an "academic education" even if only in arithmetic, than girls (Simonton, 2005). Such a curriculum is echoed in France and Germany, indicating a widespread consensus about gender in the curriculum (Maynes, 1985; Sonnet, 1993).

Workplace Culture

Divisions of labor created by a series of overlapping concerns related to space and geography, age, ideology, and custom colored the operation of the workplace. Its operational structure was also inflected by gender and this, together with other interests, reshaped the workplace into a kaleidoscope of patterns. It was influenced by wider social perceptions of gendered space and in turn helped to shape those perceptions. Fundamental to how workplace relationships functioned were ideas about honor, skill, and status as well as the sheer practicalities of working and living. There were overtly gendered debates in the worlds of work that shaped how tasks, and indeed whole areas of work, were coded as appropriate for one sex or the other. The flux and change that underpinned these worlds exacerbated these issues, since increasingly laissez-faire attitudes, a shift towards mercantile activity, and competition from unregulated areas in many handicraft industries challenged many men's view of themselves and their work.

Within most working families relations between husbands and wives were characterized by interdependence, by a partnership involving pursuit of a common goal. At all economic levels, men and women frequently operated in nominal accord to ensure that family income and status were maintained. Evidence from across Europe shows large numbers of men and women working as couples, the wife often cast in the helpmate role. This role, however, could range from maintenance tasks that we associate with housekeeping, but which included feeding apprentices and cleaning workshops, to active business responsibility operating in de facto partnership. Some women increased their activity when husbands were away, taking a more overt role in business, dealing with correspondence, negotiating with suppliers, and dispatching goods, as well as investing in their own right. Significant numbers of women were sufficiently involved in the family business to continue it when their husband died. There was, of course, a tremendous range between women in La

Rochelle *armateur* families and the small Aberdeen merchant, John McKenzie, whose relict Margaret Craig had to buy up his stock before continuing in business. Rural communities also witnessed such complementary work patterns, with the small farmer's wife responsible primarily for the house and its environs, specifically the "barnyard," while he was responsible for fieldwork and other tasks further away. Importantly, large numbers of men and women worked as singletons, as servants, apprentices, laborers, and journeymen and women. Thus the roles of men and women were determined by a multiplicity of considerations, such as age, marital status, community, and trade.

Cooperation in economic matters only partly defines gender relations. Custom combined with ideas of gender to shape the ways people worked. For example, men were more likely to take on jobs that took them away from home, such as carting, while women were more likely to work near the homestead. Yet single women were foremost amongst migrants, moving for work in service, and, like male shepherds, could be found tending animals in the high pasture in summer. Females were more closely associated with small animals, while males tended to be associated with large ones, like horses, and to take on work associated with horses, or oxen, such as plowing. However, women retained special responsibility for cows and milking. While such distinctions could be based on practicalities, such as women's long-standing responsibility for household and children, clearly ideas about gender inflected these practices.

The same could be said about gender and tools. Broadly speaking men operated machines and tools that required strength, such as scythes. But, as studies have shown, women demonstrated as much if not more capability with some tools as men, and indeed even the heavier tools, such as the Scottish heuk, could be wielded by women (Lee, 1990; Simonton, 1998). Tools are often associated with skill, strength, and status, and skill is almost always gendered. They were intimately identified with who and what people were, and they ultimately speak to the gendered ideas people had about technology.

Skill fitted into different contexts and was laden with other cultural perceptions than those of our modern world. Some of these transcended the urban community, sharing ideas and tools with the rural world, while civic and commercial roles reinforced the meanings of skill and added impetus to the way status was perceived. The "profundity of the divide between skill and lack of skill offers a key to understanding the insistent concern of those . . . whose skills were at risk, to create or consolidate their own associative structures" (Woolf, 1992: 189–90). Michael Sonenscher's examination of French *compagnonnages* (1989), and Robert Darnton's *The Great Cat Massacre* (1991), demonstrate the importance of rituals in creating symbolic inequalities to establish barriers that protected workers' fragile claims to their work. The most obvious ritual was completion of the "masterpiece," a rite of passage that gained a young man, and in some cases a young woman, the right to conduct a trade. For men it also marked the passage from youth to adulthood, a situation that was less relevant for girls. As Darnton explains, "in entering an 'estate', Jerome assimilated an ethos. He identified himself with a craft . . . he received a new name. Having gone through a rite of passage in the full, anthropological sense of the term, he became a Monsieur" (Darnton, 1991: 91). A man's tools represented his patrimony; they signified his "possession of a personal qualification." He "possessed not only the tools of the trade, but the trade itself," and it delimited the space between him and his master (Farge, 1993: 125). The tension with masters is significant.

Notions of honor shaped the identity of many men and women, particularly those in corporate communities where guild rules had held sway and frequently continued to do so. Important studies of how men operated to redefine and claim the workplace, like those by Jean Quataert (1985), Merry Wiesner (1989), and Sonya Rose (1992), have helped to articulate some of the cultural issues that define homework, skilled work, ownership of tools and notions of honor in the workplace. Gendered workplace patterns were not the result of a simple process of masculine control, or patriarchy, and the character of skill and the ways that men and women negotiated their understanding of it profoundly affected the shape of the workforce. The corporate community was situated in a discourse of skill, status, and honor, and the legacy of corporate structures in both urban and rural areas maintained much of their significance. However, new working practices undercut their solidarity so that, as the protectors of skilled labor, guilds opposed domestic industry, i.e. home-based work as opposed to the "workshop." Whereas guildsmen considered guild work to be *honorable*, other work, and therefore other workers, was *dishonorable*. The need to protect their own status and the link of domestic industry with women was central. "Skilled" work in guild shops was increasingly defined as men's work, and craft mysteries were not to be shared with women. They might work alongside women, but skilled work was still theirs to claim (Quataert, 2006; Simonton, 1998; Wiesner, 1987). In Württemberg, for example, guild controls were assiduously protected, and law supported guildsmen in their claims (Ogilvie, 1990). So in many areas guilds remained active, successfully controlling the workplace – embedding masculinity into artisan culture and claiming work that was perceived as skilled.

Apprenticeship gained women the right to trade in many "female" trades, but without political advantages. And despite some anxiety about women traders, customary practice often provided openings for women. In towns like Aberdeen and Kingston upon Thames, unregistered traders were called to account, but often only required to pay a sum to be "tolerated" for trading without recognized qualifications. And during the century, "the rights of women to purchase rather than to inherit guild status increased in Nantes" (Musgrave, 1997: 159). Certainly lack of recognized skill restricted women, and guilds were keen to limit widows' inherited privileges, and excluded women with patrimonial rights from corporation politics. Nevertheless, these strategies *situated* women in the commercial community, so that the system provided an access route for women, so long as they sought permission.

Women could establish themselves in specific niches, especially in needle trades, and operated their own corporations in Paris and in provincial French towns. They tenaciously utilized the system, which gave them tangible economic benefits, legal rights, and the privileges and structures to protect their trade. They acquired a corporate identity and a notion of female honor that derived from the female character of their trades and the independence they could enjoy. Gender was the primary focus of these female artisans, giving them a corporate identity: they worked for and with other women, and belonged to the guild as individuals not as family members. They took pride in their legal and professional autonomy and scorned the skills of women working in patriarchal workshops. And yet not all women joined corporations. The majority of Parisian seamstresses remained outside the guild, and after the abolition of corporations in 1776, seamstresses in Clermont-Ferrand proudly claimed freedom from guild control (Crowston, 2001: 291).

Political Culture

Constructions of the masculine in corporate towns and mercantile centers had resonance within the political community since men were able to claim a political position through their trading activities and positions as burghers in the corporation. Men and masters recognized their political potential, and it was tied up with their understanding of masculinity. These fraternal bonds bridged differences between journeymen, trade guilds, and merchant guilds, though within civic communities there were differences of prestige and power. Fraternal bonds also described civil society. The political world of the eighteenth century was colored by absolutism and revolution, while local politics were shaped by corporatism, custom, control, and popular action. Land, inheritance, and family had long-standing resonance and remained fundamental to politics.

The concept of citizenship gained a new significance during the century propelled by ideas embedded in the idea of Social Contract. The "rights of man" discourse mapped on to the deterioration of the absolutist rule of the patriarchal paterfamilias. Cultural production reflected a new kind of fatherhood that discarded the harsh patriarchal image and, simultaneously, absolute monarchical rule (Hunt, 1992). The shift away from reliance on political patriarchy was significant; "But because language, meaning and knowledge are social activities which alter slowly over time, patriarchalist terms continued to resonate through both public and private vocabularies" (Elshtain,1981: 125). Englishmen relied on the social contract, while Frenchmen rejected the idea of "founding fathers" and drew on the bonds of fraternity in their creation of the male citizen. "Liberty, equality and fraternity" was a central tenet. Mary Wollstonecraft and Olympe de Gouges interpreted the notion that all men were created equal to include women. At the beginning of the French Revolution it appeared that this might be the case. However, citizenship was "inflected by identity, social positioning, cultural assumptions, institutional practices and a sense of belonging," and that relationship was male (Canning and Rose, 2001: 437). These discourses, situated in differences of wealth, position, corporate customs, and the liberal thought of the Enlightenment, successfully ascribed citizenship to men. Women who intervened in public political worlds risked being perceived as acting "unnaturally" and as threatening political stability. Following the Convention's prohibition of women's societies, Prudhomme wrote: "Citoyennes, be honest diligent girls, tender and modest wives, wise mothers, and you will be good patriots. True patriotism consists of fulfilling one's duties and valuing only rights appropriate to each according to sex and age . . . not carrying pike and pistol. Leave those to men who are born to protect you and make you happy" (Prudhomme, 1789–94: no. 213,151).

The unease about women's place was also very much an anxiety about the status quo and the stability and morality of society. Thus the discourse ascribed women specific cultural responsibilities for the creation of virtue and morality, and wrote them out of the polity. William Kenrick admonished: "Let the kingdom rule itself, let the wise men and counsellors enact laws and correct them; the policy of government is a hidden thing, like a well of water in the bottom of a deep pit. Thy kingdom is thine own house, and thy government the care of thy family" (Kenrick, 1792: 16).

"On the one hand . . . politics operated on the presumption that the polity was male and that politics was men's business" (Chalus, 2005: 21). On the other, political practices provided niches for women to enter the political fray. Historians' re-examination of the political arena has shown that it was far more than formal structures and systems (Chalus, 2000; Colley, 1992; Landes, 2001; Rendall, 2006). It was a world where patronage and influence reigned. Thus connections mattered, oiling the world of preference. The politics of influence were central to how women could interject themselves into political worlds. Female activity encompassed many forms, from conversation and correspondence to support and succor, to public political stances including riot and affray. These activities paralleled men's routes, and in many instances class and community bound men's and women's actions together. By and large, women's part was played out on a personal stage, using influence with men to shape political actions, making connections and fostering political links. Politics for women was usually "first familial, then factional and only occasionally personal" (Chalus, 2000: 675).

Across Europe, coffeehouses and clubs, conversation parties hosted by women such as the salons of Paris and Berlin, and informal groups provided a space that forged writers, thinkers, and commentators. Homes and community networks equally provided a political focus, such as that of Mary Leadbeater, or of Mary Anne McCracken in Ireland in the rebellious 1790s. In Britain parliamentary politics and the emergence of embryonic political parties provided the arena for the politics of influence to flourish. In France, the salon provided a haven, and through patronage ensured that political ideas hostile to the court could be published. Conversation oiled the world of politics, and women acted as political facilitators, bringing power into their homes. They brought men together, provided a space for ideas to flourish, and assisted in building coalitions. Women used their connections, and eased the entry of new men onto the scene, sometimes being called upon for advice. They could make or break careers. "Visiting" was a form of political currency. Some visits were apparently social calls, but information gained was put to political advantage. Others were overtly political (Chalus, 2005).

Public disorder, riots, and mobs including women were not new, and collective action was a time-honored way for plebeian men and women to express their political voice. Various types of "mob" action involved women, such as those involving bread or industrial disputes, but so did the overtly political acts, like those against Jewish naturalization in London. In the Netherlands, women were active in religious, fiscal, and political uprisings, such as the Patriot Revolt of 1782–7, they were integral to disturbances against child abductions in Paris in 1750, while in 1719, the women of Nordhofen twice prevented a certain Captain von Marteauville from capturing the village herd to feed soldiers (Dekker, 1987; Wunder, 1998: 176). A feature of women's participation was their ability to move around neighborhoods, make links, spread information, and act as go-betweens. They used their knowledge of how neighborhoods worked, they understood the social machinery, and their networks enabled them to keep informed and pass on information (Farge, 1993). Thus, communication and facilitation were as much part of the political worlds of ordinary women as they were for those of the elite. Public perception frequently associated them with disorder, and control of the "feminine," the "irrational," was an underlying precept of philosophical and public consciousness. Jacobin concern with female disorder was a feature of the backlash during the French Revolution, and significantly Edmund Burke aligned London women with the violence of the Gordon anti-Catholic riots, linking atavistic behavior with the female (Kent, 1999: 119).

Intimacy

The operation of gender within intimate relationships is extraordinarily difficult to unravel primarily because they represent the ultimate in private relations. While ideology shaped the context, and law set the rules, couples negotiated practice behind closed doors. The "unspoken assumption that family is about women and children, about femininity and intimacy" both genders this intimate world at the same time as it manages to exclude masculinity (Davidoff, et al., 1999: 5). Discourses of the period constructed new views of both male and female and situated them in a child-oriented, companionate family. However, the "move towards a more child-oriented society was challenged at every stage, and never completed. . . . we are confronted at every turn by ambivalence and contradiction" (Cunningham, 1995: 62).

Learning about sexuality and gender was an important aspect of childhood and adolescence. Mme Gaçon-Dufour wrote in 1787, "Having been taught by our mothers the difference of our sex from that of men – that is, understanding, by being called a little girl or mademoiselle, that we were not at all little boys or men . . . This is how our intimate feelings of modesty are created" (Albistur and Armogathe, 1978: 131). Adolescents of both sexes derived their conjugal expectations, their knowledge of bodies, and, for girls, of childbirth through association and word of mouth. Apprentices and servants shared information and learned from mistresses and masters: "In the workshop they learned to be women at the same time as they acquired trade skills" (Crowston, 2001: 310). Male youth culture was important in conveying masculinity, and studies of *Lichtstuben* and other informal male groupings demonstrate how the activities of youth mimicked those of older men as they "copied adult male forms of participation in village politics" (Gestrich, 2005: 56). Plebeian culture was lived out in overcrowded and communal spaces, people shared beds in inns, and private space was not yet an intrinsic part of home life. If sexual intimacy was prevented by taboos and psychological distance, sexual awareness was fostered.

Though background, character, and financial potential played a part in arranging marriages, young people played an active part in courtship rituals. They utilized available spaces to get to know one another, in settings where rituals and peer pressure encouraged association. Cousins from Montauban explained that "the time they spent together and what they learned about each other formed a very tight bond of mutual inclination between them" (Darrow, 1989: 151). Wedding customs show how gender was negotiated in the process. Some communities expected the bridegroom and his mates to "fetch" the bride from home. In Wales, he "takes her by the hand, and sayeth, 'Misits, I hope you are willinge,' or kisseth her before [everyone]." These symbolic challenges forced the groom to demonstrate his manhood, his ability to "master" his wife and protect her from other males. She should show reluctance: "The Girl makes great moans & lamentations, and if she can counterfeit tears & Tearing of hair it is reckoned a merit" (Gillis, 1997: 139). These rituals demonstrated that she was sufficiently modest and not overly lustful. Weddings marked a rite of passage for young women who transferred from the father's house to the husband's, and recognizable symbols marked her passage from maiden to wife. Traditional clothing for girls, maids, wives, and widows denoted shifts in status. Hair was a particularly potent symbol. Loose it was unruly, unrestrained, and representative of unbridled female sexuality. Thus binding, plaiting, and covering were significant markers in controlling female sexuality and denoting the stages of womanhood.

Marriage was considered the natural state for adult females, and, though not so overtly, for men as well. Both appreciated that marriage and the establishment of a household was the expression of social adulthood. Religious teaching had long promoted marital love and duty, but a number of forces, including a period of relative stability, emergent notions of companionate marriage, and growing prosperity for large sections of the population, may have fostered the valorization of affection. While female subjection and male supremacy were formal elements of gender construction, clearly many men and women were able to work within or around them. Many married for love, enjoying deeply loving relationships. Where love was not deep, respect often formed a profound bond. Caroline Michaelis felt "respect and affection" for her husband, and believed "It will last because it is not excessive" (quoted in Behrens, 1982: 258). Husbands and wives each had an authentic place in marriage, and harmony was what they hoped for. They recognized the importance of mutual interests and responsibilities and did not anticipate equality.

Religious dogma had long advanced the view that in marriage woman would achieve her highest status. Newer views of Nature further sublimated that view, holding that it was part of women's nature desire the married state. "[O]nly marriage made a woman a "real" person: a person who was an authority figure to her domestics and children" (Wunder, 1998: 53, 203). She was to preserve her husband and his honor, to be his "truest" and best friend, "the participator of [his] cares, the consoler of his sorrows, his stimulator to every praiseworthy undertaking, his partner in the labours and vicissitudes of life" (Wakefield, 1798: 31–2). What was new was a particular emphasis on emotional support and a belief that she should make her husband happy by "sweetening his life with affectionate co-operation, love, care and assistance, and distract him from everyday worries" (Crampe-Casnabet, 1993: 372). Articulated differently, men too desired a household, since "[t]he domestic sphere . . . is integral to masculinity. To establish a home, to protect it, to provide for it, to control it, and to train its young aspirants to manhood, [were] essential to a man's good standing with his peers" (Tosh, 1999: 4). Men's role in marriage was also reconstructed. They were more overtly cast as breadwinner, head of household, with concomitant responsibilities. This is not to suggest that men had not perceived themselves in such a role previously, but certainly the language of masculinity, the increase of waged work, even pressures on jobs, contributed to refashioning the male. Shifts in attitudes to the paterfamilias, as the concept of the authoritarian father gave way to a more compassionate man of feeling, also fostered the construction of man as a caring father.

A variety of other factors governed the gendered relationships within marriage. Bluntly – love was not enough. Marriage relations were framed around the imperatives of family sustenance, procreation, and affection. The couple shared responsibility for maintenance of the unit, based on complementary roles and skills, whether aristocratic, merchant, or civil servant families or laboring and artisan households. Nevertheless, men held all the overt political power, and law and custom recognized the subordination of women to men. For example, though motherhood gained a new prominence, fathers still retained legal control. While marriage manuals increasingly emphasized the reciprocity of duties, law recognized husbands and wives as one, and society expected the male to be the authority in the family. "Europe lived with the paradoxical ideas that husbands and wives were equal by virtue of social estate and unequal by virtue of gender" (Gray, 2000: 40). European legal structures rested on patriarchal principles which invoked the doctrine of the unity of person, famously described by William Blackstone: "By marriage, the husband and wife are one person in law: that is, the very being or legal existence of the woman is suspended during the marriage, [and she is] under the protection and influence of her husband" (Blackstone, 1800: vol. 1, §15). Because the husband was head of household, "as the wife enters into it of her own accord, she is in some measure subject to his power; whence flow several rights and privileges, which belong to the husband with regard to his wife" (Frederician Code, 1750). At the same time, "a woman's honor is included in the wider sphere of a man's, which it is his duty to superintend" (quoted in Nye, 1993: 16). Male control of female sexuality was about his manhood, but also was tied up in protecting investment and inheritance. Male infidelity might damage domestic harmony, but was less damaging to family honor. Female infidelity, though, could be perceived as theft, particularly if a child was born of such a liaison and then usurped the inheritance of legitimate children. However, with increasing value placed on companionate marriage and family values, opinion was growing that adultery was as great a sin in the husband as the wife, and conduct that jeopardized family life was decried. Society was less tolerant of abuse and did not readily sanction separation and divorce. Nevertheless, the widely accepted sexual double standard and the belief that a woman should respect her husband even if he wronged her meant that the stain of a broken marriage was greater for a woman. If couples hoped for harmony, they did not always get it.

Single women were vulnerable to ridicule. Failures in the great game of catching a husband, they were the butt of jokes and criticism. "How utterly devoid of tenderness, & every amiable sensation must that female be, who never felt . . . a desire to engage in the duties or to share the delights, of that state, to which all human beings are invited by the voice of nature and reason" (Hayley, 1785: 13). At issue was not only their perceived failure as women but the fact that "unmastered" women were seen as disorderly and dangerous. They represented an inversion of the "natural" gender order and a threat to masculinity and male control. A greater inversion was women who posed as men. Others entered into same-sex unions. Cross-dressing reflects the long tradition of "impostors," ways of making or remaking your circumstances (Davis, 1997). Women used male clothing to go to war or empire, to look for missing husbands, or simply to take up activities which were not readily accessible to women. Their reasons varied, they were not all single, and they did not all disavow their sex, though sexual ambiguity was a feature of many who adopted male clothing (Wheelwright, 1989). Generally the punishment for female same-sex relationships was less than for male ones, and sometimes they were simply tolerated. Importantly, the focus on the penetrative sexual act privileges a male perspective, a perspective represented by the heavy punishment that a woman received if seen to be usurping a man's sexual role in intercourse. The female partner in these cases was always treated more lightly. In actuality, women expressed their feelings, erotic and otherwise, by a range of behaviors, including kissing, caressing, and passionate correspondence.

Indeed on a number of levels, gender boundaries were bent, challenged, and transgressed in popular and high culture. John Brown's anxiety of "The one sex having advanced into *Boldness*, as the other have sunk into *Effeminacy*" articulates the concern about deviance from sexual stereotypes. It explicitly notifies us of the concern about challenges to what it was to be male. Carter writes that "A male identity characterized by superficiality or delicacy was clearly at odds with the more acceptable forms of masculinity characterized by a synthesis of modern refinement and traditional responsibilities." The image of the fop depicted the effeminate male as not only blurring social distinctions but also abjuring male public responsibilities and as a man who failed to be genteel and sensible, "equally acceptable, equally masculine, in the civilized urban spaces of both leisure and work." The male homosexual, while also disturbing and undermining the emergence of the "new man," was not as significant within social discourse as the much more public figure of the fop (Carter, 1997: 55).

Conclusion

This chapter has thus far avoided the use of the overworked phrase "public–private." People did understand two overlapping realms of activity, with male predominance in one and female predominance in the other. These were of long-standing resonance; they were not, however, an ideology of separate spheres. A combination of late eighteenth-century rhetoric, middle-class activism in the nineteenth century, and twentieth-century feminism turned public and private concepts of space into, as Vickery says, "a systematic use of 'separate spheres' as *the* organizing concept in the history of middle-class women" (Vickery, 1998: 294). Indeed, activists used separate spheres in two ways during the nineteenth century – as a device to claim a specific female space and activities, but also as a binary opposition, which they could then challenge. The concept was useful for uncovering distinctions in middle-class women's lives in the nineteenth century and as a way to understand "oppression" and "patriarchy." Unfortunately, it seems to have been transposed to whenever and wherever people want to write about, and has developed a persistence that has tended to disguise more than it explains; it gets in the way of understanding the nuances and alternatives in people's experience. Separate spheres clearly were not an accurate description of the way many understood their lives; they certainly were not true across classes nor even for large sectors of the population.

Gender difference, however, was an endemic feature of eighteenth-century life. Ideologically it was defined and redefined, and though consensus was not reached, new ideas of masculinity and femininity shaped the worlds within which people operated. Lived experience both contributed to and in turn was framed by gender. Social pressures are hard to ignore, but people manufactured their lives within codes of honor, probity, and the realities of day-to-day existence. The construction of gender spoke to a perception of the masculine and the feminine as complements, each with their own role and place. Workplace and political culture interacted with the intimate worlds of love, affection, and sex framed by ideological perceptions as people created, as Gillis says, "a world of their own making."

Bibliography

Abensour, L., *La Femme et la féminisme en France avant la Révolution* (Geneva, 1923; repr. 1966).

Albistur, M. and D. Armogathe (eds.), *Le Grief des femmes: Anthologie du texts féministes du IIe empire à nos jours* (Poitiers, 1978).

Alexander, S. and B. Taylor, "In defence of patriarchy," repr. in R. Samuel (ed.), *People's History and Socialist Theory* (London, 1981).

Behrens, K., (ed.), *Frauenbriefe der Romantik* (Frankfurt am Main, 1982).

Blackstone, W., *Commentaries on the Laws of England*, ed. E. Christian (13th edn., 4 vols., London, 1800).

Bock, G., "Women's history and gender history: aspects of an international debate," *Gender & History*, 1 (1989), 7–30.

Brown, J., *An Estimate on the Manners and Principles of the Times* (London, 1757).

Brown, J., *On the Female Character and Education* (London, 1765).

Caine, B. and G. Sluga, *Gendering European History, 1780–1920* (London and New York, 2000).

Campe, J. H., *Väterliche Rath für meine Tochter* (Brunswick, 1789), extract in U. Gerhard, *Verhältnisse und Verhinderungen. Frauenarbeit, Familie und Rechte der Frauen im 19. Jahrhundert* (Frankfurt am Main, 1978).

Canning, K. and S. O. Rose, *Gender, Citizenship, Subjectivities*, special issue of *Gender & History*, 13, 3 (Nov. 2001).

Carter, P., "Men about town: representations of foppery and masculinity in early eighteenth-century urban society," in H. Barker and E. Chalus (eds.), *Gender in Eighteenth-Century England: Roles, Representations and Responsibilities* (London, 1997), pp. 31–57.

Chalus, E., "Elite women, social politics and the political world of late eighteenth-century England," *Historical Journal*, 43 (2000), 669–97.

Chalus, E., *Elite Women in English Political Life c.1754–1790* (Oxford, 2005).

Clark, A., *Working Life of Women in the 17th Century* (1919; London, 1982).

Clark, A., *The Struggle for the Breeches: Gender and the Making of the British Working Class* (Berkeley, 1995).

Colley, L., *Britons: Forging the Nation, 1707–1837* (London, 1992).

Crampe-Casnabet, M., "A sampling of eighteenth-century philosophy," in N. Z. Davis and A. Farge (eds.), *A History of Women in the West*, vol. 3: *Renaissance and Enlightenment Paradoxes* (Cambridge, 1993), pp. 315–47.

Crowston, C. H., *Fabricating Women: The Seamstresses of Old Regime France, 1675–1791* (Durham, NC, 2001).

Cunningham, H., *Children and Childhood in Western Society since 1500* (London, 1995).

Darnton, R., *The Great Cat Massacre and other Episodes in French Cultural History* (London, 1991).

Darrow, M., *Revolution in the House: Family, Class and Inheritance in Southern France, 1775–1825* (Princeton, 1989).

Davidoff, L., M. Doolittle, J. Fink and K. Holden, *The Family Story: Blood, Contract and Intimacy, 1830–1960* (London, 1999).

Davis, N. Z., *Remaking Impostors: From Martin Guerre to Sommersby*, Hayes Robinson Lecture Series, No. 1 (London, 1997).

Davis, N. Z., "'Women's History' in Transition: The European Case" (1976), repr. in J. W. Scott (ed.), *Feminism and History* (Oxford, 1997), pp. 79–104.
Dekker, R. M., "Women in revolt: popular protest and its social basis in Holland in the seventeenth and eighteenth centuries," *Theory and Society*, 15 (1987), 337–62.
Downs, L. L., *Writing Gender History* (London, 2004).
Elshtain, J. B., *Public Man, Private Woman: Women in Social and Political Thought* (Oxford, 1981).
Farge, A., *Fragile Lives: Violence, Power and Solidarity in Eighteenth-Century Paris* (London, 1993).
Forster, R., *Merchants, Landlords, Magistrates: The Depont Family in Eighteenth-Century France* (Baltimore, 1980).
Frader, L. and S. O. Rose (eds.), *Gender and Class in Modern Europe* (London, 1996).
Frederician Code (1750), in S. G. Bell and K. Offen (eds.), *Women, the Family and Freedom*, vol. 1: *1750–1880* (Stanford, 1983).
Gestrich, Andreas, "After dark: girls' leisure, work and sexuality in 18th and 19th century rural southwest Germany," in C. Benninghaus et al. (eds.), *Secret Gardens, Satanic Mills: Placing Girls in Modern European History* (Bloomington, 2005), pp. 54–68.
Gillis, J., *A World of Their Own Making: A History of Myth and Ritual in Family Life* (Oxford, 1997).
Goodman, D., "Women and the Enlightenment," in R. Bridenthal, S. M. Stuard, and M. E. Wiesner (eds.), *Becoming Visible, Women in European History* (3rd edn., Boston and New York, 1998).
Gray, M. W. *Productive Men, Reproductive Women: The Agrarian Household and the Emergence of Separate Spheres during the Enlightenment* (Oxford, 2000).
Habermas, J., *The Structural Transformation of the Public Sphere: An Inquiry into a Category of Bourgeois Society* (Cambridge, MA, 1989).
Hans, N., *New Trends in Education in the Eighteenth Century* (London, 1951).
Hayley, W., *A Philosophical, Historical, and Moral Essay on Old Maids* (3 vols., London, 1785).
Hitchcock, T. and M. Cohen (eds.), *English Masculinities, 1660–1800* (London, 1999).
Hume, D., "Of the rise and progress of the arts and sciences" (1742), in E. F. Miller (ed.), *Essays, Moral, Political, and Literary* (Indianapolis, 1987).
Hunt, L., *The Family Romance of the French Revolution* (Berkeley, 1992).
Jones, M. G., *Hannah More* (Cambridge, 1952).
Jordanova, L., *Sexual Visions: Images of Gender in Science and Medicine between the Eighteenth and Twentieth Centuries* (New York and London, 1989).
Kenrick, W., *The Whole Duty of Woman* (1753; 13th edn., Windsor, VT, 1792).
Kent, S. K., *Gender and Power in Britain, 1640–1990* (London, 1999).
Knott, S. and B. Taylor (eds.), *Women, Gender and the Enlightenment* (Basingstoke, 2005).
Landes, J. B., *Women and the Public Sphere in the Age of the French Revolution* (Ithaca, 1988).
Landes, J. B. *Visualizing the Nation: Gender, Representation and Revolution in Eighteenth-Century France* (Ithaca, 2001).
Laqueur, T. W., *Making Sex: Body and Gender from the Greeks to Freud* (Cambridge, MA, 1990).
Lee, W. R. "Women's work and the family: some demographic implications of gender-specific rural work patterns in nineteenth-century Germany," in P. Hudson and W. R. Lee (eds.), *Women's Work and the Family Economy in Historical Perspective* (Manchester, 1990), pp. 50–75.
Locke, John, *Some Thoughts Concerning Education*, vol. 37, pt. 1 (New York, 1909–14).
Maynes, M. J., *Schooling in Western Europe: A Social History* (Albany, NY, 1985).

More, H., *Essays on Various Subjects, Principally Designed for Young Ladies* (London, 1777).
Mosse, G. L., *The Image of Man: The Creation of Modern Masculinity* (Oxford, 1998).
Musgrave, E., "Women and the craft guilds in eighteenth-century Nantes," in G. Crossick (ed.), *The Artisan and the European Town, 1500–1900* (Brookfield, VT, 1997), pp. 151–71
Nye, R., *A., Masculinity and Male Codes of Honor in Modern France* (Oxford, 1993).
Offen, K., *European Feminisms, 1700–1950; A Political History* (Stanford, 2000).
Ogilvie, S., "Women and proto-industrialisation in a corporate society: Württemberg woollen weaving, 1590–1760," in P. Hudson and W. R. Lee (eds.), *Women's Work and the Family Economy in Historical Perspective* (Manchester, 1990), pp. 76–103.
Outram, D., *The Enlightenment*, (Cambridge, 1995).
Pinchbeck, I., *Women Workers and the Industrial Revolution, 1750–1850* (London, 1930; repr. 1981).
Plumb, J. H., "The new world of children in eighteenth-century England," *Past and Present*, 67 (1975), 64–93.
Prudhomme, L. M., *Révolutions de Paris, dédiées a la nation* (Paris, 1789–94).
Quataert, J., "The shaping of women's work in manufacturing guilds, households and the state in central Europe, 1648–1870," *American Historical Review*, 90 (1985), 1122–48.
Quataert, J., "Women's history at the crossroads," in D. Simonton (ed.), *The Routledge History of Women in Europe since 1700* (London, 2007), pp. x–xv.
Rendall, J., "Women and the Enlightenment in Britain, *c.*1690–1800," in H. Barker and E. Chalus (eds.), *Women's History: Britain, 1700–1850* (London, 2005), pp. 9–32.
Rendall, J. and S. Innes, "Women, gender and politics," in L. Abrams et al. (eds.), *Gender and Scottish History, 1700 to the Present* (Edinburgh, 2006), pp. 43–83.
Roper, M. and J. Tosh (eds.), *Manful Assertions: Masculinities in Britain since 1800* (London, 1999).
Rose, S. O., *Limited Livelihoods: Gender and Class in Nineteenth-Century England* (Berkeley, 1992).
Rousseau, J.-J., *Emile* (London, 1974).
Rowbotham, S., "The trouble with patriarchy," in R. Samuel (ed.), *People's History and Socialist Theory* (London, 1981).
Scott, J., *Gender and the Politics of History* (New York, 1988; rev. edn., 1999).
Scott, J., "Gender: a useful category of historical analysis," repr. in J. W. Scott (ed.), *Feminism and History* (Oxford, 1997), pp. 152–80.
Segal, L., *Slow Motion: Changing Masculinities, Changing Men* (rev. edn., Basingstoke, 2006).
Simonton, D., *A History of European Women's Work, 1700 to the Present* (London, 1998).
Simonton, D., "Women and education," in H. Barker and E. Chalus (eds.), *Women's History: Britain, 1700–1850* (London, 2005), pp. 33–56.
Simonton, D. (ed.), *The Routledge History of Women in Europe since 1700* (London, 2006).
Sonenscher, M., "Mythical work: workshop production and the compagnonnages of eighteenth-century France," in P. Joyce (ed.), *The Historical Meanings of Work* (Cambridge, 1989), pp. 31–63.
Sonnet, M., "A daughter to educate," in N. Z. Davis and A. Farge (eds.), *A History of Women in the West*, vol. 3 (Cambridge, 1993), pp. 129–37.
Stewart, W. A. C. and W. P. McCann, *The Educational Innovators, 1750–1880* (London, 1967).
Tomaselli, S., "The Enlightenment debate on women," *History Workshop*, 20 (1985), 101–24.

Tosh, J., *A Man's Place: Masculinity and the Middle-Class Home in Victorian England* (New Haven, 1999).
Vickery, A., "Golden age to separate spheres? A Review of the categories and chronology of English women's history," repr. in P. Sharpe (ed.), *Women's Work: The English Experience, 1650–1914* (London, 1998).
Wakefield, P., *Reflections on the Present Condition of the Female Sex with Suggestions for its Improvement* (London, 1798).
Wheelwright, J., *Amazons and Military Maids: Women who Dressed as Men in Pursuit of Life, Liberty and Happiness* (London, 1989).
Wiesner, M., "Guilds, male bonding and women's work in early modern Germany," *Gender & History,* 1 (1989), 125–37.
Wiesner, M., "Women's work in the changing city economy, 1500–1650," in M. Boxer and J. H. Quataert (eds.), *Connecting Spheres* (Oxford, 1987), pp. 64–74.
Wollstonecraft, M., *An Historical and Moral View of the Origin and Progress of the French Revolution* (1794), in M. Butler and J. Todd (eds.), *The Works of Mary Wollstonecraft* (London, 1989), vol. 6.
Woolf, S., "Order, class and the urban poor," in M. L. Bush (ed.), *Social Order and Social Classes in Europe since 1500* (London, 1992).
Wunder, H., *He Is the Sun, She Is the Moon: Women in Early Modern Germany* (Cambridge, MA, 1998).

CHAPTER THREE

Rural Economy and Society

MARKUS CERMAN

A Variety of "European Peasantries"

Despite considerable progress in comparative approaches in early modern economic and social history of rural societies, research remains constricted by a narrow range of theoretical categories. The influence of "grand narratives" of European history remains powerful even today, attributing "progress" and "modernity" to some and "backwardness" and "traditionalism" to other institutional arrangements governing rural societies.

There are numerous definitions of the term "peasant" and the notion of a "peasantry" in history and the social sciences. Generally, peasants are understood as owner-occupiers working on their farms primarily with their families. However, there is little agreement whether this term is adequate to encompass the wide varieties in specific situations across eighteenth-century Europe. A historian of rural England or certain areas of the Netherlands might object to this term for (tenant) farmers of these countries, who are usually conceived as promoting specialization and agrarian capitalism (de Vries and van der Woude, 1997: 202–4, 207; Hoppenbrouwers and van Zanden, 2001). Furthermore, can the same term be applied to such a diverse group as the large, progressive farms of the German northwest or the Paris Basin, the tenant farmers of former seigneurial demesnes in the German east, as well as small-scale agricultural producers with precarious property rights such as in the regions of sharecropping in the Mediterranean, or a minority of personally unfree population in the countryside of eastern or southeastern Europe? (Langton in Scott, 1998: 373–5; Scott in Scott, 1998: 1, 5).

The diversity of the European "peasantry" has many more facets. They relate to the ecological framework (see chapter 1), and to the various types of agriculture practiced in different regions of Europe. The latter ranged from intensive grain cultivation, mixed agriculture, dairy and pastoral farming to mountain and lowland agriculture, irrigation and special cultures such as fruit, olives, silk and viticulture, and finally to regions of slash-and-burn agriculture (Langton in Scott, 1998: 376–7, 383–5). Rural economies varied strongly in their degree of specialization and

A Companion to Eighteenth-Century Europe, First Edition. Edited by Peter H. Wilson.
© 2014 John Wiley & Sons, Ltd. Published 2014 by John Wiley & Sons, Ltd.

commercialization. The peasantry was also differentiated in terms of property, legal status, marketing possibilities, communal organization, and institutions. The European peasantry, characterizing eighteenth-century rural society, therefore, is a mix of European "peasantries" (Scott, 1998: 1, 3–5).

The "peasantry debate" during the 1970s and 1980s makes necessary another qualification. Using the term here by no means suggests that this was a subsistence rural economy totally averse to market orientation, commercial activities, and profit; a class of "irrational" petty producers in modern economic terms. On the contrary, historians now regard the market involvement of the rural population during the early modern period, and certainly by the eighteenth century, as having been much stronger than traditional approaches would suggest (Scott, 1998: 1–2, 7–9). The emphasis, however, shifts towards possible market failure and is not based on alleged peasant market-aversity. Thus, a definition would pinpoint this by referring to peasants as being "partially integrated in incomplete markets" (Ellis, 1993: 4). This means that limited peasant market involvement probably reflected the fact that markets did not work well, or at least disadvantaged peasants in comparison to other agents or institutions wielding extra-economic power. There were significant regional differences in market development and market involvement of rural production. A number of factors probably caused these variations in market involvement: the inherently imperfect nature of markets themselves, the influence of other institutions like the state, lack of market density, or other factors such as topography or transport infrastructure.

Given a history of misunderstandings stressing the "immobility" of pre-industrial society and economy (Le Roy Ladurie, 1981; for critical surveys cf. Béaur, 2000; Epstein, 2000; Grantham, 1998; Hoffman, 1996: 12–20), we should no longer talk about a "general tendency" of "peasant traditionalism" versus agricultural innovation. Previous historians generally accepted the self-image of eighteenth-century enlightened reformers and presented the state and elites as "innovative" structures and agents working to "improve" an inherently undynamic society and economy. More recent work no longer supports this alleged "immobility" (Scott, 1998: 2). S. R. Epstein's conclusions about early modern Italy apply just as well to the rest of Europe: "peasants responded to commercial pressures and opportunities by innovating and specializing, or alternatively by diversifying to reduce risk, on the basis of the institutionalized incentives and constraints they faced. Although the 'specializing' and the 'subsistent' peasant are obviously idealized extremes, they underline the fact that there was no such thing as 'a' peasant economy because of the considerable differences in rural incentives across space and time" (Epstein in Scott, 1998: 101).

Demography

The total population of Europe increased by more than 50 percent, from roughly 125 million in 1700 to 190–200 million in 1800. There were considerable variations within this general trend, with the north, west, and east of Europe experiencing the highest rates of growth, the Mediterranean areas the lowest, and central Europe midway between the two. Across Europe, eighteenth-century agriculture coped quite well with the rising demand for food, which in itself is an argument against Malthusian exaggerations about the limits of the *ancien régime* rural economy. A comparison of nine countries shows that output per capita increased notably during the first half of the century, and if it declined again afterwards, as in Austria or Belgium, it did not fall below the level of 1700. Based on an estimate of output volume, it seems that per capita of population agricultural output also fell in England across the century (Allen, 2000).

By 1800 the overall majority of the population lived in the countryside, i.e. outside bigger towns and urban areas. In northwestern and Mediterranean Europe the urbanization ratio was above the average (which was roughly 10 percent of the population or 13 percent, if cities of between 5,000 and 10,000 inhabitants are also included) (de Vries, 1984). These variations did not alter the general pattern that rural inhabitants everywhere constituted the bulk of the population – from 70 to 80 percent of the total in England or the Netherlands, up to 95 percent in eastern Europe.

Conditions of Agricultural Production

The strong surge in European population meant that demand for agricultural products increased significantly. Prices for agricultural goods were recovering from the seventeenth-century crisis and grew strongly after the 1730s. Until the 1790s, grain prices (measured in units of silver per quantity of grain) nearly doubled in England and northern Italy and increased by 50 to 70 percent in the Netherlands, France and Germany. Particularly dramatic peaks were reached during the Napoleonic Wars. For all those relying on the market for their food, this development caused serious problems culminating in periodic subsistence crises, generally small and regionally confined, but sometimes extensive. In the century or so after 1750 real wage levels (measured in the quantities of grain day laborers could afford from their wages) reached their low point everywhere except in the Ottoman empire. In Istanbul, real wages had already started to increase again after 1780. W. Abel estimated that by 1800, a bricklayer's family in Berlin used nearly three-quarters of their income for food only (Allen, 2001; Kriedte, 1983: 4, 105; Overton, 1996: 64, 66–8; Özmucur and Pamuk, 2002; de Vries and van der Woude, 1997: 200).

The period after the first half of the eighteenth century has usually been associated with important improvements and with the "agricultural revolution," defined as a pronounced increase in productivity caused by technical and institutional changes. These developments were most obvious in England, but also started in other parts of the continent and would last until after 1850. Recent studies tend to strengthen the case for the eighteenth century as the decisive break, without, however, neglecting or downgrading important structural changes that might have taken place since the beginning of the early modern period (Bairoch in Cipolla, 1973; Overton, 1996: 196–207).

Processes associated with the "agricultural revolution" included the reduction of fallow land and the integration of this land into more continuous crop-rotation techniques (improved three-field systems), the final abandonment of the three-field system, the introduction of new crops (most prominently maize and potatoes), an increase in fodder production (clover, turnips) instead of leaving land fallow, allowing a higher stock of cattle, a reduction of waste, an increasing use of mineral fertilizers (chalk, marl), technical changes in agricultural equipment, changes in cattle breeding, and the reclamation and amelioration of arable land. These changes were accompanied by significant institutional developments. Among these should be mentioned important changes in peasant property rights and agrarian class structure, as well as agrarian reforms ("peasant emancipation"), i.e. the dissolution of *ancien régime* institutions of lordship (Bairoch in Cipolla, 1973; Blum, 1978; Kriedte, 1983: 105–15).

English agricultural innovations ("new husbandry") became models for changes copied elsewhere in Europe during the eighteenth century. The English experience thus exemplifies what were becoming wider trends (Overton, 1996: 193–207). Large landowners controlled 75 to 80 percent of English farmland by 1850, but recent research indicates that such concentration of ownership was not a prerequisite for new techniques. In Norfolk, for instance, it was the smaller tenant and owner-occupier farmers who were the pioneers. Yield ratios seem to have been independent of farm size. The most significant case for an agricultural revolution "made" by the yeomanry (i.e. by owner-occupiers who held their land in copyhold and beneficial leases rather than short-term leases), was put forward by R. Allen in his study on the English Midlands (Allen, 1992). The advantage of larger consolidated farms probably lay in their enhanced labor productivity, which further increased output per worker. "The yeomen's revolution was primarily output-expanding; its main achievement was the doubling of corn yields. As a concomitant, labour productivity increased over 50 percent. . . . In contrast, the landlords' revolution was primarily labour-shedding" (Allen, 1992: 231).

Large consolidated farms were not unique to England. There were large-scale tenant farmers in the Île de France (Paris Basin) and the French north, who – within open field structures – led the commercial development of French agriculture during the eighteenth century and achieved comparable productivity to that of English farmers.[1] Similarly, in Lombardy there were leaseholders of commercially oriented farms (with elaborate irrigation systems in the south) engaged in specialized production also achieving high yields. The structure in Apulia is a good example for southern Italy, where inland there were large monoculture tenant farms engaged in wheat production or sheep farming (*masserie*) with wage labor, while in the densely populated areas along the coast and around towns small peasant farms concentrated on olive production. They often supplemented their income by small-scale viticulture, with fruit gardens, or by occasional fishing. The key is that both forms were closely linked to each other and strongly market-related (Epstein in Scott, 1998: 88–93). In parts of Germany, in particular in the north, owner-occupiers of large peasant farms achieved very high productivity. Even in areas customarily associated with "serfdom" there were equivalents, such as the bourgeois and peasant leaseholders of vast royal and noble demesne farms in Brandenburg (Hagen, 2002: 334–41; Müller, 1967; Wehler, 1989: 86–7).

It would be wrong to assume that consolidated tenant farms represented the only engine of agricultural innovation, or that smaller farms could not achieve the same productivity levels (Allen, 1992; Béaur, 2000; Hoffman, 1996: 190). The flexibility and adaptability of smaller farm units and peasant farmers has long been underestimated, but their role in the process of agrarian modernization is now being acknowledged. There are numerous studies pointing towards the flexibility of related institutions like open field farming and village common land (Allen, 1992; Béaur, 2000: 63–98, 167–212; Boehler in Prass et al., 2004; Epstein in Scott, 1998: 90, 104; Hoffman, 1996: 21–34; Kopsidis, 2006: 286, 296–302, 305; Moor et al., 2002;

Prass in Prass et al., 2004; Ruiz in Scott, 1998: 63; Vivier in Prass et al., 2004). This approach is particularly relevant for France, where small and medium-sized peasant farms were dominant in many regions. The gradual improvement of yields can be attributed to small changes applied by farmers over a long period (Béaur, 2000; Dewald and Vardi in Scott, 1998: 25–6, 46). Highly commercial branches, such as viticulture, are often characterized by small-scale production structures. As long as 30 years ago Jan de Vries argued that specialization and investment by medium-sized and small peasant farms mainly drove productivity improvements in maritime areas of the sixteenth- and seventeenth-century Netherlands (see now de Vries in Hoppenbrouwers and van Zanden, 2001: 78–80). Petty farmers in Flanders achieved exceptional yields per area by means of very high labor inputs (Thoen in Hoppenbrouwers and van Zanden, 2001). It has been assumed that in countries with more pronounced seigneurial demesne farming, change was primarily promoted by landlords. It is true that lords usually faced fewer institutional barriers, such as those inhibiting enclosure, or tithe and open-field production restrictions. The initial application of the Holstein *Koppelwirtschaft* on Mecklenburg demesne farms indeed derived from landlord power. However, in neighboring Brandenburg the picture is mixed. There, peasant farmers, along with bourgeois and peasant leaseholders of landlord and royal demesne farms, took part in innovations in agriculture (Müller, 1967: 52–60, 108–66; Wehler, 1989: 86–7). In other parts of Germany, in Switzerland, and in parts of Austria agricultural innovation was also driven by the activities of medium-sized peasant farms (Kopsidis, 2006: 277–374; Robisheaux in Scott, 1998: 115, 123). In Bohemia, many changes in agriculture are still seen as being pioneered by demesne farms during the eighteenth and early nineteenth centuries. In the 1840s, nearly 90 percent of the arable area used for modern crop rotation techniques was demesne land (Melville in Gunst and Hoffmann, 1982: 104). A similar description is given for eighteenth-century Hungary (Paulinyi in Mieck, 1993: 937).

Surveys using estimated aggregate data usually indicate a west–east and north–south decline in agricultural productivity (table 3.1), but it is important to remember that agricultural productivity varied strongly even regionally. Variations can only been explained through a combination of economic (such as market demand), institutional, and climatic factors, as well as influences of the physical environment (see chapter 1).

Agricultural yields increased considerably, particularly after 1750. In England, yields rose by more than 50 percent between 1700 and 1800, while between 1760 and 1812 those in Belgium increased by 15 to 24 percent depending on the type of grain. Grain yields in the most productive areas in the north of France were at around 25 hl/ha between 1760 and 1790, up from levels of around 16–18 hl/ha during the sixteenth century. Recent estimates for France highlight the importance of regional differences in long-term development and the fact that progress was not continuous. Even in countries with estimates of comparatively high aggregate yields around 1800, such as Belgium and the Netherlands, regional differences could be enormous. In 1846, land productivity in Flanders and Brabant was double that of Namur and Luxembourg, and grain yields in the most productive regions of the Netherlands could be three times as high as those in the worst in 1812. Similar regional differences can be observed from table 3.1 for areas of Germany, where maximum yields – for instance, in regions of northwestern Germany – were quite comparable to

Table 3.1 Overview of European cereal yields (in hl/ha and seed-output yield ratios) around 1800*

Country	Crop yields			Yield ratios		
	Wheat	Rye	Oats	Wheat	Rye	Oats
Austria	12.8	12.9	19.3	4.0	4.0	5.2
Belgium	19.6	20.8	25.1	11.5	12.2	13.2
Denmark	–	–	–	5.0–9.0	5.0–9.0	5.0–9.0
England	20.3	–	32.5	11.3	–	9.0
Estonia	–	–	–	5.5	3.5–6.0	3.5–6.0
France	12.2	10.8	15.2	6.4	5.5	8.2
Germany (4 depts.)	13.7	13.2	25.8	7.1	5.6	8.0
Germany (Prussian Kingdom)	–	–	–	3.75–10.8	4.0–7.9	3.0–10.7
Hungary	11.0–19.2	6.2–12.2	–	4.0–7.0	3.3–6.5	–
Ireland	19.9	–	32.9	–	–	–
Italy	6.9–8.5	7.6	9.9	4.1	4.4	5.2
Netherlands	18.9	15.4	28.8	11.2	7.5	11.1
Norway	–	–	–	4.0	4.0	4.0
Poland	–	–	–	4.8	4.2	3.4
Russia	*c.*9	*c.*9	*c.*9	3.0	3.1	3.6
Spain	7.0	4.0	9.5	4.5	–	–
Sweden	–	–	–	6.0	5.9	5.0

*Additional data: van Zanden in Bavel and Thoen, 1999, based on own calculations. For conversion of grain weights into hl yields see Overton and Campbell in Bavel and Thoen, 1999: 198–9.
Sources: Achilles, 1991: 22–3; Kahk and Tarvel in Gunst and Hoffmann, 1982: 373; Paulinyi in Mieck, 1993: 938; van Zanden in Bavel and Thoen, 1999: 359, 361, 366, 368.

western European levels. Between the individual Austrian Crown lands, wheat yields varied between 6 and more than 17 hl/ha (Achilles, 1991; Béaur, 2000: 135–66; Dejongh and Thoen, Overton and Campbell, and van Bavel in Bavel and Thoen, 1999; Dewald and Vardi in Scott, 1998: 26; Hoffman, 1996: esp. 132–42; Moriceau, 1994: 461, 878–84; Thoen in Hoppenbrouwers and van Zanden, 2001: 117–19; Overton, 1996: 82; de Vries and van der Woude, 1997: 232–4). There was also a general increase in agricultural labor productivity, rising by around 70 percent in England for instance (Allen, 2000; van Zanden in Bavel and Thoen, 1999: 369). However, labor productivity likewise displayed considerable regional variations. For example, labor productivity in the maritime western part of the Netherlands was double that of the inland eastern part around 1810 (de Vries and van der Woude, 1997: 230).

Experiences could vary not only in level, but also in timing. Some countries and regions achieved continuous growth over the early modern period. In the Netherlands, agricultural output grew faster in the period between 1510 and 1650 than between 1650 and 1810, probably because of the particularly strong nature of the seventeenth-century crisis (de Vries and van der Woude, 1997: 232–4). Fluctuations in demand, as well as feudal pressure on peasant farms, such as the requirement to provide labor services, played a major role in determining productivity in other areas of Europe (Petráň, 1973). Thus in Poland, average yield ratios in the sixteenth century were higher than in the period 1620–1750. After 1750, there was a strong increase in arable yields. In neighboring Bohemia, yields per hectare reached around 20hl/ha on demesne farms in the south and centre of the country and more than doubled between 1750 and 1850 (Melville in Gunst and Hoffmann, 1982: 104; Żytkowicz, 1971). Yield ratios in Italy remained very stable in the long run and increased steadily (by 50 percent between 1400 and 1800) due to rising labor inputs. North Italy experienced particularly strong growth: wheat yields around Rome reached 7:1, while those for barley even hit 13:1 in the first half of the eighteenth century (Abrate in Mieck, 1993: 867; Federico and Malanima, 2004: 453, 456–7).

Maize was far more important in Italy and Spain than in northern Europe, and maize yields per area were, by their nature, much higher than those of grain. Besides, the aggregate comparison is incomplete, because certain types of agriculture such as olives, rice, silk, tobacco, or cotton (prominent in France, Italy, the Ottoman empire, and Spain) are excluded from the general picture.

This survey confirms long-standing criticism that the computation of aggregate yields obscures important regional and chronological variation. In addition, research in some areas of Europe is usually under-represented in the internationally accessible literature. Thus, in his critique of prevalent approaches, J. Petráň drew attention to the fact that in areas of commercial agriculture in Bohemia yields of 1:10–12 were frequent during the sixteenth and seventeenth centuries, and even less fertile regions would reach 1:7–9. These data compare well with the better-known Dutch regions in the same period (Petráň, 1973: 107–13).

Crop yields may underestimate the extent of changes in early modern agricultural production. For instance, the introduction of certain crops like potatoes supported the subsistence basis, particularly in Ireland and the Low Countries, but also in England, Germany, and the Habsburg monarchy. Famines could trigger a widespread introduction of new crops, notably after the particularly serious one in 1771–2. A gradual intensification of agriculture through the spread of maize or rice formed an important development in Italy, Spain, and across parts of the Ottoman empire. The cultivation of maize in the Mediterranean began during the sixteenth century, intensified in the following century, and spread to other parts of Europe after 1700, for instance into Alpine areas. Equally important was the progress of regional specialization that supported productivity gains, market involvement, and commercialization. In regions of Spain (Galicia, Andalucía, Catalonia), Italy and the Ottoman empire, the specialization in viticulture or olives led to an abandonment of subsistence agriculture (Abrate in Mieck, 1993: 867; Adanir in Scott, 1998: 298; de Vries and van der Woude, 1997: 225; Epstein in Scott, 1998: 76; van Zanden in Bavel and Thoen, 1999: 366–7).

Total agricultural output during the eighteenth century grew extensively because of increases in the productive area. Thus one of the first steps towards more intensive agriculture was the improvement of the three-field system by reducing or planting the fallow over summer. In most European countries, the amount of fallow land was drastically reduced from original levels of up to 40 percent of the arable area. In areas of very low population density, where extensive forms of agriculture (temporary cultivation, *Feldgraswirtschaft*) existed, the three-field system spread during the eighteenth century (for example in the Hungarian plains: Paulinyi in Mieck, 1993: 937–8). The relative decline of transhumant pastoralism brought about some intensification. Land reclamation was widespread. Polder drainage and land reclamation were intensified in the Netherlands, but also along the German North Sea coast. About 50,000 hectares of new agricultural land were drained in the western Dutch provinces alone between 1650 and 1810 (de Vries and van der Woude, 1997: 224, 230–2). Land drainage was also widely carried out along rivers and in marshes in central and eastern Europe and in Italian coastal areas. Land abandoned or less intensively used after the seventeenth-century agricultural slump was now reclaimed for arable agriculture. In France, about 600,000 hectares of arable land was cleared after 1750 (Jones, 1988: 17). Until the first half of the nineteenth century increases in the arable areas of individual countries of 20 percent and more of the total were not rare. In addition, new arable land was colonized in parts of east-central Europe, Russia, and Ukraine, as well as Spain, where the difficult Sierra Morena was successfully settled. In Russia, 21.4 million hectares of forest were cleared in the eighteenth century. The growth of the population also meant that labor became cheaper and could be used more intensively for agriculture.

Seigneurial Structures and "Serfdom"

The majority of the eighteenth-century rural population was still embedded – at least formally – in what were ultimately "feudal" institutional arrangements. Notable exceptions included the freehold and leasehold tenants in England, the freeholders and Crown peasants of Norway, Sweden, and Finland, as well as regions of the Netherlands and the Ottoman empire. When I refer to relationships as being "ultimately feudal" no connotation of any medieval reality is intended. What I mean is that farmers and smallholders only possessed the *dominium utile*, or use-rights, of their land. In the vast majority of cases, they had secured these rights in a hereditary form. Ultimate ownership (*dominium directum*), nonetheless still belonged *de iure* to an overlord or landlord who had devolved the use-rights to "subjects" in exchange for rent obligations. Such landowners were not necessarily nobles; they also could include princes, religious institutions, municipalities, and individual commoners, including women. The owners of use-rights usually had more or less full property rights, took economic decisions, and could sell or transfer their property without interference by lords. The "feudal" burden was commuted to a customary rent that had to be paid to the landlord. The subject–landlord relationship in western and eastern Europe was thus generally tied to the land, and did not affect the personal status of individuals.

In some areas personal dependency (bondage or "serfdom"), where subjects were personally dependent on their landlord, existed. There were some limited remnants of bondage in parts of western Germany and France, but these had few practical consequences. Serfdom existed in areas of Denmark, Schleswig-Holstein, Mecklenburg, Pomerania, and Livonia (Gaunt in Scott, 1998: 330–1; Hagen in Scott, 1998: 168–9, 174–5, 177; Harnisch and Heitz in Gunst and Hoffmann, 1982: 24; Kahk and Tarvel in Gunst and Hoffmann, 1982: 366–7; Klußmann, 2003; Melton, 1988; Hagen, 2002: esp. 36–7 for the differentiated situation in Brandenburg). Personal dependency was also introduced by law in Lithuania, Belorussia, Russia, and Ukraine, but there were considerable variations, notably due to the difficulties in enforcing laws (Melton in Scott, 1998: 237–41, 246; see also chapter 14). The picture for Poland is also currently being revised. Resettlement after the seventeenth-century crisis created a growing group of free peasants numbering nearly 16 percent of the total rural population and 25 percent of the rural population in Greater Poland by 1791. Additional numbers claimed free status, while independent and commercially oriented peasant farmers dominated in the areas around Gdańsk (Blum, 1978: 30, 32; Hagen in Scott, 1998: 175–8, 182, 185–6). A substantial proportion of the Hungarian peasantry, once also considered "serfs," were in fact free to move and cannot therefore be regarded as being in personal bondage. Landlord structures remained particularly weak in the resettled large Hungarian plains before 1750 (Blum, 1978: 32–3; Király, 1975: 270, 272–3, 276; Paulinyi in Mieck, 1993: 932). Finally, strong regional differences characterized the territories of southeastern Europe. For example, the rural population of Moldavia and Wallachia contained groups subject to servile relations and others that were not. The status of peasants in some areas of the Ottoman Balkans and in central and northern Greece is said to have deteriorated when tax farmers accumulated landlord powers and formed large estates. These claims remain to be investigated in full, but it is already clear that there were considerable variations in the density of these farms, their formation, size, and methods of cultivation (Blum, 1978: 33; McGowan, 1994: 682–3, 685–6, 688).

Other regions displayed a continuum between milder forms of landlord control and the persistence of forced labor service (labor rents) and other obligations close to personal dependency, such as restrictions on individual mobility or the requirement to send children as farmhands and maids to the lord's demesne. In regions with mild landlord control, such as parts of France or central Italy, seigneurial structures scarcely constrained the rural population. Southern Spain and Castile are usually regarded as "more feudal" than Catalonia, as is southern Italy, where powerful noble families retained large estates (in the Agro Romano, 113 families owned 61 percent of the land). In Sweden, landlord structures were stronger in the southern province of Scania and in areas surrounding Stockholm. Such regional variation seems only natural given the large and composite structure of states and empires (selected examples in Harnisch and Heitz in Gunst and Hoffmann, 1982; Olsson and Sundberg in Klußmann, 2003; Dewald and Vardi, Epstein, Rebel, Robisheaux and Ruiz in Scott, 1998; Woolf, 1986: 44–50).

The preceding discussion indicates that "serfdom" is an inadequate term to characterize all landlord–peasant relationships in eastern Europe. Unfortunately, the wide variety of types of personal legal status still confuses even the current literature, compounding the traditional misconception of a "dualism" between western, supposedly "free" peasants and those in the east laboring under a "second serfdom." This term, by itself, only bears meaning within a certain theoretical framework – which, ironically, is rarely preferred by the very authors who use it in a general way in the current English-language literature. A first step to acknowledging the results of new approaches to east-central and eastern European rural societies would be to employ more useful English-language equivalents of Czech, German, Hungarian, Polish or Slovak terms, replacing "serfdom" with concepts like "demesne lordship" (*Gutsherrschaft*) or "latifundium" (Bush, 1992: 153, 157; Hagen in Scott, 1998; Hagen, 2002; Melton, 1988).

Figure 3 *Verwalter und Bauer*. Few landlords managed their estates directly, leaving them instead in the hands of stewards. This painting from mid-eighteenth-century Austria, in the former Schloss Kirchberg, shows the social distance between the steward on the left and a peasant to his right. *Photo Niederösterreichisches Archiv*

Land rents and dues provided only part of many lords' incomes, alongside returns from the demesne economy, including farms, mills, breweries, and distilleries. Additional income might derive from other rights they could possess, such as legal jurisdictions, political privileges, and economic rights including market and production monopolies (Blum, 1978: 80–94; Langton in Scott, 1998: 393). Landlords came from many backgrounds. For instance, in parts of Italy, France, and Flanders, burghers acquired former seigneurial or ecclesiastical landlordship over parts of the rural population. On the eve of the French Revolution, the bourgeoisie's share of landownership in France equaled that of the nobility at 20 to 30 percent (Béaur, 2000: 17–34, 213–42; Dewald and Vardi in Scott, 1998: 28, 30; Kriedte, 1983: 107–13). In Prussia, Sweden, and Russia, the situation of peasants on Crown and state estates was better than those on noble estates (but see Mironov, 2000: 74–5 for a different interpretation regarding Russian state peasants), even accepting the usual regional variations. After a land reform called *reduktion* in Finland and Sweden, the Crown resumed lordship over many of the nobility's peasants. However, the Swedish Crown sold much of its land to peasant farmers who became freeholders, who constituted over half of all farmers after 1800. The share of state peasants likewise increased in

Russia during the eighteenth and early nineteenth centuries (Gaunt in Scott, 1998: 325; Herlitz in Gunst and Hoffmann, 1982: 268–70, 272; Magnusson, 2000: 21–2; Melton in Scott, 1998).

We need to differentiate between lords' formal, normative powers and the practical extent of their authority. Research over the last 30 years reveals considerable discrepancies between norms and practice in central, eastern, and southern Europe, meaning we can no longer accept older claims that feudal lords exercised "absolute power." After the end of the Cold War in 1989–91, historical-anthropological and microhistorical approaches were applied to the concept of demesne lordship, considerably enriching our understanding of the situation in these regions. The results of comparative empirical research into the social aspects of lordship in the west and east revealed a differentiated continuum of manifestations rather than clear-cut "agrarian structures," and created the basis for a better understanding of the mechanisms of lordship and its extreme variation in practice. Taken together, this evidence compels us to revise our traditional concept of an agrarian "dualism" dividing Europe along the river Elbe (Bush, 1992: 153, 157; Cerman and Zeitlhofer, 2002; Hagen in Scott, 1998; Hagen, 2002; Kaak and Schattkowsky, 2003; Melton in Scott, 1988: 318; Peters, 1997; for a historiographical survey see Kaak, 1991). Comparative research based on a new conceptual framework would certainly open new frontiers and provide a better understanding of European rural societies and their respective social property and power relations, including the allegedly "liberal" countryside of England and the Netherlands (Langton in Scott, 1998: 378, 393–4; Scott in Scott, 1998: 18–19).

The burden of dues owed to landlords also varied considerably. Usually, basic payments were light and pegged at fixed cash sums unchanged over many years. In an era of grain price inflation, such as the eighteenth century, the value of dues decreased in real terms. Naturally, landlords often sought to increase existing payments or introduce new ones. Dues in kind were usually a certain percentage of the harvest, which, by nature, were inflation-proof (Antoine in Prass et al., 2004; Béaur, 2000: 213–41; see for example the regionally variable levels of harvest dues in France described in Jones, 1988: 45–9). In France, feudal dues were generally low, but landlords combined them with "commercial" rents for land from their former demesne properties which they leased to peasants, either for money or in sharecropping.

Although there is little comparative research on this matter, the current hypothesis is that the total rent burden increased from western to eastern Europe, especially if labor services are included in the calculations. As a benchmark, peasant dues and tithes are assumed to have equaled about a third of gross income (Achilles, 1991: 40; Blum, 1978: 50–64, 71–9; Harnisch and Heitz in Gunst and Hoffmann, 1982: 21–2). The burden of forced labor services per peasant farm varied between as many as six days per week in some regions and none in others. Such services were not unique to the east, although, in general, they were much lighter in western territories and affected only a very small proportion of the rural population. During the eighteenth century there was a general trend of the increasing commutation of labor services to financial payment in east-central and eastern Europe (Melton, 1988).

The agricultural boom after the 1740s led to an increase in rent burdens in those areas were commercial rents and leaseholds were common. French land rents grew by 51 percent above prices between the 1730s and the 1780s. While prices moved faster than rents during the 1760s, this trend was reversed after 1776 (Jones, 1988:

33). Lease prices likewise increased in Belgium during the eighteenth century (Thoen in Hoppenbrouwers and Zanden, 2001: 133–6). Rents represented an average of around 30 percent of gross income in France, compared to 20 to 40 percent in Holland. English rents per acre rose fourfold between 1690 and 1750, albeit from low levels, and then increased dramatically between 1790 and about 1815, following the trends of agricultural prices and income (Turner, Beckett and Afton, 1997: 148–75, 206–11).

Influenced by Physiocrat ideas and the necessity to secure the rural tax base, central governments showed greater attention to agriculture and rural social relations as the eighteenth century progressed. Reforms targeted more and more aspects of trade, economy, and society. Legal protection of the rural population improved, and the state eventually abolished the remnants of "feudalism," either through reform (see chapters 14–17, 19, 20) or, indeed, revolution (Blum, 1978: 197–400; Magnusson, 2000: 57–79; Scott, 1998; Wehler, 1989; Woolf, 1986: 69–151).

Property Rights and Rural Social Structure

An important aspect of rural life in early modern Europe is how people held their land or property. Land tenure could come through inheritance, whereby peasants owned it in perpetuity,[2] or on a temporary basis, such as leaseholds fixed for some years or the owner's lifetime. Generally, leaseholds were most widespread in England, where they coexisted with traditional customary forms of landholding such as copyholds, as well as parts of the Low Countries and Italy. However, the incidence of leases also increased in other territories, for instance when landlords dissolved or leased their demesne farms in Brandenburg and Bohemia. French peasant farmers and smallholders combined land which they held in inheritance with land they leased from landlords (Antoine in Prass et al., 2004; Béaur, 2000: 17–34; Bush, 1992: 145–6). Hereditary tenure dominated in many parts of Europe, such as in the Basque area, Catalonia, and areas of Italy, as well as in Switzerland, Austria, Germany, and in most of east-central Europe. For example, up to 90 percent of peasant farms were held this way in western Germany and Austria (Robisheaux in Scott, 1998: 111, 121, 133).

This distribution of hereditary tenure already shows that the image of a general expropriation (*Bauernlegen*) of east-central and eastern European peasant farmers and smallholders is a myth. Expropriation did climax towards the late eighteenth century, but was mainly confined to the seigneurial estates in Mecklenburg (but not the princely estates there, although peasants could still be forced to leave their farms and move to another estate). Recent studies also suggest that evictions took place in the southern Swedish province of Scania around 1800, but they stopped in the Danish duchy of Schleswig around 1720 (Melton, 1988: 324–5, 334). Even insecure forms of tenure, such as those where the landlord could evict (theoretically) at will, were in practice often extended, even over generations. The seizure of abandoned peasant land occurred more frequently and was a consequence of seventeenth-century warfare in eastern Germany, Bohemia and Moravia, Poland, and Hungary.

In the European parts of the Ottoman empire, dispossession seems to have resulted, not from direct force, but from a combination of the tax regime and the decline of both population and agricultural prices during the seventeenth century.

Tax farmers succeeded in accumulating land from abandoned farms or those seized in lieu of debt, although the Ottoman authorities tried to stop this. These large farms (*çiftlik*) were not found everywhere, and the way in which they were run varied: sometimes they specialized in animal husbandry, elsewhere they worked with wage labor or through sharecropping. It is assumed that this system promoted a more commercial and market-oriented agriculture. Nonetheless, a higher degree of peasant autonomy and dominant peasant landholding continued, for example in Ottoman Serbia, Turkey proper, and in mountainous areas of Macedonia and Greece (Adanir in Scott, 1998: 298–303; McGowan, 1994: 686–9).

Sharecropping has attracted considerable controversy. It was found in certain areas of southern France, Italy, and Ottoman Greece (French *métayage*, Italian *mezzadria*). Actual contracts varied, but usually harvests were split equally between tenants and landlords. It has traditionally been condemned as inefficient, because it did not give enough incentives to producers, and is held responsible for underdevelopment and misery among French and Italian peasants. Rather than seeing the method as simply oppressive, more recent research suggests it may have been a rational choice given the combined occurrence of market failures (especially in credit markets), lack of capital or risk aversity among peasants, and the danger of soil exhaustion (for example in viticulture). The problem with this new approach is that it suggests tenants had a free choice over contract forms, something they generally lacked in practice. Power lay primarily with the lords, and this must still be considered when assessing why certain forms developed (Béaur, 2000: 114; Bush, 1992: 144–5; Dewald and Vardi, Epstein and Scott in Scott, 1998: 10–11).

Population growth and social and economic change increased the proportion of smallholders and landless people in rural society. Peasant farmers and owners of substantial farms had already been a minority in many areas since the sixteenth century. By the eighteenth century the rural social structure in most areas was dominated by smallholders, cottagers with only small garden plots, the completely landless, and people without any property at all, such as lodgers and life-cycle servants. Gregory King already believed that half the English population were laborers, cottagers, and poor with little or no land in 1688. Another estimate puts the share of wage-dependent (i.e. proletarianized) individuals at about two-thirds of the rural population in Europe by 1800. Perhaps not all of them should be regarded as fully dependent on wage labor, as they might be integrated into labor markets only seasonally or during specific life cycles.[3] While, in some areas, large owner-occupied or tenant farms were prominent, other areas, such as Flanders, southern France, southern Spain, and parts of Italy were characterized by smallholding farms working tiny parcels of land extremely intensively. Such folk are known by a bewildering variety of local names, both in contemporary documents and in subsequent studies. Research on France, for instance, differentiates between *laboureurs*, as relatively substantial landowners, *manouvriers*, *brassiers*, or *journaliers* (smallholders), and finally a landless rural proletariat (Béaur, 2000: 99–111; Jones, 1988: 8).

In the past, the growing social stratification has been explained through theories of population pressure. This Malthusian model assumes that population growth changes the population/land ratio and hence land distribution. However, it fails to explain why property does not become less stratified in periods of population decline and why rural social structure reacted differently to demographic growth. The whole issue of a demographic "pressure," too, seems problematic, as population density varied enormously in Europe and local rural societies adapted flexibly to population growth. Thus, the inventory of such theories explaining social differentiation in English, French, and Italian rural history, or of traditions of German-language "population history," should be treated with considerable caution. In fact, recent advances in social history have proved many of the underlying assumptions to be problematic, vague, or wrong (Fertig and Zeitlhofer in Duhamelle and Schlumbohm, 2003).

A second group of theories relating to the patterns of social differentiation is closely linked to these population-based approaches and argues on the basis of differences in inheritance law and ecological conditions. According to these, impartible inheritance practices among the peasantry would create an elite of property-owning peasants and a mass of landless people, triggering the emigration of those unable to inherit land. Partible inheritance, by contrast, would cause stronger population growth and the continuous fragmentation of landownership into households holding tiny parcels of land (for assumptions of a link between partible inheritance and land fragmentation in France and Spain see Dewald and Vardi, and Ruiz in Scott, 1998; for Germany see Rouette in Prass et al., 2004).

These theories ignore both the influence of land markets and the role of individuals and institutions in determining the flexible application of existing norms, and fail to explain conflicting regional evidence. Social history has given considerable attention to rural family history, property, and inheritance over the last three decades and studies seem to agree that there is no uniform link between inheritance systems, family structure, and the development of social structure. Inheritance systems, for instance, proved to be much more varied because they are defined by the social practice of rural communities and by the strategies of peasant families. Within certain limits of institutional regulation, households and individuals adapted inheritance practices to suit their own aims and expectations. Studies now illustrate the variability of social practice, the interrelation between market and non-market mechanisms, and the limits of institutional control over these processes. The peasantry and the rural population is finally understood as an active participant in the development of early modern rural society (Béaur, 2000; Béaur in Prass et al., 2004; Bush, 1992; Cavaciocchi, 2003; Ehmer et al., 2001; Fauve Chamoux and Rouette in Prass et al., 2004; Kertzer and Barbagli, 2001; Langton in Scott, 1998: 378; Levi, 1988; Sabean, 1990; Štefanová, Velková and Zeitlhofer in Cerman and Zeitlhofer, 2002)

This criticism is a result of new approaches in economic and social history since the 1970s, particularly the theories of proto-industrialization and paradigmatic shifts within historical research. Turning attention to regions and micro-level research has shifted the focus to the lacunae in earlier, structural approaches. As a consequence, a new picture emerges of early modern rural society, one of inherent flexibility and adaptability, of constant change in its economic and survival strategies. Structural influences, such as markets, lordship, state, church, and the like are now analyzed from the perspective of the peasantry or "from the village" (Hagen in Scott, 1998).[4]

The Proto-Industrialization of the Countryside

Social differentiation illustrates that rural society was not merely made up of people owning land or engaged in agricultural activities. Many were wage or migrant laborers in agriculture but also in other sectors, such as building. Increasingly, rural households and societies were influenced by crafts whose production was geared towards supra-regional or international markets. These rural proto-industries had already emerged by the later Middle Ages, but experienced strong growth during the early modern period and especially in the eighteenth century (see chapter 4). In many regions, thousands of households joined domestic industries either full-time or as a by-employment (for example seasonally, when agricultural labor requirements were low). The spread and intensification of rural domestic industries probably changed the rural landscape of Europe more than any other economic factor in the eighteenth century.

Theories of proto-industrialization interpreted this development as the first stage of industrialization (Mendels, 1972), or as the missing link in the transition from feudalism to capitalism (Kriedte et al., 1981). Proto-industrialization was understood not only as an economic process, but as one with important demographic and social consequences for rural households and societies. Between the 1970s and the late 1990s numerous empirical studies evaluated all aspects of these theories, offering both support and criticism (Ogilvie and Cerman, 1996). This research has not only been fruitful in terms of the original theories, but has also modernized approaches in economic and social history. It has given rise to empirical in-depth studies, combining economic aspects with regional, social, and demographic developments, household and family structures, mentalities, and aspects of cultural history. Micro-historical approaches have been particularly helpful (e.g. Medick, 1996; Schlumbohm, 1994).

Although textile production was by far the most important sector, rural domestic industries worked on many other materials, such as iron and metal, leather, or wood. Most attention has been given to textiles, particularly linen, cotton, woolen and worsted, and silk production, although more recent studies have explored the organization and growth of iron and metal proto-industries in England, Sweden, and Russia (see Gaunt in Scott, 1998: 326; Hudson and Magnusson in Ogilvie and Cerman, 1996).

Rural domestic industries provided important employment opportunities for the landless and promoted regional specialization ("bifurcation") between agricultural and non-agricultural activities. Yet they also spread into zones of commercial agriculture and were not limited to sub-peasant households. This was particularly the case in more capital-intensive branches, such as silk. Income generated by domestic industries was frequently invested in land. Economic activity in both sectors was maintained as a household strategy to minimize risk and protect against crisis. This would have stabilized traditional agrarian social structure rather than bringing about change, as was recently stressed for Flanders, where many small farms would not have survived on the basis of agricultural income alone (Thoen in Hoppenbrouwers and Zanden, 2001). Other debates have been stimulated by the theories' predictions concerning gender roles, the acceleration of demographic growth, and the organization of work within rural households.

Proto-industrialization was a regional phenomenon, and it is important to acknowledge that it was not limited to western or central Europe. Other areas were important centers for the production and export of cotton, woolen, silk and linen textiles, as well as iron goods: Catalonia in Spain, parts of northern Italy, Sweden, Little Poland, the Balkan and Turkish regions of the Ottoman empire, the Urals, and those areas outside the black earth zone in Russia (Adanir, Dewald, and Vardi and Melton in Scott, 1998; Ogilvie and Cerman, 1996). Even households outside these areas of concentrated production still participated by supplying the necessary raw materials such as flax, hemp, cotton, wool, sheep, and dyeing plants.

Conclusions

This chapter has argued that the standard contrast between agricultural innovation and "peasant traditionalism" is a misleading interpretation of *ancien régime* European rural societies. New approaches have demonstrated that the long-term "immobility" of early modern rural economy and society is a myth that has many origins. Current approaches to rural households suggest that innovation and "traditionalism" should not be understood as a contradiction, but rather as two sides of the same coin. Economic decision-making at household level took place within a complex matrix of insecure and imperfect markets, concern for income security, and to minimize risk. Moreover, decisions were affected by the multifarious social, economic, political, and legal power relations governing the rural population across Europe.

Studies concentrating on a comparison of estimated aggregate statistics do represent some progress in rural history, but generally obscure the numerous important regional and national variations described above. As this chapter has suggested, it is clear that there was no single "grand design" behind rural development. Instead, productivity gains during the eighteenth century must be explained by reference to several institutional arrangements, as well as the considerable variation in form and level of rural economic development. An aggregate approach neglects these differences and obscures the presence of highly developed, commercialized, and specialized zones of agriculture or proto-industrialization in almost every part of Europe.

The increasing regional specialization was also promoted by the intensification of international and regional trade (see chapters 4 and 26). Longer-distance trade included the flow of grain through the Baltic to feed north-western Europe, the export of Danish, north German, and Hungarian cattle to neighboring countries, and that of Spanish wool to northern Europe. Examples of regional commerce range from viticulture or the Alpine pasture economy to industrial cash crops and proto-industrialization. The dimensions of this trade became increasingly global during the eighteenth century (see chapter 25).

Above all, theories of proto-industrialization stimulated a redirection of our gaze from the aristocrat's manor, banker's counting house, or reforming statesman's office and turned it towards the rural household. This "view from the village," which should be strengthened by a comparative perspective in future research, reveals that even comparatively humble men and women were important agents in the wider changes affecting the whole of Europe.

Notes

1 Cf. Béaur, 2000; Hoffman, 1996; Moriceau, 1994. Recently, the idea of a productivity gap between English agriculture and the most productive zones in France was criticized as having been overestimated by past research.

2 Sometimes, the tenure was theoretically limited to a certain number of generations, e.g. three, as in the Spanish "foros" in Galicia. For an overview see also Bush, 1992: 139–41, 144–5, Maddalena in Cipolla, 1974.

3 Bush, 1992; Mieck in Mieck, 1993: 185–6, 190–1; Tilly, 1981: 198–9. For conditions in individual countries see Béaur, 2000: 99–111; Blum, 1978: 95–115; Hagen, 2002: 391–422; Jones, 1988: 8–14; Kahk and Tarvil in Gunst and Hoffmann, 1982; 363, 372; Király, 1975: 275; Magnusson, 2000: 27–30; Melton, 1988; Müller, 1967: 79–80; Overton, 1996: 38–41, 171–82; Paulinyi in Mieck, 1993: 931; Scott, 1998; Thoen in Hoppenbrouwers and van Zanden, 2001: 115–17; de Vries and van der Woude, 1997: 233–4; Wehler, 1989: 140–77.

4 For a selection of most influential micro-historical studies, which, among other approaches, contributed strongly to overcome the gaps of "structural views" see Beck, 1993; Ginzburg, 1992; Medick, 1996; Sabean, 1990; Schlumbohm, 1994.

Bibliography

Achilles, W., *Landwirtschaft in der Frühen Neuzeit* (Munich, 1991).

Allen, R. C., *Enclosure and the Yeoman* (Oxford, 1992).

Allen, R. C., "Economic structure and agricultural productivity in Europe, 1300–1800," *European Review of Economic History*, 3 (2000), 1–25.

Allen, R. C., "The great divergence in European wages and prices," *Explorations in Economic History*, 38 (2001), 411–43.

Bavel, B. J. P. van and E. Thoen (eds.), *Land Productivity and Agro-Systems in the North Sea Area* (Turnhout, 1999).

Béaur, G., *Histoire agraire de la France au XVIIIe siècle* (Paris, 2000).

Beck, R., *Unterfinning. Ländliche Welt vor Anbruch der Moderne* (Munich, 1993).

Blum, J., *The End of the Old Order in Rural Europe* (Princeton, 1978).

Bush, M. L., "Peasant right and the peasantries of Europe under the old regime," in M. L. Bush (ed.), *Social Orders and Social Classes in Europe since 1500* (London, 1992), pp. 136–57.

Cavaciocchi, S. (ed.), *Il mercato della terra secc. XIII–XVIII* (Florence, 2003).

Cerman, M. and H. Zeitlhofer (eds.), *Soziale Strukturen in Böhmen. Ein regionaler Vergleich von Wirtschaft und Gesellschaft in Gutsherrschaften, 16–19. Jahrhundert* (Vienna and Munich, 2002).

Cipolla, C. M., *The Fontana Economic History of Europe*, vols. 2 and 3 (London, 1973, 1974).

de Vries, J., *European Urbanization, 1500–1800* (Cambridge, MA, 1984).

de Vries, J. and A.van der Woude, *The First Modern Economy: Success, Failure, and Perseverance of the Dutch Economy, 1500–1815* (Cambridge, 1997).

Duhamelle, C. and J. Schlumbohm (eds.), *Eheschließungen im Europa des 18. und 19. Jahrhunderts* (Göttingen, 2003).

Ehmer, J., T. K. Hareven, R. Wall, and M. Cerman (eds.), *Family History Revisited: Comparative Perspectives* (Newark, 2001).

Ellis, F., *Peasant Economics: Farm Households and Agrarian Development* (Cambridge, 1993).

Epstein, S. R., *Freedom and Growth: The Rise of States and Markets in Europe, 1300–1750* (London, 2000).

Federico, G. and P. Malanima, "Progress, decline, growth: product and productivity in Italian agriculture, 1000–2000," *Economic History Review*, 57 (2004), 437–64.

Ginzburg, C., *The Cheese and the Worms: The Cosmos of a Sixteenth-Century Miller* (London, 1992).

Grantham, G., "The growth of labour productivity in the production of wheat in the Cinq Grosses Fermes of France, 1750–1929," in B. M. S. Campbell and M. Overton (eds.), *Land, Labour and Livestock: Historical Studies in European Agricultural Productivity* (Manchester, 1991), pp. 340–63.

Gunst, P. and T. Hoffmann (eds.), *Large Estates and Small Holdings in the Middle Ages and Modern Times* (Budapest, 1982).

Hagen, W. W., *Ordinary Prussians: Brandenburg Junkers and Villagers, 1500–1840* (Cambridge, 2002).

Hoffman, P. T., *Growth in a Traditional Society: The French Countryside, 1450–1815* (Princeton, 1996).

Hoppenbrouwers, P. and J. L. van Zanden (eds.), *Peasants into Farmers? The Transformation of the Rural Economy and Society in the Low Countries* (Turnhout, 2001).

Jones, P. M., *The Peasantry in the French Revolution* (Cambridge, 1988).

Kaak, H., *Die Gutsherrschaft. Theoriegeschichtliche Untersuchungen zum Agrarwesen im ostelbischen Raum* (Berlin, 1991).

Kaak, H. and M. Schattkowsky (eds.), *Herrschaft. Machtentfaltung über adligen und fürstlichen Grundbesitz in der Frühen Neuzeit* (Cologne, 2003).

Kertzer, D. and M. Barbagli (eds.), *The History of the European Family*, vol. 1: *Family Life in Early Modern Times* (New Haven, 2001).

Király, B. K., "Neo-serfdom in Hungary," *Slavic Review*, 34 (1975), 269–78.

Klußmann, J. (ed.), *Leibeigenschaft. Bäuerliche Unfreiheit in der frühen Neuzeit* (Cologne, 2003).

Kopsidis, M., *Agrarentwicklung. Historische Agrarrevolutionen und Entwicklungsökonomie* (Stuttgart, 2006).

Kriedte, P., *Peasants, Landlords and Merchant Capitalists: Europe and the World Economy, 1500–1800* (Leamington Spa, 1983).

Kriedte, P., H. Medick, and J. Schlumbohm, *Industrialization before Industrialization* (Cambridge, 1981).

Le Roy Ladurie, E., *The Mind and the Method of the Historian* (1974; Chicago, 1981).

Levi, G., *Inheriting Power* (Chicago, 1988).

Lynch, J., *Bourbon Spain 1700–1800* (Oxford, 1989).

McGowan, B., "The age of the *ayans*," in H. Inalcik and D. Quataert (eds.), *An Economic and Social History of the Ottoman Empire, 1300–1914* (Cambridge, 1994), pp. 637–758.

Magnusson, L., *An Economic History of Sweden* (London, 2000).

Medick, H., *Weben und Überleben in Laichingen 1650–1900. Lokalgeschichte als Allgemeine Geschichte* (Göttingen, 1996).

Melton, E., "Gutsherrschaft in East Elbian Germany and in Livonia, 1500–1800: a critique of the model," *Central European History*, 21 (1988), 315–49.

Mendels, F., "Proto-industrialization: the first phase of the industrialization process," *Journal of Economic History*, 32 (1972), 241–62.

Mieck, I. (ed.), *Handbuch der europäischen Wirtschafts- und Sozialgeschichte*, vol. 4 (Stuttgart, 1993).

Mironov, B. N., *The Social History of Imperial Russia, 1700–1917*, vol. 2 (Boulder, 2000).

Moor, M., L. Shaw-Taylor, and P. Warde (eds.), *The Management of Common Land in North West Europe, c.1500–1850* (Turnhout, 2002).

Moriceau, J.-M., *Les Fermiers de l'Île de France: L'Ascension d'un patronat agricole (Xve–XVIIIe siècles)* (Paris, 1994).

Müller, H.-H., *Märkische Landwirtschaft vor den Agrarreformen von 1807* (Potsdam, 1967).

Ogilvie, S. and M. Cerman (eds.), *European Proto-Industrialization* (Cambridge, 1996).

Overton, M., *Agricultural Revolution in England. The Transformation of the Agrarian Economy 1500–1850* (Cambridge, 1996).

Özmucur, S. and S. Pamuk, "Real wages and standards of living in the Ottoman empire, 1489–1914," *Journal of Economic History*, 62 (2002), 293–321.

Peters, J., *Gutsherrschaftsgesellschaften im europäischen Vergleich* (Berlin, 1997).

Petráň, J., "Die mitteleuropäische Landwirtschaft und der Handel im 16. und am Anfang des 17. Jahrhunderts," *Historica*, 18 (1973), 105–38.

Prass, R., G. Béaur, C. Duhamelle, and J. Schlumbohm (eds.), *Les Sociétés rurales en Allemagne et en France (XVIIIe–XIXe siècles)* (Rennes, 2004).

Sabean, D., *Property, Production and Family in Neckarhausen 1700–1870* (Cambridge, 1990).

Schlumbohm, J., *Lebensläufe, Familien, Höfe. Die Bauern und Heuerleute des Osnabrückischen Kirchspiels Belm in proto-industrieller Zeit, 1650–1860* (Göttingen, 1994).

Scott, T. (ed.), *The Peasantries of Europe* (London, 1998).

Tilly, C., *As Sociology Meets History* (Orlando, 1981).

Turner, M. E., J. V. Beckett, and B. Afton, *Agricultural Rent in England, 1690–1914* (Cambridge, 1997).

Wehler, H.-U., *Deutsche Gesellschaftsgeschichte 1700–1815*, vol. 1 (Munich, 1989).

Woolf, S., *History of Italy 1700–1860* (London, 1986).

Zanden, J. L. van, "Early modern economic growth," in M. Prak (ed.), *Early Modern Capitalism* (London, 2001), pp. 69–87.

Żytkowicz, L., "Grain yields in Poland, Bohemia, Hungary and Slovakia in the 16th to 18th centuries," *Acta Poloniae Historica*, 24 (1971), 51–72.

Chapter Four

Manufacturing, Markets, and Consumption

Beverly Lemire

The Industrial Landscape of Europe

Daniel Defoe, the eighteenth-century champion of English trade and industry, wrote at length on this subject from many perspectives. He worried about "the French or Germans" striving to get English wool for their manufacturers through surreptitious means before it could be made into woolens or worsteds by English hands. Competition in many forms was an ongoing feature of business life in this era. Trade, by which he meant both manufacturing and commerce, was of critical importance to the nations of Europe and they each made what they could of their human and material resources. In this spirit Defoe saluted "The People of Norway and Russia [who] having nothing but Mountains and Woods . . . yet rather than not trade, and rather than not labor, they cut down their Trees, and send them abroad to build Cities, and build Navies in other Countries." Baltic timber and naval stores represented vital trade commodities and were sought out by the dynamic economic regions less well endowed, such as France, England, and the Netherlands. Commerce in raw and manufactured materials preoccupied governments in war and peace and Defoe felt it a truism worth repeating that "Trade invigorates the World" (Defoe, 1967).

By 1700 significant forces were reshaping regions and communities. Luxury trades, like silk textile production, had earlier taken root in Italy; but well before 1700 Italy had lost its monopoly in this and other luxury manufactures, which had spread west and north. A successful silk industry had taken root in France where it was a pampered and cosseted trade, beloved of French ministers, who saw in it a means to dominate luxury commerce in Europe, a trade with a vaunted political aesthetic that complemented the authority of the Bourbon kings. However, the political and religious turmoil of the seventeenth century resulted in the forced migration of groups like the French Protestant Huguenots, whose talents were welcomed in Prussia, the Netherlands, and England. Religious upheavals encouraged the diffusion of luxury trades to the great cities of Europe where newly arrived craftsmen began working at silver- and goldsmithing, as well as silk weaving, augmenting the expertise of their new nations and eroding the advantage previously enjoyed in other regions of

A Companion to Eighteenth-Century Europe, First Edition. Edited by Peter H. Wilson.
© 2014 John Wiley & Sons, Ltd. Published 2014 by John Wiley & Sons, Ltd.

Europe. Networks of family ties and religious connections facilitated the circulation of skills and knowledge across Europe, allowing migrants like Huguenot refugees in England and their co-religionists in Prussia to flourish (Luu, 2005).

The provision of luxury commodities, like silk, had been a significant source of wealth for trading communities since the advent of the Silk Road trade route with China. The earlier transmission of knowledge about silk production from China to Italy and the subsequent cultivation of the silk industry in France, as a matter of government policy, acknowledged the singular importance of this commodity. Silk was a social marker, but one impossible to limit to the secular and ecclesiastical elite, despite sumptuary legislation relating clothing to social status. Though neither England nor the Netherlands was burdened by sumptuary laws in 1700, most of Europe functioned within this system of legislated restraint, while at the same time the manufacture and trade in silk was actively encouraged by governments well aware of the value of this commodity to their national exchequers.

Aside from silk, other luxury trades prospered in Europe's great cities, including carriage-making, book-binding, instrument-making, tailoring, and wig-making, providing the sorts of goods deemed essential by the nobles and wealthy merchants who frequented cities for political or mercantile ends. These sectors absorbed a considerable workforce and the talents and taste of these artisans (or their absence) determined the reputation of the city. Paris, of course, stood at the apogee of luxury trades, with a concentration of superior craftsmen and women cooking, gilding, stitching, and decorating, serving the court, the rising bourgeoisie, and Paris's countless visitors. French tastes and French luxury manufactures were pre-eminent throughout eighteenth-century Europe, representing the model against which other luxury producers gauged their success (Coquery 2004; Fox and Turner, 1998). The skilled workers who created the gilt, leather-bound books or the exquisite mantel clocks labored in workshops, most of which were still controlled by guilds which established the context for the training and organization of labor and ensured the quality of the finished products. Guilds were most powerful and most persistent in continental Europe. Their power was much less in the British Isles, and was further eroded over the eighteenth century and ultimately extinguished by 1813 with the repeal of apprenticeship laws. Guilds retained the power in many regions to reject new technology, in favor of older forms of manufacture, valuing the tried and true which assured reliable standards of goods. Women were typically excluded from guild membership, as skilled manufacture was designated a male attribute. Guilds affected this sort of political authority as a result of their central role in municipal government, where their institutional authority persisted throughout the century, even in the face of significant pressures for change.

However, even as guilds shaped working conditions and enforced quality production in cities throughout continental Europe, in many other rural and suburban locales other patterns of work prevailed. These industries were among the most dynamic manufacturing sectors of Europe, and the modes of production entrenched in these regions produced important new types of commodities and important new patterns of work.

Long before 1700 manufacturing had been relocated from urban to rural or suburban locales, outside the control of city guilds and the mandate of municipal corporations. The rationale for this move was simple. Merchants and manufacturers wanted to reduce costs by employing cheaper, semi-skilled rural labor – men, women, and children – putting out the raw materials to be made up by families in domestic settings. This form of manufacturing was termed a putting-out system, domestic or cottage manufacturing; but approximately 30 years ago this phenomenon was also termed proto-industrialization. Re-examinations of this process in the 1970s led some to hypothesize that proto-industrialization was an essential preliminary stage in economic development, involving distinct economic and social features within a specific community and being an essential precursor to industrialization (Kriedte, Medick and Schlumbohm, 1981; Mendels, 1972). Further research found almost as many expressions of proto-industry as there were communities involved. Moreover, every region that benefited from domestic manufacturing in one period did not necessarily slide effortlessly into industrialization at a later date, leading many to doubt the efficacy of this analytical concept, and one historian to suggest that proto-industrialization was "a concept too many" (Coleman, 1992). Earlier classic works, like that of Joan Thirsk on rural industries in the English countryside, outlined the complexity of this process and critical features of domestic industry which enabled it to thrive in pastoral districts where the rural poor more readily blended agriculture and manufacturing into seasonal schedules. But Thirsk also noted the ambiguities inherent in this form of manufacture, which could never ascribe with "certainty or finality" explanations for the growth of rural industries in one locale as opposed to another (Thirsk, 1961). What is indisputable, however, is the vitality of many industries outside Europe's cities, an important feature of the eighteenth-century economy that persisted throughout the century.

Rural industries could be found in numerous regions of Europe, from northern Italy and the Rhineland, to Silesia in eastern Europe; they arose across a broad swath of France, from the mouth of the Garonne in Bordeaux around the north coast, through Nantes and Rouen, to the Netherlands, to Ulster and the east coast around Dublin in Ireland, and through the lowlands of Scotland, and in England they could be found in the northwest and in the Midlands. In these locales and others, a range of commodities was produced, including buckles, lace, ribbons, hats, and textiles of many sorts. The new types of textiles emerging from these locales – such as mixed-fiber fustians, light worsteds, linens, and cotton/linen blends – were generally cheaper and lighter, and they added a new dynamism to the marketplace. Textile manufacture represented one of the principal sources of employment of the eighteenth century, and developments within this sector had major effects on local and even national economies. For example, expansion in the Rhineland fustian and linen trade enhanced prosperity and improved standards of living in that region, attracting new workers who were not subject to the restrictions based on sex or patterns of training such as continued to apply in guild-controlled workshops. The districts where domestic manufacturing developed became zones of relative prosperity. The labor contributed by women and children added important earnings to family budgets, in many cases matching the wages earned by the husband, and doubling family income.

Jan de Vries terms this period of expanding domestic manufacture in Europe the "industrious revolution," noting the crucial decisions made in households to expend more labor, rather then enjoy more leisure (de Vries 1993). In some communities, certain trades were at a premium and workers received compensation accordingly. This was the experience of handloom weavers during the late eighteenth century in

Britain. The demand for spun yarn led to improved spinning technology after the 1760s, with the use of multi-spindle spinning equipment called the spinning jenny. With yarn now in greater abundance, more handloom weavers were wanted, and many entered the trade lured by high wages. Contemporaries recalled the thriving communities of textile workers in the later eighteenth century, including handloom weavers, who prospered for a generation or two in particularly auspicious conditions, before power looms moved weaving into factories. In these halcyon days, textile workers were described as "well clad, – the men with each a watch in his pocket, and the women dressed to their own fancy – every house well furnished with a clock . . . handsome tea services in Staffordshire ware . . . and Sheffield wares for necessary use" (Radcliffe, 1828: 12). These workers could afford to dress themselves and their dwellings in the products emanating from other manufacturing districts.

The advantages of domestic manufacturing were many. Goods were produced in a range of qualities and prices, and the absence of quality control by guilds ensured that customers of all social ranks would find articles they could afford. Underemployment gave way to by-employment in many regions of Europe, blending the seasonal demands of agriculture and the marketplace. For merchants and manufacturers who organized production the advantages of this system came in reduced labor costs and an enhanced flexibility in directing production. But they often chafed at the independence of their workforce, many of whom could not be compelled to work faster or longer hours when other tasks or social obligations pulled them from their loom or their anvil. At the same time, the manufacturer could not directly oversee production and could not manage the disposal of raw materials put out to the villagers. Manufacturing processes inevitably resulted in waste, like the ends of warp threads tied to the beam on the loom (long considered a perquisite of the weaver). This sort of waste had value and could be sold or traded for other commodities in the vast, informal marketplace typical of the era. Tensions persisted between workers and manufacturers about legitimate access to waste materials. Manufacturers complained about workers' embezzlement, and governments responded with intermittent legislation attempting to halt traditional practices. Employers made every effort to ensure the full quantity of raw material made its way into the finished product, with limited success. Despite these efforts, waste from virtually every manufacturing process was carefully hoarded and used by artisans and laborers as an additional source of income (Styles, 1983).

The new technologies that developed in the textile industries from the 1750s onwards enabled production to be moved from cottages and sheds into mills or factories under the watchful eye of supervisors, foremen, and owners. England was the first nation to experience mechanized industrial production, and this process arose first in the cotton sector. The British model of more highly capitalized industrial production applied new technology, organized labor into new forms and larger units, and dramatically expanded output. These new patterns of industrial manufacturing were regional, not national. From England they spread to the Scottish lowlands and then to various regions on the continent. However, domestic patterns of production persisted in tandem with factories both in rural areas as well as in the growing suburban industrial sectors. Inside the mills and factories owners introduced greater labor discipline with specified hours of work, a challenge to older practices. Employers also sought to end what they saw as costly pilfering, with a regular money wage as payment for work. The size of the new industrial sites, the unvarying tempo of the machines, and the disciplinary regime that commonly accompanied this employment sometimes produced covert or overt resistance, with workers negotiating for compensation, sometimes along the lines of older practices and perquisites. The transition from workshop and domestic manufacturing to factory and mill was gradual, taking place over generations. Mills produced sometimes bleak working conditions for the first generations of workers, many of whom were children; and authorities in the late eighteenth century were slow to address the politics of working conditions under such new and unprecedented circumstances. The new communities of workers built labor organizations in response to industrial experiences. Only in the nineteenth century would conditions of industrial labor become the subject of general public concern. In the interim, the last years of the eighteenth century saw the building of mechanized spinning factories using water-powered technologies on a scale never previously witnessed, with a level of output never previously achieved. These would soon be followed by steam-powered technologies applied to weaving as well as spinning.

Fortunes were made by some ambitious entrepreneurs, like Richard Arkwright (1732–92), who left his early trade as a wig-maker, recognizing the advantages of the new spinning technology being developed by John Kay. In 1771, with his partners, he opened a mill which employed the newly invented water frame; water-powered spinning machinery could now produce yarn at great speed and of good quality. Building mills in the Midlands, Lancashire, and Scotland, Arkwright epitomized the successful, newly made man in the most dynamic of industries, the cotton trade, amassing a fortune of approximately £500,000 on his death, an extraordinary sum for that era. Less successful, but equally representative, Samuel Crompton (1753–1827) had worked on a spinning jenny under his mother's eye from about the age of 15. Musical and mechanically adept, Crompton later combined the technology of the spinning jenny with the water frame to produce a more effective machine for the production of fine yarns, called the mule. The yarns he produced were of exceptionally fine and uniform quality. But he was not as adept or ruthless as Arkwright and accumulated relatively little wealth, despite the general adoption of his mule spinning technology within the industry.

With considerable experience in calico printing and trade connections to supplies of American raw cotton, Barcelona was well positioned when two French machine-makers brought spinning jenny technology to that city in 1784. An extensive period of experimentation was followed by some organizational turmoil as the new venture developed. The success of the spinning mill depended on many things, including the finding of an appropriate site, the more careful selection of raw materials, and stringent monitoring of workers' output. The transfer of technology was not without problems; nevertheless, this became a profitable industry within a five-year period, the first industrial site in Spain. Over the 1790s, spinning jennies were set up in many parts of the region, with local entrepreneurs confident of their potential success (Thompson, 2003).

Inspiration, invention, and dedication did not guarantee achievement in an era of significant risks for entrepreneurs. Arkwright and Crompton were among the growing generations of European men from the middle classes who saw their opportunities in industry. Both of these men were born in Lancashire, in northwest England, long the center of domestic textile manufacturing. Both had faced attacks by regional communities antagonistic to new machinery that could possibly jeopardize their earnings – other neighborhoods embraced the potential of the new equipment. Both were deeply aware of the markets they served and the growing demand they sought to meet. The dynamism of the area encouraged the growth of the inland city of Manchester and the port of Liverpool, both of which prospered over the eighteenth century through the robust expansion of the regional textile trade. The unanticipated industrial development that followed made these cities magnets for labor from Britain and Ireland, attracting as well the capital and talents of those seeking to advance themselves. These cities grew in the service of markets, national and international. As with many urban centers in Europe – Nantes, Marseilles, Seville, Barcelona, Amsterdam, Bristol, Glasgow, and London – the combination of regional manufacturing, the processing or distribution of colonial products, and entrepôt functions enabled these cities to prosper. At the same time, these centers attracted entrepreneurs, artisans, and professionals, skilled and unskilled laborers in the hundreds of thousands. The growing urban communities represented complex new environments, increasingly literate, increasingly cosmopolitan, with national and international links enhanced through shipping, commercial, religious, military, and intellectual enterprises.

Markets

Every city exerts pressure on the surrounding countryside. Cities must be fed and have their thirst quenched. Their people must be clothed, shod, housed, and entertained. Northern cities require heat for their residents during the winter months, and all cities, but particularly capital cities, require the labor of many hands to serve those assembled to govern the country whether through church synod, law court, or the courts of kings and princes. Financial exchanges were also important features of capital cities, where those with assets looked for opportunities to invest, not in land, as had been traditional, but in trade, or invention, or established financial institutions like banks. Bank of England stock was a sound conservative investment vehicle that appealed to generations of eighteenth-century investors. Perhaps as many as invested in lottery tickets – a venture that roused passions wherever they were sold in Europe. Speculation vied with commercial intelligence for available funds. A new phenomenon took shape in this era with the growth of investments, investors, and brokers. Amsterdam developed the model, establishing the first stock exchange (or bourse) in the early 1600s, a form much copied over the next several centuries. In the early 1700s, the Bourse du Commerce in Paris replaced an earlier convent for wayward women on that site – the ethics of both the new and older types of exchange confounded moralists of that age. London's stock exchange was slower to formalize. Its brokers were expelled from the Royal Exchange for rowdiness about 1700 and congregated for decades in Jonathan's Coffee House in Change Alley, before their own building in Sweeting's Alley was erected in the 1770s. Whether it was Copenhagen or Amsterdam, London or Paris, eighteenth-century capital cities attracted speculators and projectors large and small. Financial markets attracted a wider range of investors, men and women from the propertied classes, who now bought stocks and insured their property against losses, all of which employed a growing sector of

Figure 4 "The Bubblers Medley," a satire on the South Sea Bubble published by Thomas Bowles, London 1720. *City of London Libraries and Guildhall Art Gallery*

professionals in the movement and management of wealth. Financial scandals and stock collapses rebounded from one nation to another over the eighteenth century – England's South Sea Bubble in 1720; France's Mississippi Bubble of the same year – both tested the resilience of governments, markets and investors. The French distrust of national banks and paper currency would last several generations; but this distaste was not general throughout Europe and the English were one group that continued to be enamored of the potential of paper investments and the promise of dividends.

In the eighteenth century city folk were a minority of the population of Europe; but the impact of cities was disproportionate to their actual size. The impact of urban culture, as well as urban financial clout, rippled out from cities into neighboring regions. Cities drew immigrants from near and far, as opportunities arose or regional pressure compelled migration. Some of the fastest-growing cities were to be found in the northwest of the continent, attracting residents nationally and internationally. Within Europe, London was the largest city, swelling from half a million in 1700 to approximately a million inhabitants by 1800. Paris began the century at between 400,000 and 500,000 people and grew to approximately 750,000 on the eve of the revolution; however, the turmoil of the end of the century induced a decline to about 550,000 by 1800. Amsterdam had been commercially dominant in seventeenth-century Europe, but, battered by wars with France and England, facing intense commercial competition, it could only maintain its international trading and commercial stature. These great cities did not stand alone. Every corner of Europe boasted municipalities of various sizes, vital to their hinterlands, essential to the business and culture of the region or kingdom, though their origins and histories varied widely. St. Petersburg was newly established by the fiat of Peter the Great in 1703, its glory built out of marshland. Vienna, having survived a last assault by Ottoman forces in 1683, enjoyed a political and cultural revival in the eighteenth century as the permanent capital of the Habsburg dynasty. Lisbon, capital and ancient port city of Portugal, was part of a vital trading network on the Atlantic Ocean and was largely destroyed by a cataclysmic earthquake in 1755. It was rebuilt within years of that catastrophe. Europe's cities, whatever their size or disposition, were linked together by networks of business and personal contacts among urban residents, some of whom shared religious, family, or ethnic ties. Routine correspondence, trade, and travel facilitated a more cosmopolitan Europe, with as many connections of culture and commerce as there were religious and political divisions.

The commercial and professional classes were of particular importance to the flavor and function of urban life. In fact, their influence helped define and redefine the eighteenth-century city. Most within the amorphous middle classes depended on education for their future opportunities, and particular attention was given to the training of sons. Schools and academies were opened in growing numbers to provide instruction in the practical skills essential for advancement. These schools trained young men needing to earn a living, emphasizing languages, mathematics, and the mechanics of trade (legal and cultural). Those families without the resources for schooling hoped for advancement through practical apprenticeships. Molière made the newly enriched man an object of mockery in his widely performed play *Le Bourgeois Gentilhomme* (1670); this ridicule is hardly surprising as Molière wrote to entertain the court. But this production had a wider appeal, just as the subject of the thrusting, middle-ranked male occasioned comment in other literary traditions. Wherever trade flourished the middle ranks multiplied, their numbers increased, and the complexity of this overlapping hierarchy became a subject of discussion and occasional dispute.

Not surprisingly, Daniel Defoe celebrated trade and those who labored for profit. "Trade," he asserted, "is so far here from being inconsistent with a gentleman, that, in short, trade in England makes gentlemen, and has peopled this nation with gentlemen; for, after a generation or two, the tradesman's children, or at least their grandchildren, come to be as good gentlemen, statesmen . . . judges, bishops, and noblemen, as those of the highest birth and the most ancient families" (Defoe, 1724). The middle classes aspired to wealth, or at least to comfort. Their ethic was generally speaking one of diligence, timeliness, and thrift, exemplified in the maxims coined by Benjamin Franklin for his *Poor Richard's Almanac*: "Light purse, heavy heart"; "He is ill cloth'd, who is bare of Virtue"; "He that buys upon Credit, pays Interest for what he buys"; "The favour of the Great is no inheritance"; "You may delay, but *Time* will not" (Franklin, 1733). Readers of these and the many other instructional texts hoped to raise themselves and their sons to achieve worldly success, however modest. The middle classes were intensely aware of challenge posed by their ambition and the significant risks with which they lived. Wars, weather, business cycles, and politics all imperiled the financial stability of men and women in trade. Failure for whatever reason took place in a context where there was unlimited liability for business debts. For women in business there were the added challenges of legal systems and social practices less equitable to married women than to men. An English case illustrates the objective difficulties. Mary Holl, though married, ran her London millinery business as a *femme sole*, in effect with the legal status of a single woman. In 1775 she had a profit of over £60 from her shop; but within months she was troubled by creditors and facing bankruptcy, not because of decisions she had made, but because on her husband's bankruptcy in his separate trade his creditors conspired to seize her assets. Mary despaired: "My business is quite ruined, for I have nothing to sell, & now no Credit or money to buy" (Hunt, 1996: 141). Business depended on interconnecting networks of credit, for little business was done with cash, and in this commercial nexus personal reputation was critical. New enterprises typically relied on investment from family and friends and, for male enterprises, the practical assistance of female relatives. A good name and recommendations were equally essential ingredients to advancement.

The middle classes represented an important growing market for goods and services, and they also organized and profited from the networks of trade that crisscrossed Europe and beyond. It was they who staffed the growing numbers of shops that lined major streets in Europe's cities and towns; it was they who directed overseas and long-distance commercial enterprises. Shopkeeping became an increasingly important part of commercial life over this century, with the shops themselves evolving as improved lighting and better display modes became more common. Paris shops were filled with delectable goods, and the Baroness Oberkirch observed woefully in 1789 that, "when leaving Paris, you need carts" to carry away all the irresistible wares (Coquery, 2004: 71). Over the century retailing became more differentiated and advertising more sophisticated, as retailers learned new methods to publicize their wares; each innovation in turned employed more men and women in the middle classes, or those who aspired to join their ranks. Napoleon's cut at the English as "a nation of shopkeepers" was a designation many English embraced. London gloried in its rising reputation as a retail center, with glass-fronted shops and lighted shopping precincts that delighted its citizens and foreign visitors. High street shops presented the best and most luxurious face of retailing; they were outnumbered many times over by basic chandler shops and general retailers, street stalls, and informal establishments operated out of the front rooms of lodgings in less salubrious districts. These, too, served essential purposes, employing vast numbers in petty retailing and bringing a lower quality of new and secondhand wares to laboring peoples. And if eastern Europe had both smaller cities and a less extensive array of shops than could be found in most western regions, all parts of Europe were served by an intersecting complex of pedlars. Itinerant retailing continued to be one of the most important aspects of commercial life throughout the eighteenth century, bridging bulk trade in commodities and fixed retail concerns.

The authorities disliked pedlars. Pedlars moved around too readily, often carrying smuggled or illicit goods, sometimes moving stolen items, and occasionally circulating proscribed pamphlets or literature. Unlike merchants who ran fixed shops, they were difficult to tax. Shopkeepers were perennially jealous of the lower costs of doing business enjoyed by pedlars, and in every community tried to have these competitors barred from trading. But pedlars were essential commercial agents, serving rural and poor customers, typically trading on credit, accepting local produce in one area to sell on in another, weaving even the most remote hamlets into the wider commercial web. Typically pedlars working in teams originated in mountainous regions of Europe – the Alpine districts, the Pyrenees, and Scotland – moving out in circuits through the low-lying, more populated rural communities, tying these together with towns, villages, and larger cities to form a dense commercial network. Skilled in avoiding tolls and customs agents, these mountain folk began by establishing bases in convenient towns and from these epicenters developed extensive routes building on familial ties and making key local connections. Scottish pedlars were to be found in Poland, Denmark, Norway, and Sweden; Italians from the lake regions crossed the Alps to cultivate German markets during the eighteenth century. Flexible and adaptable, they responded to opportunities. Peddling hierarchies developed, with new apprentices learning the routes, attending fairs, hoping at some time to establish themselves in larger towns through an auspicious marriage, as their masters had done (Fontaine, 1996). Pedlars facilitated the development of markets, moving goods from region to region and across social classes. Village shopkeepers were often happy to blend their trade with that of itinerant dealers, accepting goods in exchange for others, picking up special items not otherwise available. Pedlars do not fit a neat trajectory of retail modernization, and they continued as an important segment of retailing through the nineteenth century, without benefit of fixed prices, fixed premises, or new modes of retail display. Their longevity may well be explained by their importance in rural regions and their willingness to barter and sell cheap goods on credit. Altogether, pedlars added a vital dynamism to the marketplace, breaking down rural isolation, and building national and international markets.

The Practice of Consumption

The eighteenth-century European market was larger and more diverse than its predecessors, even though new patterns and practices were clearly presaged in earlier periods. Capital markets were becoming more extensive and sophisticated, if still imperfect. The scope of international and colonial trade was one of the hallmarks of this era. Before the era of income tax, investments in slaving voyages or sugar plantations could yield exceptional profits for those not squeamish about the morality of these ventures. By the mid-eighteenth century Quakers forswore these investments on moral grounds, encouraging their adherents to invest elsewhere. By the 1780s politics animated the question of slave-produced sugar, adding another dimension to the complexities of the consumer process. Markets were the focus of intense interest during the eighteenth century, being theorized in new and interesting ways by the French *philosophes* and the Scot, Adam Smith, for example. It was Adam Smith, in *The Wealth of Nations* (1776), who opined that "Consumption is the sole end and purpose of production." A more recent rethinking of markets and their functions has renewed interest in the role of the consumer and the importance of practices that took place before and after exchanges were made.

In the past 20 years historians have identified and examined a complex social, economic, and cultural matrix that has been described as the rise of consumerism (Berg, 2005; Fairchilds, 1993; Lemire 1991, 1997; McKendrick et al., 1983; Roche,

1994, 2000; Weatherill, 1988). This new historical template rejected classic theories of economic development which privileged work over all other activities or emphasized formal industrial or political developments at the expense of wider and more complex social agendas. Material life became a focus of inquiry and new questions were posed about the agency of women and men; disparate priorities were interrogated within complex social ranks, where religion, locality, ethnicity, age, and gender figured as much as one's place in the social hierarchy. Women's history clearly influenced this new historical project, as attention was given equally to the practices of women and of men, from all social backgrounds. For eighteenth-century England, a new focus on the consumption of goods and their meanings has reoriented the study of the eighteenth century. Similarly, the extensive work on probate inventories in the Netherlands has made clear the material transformations underway in this region of Europe (Schuurman, 1988). And while regional variation was central to the understanding of shifting consumer practices, commodities were also examined with greater attention to their social and cultural meanings over time.

Eighteenth-century England was the first nation to which the idiom "consumer revolution" was applied; but researchers very soon revealed the diverse practices of consumerism within urban and rural contexts. The timing of this phenomenon was variable, with authors arguing for a new consumerism for sixteenth-century Italy and the seventeenth-century Netherlands (Jardine, 1996; Schama, 1991). In fact, Joan Thirsk's ground-breaking observations on the origins of popular consumerism in England – both new trades and new customers – arose from seventeenth-century evidence (Thirsk, 1978). The roots of consumerism in Europe are deep, with manifestations first in the dynamic trading communities of Italy and, later, the Netherlands, England, France, and elsewhere. Rural and urban populations did not value all commodities equally; variability was common, as too was the growing array of commodities from which to choose. Not only were Europeans served by their own manufactures, but the wealth of Asian and colonial products refashioned society, culture, and economy. Consider coffee. In the eighteenth century, coffeehouses spread throughout metropolitan Europe, epitomizing the new consumer forms and evolving social practices of consumption. Coffeehouses provided a new kind of public space for the consumption of caffeinated liquids, along with discussions of news and affairs or expressions of wit and literary aphorisms. These venues took on the distinctive features of their locales from Venice to Vienna, Prague to Paris. Coffee had become an essential staple by the eighteenth century, no longer a foreign oddity, but the stuff of innumerable breakfasts and the essential refreshing liquid of businessmen, virtuosi, and growing throngs with a taste for the beverage. Zimmerman's Coffee House, Leipzig, hosted the performance of Bach's Coffee Cantata in the early 1730s, coffee figuring as the point of contention between a rebellious daughter and an authoritarian father. In a satiric tribute to the power of this new consumable, Bach's librettist opined that cats would stop hunting mice sooner than women would give up coffee. The Italian Francesco Procopio arrived in Paris from Italy in the 1680s with two skills: the first, knowing how to make ice cream and the second, knowing how to make coffee. His Paris café became the meeting place for the literary and theatrical world and retained that distinction for generations. Coffeehouses served more commercial ends as well as hosting the literati. The insurance company Lloyd's of London got it started at an establishment named for the owner, Edward Lloyd. Lloyd began producing a newssheet of ships and cargoes for his clients, encouraging the patronage of investors, shipowners, and underwriters, some of whom eventually set up business there in 1771, taking the name of the coffeehouse. Coffee, tea, chocolate, and sugar changed the diet of Europeans, reshaped the economies of Europe, and transformed the material culture at the same time (Mintz, 1985). Coffee and sugar became so essential to everyday life that they even figured in the politics of revolutionary France when they became the focus of riots in 1793, needs that had to be met (Jones and Spang, 1999).

The role of trade was central to the expansion of the European economy and in the expanding capacity of Europeans to consume. Europe's direct contacts with the Americas and with Asia were two centuries old by 1700, and by this era most of Europe had established trading companies to profit from Asian commerce; most also sought to profit from the slave trade between Africa and the Americas, where colonial products like sugar were produced on plantations with slave labor. Even those states with the smallest colonial American toe-holds, like Denmark and the Netherlands, used this fact to negotiate a claim to the lucrative trans-Atlantic slave trade. Europe had forcibly positioned itself at the center of a world trade system that brought the most desirable commodities from Asian manufacturers, securing goods like Indian printed cottons to exchange in West Africa for slaves destined for plantations across the Atlantic.

The impact of Asian and colonial trade was apparent in Europe not only through the circulation of new commodities, but also in the development of new industries, many of which attempted to copy Asian manufactures. Porcelain, silk, and printed cottons epitomized the best of Asian-made consumer goods, with a wide range of qualities, many price points, and traits that could not be easily matched by European copyists. Europeans struggled to find the secrets of "Turkey red," for example, and they strove for a century to discover the secrets of the dyes used in the printed textiles that came from India. Printed cottons, known as calicos, were the rage across Europe amidst all social classes – color-fast, repeated washings only improved their appearance. Recurring legislative prohibitions against the use or wearing of cotton did not extinguish this popular taste, only giving encouragement to local industries. Asian trade goods not only stimulated consumer appetites in Europe, but set the standard of mass-produced commodities, inspiring efforts to match the techniques and industrial capacity of the East.

Was an interest in consumer goods restricted solely to the wealthy elite or the affluent middle classes? Not at all. The wealthy, as in all ages, enjoyed luxuries large and small. But the history of consumption was more complex than that. Lorna Weatherill demonstrated for Britain that the social hierarchy and the consumer hierarchy were not identical or interchangeable. The emulation theory is a crude explanatory mechanism in the study of consumerism, inadequate to explain the complexities of the processes. Using a detailed analysis of probate inventories from 1675 to 1725, Weatherill uncovered nuances of consumer behavior that differentiated the various social groups. It is hardly surprising that 61 percent of the gentry sampled owned silver, for example; but 51 percent of the men in high-status trades and professions likewise owned goods of this sort. Books, on the other hand, were listed for 45 percent of all high-status tradesmen and only 39 percent of gentry – apparently literacy carried more cultural and practical meanings for tradesmen than for gentry.

Among those in the middling, less affluent, social category the differences to be found between rural and urban households were even more marked. There were sharp differentiations in material priorities between large-scale yeomen farmers and tradesmen from the middle rank: books, clocks, table linen, pictures, curtains, and saucepans were found in far greater quantities among the urban or town-based tradesmen than among farmers. Novelties associated with drinking the new caffeinated beverages like tea, coffee, or chocolate were not generally owned by those who died before 1725. However, the ownership of china was clearly more in evidence among tradesmen than any other social group. Both high-status and intermediate-status tradesmen and professionals possessed more china than did the gentry, while among large- and small-scale farmers china was virtually absent from post-mortem lists of property (Weatherill, 1988: 168).

Most parts of Europe have benefited from detailed investigations of shifting consumer practices and changing commodity cultures (Cavallo, 2000; Deceulaer, 2001; Moreno 2006; Riello 2006; Roche, 2000). Without doubt those living through the eighteenth century witnessed unprecedented changes in their physical environment and grappled with the meanings and importance ascribed to new and changing materials entering their lives. Some eschewed change; others embraced it. The ownership of clocks and the wearing of watches by literate professional or commercial men are understandable as a testament to their ideals; the rationality of time and its value were taught the young in these social groups from an early age. Time discipline was enforced and accepted among the middle ranks. So too were literacy, privacy, and particular types of hospitality, all of which were reflected in the furnishing priorities of bourgeois husbands and wives. Servants, artisans, journeymen, and clerks likewise bought a wider array of goods from generation to generation over the eighteenth century. Moreover, their strategies for acquiring, using, and disposing of commodities took different forms from the strategies of those who could employ formal credit instruments and who functioned in a more monetized sector of the economy.

Pawning and the secondhand trade were two of the most important mechanisms that facilitated consumerism among the laboring classes. Clothing and textiles were particularly favored as alternate currencies, easily bartered for other commodities and easily pawned or sold. Textiles in whatever form, including waste from production processes, were readily accepted by shopkeepers, pedlars, and other retailers and offered important flexibility for the working poor and even some middle-class families. Pawnshops, formal and informal, proliferated in every urban setting, although with national and regional variations. Previously, in Catholic nations a religious order had encouraged the founding of *monts de piété*, or charitable pawnshops, where the interest charged was limited; in the Netherlands municipal authorities opened similar establishments. In Britain, successive governments reluctantly accepted the necessity of pawnshops, legislating these establishments in an attempt to restrict the circulation of stolen goods. Pawnbrokers' records offer evidence of the growing range of items owed by ordinary people who did not make wills and did not leave probate accounts. In whatever country they were found, in whatever form they took, pawnshops were indispensable to plebeian budgeting, allowing vital credit and the balancing of material priorities (Fontaine 2002; Lemire 2005).

The circulation of secondhand wares was similarly essential. This was still an occasional practice among the elites. But the purchase and resale of used goods was a habitual practice within less exalted circles, producing a vast international network of trade in secondhand commodities, especially clothing and textiles. It was commonplace, for example, for new earthenware or pottery to be bartered for used garments. Every household, however modest, might have linens or outer garments they could spare in order to acquire a teapot, cup and saucer, or dish of a particular pattern. Practices like this allowed access to products that otherwise would have been beyond the resources of the less affluent. Street dealers moved through affluent neighborhoods and through alleys and courtyards peopled by working men and women, buying, trading, and bartering to acquire stock. Women readily found commercial space in this sector, especially at the lowest level of the trade. Working women were knowledgeable about domestic commodities and they had community networks through which they could work. Moving from one hand to another, stocks of secondhand wares accumulated, and specialist national and international dealers shipped vast quantities of apparel from one region to another where market advantage could be found. Over the century, in England, for example, livery became harder to resell, as working men would not willingly wear a coat that suggested a servile status. But, shipped to the Low Countries, where the cultural significance of a badge or particular coat colors were unknown, these garments became potentially profitable once again.

The secondhand market augmented the range of goods available for sale, both in terms of price and quality. Not all items that arrived in this mart came there legitimately. The resale of stolen goods was a persistent, intractable problem, in part because of the size of the secondhand market. In Paris, the theft of clothes and linens represented 24 percent of cases tried at a central court from 1721 to 1741, and 37 percent from 1770 to 1790. Easily accessible, easily sold, and widely recognized for their almost instant mutability as these goods were, Roche argues that the authorities responded with greater severity to this type of property crime in Paris as the century advanced (Roche, 1994: 337–8). The thefts themselves are also suggestive of the various motivations behind these peculations, as not all the goods stolen were sold on; in many instances the opportunistic thief was caught with the stolen coat on his back or the hat on his head. The desire to cut a fine figure inspired at least some of those who stooped to thieve. Only a portion of these men and women arrived in court.

The material world of the eighteenth century was complex and shifting. Tradition still played an important role in many aspects, like the giving of gifts to friends and kin, the disbursal of favors to mourners at funerals and exchanges arranged between patron and client. But here too there was change, and some followed what they saw as more rational practices, discarding customary forms. The tensions between custom and modernity were evident in many facets of European life, not least in the fields of manufacture, markets, and consumerism. The periodic calls by food rioters for a "fair price" reflected community antagonism towards national markets and the movement of grain from one district to another for the maximization of profits. Yet national and international markets were established and consolidated in this era despite repeated efforts to constrain trade. Legislative antagonism towards imported Indian cottons, for example, which had threatened the established advantage of wool, led to trade barriers and legal prohibitions in much of Europe at the beginning of the century. Those barriers could not be enforced. Imitations of Indian cottons, made by European entrepreneurs, ultimately produced equivalent industries in Europe, initiatives ultimately welcomed by governments. But the form of manufacturing that followed and the spread of factories antagonized many common folk. Meanwhile, moralists fussed about the widening use of tobacco by laboring people, and cantatas were sung about the seductive powers of coffee. The eighteenth century involved a perpetual and imperfect negotiation between novelty and custom.

Bibliography

Berg, M., *Luxury and Pleasure in Eighteenth-Century Britain* (Oxford, 2005).

Blondé, B., et al. (eds.), *Buyers, Sellers and Salesmanship in Medieval and Early Modern Europe* (Turnhout, 2006).

Cavallo, S., "What did women transmit? The boundaries of domestic and personal property in seventeenth- and eighteenth-century Italy," in M. Donald and L. Hurcombe (eds.), *Gender and Material Culture in Historical Perspectives* (London, 2000), pp. 38–53.

Clark, P. (ed.), *Small Towns in Early Modern Europe* (Cambridge, 1995).

Coleman, D., "Proto-industrialization: a concept too many," in D. C. Coleman (ed.), *Myth, History and the Industrial Revolution* (London, 1992), pp. 107–22.

Coquery, N., "The language of success: marketing and distribution of semi-lux goods in eighteenth-century France," *Journal of Design History*, 17 (2004), 71–89.

Crossick, G. (ed.), *The Artisan and the European City, 1500–1900* (Aldershot, 1997).

de Vries, J., "Between purchasing power and the world of goods: understanding the household economy in early modern Europe," in J. Brewer and R. Porter (eds.), *Consumption and the World of Goods* (London, 1993), pp. 85–132.

Deceulaer, H., "Urban artisans and their countryside customers: different interactions between town and hinterland in Antwerp, Brussels and Ghent (18th century)," in B. Blondé, E. Hanhaut, M. Galland (eds.), *Labour and Labour Markets between Town and Countryside (Middle Ages–19th Century)* (Turnhout, 2001), pp. 218–35.

Defoe, D., *A Plan for English Commerce* (2nd edn., London, 1730; repr. New York, 1967).

Defoe, D., *The Complete English Tradesman* (London, 1724), http://www.gutenberg.org/files/14444/14444-h/14444-h.htm#CHAPTER_XXV, accessed 23 October 2006.

Epstein, S. R. (ed.), *Town and Country in Europe, 1300–1800* (Cambridge, 2001).

Fairchilds, C., "The production and marketing of populuxe goods in eighteenth-century Paris," in J. Brewer and R. Porter (eds.), *Consumption and the World of Goods* (London, 1993), pp. 228–48.

Fontaine, L., *History of Pedlars in Europe* (Cambridge, 1996).

Fontaine, L., "Women's economic spheres and credit in pre-industrial Europe," in B. Lemire, R. Pearson, and G. Campbell (eds.), *Women and Credit: Researching the Past, Refiguring the Future* (Oxford, 2002), pp. 15–32.

Fox, R. and A. Turner (eds.), *Luxury Trades and Consumerism in Ancien Régime Paris* (Aldershot, 1998).

Franklin, B., *Poor Richard, 1733. An Almanack for the Year of Christ 1733* (Philadelphia, 1733). http://usinfo.state.gov/usa/infousa/facts/loa/bf1733.htm, http://usinfo.state.gov/usa/infousa/facts/loa/bf1737.htm, http://usinfo.state.gov/usa/infousa/facts/loa/bf1758.htm, accessed 23 October 2006.

Grazia, V. de (ed.), *The Sex of Things: Gender and Consumption in Historical Perspective* (Berkeley, 1996).

Hunt, M., *Commerce, Gender and the Family in England, 1680–1780* (Berkeley, 1996).

Jardine, L., *Worldly Goods: A New History of the Renaissance* (London, 1996).

Jones, C. and R. Spang, "*San-culottes,* san café, san tabac: shifting realms of necessity and luxury in eighteenth-century France," in M. Berg and H. Clifford (eds.), *Consumers and Luxury: Consumer Culture in Europe 1650–1850* (Manchester, 1999), pp. 37–62.
Kriedte, P., H. Mendick, and J. Schlumbohm, *Industrialization before Industrialization* (Cambridge, 1981).
Lemire, B., *Fashion's Favourite: The Cotton Trade and the Consumer in Britain, 1660–1800* (Oxford, 1991).
Lemire, B., *Dress, Culture and Commerce: The English Clothing Trade before the Factory, 1660–1800* (Basingstoke, 1997).
Lemire, B., *The Business of Everyday Life: Gender, Practice and Social Politics in England 1600–1900* (Manchester, 2005).
Luu, L. B., *Immigrants and the Industries of London, 1500–1700* (Aldershot, 2005).
McKendrick, N., J. Brewer, and J. H. Plumb, *The Birth of Consumer Society: The Commercialization of Eighteenth-Century England* (London, 1983).
Mendels, F., "Proto-industrialization: the first phase of the industrialization process," *Journal of Economic History*, 32 (1972), 241–61.
Mintz, S. W., *Sweetness and Power* (New York, 1985).
Moreno Claverías, B., "Révolution de la consommation paysanne? Modes de consommation et différenciation sociale de la paysannerie catalane, 1670–1790," *Histoire & Mesure*, 21 (2006), 141–83.
Radcliffe, W., *Origin of the New System of Manufacture, commonly called "Power-Loom Weaving" and the Purposes for which this System was invented and brought into use, fully explained . . .* (Stockport, 1828).
Riello, G., *A Foot in the Past: Consumers, Producers and Footwear in the Long Eighteenth Century* (Oxford, 2006).
Roche, D., *The Culture of Clothing: Dress and Fashion in the Ancien Régime* (Cambridge, 1994).
Roche, D., *A History of Everyday Things: The Birth of Consumption in France, 1600–1800*, trans. B. Pearce (Cambridge, 2000).
Schama, S., *The Embarrassment of Riches: An Interpretation of Dutch Culture in the Golden Age* (London, 1991).
Schuurman, A. J., "Probate inventory research: opportunities and drawbacks," in M. Baulant, A. J. Schuurman, and P. Servais (eds.), *Inventaires après-décès et ventes de meubles: Apports à une histoire de la vie économique et quotidienne XIVe–XIXe siècles* (Louvain, 1988), pp. 19–57.
Stein, R. L., *The French Sugar Business in the Eighteenth Century* (London, 1988).
Styles, J., "Embezzlement, industry and the law in England, 1500–1800," in M. Berg (ed.), *Markets and Manufacture in Early Industrial Europe* (London, 1983), pp. 173–210.
Thirsk, T., "Industries in the countryside," in F. J. Fisher (ed.), *Essays in Economic and Social History of Tudor and Stuart England* (Cambridge, 1961), pp. 217–33.
Thirsk, T., *Economic Policy and Projects: The Development of a Consumer Society in Early Modern England* (Oxford, 1978).
Thomson, J. K. F., "Transferring the spinning jenny to Barcelona: an apprenticeship in the technology of the Industrial Revolution," *Textile History*, 34 (2003), 21–46.
Weatherill, l., *Consumer Behaviour and Material Culture in Britain, 1660–1760* (London, 1988).
Wiesner, M., *Women and Gender in Early Modern Europe* (2nd edn., New York, 2000).

CHAPTER FIVE

Towns and their Inhabitants

MARC SCHALENBERG

Introduction

Eighteenth-century Europe had a diverse urban landscape, ranging from the cultural attractions, fashionable circles, and general polyphony of London, Paris, Vienna, or Rome to the rather static strongholds of vested interests and established routines in Sicilian, Polish, or Irish small towns – and indeed most everywhere across the still thinly populated continent. The rhythm and the values of the countryside, as portrayed in chapter 3, clearly dominated. Yet towns and cities acquired greater significance in the course of the century, both quantitatively and qualitatively, while their relationship to their rural hinterlands remained complementary rather than contradictory (Clark and Lepetit, 1996).

Bigger urban centers enjoying a prominent political, economic, or cultural role have long been the focus of research. Treatment of "provincial" or "small" towns (Borsay, 1989; Clark, 1995; Gräf, 1997; Keller, 2001) is, by contrast, a much more recent phenomenon in urban historiography, undoubtedly favored by the rise of social history with its interest in the "normal" rather than the "exceptional." A particularly pointed – and hence controversial – treatment of the political implications of a parochial, often xenophobic, small-town world is Mack Walker's portrait of German "home towns" as an incubator of an ideology that could eventually be played upon by the Nazis (Walker, 1971; see also Friedrichs, 1997). At the other end of the spectrum, German cities were hailed as a breeding ground of civil society (Ribhegge, 2002).

This may be an extreme case, but approaching urban history from very different angles and arriving at opposite conclusions is rather the rule than the exception. What follows can only cover a fraction of the numerous issues and judgments on early modern towns. Opinions diverge even on what exactly constitutes a "town." Definitions vary according to the emphasis on legal status (such as a civic charter), the function (economic, political, cultural) it performs for the surrounding area, or simply the number of inhabitants (with 5,000 taken as a general minimum). This chapter uses a pragmatic combination of the three. In accordance with most of the

A Companion to Eighteenth-Century Europe, First Edition. Edited by Peter H. Wilson.
© 2014 John Wiley & Sons, Ltd. Published 2014 by John Wiley & Sons, Ltd.

literature, "town," "city," and the derived adjective "urban" are taken to denote the same thing, even though the connotations of related terms like "citizen," "civil," "bourgeois," "burgher," or "urbanity" may differ.

Statistics

As far as the quantitative aspects of urbanization are concerned, historians are still indebted to the extensive and thorough research carried out in the 1960s, 1970s, and 1980s by scholars such as Pierre Goubert, Maurice Garden, Chandler and Fox, Wrigley and Schofield, Arthur Imhof, or, on a European scale, Brian Mitchell, Paul Bairoch, and Jan de Vries. The seemingly easy task of counting the number of inhabitants is mired with methodological problems that lie beyond the scope of this chapter. The principal difficulty is the lack of reliable census data. Outside Scandinavia, national censuses were not conducted prior to 1800, forcing historians to use more ambiguous sources such as tax cadastres, parish registers, and communal records.

Nonetheless, it is possible to compile a fairly reliable list of the "top ten" European cities around 1700. Constantinople tops the list at 700,000 inhabitants, though some question whether this city (modern Istanbul) can be considered fully European. The others, in descending order, were: London (550,000), Paris (530,000), Naples (207,000), Lisbon (188,000), Amsterdam (172,000), Rome (149,000), Venice (144,000), Moscow (130,000; with similar qualifications to Constantinople), and Milan (124,000) (all figures in Chandler and Fox, 1974: 17). The list indicates clearly that the traditional centers in southern Europe still held their own before the onset of industrialization and the growing dominance of North Atlantic over Mediterranean connections (political, economic, cultural). The overall number of Europeans living in towns of more than 5.000 inhabitants in 1700, excluding Russia, has been estimated at 13.2 million (or 12.9 percent of the entire population), which in a century of demographic growth rose to 16.4 million (or 13.8 percent) in 1750 and to 20.9 million (still 13.8 percent) in 1800 (Bairoch et al., 1988: 254). London now clearly led the list with 861,000 inhabitants, followed by Constantinople (570,000), Paris (547,000), Naples (430,000), Moscow (238,000), Lisbon (237,000), the imperial capitals of Vienna (231,000), and St. Petersburg (220,000) as "newcomers," stagnant Amsterdam (201,000), and another fast-growing novice, Berlin (172,000). Jan de Vries has criticized Chandler and Fox's methods and produced slightly different figures, with Vienna and Amsterdam outranking Lisbon in 1800, whereas Dublin, Madrid, and Rome still outdid Berlin (de Vries, 1984). Such differences illustrate the methodological problems, in this case whether to include the garrison – which was large in the Prussian capital – among a town's inhabitants. Either way, the ascent and dominance of (monarchical) political centers in eighteenth-century Europe at the cost of older (republican) commercial centers is obvious.

Traditionally, urbanization has been linked to industrialization, with the "industrial town" centered around factory production seeing its apogee in the nineteenth century. Early traces of this major new city type can be recognized in the eighteenth century, most notably in the British centers of early industrialization such as Manchester (rising from 9,000 in 1700 to 70,000 in 1800), Liverpool (from 6,000 to 78,000), Leeds (from 6,000 to 53,000), or Glasgow (from 13,000 to 77,000; all figures in de Vries, 1984: 270–1). The first truly "urban" nation in Europe was, however, the Netherlands, and the province of Holland in particular, where a remarkable 61 percent of the population already lived in towns of at least 2,500 inhabitants as early as 1675. In Amsterdam, moreover, the Netherlands could not only boast a proper metropolis by contemporary standards, but also the first instance of what would become known as a *Randstad*: an integrated urban network that was more than a string of towns along a trading route (as, for example, along the via Emilia north of the Apennines or down the Rhine valley). From this high level, a "gradual deurbanization" (de Vries and van der Woude, 1997: 60), concomitant with a general demographic stagnation, occurred over the eighteenth century. Nonetheless, the number of town-dwellers remained at a much higher percentage than in the rest of Europe. England eventually overtook the Netherlands and Brabant in the early nineteenth century, although London already outstripped Amsterdam much earlier.

At the other end of the scale were the *Ackerbürgerstädte*, where the inhabitants lived in an urban setting but pursued a still largely rural lifestyle. Such settlements dominated regions with low population density. Still, as has been shown for Finland and Sweden, these "privileged villages" were regarded as models for their thoroughly rural environment, as their more knowledgeable inhabitants produced higher crop yields (Imhof, 1976: 859–61). This function as a hub of knowledge, communication, and information naturally grew in proportion to the size of the city; the existence of educational institutions or publishing houses is a good indicator in that respect.

Population figures depended on the three main factors generally identified by historical demographers: fertility, mortality, and migration. Fertility remained high in the eighteenth century (about four to six births per woman), but so did mortality. The latter particularly affected infants, but also adolescents and adults, for a number of reasons: wars, drought, or other natural catastrophes (of which the 1755 earthquake at Lisbon was probably the most infamous), epidemics, and generally inadequate medical and sanitation facilities.

The most dynamic aspect of urban demography was migration, which brought people into towns in search of employment and personal advancement. In addition to proximity, factors affecting migration included existing family ties and recommendations or cultural affinities, including religious ones. The latter could override distance. For example, nearly 40 percent of immigrants to eighteenth-century Koblenz, a bastion of Catholicism, were Catholic males who had come from over 50 kilometers away, whereas Protestants, often living much closer, rarely tried their luck there (François, 1982: 42–51, 191). In contrast, further down the Rhine, the town of Krefeld, which fell to Prussia in the early eighteenth century, turned into a multiconfessional and more business-minded city; it soon became an important center for textile manufacturing, attracting new inhabitants from near and far (in more or less concentric circles). The same can be said for Lyons, its more populous French counterpart in terms of large-scale textile manufactures (Garden, 1975: 118–19).

Infrastructure

The emergence of a proper urban system, so much stressed by de Vries and others, had its preconditions in an efficient transport and communication infrastructure. The railways, which were to revolutionize traveling and the economy in the nineteenth century, were only in their very infancy at the end of the eighteenth, with rather short tracks to carry wagons in coal mines. Even more of a gimmick – although hailed by thousands of curious bystanders – were the experiments with hot-air balloons by the Montgolfiers in the 1780s. Canals were a more widespread and practicable option, used already for inner-city transportation, but extended during the eighteenth century into more long-distance networks. An equivalent on land were the *chaussées* (or turnpike roads), which greatly eased and accelerated traveling; they also fostered the emergence of a radial pattern of roads from the capital or other centers. Improvements in coach construction and a more efficient use of horses brought people, (lighter) goods, mail in particular, and not least cities into closer communication.

A sign of the growing size of cities and the mobility of their populations was the introduction of house numbers, starting in Madrid in 1750 and soon adopted by Britain, France, and the Habsburg monarchy (Tantner, 2006). A consecutive order for the entire city or administrative parts of it – such as the *sestieri* in Venice – was preferred for military reasons, including the French occupation of many cities in the 1790s and 1800s. More often, however, and more in touch with the spirit of place, houses were given ascending numbers street by street; their names were in turn indicated by signposts, which added a further means of orientation and control inside the city. *Enseignes*, as signposts were called in France, of a more private and commercial character hanging on the streets were often a matter of dispute between tenants and public authorities. Paving was less controversial, as its immediate benefits were obvious. To further enhance security and "enlightenment" in a literal sense, nightly street lighting was introduced at varying speed and intensity over the whole century, increasingly replacing torches by proper street lamps (fueled by oil and wax) and eventually by gas lanterns, as introduced in London in 1809. There were even some attempts at public waste disposal.

But progress was not universal. Eighteenth-century towns already experienced traffic congestion that was just as damaging to their fabric and health as that of the twentieth and twenty-first centuries. The first pavements (*trottoirs*) only appeared at the very end of the century, while traffic jams and accidents caused by carriages were commonplace. This was worsened by early forms of public and taxi transport in the form of *fiaker*, notably in the bigger cities. In addition to horses, cattle were driven down the street for sale or slaughter, adding distinctive noises and odors to the urban scene. Warmth, but also dirt, was brought into towns by the burning of wood and coal, and underground canalization was not yet thought of. Inner-city cemeteries, often surrounding parish churches, were not removed to the outskirts before the 1790s. Many denizens bathed and fished in the same water used to wash clothes and carry away sewage.

Rather more thought and sophistication were devoted to the built environment, which revealed not only layers of sandstone and brick, but also social stratification. The prevailing urban notion of "embellishments" (*embellissements*), as defined by city or state authorities or, particularly in Britain, by private investors, could result in coherent and compact architectural ensembles along avenues, squares, crescents, terraces, and arcades, sometimes complemented by parks or monuments. The creation of wide-open spaces, deemed conducive both to hygiene and status, could square with existing property rights or other interests in keeping intact "grown" structures. Princely residence towns, including medium-sized ones such as Nancy, Kassel, or Karlsruhe, were therefore particularly prone to reinvent or brush up their urban fabric in "geometrical" fashion. The (neo-)classical style often chosen can be read as a conscious attempt to replace what was considered too vernacular and hence parochial an appearance. More research is needed here, but it appears that such considerations motivated what came to be known as the "middle classes" in English provincial towns, as much as prestige-seeking continental princes (Sweet, 1997).

England also led the way in demolishing town walls, a practice that spread to the continent during the century. Tax collectors and military experts opposed this (and had their way in Vienna until 1857), whereas more open-minded citizens hoped for spatial, economic, and cultural improvements. In line with the latter's predictions, the practical uselessness of existing fortifications was revealed rather drastically by Napoleon's armies in the early nineteenth century. The importance of space is demonstrated by those towns that lacked it, such as Amsterdam with its canals, or, more strikingly, Venice in its lagoon, both of which experienced a relative decline during the eighteenth century.

Generally, the infrastructure of a city was influenced by its function. The plethora of princely residence towns in the Holy Roman Empire as well as the bigger European state capitals, dominated by princely and other palaces, usually boasted the devices that courtly distraction and security demanded: banquet and concert halls, squares, parks, *orangeries*, stables, an arsenal, and guard-houses, to list but the most essential. The provision of purpose-built and potentially "public" locations for education and amusement (such as museums, theaters, *vauxhalls*, and other pleasure gardens) was a characteristic concern of eighteenth-century reformers and – depending on the political system – of private businessmen. Trading, and notably port, cities were eager not to fall behind in cultural attractions, but the mechanisms of funding and the sorts of entertainment and personnel engaged to supply these necessarily differed from the political centers. Spas represented an interesting hybrid type, mostly situated in rather confined settings close to hot springs or to the sea, and became increasingly popular with the nobility, affluent artists, and gamblers. In a way, they combined the conventions and amenities of a stratified urban society with freedom from its constraints and a rural setting. The "urbanity" of spas was lacking in most of the small-scale market towns, which could legally claim "urban" status and which fulfilled a well-defined role for their inhabitants and those living in the rural surroundings, but they mostly did not aspire to a share of the latest national or international fashions.

Social Structure

Seen as a whole, eighteenth-century towns were remarkably compact and "mixed" places. Still, their *quarters* (which could, in fact, number four, but also more) differed fundamentally with regard to their standing, and larger communities saw an unprecedented trend towards further social segregation. In Renaissance Florence, for example, the grand houses (palazzi) of powerful families were to be found across the city, while prominent squares adjoined back alleys. During the eighteenth century, however, cities became more segregated as parts, usually to the west and south of the historic centers, emerged as fashionable quarters, driven by speculation and the desire of noble or wealthy families to literally set themselves apart. Classic examples include London's West End, the Faubourg Saint-Germain and Faubourg

Saint-Honoré in Paris, and Edinburgh's New Town (although that was sited to the north, reminding us that there is not only a social, but also a physical, geography to be taken into account). In mercantilist states like Prussia we can observe similar developments, although the building of Friedrichstadt and Dorotheenstadt in Berlin left little room for individual marks of distinction. Most houses and palaces were built following the king's blueprint and allotted to subjects of his choosing. Other towns also displayed fine gradations in access to privilege and protection (for German examples, see Rosseaux, 2006: 54–6).

"Residence" in the capital could mean a largely symbolic presence of courtiers and noble families, who rarely cut their ties to the countryside (though with some exceptions in southern Europe). But then a pied-à-terre, often an exclusive *hôtel* or *palais* in a fashionable quarter of the capital, and an even grander country house, were not mutually exclusive, but served different occasions and seasons. The general desire among aristocrats to run a "court" of their own is clearly reflected in the number of servants and suppliers they employed, leading to a chronic (over)stretching of financial resources. The Paris-based Fitz-James family alone made use of no fewer than 158 clothing suppliers and 144 concerned with housing matters (Coquery in Crossick, 1997: 98). Other noble families were eager to distinguish themselves with elaborate interior decoration, or refined tastes in food and wine. Although not all suppliers lived in the same quarter as their discerning clientele, it was clearly an advantage to do so. So luxury as well as leisure goods and services came to occupy – literally as well as figuratively – an increasing number of people in towns, and they were instrumental in shaping social geographies.

While the family, often comprising three generations or more, was the "normal" basic unit in social life, eighteenth-century cities saw a growing number of public or semi-public meeting-places and associations. These were overwhelmingly reserved for men. Though educated aristocratic or wealthy women figured as salon hostesses (*salonnières*), society defined the home as the proper sphere for female activities and aspirations. This was true even for unmarried women, notably prostitutes in *maisons closes* or nuns in convents. Gender historians have pointed to the socio-cultural conditions and occasional exceptions, but the rise of "bourgeois" ideals reinforced the concept of "separate spheres" where women were supposed to keep house, raise children, care for their husband and, possibly, engage in charitable activity.

Charity in eighteenth-century towns was generally a much more "private" affair than later on, when communal support and the "welfare state" became more important. Begging was ubiquitous, and was sanctioned to varying degrees (legally as well as culturally). Soup kitchens were a common means of relieving the worst distress of hunger, while infirmaries, including foundling hospitals and orphan homes, were mostly run by private or religious foundations. It was not until the later eighteenth century that enlightened ideals encouraged the development of institutions intended to provide "public" assistance, such as the general poor house (Allgemeine Armenanstalt) founded at Hamburg in 1788, or the general hospital (Allgemeines Krankenhaus) in Vienna (1784).

We should be careful not to over-emphasize these developments as ongoing secularization or the emergence of a modern public sector. Religion remained very important. Towns were dominated by churches both visually and acoustically (and morally, it was hoped by the clergy), and confessional allegiances – and sometimes rifts – loomed large. Although these rifts were not comparable with the excitement and violence of the confessional (civil) wars of the sixteenth and seventeenth centuries, religion could still be a powerful instrument of internal discrimination or indeed of external control. "Jesuit" Cologne, far from being an introspective city in other respects, became notorious for its intransigent attitude towards non-Catholics. The Lutheran establishment in Hamburg repressed the city's Catholic minority until the Jesuits and emperor answered their appeals in the early eighteenth century. The threat of sanctions and even military intervention forced the Hamburg Senate to pay compensation, as well as provide a sumptuous residence for the imperial ambassador (Whaley, 1985: 70–6). This example also reminds us of the multifarious and intricate issue of political iconography, so palpable in the early modern city and itself an indicator of the relevance of rank and honor as cultural codes.

The urban economies continued to be dominated by the vested interests of merchants' and artisans' guilds, especially in smaller and medium-sized towns, and more so on the continent than in Britain. While guilds had long been subject to state regulation, it took the French Revolution, with its comprehensive assault on corporate rights, to begin the process – at hugely different speeds – of dismantling the complex framework of guilds and their privileges. Clubs and associations of all sorts were already forming, primarily as a new form of sociability, but occasionally challenging the roles of the older corporations. This could result, as has been shown for Toulouse in southwest France, in a "cosmopolitan" widening of horizons that simultaneously entailed the city elites distancing themselves further from their less well-to-do neighbors (Schneider, 1989). More typically, however, guilds remained firmly in place, providing social and material security for their members, overseeing production standards, and generally representing their trade within the city. This representational role assumed physical form. The guild halls in Zurich, for example, stand second only to the city's churches in size and appearance.

Quantitative evidence also demonstrates the dominance of traditional trades. Artisans and petty merchants formed almost two-thirds of the burghers of the medium-sized Rhenish residence town of Koblenz (François, 1982: 188). In bigger trading cities like Lisbon commerce naturally played a more significant role, revealing at the same time the differentiation in wealth and habits of consumption. While you could purchase exclusive china or colonial products on the banks of the river Tejo, the lion's share (55 percent) of all traders in the 1760s specialized in foodstuffs (Rocha in Coquery, 2000: 134). Little training and only modest investment were required to start such small-scale shops that often served as places of gathering and communication in specific neighborhoods.

The study of neighborhoods has proved most fruitful for urban historians and has benefited from exchanges with sociologists and anthropologists. Its relevance derives from both social and physical factors, as pre-industrial cities were built rather more densely, particularly in southern Europe, but also north of the Alps. The closeness in living together often added to a sense of community, as reflected, for example, by the *contrade* as important political and social units in Tuscan cities; these districts could also form the base for social control. Surely, a completely "private" sphere was very hard to find in towns (except, perhaps, in more exclusive enclosed gardens), while enlightened discourse was not the only talk in the ubiquitous "public" sphere.

Neighborhoods excluded as well as included. Some outsiders were criminalized, or incarcerated in one of the many workhouses intended for their moral re-education. There were other, more subtle, ways to delineate honest and "deviant" behavior. Examples of "no-go areas" include the city executioner's house and the legally sanctioned enclaves surrounding ecclesiastical foundations (Friedrichs, 1995: 4, 30ff.). Thus, in one way or another, social determinants such as gender, religion, family background, profession, age, or reputation found their expression in the ways inhabitants used and were assigned places in their towns.

Cultural Life and "Urbanity," Comfort and Commodity

The self-confidence of a social and cultural elite considering itself at the forefront of Enlightenment and refined manners often produced smug arrogance masking moral corruption and gaping social inequalities. Still, the bigger urban centers proved very attractive to the *république des lettres*, as well as pan-European business and aristocratic connections.

Probably the most cosmopolitan place in eighteenth-century Europe was Rome, a chaotic, decadent, but singularly colorful and "coded" city that otherwise lacked a national role in a yet to be united Italy. Containing the remnants of two millennia of Mediterranean civilization and the ideas that this entailed, the *città eterna* hosted a unique blend of "Grand Tourists," pious pilgrims, monks and nuns, papal courtiers, diplomats, gamblers, artists, dilettanti, and serious scholars. The exchange of knowledge, fashions, rumors, and favors took place at countless receptions or in *conversazioni* circles, on one of the lively piazzas in the city center or in remote hideaways in the Campagna. Much as in London or Paris, native people were almost in a minority, despite the impressive palazzi and *giardini* of Roman noble families. Unlike the great majority of the population, whose career ambitions were in one way or another centered around the Vatican, this traditional urban elite rarely took an active part in the papal administration, except at its highest levels in the college of cardinals and the Holy See itself (Gross, 1990: 48–9).

Paris, which liked to fashion itself as "Rome moderne," likewise assumed the role of a melting-pot for inhabitants from different backgrounds, albeit in a less meritocratic way than in the USA a century later. Among others, David Garrioch, Daniel Roche, and Robert Darnton have disentangled the networks of people, communication, suspicion, and fortune in the French capital. New arrivals were typically less wealthy, in search of a job, and envisaging a more permanent stay than the Grand Tourists in Rome. Social acceptance and advancement were not impossible, but certainly required an understanding and adoption of the specific social grammar, and, because of the city's complexity, a "primacy of neighborhood and the local community" (Garrioch, 1986: 16–55) was pertinent even in Paris.

Vienna was the primary seat of Habsburg imperial government and representation and emerged as a very Baroque capital in the decades following the repulse of the Turks from its gates in 1683. The court set the tone, both socially and economically, though the city council and especially the guilds retained some of their traditional privileges. Wine-making and construction work were the only really "productive" sectors of the local economy, which was otherwise dominated by the consumption needs of the court, military, and administration (Spielman, 1993: 47). A plethora of bureaucratic bodies associated with the city, empire, and Habsburg monarchy regulated public life to a degree unheard of in other major cities. Concern to preserve the defensive *glacis* (clear field of fire) encircling the city constrained construction within the walls, making Vienna more compact than most other cities, except Naples, with what were, by the standards of the time, high-rise buildings and few open spaces apart from that around the Hofburg palace. This also resulted in less social segregation, since aristocrats and burghers, drawn from across the monarchy, lived in close proximity to their servants. Nonetheless, the wealthier aristocrats sought to distinguish themselves by building lavish palaces immediately outside the defensive ring.

London was already the "unique city" (Rasmussen, 1988), as Europe's largest by the mid-eighteenth century. It also saw the erection of exquisite town palaces, but even aristocrats "most often chose to live in fairly simple terrace houses, which contrasted oddly with the opulent city residences of their fellow-noblemen on the continent of Europe" (Rudé, 1971: x). The reasons were cultural rather than financial, since London already profited from a truly global hinterland and was particularly instrumental in redefining ambitions, manners, and tastes in Dr. Johnson's time. It absorbed and spoiled much talent, but also spurred a spirit of emulation in bigger provincial towns, the cultural life of which was flourishing by the 1770s (Borsay, 1989: 311). The British capital was probably the most important European center for banking and insurance, as well as the definition and distribution of "material culture," be it furniture, carpets, silver, cloth and clothing, wine, coffee and countless groceries. In contrast to the mercantilist protectionism in most continental capitals, London succeeded early in becoming an international center of commerce, even though the notion of "free trade" is an anachronism for this period.

British examples have helped inspire the history of consumption, pioneered by John Brewer and Maxine Berg, that has enriched urban economic history by integrating social and cultural factors. The approach has been applied successfully to France by Daniel Roche and by Natacha Coquery, who is concerned with the place of shops in the urban fabric and (social) geography (Coquery, 1998, 2000). The depiction of public life in cities itself became a sought-after commodity, involving artists such as Canaletto (two relatives working in places as diverse as Venice, Saxony, Poland, and England), Piranesi (mainly in Rome), Rosenberg (in Berlin), or even Hogarth with his satirical presentation of London's vices. Innumerable lesser-known engravers and printers provided customers with city views. Besides, the emergence of the novel as a new literary genre owed much to the urban environment (which it frequently portrayed in return). The rise of the newspaper and journal press, one of the great economic success stories of the eighteenth century, would have been inconceivable outside cities. Visual and textual sources present considerable problems for interpretation, but some historians have moved on to explore the urban sound world, suggesting that acoustic sensibilities changed fundamentally around mid-century, prompting legislation to reduce noise and to select new sites and designs for buildings such as hospitals (Gutton, 2000: 84–94; see also Garrioch, 2003; Smith, 1999).

A European City?

Much research remains to be done, and it is still difficult to draw general conclusions about eighteenth-century towns and their inhabitants. The topic is wide and, indeed, it is hard to conceive of an aspect of European history entirely without an urban dimension. Cities shaped contemporary realities and imaginations, but leaving aside the most stubbornly introverted small towns, they were far from static entities themselves. Each was individual and specific, but also in constant exchange with the surrounding countryside, and with other cities nationally and internationally.

Even with more space than is available here it would be difficult to state whether there was such a thing as a typically "European city" in this period and beyond, nor is it easy to delineate the geographical area in which such settlements might be found. Over a decade ago, Christopher Friedrichs, in his magisterial synthesis, named Aberdeen and Dubrovnik, Lisbon and Tallinn, as border towns of "a common urban civilization," irrespective of major differences in their size and individuality (Friedrichs, 1995: 7). While there may be good arguments for such a stance, it seems appropriate not to forget that the eighteenth-century urban fabric contained much that was "non-European": Turkish baths in Budapest, *lonja* buildings on Moorish designs in southern Spain and *chinoiseries* – the Chinese-inspired decorations that were the last word in fashionable taste across a wide social spectrum. Such curiosity and openness to external influences was, after all, integral to a time and a continent, the elites of which deemed themselves not only enlightened, but urbane.

Bibliography

Bairoch, P., J. Batou, and P. Chèvre, *La Population des villes européennes de 800 à 1850* (Geneva, 1988).

Berg, M. (ed.), *Markets and Manufactures in Early Industrial Europe* (London, 1991).

Bermingham, A. and J. Brewer (eds.), *The Consumption of Culture, 1600–1800: Image, Object, Text* (London, 1997).

Borsay, P., *The English Urban Renaissance: Culture and Society in the Provincial Town, 1660–1770* (Oxford, 1989).

Brewer, J. and R. Porter (eds.), *Consumption and the World of Goods* (London, 1993).

Chandler, T. and G. Fox, *3000 Years of Urban Growth* (New York, 1974).

Chartier, R., G. Chaussinaud-Nogaret, H. Neveux, and E. Le Roy Ladurie, *La Ville des temps modernes: De la Renaissance aux révolutions* (Paris, 1988).

Clark, P. (ed.), *Small Towns in Early Modern Europe* (Cambridge, 1995).

Clark, P. (ed.), *The Cambridge Urban History of Britain*, vol. 2: *1540–1840* (Cambridge, 2000).

Clark, P. and B. Lepetit (eds.), *Capital Cities and their Hinterlands in Early Modern Europe* (Aldershot, 1996).

Coquery, N., *L'Hôtel aristocratique: Le Marché du luxe à Paris au XVIII siècle* (Paris, 1998).

Coquery, N. (ed.), *La Boutique et la ville: Commerces, commerçants, espaces et clientèles XVIe–XXe siècle* (Tours, 2000).

Craig, M., *Dublin, 1660–1860* (London, 1992).

Crossick, G. (ed.), *The Artisan and the European Town, 1500–1900* (Aldershot, 1997).

Csendes, P. and F. Opll (eds.), *Wien. Geschichte einer Stadt*, vol. 2: *Die frühneuzeitliche Residenz (16.–18. Jahrhundert)* (Vienna, 2003).

de Vries, J., *European Urbanization 1500–1800* (Cambridge, MA, 1984).

de Vries, J. and A. van der Woude, *The First Modern Economy: Success, Failure, and Perseverance of the Dutch Economy, 1500–1815* (Cambridge, 1997).

François, E., *Koblenz im 18. Jahrhundert. Zur Sozial- und Bevölkerungsstruktur einer deutschen Residenzstadt* (Göttingen, 1982).

François, E., *Die unsichtbare Grenze. Protestanten und Katholiken in Augsburg, 1648–1806* (Sigmaringen, 1991).
Friedrichs, C. R., *The Early Modern City 1450–1750* (London, 1995).
Friedrichs, C. R., "But are we any closer to home? Early modern German urban history since *German Home Towns*," *Central European History*, 30 (1997), 163–86.
Garden, M., *Lyon et les Lyonnais au XVIIIe siècle* (Paris, 1975).
Garrioch, D., *Neighbourhood and Community in Paris, 1740–1890* (Cambridge, 1986).
Garrioch, D., "Sounds of the city: the soundscape of early modern European towns," *Urban History*, 30 (2003), 5–25.
Girouard, M., *Cities and People: A Social and Architectural History* (New Haven, 1985).
Gräf, H. T. (ed.), *Kleine Städte im neuzeitlichen Europa* (Berlin, 1997).
Gross, H., *Rome in the Age of Enlightenment:The Post-Tridentine Syndrome and the Ancien Régime* (Cambridge, 1990).
Gutton, J.-P., *Bruits et sons dans notre histoire: Essai sur la reconstitution du paysage sonore* (Paris, 2000).
Hembry, P., *The English Spa, 1560–1815: A Social History* (London, 1990).
Hohenberg, P. M. and L. H. Lees (eds.), *The Making of Urban Europe 1000–1994* (Cambridge, MA, 1995).
Imhof, A. E., *Aspekte der Bevölkerungsentwicklung in den nordischen Ländern 1720–1750* (2 vols., Bern, 1976).
Jersch-Wenzel, S., *Juden und "Franzosen" in der Wirtschaft des Raumes Berlin-Brandenburg zur Zeit des Merkantilismus* (Berlin, 1978).
Keller, K., *Kleinstädte in Kursachsen. Wandlungen einer Städtelandschaft zwischen Dreißigjährigem Krieg und Industrialisierung* (Cologne, 2001).
Knittler, H., *Die europäische Stadt in der frühen Neuzeit. Institutionen, Strukturen, Entwicklungen* (Vienna, 2000).
Meyer, J. and J.-P. Poussou, *Études sur les villes françaises: Milieu du XVIIe siècle à la veille de la Révolution française* (2nd edn., Paris, 1995).
Mitchell, B. R., *European Historical Statistics 1750–1975* (2nd edn., London, 1981).
Norberg, K., *Rich and Poor in Grenoble, 1600–1814* (Berkeley, 1985).
Rasmussen, S. E., *London: The Unique City* (3rd edn., Cambridge, MA, 1988).
Rausch, W. (ed.), *Die Städte Mitteleuropas im 17. und 18. Jahrhundert* (Linz, 1981).
Ribhegge, W., *Stadt und Nation in Deutschland vom Mittelalter bis zur Gegenwart. Die Entstehung der Ziviligesellschaft aus der Tradition der Städte* (Münster, 2002).
Roche, D., *Le Peuple de Paris: Essai sur la culture populaire au XVIIIe siècle* (Paris, 1998).
Roche, D. and G. Chabaud (eds.), *La Ville promise: Mobilité et accueil à Paris (fin XVIIe–début XIXe siècle)* (Paris, 2000).
Roeck, B., *Lebenswelt und Kultur des Bürgertums in der Frühen Neuzeit* (Munich, 1991); expanded English translation, Leiden, 2006.
Rosseaux, U., *Städte in der frühen Neuzeit* (Darmstadt, 2006).
Rudé, G., *Hanoverian London, 1714–1808* (Berkeley, 1971).
Schilling, H., *Die Stadt in der frühen Neuzeit* (Munich, 1993).
Schneider, R. A., *Public Life in Toulouse, 1463–1789: From Municipal Republic to Cosmopolitan City* (Ithaca, 1989).
Schultz, H., *Berlin 1650–1800. Sozialgeschichte einer Residenz* (Berlin, 1992).
Smith, B. R., *The Acoustic World of Early Modern England: Attending the O-Factor* (Chicago, 1999).
Spielman, J. P., *The City and the Crown: Vienna and the Imperial Court, 1600–1740* (West Lafayette, 1993).
Sweet, R., *The Writing of Urban Histories in Eighteenth-Century England* (Oxford, 1997).
Sweet, R., *The English Town, 1680–1840: Government, Society and Culture* (Harlow, 1999).

Tantner, A., *Ordnung der Häuser, Beschreibung der Seelen. Hausnummerierung und Seelenkonskription in der Habsburgermonarchie* (Innsbruck, 2006).

Walker, M., *German Home Towns: Community, State and General Estate, 1648–1871* (Ithaca, 1971).

Whaley, J., *Religious Toleration and Social Change in Hamburg, 1529–1819* (Cambridge, 1985).

Wrigley, E. A. and R. S. Schofield, *The Population History of England, 1541–1871: A Reconstruction* (Cambridge, MA, 1981).

Chapter Six

The Eighteenth-Century Nobility: Challenge and Renewal

Hamish Scott

Joseph Haydn was a musical superstar of later eighteenth-century Europe. His orchestral compositions and string quartets, which established the genre, earned him a pivotal position in the development of Western music. He was also *Kapellmeister* to the aristocratic family of Esterházy for almost three decades. The Esterházy ruled a vast latifundium in northern Hungary, at its greatest extent some 4,800 km^2 in size, within which their authority was all but absolute and which they exploited through an efficient estate administration. They were also celebrated cultural patrons, especially Prince Nicholas "the Magnificent," head of the House from 1762 to 1790. Haydn, like all the other servants, was obliged to wear the Esterházy family's distinctive light blue livery and had to appear before Prince Nicholas every morning, to inquire what musical entertainment might be required. Before he could undertake any commissions for other patrons, he needed the permission of the head of the family, while his career in Vienna and more widely in Europe during the final two decades of his life was only made possible by his release from his formal contract after the Prince's death in 1790.

These circumstances epitomize the Janus-faced nature of eighteenth-century Europe and of Haydn's position in that world. Though some of his compositions point towards the modern age, his own career testified to the extensive and continuing role of a traditional social group. This same dichotomy is evident in the history, and even the historiography, of the eighteenth-century nobility, which both look backward into the traditional society of Old Europe, and simultaneously forward to the more modern world ushered in by the French Revolution.

The dramatic events in France after 1789 have exerted a considerable influence on writing about the old regime's nobility. The established tendency to view the eighteenth century simply as an extended preparation for the French Revolution, together with the onslaught which it faced during the 1790s, for long encouraged historians to see the nobility as a declining and outmoded group within society and state. The future, it was assumed, lay with the middle classes, who would dominate the nineteenth century. A recognition that this was far from true has led to a rehabilitation of the eighteenth-century nobility during the past generation. Instead of

A Companion to Eighteenth-Century Europe, First Edition. Edited by Peter H. Wilson.
© 2014 John Wiley & Sons, Ltd. Published 2014 by John Wiley & Sons, Ltd.

viewing it as a declining social caste preparing for a well-merited nemesis, its coherence, strength, and resilience are now recognized.

Indeed, it was stronger in the 1780s than a century before in important respects. Though a privileged group which tenaciously defended an established position, it was surprisingly open to new forces and ideas. Many nobles participated in and even launched manufacturing enterprises and commercial developments, and benefited significantly from them. In the longer perspective the Enlightenment, with its emphasis on social utilitarianism, natural rights, and individualism, challenged the whole basis of nobility, which rested upon inherited privilege, presumed inequality, and corporate status, and would undermine the elite almost completely. Yet many eighteenth-century noblemen and noblewomen participated enthusiastically in the new intellectual currents and facilitated their circulation and discussion through literary societies, provincial academies, and *salons*. For many noble families, the last hundred years of the old regime were a period of social dominance, economic prosperity, and even political power. They were also decades of significant change, which made the elite better able to retain its authority in the next century and beyond. A Sicilian nobleman who was also a noted novelist, Giuseppe Tomasi, duke of Palma and prince of Lampedusa (1896–1957), would declare in his celebrated novel of nineteenth-century aristocratic life, *The Leopard*, that in order for everything to stay the same, everything also had to change. The validity of his aphorism is increasingly apparent to historians of the old regime's nobility.

Composition and Consolidation

Nobility was a hereditary and privileged status enjoyed by those born legitimately of noble parents or ennobled, either by a monarch – sometimes in return for a cash payment – or, much less commonly, by a representative body: as was the case in Poland-Lithuania until its extinction in 1795, and in Sweden during the "Age of Liberty" (1720–72) when the *riksdag* and not the king ruled. By the eighteenth century many more nobles were born than were raised to that status during their own lifetime. The nobility's privileges were social, political, and legal in nature, and collectively were impressive. Nobles alone were entitled to carry a sword (the badge of their role as the fighting caste); significantly, impoverished members of Poland-Lithuania's numerous nobility (the *szlachta*) carried wooden sabers, when they were too poor to afford the real thing. They alone were entitled to employ titles and distinctive forms of address (such as that of "Don," which was widespread in the eighteenth-century Spanish monarchy), to display their coats of arms on their carriages and over the portals of their residences, and to dress their servants in a distinctive livery. More generally they were entitled to a position of honor in any religious or secular ceremony they attended, and would normally have their own private gallery or pew in the local church, often decorated with their family coat of arms. Where representative institutions survived, nobles were always in a very powerful and often dominant position within them. Indeed, in Hungary (then part of the Austrian Habsburg monarchy), the magnates alone were entitled to attend the kingdom's diet. More generally noblemen dominated government and political life, with the majority of public offices reserved for them either legally or in practice, and in Catholic countries they also predominated in the upper levels of the church.

These privileges also took more tangible forms. The most celebrated was the exemption from the principal direct tax (the *taille*), which the nobility enjoyed in large areas of France, long believed to be a major cause of the revolution since it prevented a fairer distribution of the tax burden and so contributed to the old regime's financial problems, which ultimately caused its collapse. In fact the eighteenth-century French nobility paid some direct taxation, in the form of the *capitation*, the *dixième*, and similar levies: the problem was that of massive under-assessment and under-payment, not complete exemption. The pattern in France was to be found in several European states, where the nobility enjoyed exemption from certain forms of direct taxation, though the situation was complex and generalizations are difficult, except for the obvious conclusion that everywhere they were under-taxed in terms of their income and wealth. During the eighteenth century, these surviving fiscal exemptions were attacked by hard-pressed governments, which made inroads into them. Nobles benefited enormously from their positions as landowners and seigneurs, enjoying diverse forms of income and the right to hunt over arable land and to monopolize fishing in that locality. Finally they enjoyed extensive juridical privileges: trial in separate courts usually composed of their peers and, if convicted, a different range of punishments than commoners, freedom from arrest except in well-defined circumstances, freedom from some forms of civil action, such as for debt. Above all they long possessed the right to administer justice, an important source of income and prestige within the local community, and resisted efforts by central government to encroach upon this role, often successfully. In many countries this function would survive beyond the eighteenth century, exemplifying the nobility's wider social dominance. Old regime Europe consisted of numerous intensely localized societies, which were sustained by poor communications and long remained surprisingly resistant to the forces of commercialization and the intrusions of state power. Towns, and the more advanced regions in northwestern Europe, were obvious exceptions to this generalization. Over most of the continent, however, society remained very traditional. Deference survived, and with it the authority and leadership of Europe's nobilities.

Nobility was also characterized by a distinctive lifestyle, primarily involving the enjoyment of landed estates, and keeping up appearances was crucial for all its members. Leading aristocrats such as the Esterházy buttressed their exalted status through architectural and cultural display, while provincial noble families built town houses and rural residences on a new scale. By the eighteenth century the similarities between individual national nobilities, particularly at the highest level, were increasing, and a more truly "European" elite was taking shape, as growing contacts enhanced awareness and advanced homogeneity. The aristocratic "Grand Tour," which flourished during the seventeenth and eighteenth centuries and through which young noblemen were sent round Europe in the nominal care of a tutor, to study history, culture, and languages and to mix in court society, together with growing intermarriage, both fostered this development. It was also encouraged by the publication and circulation of treatises on the nobility, and by the spread of the French language and culture from Louis XIV's reign (1643–1715) onwards. Yet even in the 1780s such internationalization was still in its infancy. Europe was still dominated by individual national nobilities, whose structures were produced primarily by that country's extended and distinctive historical evolution.

This was most evident in the size of individual elites as a proportion of total population. In certain countries, usually located near the continent's periphery, the status of nobility had been particularly readily awarded or recognized by rulers in the past. It was the case especially in the Spanish monarchy, the kingdom of Hungary and Poland-Lithuania, where nobles made up as many as 5 or 6 percent of the total population. These countries all contained a large and often impoverished lesser nobility, the obstacles to entering which were relatively slight for impostors, and this further boosted numbers. These figures were unusual, however. Elsewhere, the nobility made up a very small proportion, no more than 1 or 1.5 percent and sometimes far less than that. In Hanoverian England, where exceptionally a father's noble status was usually transmitted only to his eldest son – in contrast to continental Europe where all the legitimate children of noble parents received their nobility – the new British peerage created by the Union with Scotland in 1707 contained fewer than 200 individuals during the mid-eighteenth century, when the total population was some 7 or 8 million. A spate of creations increased this total to 267 by 1800. The separate nobilities of Scotland and Ireland added a few hundred families, but the general point about the smallness of Britain's elite remains. Yet there, as throughout Europe, the nobility's influence was wholly disproportionate to its numerical size.

During the second half of the eighteenth century the number of nobles began to decline, sometimes quite sharply. The numerical reductions were especially striking at a period when general population levels were increasing rapidly. Governments, anxious to limit the privileges enjoyed by most nobilities and so increase their own fiscal revenues, and also to uphold the more rigid definitions of elite status which had become established, carried out inquiries into the nobility, and these invariably reduced numbers. Even more important than such investigations were the economic pressures upon the lesser nobility in particular, squeezed between the increasing expenditure needed to sustain the necessary lifestyle in an age of sharply rising prices, and incomes which could only with difficulty be raised, particularly when that status conferred diminishing social benefits and was increasingly questioned by some contemporaries. The consequent reduction in the size of the lesser nobility strengthened the established tendency for a compression of the elite, as the aristocracy and middle ranks became numerically more important, as well as socially, economically, and politically preponderant. The sharpest decline was evident in the Spanish monarchy. The government – in keeping with the newly statistical spirit of the age – carried out a series of censuses, which reveal a fall from around 800,000 (1750), to 722,794 (1768), 480,000 (1787), and 403,000 (1797), a drop of almost 50 percent during the second half of the eighteenth century.

The nobility as a social group everywhere resembled a pyramid, the steepness of the gradient depending upon the proportion which can be classified as lesser nobles. Though there were a considerable number of gradations of status and wealth, which varied from country to country, certain generalizations are possible. The main subdivisions were into an aristocracy, a more sizeable middling nobility, and a large – sometimes very large – lesser nobility. At the apex were a group of families of real power and immense wealth, such as the Esterházy with their latifundium in northern Hungary, the Bourbon-Penthièvre in France, who were in control of at least 254 parishes, with 150,000 people, or the Radziwill, who ruled properties in the eastern regions of Poland-Lithuania approximately equal in territorial extent to present-day

Belgium. These lineages were of national and even international importance, and were accustomed to play a major political role, probably living part of each year in the capital where they would also own a substantial residence. During the seventeenth century a process of social centralization had been evident at the higher levels of the nobility. A very good example had been the rise of Vienna in the Austrian Habsburg monarchy, after the relief of the second Ottoman siege in 1683. Thereafter, as the dynasty and the government became fully identified with the city, which more clearly than ever was the capital, the leading noble families had built the white stucco palaces which still dominate the skyline, to facilitate their access to the Habsburg court and their own role as advisers and ministers to the dynasty.

The nobility in the Habsburg monarchy, like its counterparts throughout Europe, had been created by a distinctive historical evolution, extending back across several hundred years. Here, as elsewhere, the seventeenth century had been decisive. A number of well-placed families, loyal to Catholicism and to the dynasty, had secured substantial landholdings during the upheavals of the Thirty Years War (1618–48) and the reconquest of Ottoman Hungary in the 1680s and 1690s, together with the higher titles of nobility – prince, count, and baron – and the accompanying social and political influence. This evolution had parallels throughout Europe: the Spanish monarchy had witnessed a significant expansion of the grandees and France the rise of the *ducs et pairs*, at the aristocratic peak of the noble hierarchy. In Restoration England after 1660, the peerage recovered notably after its temporary demise during the Civil Wars, when the House of Lords had been abolished. The aristocracy's landed power was little diminished, while its social and political influence was first restored after 1660 and then consolidated by the revolution of 1688–9, which made it a partner in government with the monarchy. The eighteenth century was a golden age for the British peerage, when economic wealth, social power, and political influence were all at their zenith. A similar evolution occurred in Portugal. There, the recovery of political independence from Spain during the War of Independence (1640–68) and the accession of the new Braganza dynasty – hitherto itself a prominent Portuguese noble family – had been followed by a notable reconstitution of the aristocracy. It was distinctive in one respect: landholding was proportionately far less important as a source of income for Portugal's great nobles than royal grants of pensions and other revenues. Otherwise it paralleled developments elsewhere, as a relatively small group of well-placed families monopolized Crown favor, acquiring wealth, status, and the titles to match.

These and similar developments ensured that the eighteenth-century nobility in much of Europe was stratified to a novel extent. The elite, increasingly known as an "aristocracy," was distinguished by its control of substantial resources, titles, and social and political authority, and was everywhere apparent. Below it were the middling nobility, which consisted of families of moderate wealth and social standing, though their influence did not extend far beyond their own province and even locality. Aware of national issues and with contacts upwards into the aristocracy, families of middling rank had rather more limited horizons than their peers whose clients they often were. At the base of the pyramid was a sizeable petty nobility, deeply traditional in outlook, frequently impoverished, and sometimes landless: groups such as the *hobereaux* in France, many *hidalgos* in the Spanish monarchy, and the overwhelming majority of the *szlachta* in Poland-Lithuania. Far fewer sources survive for the lesser nobility, and knowledge of them is often scanty. Such families were little distinguished from the poorer members of society, at least in economic terms, and they faced an unending struggle to uphold their own noble status. They were unable to buy land, launch their children into a career or marriage, or even maintain an adequate standard of living. Poland-Lithuania, Hungary, and the Spanish monarchy all contained a numerous petty nobility, as did certain French provinces, above all Brittany and Normandy. One key development during the eighteenth century was that significant numbers of poorer nobles gave up the attempt to maintain their privileged status and declined into the ranks of the commonalty, contributing to a sharp reduction in the size of many national elites.

The precise gradient of the noble pyramid varied from country to country, and even from province to province. One fundamental reason why this was so was the nature of inheritance systems. In those countries – most of Europe by this period – where male primogeniture was the norm, a father's wealth and especially his lands passed on his death to his eldest son. Younger sons received far less, while daughters could only expect a dowry when they married, or its equivalent if they entered a Catholic religious institution. In many countries this was guaranteed by the existence of a formal entail: variously known as a *Fideikommiss* (the Habsburg monarchy), *fedecommesso* (Italian peninsula), *mayorazgo* (Spanish monarchy), *majorat* (parts of France), or Strict Settlement (post-1660 England). Such arrangements were legal trusts, breakable only with considerable difficulty, which protected family lands and sometimes even moveable wealth, while guaranteeing a regular income to each generation. Even more importantly, entails created a fixed order of succession and thereby a degree of insurance against demographic extinction, always a potent threat to a noble line. These arrangements were far from universal, even where primogeniture was established. Only well-off families, as a generalization, set up formal trusts, which were costly to administer and could be troublesome to operate, being everywhere a fertile source of the litigation which Europe's nobilities pursued with vigor. The only important exception was Spain, where *mayorazgos* were widely established by lesser nobles, due to their iconic status as a badge of nobility.

There were significant areas of Europe where partible inheritance – the division of a father's wealth among all his male offspring – was the norm. This was the case in Russia and Poland-Lithuania (in both countries only a tiny number of entails were permitted), and in much of the Holy Roman Empire. While agreements between sons to keep the family lands intact were common, the combined impact of partible inheritance and a relatively poor agricultural economy militated against much stratification within the nobility in these regions. Instead there was less social and economic distance between the greatest lord and the poorest noble. This was certainly the case in Brandenburg-Prussia, where in 1780 only one *Junker* family (the counts von Arnim auf Boitzenburg) had wealth on the same scale enjoyed by the top one hundred families in the Habsburg monarchy. The von Arnim owned around 11,000 acres of land, with approximately 100 farms, while in Bohemia alone no fewer than 16 aristocratic families had at least 2,000 farms each. A rather different pattern can be identified in Poland-Lithuania and Russia, where no stable aristocracy had emerged by the end of the eighteenth century, though individual families enjoyed immense power and considerable wealth, which took the form of control over communities and people rather than simple landed property, in a region of Europe where land was plentiful and labor scarce. The Zamoyski landholdings were unusually concentrated, extending over some 4,000 km^2 in the palatinate of Lublin (central Poland) and, by the 1770s, had a population approaching 100,000, with 10 towns, 220 villages, and 100 manors.

The discussion of inheritance arrangements has also highlighted that the nobility was an aggregate of families rather than of individuals. The importance of social and economic individualism during the past two centuries makes this crucial factor difficult to explain to a contemporary reader. Nobility was a collective, not an individual, status, and noblemen and noblewomen were subordinate to several larger and overlapping wholes: the family, the lineage, and the House. Their status derived from membership of the wider lineage, to which individuals were entirely subordinate. A marriage or a son's career concerned the family as a whole, not merely the individual, who might at most enjoy a veto. Noblemen and noblewomen lacked what would now be called "agency," in the sense of influence over their own destinies. Individual preferences were always subordinate to family strategy, which was drawn up by the senior figures in the House, frequently meeting in a regular and semi-formal council. Within such discussions older noblewomen would often play a decisive role, especially where marriages were concerned. Nobility was an essentially masculine attribute, which adhered in the male line and was transmitted from father to son. Daughters occupied a wholly subordinate position, though – as in Russia and the Spanish monarchy – they could have extensive legal rights where inheritance was concerned. Less formally, female family members exercised considerable influence. They might personally conduct negotiations for a marriage, and often ran the family estate and supervised the education of the children, either during their husband's absence at court or on military campaign, or after his death: widowhood was, as it had long been, the period when a noblewomen's influence and power were at their peak.

In the middling and higher nobility in particular, family strategy dictated the roles of all the children. The key requirement was to secure the succession through the marriage of the eldest son and the birth of a male heir. The concentration of expectations and resources upon the first-born son inherent within a system of primogeniture could be accompanied by informal restrictions upon the marriages of cadets. Instead younger sons would be assisted into a career which did not imperil noble status, as direct participation in commerce might do. In Catholic countries the church remained the major destination for second sons in particular, and the nobility was entrenched in its upper echelons. In many German cathedral chapters places were formally reserved for noblemen, as were most bishoprics and prelacies in Poland-Lithuania. In 1789 every single French bishop and archbishop was a nobleman, as were most heads of monasteries. The other traditional destination for younger sons was the army, and this became even more important during the eighteenth century. The expansion of government also offered careers, though it could demand previous training. Daughters would be provided with a dowry upon marriage, and the rise in the value of these during the early modern period contributed to the numbers who remained single: as many as 42 percent of the sisters of French *ducs et pairs* in the early eighteenth century. Those who remained unmarried would stay in the family home, perhaps becoming responsible for the education of the younger children or, if they were Catholic, might enter a religious institution.

Vast differences of gender and wealth characterized Europe's nobilities, and these may have increased during the eighteenth century. Yet there were also important sources of coherence and unity. The vertical bonds of patronage and clientage, extending down from the aristocracy into the provincial nobility, and even from middle-ranking families into the lesser nobility, promoted integration. Even more important, however, was the notion of nobility itself. A member of the lesser nobility and a great aristocrat might be separated by wealth and status from each other and move in quite different social circles, but each regarded themselves as members of the same order or estate, and so distinct from all other groups within society. What divided them, in other words, was still viewed as less important than what united them. This was exemplified by the actions of some French aristocrats when the Estates General met after a long gap in 1789. Appalled by the evident poverty of some lesser nobles who had come to Paris, they bought new clothes and subsidized better lodgings for their fellow noblemen, determined that the honor of the second estate should not be compromised. The small royal pensions discreetly paid to a few impoverished British peers had the same broad aim, that of keeping up appearances.

By the final decades of the eighteenth century, at least in the more advanced economies of western Europe, the early signs of what would become the transition from order to class, which would transform the nobility during the next century, were becoming apparent. But these were everywhere less important than the real unity imparted to Europe's nobilities by a sense of membership of what was still seen in a very traditional way as the fighting class, and by the privileges which this conferred, privileges which still defined the noble caste at the very end of the old regime.

Economic Power

One important foundation of the nobility's strong position was its wealth and economic power. Only in the two most advanced economies, those of England and the Dutch Republic, did the bourgeoisie rival and even eclipse the resources it controlled. The eighteenth century, and especially its final decades, was a period of rapid economic expansion, demographic growth, and rising prices and rents. In Brandenburg-Prussia, for example, grain prices trebled between around 1730 and 1800, and increases of this magnitude could be found throughout Europe. Many nobles did very well indeed out of the upturn: on the lordship of Stavenow in the Prignitz (northwest Brandenburg) a combination of agricultural improvement and skilful management increased the owner's annual income more than threefold between 1719 and 1808. In Extremadura (along the Spanish border with Portugal) income from the estates of the dukes of Feria tripled between the 1720s and 1770s. Not everyone did so well out of the economic upturn: one reason why significant numbers of lesser nobles gave up their privileged status was their inability to bear its increasing costs, at a period when the benefits themselves were becoming less apparent. In this way wider economic trends confirmed established developments and accelerated the stratification in progress.

At the nobility's apex there was an elite of super-rich families, such as the Esterházy in the Habsburg monarchy, the Radziwill in Poland-Lithuania, or the Condé in France, who enjoyed a level of resources and a standard of living which rivaled those of minor rulers elsewhere in Europe. The scale of that wealth was remarkable: in the 1780s the leading French aristocratic family of Conti owned landed resources valued at 29 million *livres* and enjoyed an annual income estimated at 3.7 million *livres*; their relatives the Condé possessed estates worth 32 million *livres* at the beginning of the century; while the plutocratic Bourbon-Penthièvre controlled 100 million *livres* of land on the eve of the revolution. To put such figures into perspective, it has to be remembered that better-off peasants and artisans might have annual incomes of a few hundred *livres*. In eighteenth-century France most aristocratic families had properties valued at between 1 million and 2 million *livres*, while collectively nobles owned some 25–30 percent of the land. In eighteenth-century Denmark, approximately half of the land was controlled by the nobility. In most European countries a group of families controlled extensive estates, which usually were scattered across several provinces, though the majority would be consolidated into one or two large blocks of land. The Condé, for example, seem to have had properties in no fewer than 10 provinces, though this was unusual and owing to their vast landholdings. This reflected both the haphazard way in which these properties had been acquired in previous generations and past centuries and the rigidities of the early modern land market, which inhibited efforts to consolidate noble estates. The coherence of the Zamoyski estates in central Poland-Lithuania was quite exceptional.

Great latifundia were the exception rather than the rule, however. Most noble landholdings were more modest and could be very small indeed. Though precise figures do not exist, estimates have been made for East Prussia, which rest upon a division of noble estates into three categories: one-quarter were large (2,500 acres and above); one-half were medium-sized (500–2,500 acres); and one-quarter were small (less than 500 acres). For Brandenburg around 1800, a broadly similar breakdown was reached based upon value rather than extent: 20 percent can be classified as large estates, around 66 percent as medium-sized, and around 14 percent small estates. These figures are only, at best, of the right order of magnitude, but they offer an approximate guide to landholding patterns.

The scale of the landed property controlled was – usually – an index to the standing of a particular family. Russia was distinctive, since wealth took the form of enserfed peasants rather than landed acres, which were near-valueless without the labor to work them. The leading Russian aristocratic family, the Sheremetev, seems to have owned over 100,000 serfs. Most noble families in Russia owned far fewer peasants, and some none at all. In a handful of predominantly urban polities – Venice is the leading example – investments and other moveable wealth might be more important in the make-up of a family's resources. But even Venetian nobles had eagerly sought to acquire land on the republic's mainland territories. Only in Portugal did the aristocracy depend more upon the Crown than upon their own estates for income by the eighteenth century, and even there families all had some landed possessions. Everywhere rolling acres were – as they had long been – an essential prerequisite of noble status. When England's naval hero Horatio Nelson was ennobled, he was also given the necessary landed estates without which the new Lord Nelson would have been incomplete: exactly as, almost a century before, the duke of Marlborough had been given Blenheim.

The principal noble resource was usually landed property. Though its relative importance may have declined during the eighteenth century, as commercial activities and state service increased in significance, landholding retained its primacy until the French Revolution and far beyond. Noble estates – like family finances in general – were run by specialized individuals and even councils, who administered the patrimony with distinctive aims in mind, above all that of maximizing income for the family's wider objectives. The economic aims of noble families can all too easily be a source of considerable misunderstanding. Unlike more modern approaches to income and wealth creation, they were dictated not by purely economic considerations but by rather different social, cultural, and even political factors, and should not be viewed through the lens of economic rationality, but in terms of more traditional, non-economic imperatives. The *Encyclopédie* famously defined "economy" as "the wise and legitimate management of the household," a long-established approach and one which certainly applied to the economics of noble power. The estate management of the Esterházy, efficient but deeply traditional, had parallels throughout Europe. Income, always less important than consumption, would be partly in kind, and would either be consumed locally or sold to raise cash; in the less commercial regions of southern, central and eastern Europe, a higher proportion would be in this form. The demand side was also distinctive. A noble family would need money both for routine living expenses, which given the obligation to "live nobly," to keep up appearances through conspicuous consumption, and to entertain on a substantial scale, could be considerable, and for a variety of erratic but large-scale expenditures: a building project, a funeral, a daughter's dowry, the costs of launching a son on his career. The substantial sums involved often could only be raised by large-scale borrowing. Debt frequently was an index not of economic difficulties, far less impoverishment, but of wealth and prosperity.

During the eighteenth century families, with ever-increasing financial commitments and faced by rising prices, sought to maximize income from their estates. The success with which established sources of revenue were exploited and new ones developed in France led both contemporaries and historians to talk of a "seigneurial reaction," but in some degree this could be found across much of Europe. In central and eastern Europe the later seventeenth century and the eighteenth century saw a notable increase in the power of landlords over their peasants and in their ability to exploit them, as the system of *Gutsherrschaft* ("manorial lordship") became widely established. Its distinguishing characteristics were that a nobleman had a relatively large demesne, which he farmed directly with the aid of unpaid labor from the peasants who were now completely dependent upon him, while the peasant/serf was tied to the lord's estate and was legally unfree, being unable to move or to marry without the nobleman's permission, and was also subject to his judicial authority.

The pressures upon incomes also encouraged a more extensive exploitation of the increasing commercial opportunities. Nominally, direct involvement in trade and commerce could imperil nobility, since it "derogated" from an individual's privileged status. The threat of derogation, however, had never been very potent. The formal laws which expressed it incorporated a series of cultural values associated with nobility and set out what constituted "menial" conduct, leading to the loss of noble status. By the eighteenth century derogation was becoming less of an obstacle to involvement in commercial activities, both in practice and in law. In France, which since the mid-sixteenth century had possessed one of the most extensive series of legal provisions, the threat of derogation was removed in stages from different kinds of commerce: maritime trade (1669), naval construction and arms production (1681), maritime insurance (1686), wholesale commerce (1701), and manufacturing and banking (1767). These successive liberalizations were motivated by concern at the number of merchants who were "living nobly," with the implied threat that their commercial activities could be abandoned, and by a wider desire to promote French economic development. The same aims lay behind both the ennoblement of wholesale merchants in Portugal (1770) and the decree of 1783 in Spain which granted noble status to families active in commerce or manufacturing for three successive generations.

Many countries in any case had never had a formal code of derogation. Actual participation in the retail trade was frowned upon, but other commercial activities were permitted, either formally or tacitly. A proportion of noble income always took the form of the produce of their own lands, both foodstuffs and natural products such as timber, and trade in these had always been possible. During the eighteenth century involvement in commerce and manufacturing grew, due to expanding opportunities and increased pressure upon noble incomes. In France a small number of well-placed families profited spectacularly from economic expansion. The Condé invested so successfully in iron manufacturing in Brittany that profits doubled to a massive 50 percent of the family's income. In that province almost all metalworking was controlled by nobles, while in neighboring Normandy 84 percent of forges were in their hands. The nobility owned around half of all metal works in France. Similar examples of increased involvement in manufacturing can be found throughout Europe, sometimes on a very considerable scale. By mid-century over 40 percent of income from noble estates in Bohemia came from such enterprises. The remarkable growth of woolen manufacturing on the Waldstein estates was a case in point. In the second decade of the eighteenth century Count Johann Joseph Waldstein brought in Dutch and English specialists to establish the production of woolen cloth, based on forced peasant labor. It succeeded so spectacularly that, 50 years later, the Waldstein enterprise had 27 looms and over 200 spinning wheels.

The third source of noble income was state service, and it also gained in importance during these decades. Throughout Europe nobilities were the backbone of the expanding administrative structures of this period. The new nobility established in Denmark after 1660 was specifically designed to serve the absolute monarchy which had seized power from the noble-dominated diet, and in the eighteenth century this group came to dominate the Danish elite in a way which had parallels elsewhere. Noblemen predominated in local government and even in the central agencies; they provided the overwhelming majority of military officers and diplomats. They did so very largely because they alone were believed to possess the necessary qualities to fill these roles, and because of the lack – in most countries – of a sufficiently sizeable bourgeoisie. Only the nobility could provide the specialized personnel in the numbers now needed, and they were rewarded for their service. Income – however erratically paid – was more and more important for noble lineages and especially for younger sons, who secured a vocation – that of arms – which affirmed noble status, an opportunity for service and a career, and a source of income which the consequences of primogeniture denied them within the family itself.

The Nobility and the State

Armies exemplified this central role in the absolutist state. Europe's monarchies maintained large standing armies, while the more sophisticated command structures further increased the demand for officers. It was universally believed these could only come from the nobility, still seen as the fighting caste. The scale is apparent from the cases of Brandenburg-Prussia, where the officer corps in 1740 was slightly more than 3,000, but by 1806 had grown to between 7,000 and 8,000, of whom only around 700 seem to have been non-noble, concentrated in the technical branches. The Russian officer corps increased even more rapidly, multiplying fivefold during the century after 1725 from some 5,000 (in itself a great increase on the numbers a few decades earlier) to 9,000 (1762), to around 16,000 (1796), and to 27,000 by 1825, once again almost entirely noble.

Service, still viewed as primarily military, was anticipated by both rulers and their elites. "Noble status," declared Frederick the Great, "can only be gained by the sword, by bravery and by other outstanding behavior and services. I will tolerate as vassals only those who are at all times capable of rendering me useful service in the army and those who because of exceptionally good conduct and exceptional service I choose to raise into the Estate of the nobility." This was an extreme statement, penned at the close of Prussia's fight for survival in the Seven Years War (1756–63), but the sentiment was shared by an overwhelming majority of the king's contemporaries, noble and non-noble alike. The impoverished lesser nobility, above all in central and eastern Europe, saw a military career as a potential source of income and flocked to the colors. The proportion of *Junker* estate-owners who served in Brandenburg-Prussia's army almost doubled between 1713 and 1800, though simultaneously there was a fall in the length of their military careers. The establishment of cadet corps, in which sons of poor nobles could be trained, strengthened this link: these were established in Prussia in 1717 and in Russia in 1731. Similar foundations, such as those in Portugal (1757) and France (1776), strengthened the identification between elite and warfare which was evident throughout Europe. In France the celebrated Ségur Law of 1781 sought to tighten the traditional nobility's firm grip upon the officer corps by requiring any would-be officer to demonstrate no fewer than 16 quarterings of nobility, that is four complete generations of noble forebears. Long associated with the idea of an "aristocratic reaction," it was also motivated by the widespread assumption that military qualities were primarily to be found in noblemen.

Government was the second area of state activity where the nobility played a quite crucial role. In many countries, a distinction has to be made between central agencies and local bodies. The expansion of government, as rulers began to pursue more interventionist domestic policies, meant that administrators were now required to devote an increasing amount of time to their duties and even to possess previous education or training. Both demands militated against the continued involvement of large numbers of the traditional nobility. Instead, the expansion and professionalization of royal government across much of Europe from the second half of the seventeenth century onwards had the effect of reducing the involvement of aristocrats, who came to be replaced both by members of the middle and even lesser nobility, and by a new group of nobles who owed their privileged status to their role in government and especially the law courts: the *noblesse de la robe* and the *noblesse de la plume* in France, the *togado* in the Spanish monarchy, and the *nobiltà di toga* in the Spanish-controlled kingdom of Naples. The new Bourbon rulers of the eighteenth-century Spanish monarchy quite deliberately reduced the role of the grandees, so influential in the councils in the final decades of Habsburg rule, and encouraged the development of a new administrative nobility, often consisting of individuals with a background in law.

Throughout Europe the highest state positions were still occupied by members of the titled nobility, with the important difference that they had usually been advanced into the aristocracy as a reward for their service. This was so for Wenzel Anton von Kaunitz, Austrian Chancellor for almost four decades after 1753, who was originally a member of a family in the service nobility of Moravia (part of the kingdom of Bohemia), and was created prince in 1764. An identical upward trajectory was that of the duc de Choiseul, France's leading minister from 1758 to 1770. Originally from the duchy of Lorraine, Choiseul was only raised to the rank of *duc et pair* in 1758, when he became foreign minister. Even in Britain, where the House of Commons was growing in political importance and self-confidence, and provided the more important and long-serving prime ministers, the peerage provided a majority of most cabinets and continued to do so until the second half of the nineteenth century.

The nobility, and especially the aristocratic elite, consolidated its hold during these decades over one significant dimension of central government activity: the new-scale resident diplomacy which spread across much of Europe. States now began to maintain continuous and reciprocal diplomatic relations during peacetime, and to fill these permanent embassies with noblemen to a novel extent. Rulers did so because they believed nobles would have the dignity and social poise needed to represent them, still a diplomat's major function. The protean diplomatic services of eighteenth-century Europe were aristocratic redoubts, as statistical analyses have demonstrated. In the kingdom of Sardinia, as the composite monarchy ruled from Turin and consisting of the island of that name together with Savoy and Piedmont on the north Italian mainland was known, out of 54 diplomatic appointments made at this period no less than two-thirds (36) went to members of the traditional nobility and 15 to families ennobled more recently. Only three posts were filled by commoners, and these men were ennobled while serving as diplomats. Spanish diplomacy was even more blue-blooded. Between 1700 and 1808, 167 individuals headed diplomatic missions. Around 30 of these men were grandees, who inevitably dominated the most prestigious embassies, while the rest were drawn overwhelmingly from long-established noble families. The social elite's grip on Spanish diplomacy actually increased during the eighteenth century: the traditional nobility provided 76 percent of all ambassadors and envoys from 1700 to 1759, but after Charles III's accession the figure rose to a remarkable 86 percent.

The final area dominated by the nobility down was local administration, which long remained deeply traditional in nature and personnel. This has been obscured by later scholarship which, since the seminal writings of the German sociologist Max Weber around 1900, has concentrated on the state's central agencies. Once more the lack of any alternative source of personnel contributed significantly to the nobility's dominance of local administration. Brandenburg-Prussia provides an excellent example. The key post of district commissioner (*Landrat*) became the preserve of the local *Junkers*, at least from the significant administrative reforms of Frederick William I (r. 1713–40) onwards. These men collected taxation, supervised the cantonal system of military recruitment and, generally, were responsible for royal government in their locality. Chosen by their fellow *Junkers* and usually confirmed by the king, these men were only partly salaried officials and sometimes received no income at all. Their administrative role was an extension of the wider social dominance which the *Junkers* – exactly like their counterparts throughout Europe – continued to enjoy well into the nineteenth century.

The lesser nobility's role was even greater in Russia, where the formal obligation to provide service was only abolished in 1762. In vast expanses of European and Asiatic Russia personnel were few and far between, and the reach of the state – measured in terms of the capacity to tax and to conscript its subjects – was very limited indeed. Such local government as existed was provided by noblemen, acting as the unpaid or underpaid agents of a remote emperor whom these men believed it was their duty to serve. A similar pattern was evident in the much more compact surroundings of Hanoverian England, where the peerage and the gentry served in local government in a variety of capacities, formal and informal, usually without any payment at all, and so helped to make the British state one of the most efficiently run in all of Europe. The key office was that of Lord Lieutenant, and here the aristocracy's dominance was overwhelming. Out of 200 men appointed to the post during the eighteenth century, a mere 14 were not peers or the sons of peers.

Conclusion

The nobility's enduring role in government highlighted both the strong position it occupied and its own coherence and resilience. It was not that signs of the challenges which lay ahead were lacking, not least the ideas of the Enlightenment. Eighteenth-century reformers, with vested interests of all kinds as their target, were beginning to undermine the established legal foundations of the second estate. One example was the campaign against mortmain, that is to say perpetual entails of land to the Roman Catholic Church, which inevitably raised questions about noble use of such devices. In Spain the *mayorazgo* was one principal target, now seen as a block on the land market and so an obstacle to economic progress. Symbolically, in 1789 the first relaxation was made in its operation: legislation was introduced to permit its division among all children, female as well as male. Simultaneously the crown prohibited the establishment of any new *mayorazgo* without a specific royal license, with the declared purpose of promoting economic development. In that same year the outbreak of the revolution on the northern side of the Pyrenees appeared to offer a more direct challenge to the nobility than enlightened reformers ever did.

In the 1780s, however, the elite's strength and coherence were still more impressive than the cracks, which were beginning to appear in the imposing edifice of noble power. Changes within the nobility itself contributed to this resilience. The loss, in some countries, of large numbers of lesser nobles enhanced unity, and accelerated the transition from nobility to aristocracy, especially in western and central Europe. But it was more the immense social, economic, and political power of the elite which ensured not merely its survival, but its continuing importance in the rather different world ushered in by the French and industrial revolutions. That continuity was to be even more evident in central and eastern Europe, where aristocratic power would remain largely intact until World War I. Joseph Haydn's celebrated patrons, the Esterházy, would remain among the largest landowners until the Austro-Hungarian monarchy was swept away in 1919, still ruling from the family's impressive seats at Eisenstadt and Esterhaza, exactly as their eighteenth-century predecessors had done in such splendor.

Bibliography

The following is a select list of works in English.

Astarita, T., *The Continuity of Feudal Power: The Caracciolo di Brienza in Spanish Naples* (Cambridge, 1992).

Augustine, W. R., "Notes towards a portrait of the eighteenth-century Russian nobility," *Canadian-American Slavic Studies*, 4 (1970), 373–425.

Bien, D., "The army in the French Enlightenment: reform, reaction and revolution," *Past and Present*, 85 (1979), 68–98.

Bien, D., "Aristocracy," in F. Furet and M. Ozouf (eds.), *A Critical Dictionary of the French Revolution* (1988; English translation, Cambridge, MA, 1989), pp. 616–28.

Cannon, J. A., *Aristocratic Century: The Peerage of Eighteenth-Century England* (Cambridge, 1984).

Chaussinand-Nogaret, G., *The French Nobility in the Eighteenth Century* (1976; English translation, Cambridge, 1985).

Cooper, J. P., "Patterns of inheritance and settlement by great landowners," in J. Goody, J. Thirsk, and E. P. Thompson (eds.), *Family and Inheritance* (Cambridge, 1976), pp. 192–327.

Dickson, P. G. M., *Finance and Government under Maria Theresia, 1740–1780* (2 vols., Oxford, 1987), vol. 1, ch. 5.

Gates-Coon, R., *The Landed Estates of the Esterházy Princes* (Baltimore, 1994).

Hagen, W. W., *Ordinary Prussians: Brandenburg Junkers and Villagers, 1500–1840* (Cambridge, 2002).

Janssens, P. and B. Yun-Casalilla (eds.), *European Aristocracies and Colonial Elites: Patrimonial Management Strategies and Economic Development, 15th–18th Centuries* (Aldershot, 2006).

Lukowski, J., *The European Nobility in the Eighteenth Century* (Basingstoke, 2003).

Raeff, M., *Origins of the Russian Intelligentsia: The Eighteenth-Century Nobility* (New York, 1966).

Scott, H. M. (ed.), *The European Nobilities in the Seventeenth and Eighteenth Centuries* (2 vols., 2nd, expanded, edn., Basingstoke, 2007).

Serna, P., "The noble," in M. Vovelle (ed.), *Enlightenment Portraits* (1992; English translation, Chicago, 1997), pp. 30–84.

Storrs, C. and H. M. Scott, "The military revolution and the European nobility, *c.* 1600–1800," *War in History*, 3 (1996), 1–41; repr. in J. Black (ed.), *Warfare in Europe, 1650–1792* (Aldershot, 2005), pp. 3–43.

Chapter Seven

Poverty

Peter H. Wilson

The Rise of the Poor

Poverty blighted the lives of the majority of eighteenth-century Europeans. Their century has become associated with scientific progress, the rise of the "middle classes," and the spread of consumer culture, but it also witnessed the culmination of a long-term growth in poverty and sharper social stratification. These structural changes had their roots in the late fifteenth century and helped characterize the period now labeled by historians as "early modern," running (depending on definition) from around 1450 to between 1789 and 1840. The conclusion of these trends in the eighteenth century ran parallel to the beginnings of another fundamental socio-economic shift that would produce the classes associated with nineteenth- and twentieth-century "modernity." These processes caused considerable alarm as reality diverged ever more sharply from what people thought society should be like.

The rise of the poor had deep, complex origins that lie outside the scope of this volume, but were linked to the structural shifts in European society following the Black Death in the fourteenth century and the subsequent agrarian depression. The population recovery accelerated from the 1470s, leading to sustained demographic growth in most parts of Europe across the sixteenth century. There were not simply more people, but they were often living and working differently from their medieval forebears. The growing urban population in many parts of Europe changed the balance between town and country, and even rural areas were integrated into more extensive market networks. Europe's relationship with the wider world also changed with the onset of sustained colonial trade, settlement, and exploitation, while the climate changes around 1580 posed further challenges (see chapter 1). The impact of these factors was felt unevenly throughout society, as some individuals, groups, and communities profited, while others suffered. The overall effect was to sharpen social distinctions and produce a more complex and highly stratified society. The differences between rich and poor not only widened, but wealth became more concentrated in the hands of relatively fewer people, enlarging the numbers who were considered poor.

A Companion to Eighteenth-Century Europe, First Edition. Edited by Peter H. Wilson.
© 2014 John Wiley & Sons, Ltd. Published 2014 by John Wiley & Sons, Ltd.

The growth in both the overall numbers of poor and of new kinds of poverty fostered a distinctly early modern language and range of institutions that persisted into the early nineteenth century. A new and increasingly sharp distinction was drawn between the so-called "deserving" and "undeserving" poor. Though lacking in material wealth, the former remained an accepted part of settled society entitled to the assistance of their more fortunate neighbors, in contrast to the latter, who were stigmatized, segregated, and increasingly targeted for punishment. The authorities identified a new crime of "vagrancy" to encompass the "masterless" sections of the population who either refused or were unable to conform to the new ideal of the obedient, thrifty, God-fearing subject. The new language in part represented a further development of the medieval attitude to poverty as related to lifestyle rather than economics. The deserving encompassed those afflicted by accident and misfortune: widows, orphans, the sick and disabled. The undeserving were "rogues" or "sturdy beggars" who only had themselves to blame for their present predicament.

This distinction shaped the development of new institutions to tackle poverty. The church remained important, even into the eighteenth century, but the medieval practice of alms-giving was undermined by the new attitudes to religion and morality associated with the sixteenth-century Reformation. Protestantism challenged the theological value of good works that implied the poor existed as a route to salvation for the rich, who would be rewarded in heaven for assisting their less fortunate neighbors on earth. Meanwhile, the moral element already inherent in medieval Christian attitudes emerged more strongly, as both Protestant and Catholic theologians stressed the presumed relationship between poverty and the failure to conform to the new ideal of the obedient subject. Traditional alms-giving and other charity organized through the church in any case proved inadequate to cope with the growing numbers of the poor, further encouraging the intervention of the secular authorities to coordinate existing measures and introduce novel initiatives.

These measures were not fully in place when European demographic growth stalled around the beginning of the seventeenth century, while some areas experienced a decline associated with major international conflicts, notably the Thirty Years War (1618–48). Further prolonged warfare in much of Europe between 1667 and around 1720 undoubtedly delayed recovery. The population of many areas of western and central Europe only returned to its pre-1618 level around a century later. Renewed growth set in around 1730 and was only temporarily slowed by the mid-eighteenth century wars, whose impact was felt primarily through social and economic dislocation rather than overall casualties. The impact of war and population growth intersected with economic changes, such as the development of new forms of manufacturing (see chapter 4), to shift European society from its early modern structure to that of the modern industrial age.

Social Structure

Most commentators around 1700 still saw society as divided into estates or social orders, though views differed in Russia (see chapter 14). Estates emerged in the early eleventh century as status became more closely related to social function. The first estate of clergy (*oratores*), were distinguished by their proximity to God and role in assisting humanity's salvation. The second estate of nobles (*bellatores*) defended society and provided leadership. The third estate of peasants (*laboratores*) worked to provide for society's material needs. The rapid growth of towns greatly complicated this structure in the later Middle Ages by creating a new group of urban burghers distinct from the peasantry. The subsequent rise of the state promoted other distinct groups, notably soldiers and officials.

Such distinctions were rooted in the biblical presentation of a divinely ordained social hierarchy reflecting the inherent imperfections of the human condition since the fall from grace. Social inequalities were thought to reflect natural variation between individual abilities and the moral value of different activities. True equality could only be found in heaven. Yet, the temporal hierarchy was intended to be harmonious to facilitate the good Christian life. Egalitarianism was widely associated with anarchy, since there would be nothing to prevent the strong from exploiting the weak. Theologians and political theorists repeatedly presented an idealized model of the state as a family, ruled by a firm yet benevolent father of the people. The "lower orders" were regarded as children, lacking in reason, only interested in external appearances and unable to grasp the true workings of the world. They had to be protected from temptation, both physical and spiritual, to keep them on the true path towards a productive and Christian life.

The ideal of social estates was riddled with contradictions that no theorist or commentator managed to resolve. All people were humble sinners, yet occupied very different stations in worldly existence with substantially different life chances. The inequalities were underpinned by law and the intervention of church and, increasingly from the sixteenth century, state. The Prussian General Legal Code (Allgemeines Landrecht) of 1794 attracted considerable attention as a model of enlightened legislation, but still divided society into four estates of clergy, nobility, burghers, and peasants. The legal distinctions enshrined the fundamental early modern norm of "each to his own." Each social estate was a corporate group with its own special rights and freedoms; "liberties," not uniform Liberty. The differences were expressed by specific behavioral norms, collective honor, and a distinct corporate culture. One example persisting into the eighteenth, and indeed early nineteenth, century was the different forms of address and clothing of different groups, intended to make each easily recognizable in social encounters.

Estates society thus did not embody a sharp contrast between those without rights and a privileged elite. Neither was it a finely graduated hierarchy. It is virtually impossible to depict it in a clear diagram, though many have tried, usually using some form of pyramid (e.g. Saalfeld, 1980). There were not only varying degrees of rights and status between and within the main estates, but also distinct subgroups and important gender differences. Power and status could also vary according to situation, since a person's rights were not uniformly accepted in every occasion or location. More fundamentally, society was not static, but shifted with the various changes noted above in the discussion of the rise of the poor. Attempts to define the social order also helped change it. This is most apparent in the growth of secular social regulation associated with the rise of the state that sought to reduce all groups to a common category of subjects (Blickle, 1983). As we shall see, the role of the state in social change remains hotly debated. Nonetheless, it is clear that state intervention fundamentally affected how society was interpreted. The drive for fiscal efficiency led governments to override established social distinctions that had allowed some groups to escape taxation or military service. The Spanish monarchy refused to recognize the tax exemption of many of the lesser nobility during the eighteenth century, while Prussia did the same in the areas it annexed from Poland after 1772. People were increasingly categorized according to their relationship to public finance either as a taxpayer or a recipient of official welfare. Such "rational" criteria shifted the emphasis from morality and honor to material wealth and an individual's place in the economy. A person's status in their community increasingly rested on their material rather than social or spiritual contribution. Estates society thus assumed certain class characteristics as, already before 1800, economic role came to replace social function in some parts of Europe (Dipper, 1991: 77–80). These changes accelerated from the mid-eighteenth century due to the convergence of demographic, political, economic, and philosophical factors.

Poverty and Marginality

The writing on poverty and social change was long dominated by macroeconomic explanations that related the rise of the poor to the shift from feudalism to capitalism, and linked eighteenth-century developments to the agrarian and industrial revolutions. The other major theme was to trace the relative roles of church and state in poor relief and social control, and to investigate the differences between Catholic and Protestant countries and assess whether state welfare proved more effective than private charity. Writing since the 1980s has been more aware of the presence of modernization narratives in such research: poverty was being presented as a by-product of economic progress or as a problem overcome by the rise of the welfare state. This awareness stimulated new approaches that generally concentrated on the poor themselves by examining their attitudes and survival strategies. The range of source material was widened from economic statistics and official papers to include literary texts, images, and court records.

Important methodological problems remain, not least that of defining poverty and social marginality. Modern definitions do not match those used in the eighteenth century. Many people in the eighteenth century lived in conditions considered acceptable at the time, but which would fall well below today's official standards. Poverty was also relative. A noble or burgher who could not live up to the expectations of his peers was likely to be considered poor, yet might still live comfortably compared to a rural parson or a day laborer. It was not until the nineteenth century that "objective" criteria predominated in defining a "poverty threshold" (Geremek, 1988). This is generally related to income, either assessed through tax records or calculated as a proportion of disposable income needed to buy staple foods. Those families who spent 80 percent or more of their disposable income on bread are generally considered poor by historians. While useful, these material assessments are increasingly supplemented and even displaced in more recent work by more subjective criteria relating to the contemporary concepts of status and honor.

Subjective factors can be labeled loosely as "cultural" and play a useful role in understanding marginality. Marginality overlapped, but was not necessarily synonymous with poverty. Stigma and prejudice could prove more important than material factors in placing an individual on the margins of settled estates society. Marginality is thus best defined as the absence of the material and social capital that anchored other people in settled society. Those on the margins lacked legal status, political power, property, income, professional or educational qualifications, and, above all, social prestige (Hippel, 1995: 4–7, 14–15, 66–7).

The problems of definition are reflected in the varying assessments of the number of poor and marginal Europeans, since different criteria produce different figures. Calculations using tax and other statistical data suggest that between 25 and 30 percent of Germans formed the core of settled society around 1800. Of these, 1 percent were nobles, 3 to 5 percent were urban patricians and other privileged groups, and 10 to 12 percent were urban burghers. Since the latter generally had to meet certain legal and fiscal obligations, they enjoyed both a minimum of material comfort and social privileges. Another 11 to 13 percent were urban residents without burgher status, many of whom were certainly poor, but not necessarily marginal. The remaining 57 to 64 percent were rural inhabitants, of whom 20 to 25 percent had no fixed property (Saalfeld, 1980). There is considerable evidence to suggest that Germans enjoyed more secure material circumstances than many of their European neighbors, including the French. Around 35 percent of western and southern European peasants had little or no property. At least half of Europeans can be classed as poor according to these criteria, with the proportion rising in rural areas and during time of war, dearth, and other crises. The marginal population numbered one-fifth to one-quarter, of whom a substantial proportion lacked a fixed abode or lived on the streets.

Such statistics can be improved on by further research, but they in any case only tell part of the story. The poor and marginal were not an amorphous, undifferentiated mass. Distinctions depended on perspective, since status and honor were not always understood in the same way. Three major groups can nonetheless be identified within the marginal population. One was composed of those engaged in "dishonorable" trades involving contact with those lacking honor, or work in particularly unpleasant conditions or in places or with items considered ritually polluting: gravediggers, hangmen, bailiffs, jailers, prostitutes, skinners, knackers, cesspool cleaners, mole catchers and charcoal burners. A second group were stigmatized on account of their ethnic origin, such as gypsies, or religion, such as the Jews. The third included the rootless without a fixed abode. Some of the latter could still be semi-respectable, at least in the eyes of some of their contemporaries: peddlers, knifegrinders, itinerant musicians and entertainers. Others were more generally suspect, such as demobilized soldiers, beggars, and, especially, the tiny minority of robbers and professional criminals.

Many of those on the margins lived next to the more respectable settled poor. The latter were increasingly segregated from their richer neighbors and pushed to the margins of communities by rent rises and urban development. The inhabitants of many eighteenth-century towns were already segregated according to wealth, forming the basis for the socially distinct districts that would characterize life across nineteenth-century Europe (Norberg, 1985).

Marginality could be determined by birth. Illegitimacy was a stigma running throughout estates society, affecting noble and peasant alike. Marginal groups tended to be self-recruiting, as children acquired the stigma of their parents. Poverty and illness could push people into entering one of the dishonorable trades. Underemployment was the principal cause of vagrancy that rose when a major trade entered a downturn or soldiers were discharged after a war. However, poverty was frequently

Figure 5 Invalid soldier, etching by Joseph Franz von Goez, 1784. Discharged soldiers and deserters formed a significant proportion of those arrested for vagrancy. *Bayerisches Armeemuseum*

compounded by prejudice, because those considered "disorderly" or "reprobate" were less likely to be helped by the authorities or their neighbors.

There were many for whom daily existence was a constant struggle. Day laborers, cottagers, and others whose livelihood provided only the bare minimum were vulnerable to price fluctuations and their situation could deteriorate rapidly. However, poverty generally changed with individual circumstances. Robert Schwartz has identified a life-cycle of poverty as people were more at risk at certain stages of their lives (Schwartz, 1988). The first stage came in early childhood and could affect the entire family as it struggled to feed those members who could not yet earn an income. Childbirth was an added risk, as the death of a mother both removed a potentially important breadwinner and could reduce the father's chances of work. Abandoned children, or "foundlings" constituted one of the largest groups receiving official welfare during the eighteenth century. The number of children abandoned each year in Paris rose from 3,000 in the seventeenth century to 7,600 by 1772, while the national total in France reached 40,000 in the 1780s. Foundlings formed between 9 and 16 percent of baptized births in major cities like Brussels, Madrid, and Venice. Despite the official attention, their survival chances remained poor, with 60 percent of the French *enfants trouvés* dying each year (Hufton, 1974: 334–49).

The chances of avoiding poverty improved with adolescence, especially once an individual reached the age of 15 and could find sufficient work to survive unaided if necessary. A healthy person could enjoy perhaps 20 years of relative security provided they remained unmarried. Poverty frequently returned with marriage and the start of a family around the age of 35. Official welfare was hard to obtain at this stage, though widows might receive some relief. This middle stage of poverty could last 10 to 15 years, depending on the size of the family and the number of children surviving as dependants. Relative security might return once the healthy children reached the age of 12 and could work unsupervised to supplement family income. The third stage of poverty generally began with the onset of infirmity around 60, itself accelerated by malnourishment and overwork.

Many of the "respectable" poor were little better off than those living on the margins. Respectability was defined more by cultural than material criteria. It depended on the assessment of an individual's "character" by their neighbors and the authorities, and was based on subjective judgments of their honesty, morality, skill, and dedication to their trade, behavior and ties to the local community. Some on the margins might also find acceptance, at least in certain circumstances: widows, the sick, and those hit by misfortune obviously beyond their control, such as flood or fire victims. Others were stigmatized socially, but still possessed some material wealth. Records of arrested beggars indicate that most carried no money when apprehended. A minority made enough to lodge in inns and indulge in habits like snuff-taking and smoking. A few lived well: one German was estimated to make 1,000 thaler a year in 1789 (Ulbricht, 1994: 165).

Attitudes, like material conditions, remained in flux. Prejudices changed over time, affecting both the numbers who were considered poor or marginal, as well as their experience. Poverty was related to work in the late Middle Ages, with all those laboring to secure their daily existence considered poor. Many kinds of manual work gradually acquired respectability, thanks to the efforts of craft guilds and of the authorities quick to appreciate potential sources of revenue, and to new social and moral values usually, though not entirely accurately, summed up as the "Protestant work ethic." The growth of markets and new forms of wealth creation also changed attitudes. This process continued in the eighteenth century, particularly among those asserting themselves as "professionals," such as lawyers, medical practitioners, and state officials. The state intervened to promote the collective interests of those groups it deemed the most valuable. Soldiers are a good example, because their role as licensed killers made them morally suspect to many, while their low and generally static pay placed them in the ranks of the poor. Most European governments made some efforts over the eighteenth century to improve soldiers' social status, particularly during the long peace after 1763. These efforts included new, and more regular, issues of uniforms, the inclusion of military personnel in officially sanctioned prayers, the construction of barracks, and the admittance of officers in uniform, rather than court dress, to the ruler's residence. New political and philosophical ideas contributed to this, notably the revived interest in the concept of "citizens-in-arms" that was expanded from the civic duty of enfranchised burghers to defend their home town and applied to regular soldiers as well. The parallel debate on the state and individual expanded the concept of the "nation" to include peasants alongside nobles, intellectuals, and the richer burghers. Peasants were transformed from figures of fun, ridiculed for their supposed ignorance and clumsy rustic ways, to be celebrated as embodying true national virtues (Gagliardo, 1969).

Surveillance, Control, Relief

The rise of the poor was accompanied by an expansion of official efforts to monitor, control, and remedy poverty. Surveillance had its roots in the fifteenth-century response to urbanization and the agrarian recession, and was further stimulated by the heightened emphasis on morality that accompanied the religious changes after 1517. The development of state institutions during the seventeenth century raised the desire to regulate and the ability to do so, but it was not until the eighteenth century that the full panoply of early modern measures was deployed. These lasted until the break-up of the old social order in the economic and political changes of the 1840s, when it became obvious that established methods could not cope with the new conditions.

The purpose of official surveillance was to categorize the population according to the early modern definitions of the deserving and undeserving poor. The latter were to be controlled to reduce their numbers through punitive measures forcing them to conform to official norms. The former were to receive relief to enable them to resume their role as obedient, constructive members of the community. These objectives were to be achieved through regulations identifying unacceptable behavior and specifying appropriate punishments. Such regulation was generally known as "policing" and was largely intended to preserve the idealized hierarchy of the social estates, resolve their problems, and ensure that each estate could exercise its officially sanctioned liberties (Stolleis, 1996). The regulatory element persisted into the eighteenth century, but had already been supplemented by a growing drive to reshape society in the interests of the authorities. This drive had many motives, including the desire to raise more revenue to fund the state's expanding activities and costly military competition. However, it was also intended to solve poverty by encouraging or coercing the poor to "improve" their condition.

This latter aspect has generated considerable debate. One of the most influential interpretations was the concept of "social discipline" proposed by Gerhard Oestreich, who in turn developed ideas already advanced by Max Weber and Norbert Elias (Schulze, 1987). Oestreich rejected Karl Marx's view that social change was promoted primarily by the emergence of new forms of production associated with the growth of capitalism. Instead, change followed state intervention that reshaped society and made capitalism possible by "disciplining" its potential workforce. Intervention began as regulation and developed into social disciplining. The latter involved subordinating the state's servants and military personnel to its authority ("staff disciplining") and then using them to mold society according to the officially sanctioned moral and material criteria exemplified in the ideal of the thrifty, obedient subject.

Oestreich's interpretation has attracted considerable criticism from those who point out, rightly, that many official measures were counterproductive, repressing human creativity and causing new problems. He has also been accused of perpetuating the conservative view of a benign paternalist state that supposedly only had its subjects' best interests at heart (Rebel, 1991). Others reject the idea that state regulation made any impact, arguing that social norms emerge through more complex interactions and are not imposed solely from above. This interpretation was inspired by Michel Foucault, who proved particularly influential in the 1980s and 1990s with his critique of enlightened reform and attempt to "deconstruct" the language of official regulation (e.g. Foucault, 1979). The limitations of his approach have become more obvious with growing skepticism about the postmodernist philosophy to which it belonged. Language is indeed a form of power, but "discourse" alone does not shape reality. Foucault's refusal to identify motive forces behind change renders his approach ahistorical. The people he wrote about appear to be trapped in a prison of their own incessant making and remaking. Labels alone cannot be blamed for "creating" deviancy or "inventing" crime that were not imaginary problems for those who experienced them. State and church institutions were certainly not socially neutral, but neither were they exclusively devices of social control. Much of the regulation was devised and enacted locally. It responded to and reflected pressures from within society (Wegert, 1994). The state relied on cooperation within society to be effective. Some measures were constantly reissued, indicating they were repeatedly ignored. Others were enforced, but only with considerable effort, while some required little or no official involvement, suggesting they met with broad approval (Schlumbohm, 1997).

It was not until the eighteenth century that the early modern state obtained fairly reliable data about the majority of its subjects. Even this information contained considerable gaps and ambiguities, while the way in which it was collected certainly influenced how it was presented, understood, and utilized. States had been collecting more regular and detailed population statistics since the fifteenth century for use in tax-collecting, raising recruits, and enforcing the new emphasis on marriage that accompanied the Reformation. These became more sophisticated in the eighteenth century as the central authorities co-opted greater numbers of local officials in more uniform administrative structures. Co-option gave central government access to detailed local knowledge, since village headmen, parish overseers, and others on the ground generally knew everyone in their community personally. Record-keeping became more consistent as standardized, printed forms were introduced for local officials to fill in specific details, such as an individual's name, place of birth, and age.

Personal papers became increasingly important to the poor and marginal population, who were required to show passports to travel, begging licenses, or references from previous employers. The English Act of Settlement of 1662 ordered migrants to carry certificates from their home parish, to which they would be obliged to return if they needed official relief. Other countries enacted similar legislation during the later seventeenth and early eighteenth centuries, for example Brandenburg-Prussia in 1696.

Modern-style policing remained restricted to capital cities like Paris or Vienna, with their networks of secret informants, detectives, patrolmen, and guards. However, even small towns had nightwatchmen and gatekeepers to check those sleeping rough or entering the community. Most continental states developed armed, mounted police from the early eighteenth century. The French *maréchaussée*, or highway patrol, established in 1720, is the best known, but even small German territories like Baden-Durlach or Lippe-Detmold had units of "land riders" (*Landreiter*) or hussars from the late seventeenth century. These gendarmes could be reinforced by units of the regular army, notably for large-scale sweeps of the countryside to round up vagrants and criminals. A systematic drive between 1767 and 1773 netted 71,760 people in France, who were herded into the newly established *dépôts de mendicité* (Metz, 1985: 6–7). As with other aspects of eighteenth-century state policy, there were clear limits to the effectiveness to these measures. The *maréchaussée* only had 3,500 personnel to patrol a country with over 25 million inhabitants. Their significance lay not so much in the numbers of criminals apprehended, as in their presence as a demonstration of the state's will to enforce order (Cameron, 1981).

Even the improved record-keeping leaves historians with insufficient evidence to gauge the true extent of crime. There are always discrepancies between reported, recorded, and actual levels. Nonetheless, evidence suggests a relatively low level of physical violence. Violent crime constituted only 5 percent of cases in eighteenth-century Amsterdam, though the incidence in rural areas was around 21 percent. There were only 136 cases of violent crime, including just 10 murders, in Frankfurt between 1741 and 1805 when the city had well over 40,000 inhabitants. Physical violence was predominantly male, with men constituting 93 percent of those accused in Frankfurt, together with 76 percent of their victims. Crimes against property, including theft, formed the largest single category before the courts, making up 49 percent of cases in Amsterdam (Diederiks, 1982; Eibach, 1998).

Punishments were harsh. Over a hundred vagrants were executed and several thousand exiled, beaten, or imprisoned in the workhouse across the eighteenth century in the electorate of Mainz (Härter, 1999: 375). The principle of "each to his own" underpinning Estates society ensured that "foreign" delinquents were handled more severely, with itinerants from outside the community far less likely to receive assistance than locals. Men and women were treated differently. The official practice in France and other Mediterranean countries during the first half of the eighteenth century was to send male vagrants to work as oarsmen on navy galleys, while women were incarcerated in workhouses. Western European states also deported criminals and vagrants to their colonies, reflecting the prevailing belief that these "dependencies" were subordinate adjuncts to the metropolitan homeland that was reserved for the "best" inhabitants.

Workhouses originated with the Bridewell, founded in London in 1550, though the Dutch *tuchthuizen* (houses of correction) proved more influential on the continent, where they were copied in Bremen in 1609 and spread across central Europe over the seventeenth century. Catholic countries were generally slower to introduce them than their Protestant neighbors. The first Habsburg workhouse was opened in Vienna in 1671, with others following in the major cities during the first third of the eighteenth century. Spain began rather later in 1750, but had 25 establishments by 1798. France started much earlier with the Hôpital Général, which opened in Lyons in 1614 with 1,500 inmates. It was copied in Paris in 1656, whose workhouse already held 7,000 inmates six years later when an edict ordered one to be built in every major town. Workhouses were funded partly through endowments, but were intended to finance themselves through the labor of their inmates. Actual returns always fell well below expectations, but the system was extended to other forms of "in-house" poor relief, such as orphanages, where the young charges were set to work, usually in some form of textile production. These institutions reflected the moral status attached to work, which was expected to reform the characters of those made to do it. The spread of the workhouse transformed the concept of a hospital from a refuge for the sick and homeless into an institution for moral control and social discipline.

Despite the existence of centrally devised schemes such as the French workhouses, most policing, punishment, and relief remained in the hands of local communities. Even in England, with its famed national "poor law" since the later sixteenth century, municipal and parish officials remained crucial to the delivery of relief. Other Protestant countries introduced similar legislation, such as Denmark, where it began in Copenhagen in 1708 and was extended nationally by 1784. These systems relied on locally assessed and collected taxes ("poor rates") to support each community's own deserving poor. The church remained more important in Catholic countries, but here too matters varied considerably on the ground as different religious orders and institutions undertook their own work. Contemporaries were well aware that poverty produced different needs that could not be met by a standard, regimented system. The same applied to crime, where most minor offences and disputes were resolved locally outside the official judicial system. However, there was a general trend to place both justice and relief under centrally sanctioned systems. In part, this reflected the state's desire to extend its supervisory role into previously private spheres, but it also responded to local demands, such as the dissatisfaction felt in France with the seigneurial courts and popular justice (Reinhardt, 1991).

Growing state involvement made welfare a more regular and substantial element of central government expenditure. The French controller-general, Neckar, estimated in 1780 that at least 18 to 20 million *livres* were generated annually to support the country's network of 700 *hôpitaux généraux* that housed 40,000 mostly elderly inmates, together with 25,000 sick, as well as 40,000 foundlings who were largely lodged separately in foster homes and boarding houses (Metz, 1985: 8). While official relief only reached a small proportion of those in need, the numbers could still be substantial, as in Berlin, where 8 percent of the population received welfare in 1785 (Sachße and Tennstedt, 1980: 101–2). State measures were not only punitive, but played a significant role in promoting the modern language of rights and entitlement. A Danish edict of 1683 established the right of paupers to state relief, though obliged them to be available to work on public projects. Brandenburg legislation in 1696 required parishes to provide work for the deserving poor.

Survival Strategies

Recent research has increasingly shifted away from official measures of control and relief to examine how the poor and vulnerable managed to survive. Access to public relief was generally restricted and intermittent, and it formed only part of what has been labeled the "economy of makeshifts" (King and Tomkins, 2003). The poor were not helpless victims of impersonal forces or state repression, but possessed a variety of strategies that could be employed to overcome daily difficulties. Their own networks of family, friends, neighbors, and employers were of major significance, as was personal knowledge garnered through experience. Long before Foucault, they already deconstructed the official discourse to modify their behavior and frame their case in a manner more likely to gain acceptance from the guardians of order and dispensers of public relief. The same applied to individual encounters where, for example, beggars adopted a demeanor to evoke sympathy and secure alms and shelter. They also accessed specialized skills, such as forgery to obtain false documents in order to travel or obtain employment. Beggars and other itinerants frequently carried two sets of clothes. Rags were donned to attract sympathy, while a finer suit was worn where they needed to pass as "respectable," for example to gain entry to a town. The fine suit also constituted an emergency reserve, since it could be sold or exchanged for food or shelter. They communicated using specialized terms, or argot, and could sometimes draw on specific skills, like lock-picking, for certain tasks. Those on the road relied on local knowledge of safe places and routes to travel without risking arrest, as well as those locations where charity might be more forthcoming.

Evidence for such behavior and knowledge attracted considerable interest from the late 1960s as some historians advanced claims it constituted a distinct "counter culture" in opposition to the officially sanctioned norms of settled society (Hobsbawm, 1969; Küther, 1987). Much attention focused on bandits and others who more obviously defied the authorities and sometimes passed into popular memory as folk heroes. This discussion was related to the then fashionable concept of the state as a repressive instrument of social control that suppressed individual creativity and promoted bourgeois morality. Clearly influenced by the political aspirations of those writing in the 1960s and 1970s, this idealized construct of the "social bandit" has not withstood subsequent research. There were cases of bandits stealing from the rich and giving to the poor, but little evidence that this was motivated by anything other than personal whim or simple expediency, and certainly nothing to suggest it formed part of a coherent oppositional culture (Danker, 1988).

The debate has shifted to what the poor and marginal may have thought of themselves and the extent to which they shared the norms and beliefs of their more settled neighbors. The economy of makeshifts entailed an element of solidarity, but little to suggest that it constituted the potential basis for a more egalitarian society. For example, itinerants' collective culture imitated the rituals and practices of the craft organizations and journeymen's associations to which many vagrants had once belonged and frequently hoped to rejoin (Ulbricht, 1994).

Protest was related to poverty, especially in times of price fluctuation or when conditions were widely perceived as unjust (see chapter 30). Rioting and other forms of protest were ways of pressuring the authorities to take action, such as distributing grain from government magazines, banning food exports, or at least regulating prices. Migration was another option, and reflected the fact that poverty was not necessarily permanent, but was a condition that most sought to escape. Seasonal migration was common in mountain communities, such as those in the Alps, Pyrenees, Apennines, or the French Massif Central, where thousands temporarily left their communities to work in the fields of the richer lowlands. Necessity drove others to leave their homes permanently. The most common form was migration from rural areas to regional market towns and other urban centers that appeared to offer better prospects. Emigration became a more common feature during the eighteenth century, especially as the demographic growth ran parallel to European colonial expansion, notably in North America. Large numbers of Germans, Scandinavians, and Britons emigrated to the British colonies in North America, as did generally smaller numbers from France and Spain to their respective possessions in Canada and Central and South America. Others, notably from central Europe, were encouraged to emigrate to

Hungary and Russia by the Habsburg and Romanov governments, while Spain attempted to attract settlers to its under-populated regions.

Bibliography

Blickle, P., "Untertanen in der Frühneuzeit. Zur Rekonstruktion der politischen Kultur und der Sozialen Wirklichkeit Deutschlands im 17. Jahrhundert," *Vierteljahresschrift für Sozial- und Wirtschaftsgeschichte*, 70 (1983), 483–522.

Cameron, I. A., *Crime and Repression in the Auvergne and the Guyenne 1720–1790* (Cambridge, 1981).

Danker, U., *Räuberbanden im Alten Reich um 1700* (Frankfurt am Main, 1988).

Diederiks, H., "Punishment during the ancien régime: the case of the eighteenth-century Dutch Republic," in L. A. Knafla (ed.), *Crime and Criminal Justice in Europe* (Waterloo, 1982), pp. 273–96.

Dipper, C., *Deutsche Geschichte 1648–1789* (Frankfurt am Main, 1991).

Dülmen, R. van, *Theatre of Horror: Crime and Punishment in Early Modern Germany* (Cambridge, 1990).

Eibach, J., "Städtische Gewaltkriminalität im Ancien Régime. Frankfurt am Main im europäischen Kontext," *Zeitschrift für historische Forschung*, 25 (1998), 359–82.

Evans, R. J. (ed.), *The German Underworld: Deviants and Outcasts in German History* (London, 1988).

Foucault, M., *Discipline and Punish: The Birth of the Prison* (Harmondsworth, 1979).

Gagliardo, G., *From Pariah to Patriot: The Changing Image of the German Peasant 1770–1840* (Lexington, KY, 1969).

Gall, L., *Von der ständischen zur bürgerlichen Gesellschaft* (Munich, 1993).

Geremek, B., *Geschichte der Armut. Elend und Barmherzigkeit in Europa* (Frankfurt am Main, 1988).

Härter, K., "Sozial Disziplinierung durch Strafe? Intentionen frühneuzeitlicher Policeyordnungen und staatliche Sanktionspraxis," *Zeitschrift für historische Forschung*, 26 (1999), 365–79.

Hippel, W. v., *Armut, Unterschichten, Randgruppen in der Frühen Neuzeit* (Munich, 1995).

Hobsbawm, E., *Bandits* (London, 1969).

Hufton, O., *The Poor of 18th Century France, 1750–1789* (Oxford, 1974).

Jütte, R., *Poverty and Deviance in Early Modern Europe* (Cambridge, 1994).

King, S. and A. Tomkins (eds.), *The Poor in England 1700–1850: An Economy of Makeshifts* (Manchester, 2003).

Küther, C., *Räuber und Gauner in Deutschland* (2nd edn., Göttingen, 1987).

Metz, K. H., "Staatsraison und Menschenfreundlichkeit. Formen und Wandlungen der Armenpflege im Ancien Régime Frankreich, Deutschlands und Großbritanniens," *Vierteljahrschrift für Sozial- und Wirtschaftsgeschichte*, 72 (1985), 1–26.

Norberg, K., *Rich and Poor in Grenoble, 1600–1814* (Berkeley, 1985).

Rebel, H., "Reimagining the *oikos*: Austrian cameralism in its social formation," in J. O'Brien and W. Roseberry (eds.), *Golden Ages, Dark Ages* (Berkeley, 1991), pp. 48–80.

Reinhardt, S. G., *Justice in the Sarladais 1770–1790* (Baton Rouge, 1991).

Saalfeld, D., "Die ständische Gliederung der Gesellschaft Deutschlands im Zeitalter des Absolutismus. Ein Quantifizierungsversuch," *Vierteljahrschrift für Sozial- und Wirtschaftsgeschichte*, 67 (1980), 457–83.

Sachße, C. and T. Tennstedt, *Geschichte der Armenfürsorge in Deutschland* (Stuttgart, 1980).

Schlumbohm, J., "Gesetze, die nicht durchgesetzt werden. Ein Strukturmerkmal des frühneuzeitlichen Staates?," *Geschichte und Gesellschaft*, 23 (1997), 647–63.

Schulze, W., "Gerhard Oestreichs Begriff 'Sozialdisziplinierung in der Frühen Neuzeit'," *Zeitschrift für historische Forschung*, 14 (1987), 265–302.
Schwartz, R., *Policing the Poor in Eighteenth-Century France* (Chapel Hill, 1988).
Stolleis, M. (ed.), *Policey im Europa der Frühen Neuzeit* (Frankfurt am Main, 1996).
Ulbricht, O., "The world of a beggar around 1775: Johann Gottfried Kästner," *Central European History*, 27 (1994), 153–84.
Wegert, K., *Popular Culture, Crime and Social Control in 18th-Century Württemberg* (Wiesbaden, 1994).
Woolf, S., *The Poor in Western Europe in the Eighteenth and Nineteenth Centuries* (London, 1986).

Part II

Cultures

Chapter Eight

The Public Sphere

Michael Schaich

Few features have been more commonly invoked to characterize the eighteenth century than what is generally referred to as the rise of the public sphere. The spread of new forms of sociability reified in literary circles, Masonic lodges, salons, and coffeehouses and the proliferation of a highly diversified print culture are invariably quoted when it comes to defining some of the developments that set the period apart. These new venues and channels of communication transcended the private realm of the household or the family and carved out a public space in which men, and to a limited degree also women, could engage in debate about topics of shared interest, be they of a literary, artistic, economic, or political nature. Almost of necessity the discourse of private individuals coming together as a public assumed a sharp edge in the predominantly absolutist political system of eighteenth-century Europe, whose workings were, at least in theory, shrouded in secrecy. New areas of the social and political world were opened up to a wide audience. Knowledge to which only the political and social elites had been privy now became part of the public domain. Debate gave rise to public opinion which some enlightened writers elevated to the guiding principle for how affairs of state and society were to be conducted rationally. In their view the public constituted a tribunal which could summon monarchs and governments to appear in its court and to justify their decisions in the hard and unforgiving light of critical scrutiny.

This notion of the public sphere has informed modern scholarship since the first publication of Jürgen Habermas's seminal study *The Structural Transformation of the Public Sphere* in 1962. Embedded in a critique of late capitalist mass culture and the decline of public reasoning, it advanced the argument that the eighteenth century saw the ideal embodiment of a bourgeois public sphere. As Habermas came to be understood, that was the time when the courtly "*publicness* (or *publicity*) of *representation*" (Habermas, 1989: 7) which was specific to feudal society and represented power in symbolic forms was supplanted by new modes of communication. First in Britain from the 1690s, then in France from the middle of the century, and finally in Germany from its last decades, a public exchange of ideas governed solely by rational argument and free of any restrictions of social status or political pressure

A Companion to Eighteenth-Century Europe, First Edition. Edited by Peter H. Wilson.
© 2014 John Wiley & Sons, Ltd. Published 2014 by John Wiley & Sons, Ltd.

came into being. Disinterested discourse held sway in the coffeehouses and salons, moral weeklies and sentimental novels which Habermas identified as the arenas where the new rules of engagement were played out. It is hardly surprising, therefore, that the public sphere acquired a subversive character undermining autocratic forms of government, religious orthodoxies, and traditional social values.

In a more profound sense, Habermas's model is predicated on the assumption that the rising modern state, as exemplified in the absolutist governments of seventeenth- and eighteenth-century Europe, appropriated all authority previously wielded by intermediate and local powers, thereby relegating its subjects to the private domain and opening up a divide between state and civil society. Nascent capitalism, with its networks of goods, artworks, and information, further deepened this divide. At the same time, however, it prepared the ground for the public sphere situated at the intersection of the state and the private realm that came to be occupied by propertied men. The new bourgeois family, which had developed in tandem with the ascent of the absolutist state, also shaped public discourse. Deprived of the economic and judicial functions which it had previously exercised, the family evolved into a private institution based on emotional attachment and intimacy, free from state intrusion and separate from the demands of the economic process. Its norms and moral values, however, were crucial in defining public deliberations. At first applied only to debates about literary and cultural subjects, with the passage of time they spilled over into politics, culminating in demands for a fundamental reform of the *ancien régime*. The bourgeois public sphere emerged from the domestic realm and came into its own. It was both the medium through which civil society could formulate its aims and the means of attaining them.

Although Habermas's notion of the public sphere bore strong normative overtones and had primarily been intended as a fundamental critique of communication processes in fully developed capitalist societies, historians of early modern Europe were quick to engage with the new master-narrative. Enthralled by the compelling conceptual framework, they set out to trace the shifting boundaries between public and private during the premodern period. Since the publication of the English translation of Habermas's book in 1989, and a new German edition containing an extensive foreword by Habermas in 1990, in particular, a vigorous debate has started. The concept has been scrutinized in the light of new historical evidence, applied to countries and periods which had hitherto been outside its pale, and, more often than not, adjusted or even rejected. In the process it has sometimes been altered beyond recognition and skepticism about its original tenets seems to prevail among historians. Yet the notion of the public sphere in a vastly modified form still provides a comprehensive frame of reference which helps us to understand crucial processes of eighteenth- (and seventeenth-)century European history. The following will outline the changes made to the original concept and attempt to assess where the debate has taken us. In doing so, it will concentrate primarily on the examples of Britain, France, and the German-speaking areas of Europe.

Coffeehouses, the Associational World, Print Culture

Research on the public sphere initially concentrated on social spaces in which individuals could assemble to discuss matters of common interest. Habermas himself had already pointed to new modes of social organization such as coffeehouses, salons, and reading societies as arenas for public reasoning. Since then, extensive research has confirmed that the eighteenth century saw the emergence and proliferation of various forms of sociability which allowed social interaction and communication on an unprecedented scale.

Foremost among them is the coffeehouse, which has acquired an almost iconic status in all discussions about the public sphere. Since its first appearance in Europe in the middle of the seventeenth century, the coffeehouse has been seen as a congenial setting for public debate. Some contemporaries, and representatives of authority in particular, imagined it as a seditious haunt given to atheist discourse and disrespect for all authority. Others praised it as a vehicle for free discussion and precursor of the freedom of expression. An anonymous German tract of 1690 described the coffeehouse as a place "where everyone can express his opinion without fear," while half a century later the political writer James Ralph associated it with the "light of reason" and "the power of reflection" (quoted from Albrecht, 1992: 59; Cowan 2005: 148). These beliefs were derived from a set of features which distinguished coffeehouses almost from the start. First of all they were socially inclusive. Everybody who could afford the hot beverages on offer, usually chocolate and tea as well as coffee, was admitted. What is more, however, within the coffeehouse all distinctions of rank, wealth, or office temporarily ceased. For the duration of their presence all patrons were supposed to treat each other as equals. Only when they met in the public space of the coffeehouse as private men was the stage set for uninhibited and civil conversation.

In addition, coffeehouses were closely tied up with the world of information. Well provided with local and foreign newspapers, journals, and pamphlets they were ideal locations for reading and discussing the latest news and transacting business. Cultural events, political affairs, and commercial activities formed the basis of discussion. As places where information circulated, coffeehouses also maintained close links with journalism. In Restoration England coffeehouse hacks produced manuscript newsletters, while at the beginning of the eighteenth century the moral weeklies commended coffeehouses as the breeding ground of an urbane and polite culture. In French cafés literary careers could be made by meeting and currying favor with influential figures in the world of letters, while in German towns they served as editorial offices for many a journal. Besides, voluntary associations and political groups often chose coffeehouses as meeting-places. James Harrington's famous Rota Club, which came together in the Turk's Head Coffeehouse in London in the dying months of the Interregnum, is an early example.

Faced with such hot spots of seemingly unbridled discourse, authorities all over Europe repeatedly issued edicts against inflammatory speech and sometimes put coffeehouses under surveillance, although they were at least equally worried about the damaging effects that the consumption of coffee might have on social discipline. The proliferation of coffeehouses, however, could not be stopped. In the imperial capital Vienna their number rose from 37 in 1737 to more than 80 in 1791. In contrast, Paris had 280 coffeehouses in 1720, 600 in 1750, and 900 in 1789. Yet not even Paris could match London, which as early as 1663 already counted 82 of these venues. For the years around 1700, estimates range from several hundred to 2,000–3,000. Most of these coffeehouses, of course, did not correspond to the ideal outlined above.

Such huge numbers can be explained solely by the inclusion of humble establishments which bore only a remote resemblance to the sophisticated and dignified meeting-places discussed by modern scholars. Even the latter did not always live up to elevated notions of the coffeehouse. It is hard to imagine, for example, that in a century as status-conscious as the eighteenth, distinctions of rank were invariably laid aside once the threshold of a coffeehouse was crossed. Not surprisingly, in some countries such as England and the German-speaking world the social elites increasingly withdrew from coffeehouses into private members' clubs in the later part of the century in order to maintain exclusivity, leaving artisans and tradesmen to their own devices.

Recent research has also shown that the coffeehouse was far from unique in providing a venue for public debate. The tavern has been discovered as a crucial public arena, in particular, in rural areas or towns where coffeehouses were sparse (Freist, 2005; Kümin and Tlusty, 2002). In England and the German-speaking countries, although apparently not in France, taverns, alehouses, and inns were frequented not only by the lower classes but also the respectable groups of society, although they were sometimes spatially segregated. But then, coffeehouses too had separate rooms and, in Britain from the early eighteenth century, private booths which allowed retreat from other groups of customers. Voluntary associations, therefore, were as likely to assemble in a tavern as a coffeehouse. In 1717 the first annual meeting of London Freemasons took place at the Goose and Giridion alehouse, while in 1737 the first German lodge came together in a Hamburg tavern. At a more basic level taverns were hubs of political and religious debate which often also provided newspapers for their patrons. It was not without reason that authorities were equally worried about what went on in taverns and coffeehouses and sent spies to eavesdrop in both locations. At the same time they used public houses as convenient places to publish decrees and mandates. The list of premodern settings for public debate, however, does not stop with taverns. Increasingly, historians are becoming aware of further public spaces such as churches, squares, and town halls (Rau and Schwerhoff, 2004). These findings put the undisputed role of the coffeehouse in the rise of the public sphere into a wider perspective.

In addition to these rather informal venues, a vast array of associations ranging from reading clubs and philanthropic and religious societies to academies, debating societies, and Masonic lodges constituted public debate in eighteenth-century Europe. Distinct from old-style corporations, guilds, and religious fraternities in that membership was voluntary and not ascribed, they mushroomed throughout the century, with the last decades seeing a further exponential increase in range and number. In London alone, by 1750, 20,000 men met daily in associations. Half a century later every third English townsman belonged to at least one society on average, a picture that was mirrored in central Europe where, according to conservative estimates, there were more than 500 reading societies alone at the end of the century. The expansion of the associational world was, of course, closely linked with other prominent trends discussed fully elsewhere in this volume, such as urban growth, population increase, and the emergence of a commercialized consumer culture which brought with it new public amenities aimed at the middle and genteel classes, the core membership of clubs and societies. What made associations stand out and attract the interest of historians, however, was their role in bringing about civil society. Closely linked with the moderate mainstream of the Enlightenment and largely urban-based, they served as channels for the dissemination of ideas and agencies for reform within the framework of the old regime. In particular, they debated and promoted political change, agrarian innovation, educational reform, moral correction, and the refinement of manners and taste. They have even been ascribed the emancipating effect of encouraging social equality and political participation.

No part of the associational world has received more attention in this respect than Freemasonry. Originating in early eighteenth-century England, this movement soon took root all over Europe, even in Catholic countries, despite the papal indictment of 1738. France, for example, counted around 600 lodges in 1789, while in Germany more than 500 lodges had been founded in the preceding half-century. Since Freemasonry was surrounded by an air of secrecy some historians saw it inhabiting "a sphere of autonomy *vis-à-vis* the state and its institutions" (van Horn Melton 2001: 253) in which freedom of thought, religious toleration, and social equality could be exercised. The egalitarian nature of Freemasonry was particularly apparent in its elaborate initiation rites, which stripped new members of their outward attributes of social rank and privilege and presented them to their fellow Freemasons as mere human beings or "brothers." That Freemasons practiced the principle of election, were obliged to give public speeches, held office for particular periods of time, took minutes of proceedings, and kept records was further interpreted as proof of the existence of democratic techniques. Several historians, among them Margaret Jacob, have therefore argued that Freemasonry was instrumental in developing a modern sense of civil society leading, ultimately, to democracy.

The reality of Masonic life, however, was more sober (Clark, 2000: 309–49; van Horn Melton 2001: 252–72). Complaints about the persistence of hierarchical structures within lodges, about aristocratic members who were spared part of the initiation rites or fast-tracked to higher degrees, abounded and repeatedly erupted into internecine feuds. Comparatively high induction and membership fees as well as the considerable cost of a Freemason's attire and participation in the social life of lodges excluded all but the better-off and secured a relatively homogeneous membership. The alleged subversiveness of Freemasonry has also been debunked as a myth, as a look at membership lists clearly demonstrates. Within the Holy Roman Empire the higher echelons of the state bureaucracy and numerous princes, among them Frederick II and Joseph II, formed a sizeable portion of overall membership. In Britain the future George IV was the most prominent but by no means only Freemason in the royal family, while in France the two brothers of Louis XVI donned the apron. Whereas royalist and loyalist lodges were a common phenomenon throughout Britain, France, and the German-speaking world, deist, atheist, or politically radical lodges were few and far between, although it has to be said that many British Freemasons, for example, sided with John Wilkes and his supporters in the 1760s. In addition, with such notable exceptions as the order of the Illuminati, lodges cannot really be labeled secret societies. British lodges, for example, announced the time and place of their meetings in newspapers, published membership lists, and held lavish street processions. Even in countries where Freemasons renounced this sort of publicity Freemasonry did not go unnoticed, nor was it intended to. Lodges owned houses or met in dedicated rooms in taverns, and celebrated sumptuous feasts and banquets. It was not the existence of a lodge that was kept secret but the rituals performed within it and the traditions of esoteric learning supposedly handed down by Freemasons since antiquity or the Middle Ages.

Access to exclusive knowledge was also one of the attractions of Freemasonry. Combined with Masonic rituals which imbued members with a sense of spirituality, this must have appealed to those who had become disenchanted with official forms of learning and piety, and were on a quest for a superior meaning to life. Apart from these otherworldly pursuits, however, the daily activities of lodges revolved around practical concerns: self-education, charity, the provision of hospitality and mutual aid for fellow Freemasons and, not to be belittled, conviviality. Eating, drinking, singing, smoking, and gambling in congenial company formed an integral part of the Masonic and, indeed, associational experience in general. In this and most other respects, lodges did not differ greatly from the rest of the associational world. The demand for good fellowship and entertainment was at least as important as the enlightened obsession with utilitarian measures or intellectual debate in explaining the success of clubs and societies.

Their upsurge must also be seen against the backdrop of changes in the print trade and book market which are outlined more fully elsewhere in this volume. Suffice it to point out a few universal trends which are indicative of the expansion of the public sphere. To start with, the eighteenth century witnessed what contemporaries described as a "reading frenzy," an insatiable appetite for books and journals which enthralled the upper as well as the middle classes. In line with growing literacy rates, this trend was already discernible in the early parts of the period only to gain further pace as time passed. In response to increasing demand the supply of reading material multiplied. As early as the beginning of the century, in France, England, and even central Europe, the domination of the book market by academic publications, proverbial large tomes written in Latin, had broken down. By 1700 a new transnational trade had come into existence which specialized in elevated entertainment, exchanging, often in translation, satires, poetic works, and tales. It was to grow even more rapidly with the advent of the novel. Other segments of the book market expanded as well, generating new types of publications such as travelogues, dictionaries, encyclopedias, and popular scientific works, to name but a few genres which were to become characteristic of the age of Enlightenment. In addition, a varied range of journals and periodicals developed catering to different audiences. The moral weeklies which had found their ultimate expression in Addison and Steele's *Tatler* and *Spectator* embarked on a triumphant progress through continental Europe leaving numerous translations, imitations, and adaptations in their wake. The press in the Holy Roman Empire is characterized by the so-called Intelligence Gazettes, which had been published since 1722 and were suggestive of the reform-oriented mood of the Enlightenment. They included primarily advertisements for goods and services, but also provided an important arena for debate about domestic reform. In their various ways these and numerous other types of publications, together with voluntary associations and more informal venues, gave the public sphere its material expression.

Social Composition and Gender

If the debate on the role and function of societies, coffeehouses, and journals can be seen as an organic extension of Habermas's original concept, a number of its key

Figure 6 William Hogarth, *The Election: Canvassing for Votes*, 1755. Taverns were frequently used for political meetings. © *Courtesy of the Trustees of Sir John Soane's Museum, London/The Bridgeman Art Library*

aspects have been vigorously rebutted. One of the first assertions that was criticized was the allegedly bourgeois nature of the public sphere. Detailed investigations into the membership of associations and subscription lists of journals have shown that those active in the public sphere did not come mainly from a bourgeois background or, indeed, the affluent circles of merchants, bankers, and manufacturers which were at the heart of Habermas's argument. Even in Britain, one of the most commercialized societies of eighteenth-century Europe, clubs and societies recruited their members from a broad coalition of landed (nobility, gentry), professional (lawyers, doctors, clergy), and commercial (artisans, bankers, merchants) interests with great variations according to region and type of association. A similar picture emerges in France, where lawyers, officials, noble officers, aristocrats, and, only to a lesser extent, merchants and bankers made up societies, while in the Holy Roman Empire primarily civil servants, clergy, aristocrats, and academics are to be found in membership and subscription lists. It was not the rising bourgeoisie, but a mixture of the genteel and middle classes that laid the social foundations of the public sphere. By intermingling, they forged a new elite of the educated with shared habits and values.

This process entailed a widening gap between the upper classes and the rest of society which obscured the fact that there also existed a "plebeian public sphere," a term used, but not further explored by Habermas (Habermas, 1989: xviii). Its outlines have only been traced by studies of popular culture and protests of the lower orders (Farge, 1994; Luebke, 2004; Würgler, 1995). From their findings it emerges that the common folk made ample use of printed pamphlets to voice their grievances. Political sentiments were also expressed through ritualistic behavior, collective political actions such as mass rallies, and the collection of signatures, placards, and, of course, rumors and mutterings on the street. In addition, these studies show a high degree of awareness of governmental decisions and a strong sense of political interest on the part of ordinary people even in rural areas. Including demotic politics in Habermas's model thus led to a substantial extension of the public sphere, in terms not only of social composition but also of the media and channels used for political debate. Symbolic forms of political discourse and oral culture, which had fallen by the wayside because of an exclusive focus on the written word, were reinstated.

Another obvious lacuna in Habermas's concept, and one to which he later readily confessed, was the role of women. Ironically, some feminist historians indirectly justified this omission by claiming that the public sphere was "essentially, not just contingently, masculinist" (Landes, 1988: 7), relegating women to the domestic domain. This notion seemed to chime well with the view that a separation of gendered spheres took place during the eighteenth century. While men were engaged in public life, women had to retreat into the private realm of household and family. Other historians, however, have rejected this hypothesis as reflecting merely the dominant normative discourse about public and private in the eighteenth century. Instead, they recovered the story of a more active engagement of women in the public sphere. Many women who successfully negotiated contemporary discourses in their writings have been brought to light. One does not have to refer to a Francis Burney, Mme de Beaumont, or Sophie de la Roche to indicate the considerable success female authors could enjoy. The example of less famous figures such as Marianne Ehrmann, one of the first women journalists in late eighteenth-century Germany, who was able to live from her writing and support a family, albeit with difficulty, is even more suggestive of the increasing number of independent female literary careers.

Women also played a role in the new forms of sociability. Various public spaces such as pleasure gardens, promenades, and theaters were frequented by both sexes. The French salons, public spaces in private settings, are well known for their often aristocratic hostesses who not only excelled in conversation and erudition, but embodied an ideal of polite sociability central to the self-definition of a civilizing Enlightenment (Goodman, 1994; Lilti 2005). At around the same time, Freemasons allowed women entrance into their world, particularly in France and the Netherlands. So-called adoption lodges admitted female members and introduced rituals adapted to their needs. In the liberal setting of late eighteenth-century Britain, women could even participate in political discourse in London debating societies. A claim has also been made for the presence of women in British coffeehouses. But, as has recently been argued (Cowan, 2001), apart from female proprietors and servants, women, especially gentlewomen, were only likely to patronize certain types of coffeehouses such as those in spas and resorts, which were more conspicuous for leisure and entertainment than discourse, or on certain occasions such as auctions, which served to furnish the household. This restricted female presence certainly did not imply active participation in coffeehouse debate.

Such qualifications also give reason to caution against an all too enthusiastic assessment of the part played by women in the public sphere. Despite the examples given above, the associational world on the whole remained a male preserve. Adoption lodges, for example, were few and far between, while the overwhelming majority of clubs and societies excluded women from membership. Even in the literary world, their involvement was greatest when pursued from the privacy of their home. Rising literacy rates led to the reading mania mentioned above. Women poring over novels became almost proverbial in the eighteenth century. Notwithstanding a number of forays by women into the public sphere, gender hierarchies continued to shape active participation in general discourse.

Religion and State

Gender and popular culture, however, were not the only gaps in Habermas's story. In modern research there is a growing appreciation of the significance of religion in the rise of the public sphere. In line with new approaches that stress the resilience of Christian beliefs in a supposedly secularizing period, various modes of communication have been unearthed which were firmly rooted in a world dominated by churches and faiths. Chief among them is the pulpit, which arguably reached larger audiences than the printed word, crossing social boundaries. Despite appearances, religious books, too, were still widely distributed. The proportion of theological and religious works among new publications may have decreased over the century, but in absolute numbers their output rose, not least in France. In addition, the age of Enlightenment witnessed the publication of numerous religious journals. Outstanding examples, such as the Jansenist *Nouvelles ecclésiastiques* or the Pietist *Sammlung auserlesener Materien zum Bau des Reichs Gottes*, enjoyed a remarkable circulation and outlived many of their more secular counterparts. And finally, the associational world of lodges, reading societies, and academies was augmented by Pietist conventicles and Anglican religious societies. There was, then, a part of the public sphere which was essentially religious.

Against this background it is hardly surprising that religious controversies equaled or even surpassed the better-known debates of the Enlightenment with regard both to the number of interventions they stimulated and the vigor with which they were fought. In the Holy Roman Empire the acrimonious arguments between Pietists and orthodox Lutherans from the 1670s to the 1720s were instrumental in broadening public debate, as were the concomitant clashes between latitudinarians and High Churchmen in England. Public religious strife, however, was not confined to the turn of the century. As late as the 1770s and 1780s the exorcisms performed by the Catholic priest Johann Joseph Gassner in south Germany instigated one of the most sensational disputes of the age (Midelfort, 2005). If discussions about faith and theology contributed to extending public discourse, recent research has gone even further and identified causal links between developments in religious history and the public sphere. Pietism has been credited with the introduction into scholarship of a dialogical model which helped to establish new forms of learned discourse based on the idea of scrutiny. In a similar manner historians have traced the notion of public opinion as an independent tribunal back to the Jansenist movement. Defending dissenting priests against church prosecution in the 1720s and 1730s, lawyers appealed to the public as a higher authority, thus inaugurating a key element of a critical public. As such observations imply, one of the seemingly most traditional features of the century proved to be crucial in engendering one of its most dramatic changes.

And yet religion was not the only driving force behind the public sphere. The early modern state has likewise emerged as a major player. This is rather paradoxical in view of the oppositional relationship between state and public in Habermas's initial concept. Such a contention, however, could hardly be sustained in the face of mounting evidence to the contrary. A number of historians have made it clear that public sphere and state were closely intertwined throughout the eighteenth and even seventeenth centuries. The coffeehouse is a case in point (Cowan, 2005: 147–92). In Restoration England parts of the state apparatus under the leadership of the Crown may have been hostile towards coffeehouses. Others, especially fiscal, local, and church authorities, however, treated them as an integral part of the social and political order. Eager to generate income and regulate trade in an orderly manner, they levied excise tax on the consumption of exotic goods and licensed coffeehouse proprietors, thus conferring the all-important seal of legitimacy and respectability on establishments which suffered from the ill repute of being seditious haunts. In addition, local government organizations and parish vestries convened meetings and sessions at coffeehouses. Judicial hearings were even held there. The link between state and public sphere is all the more obvious in the case of the French provincial academies. Promoting the natural sciences and projects of practical reform, they received official sponsorship. As has been stated above, the vast majority of Masonic lodges also lacked subversive traits. As with all other associations, the presence of numerous civil servants, noblemen, and princes made opposition look rather unlikely. On the contrary, as has been argued, the intermingling of old and new elites in clubs and societies allowed the *ancien régime* to integrate the middling sort more effectively.

The world of print betrays an equally strong state influence. As early as the Civil War and the Interregnum, British politicians on both sides of the political divide acquired a strong sense of the power of public opinion (Peacey, 2004). The parliamentarian regimes after 1649, in particular, were adroit at pursuing an active press policy. They enlisted the services of newspaper editors, hired writers supplying them secretly with information, and used press licensors to edit texts before publication. In view of the extraordinary political circumstances of the 1640s and 1650s this may seem rather exceptional. Nothing, however, could be wider of the mark. Throughout the seventeenth and eighteenth centuries, in republican as well as autocratic states, governments as a rule attempted to mold public opinion. Especially at times of war or high political crisis, princes issued declarations and pamphlets to justify decisions, while their governments leaked information to journalists. Newspapers, to whose fundamental role in the rise of the public sphere we will return below, were a particularly sought-after tool.

In France the first newspaper, Théophraste Renaudot's *Gazette*, was closely controlled by Richelieu and his staff, who steered the flow of information distributed through its channel. The same holds true for many newspapers in the Holy Roman Empire. Court cities were especially fertile ground for journalists. Officials willingly supplied them with intelligence about court life and political decisions in an attempt to sway opinion. The Viennese *Ordentliche Post Zeitung* reported extensively on court affairs, effectively becoming a propaganda instrument for the emperor. To be sure, feeding journalists with information was not always a successful way of doing politics. Once news had entered the public domain it was impossible to control. By way of other media it could reach audiences, such as the lower orders, for which it had not been intended in the first place. Nor was all news leaked in support of government policies. But there was a growing awareness among officials that they disregarded the public sphere at their peril.

Some governments relaxed the secrecy formerly surrounding decision-making and welcomed wider discussion of their plans, especially as they embarked on major internal reforms after the Seven Years War had exposed the inadequacies of existing economic, financial, and administrative structures. Too weak and ossified to generate reform entirely alone, the absolutist state had to draw on public debate to muster the expertise and popular support needed to carry out essential changes to society. In the 1780s, while drafting the General Code (1794), Prussian officials discussed crucial aspects of their work in one of Berlin's most famous associations, the Mittwochsgesellschaft, before going on to print a first draft and invite the public to opine on it. As Johann Friedrich Zöllner, a member of the Superior Consistory in Berlin, put it: comments on the General Code "were accepted gratefully as a contribution for illuminating an important issue from all sides" (quoted from Sauter, 2004: 545 n. 7). In an almost identical move, in 1786 the Danish government submitted its plans for rural reform to public scrutiny by publishing the minutes of the commission set up to look into these issues (Munck, 1998; see also chapter 9 below). Prussian and Bavarian censors even protected enlightened reform discussion until the mid-1780s in the interests of administrative efficiency.

It has to be said, of course, that government strategies and domestic policies became major topics of debate not only at the behest of authorities and civil servants. Some journalists, such as the Göttingen professor August Ludwig Schlözer, made a reputation out of uncovering judicial blunders, administrative shortcomings, and politically driven persecutions. Many of the debates conducted within the associational world and on the pages of journals, however, have to be understood as part of a wider discussion aimed at a general overhaul of the old regime, transcending the boundaries of the state and pervading the public sphere. As a result, the seventeenth century, and even more so the eighteenth, saw state bureaucracies engage in public debate in a variety of ways and on a large scale. Against this background it is certainly more appropriate to imagine the public sphere as an extension or even creation of the state, as some have argued (Blanning, 2002: 13), than as its opposite.

Chronology

Harking back to the seventeenth century to capture essential turning points in the history of communication, however, also lays bare a fundamental flaw in many concepts of the public sphere. For a long time, historians following in the footsteps of Habermas have associated the rise of public debate with the enlightened discourse of the eighteenth century. Yet recent research has thrown this model into disarray, pushing the origins of the public sphere further and further back.

Some revisionists point to the sixteenth-century Reformation, with its outpourings of pamphlets and controversies about issues of faith and doctrine or, in the English example, to the Elizabethan reign, when both Protestants and Catholics debated the politico-religious settlement through a wide range of media which transcended the confines of the court and the political elite. One could also draw attention to manuscript news bulletins written by professional scribes and intended for merchants, bankers, and princely courts or, indeed, to the printed biannual and annual summaries of recent news, the so-called *Messrelationen* or trade fair reports. These had been published in the Holy Roman Empire since 1583 on the occasion of the big fairs in Frankfurt and Leipzig and covered events in the whole of Europe. Taken together these trends certainly indicate both growing interest and wider distribution of news well before 1600. But even in their entirety they did not amount to a fundamental change in the patterns of communication. The new media were restricted to certain segments of society, that is, they were "public" in a very limited sense, while the controversies only fitfully constituted public debates. They may be seen as precursors of the public sphere, but they lacked the universal and permanent character which is peculiar to the concept.

When, then, did a lasting and unified public sphere supplant the short-term and episodic publics of the past? In recent research the early seventeenth century emerges as a watershed. A radical innovation in the reporting of current news, the birth of the newspaper made possible by changes in the infrastructure of communication seems to have brought about the rise of the public sphere. As Wolfgang Behringer has argued in a seminal study on the postal system of central Europe, around 1600 structures were in place that guaranteed both a constant flow of topical news and its public diffusion (Behringer, 2003: 303–436; see also Behringer, 2006). By that time the imperial post had been restructured after a period of organizational failure and put on a firm footing. Just as in the past, but in a more efficient and reliable way, relays of mounted couriers divided up long distances into convenient sections and swiftly transported letters and news on an ever-expanding network of postal routes. Crucially, the postal service was now open to the general public and no longer the exclusive preserve of princes and bureaucracies. This removed the main obstacles to the formation of a permanent and public universe of communication. All those involved in the information business could gain access to a regular supply of news. Once the conditions were right, the next step was soon to follow. In 1605 the first weekly newspaper was printed in Strasbourg. Within a few decades numerous newspapers sprang up all over the Holy Roman Empire, invariably dependent on the postal system which alone could guarantee the speedy delivery of the coveted raw material. The same mechanisms were at work in other parts of Europe. The rage for current news spread to the Dutch Provinces, the Spanish Netherlands, and France in the 1620s and early 1630s. In England, on the other hand, despite first attempts to introduce serialized news reports from 1622, half-hearted reforms of the postal system delayed the process. The transition from occasionally published news tracts to topical reports at regular intervals was only complete in 1641 with the publication of so-called newsbooks, which were indistinguishable from newspapers in all but format.

The 1620s and 1630s, however, already saw the emergence in various parts of Europe of communicative spaces which allowed audiences to enter into debate about themes familiar to all of them. It was precisely this quality that proved to be the decisive leap in constituting a public sphere: newspapers created a sounding board for public argument. They familiarized a wide and potentially universal audience with segments of societal and political reality which had hitherto been available only in private letters, manuscript news bulletins reserved for a tiny elite, and the occasional pamphlets or broadside ballads whose frequency would increase once noticeable events happened, but fall back to a low level as soon as they had passed. In contrast, the regular supply of news resulted in a new quality of political awareness which allowed contemporaries to see political events unfold almost in front of their eyes and draw their own conclusions. Newspapers equipped their readers for debates in taverns, literary circles and, later on, coffeehouses, which significantly staked their claim to a leading role in the public sphere in the provision of topical information. Even illiterate groups could participate, as newspapers were often read out loud. It did not, therefore, matter that, with the notable exception of some of the English newsbooks in the 1640s and early 1650s, newspapers before the French Revolution did not contain editorials or leaders but dry, factual intelligence. What was important was not the debate conducted in their pages but the supply of information, which served as a catalyst of debate. It was likewise of minor significance that, as a rule, newspapers could not report about domestic issues since they touched on the workings of government. With a few exceptions, again most prominent among them English newsbooks, coverage was restricted to war and diplomacy, dynastic affairs, events at princely courts, parliamentary debates in foreign countries, trade news, and religious topics. Reports of this kind, however, mattered to contemporaries. In a world of divinely ordained monarchs, almost constant warfare, and religious strife they contained highly relevant information.

All these indications, then, point to the news revolution of the early seventeenth century as the decisive moment in the emergence of the public sphere which, contrary to Habermas's theory of a progression from literary to political subjects, was political from the start. Other factors, of course, also contributed to its development. The meteoric rise of current news reporting was certainly driven by the hunger for information sparked by the Thirty Years War and other major conflicts. New forms of conducting international affairs in a legalized manner also helped increase the flow of and demand for information, as did the changes in the pursuit of knowledge that made up the Scientific Revolution. In addition to such general factors, specific developments were at work in individual countries. In England, for example, the breakthrough in the development of a modern public sphere which, after the first inklings in the 1620s, is most commonly dated to the 1640s, was not solely down to the publication of newspapers. Exceptional political circumstances and the concomitant war of words produced an explosion in the number of pamphlets and printed petitions, which played an equally important part in creating the space and the rules for public debate (Lake and Pincus, 2006; Raymond, 2003: 128–60; Zaret, 2000). Nonetheless, it was the sustained publishing of topical news, albeit in different formats, that enabled the formation of public opinion. Ultimately, we "can clearly trace in the seventeenth century the rise of a public in the sense of a supra-local social unit connected through communication via printed media and both interested in political matters and able to debate them" (Gestrich 2006: 424).

Conclusion

These changes to the established chronology have profound implications. First of all, it is no longer possible to portray the public sphere as the product of developments in western Europe which, later on, were eagerly adopted in the rest of Europe as the traditional bias towards Great Britain, the Dutch Republic, and France has it. Rather, its emergence and growth may be imagined as a kind of relay race with countries passing the baton on from one to the other. The origins of the public sphere lay in the newspaper revolution of central Europe, whose political fragmentation and lack of central coercive power was more conducive to such an innovation than the emerging nation-states to the west. In the course of the seventeenth century, however, the focus shifted to the Anglo-Dutch universe with its advanced commercial and political structures to which the unparalleled spread of coffeehouses and the birth of Freemasonry testify. France made its presence felt more strongly only in the eighteenth century with the creation of the salon and a radicalized print culture. Different countries thus contributed in different ways and at different times to the emergence of a debating public.

The new chronology also changes the place of the eighteenth century in the story. A number of features remain specific to the period. Although the roots of the associational world went back to before 1700, new types of associations such as Masonic lodges came into being only after that date. The overall number of clubs and societies, moreover, multiplied hugely throughout the century, and they even reached the provinces. The same holds true for coffeehouses, journals, and newspapers. The entrance of women into the public sphere in more than token numbers also only happened after the early eighteenth century. In addition, the closing decades of the century were characterized by an opening up of spaces which had hitherto been closely guarded from public penetration. Public debate turned increasingly to domestic politics, which in the past had been part of the arcane sphere of the state. Nevertheless, against the backdrop of developments in the previous period the overwhelming impression of the eighteenth century is one of quantitative proliferation and differentiation. The fundamental principle of public reasoning about matters of common interest had already been established before 1700. Although the eighteenth century without any doubt occupies a central place in any narrative of the public sphere, its essence can only be grasped in a wider chronological framework. The public sphere may traditionally have been invoked to explain the newness of the eighteenth century, but it seems more appropriate to conceptualize it as a fundamental process in European history stretching over at least two centuries.

Bibliography

Albrecht, P., "Kaffeetrinken. Dem Bürger zur Ehr – dem Armen zur Schand," in R. Vierhaus (ed.), *Das Volk als Objekt obrigkeitlichen Handelns* (Tübingen, 1992), pp. 57–100.

Barker, H. and S. Burrows (eds.), *Press, Politics and the Public Sphere in Europe and North America, 1760–1820* (Cambridge, 2002).

Behringer, W., *Im Zeichen des Merkur. Reichspost und Kommunikationsrevolution in der Frühen Neuzeit* (Göttingen, 2003).

Behringer, W., "Communications revolutions: a historiographical concept," *German History*, 24 (2006), 333–74.
Blanning, T. C. W., *The Culture of Power and the Power of Culture: Old Regime Europe 1660–1789* (Oxford, 2002).
Chisick, H., "Public opinion and political culture in France during the second half of the eighteenth century," *English Historical Review*, 117 (2002), 48–77.
Clark, P., *British Clubs and Societies 1580–1800: The Origins of an Associational World* (Oxford, 2000).
Cowan, B., "What was masculine about the public sphere? Gender and the coffeehouse milieu in post-Restoration England," *History Workshop Journal*, 51 (2001), 127–57.
Cowan, B., *The Social Life of Coffee: The Emergence of the British Coffeehouse* (New Haven, 2005).
Ellis, M., *The Coffee-House: A Cultural History* (London, 2005).
Farge, A., *Subversive Words: Public Opinion in Eighteenth-Century France* (Cambridge, 1994).
Freist, D., "Wirtshäuser als Zentren frühneuzeitlicher Öffentlichkeit. London im 17. Jahrhundert," in J. Burkhardt and C. Werkstetter (eds.), *Kommunikation und Medien in der Frühen Neuzeit* (Munich, 2005), pp. 201–24.
Gestrich, A., *Absolutismus und Öffentlichkeit. Politische Kommunikation in Deutschland zu Beginn des 18. Jahrhunderts* (Göttingen, 1994).
Gestrich, A., "The public sphere and the Habermas debate," *German History*, 24 (2006), 413–30.
Goldenbaum, U. (ed.), *Appell an das Publikum. Die öffentliche Debatte in der deutschen Aufklärung 1678–1796* (2 vols., Berlin, 2004).
Goodman, D., *The Republic of Letters: A Cultural History of the French Enlightenment* (Ithaca, 1994).
Habermas, J., *The Structural Transformation of the Public Sphere: An Inquiry into a Category of Bourgeois Society* (Cambridge, MA, 1989).
Hellmuth, E. (ed.), *The Transformation of Political Culture: England and Germany in the Late Eighteenth Century* (Oxford, 1990).
Hesse, C., *The Other Enlightenment: How French Women Became Modern* (Princeton, 2001).
Jacob, M. C., *Living the Enlightenment: Freemasonry and Politics in Eighteenth-Century Europe* (New York, 1991).
Johns, A., *The Nature of the Book: Print and Knowledge in the Making* (Chicago, 1998).
Kümin, B. and B. A. Tlusty (eds.), *The World of the Tavern: Public Houses in Early Modern Europe* (Aldershot, 2002).
Lake, P. and S. Pincus, "Rethinking the public sphere in early modern England," *Journal of British Studies*, 45 (2006), 270–92.
Landes, J. B., *Women and the Public Sphere in the Age of the French Revolution* (Ithaca, 1988).
Lilti, A., *Le Monde des salons: Sociabilité et mondanité à Paris au XVIIIe siècle* (Paris, 2005).
Luebke, D. M., "Signatures and political culture in eighteenth-century Germany," *Journal of Modern History*, 76 (2004), 497–530.
Midelfort, H. C. E., *Exorcism and Enlightenment: Johann Joseph Gassner and the Demons of Eighteenth-Century Germany* (New Haven, 2005).
Munck, T., "Absolute monarchy in later eighteenth-century Denmark: centralized reform, public expectations, and the Copenhagen press," *Historical Journal*, 41 (1998), 201–24.
Peacey, J., *Politicians and Pamphleteers: Propaganda during the English Civil Wars and Interregnum* (Aldershot, 2004).
Rau, S. and G. Schwerhoff (eds.), *Zwischen Gotteshaus und Taverne. Öffentliche Räume in Spätmittelalter und Früher Neuzeit* (Cologne, 2004).

Raymond, J. (ed.), *News, Newspapers, and Society in Early Modern Britain* (London, 1999).
Raymond, J., *Pamphlets and Pamphleteering in Early Modern Britain* (Cambridge, 2003).
Sauter, M. J., "Preaching, a ponytail, and an enthusiast: rethinking the public sphere's subversiveness in eighteenth-century Prussia," *Central European History*, 37 (2004), 544–67.
van Horn Melton, J., *The Rise of the Public in Enlightenment Europe* (Cambridge, 2001).
Würgler, A., *Unruhen und Öffentlichkeit. Städtische und ländliche Protestbewegungen im 18. Jahrhundert* (Tübingen, 1995).
Zaret, D., *Origins of Democratic Culture: Printing, Petitions, and the Public Sphere in Early-Modern England* (Princeton, 2000).
Zaunstöck, H. and M. Meumann (eds.), *Sozietäten, Netzwerke, Kommunikation. Neue Forschungen zur Vergesellschaftung im Jahrhundert der Aufklärung* (Tübingen, 2003).

Chapter Nine

Enlightened Thought, its Critics and Competitors

Thomas Munck

Until the 1970s, there was broad agreement about what the eighteenth-century Enlightenment was: an intellectual challenge to traditional authority and established values, driven forward by a relatively small but imaginative group of French-speaking thinkers (the *philosophes*). Their searching philosophical doubts and their interest in the rational analysis of knowledge consolidated the gains of the seventeenth-century scientific and intellectual revolution (notably the work of Locke and Newton), but also extended the scope and range of intellectual inquiry into new areas. The French Enlightenment was strong on individualism and iconoclasm (clear both in fictional and non-fictional writing), but its focal points were not in doubt. Montesquieu's magisterial political analysis provided intellectual foundations for both the American Revolution and the early constitutional phase of the French Revolution. A new form of economic analysis, established by the physiocrats around Quesnay and Turgot, had offered fresh answers to the fiscal and economic challenges faced by the *ancien régime*. Meanwhile, prolific writers such as Voltaire could sustain a vast circle of correspondents who looked to France for validation and inspiration. The perpetual rebel Rousseau, on the other hand, placed himself demonstratively at the edge of these movements, his rejection of Paris patronage a colorful reminder of the importance of dissent and controversy amongst the *philosophes*, his championing of the "common man" a herald of what was to come. Taken as a whole, this Enlightenment could be seen as rational and largely "progressive," its audience found mostly amongst the thoroughly Francophile European educated elite. Its significance lay in the way it challenged some fundamental European traditions – questioning established church hierarchies which appeared to perpetuate institutionalized abuses, picking at popular beliefs which sustained irrational superstitions, warning against the more specific dangers of political "despotism" (often illustrated by means of eastern European or oriental examples) or the exploitative legal systems which reinforced privilege and inequality, and of course attacking related but more specific iniquities such as intolerance or the arbitrariness of censorship controls.

As we shall see, some of these generalizations now require qualification even from a solely French perspective. More fundamentally, however, detailed European

A Companion to Eighteenth-Century Europe, First Edition. Edited by Peter H. Wilson.
© 2014 John Wiley & Sons, Ltd. Published 2014 by John Wiley & Sons, Ltd.

comparisons have revealed much greater complexities in the wider Enlightenment. An important collection of papers (Porter and Teich, 1981) placed the Enlightenment firmly in "national" context, with Roy Porter himself leading the way in arguing that England, too, had an Enlightenment of its own. By that stage it had already become clear that the Scottish Enlightenment had a very distinctive profile in Europe: Adam Smith's authoritative analysis of the economic structures of modern society was noted internationally, as was the devastating challenge to philosophical systems offered by his friend David Hume. The German-speaking lands offered distinctive perspectives of their own – Kant an attempt to restore some of the cognitive unity now challenged from all sides, Herder a deep-rooted critique of French cultural values, and both Mendelssohn and Lessing powerful new perspectives on European self-perceptions. Even at a level of characterization as brief as this, intellectual unity seems elusive; it becomes quite unconvincing if we also try to add younger (pre-Romantic) writers such as Goethe and Schiller into an Enlightenment framework, let alone those (such as Hamann or Jacobi) who reacted against the alleged pantheism or "nihilism" of their more radical contemporaries and tried to shore up unquestioning faith (in what has sometimes been called a "counter-enlightenment"). In Italy, too, wide differences of approach are clearly apparent: Giannone's challenge to the temporal authority of the church was consonant with that of earlier critics elsewhere in Europe, whereas Beccaria's radical critique of crime and punishment took a fundamentally different and original turn. The English-language writings of North American thinkers illustrate how the social context could substantially modify the agenda. Further examples could be added, exemplifying Swiss and Swedish scientists, Russian social critics, or Iberian reformers who sometimes were widely recognized in Europe-wide circles and sometimes relate more specifically to their own cultural context, but equally often do not fit particularly well into any simple explanatory scheme. Recognizing this great diversity has allowed historians to see the Enlightenment much less as a specific reform movement, much more as a process rooted in particular local and cultural circumstances.

The traditional view of the Enlightenment has also faced a more fundamental challenge. Postmodernism began to have an impact on various academic disciplines in the 1970s, history amongst them. To French postmodernists such as Lyotard and Foucault, the Enlightenment seemed to represent a deceptive watershed on the way towards the illusion of a modern, democratic, but also doctrinaire world in which one particular set of European values had been imposed on all. Although postmodern historians and theorists have tended to be imprecise in defining who imposed exactly what during the eighteenth century, scholars in cognate disciplines adopted the phrase "Enlightenment Project" as a generalized pejorative label to describe the roots of a variety of modern developments regarded as at best naively optimistic, at worst exploitative, or even (since the French Revolution) potentially totalitarian. Historians who have worked on eighteenth-century texts and sources in detail do not, on the whole, find the postmodernist critique convincing or even plausible – on the contrary, some would argue, the Enlightenment was itself already postmodernist in its denial of our ability to identify absolute truth, and in its fertile epistemological disagreements (Gordon, 2001). But the debate has forced more traditionalist historians to review their own assumptions about the Enlightenment; and, more specifically, has helped to bring about a much closer scrutiny of the language and communicative strategies of the Enlightenment writers themselves, the elusive significance of the "text" in early modern Europe, not to mention the sheer diversity of methods and aims amongst those who considered themselves "enlightened" in one way or another across Europe.

If historians now find it more difficult to define the Enlightenment as a whole, these criticisms have not dampened their ability to gain fresh perspectives on the period. Despite the difficulties of locating reliable evidence on the history of reception, the observable impact of the Enlightenment has been extended well beyond the elite, beyond "bourgeois" sociability, into the socially far more composite crowds that flocked to see Beaumarchais' play *The Marriage of Figaro*, or the casual customers reading (or listening to others reading out) newspapers in the coffee shops and inns of every city (Munck, 2000). The prejudices of gender, race, and social privilege have been scrutinized, and the ineffectiveness of Enlightenment aspirations for social reform re-examined. The contours of public opinion, urban sociability, and the "public sphere" now provide a much clearer context for the role of individual writers and specific controversies (Baker, 1987; Ozouf, 1988; van Horn Melton, 2001), and we are beginning to appreciate the "social history of language" – the malleable complexities of the way languages were used in this period (Burke, 2004). Intellectual origins generally, and the more radical strands in the early Enlightenment in particular, have been subjected to renewed and very close scrutiny (Israel, 2001). There are also signs that a more thorough understanding of cultural diversity within Europe will allow significant and innovative comparisons to be made (Robertson, 2005). The Enlightenment has become more complex, and perhaps more inclusive of aspects of the eighteenth century which go beyond the history of ideas alone.

From Seventeenth-Century Intellectual Origins to the French Revolution

Across eighteenth-century Europe, there were interesting differences in actual terminology. In most European languages verbs equivalent to "enlighten" were well established in the early modern period, the original religious connotations often in effect widened to incorporate other fields of human understanding. Nouns such as the French "lumières," in the plural, served both as a specific word for light, and as a more abstract concept of intellectual clarification. The Germans used "Aufklärung" consistently during the later eighteenth century, but usually in the sense of a process ("enlightening") rather than as a label for a philosophical movement or historical period. In English, the abstract noun "enlightenment" was not used at all until the later nineteenth century, although "illumination" was current by 1799 (Schmidt, 2003). Whilst such semantic differences may appear accidental, they illustrate differences in eighteenth-century usage which are reflected in the work of more recent historians.

The Enlightenment remains firmly rooted in the intellectual revolution of the seventeenth century – and in particular in the way Hobbes, Locke, and Bayle used new scientific and philosophical techniques for a rational analysis of human society itself. But this can be interpreted in different ways: Jonathan Israel has made a striking case for Spinoza as a key originator of the radical Enlightenment, which leads him to argue that "by the 1750s, all major intellectual innovations and accomplishments of the

European Enlightenment were well advanced if not largely complete" (Israel, 2001: 20). Such a chronological delimiter may help us to clarify key components in the Enlightenment, notably the challenge to the religious authority of the church (to which we shall return). But major social and political controversies took rather longer to emerge – in effect developing around mid-century, following the publication of Montesquieu's most important work, *The Spirit of the Laws*, in 1748, the launching of the great French *Encyclopédie* three years later, and the appearance of a range of major and controversial works in the later 1750s and early 1760s. A more natural end-point of the Enlightenment might therefore be found in the period 1776–84, with the death of key figures including Hume, Voltaire, Rousseau, Diderot, and Lessing, and the full flowering of the more emotionally charged and turbulent "storm and stress" period in German culture. During these years a new generation of angry rebels (taking a lead notably from Herder) distanced themselves from what they saw as the genteel decadence and hypocrisy of French elite culture, became absorbed in non-Christian cultural roots (such as those apparently portrayed in Macpherson's *The Works of Ossian*, which had been published in 1765), explored the human inner self (as in C. P. E. Bach's later keyboard sonatas, or the writings of Goethe and Schiller from the 1770s onwards), and began a more critical re-examination of European history through the works of Raynal and Gibbon after 1770.

From the perspective of social and political reform, however, the 1780s brought further significant developments, culminating in the French revolutionary decade from 1789 and its dramatic impact on the domestic politics of nearly all European countries. Disenchantment with the old order in France had built up since the 1770s, fueled partly by the critical writings of the *philosophes*, partly by an increasing public awareness of political and fiscal problems at the heart of government. When the Estates General met in 1789 hopes for constitutional and social reforms were high, with the agenda firmly rooted in the moderate Enlightenment. By 1792, however, only a few of the most pressing problems had been addressed effectively, and the revolution took an increasingly destructive direction. A balanced monarchy such as described by Montesquieu became unworkable, judicial processes were increasingly short-circuited by popular violence, economic improvement was undermined by wartime emergencies, and basic human rights came once more under threat. To most European observers, the Terror was a horrible perversion of enlightened values; it also brought the premature death of the last surviving French *philosophes*, Condorcet and Lavoisier. European governments everywhere reacted with repressive tactics ranging from tightened censorship to show trials of suspected sympathizers. By 1795 the intellectual and cultural map of Europe had changed beyond all recognition. One of the greatest minds of the Enlightenment, Kant, was threatened with reprisals in 1793 and forced to abandon key areas of rational inquiry; the polemicist Thomas Paine was ostracized wherever he went, his writings banned, and his own life nearly taken by a revolution which had made him an honorary citizen and member of the National Convention only two years earlier.

Enlightenment and Religion

In earlier historical accounts, one particular confrontation constituted the defining feature of the Enlightenment: the conflict between the doctrinal authority and collective "superstitions" allegedly perpetuated by the church, pitted against the "emancipated" rationality and critical scrutiny of the individual freethinker. More recent discussion of national contexts has done much to qualify such assertions: religious controversies seem more subdued in most of Protestant Europe compared with France or Italy, and, more fundamentally, it is no longer clear that religious belief and Enlightenment actually represented conflicting opposites in eighteenth-century consciousness. Matters of both ideological interpretation and institutional church reform can readily be traced back through the wonderful array of religious dissenters in the seventeenth century, to the Reformation, and into late medieval heresy. The more deeply skeptical challenges, too, seem to have been unavoidable by-products of a succession of distinguished attempts, from Erasmus to Descartes, actually to dispel doubts which might undermine religious beliefs, and to address matters of faith and certainty through rational and verifiable argument. By the later seventeenth century, efforts to suppress religious "deviance" by means of either military force or open persecution for heresy were slowly becoming recognized as counterproductive; but although the political context was changing, the intellectual issues were as divisive as ever.

In the 1680s and 1690s Locke completed and published a number of works in which reason tended to predominate over faith as a foundation for knowledge, and he also tackled specific issues such as education and toleration. His writings were widely noted (if not always read or fully understood) across Europe in the following decades, and alongside the scientific works of Newton came to be accepted as a key source of inspiration for the Enlightenment. So was the *Historical and Critical Dictionary* first published in 1697 by the French Huguenot exile in the Netherlands, Pierre Bayle, whose sophisticated discussion of major religious and philosophical questions, in the format of a reference work, broke new ground. Equally fundamental was the examination of the Bible itself as a historically conditioned text – a task already suggested by Spinoza, but pursued so vigorously by the French Oratorian scholar Richard Simon that his publications (1678–92) angered traditionalists in both the Catholic and Protestant churches. His work facilitated closer scrutiny of the innumerable variant translations of both the Old and New Testaments, and encouraged a more critical approach to biblical scholarship which proved crucial in laying new foundations. None of these three pivotal thinkers intended to cast doubt on religious faith as such. But taken in conjunction with John Toland's provocatively anticlerical tract of 1696, *Christianity not Mysterious*, the absolute intellectual authority of the church seemed visibly open to question. Ultimately, if God's revelation was imperfectly understood (and imperfectly transmitted), and there appeared to be no obvious rational way of answering key questions, how could one particular version be regarded as unchallengeable truth enforceable through censorship, prosecution, or repression, at the expense of alternative interpretations?

In northwestern Europe, increasingly open (if guarded) discussion of these points, combined with a growing interest in comparisons between different religious systems (as for example in Montesquieu's brilliant *Persian Letters* of 1721), were certainly part of enlightened debate. Very few, however, went as far as La Mettrie in proposing a totally materialist world-view in his *Machine Man* (1747), or the Baron d'Holbach in making an explicitly atheist case in his *System of Nature* (1770) – and neither put his name to his book. A more moderate stand, commonly known as deism (belief in

God, but rejection of both divine revelation and divine intervention, and hence of mediation by the church) may well also have been much less common during the eighteenth century than has often been assumed (Barnett, 2003), but labels of this kind were used rather too freely (and pejoratively) for us to make precise distinctions amongst those with a more latitudinarian approach to faith. What gradual abandonment of traditional religious observance we see is likely to have been the result of a number of different factors, including the relaxation produced by growing economic prosperity and changes in popular sociability. Equally significant was the continuing interest in alternative forms of worship (notably amongst the Dissenters in England, and in the colorful array of internal reform movements in other sections of the Catholic and Protestant churches in Europe). To some traditionalists, attempts at religious regeneration may have seemed nearly as dangerous as deism or "naturalism" (loosely equated with pantheism, and ascribed to Spinoza). But research on the complex evolution of internal dissident movements such as Jansenism in France (Doyle, 2000; van Kley, 1996) has shown that the major shifts in the religious landscape that took place during the eighteenth century probably had more to do with the interminably creative quarrels between devout and sincere Christians of different persuasions than with any fundamental rational subversion of core religious belief by radical *philosophes*. If that is the case, the modern term "counter-enlightenment" (as applied to those seeking a consolidation of religious beliefs against criticism) may be misplaced, focusing on the lesser of two confrontations. In practice, however, disagreements amongst strong-willed believers were liable to raise a broad range of questions not just about ultimate authority in matters of faith, but also about the temporal power of the established clergy and their economic privileges, the policing of public morality, educational improvement, and the role of the individual in society, as well as about institutional reform itself. France is the most striking example of how inseparable dissident religion and political resistance were, right through the eighteenth century; but clear precedents had already been set in England (Haakonssen, 1996), and no part of Europe remained immune to such fundamental ideological problems.

Although none of these issues was likely to be resolved easily, tangible progress was made in one specific area. Religious toleration, the bounds of which had been explored for many generations, became a matter of political opportunity following the suppression of Huguenot rights in France in 1685 and the resettlement of many skilled and productive communities all over Protestant Europe. In parts of the Holy Roman Empire, disunity gradually paved the way for limited toleration; for different reasons, the incomplete relaxation of religious controls in England and the Netherlands seemed more secure after 1689. Voltaire and many others added to the public debate. However, the process was never linear, and the persistent re-emergence of popular hostility to Catholic emancipation in England (dramatically so in 1778–80), or the unpopularity of limited civil protection for Jewish communities (attempted notably by Frederick II in Prussia in 1750, and by the British government three years later) warn us against any assumption that European society was generally becoming open-minded. Other governments moved in the same direction, mostly for purely practical reasons, but invariably with hesitation. Even the French Crown was eventually brought round to the idea in 1788, under strong *parlementaire* pressure, but the legislative misjudgments of the revolutionary government of 1790, compounded by the violent de-Christianization campaigns of Year II, ensured that religion remained a deeply divisive political issue in France for generations to come. Interestingly, however, the battle over toleration was not always fought at state or street level: sometimes individual friendships were broken in ways that made bitter headline news, as happened when the German philosopher Friedrich Jacobi triggered the so-called "pantheism controversy" in 1785. His main point was to accuse the great playwright Lessing (who had died four years earlier) of being a furtive Spinozist (meaning by this time in effect an atheist). But in so doing he not only outraged Lessing's old friend, the remarkable Jewish philosopher Moses Mendelssohn (who died prematurely in the middle of the dispute), but also stirred up a storm over the threat posed both to religious faith and to the moral values that kept society together. A whole array of German intellectuals, from Goethe to Hamann and Herder, were drawn into the dispute on one side or the other. The issue was acutely relevant, since freedom of speech and religious toleration were (rightly) expected to be rescinded after the death of Frederick II (1786).

Not all areas of intellectual activity were quite so vulnerable to political accident, however. It is one of the hallmarks of the Enlightenment that a number of academic disciplines developed into a recognizably modern form during this period. Amongst them was a cluster of subjects which the Scots described as "the science of man": those disciplines now generally described as the social sciences, where a break with past assumptions, and the use of empirical observation as a basis for innovative analytical frameworks, seemed particularly fruitful. Greater room for maneuver also allowed the natural sciences to flourish, bolstered by the fashionable popularity of spectacular experiments such as those of Benjamin Franklin on electricity, the monumental Natural History published by Buffon between 1748 and 1789, or Montgolfier's trendy balloon-flying in 1783. That said, the potential for deep cultural antagonisms had clearly not disappeared. Outstanding innovative thinkers such as David Hume in Scotland or Joseph Priestley in England paid a high price for scholarly freedom in terms of lost career opportunities, prejudice, and popular hostility. In France, Lavoisier found to his cost that scientific methodology, when extended into the mechanics of government, was no defense against political denunciation.

Power, Propaganda, and Reform

Although the specifics of domestic and international politics are discussed elsewhere in this volume, it is appropriate at this point to note the extent to which public opinion (enlightened or otherwise) came to play a growing part in eighteenth-century government. The term "enlightened absolutism" (or its misnamed variant, "enlightened despotism") has been regarded as a convenient shorthand for a stage in the process of state formation where political authority typically abandoned many of its "divine right" claims in favor of a modest degree of openness and public accountability. Such change was gradual and at times hesitant, but in the years after 1763 evolved in directions which would have been unthinkable to the generation of Louis XIV. To some extent, the reasons for change can indeed be found in the impact of enlightened thinking on the rulers and political elites of Europe, but it was rarely a straightforward process. The long reign of Louis XV in France is an interesting case in point: historians have shown the extent to which royal mediocrity could be

Figure 7 François Boucher, *Madame de Pompadour*, 1756. © *Wallace Collection, London, UK/ The Bridgeman Art Library*

counterbalanced by shrewd ministers and advisers (including the king's mistress, Madame de Pompadour – shown in one contemporary portrait literally leaning on a pile of books which includes a volume of Diderot's *Encyclopédie*), but have at the same time highlighted the increasing damage done by the disparity between the monarchy's traditional claims to divine authority and its visibly sordid reality. The notion of a "desacralization" of the monarchy (Merrick, 1990) has not gained unqualified acceptance amongst historians, but the change in public reactions is illustrated graphically by the way in which a new statue of Louis XV, erected at a strikingly low-key ceremony in 1763, was soon defaced by graffiti. Neither Louis XV, nor his unfortunate successor Louis XVI, ever fully understood the realities of the political life in which they should have been able to take a leading role; others, however, were able to exploit the changes very effectively. By the time the rebellious American colonies were drafting their new constitution in the 1780s, the realities of what we might now call "enlightened reform" were gaining rapid acceptance in many parts of Europe.

As we would expect, the potential for effective government in eighteenth-century Europe remained severely curtailed by a whole range of obstacles, including the lack of resources, inadequate information, and the minuscule central bureaucracy of most states. Nevertheless the relatively peaceful decades from 1721 to 1740, and the growing economic prosperity and domestic stability which resumed intermittently after 1763, brought a renewed interest in domestic reform. Some of the impulses were entirely traditional, notably in areas such as mercantilist economic and infrastructural development, fiscal reform, administrative rationalization, and improvements in bureaucratic management (all often grouped together in the German-speaking lands under the term "cameralism"). More directly visible, but still traditional in origin, were improvements in agriculture – notably in field systems, crop rotation, and animal husbandry. In such areas public debate and rational discussion played an increasing role. It is no accident that Adam Smith gained a widespread following for his analysis of trade patterns, social relations, and the proper role of government – all highly relevant both in government circles and in the numerous academies and reform societies which sprang up in all the major cities of western and central Europe. Effective implementation depended not just on the stability and security which sound government might provide, but also on a broader public commitment which could ensure effective realization at a time when the constraints of property rights and the rigidity of social relations still posed formidable obstacles to change. It is worth noting how successful many of the German states, some of the Italian ones, and both Scandinavian kingdoms were in integrating practical reform initiatives into government policy, often by employing some of the key thinkers as government officials.

The Enlightenment added other issues to the political agenda. Law reform itself had been part of enlightened thinking at least from mid-century onwards, but – since the functions and privileges of legal officeholders often came into question as soon as the law itself was changed – obstruction was guaranteed. The legal profession itself was regarded by the general public with a mixture of cynicism and hostile alienation satirized both in contemporary literature and in the prints of Hogarth – not without justification, it seems, given the lack of proper professional standards and the scope for procedural manipulation reflected in the records which survive for countless local courts in many parts of Europe. In France, the complexities created by incompatible legal systems in north and south, compounded by an inordinately complicated mosaic of jurisdictions, were clearly recognized by commentators from the 1720s onwards; but pervasive venal officeholding ensured that not even the major battles between the *parlement* of Paris and the Crown (1771 and 1788) led to durable results. Further east, the occasionally intemperate interference by Frederick II in his otherwise more professional judiciary suggested that too much state control could be as problematic as too little. That said, the Europe-wide discussion generated by Beccaria's remarkable tract *On Crimes and Punishments* (1764), and the impact of John Howard's damning indictments of penal practice in his *State of the Prisons* (first published in 1777), were not without practical results. Countless government decrees on judicial and penal reform demonstrate worthy intentions; but perhaps more informative is the public reaction to revelations of systemic failures and judicial malpractices in Voltaire's portrayal of the Calas affair of 1762, or in the ever-popular judicial memoirs and trial briefs published in France in the 1770s and 1780s (Maza, 1993). It is also instructive to observe how the politically determined trials of Struensee in Denmark in 1772, and of Radischev in Russia in 1790, created adverse publicity across Europe. Visibility is not the same as accountability; but no one could be sure any longer that major legal malpractice would remain unnoticed.

The implementation of reform, and the publicity it generated, had the capacity to change the nature of politics itself. This became particularly visible in the distinction which emerged between technical agricultural improvement (now commonplace across many parts of Europe) and a more intrusive mediation in that personal and legal relationship between landowner and peasant which was at the very heart of *ancien régime* social privilege and inequality. Several European governments made serious attempts to legislate, and Joseph II can be said to have put his own authority on the line in an attempt to regulate seigneurial power. More permanent change was achieved in Denmark, and its Rural Reform Commission of 1786 can serve as an example of how the nature of national politics was changing. First of all, we might note that this commission was vested with the not inconsiderable theoretical powers of an absolute monarchy, made real through a cohesive ministerial team and the direct backing of the heir to the throne. Yet the commission had 16 members chosen to represent all the major interests within the landowning elite, conservatives and uncompromising free-marketeers as well as cameralist reformers, and it proceeded to consult widely about the legal, economic, and social implications of its proposals. Startlingly, the Crown not only gave free rein to a public debate conducted through pamphlets and journals, but also decided to publish the minutes of the commission itself (Munck, 1998). The seriousness of the confrontation became apparent from 1789, when disturbances occurred in many parts of the kingdom in expectation of lightened labor services and other reforms. Even more dramatic, however, was the response by the Crown, the following year, to a collective private petition against the reforms ostensibly signed by 103 landowners. The chief legal adviser to the Crown, Colbiørnsen, published the full text of the petition, in parallel text with a witheringly detailed commentary. The combination of preparatory public debate, public consultation, legal pressure, and sustained supervision for a decade (the commission met formally on no fewer than 134 occasions, and drafted a formidable array of detailed memoranda and legislative proposals), together with local implementation through arbitration, produced settlements which were more of a compromise than such an impressive litany might suggest. But the fundamental enlightened aspirations driving the reformers were explicitly stated from the start, and the mutual dependency of government and public opinion in the achievement of change soon became clear for all to see.

Print, Freedom of Expression, and Public Debate

Traditional histories of the Enlightenment have relied almost exclusively on printed texts for the bulk of their evidence. This is hardly surprising given the difficulty of reconstructing oral culture and communication convincingly (Farge, 1994), and, to a lesser extent, of using eighteenth-century theater and visual culture for these purposes. In any case, print remained the most accessible (and most reliable) medium for the dissemination of ideas – both for those who saw themselves as enlightened, and those who were critical of the new ideas, or even indifferent to them. Recent research on the use of print in the early modern period, however, has highlighted a number of problems that can be outlined as follows. First, we cannot assume that what we regard as the major classics of the Enlightenment (the substantial works by authors who are recognized today) represent what contemporaries would have recognized as the most important or influential works. Second, we cannot even assume that books were the mainstay of communication in print: pamphlets, newspapers, and journals may well have had a significantly wider readership. Third, despite much recent research, there are a number of unresolved questions regarding the reception of print: how print was actually "used" amongst those readers who did not themselves leave much evidence, notably the lower levels of urban society and the majority of the rural population, where even the extent of functional reading skills (let alone inclination) is difficult to map accurately. Fourth, whatever texts we study, we have to recognize that prevailing censorship restrictions and social conventions meant that many authors were forced not only to temper their arguments in print, but also to exploit what means they had of ensuring that users would read "between the lines." Given also the practical complexities of printing techniques and distribution networks throughout this period, eighteenth-century texts cannot be regarded as constituting the "firm" evidence that we might wish.

The reflection of the Enlightenment that we see in print is thus both selective and ambiguous. A large proportion of new texts remained confined to the traditional genres, for which there was a steady demand across society, not least in provincial markets: devotional literature, catechisms, collections of psalms, and (where permitted) reprints of bibles. To these were added a gradually increasing output of texts relating to history, genealogy, antiquarianism, the classical world, travel, and topography – all of them relatively "safe" provided the author did not get too close to the contemporary world. Far more controversial were the newer genres of fiction, including plays, moral tales, and (from the early eighteenth century) the novel. Fiction was difficult to censor, precisely because it could be disguised in allegorical terms and made to appear totally unrelated to contemporary society. But one of the reasons for the rapid growth in the market for novels (initially in western Europe, but in the last third of the century also elsewhere) was precisely the fact that interpretation was in the mind of the reader, learned or not, male or female, of any age. Increasingly, other types of printed material also gained ground, amongst them serials (such as *The Spectator*) intended for a general audience, as well as the regular newspapers (weekly, bi-weekly, and soon daily) which sought to meet an apparently insatiable demand for gossip, personal and commercial advertisements, local and trade information, international news, and, most contentiously, domestic national political news. Equally difficult to manage was the surge in pamphlets and other short (usually single-subject) publications which increasingly accompanied major domestic developments: these turned into a torrent in France during the Maupeou crisis (1770–4) and in the run-up to the meeting of the Estates General in 1789, but seem to have been equally popular in Denmark after the abolition of censorship in 1770, and in Sweden in connection with the frequent meetings of the Riksdag (parliament) from mid-century onwards. There were other types of publication peculiarly relevant to the growing public of the Enlightenment. A large-scale reference work designed for a general readership, Diderot's *Encyclopédie* of 17 volumes of text (1751–65), with 11 volumes of plates (completed in 1772), was initially purchased by a wealthy elite readership, but was soon pirated in smaller and cheaper editions, reaching an estimated circulation of 25,000 copies by 1789 (Darnton, 1979: 33–7). Equally interesting is the growth in single-volume dictionaries, language manuals, and other instructional material designed to give readers access to texts and issues normally beyond their reach (or not available in their native language).

Quantification of all these changes remains problematic, since it is rarely possible to establish either the size of individual print-runs or the identity of purchasers (other than of those who subscribed). Nevertheless, we can get some idea of the success of particular publications from the frequency of reprints and the appearance of translations, pirated copies, or thinly disguised imitations (as happened to best-sellers such as Defoe's *Robinson Crusoe* of 1719). Equally striking is the disproportionate increase in cheaper small-format publications (octavo, duodecimo, and even smaller) so noticeable in many parts of Europe after 1763, and clearly intended for a socially wider readership. Expensive books (and those in Latin) were of little concern to the authorities since the readership would be small. For more accessible texts, however, governments continued to rely on pre-publication censorship and import regulation. Originally, controls were operated by members of university theology faculties and their delegates, various ecclesiastical authorities, or (in most of Catholic Europe except France) the Inquisition itself. Increasingly, however, censorship became more political, and the staff in part secular. We should remember that regulation could work both ways: gaining official approval for a text could be hugely lucrative, and if the approval included some kind of formal copyright privilege the publisher could, at least for a time, monopolize a captive market. Copyright entitlements, however, were rarely enforceable, and only in Britain were publishing conditions sufficiently stable to allow authors to secure a significant share of the profits for themselves. In the rest of Europe it was difficult to make a predictable living from the pen – even if shrewd publicists (or accidental ones, such as Rousseau) could do quite well both in negotiating particular deals with their publishers, and in exploiting the publicity value of an official suppression of their work. In France, where censorship has been studied in detail, the system had by mid-century become so convoluted and inconsistent that the authorities themselves routinely connived at substantive circumvention and profited from the numerous loopholes.

Disapproval of censorship, from the 1760s onwards, was rarely straightforward. Many of the more radical French writers railed against the unpredictable censors whom they faced (Birn, 2005; Furet, 1984), and the significant prison sentences that could arise from evasion, but did not expect a totally free market. In the Netherlands and Britain, the disappearance of pre-publication censorship was largely fortuitous, and libel laws provided an alternative (Gibbs, 1987; Johns, 1998). Explicit removal of censorship, significantly, was first attempted in Sweden (1766) as a result of specific domestic political circumstances, closely followed for more theoretical reasons in Denmark (1770). In both cases the impact on print culture was dramatic, but changes in political circumstances in each country in 1772 led to gradual erosion of this freedom. Joseph II found the results of his reforms (1781) equally difficult to manage, and other states were more cautious. In revolutionary France effective freedom of print only lasted for four years (1789 to early 1793). In Prussia, public discussion of censorship in the 1780s was ambivalent (Hellmuth, 1998), and further restrictions were in fact imposed already in 1788.

As always in the Enlightenment, there was no ready-made divide between "reformers" and "conservatives," or even between subversives and censors: cases of individuals serving in both capacities are not hard to find. We should also remind ourselves that eighteenth-century governments themselves became quite adept at using print for their own purposes. Walpole's administration in Britain in the 1720s and 1730s openly manipulated the rapidly growing newspaper industry, both by harassing critics and by paying supporters who might portray government policy in favorable light. The French government hired major writers (including Voltaire) to help undermine the *parlement* of Paris during the Maupeou crisis of 1770–4. And, as we noted earlier, the Danish government made effective use of print to win over public opinion in its campaign for rural reform in the years after 1786. What is perhaps even more remarkable is the extent to which control of daily domestic news could be exploited for specific purposes, in ways that seem to herald the "spin" so essential to modern governments. In most European countries newspapers were severely restricted in their ability to provide substantive reports on domestic political events, and officially authorized newspapers tended to concentrate on court news and official announcements. Below the surface, however, the growing demand for news could be exploited in intriguing ways. In France, where restrictions on domestic reporting were very tight, the foreign minister from 1774 to 1787, Vergennes, allowed detailed "leaks" to reach the French-language newspapers across the border, notably the *Gazette de Leyde*: its reputation for accuracy in effect allowed the French government to test public opinion by observing the reaction to such "illegal" but accurate information amongst those less volatile wealthier Frenchmen who could afford to subscribe to an international newspaper (Popkin, 1987). The role of the *Berlinische Monatschrift* (*Berlin Monthly*) from 1783 was not altogether different: although the relative freedom of the press in Prussia allowed it room for maneuver, its readers were not told that it represented a selection of views aired in the monthly meeting of the secret Mittwochsgesellschaft, whose members and correspondents included some of the key advisers to the king as well as some of the greatest enlightened thinkers in Germany. In other words, print could be used both by the state and by others, for a great variety of purposes, and by the later eighteenth century it is clear that many governments recognized that attempts to control the press were less effective than efforts to use print to influence public opinion.

Sociability, Gender, and the Individual

The Republic of Letters (the informal network of scholars and intellectuals around Europe) pre-dated the Enlightenment by a long way, and it is no accident that when Pierre Bayle in 1684 launched a trend-setting journal devoted to scholarly news and reviews for a wider readership, he called it *Nouvelles de la République des Lettres.* Many more review journals followed during the eighteenth century, some of them precursors of modern academic journals, others intended for a more general readership. But there were now several alternative forms of communication available to the generalist. For those of a gregarious disposition, and sufficient reputation, the salons came to play a central role in elite sociability after mid-century (first in France, but soon imitated with varying degrees of success elsewhere in the major cities of Europe). Most salons were hosted by aristocratic women, whose main role was to ensure that an informal but lively intellectual atmosphere prevailed at her weekly gatherings of friends, where everyone (but especially men) could discuss literature, philosophy, and other current ideas freely without the formalities of social rank and etiquette that prevailed in more formal gatherings. Some salons, such as those hosted by Madame de Geoffrin, Mlle de Lespinasse, or Madame Necker, gained a very high reputation and attracted some of the most famous thinkers of the age. Others challenged social conventions (within the strict bounds of good taste), and might even provide women with a measure of freedom they might not have in other contexts (Goodman, 1994).

In reality, however, the Enlightenment barely noticed the glaring problems of gender inequality. The marquise du Châtelet won recognition as a mathematician and physicist, and Lady Mary Wortley Montagu as a travel writer in Constantinople. But solitary voices questioning convention and complacency (from Montesquieu in his *Persian Letters* to Etta Palm d'Aelders and Olympe de Gouges in 1790) do not appear to have made much of an impression on contemporary prejudices. As with the issues surrounding slavery and race discrimination, it seems that the significant progress made from the 1770s onwards in the construction of public concepts of political and individual rights applied solely to white adult males – a curious selectivity sanctioned by the self-proclaimed egalitarian of the age, Rousseau, himself. As the fate of individual female activists, and the diary of the studiously respectable Madame Roland, confirm, prevailing norms of gendered behavior remained very conservative during the early years of the revolution, and women continued to face great difficulties in becoming accepted as serious authors (let alone active participants in debate) in their own right. Mary Wollstonecraft argued the case with great moderation and sensitivity in her most important work, *Vindication of the Rights of Woman* (1792), but those French women who tried to organize themselves into a more active campaigning group the following year (the Society of Revolutionary Republican Women) faced hostile prejudice on such a scale that the emergent Jacobin government could easily dismantle their organization and silence its leaders with threats of prosecution for disorderly conduct.

Full discussion both of gender issues and of the growing awareness of public and private sociability will be found elsewhere in this volume (chapters 2, 8, and 12). In the present context, however, we should note that appreciation of the complex social context has made it more difficult to evaluate the significance of a particular individual (or work). Equally, the origins of major political ideas (such as the notion of a written constitution, the demand for the removal of aristocratic fiscal privilege, or the right to vote without restrictions of property or gender) can rarely be traced back in a simple, linear way. Public opinion itself can no longer be taken for granted. Are we right in thinking that Rousseau really did initiate a new vision of society, even when some of his key works (including the *Social Contract* of 1762) do not seem to have sold particularly well at first? Why did the Finnish polemicist and parish priest Anders Chydenius make no international impression with his well-written publications on free trade and economic reform, when Adam Smith was widely recognized (and translated) a few years later? Since the most important writings of Kant are very difficult to follow (in any language), can we assume that he became known more through his teachings, through his more accessible short pieces, or by way of the explanatory comments of his followers, such as Karl Reinhold?

There are no easy answers to these questions, but they prompt some interesting observations about the diffusion of ideas during the eighteenth century. Work on the reception of particular books, paintings, or musical compositions goes back a long way, but the subject was brought into relief from the 1970s onwards when actual patterns of book distribution and reading in France were re-examined (Chartier,

1987; Darnton, 1971 onwards). Darnton used the detailed records of publishers, book traders, and the police to demonstrate that the best-sellers of later eighteenth-century France included works which later generations have dismissed as insignificant, derivative, or vulgar (scandal and pornography prominent amongst them). More work is needed in this field (Mason, 1998), but here again the European comparative context can bring unexpected results. The French Enlightenment was widely appreciated in its original language, at least amongst the European elite; German-language publications probably had a more limited readership outside central Europe and southern Scandinavia, while neither Italian nor English were international languages in any real sense. When we look at patterns of translation (in those parts of Europe that had no Inquisition and no formal index of prohibited books), however, there are some surprises. Translations into English, French, and German often appeared fairly quickly, while Dutch translations seem more selective, and Danish and Swedish ones more so still. It is striking that, for example, Montesquieu's *Persian Letters* never appeared in Danish, Swedish, or Dutch, and that while his *Spirit of the Laws* was available in English already in 1750, in German in 1753, in Danish and in Dutch in 1771, it was not translated into Swedish. Rousseau's *Discourse on Inequality* was widely translated and recognized, but his *Social Contract* appeared only in English during his lifetime (German, Dutch, and Danish translations were delayed until the 1790s). It comes as no surprise that David Hume was recognized abroad above all for his historical writings, but we might speculate why, given that his *Natural History of Religion* (1757) appeared almost immediately both in French and in German, as did his controversial posthumous *Dialogues concerning Natural Religion*; there were no Scandinavian translations of either. Part of the answer no doubt lies in the religious sensitivities of these areas, and indeed in the business calculations of the printers themselves. Once more research has been done on the journals and periodicals of the European Enlightenment, however, we may well have a more fine-grained impression of what the reading public really knew about. It is clear, for example, that one of the least translated works of the period, d'Holbach's extreme atheist *System of Nature*, was indeed noticed (with abhorrence) in the journals of the time. And it is no surprise to find one of the more colorful parts of the *Persian Letters*, the story of the Troglodytes, in a popular reader's digest in Swedish in 1771.

Overall, then, the Enlightenment has become far more difficult to sum up in a succinct definition: like its most famous product, the *Encyclopédie*, the Enlightenment was composite, imperfect, and full of contradictions. It certainly encompassed men (and a few women) whose intellectual and imaginative flair had enough scope and opportunity to make a significant impact on how contemporaries saw their world. It witnessed a substantial shift in the relative balance between inherited belief-systems and individual judgment, but the results were neither particularly coherent nor invariably above rational dispute. There never was a cohesive enlightened "program," nor any convincing agreement about reform priorities. But there was a great deal more argument about what these might be, and ultimately a clearer recognition that diversity need not undermine social cohesion. Inevitably, the parameters both of social and of political organization changed irreversibly: if in the end the Enlightenment sometimes appeared destabilizing, it certainly lacked neither intellectual challenge nor the capacity to make everyone reflect on the nature of change itself.

Bibliography

Baker, K., "Politics and public opinion under the old regime," in J. R. Censer and J. D. Popkin (eds.), *Press and Politics in Pre-Revolutionary France* (Berkeley, 1987), pp. 204–16; repr. in revised form as "Public opinion as political invention," in K. M. Baker, *Inventing the French Revolution* (Cambridge, 1990), pp. 167–99.

Barnett, S. J., *The Enlightenment and Religion: The Myths of Modernity* (Manchester, 2003).

Birn, R., *Book Censorship in Eighteenth-Century France and Rousseau's Response*, Studies on Voltaire and the Eighteenth Century, ns 1 (Oxford, 2005), 223–45.

Burke, P., *Languages and Communities in Early Modern Europe* (Cambridge, 2004).

Chartier, R., *The Cultural Uses of Print in Early Modern France* (Princeton, 1987).

Darnton, R., "The high Enlightenment and the low-life of literature in pre-revolutionary France," *Past & Present*, 51 (1971), 81–115.

Darnton, R., *The Business of Enlightenment: A Publishing History of the* Encyclopédie *1775–1800* (Cambridge, MA, 1979).

Darnton, R., "The forbidden books of pre-revolutionary France," in C. Lucas (ed.), *Rewriting the French Revolution* (Oxford, 1991), pp. 1–32.

Doyle, W., *Jansenism: Catholic Resistance to Authority from the Reformation to the French Revolution* (Basingstoke, 2000).

Farge, A., *Subversive Words: Public Opinion in Eighteenth-Century France* (Cambridge, 1994).

Furet, F., "Book licensing and book production in the kingdom of France in the eighteenth century," in id., *In the Workshop of History* (Chicago, 1984), pp. 99–124.

Gibbs, G. C., "Government and the English press, 1695 to the middle of the eighteenth century," in A. C. Duke and C. A. Tamse (eds.), *Too Mighty to be Free: Censorship and the Press in Britain and the Netherlands* (Zutphen, 1987).

Goodman, D., *The Republic of Letters: A Cultural History of the French Enlightenment* (Ithaca, 1994).

Gordon, D. (ed.), *Postmodernism and the Enlightenment: New Perspectives in Eighteenth-Century French Intellectual History* (New York, 2001).

Haakonssen, K. (ed.), *Enlightenment and Religion: Rational Dissent in Eighteenth-Century Britain* (Cambridge, 1996).

Hellmuth, E., "Enlightenment and freedom of the press: the debate in the Berlin Mittwochsgesellschaft, 1783–1784," *History*, 83 (1998), 420–44.

Israel, J., *Radical Enlightenment: Philosophy and the Making of Modernity 1650–1750* (Oxford, 2001).

Johns, A., *The Nature of the Book: Print and Knowledge in the Making* (Chicago, 1998).

Mason, H. T., *The Darnton Debate: Books and Revolution in the Eighteenth Century*, Studies on Voltaire and the Eighteenth Century, 359 (Oxford, 1998).

Maza, S., *Private Lives and Public Affairs: The Causes Célèbres of Prerevolutionary France* (Berkeley, 1993).

Merrick, J., *The Desacralization of the French Monarchy in the Eighteenth Century* (Baton Rouge, 1990).

Munck, T., "Absolute monarchy in later eighteenth-century Denmark: centralized reform, public expectations, and the Copenhagen press," *Historical Journal*, 41 (1998), 201–24.

Munck, T., *The Enlightenment: A Comparative Social History, 1721–1794* (London, 2000).

Ozouf, M., "'Public opinion' at the end of the old regime," *Journal of Modern History*, 60 (supplement, 1988), S1–21.

Popkin, J. D., "The *Gazette de Leyde* and French politics under Louis XVI," in J. R. Censer and J. D. Popkin (eds.), *Press and Politics in Pre-Revolutionary France* (Berkeley, 1987), pp. 75–132.

Porter, R. and M. Teich (eds.), *The Enlightenment in National Context* (Cambridge, 1981).
Robertson, J., *The Case for the Enlightenment: Scotland and Naples 1680–1760* (Cambridge, 2005).
Schmidt, J., "Inventing the Enlightenment: anti-Jacobins, British Hegelians and the *Oxford English Dictionary*," *Journal of the History of Ideas*, 64 (2003), 421–43.
van Horn Melton, J., *The Rise of the Public in Enlightenment Europe* (Cambridge, 2001).
van Kley, D. K., *The Religious Origins of the French Revolution: From Calvin to the Civil Constitution of the Clergy, 1560–1791* (New Haven, 1996).
Venturi, F., *Italy and the Enlightenment: Studies in a Cosmopolitan Century* (London, 1972).

CHAPTER TEN

Medicine, Medical Practice, and Public Health

MARY LINDEMANN

In the realms of medicine and public health, the eighteenth century often seems uncomfortably perched between the modern and the premodern worlds. During the eighteenth century older traditions (such as Galenism) and older realities (such as the omnipresent threat of plague) ended, and new developments (such as demographic analysis and clinical teaching) took hold. Moreover, while it would be wrong to reduce medicine or public health to epiphenomena of broader historical forces, still such forces strongly influenced the course that medicine, medical practices, and public health took in the eighteenth century and any survey must take these into account. Conversely, medicine and health became ways in which other social, political, and cultural institutions came to be understood and their purposes expressed, as in the phrase a "healthy economy" or a "diseased society."

The Medical Environment

Eighteenth-century Europe has often been portrayed as a fearfully dangerous place. Life expectancies were low, infant mortality enormous, disease rampant, cures uncertain, and surgery frightful. While obvious truth adheres to all these perceptions, each requires considerable modification in order to comprehend more perfectly the constraints and the possibilities of the world which eighteenth-century Europeans inhabited. Perhaps far more than in any previous century, the eighteenth century was an age of optimism that combined with – and probably derived from – growing economic prosperity, increasing consumer possibilities, and an ineffable but definite faith (nurturing, and nurtured in turn by, the Enlightenment) that human action could alter things previously accepted as providential. Fatalism in the face of ubiquitous disease pertained only within limits. The belief that people in the eighteenth century were always ailing is likewise a misconception. As James Riley has pointed out, the possibility of *becoming* ill was great, yet that of *being* ill was less because most infectious or epidemic diseases were acute and of relatively short duration, rapidly ending in either recovery or death (Riley, 1989: 156–8). While one should not underestimate the effect of chronic afflictions (gout, strangury, ulcerated varicose

A Companion to Eighteenth-Century Europe, First Edition. Edited by Peter H. Wilson.
© 2014 John Wiley & Sons, Ltd. Published 2014 by John Wiley & Sons, Ltd.

veins, gall-, bladder-, and kidney-stones), or the debilitating effects of parasitical infections (worms, for instance), infectious diseases remained the great killers of eighteenth-century Europe. Yet here, too, things had changed since earlier times, and one reason for the more hopeful tone sounded in the eighteenth century was that (western) Europe had emerged from beneath "the shadow of the plague" (Brockliss and Jones, 1997: 356). The last great epidemic of plague in western Europe struck Marseilles in 1720. Thereafter, it remained confined to eastern and southern Europe and it took a frightful toll in Moscow in 1771–2. But for most of Europe plague was gone. Yet other epidemics continued to strike European populations throughout the century and to account for high mortality rates. The most important were smallpox, influenza, diphtheria, and tuberculosis.

The World Health Organization's eradication campaign of the 1960s and 1970s banished smallpox from the environment, and it now exists only in laboratories. During the eighteenth century, however, this acute viral infection formed, in the words of the nineteenth-century historian Thomas Macaulay, "the most terrible of all the ministers of death." Already in the sixteenth century, smallpox existed throughout the Old World (and soon, in the New World as well) and accounted for about 10–15 percent of all mortality. It had, however, become essentially a disease of children, with 80 percent of its casualties under the age of 5. Most people contracted the disease when young and then either survived – with a permanent immunity – or died. Still, the number of adult smallpox deaths was never insignificant and many victims suffered serious sequellae. This "speckled monster" struck horribly in several royal families, scourging the Austrian Habsburgs, the Spanish Bourbons, and the Russian Romanovs. Those who survived were often badly scarred or blinded. Treatments had little effect, and case mortality ranged between 10 and 50 percent depending on the lethality of the dominant infective virus. The number of deaths attributed to smallpox, however, may well have been elevated by a tendency to confuse it with measles and other exanthematous (rash-producing) diseases, such as scarlet fever and scarlatina.

Smallpox remained deadly, yet even in the early decades of the century Europeans were beginning to experiment with preventing it, by inoculating. The practice of inoculation came to Europe from the Middle East by several pathways and offered for the first time in history a human-made way to prevent (admittedly not *cure*) disease. By inserting a smallpox scab and some pustulous material into a superficial incision in the arm or leg, the inoculator induced a real case of smallpox, but generally one milder than that naturally acquired. Successfully inoculated individuals enjoyed protection for life. The procedure was not entirely safe – inoculees occasionally died or suffered serious wound infections, and they could also spread smallpox – but it proved a reliable means of avoiding the disease. Reaction to inoculation was mixed, however. Some opponents raised religious or moral objections (for example, inoculation supposedly thwarted the will of God). More serious epidemiologically was the fact that inoculees could trigger an epidemic. Thus when the English provincial physician Edward Jenner (1749–1823) developed vaccination, it was more rapidly accepted than inoculation had been. The word "vaccination" came from the Latin *variolae vaccinae* or "smallpox of the cow." From milkmaids in his area Jenner had learned that those who had had cowpox remained immune from smallpox. In fact, immunity was limited and periodic revaccination was necessary. Still, both practices combined to reduce significantly deaths from the disease and *may* also have contributed to a general decline in mortality rates.

Like smallpox, influenza and diphtheria are age-old diseases of Europe, Africa, and Asia. The spread and impact of influenza have always been hard to document, but at least three pandemics of influenza occurred in the eighteenth century: in 1729–30, 1732–3, and 1781–2. In addition good evidence supports the suspicion that several other major outbreaks bracketed these pandemics. Unlike smallpox, however, influenza usually kills few although many fall ill. While most people considered smallpox and diphtheria contagious, contemporaries did not perceive tuberculosis as a "catching" disease but an individualized one based on a constitutional weakness. In the eighteenth century, the "world's greatest epidemic of tuberculosis" began and rapidly spread in increasingly crowded urban environments. Indeed, tuberculosis might have affected much of the population, albeit in a subclinical (non-symptomatic) form, although case mortality and actual morbidity are extremely difficult to extract from the existing historical records. In addition, bacillary dysentery (the "bloody flux") affected adults and children alike, although the latter, as well as the elderly and weak, succumbed most often. It, too, was regarded as epidemic in the eighteenth century. Mosquito-spread malaria, on the other hand, was not, and was counted among the "fevers" that appeared in multiple forms and under various names – in this case, as an intermittent or relapsing fever – whose presence in some areas was almost ubiquitous. Malaria, although a significant disease in Roman times, had receded in the Middle Ages only to revive in the seventeenth and eighteenth centuries as Europeans began to settle previously uninhabited parts of their continent, penetrating marshy areas and building canals for transportation and irrigation. Yet, in the end, malaria remained more a problem abroad – in the European colonies – than at home. Rashes distinguished other fevers, such as typhus or "spotted fever." These occurred most commonly in large groups of people who crowded together under poor hygienic conditions. Thus, such fevers appeared under a variety of names, such as jail, ship, or camp fever. Typhus decimated armies, and the troops Napoleon took to Russia in 1813 suffered dramatically.

Syphilis first appeared in an epidemic form in Europe in the late fifteenth century when it spread rapidly through a virgin population (i.e. a population for whom the disease was new). Thereafter, it became a permanent feature of the European disease landscape. For a long time, it was unclear whether this *morbus gallicus* (or French disease as it was then known; in the eighteenth century, the commonest name was *lues venerea*) was one disease or two. The differentiation of *lues venerea* into gonorrhea and syphilis began with the work of Giovanni Battista Morgagni (1682–1771) in the 1750s and 1760s. Although, in demographic terms, syphilis was in no way as important as smallpox, few diseases gripped the eighteenth-century European psyche as fiercely and few enjoyed so much attention from all sorts of healers who offered discreet assistance. Newspaper advertisements, for example, promised cures under euphemistic names such as Kennedy's Lisbon Diet Drink. Such concoctions seemed far more palatable than the traditional (and toxic) mercury-salivation therapy.

There can be no doubt that epidemic disease imprinted its image on generations of Europeans. But epidemics are – by definition – unusual (if, in the early modern period, depressingly frequent). People suffered from a much larger range of chronic, debilitating, and painful afflictions, as well as annoying ones. We still live with many of these today, such as cancers, arteriosclerosis, and other degenerative diseases, although the shorter lifespan in the eighteenth century may have lessened their demographic impact and visibility. The list is virtually unending. Coughs and colds were omnipresent, as well as diarrheas that were often imperfectly distinguished from dysentery. Metabolic disorders, such as the porphyria from which George III probably suffered, were poorly understood and misdiagnosed; George III was thought mad and treated accordingly. Diet deficiency illnesses, such as rickets and scurvy (the first resulting from insufficient vitamin D and the second from a lack of vitamin C in the diet) afflicted many. Sailors, who lacked fresh foods for long periods of time, were particularly prone to the latter. When Europeans discovered that adding lemon or lime juice, or cider, to rations solved the problem, scurvy virtually disappeared in the navies that took these precautions. Skin ailments, such as the "itch," the "scald," or vermin infestations, were exceedingly common in an age of primitive hygiene and where wool was still often worn next to the skin. (Lice and fleas could, of course, be the vectors in the spread of other diseases, such as typhus.) Impaired circulation and heart disease could produce angina, dropsy (edema), or ulcerated varicose veins. Gout was widely thought to plague those who ate gluttonously, but the fatted rich were not its only victims. Besides cataracts (which surgeons were relatively effective in treating), eye ailments such as runny eyes, conjunctivitis, and pink-eye, as well as colorfully named ailments such as "wry-neck," made the lives of our eighteenth-century ancestors uncomfortable and often rendered their appearance unsightly. Accidents occurred frequently in an age of open hearths, horse-drawn vehicles, and unregulated industries. Surgeons could quite successfully set broken limbs or even sew up gaping wounds (although wound infection was always to be feared), but complicated fractures that pierced the flesh, serious burns, tumors deeply embedded in the body cavities, or wounds in the chest or abdomen almost always resulted either in an amputated limb or death.

Thus, in many ways, the eighteenth century was just as perilous as previous ones despite the disappearance of some older killers. General, if slow, improvements in nutrition, greater overall affluence, and a growing range of material comforts perhaps made life seem less harsh and dangerous. Non-medical innovations – such as the development of sick funds, pension schemes, annuities, life and fire insurance, and joint-stock companies – also helped deflect the slings and arrows of outrageous fortune. Although famine had mostly disappeared from large parts of Europe in the eighteenth century, hard times had not. In fact the numbers of the *potential* poor (or the laboring poor) rose as the inevitable by-product of a precocious, yet unstable, world economy that had rained unheard-of riches down on many. Global depressions and economic crises sent thousands of workers spiraling down into beggary. Ill health exacerbated their plight and sped their fall.

Patients and Practitioners

If cures were scarce and surgery painful, still, few sufferers went down without a fight. Almost everyone secured aid or helped him- or herself in illness. The range of available practitioners was enormous and heterogenous. Yet medical care almost always began at home, and that had been true for millennia. Self-help, followed by the assistance of family members, neighbors, and friends formed the first recourse for almost everyone and most people felt confident that they knew what was best for them. Praying, visiting a shrine, supplicating saintly intervention, or venerating a relic might all count in the calculus of self-help. Prayer and medical advice (including that of physicians, apothecaries, or surgeons) were by no means mutually exclusive efforts even in a progressively secularized century. Moreover, new religious directions in the late seventeenth and the eighteenth centuries had implications for healing. Revivalism within Protestantism – in the form of Pietism centered in Germany or in the English version of John Wesley's Methodism – made healing an integral part of religion. The Pietist-influenced university in Halle (then part of Prussia) shipped medicines, advice pamphlets, and missionaries to far-flung colonies, including those in the East Indies and the Americas. Wesley strongly criticized the orthodox medicine of his day and published his own medical manual, *Primative Physick*, that proved a hardy perennial, appearing in various editions from 1774 to 1880. Magical curing had by no means died out, but was rapidly becoming unfashionable or at least unmentionable. Some people rushed to try almost anything that promised amelioration of their cares and rarely preferred one cure to another except on their own perception of "what worked." Others were more skeptical and trusted no physicians or healers. Individual variation in medical choice was – and is – always great. In the eighteenth century, a plethora of practitioners and practices, drugs and regimens, were accessible to almost all. The rise of a vigorous and profitable medical entrepreneurship – the burgeoning availability of new medicines (especially proprietary ones) and the wild popularity of spas, for instance – had much to do with the growth of a producing and consuming society, especially in the western part of the continent. In the eastern and southern parts of Europe, the cornucopia of drugs was less full and the impact of advertising, as well as the sheer proliferation of goods and services, less pronounced, although the wealthier segments of these areas certainly participated in medical consumerism when feasible.

Once the decision was made to move beyond a close circle of family and friends, the eighteenth century offered a wide range of medical practitioners from which to choose. An assertive spirit of enterprise, growing commercialization, and the rise of advertising vastly multiplied the choices at one's fingertips. Most sufferers were medically promiscuous, moving from one practitioner to another if a cure failed to take, or consulting several practitioners simultaneously. Although guilds existed for some medical practitioners (and these varied in membership, size, and organization from place to place) and physicians were generally academically trained (that is, at universities), little sense of professional superiority guided medical decision-making. Indeed, the idea of a medical *profession* (which sociologists often define as "an occupation that regulates itself through systematic, required training and collegial discipline; that has a base in technical, specialized knowledge; and that has service rather than profit orientation, enshrined in its ethics": Starr, 1982: 15) was at best imperfectly elaborated. Only toward the end of the century, and more in the urbanized western parts of the continent, did physicians begin to develop the social and cultural authority that coincides with a modern view of professionalism. In addition to physicians, a whole array of other medically licensed and often superbly trained medical practitioners catered to the demands of a public ready and able to patronize them. Apothecaries acted as doctors, distributing advice as well as medication and taking fees for both, although generally their writ extended only as far as supplying simple and complex (that is, compounded) medicines. In England, however, where medical regulation remained weaker and control over practices (especially outside London) less crisp than in some continental states, apothecaries or surgeon-apothecaries came to function virtually as general practitioners. Surgeons, too, enjoyed better training over the course of the eighteenth century and in some places (again England and Scotland stand out), by the end of the century, boundaries between surgeons and physicians had been largely erased.

Proximity, perhaps more than expertise or perceptions of qualifications, determined medical choice. While obviously some cures and the fees of some practitioners put them out of the reach of many, even ordinary people spent what appear to have been exorbitant sums to regain health or heal wounds. Likewise, neither infants nor children nor the aged were neglected. Generally speaking, urban environments had more trained and licensed personnel – physicians, surgeons, barber-surgeons, apothecaries, and midwives – than rural areas. In addition, a whole range of empirics and traveling healers plied their trade, and in many parts of Europe (if not everywhere) the competition for clients was intense. This "medical marketplace" (a term coined by Harold Cook some 20 years ago: Cook, 1986) presented a dazzling array of healing options: tooth drawers and dentists; root-wives and oil- and *orviétan*-peddlers (*orviétan* was a composite secret remedy); oculists and corn-cutters; as well as all the other practitioners that existed in their multitudes throughout Europe. Mary Fissell perceptively observes that "[s]omeone who fell ill in eighteenth-century England found a profusion of health-care practitioners eager for his or her custom" (Fissel, 1991: 37). But England was hardly unique in this regard. "Cunning" men and women (who practiced sympathetic or magical cures) continued to exist and were consulted, although probably less frequently and less openly than in the past. Moreover, their venue was the village and, as more people migrated to cities, their clientele may have vanished. While social standing might make some difference in determining who consulted which practitioners (male midwives, for instance, became fashionable among the upper crust by the late eighteenth century), lords and ladies as much as cowherds and goose-girls shopped around, sampled the cures, and solicited the advice of many healers. Governments often warred relentlessly on the practice of "illicit healing" but their campaigns hardly stopped it. Yet the definitions of "quacks," or the separation between "licit" and "illicit" healers, shifted rapidly, and historians now recognize that "the frontiers between orthodox and unorthodox medicine have [always] been flexible," so changeable indeed that "one age's quackery has often become another's orthodoxy" (Bynum and Porter, 1987: 1). Clearly, the medical marketplace of the eighteenth century was a free-wheeling place. The astrological medicine of a divine like Richard Napier (1553–1634), however, had practically disappeared in a general revulsion against the religious "enthusiasm" that had disrupted European societies in the early to mid-seventeenth century. While healers of all stripes had *always* characterized the European medical world, that world became more complex in the eighteenth century with the rise of a more aggressive medical entrepreneurship that produced medicines in bulk, shipped them to foreign lands, and puffed them in the darling media of the day: the newspapers. Jean Ailhaud (1684–1756) and his son, for example, built a fortune from the sale of their "purgative powders" as a universal remedy. Their marketing network crossed borders and worked through a well-coordinated system of distributors. Particularly in western

European countries (Britain, France, the Germanies and the Italies), fashionable life combined with the quest for health and spas provided not only solace of body but also a stage on which to play a life. The actual number of practitioners is difficult to determine, and greatly depends, of course, on how one counts. If one accepts an expansive, but quite accurate, definition of medical practitioners as those who earned their living in whole or in part through healing, then huge numbers practiced medicine in the eighteenth century. If we add self-help and the assistance of family and friends, the figure becomes truly staggering. However, it is not easy even to get a good impression of the number of licensed or academically trained practitioners, such as surgeons and physicians. It is probably safe to say that the numbers in western European countries expanded significantly in the eighteenth century and it now appears that by the end of the old regime the majority of Frenchmen may have been in a position to consult an authorized healer (Ramsey, 1988: 62). This held equally true in England and in many parts of the Germanies and the Italies, as well as in urban (compared to rural) areas. The Scandinavian countries, for instance, were probably not as well stocked with physicians (for example), but availability rose there as well, especially in cities such as Copenhagen and Stockholm. Even in Russia, some physicians and surgeons (often transplanted Germans or Balts) could be found, whereas they had been virtually non-existent a century earlier.

The eighteenth century might also have experienced greater "gendering" of certain medical activities. If one surveys the entire range of medical practice, one finds that more women than men practiced medicine, that is, if one employs the broad definition introduced above and counts mothers, aunts, sisters, and daughters who attended their families, and gentlewomen who treated their households and servants. And until the late eighteenth century midwives delivered the vast majority of children. Even with the appearance of the male midwife (the physician or surgeon trained as an *accoucheur*) in the mid- to late eighteenth century, only among the upper and middle ranks of society did they quickly became popular. Geographical differences also pertained: male midwives were far more common in England and France than in the German states or the Scandinavian countries. In these latter two areas, midwives obtained considerably more sophisticated instruction usually, although not invariably, under male tutelage. Yet they were never edged from the birthing chamber entirely. In southern Europe, the number of male midwives remained tiny, as it did in eastern Europe as a whole. Nursing did not become a secular career until much later, but nursing (religious) orders – male as well as female – assumed critically important roles in running many hospitals and, of course, most home nursing was done by women. Thus, even at the end of the century, women had by no means been banished from the realm of medical care, even if men were coming to monopolize some parts of it. Of course, women were generally excluded from both academic education and guild membership.

Once the practitioner came to the patient's bedside (and not all did, for many consultations were epistolatory or went through intermediaries), his or her therapeutic options remained relatively limited. Moreover, little distinguished the practice of home doctors, physicians, surgeons, and those denigrated as quacks and charlatans from the others. Bleeding, purging, and sweating formed treatments of choice for a wide variety of afflictions and were applied, for instance, to reduce fever, relieve edema, cure apoplexies, and halt epileptic fits. Palliatives, such as cooling poultices and strengthening tonics, were favored by home nurses and were prescribed by physicians. The medical armamentarium was stocked full of simple and compound medicines and positively bulged with the addition of many new specifics and panaceas (universal remedies) by late century. Still, few were effective, at least in our terms. Herbal remedies, known since antiquity, remained popular, and a goodly number proved beneficial. Willow bark, for instance, is indeed a good febrifuge (fever-reducer) because it contains salicylate, an analgesic. Since the sixteenth century, the quantity of chemical medicines available had grown enormously. Physicians and surgeons, for example, typically ordered mercury for syphilitics. Antimony (in its natural sulfide) was found in a range of medicines and also as an ingredient in cosmetics. Calomel (mercurous chloride) was an effective, albeit harsh, purgative. All could be extremely toxic, as were the arsenic and strychnine many medications contained. Likewise age-old, but still commonly used in the eighteenth century, were hemlock, opium, wine, hellebore, and mandragora. All reduced pain but could also kill, even in relatively small overdoses. The New World promised much in the way of drugs, but produced less. Perhaps most important were Peruvian or Jesuit bark (cinchona) and ipecacuanha. The first lowered the fever of malaria, while the second was an effective emetic and anti-congestant. Eighteenth-century investigators also discovered new drugs closer to home. European foxglove (digitalis) proved efficacious for watery edema (dropsy) and heart failure.

Medical Theory and Medical Education

The late sixteenth and early seventeenth centuries generated a great deal of knowledge in several fields related to medicine. Dissection, by no means unknown in the Middle Ages, became more usual in the sixteenth and seventeenth centuries and created a vast storehouse of information about the structure of the human body. Early inquiries into physiological processes (known then as "animal economy"), such as Sanctorius Sanctorius (1561–1636) on metabolism (using his own invention, the "weighing chair") and William Harvey's (1578–1657) discovery of the circulation of the blood and his work on reproduction (Harvey argued that all life sprang from the *ovum* or egg), offered new ideas about how the body worked. The talented microscopists of the seventeenth century, such as the Dutchman Anton van Leeuwenhoeck (1632–1723) and the Englishman Robert Hooke (1635–1703) revealed many hidden wonders. Little that resulted from this accretion of knowledge proved of immediate practical use; it had hardly any impact on therapeutics. Yet the "new science" of the seventeenth century carried over into the eighteenth, and strongly molded Enlightenment views on the world, imparting a greater sense that disease could be conquered, life expectancies raised, and human happiness augmented.

The Galenist and humoralist thinking that had shaped ideas about the body, health, and medicine for centuries was very slowly losing its grip. (Most people, lay and learned alike, still accepted that health depend on an equilibrium of humors – black bile, yellow bile, blood, and phlegm – and that disease was born when something disrupted the balance or when one or the other humor "putrefied" or became "morbid"). No single medical theory, however, became immediately dominant or assumed medical orthodoxy. Rather, several rival medical schools developed, each

Figure 8 Het Hospital. Female involvement in medical practice could extend to senior levels, as this Dutch engraving indicates. *National Library of Medicine, USA*

with its own set of ideas (its own *system*), its champions and detractors, and its institutional affiliation. While it is simplistic to suggest that the camps divided neatly into those of mechanism and vitalism, that dichotomy catches critical differences. Those who adhered basically to mechanistic beliefs seem perhaps closest to the science of the seventeenth century and especially to the thinking of Isaac Newton (1643–1727) and René Descartes (1596–1650). The great Dutch professor and clinical teacher Hermann Boerhaave (1668–1738) was one of the earliest and most influential physician-professors who applied physics to medicine and human physiology, arguing for a mechanistic understanding of disease as a matter of disturbed hydraulic (fluid) balances. Boerhaave's presence at the University of Leiden (in the Dutch Republic) from 1702 until his death, made Leiden a center of mechanism (or, as it was often called, *iatromechanism*). Similarly, the German physician Friedrich Hoffmann (1660–1742) believed that "[m]edicine is the art of properly utilizing physico-mechanical principles, in order to conserve the health of man or to restore it if lost" (Broman, 2003: 469). Both pooh-poohed the concept of "purpose," which they associated with occult, "unscientific" beliefs. Some of those close to mechanism emphasized nerves over vessels, such as William Cullen in Edinburgh (1710–90) or Albrecht Haller (1708–77) and Johann Friedrich Blumenbach (1752–1840) in Göttingen. These men stressed that disease was rooted in spasms of the nervous system or in too much, or too little, stimulation. Few, however, followed Julien La Mettrie (1709–51; *L'Homme machine*, 1754) in claiming that even thought and soul were material.

Far more prevalent than radical materialism was dissatisfaction with cold mechanism. The so-called "vitalists," men like the Halle professor Georg Ernst Stahl (1659–1734), refused to view human beings as mere collections of mechanical parts and chemical substances. They believed that an "anima" – something like a God-given soul – formed the vital element that endowed human beings with life and motion. Of course, a large number of medical thinkers and physicians found comfortable spots for themselves between these two poles. More than just a handful, like the "English Hippocrates" Thomas Sydenham (1624–89), for example, or "Father Heim," the Berlin physician Ernst Ludwig Heim (1747–1834), felt that no theory adequately explained life (or health and illness) and that no theories helped much at the bedside. Typically, Heim was far better known for his practice than his writings.

Professors of medicine at prominent European universities nevertheless wrote extensively, developed theories, and experimented on the workings of the human body. The Göttingen professor Haller indefatigably pursued his investigation of nervous fibers, for example. The other duty of professors, of course, was to teach. Still, only a small part of medical education (and not merely the education of physicians) in the eighteenth century was accomplished at universities. Many people trained in an apprenticeship and that included some doctors (especially in the colonies). Medical occupations with a guild or corporate structure – apothecaries, surgeons, barber-surgeons – specified a course of apprenticeship approximating that of other artisanal occupations. Midwives, too, generally learned their craft in an apprentice-like framework, although they, like most women, enjoyed no guild membership. One should not assume that these non-academic methods produced inferior practitioners or that they conveyed no systematic or theoretical material. Especially in the eighteenth century one can also discern new initiatives that wrought changes in this venerable, and by no means ineffective, system. In each case, the location of training began to shift, from the side of the master surgeon (for example) to a school devoted to surgery, often established by states, but in many places founded as commercial enterprises. Such theoretical, "school" training did not replace "learning by doing," but came to form a complementary and more frequent part of it. To a large extent this process also affected the medical training of physicians, especially in France and England, where private medical schools and courses (especially in Edinburgh and London) existed alongside university training. Surgeons, too, attended private classes. By the end of that century, most territories mandated that midwives, in order to receive their licenses, had to attend lectures on midwifery given at universities, in special surgical schools, or in lying-in wards. The newly founded lying-in hospitals thus served several purposes equally near and dear to the goals of good government and Enlightenment: (1) to provide better care for destitute women; (2) to reduce infant mortality; and (3) to train *accoucheurs* and midwives more rigorously. While such wards and hospitals probably had little significant impact on infant mortality as a whole, they opened up better opportunities for instructing midwives and, in particular, for educating the new male midwives, who appeared in greater numbers after mid-century. Obviously, such developments did not proceed at an equal pace throughout Europe. England, France, some of the Italian and German states, and parts of

Scandinavia spearheaded these innovations. Such changes took place less rapidly in southern and eastern Europe, but were by no means totally absent there.

Universities, of course, continued to churn out physicians, but the universities that assumed pride of place in the mid- to late eighteenth century were Leiden and Edinburgh, where the emphasis lay on bedside teaching and where professors had began to "walk the wards" with their students. (Similar institutions or practices also existed, for instance, in Halle, Strasbourg, Aix-en-Provence, Avignon, Vienna, Pavia, and so on.) One should, however, not overestimate the amount and type of clinical teaching that took place. The opportunities for hands-on experience remained relatively limited. Boerhaave, often considered the father of bedside teaching (an appellation he only partially deserves as one can trace clinical teaching to the 1540s and the work of Giambatista da Monte [1498–1551] in Padua), gave his students relatively little chance to "practice." Rather, he presented a single patient to students and then discussed the particular case. Still, by the 1780s and 1790s and in many places throughout Europe, clinical experience for ongoing physicians became more available, although until the very end of the century the number of patients involved remained relatively small and the principal goal was that of disseminating what was already known to ongoing students.

What happened at the Paris clinic at the close of the eighteenth century differed quantitatively and qualitatively. Paris's huge population produced an equally enormous number of hospital patients, at any one time there were some 20,000. Students there could observe an extraordinary variety of cases. Also new were the postmortems, which emphasized pathological anatomy. Thus, the Parisian clinic not only disseminated information and taught skills to ongoing medical students, but it also produced knowledge.

Institutions

The concept of a medical "institution" in eighteenth-century Europe must be understood broadly: some had walls, some did not. Typical was the proliferation of institutions and the amplification of purposes and goals envisioned for them. The century witnessed the renovation of old facilities, the construction of new ones, and the expansion of others. In addition, newer institutions – such as out-patient facilities (or dispensaries), lying-in wards or maternity hospitals, and medical care for the sick poor – sprang up. The impetus for these often came from governments, but with increasing frequency private individuals or groups provided the energy and the funding. A more worldly-directed religious sentiment combined with a sense that society and individuals could better unacceptable conditions, improve health, and prolong life. The leisure enjoyed by the possessing classes drove a voluntarism that contributed to the planning, founding, and maintenance of numerous philanthropic and benevolent institutions, such as the voluntary or subscription hospitals.

The hospitals of the medieval and early modern world were never mere "gateways to death," as they were once portrayed. Most hospitals at least attempted to provide medical care, and all extended some modicum of shelter and better nourishment that were extremely valuable to those wishing to recover their health or simply seeking refuge in hard times. It is also false that such early hospitals only catered to the absolutely destitute, although there is no denying that more of the poor – or laboring poor – entered their doors than did better-off artisans or the truly wealthy, for example. Six changes characterized the hospitals of the eighteenth century, although significant precedents existed for all: (1) hospitals became more exclusively devoted to caring for the acutely ill; (2) more specialized hospitals (such as "lock" hospitals for those with venereal disease, lying-in wards or hospitals for parturient mothers, or separate institutions for the mentally disturbed) were established; (3) founders and administrators expressed greater concern over mortality rates and a concomitant regard for hygiene within institutions (introducing novel methods of ventilation and altering hospital structures and ward layouts, for example); (4) hospitals engaged more medical personnel (and more varied personnel as well); (5) hospitals evolved into teaching facilities, and this development quickened toward the end of the century, leading to the "birth of the clinic"; and (6) there was considerable experimentation with programs to provide medical care *outside* of hospital walls, either as visiting care for the sick poor or in freestanding dispensaries and out-patient clinics.

Under the impact of utilitarianism and mercantilism many states and individuals became increasingly disturbed by the apparently high mortality rates in hospitals. In addition, those involved in medical education and who wished to improve medical training in order to foster the "health of the people" tended to regard the existing multi-purpose, huge edifices (or clusters of buildings) inherited from the medieval world as an inadequate way of caring for the sick or training medical personnel. The charitable purposes of hospitals continued to be recognized, but the dilemma remained of how to care for the needy and deserving without encouraging indolence and deceitfulness. In England, the Westminster Infirmary that began admitting patients in 1720 became the model for the voluntary hospital (a hospital founded by private initiative and financed by charitable giving). Everywhere the energy and effort involved came from well-to-do laypeople and clergymen, who then managed the enterprise and recommended patients for admission. Thus the voluntary hospital provided a socially satisfying activity for (often religiously connected) benevolence. It was a rational form of charity that fitted well into the mercantile, wealthy middle-class world that had called it into being. Hospitals endowed by individuals, such as that set up by Suzanne Necker (1739–94) in Paris or established by Johann Christian Senckenberg (1707–72) in Frankfurt am Main, were also symptomatic of eighteenth-century enterprise. Such institutions were generally small, well-staffed, and comfortable. Royalty and states quickly followed these models and set up their own new hospitals, albeit cast on a much larger scale. The princes, dukes, and top bureaucrats who ruled German territories often sought to improve the health of their populations and preserve or extend their lifespans, thereby contributing to the state's economic prosperity and its secular and military power. They, too, founded new hospitals or drastically reformed older ones to achieve these goals. The general hospital in Vienna established by Joseph II was one such endeavor, but one can document similar projects in Italy, Spain, the Netherlands, France, Sweden, and – later – Russia. All these hospitals tended to employ a larger medical staff including doctors, surgeons, apothecaries, midwives, and nurses. Hospitals in Catholic countries were often excellently served by nursing orders. In addition, as we have seen, many hospitals initiated the training of medical personnel by opening their wards to students and their mentors. Overall, private–public cooperation expanded beyond the realm of hospital foundations.

(Voluntary hospitals were, obviously, *private* institutions erected and maintained for *public* benefit.)

Another important model for hospitals and hospital reform in the eighteenth century was the military hospital. By the eighteenth century, medical care and hospitals formed well-established parts of the military system. Contrary to what most people tend to believe, military medicine achieved good standards and military hospitals frequently proved paragons of orderliness and efficiency. Indeed, military establishments often inaugurated the improvements civilian hospitals later adopted. The turmoil of the great Valois–Habsburg conflicts of the sixteenth and seventeenth centuries spurred the building of military hospitals in Austria, Spain, and France. Veteran hospitals came later, and Louis XIV's creation of the famous Hôtel des Invalides in Paris in 1670 stands as one splendid example. Countries that led in centralizing and consolidating government activities – France, Spain, and some German territories – also took the lead in establishing military hospitals. Less centralized states, such as England and the Netherlands, however, set up theirs a bit later. Recent evaluations of the role of military hospitals in medical progress have struck a particularly positive note, seeing in them places where "the fundamentals of a creative and investigatory anatomy-clinical medicine were falling into place long before the 1790s" (Brockliss and Jones, 1997: 700).

A further innovation in institutional care was the rise of specialty hospitals; good examples are asylums for the insane and separate facilities for lying-in women. The horrors of mammoth, catch-all madhouses revealed by the English reformer John Howard (1726–90) in several publications at the end of the century were not fantasies. Yet, by the time he wrote, care for the insane had already been inching toward more humane methods for decades (culminating in the legendary striking off of chains by Philippe Pinel [1745–1826] at the Salpêtrière hospital for female lunatics in Paris in 1800). That transformation, too, reflected the optimism of the age. As ideas about mental illness changed from regarding insanity as a physical ailment to seeing it more in the Lockian perspective of a false association of ideas, the possibility of cure began to appear as a realistic goal. Therefore, the principal function of the insane asylum shifted from rendering lunatics harmless to an equally important duty, that of returning them cured to their families and to society as productive members. The mad were not brutes, and would respond to considerate handling. The harsh regimens once applied to "treat" the mad – strong purgatives, bleeding, emetics, as well as blows and chains – yielded to mixtures of kindness and useful employment, such as gardening. One prominent reformer, William Battie (1703/4–76), argued that management did more than medicines to help the insane. This project of moral management – the use of psychological rather than physical techniques – soon spread throughout Europe. Equally important, it was believed, was the construction of special or segregated wards or houses where the mad might be confined for their own benefit and not merely to secure society from them. Private madhouses – charitable as well as commercial ones – shot up like so many mushrooms, especially in the fertile English soil where many opened at the end of the seventeenth century. France, and also Germany and Italy (and again, particularly in cities), boasted numerous such institutions. Conditions in them varied from abominable to excellent, but the whole apparatus concretized an Enlightenment emphasis on private enterprise, commercialism, and charity turned to public benefit. Not only the insane, but also the deaf, mute, blind, and autistic drew new interest in these decades, and several physicians, clergymen, and educators attempted to school them by novel methods.

Innovation, however, by no means ceased once new hospitals were built and the worst abuses remedied. Dispensaries (proto-outpatient clinics) were established in cities to provide inexpensive, rapid treatment for the working poor, that is, for those who owned little more than their labor but who were neither beggars nor destitute. As early as 1630, the French physician Théophraste Renaudot (1586–1653), set up a *bureau d'adresse* in Paris that treated the sick poor for free and acted as a clearing house for those seeking work. Thus one institution alleviated two causes of impoverishment: illness and lack of work. Physicians and surgeons donated their time and expertise in dispensaries as well as in similar programs, while others – clergy, successful professionals such as lawyers, bureaucrats (in their private life), and merchants – contributed their administrative and financial skills to, as well as the necessary capital for, the running of such institutions. Even more radical, perhaps, in its approach to the problem of the sick poor were proposals for home care or visiting care that several cities implemented. Many of those disquieted by what they viewed as the unacceptably high mortality rates in hospitals (and disturbed as well by the cost of hospital building and maintenance) sought a domiciliary solution whereby doctors, surgeons, and midwives visited patients in their lodgings. Although such aid was generally limited to the sick poor and those actually on relief rolls, the primary purpose lay in extending timely assistance to the laboring poor, thus preventing them from succumbing to an illness that could mean economic ruin. Other benevolent societies focused on particular groups. One such example was the Philanthropic Society of Paris (established in 1780), which procured aid for artisans and shopkeepers when they fell ill. Likewise, organizations such as the London Lying-In Charity for Delivering Poor Married Women in Their Own Habitations (1758) or the French Society for Maternal Charity (1788) assisted only respectably married women, thus not only providing medical assistance but also advancing a sense of middle-class morality.

State and Society

Novel initiatives in public health hallmarked the eighteenth-century state. Although what was done stood on the groundwork of older achievements and methods, the scale of these endeavors so massively exceeded previous efforts that one can consider them new. State action geared up enormously in the realm of public health and often paired with private undertakings. The emergence of a bourgeois public sphere not only fostered new networks of communication; it also generated public programs of which health care formed a very prominent one. If state and non-state endeavors often moved on parallel tracks, they also often crossed and worked toward the same goals. Those institutions discussed above – such as voluntary hospitals or privately funded medical care for the laboring poor – are an excellent illustration of how private institutions fulfilled social functions and how important the public–private hybrid had become in the realm of health.

During the seventeenth century the science of demography, too, became a practical endeavor. States became ever more interested in the size of their populations as an accurate measure of economic wealth and political power. (This point of view was sometimes formalized as the doctrine of populationism.) The "bookkeeping of state" began with censuses whose utility governments quickly recognized and which they then conducted with greater regularity in the seventeenth and eighteenth centuries. Mortality data, generally first collected in conjunction with plague, was soon aggregated to reveal broader patterns. Morbidity, too, came to be assessed numerically, if less frequently and considerably less reliably. Just as important as the gathering of information was its analysis. Beginning about the middle of the seventeenth century, private individuals – such as William Petty (1623–1687) in England (who coined the apt phrase "political arithmetic") or, later, the pastor Johann Süssmilch (1707–67) in Breslau – sought to discover the rules of mortality in order to facilitate rational state planning, for instance in gauging the prospective pool of recruits for the armed forces. For most of the century, this budding science of demography – and the populationism that accompanied it – concerned itself with augmenting the size of the population in order to enhance a state's power and status vis-à-vis its competitors. Men like Petty and Süssmilch thereby hoped to learn how to counter the decline of population that they accepted as a fact of life by avoiding "excess" deaths. Not until the end of the century did another political arithmetician, Thomas Malthus (1766–1834), suggest that the real danger lay in *over*population.

What, then, did the state do to protect the health of its people? Governments and their constituencies came to acknowledge that the state could – and should – intervene in a far broader range of instances than once thought desirable or possible. Even in countries like England, where state power and administrative centralization loomed less large than in many continental polities, authorities at all levels became increasingly active in the realm of public health. Although no one actually enforced a thoroughgoing state intervention into the lives of its subjects and citizens in *all* matters of health and public welfare from "womb to tomb," as advocated by Johann Peter Frank (1745–1821) in his multi-volume *Complete System of Medical Police* (1779–1819), the activities of government in the realm of health nevertheless mounted dramatically. These efforts created what James Riley has called "the eighteenth-century campaign to avoid disease." This program rested on a "new Hippocratism" (a sort of environmentalism) as the basis for public health (Riley, 1987). To be sure, states had always been in the business of public health to a greater or lesser degree. Long before the first wave of plague struck western Europe in the mid-fourteenth century, cities and territories had regulated aspects of public health by setting up hospitals or hiring physicians. In the eighteenth century, however, these exertions became more vigorous and their scope more comprehensive. Moreover, this new Hippocratism, in altering the understanding of how diseases spread – from personal contact, through the air, or from one's surroundings – suggested that changes in the environment (in what the Hippocratic writings referred to as "airs, waters, places") could significantly improve health. Admittedly, this orientation was not original to the eighteenth century. Two ways of explaining disease have always been present in Western society: contagionist and miasmatic (or anti-contagionist). Indeed, "much of epidemiological thought between classical antiquity and the present can be usefully understood as a series of shifting rearrangements of these thematic building blocks" (Rosenberg, 1992: 295). There persisted a clear tendency to understand some diseases, such as smallpox, as spread by contact with infected persons. But the idea that epidemics arose from environmental causes made "bad air," polluted or standing water, and "noxious odors" the main objects of public health action. Such approaches generated a convincing rationale for intervention and suggested an agenda. Public health became, therefore, mostly a program of prevention. Governments drained swamps, eliminated polluted areas in cities, provided for potable water, and banned offensive trades from densely populated areas. Such clean-up campaigns could do little against pathogens like the smallpox virus, but they probably had a widespread salutary effect on preventing diseases, like dysentery, that were spread by infected water.

Still, public health in the 1700s was not only about what would come, in the next century, to be called "sanitary engineering." Governments launched programs to augment the supply of medical practitioners and, especially, to furnish medical care to rural populations. Physiocratic teachings – which emphasized that the wealth of the state depended to a large degree on agriculture – undergirded these efforts. Many continental states dispatched trained medical personnel (physicians, but also surgeons, apothecaries, and midwives) to more remote areas, providing them a salary in addition to what they earned in private practice. These men and women acted not only as practitioners but also as government agents responsible for reporting on health conditions in their districts. Other measures included, for example, in France, the provision of remedies in the *boîtes des remèdes* intended for distribution in the provinces.

Increasingly as well, governments got into the business of health advice. Self-help manuals had existed for centuries, but now governments either commissioned their publication or parceled out ones considered suitable for "the people." Bernard Faust's *Catechism of Health* (*Gesundheits-Katechismus*, 1794) was introduced in schools in Hesse, for instance. Some observers roundly criticized such "popular medical enlightenment," believing that it did more harm than good. Nonetheless, it became a common policy. Moreover, the state got involved in education in other ways as well. We have seen how governments founded schools for the training of medical personnel who were not physicians. Particularly frequent was the establishment of institutions for military surgeons (such as the Pépinière that opened in Berlin in 1795) or midwives (such as the midwifery school set up in Hanover in 1751). But the expansion of health education did not halt there. Several countries, including Sweden and some of the Italian and German states, added basic medical training to theological curricula to make pastors and priests better able to assist their congregations physically as well as religiously. Louis XV of France licensed the midwife Madame du Coudray to travel throughout France, offering instruction in delivering babies safely (always a populationist concern). Over the years of her "mission" she taught more than 5,000 women and perhaps as many as 500 physicians and surgeons.

In conclusion, then, the eighteenth century both built on the ideas and institutions it had inherited from earlier periods and added its own significant contributions as well. Perhaps the most important underlying cause of new initiatives in medicine and public health in these years lay the changing character of European economy and society. While mortality rates did not appreciably decline (or begin to decline) until the very end of the century, a growing number of practitioners and practices offered hope in many ways. But it was not only hope that was dished up – so, too, was a wide panoply of places and projects – hospitals, dispensaries, and other charitable institutions – that promised assistance for those clinging to the lower rungs of the social ladder. And in the bustling emporium that Europe was becoming in these decades, a whole range of people – from the affluent to the not-so well-off – could seek to regain their health from many purveyors and in many locations.

Bibliography

Alexander, J. T., *Bubonic Plague in Early Modern Russia: Public Health and Urban Disaster* (new edn., New York, 2002).

Brockliss, L. and C. Jones, *The Medical World of Early Modern France* (Oxford, 1997).

Broman, T. H., "The medical sciences," in D. C. Lindberg and R. L. Numbers (eds.), *The Cambridge History of Science*, vol. 4: *The Eighteenth Century*, ed. R. Porter (Cambridge, 2003).

Bynum, W. F. and R. Porter (eds.), *Medical Fringe and Medical Orthodoxy, 1750–1850* (London, 1987).

Cavallo, S., *Charity and Power in Early Modern Italy: Benefactors and their Motives in Turin, 1541–1789* (Cambridge, 1995).

Conrad, L. I., et al., *The Western Medical Tradition: 800 BC to AD 1800* (Cambridge, 1995).

Cook, H. J., *The Decline of the Old Medical Regime in Stuart London* (Ithaca, NY, 1986).

Cunningham, A. and R. French (eds.), *The Medical Enlightenment of the Eighteenth Century* (Cambridge, 1990).

Duden, B., *The Woman Beneath the Skin: A Doctor's Patients in Eighteenth-Century Germany*, (Cambridge, MA, 1991).

Fissell, M. E., *Patients, Power, and the Poor in Eighteenth-Century Bristol* (Cambridge, 1991).

Foucault, M., *The Birth of the Clinic* (London, 1973).

Gelbart, N. R., *The King's Midwife: A History and Mystery of Madame du Coudray* (Berkeley, 1998).

Gelfand, T., *Professionalizing Modern Medicine: Paris Surgeons and Medical Science and Institutions in the 18th Century* (New York, 1980).

Gentilcore, D., *Healers and Healing in Early Modern Europe* (Manchester, 1998).

Gentilcore, D., *Medical Charlatanism in Early Modern Italy* (New York, 2006).

Hopkins, D. R., *The Greatest Killer: Smallpox and History* (Chicago, 2002).

King, L., *The Medical World of the Eighteenth Century* (Chicago, 1958).

King, L., *The Philosophy of Medicine: The Early Eighteenth Century* (Cambridge, MA, 1978).

Kiple, K. F. (ed.), *The Cambridge World History of Human Disease* (Cambridge, 1993).

Kiple, K. F., *The Cambridge Historical Dictionary of Disease* (Cambridge, 2003).

Lawrence, S. C., *Charitable Knowledge: Hospital Pupils and Practitioners in Eighteenth-Century London* (Cambridge, 1995).

Lindemann, M., *Health and Healing in Eighteenth-Century Germany* (Baltimore, 1996).

Lindemann, M., *Medicine and Society in Early Modern Europe* (Cambridge, 1999).

McGrew, R., *Encyclopedia of Medical History* (New York, 1995).

McNeill, W., *Plagues and Peoples* (rev. edn., New York, 1997).

Marland (ed.), H., *The Art of Midwifery: Early Modern Midwives in Europe* (London, 1993).

Porter, D. and R. Porter, *Patient's Progress Doctors and Doctoring in Eighteenth-Century England* (Stanford, 1989).

Porter, R. (ed.), *Patients and Practitioners: Lay Perceptions of Medicine in Pre-Industrial Society* (Cambridge, 1985).

Porter, R., *Health for Sale: Quackery in England, 1660–1850* (Manchester and New York, 1989).

Porter, R., *The Greatest Benefit to Mankind: A Medical History of Humanity* (New York, 1997).
Ramsey, M., *Professional and Popular Medicine in France, 1770–1830: The Social World of Medical Practice* (Cambridge, 1988).
Razell, P., *The Conquest of Smallpox: The Impact of Inoculation on Smallpox Mortality in Eighteenth-Century Britain* (Southampton, 1977).
Riley, J. C., *The Eighteenth-Century Campaign to Avoid Disease* (New York, 1987).
Riley, J. C., *Sickness, Recovery, and Death* (Iowa City, 1989).
Risse, G., *Hospital Life in Enlightenment Scotland: Care and Teaching at the Royal Infirmary of Edinburgh* (Cambridge, 1987).
Rosenberg, C., *Explaining Epidemics and Other Studies in the History of Medicine* (Cambridge, 1992).
Rosner, L., *Medical Education in the Age of Improvement: Edinburgh Students and Apprentices, 1760–1820* (Edinburgh, 1991).
Starr, Paul, *The Social Transformation of American Medicine: The Rise of a Sovereign Profession and the Making of a Vast Industry* (New York, 1982).
Weiner, D., *The Citizen-Patient in Revolutionary and Imperial Paris* (Baltimore, 1993).
Wellman, K., *La Mettrie: Medicine, Philosophy, and Enlightenment* (Durham, NC, 1992).
Wilson, A., *The Making of the Man-Midwife: Childbirth in England, 1660–1770* (London, 1995).

Chapter Eleven

Religion

Joachim Whaley

Problems and Approaches

Earlier generations of liberal-minded historians took it as axiomatic that the century of the Enlightenment saw the decline of religious belief and the secularization of European society. Enlightenment promoted rationalism; new science undermined the basis of traditional belief; Christianity was edged out of the central position it occupied in Western society by the rise of a new "paganism." The vitriolic campaigns of Voltaire were seen as typical of the age. His denunciation of the traditional belief in providence, his campaign for toleration, and his crusade against the Christian churches, especially the Catholic Church, were taken to be pure expressions of the new tendencies, setting a standard of high progressiveness against which to judge the thoughts and endeavors of others (Gay, 1964). British thinkers in particular were rarely reckoned to be part of the Enlightenment. The French Enlightenment was viewed as the "gold standard." For it was only in France that criticism led to action and that the *ancien régime* was swept away by the revolution of 1789.

Over the last few decades scholars have significantly revised this "progressive" Franco-centric view. They have discovered the existence of indigenous Enlightenment traditions in many parts of Europe, and the notion of a direct causal relationship between Enlightenment and revolution in France has been challenged. Other Enlightenment traditions inspired by the ideas of John Locke and the Dutch Jewish philosopher Benedict de Spinoza (1632–77) have been depicted as more influential than, and independent of, developments in France (Israel, 2001).

The perspective is still often "progressive." The history of the radical Enlightenment is written as the history of the "making of modernity" (Israel, 2001). The history of the British Enlightenment is written as the "creation of the modern world" by British thinkers from the late seventeenth to the early nineteenth centuries (Porter, 2000). The key themes are the assault on Christianity and its marginalization in European society. Secularization, desacralization, and disenchantment are widely taken to describe fundamental aspects of the European experience between the seventeenth and the nineteenth centuries.

A Companion to Eighteenth-Century Europe, First Edition. Edited by Peter H. Wilson.
© 2014 John Wiley & Sons, Ltd. Published 2014 by John Wiley & Sons, Ltd.

By contrast, research focused on the role of religion has frequently raised doubts about the older-style narrative of progress. The study of eighteenth-century religion has been characterized by a rich profusion of novel approaches. "New" histories of religion have applied methods and terminology from sociology, anthropology, economic history, ethnology, and folklore studies and, more recently, gender theory. Many of these new approaches have been criticized for their essentially secular intent. They sometimes fail to take the human religious experience seriously; some treat religion merely as a vehicle for the expression of secular or material ambitions or as a tool employed by rulers for worldly purposes.

Problems of interpretation also abound. Anthropological and ethnological approaches, for example, typically seek to illuminate the religious behavior of individuals and small groups, to trace the development of religious practices at the household, local, or regional level. Yet it is not easy to relate such information to the wider history of Christianity in Europe or to construct a picture of long-term trends in the history of religious belief and practice. Since the 1920s, the French Annales school of historians has called for the study of *mentalités* over the *longue durée*. This involved the study of mindsets and attitudes as the intellectual-emotional-psychological bedrock or infrastructure of European society over the past millennium. Much fascinating research has illuminated key aspects of the history of religion, such as attitudes to birth and childhood, to love and marriage, or to death and the afterlife. Yet it has not so far produced any real certainty on the question of whether the eighteenth century really did see a process of secularization or de-Christianization, either as a fundamental social process or as something that only affected small elites.

Feminist theory has also proved interesting yet problematic. Most "feminist" research has focused on the Reformation, on aspects of Protestantism, and on the late eighteenth and the nineteenth centuries. Studies of the role of women in the Reformation, on pastors' wives, female Pietists, and women members of literary salons in the eighteenth century abound. Yet the argument that religion became "feminized" rests largely on the evidence of the nineteenth century, when women increasingly became the mainstay of Christian practice and the transmitters of belief to the family (Hersche, 2006: 86). The role of women in eighteenth-century Christianity is not yet fully understood.

Theories of State and Religion

Most new approaches in recent decades have involved broadly social and cultural treatments of the themes of secularization and de-Christianization. In the 1980s and 1990s a number of German historians sought to combine the themes of modernization, Christianization, confessionalization, and state formation into an all-embracing theory of the development of European society from around 1530 to roughly 1730. The Reformation and the Counter-Reformation, they argue following French scholars such as Jean Delumeau, marked the beginning of a thorough Christianization of European society for the first time, as reformers imposed their reform agendas on a population that had practiced an essentially heathen religion under the umbrella of the medieval Catholic Church. At the same time they linked the development of confessional churches in the sixteenth century with the process of state formation and the extension of social discipline over the population at large by secular authorities by means of ecclesiastical institutions and religious norms. Heinz Schilling and Wolfgang Reinhard argue that these developments were common to all three major Christian churches (Catholic, Lutheran and Calvinist) across Europe as a whole (Klueting, 2003).

A popular variation on their theme is the counter-argument by Winfried Schulze that the central lesson learned by Europe's elites during the confessional conflicts of the sixteenth century was the need to free human existence from the tyranny of the confessions and to develop secular or political solutions to the key problems of human coexistence in society (Schulze, 1987). Though conceived as a critique of the confessionalization thesis, Schulze's basic idea is not so different: he too sees the construction of the "modern" state as the key theme of European history since the late sixteenth century, with secular governments seeking increasingly effective ways of imposing discipline on society. That involved moral and behavioral norms often formulated within Christian theological systems, albeit applied by secular rulers for essentially secular purposes.

Schilling and Reinhard both focused on the period before 1650 and had little to say about developments thereafter. The notion of a long confessional era from 1530 to 1730 begs the question of how to characterize the eighteenth century. Furthermore, if confessionalization really was the Europe-wide motor of modernization in all three Christian churches, it becomes difficult to understand why in the eighteenth century Catholic Europe came to be perceived as backward, or indeed why there were such differences within what should, according to the theory, be confessional blocs with relatively uniform experiences. Not all Protestant areas were progressive; not all Catholic areas were backward.

The confessionalization thesis found at least one notable English champion in the person of J. C. D. Clark, who argued that Hanoverian England was a hegemonic confessional state (Clark, 1985). Following extensive debate, Clark later modified his original claims and emphasized "the dominance of certain ideas of what society's problems were and how they should be addressed" rather than the prevalence of a "uniformly successful popular morality or piety" or "denominational uniformity" (Clark, 2000: 34). Thus qualified, the term has fairly general applicability throughout Europe. To varying degrees, all eighteenth-century European states designated or maintained official or established churches and strictly regulated the terms under which those who subscribed to other churches or faiths might be permitted to live and work.

More recently two historians have focused on eighteenth-century Catholicism. Philippe Goujard's study of France, Spain, Italy, and Rhineland Germany develops a new approach to what he calls "French originality" (Goujard, 2004). The secularization of French society, he argues, pre-dates the French Revolution. The influence of the clergy had declined radically in the decades before 1789 and in some areas it collapsed completely. The emerging bourgeoisie refused to accept the second place accorded it in the social order by the church; at the same time friction developed between the clergy and the mass of the peasantry. The church, he suggests, was discredited by the bitter internal struggle between Jansenists and anti-Jansenists conducted under the sarcastic gaze of the *philosophes.* As the church lost ground and forfeited its monopoly on the expression of opinion, its former role was assumed by academies, by Masonic societies, and by the new bourgeois class of writers. The advocate took the place of the priest as the local notable. Opinion supplanted belief: public opinion itself became sacralized; religious belief became private opinion.

In other Catholic countries, according to Goujard, this process was reversed. In Spain, Italy, and Germany enlightened rulers sought to transform the state without fundamentally disturbing the existing social order. However, they failed either to improve the lot of the mass of the population or to make much impact on popular beliefs and religious practices. The bourgeoisie, which shared their enlightened ideals, was a weak ally. In the Mediterranean lands it was constrained by the iron grip of the aristocracy. In Germany the bourgeoisie lacked nothing in intellectual originality and radicalism, yet it was unable to transcend the rigid structures and rules of a deeply conservative society of estates. Enlightened rulers and their meager intellectual supporters succeeded only in marshaling against themselves social groups that opposed their rationalist reforming agendas. The clergy were the natural leaders of these diverse popular coalitions and, in assuming leadership, they reinforced their spiritual authority. The same coalition that thwarted enlightened absolutism then shortly afterwards rallied to fight the revolution when the French tried to export it to their neighbors. The counter-revolution, Goujard suggests, was already in people's minds when the revolution exploded.

Goujard suggests that de-Christianization was more pronounced in France than elsewhere in the nineteenth century. However, studies of religious observance in Germany and elsewhere in the later eighteenth century reveal similar patterns of change (Greyerz, 2000: 318–24; Pammer, 1994; Schlögl, 1995). At least some of the apparent difference between France and other countries may be explained by the fact that French historians have been investigating this theme intensively for at least 30 years (Vovelle, 1973). The formal abolition of Christianity by the Jacobins in 1793–4 had no parallel elsewhere, and religion undoubtedly played a key role in the German, Spanish, and Italian resistance to France in the 1790s. Yet religion also played a role in the French counter-revolution.

Different perspectives emerge from Peter Hersche's study of European society and culture in the age of the Baroque. This is aimed explicitly against the German confessionalization theorists and takes a broad view of the development of European Catholic society from about 1600 to the present (Hersche, 2006). Hersche dismisses the idea that post-Tridentine Catholicism was a "modernizing" force. On the contrary, Baroque Catholicism was constructed following the failure of the reforms envisaged at Trent. Contradicting Reinhard, Hersche insists that developments in Catholic and Protestant Europe were dissimilar. The reformers aimed to do too much too quickly. The congregations resisted the implementation of Tridentine decrees; the new seminaries failed to produce enough priests, and church institutions failed at every level from the diocesan synods to the parishes. Consequently the church was obliged to turn back to medieval forms of religiosity and Catholic Europe developed ecclesiastical, social, economic, and cultural forms that were the explicit antithesis of the modernizing, disciplining values of the Protestants.

The Catholic Enlightenment, Hersche argues, was fired by an acute awareness of the backwardness of Catholicism and by the ambition to catch up: it aimed to succeed where the Tridentine reformers had failed. This aggressive "anti-Baroque" movement met with staunch resistance from the laity and many lower clergy. Revulsion against the radical atheism of the French Revolution then combined with resentment at the ecclesiastical reforms of the Napoleonic period to give force to the anti-Enlightenment groups that had formed before 1789. The 1830s then saw the emergence of a "neo-Baroque" that persisted until the Second Vatican Council (1962–5) unleashed a new onslaught on traditional piety.

A Common European History?

Views on the history of religion in eighteenth-century Europe vary according to their geographical and chronological perspective. Geographical variables are most apparent in the case of Catholic Europe, where approaches that focus on explaining the singularity or originality of France have often lead to schematic treatment of other countries. Differing chronological perspectives are also significant. Some view the eighteenth century as the tail end of developments that unfolded principally in the sixteenth and seventeenth centuries. Others view it as the prelude to the nineteenth and twentieth centuries. This makes it essential to consider a "long eighteenth century" that starts well before 1700 and that finishes well after the revolutionary/ Napoleonic era, 1789–1815.

Some broad developments are common to both Catholic and Protestant Europe. First, all states were, to one degree or another, confessional states. Secondly, both Catholic and Protestant churches had to deal with challenges "from below." That could mean either popular resistance to attempts to impose a new official version of the faith and its forms of worship or revivalist movements and new forms of piety that often also involved a turn away from the official church. Thirdly, the eighteenth century saw two distinct reactions "from above." In the early eighteenth century official or orthodox authorities frequently tried to thwart or manage challenges from below. After 1750 both Catholic and Protestant churches saw efforts at enlightened reform. Fourthly, those responses and the reactions to them were profoundly affected by the upheavals of the period 1789–1815. That in turn created a new framework for the renewal of European Christianity in the nineteenth century. Within those broad parameters, however, similar movements frequently had different meanings and impacts in different contexts. Something of those national and regional variations will be indicated in what follows.

Catholic Europe

There was only one Catholic Church but there were many Catholicisms. A recent authoritative survey of the period 1540–1770 has defined three broad zones (Hsia, 2005: 43–95). The churches in Portugal, Spain, and Italy formed the "triumphant church"; Poland, the Catholic Netherlands, France, Germany, Austria, and Bohemia comprised the "militant church"; the oppressed Catholic communities of England, the Dutch Republic, Ireland, and Hungary made up the "martyred church." The zones are defined in terms of the struggle against Protestantism: "triumphant" where there were no Protestants or where Protestantism was defeated early; "militant" where the struggle against Protestantism was ongoing into the eighteenth century; "martyred" where Protestantism was dominant.

Mediterranean Catholicism was distinctive. The absence or early extirpation of Protestantism was one important feature. In Spain and Portugal the bond between church and monarchy was also reinforced by the early "nation-building" experience of an internal crusade and a subsequent overseas imperial mission. Both countries developed a powerful Inquisition that began to "discipline" the church before the Tridentine reforms were published in 1564.

Spain regarded itself as *the* Catholic nation. The Tridentine reforms failed to transform the church. This led to the perpetuation of the traditions of the late fifteenth-century "Reconquest" of Spain from Islam and the Moors. These traditions were also applied to a new imperial mission from the sixteenth century. The Spanish church embraced a wide variety of different enterprises and functions. The Jesuits pursued a continuing program of Tridentine Catholic renewal. However, a plethora of older forms of popular piety also flourished and developed new institutional forms and modes of expression. Massive investment not only in ecclesiastical buildings but in religious art, devotional trinkets, or in ritual procedures such as masses said for the dead comprised a significant "industry." The accusation by enlightened critics that Spain, like other Mediterranean societies, was "priest-ridden" and afflicted by the clergy as by a plague of leeches, underlined the extent of the phenomenon. The remedy that was applied both failed to solve it and created new problems in addition.

In Portugal seventeenth-century Catholicism was characterized by strong messianic and millenarian tendencies. These were spawned by the powerful sense of imperial mission that also generally characterized the restored monarchy from 1640. The continuing crusade against Jewish converts also focused clerical energies into the eighteenth century. At the same time the monarchy patronized the Jesuits, who both introduced elements of new Tridentine discipline at home and became a dominant force in the missionary enterprise abroad. The church fulfilled vital economic functions, and investment in church buildings and new monasteries reached an extraordinary peak between 1720 and 1750. By the eighteenth century, however, the ecclesiastical system had become bloated and conflict-ridden. Equally seriously, the clergy were beginning to lose control of the confraternities, some of which enjoyed royal protection and claimed exemption from clerical control. By the 1750s it seemed increasingly obvious to some enlightened critics that the system was ripe for reform. Pombal's expulsion of the Jesuits from Portugal in 1759 was one of the first serious blows struck against the order.

In Italy there was no central monarchy and no imperial mission (Hsia, 2005: 54–60; Ward, 1999: 39–52). However, the sense of representing the "true" Catholic Church was reinforced here by the fact that the Italians established an exclusive hold on the leadership of the church and its central institutions. The pattern of a devout north and a more indifferent south which became characteristic of all the Mediterranean countries in the nineteenth century was already emerging long before 1700 (Carroll, 1992). In Italy, unlike Spain and Portugal, this prompted a whole series of internal missions, starting in the late sixteenth century and continuing vigorously into the eighteenth century.

In northern Europe the protracted struggle against Protestantism and the engagement of the state in campaigns of systematic Catholicization or re-Catholicization had in many areas resulted in the development of more organized and controlled forms of church. At the same time, the continuing proximity to Protestantism could, depending on circumstances, either intensify dogmatic and demonstrative forms to underline differences and reinforce boundaries or moderate them in efforts to "compete" against the attraction of an internal Protestant movement. The German territories provide perhaps the most extreme form of the first case; France is an example of the second.

By the late seventeenth century the Peace of Westphalia had brought a high degree of stability to the Holy Roman Empire (Maurer, 1999: 3–6, 21–2). The end of a long period of confessional conflict marked the beginning of an equally lengthy period of consolidation. A similar development took place in the Austrian lands (including Bohemia and, with a delay of roughly half a century and even then less completely, Hungary), where Protestantism had all but taken over by the end of the sixteenth century. To that extent the Thirty Years War was both a confessional struggle as well as a constitutional conflict. Re-Catholicization made significant advances before 1648; thereafter both Habsburg political authority and the religious and intellectual foundations of the monarchy were more firmly established than ever before (Evans, 1979). A similar pattern unfolded in the Spanish Netherlands (Hsia, 2005: 65–8). In Poland the relatively tolerant pluralism established by the Warsaw Confederation of 1573 (at least for the nobility and other estates) gave way to an attempt at re-Catholicization after about 1650 that endured, without ever achieving real success, until the late 1760s.

In the Habsburg lands and the German territories the Tridentine reform program was at least partly implemented. The Jesuits played a central role and formed a core reforming elite with huge political influence and control over the upper echelons of the educational system. Yet nowhere were they able to impose their agenda on society as a whole. As in the Mediterranean world, they had to compromise with the wishes of the laity and were obliged to "develop strategies to mobilize and direct popular religiosity" (Hsia, 2005: 223). Internal missions to rural areas led by revivalist preachers were a regular feature of the larger German Catholic territories in the eighteenth century. The church authorities sought to control places of pilgrimage and to regulate the cult of saints. Much effort was devoted to channeling popular passions into the cult of the Virgin Mary, as central a figure in eighteenth-century Catholic devotion in Bavaria as in Italy. The century after 1650 also saw massive investment in building: new churches and monasteries and hugely ambitious programs for the rebuilding ("baroquization") of existing gothic structures (Beales, 2003; Hersche, 2006).

French Catholicism developed in distinctive ways. In the late sixteenth century many contemporaries believed that the French religious wars, along with the parallel conflict in the Netherlands, were the most acute confrontation between Catholicism and Protestantism. Gallicanism was a more radical form of anti-curialism than any found in the German *Reichskirche* until after 1750. Paradoxically perhaps, forthright rejection of the authority of Rome enabled the implementation of Tridentine-style reforms. Between 1642 and 1700 nearly one hundred seminaries were founded, resulting in a far greater concentration than in any other European country. A well-trained and disciplined lower clergy developed which assumed many of the conscientious attributes of the Protestant ethic (Hersche, 2006: 132). The bonds between clergy and parishioners were also reinforced; by royal decree of 1695 communities were forced to construct rectories for their priests. The Gallican tradition also allowed

France to participate in the great expansion of monastic foundations that was common to European Catholicism as a whole (Beales, 2003: 84–111).

The need to confront the Huguenot challenge had also shaped French Catholicism. In 1700, for example, Joseph Addison observed that French Catholicism was less characterized by ceremonies and superstition than that of Naples or Spain, because the French had undergone a "secret Reformation," not least due to the permanent competition with the Huguenots (Hersche, 2006: 126). The Huguenots were expelled following the revocation of the Edict of Nantes (1598) in 1685, but nearly a century of uneasy coexistence with this politically adroit, economically successful, and intellectually sophisticated minority had left its mark on the dominant Catholic Church. Jansenism and its parallel movement among the lower clergy, Richerism, promoted essentially Tridentine values. It was ascetic, rationalist, and cerebral, as well as pious enough to be attractive to Protestants, and it generated an unusual profusion of spiritual literature as well as the adoption of the vernacular Bible, Mass, and breviary. "Gallican" music focused on simple motets with few voices rather than the grandiose Roman style that found favor in Vienna and the German courts. "Gallican" churches were austerely classical compared with the boundless profusion of post-Bernini Baroque elsewhere. Baroque styles only took root on the periphery: in the Basque country, Roussillon and Provence, the Dauphiné, Franche Comté, Lorraine, Picardy, Artois, and Hainaut (Hersche, 2006: 145–6). On the other hand, the convulsionary cult that erupted at Saint-Médard in Paris in 1727 and that flourished until the cemetery was closed by royal decree in January 1732 demonstrated that the French public was just as avid for miraculous religious experience as its counterparts in Spain or south Germany (McManners, 1998: vol. 2, pp. 436–55).

Despite the differences between the various European Catholic traditions, they all went through the same mill of Enlightenment criticism from the 1740s. Both Protestant and Catholic observers increasingly commented on the inherent backwardness of Catholic societies. Feast days struck them as unproductive leisure time rather than as a valuable spiritual investment. Investment in churches, or church art, or devotional practices involving votive candles or masses for the dead were denounced as a simple waste of money, at worst deluded or even fraudulent practices. The chorus of condemnation of the monasteries as temples of idleness echoed the most virulent anticlericalism of the Reformation. The campaign against the Jesuits, ironically actually pro-Enlightenment in many parts, marked the culmination of state-driven reform of the national churches, with the Papacy acquiescing in a general ban in 1773 to the jubilation of Catholic reformers, and Protestants, throughout Europe. In Spain, Portugal, Italy, Austria, and many of the German territories enlightened reforms attempted to remedy the defects of the church. Many of the reformers were driven by anti-curialism and inspired by a kind of rigorism and piety similar to that espoused by the Jansenists whom the French Crown had suppressed (Outram, 1995: 43–4). The reforms everywhere remained incomplete. There was widespread clerical resistance; the laity stubbornly refused to abandon its old "irrational" and "superstitious" forms of worship. In southwest Germany in the 1770s and 1780s, for example, as enlightened reformers were seeking to bring rational order to religion, thousands flocked to be cured in mass exorcisms performed by the traditionalist priest Johann Joseph Gassner (Midelfort, 2005).

Was France really different? Not long after Gassner's appearance amongst the simple folk of southwest Germany, Franz Anton Mesmer (a Swabian "scientist" who had pronounced Gassner to be a sincere possessor of unusual levels of animal magnetism) enjoyed a similar success in Parisian polite society (Darnton, 1968). Belief in supernatural forces transcended national and class boundaries. The reform of the monasteries begun by the royal *commission des réguliers* in 1766 also paralleled developments elsewhere (Beales, 2003: 169–78). The coruscating criticism of Voltaire and others undoubtedly gave impetus to the reformers. Yet a tradition of aggressively secularist French historical research has often ignored the persistence of the church and the clergy as a political, religious, and moral force in France up to and during the revolution. Goujard's argument that by 1789 the *avocat* had supplanted the *curé* seems to overlook the fact that the monarchy's defeat in the assembly of notables in 1787 was led by archbishops and that the clergy led the way into constitutional reform (McManners, 1998: vol. 2, pp. 661–744; Ward, 1999: 235). They were not the only victims of the upheavals that followed.

Protestant Europe

Protestant Europe was even more fragmented and diverse than Catholic Europe. A great range of traditions had developed across a wide variety of states. Lutheranism predominated and much of the rest adhered to Calvinism, but those broad confessional blocs accommodated many divergent and often opposing tendencies. The unity of Protestantism was often only manifest in confrontation with or in solidarity against Catholicism. Even in the Holy Roman Empire, the various Protestant territories developed distinctive theological and political traditions. If over Europe as a whole Lutheranism tended to be more cohesive, that was largely because of its prevalence in some of the larger territorial states and, above all, because of its widespread retention of an episcopal church structure. The link between German and Scandinavian Lutheranism created a supranational network, while German Lutheran universities also attracted students from Baltic, Slavic, and Hungarian Protestant communities (Hope, 1995).

Calvinism, by contrast, with its emphatically non-episcopalian traditions, was more open to the development of idiosyncratic regional and local traditions which militated against the maintenance of any overall solidarity over and above a common adherence to certain basic articles of faith (Aston, 2002: 34–5). Alongside the Lutheran and Calvinist churches with their various affiliations, a plethora of minor groups such as Anabaptists, spiritualists, and other sectarians and Dissenters also survived. These were often persecuted, or driven to emigration to the greater freedom of North America, though the eighteenth century also saw a greater toleration of such groups in Europe, not least for economic reasons.

Despite the variety within Protestantism, the pattern in the eighteenth century of challenge "from below" or from within followed by a challenge "from above" or from outside was fairly uniform. The most important challenge to established Protestantism was German Pietism. There is little agreement on the origins of this movement (Greyerz, 2000). Some seek its origins in late sixteenth-century Dutch and German calls for "further Reformation" or a "Reformation of life." Others underline the influence of English Puritanism. Some insist that Pietism originated before the Thirty Years War (Pre-Pietism); others see it as a reaction to the devastation wrought by the war. Some argue that it developed entirely within the Lutheran Church as a reaction to an ossification of dogma and ritual that set in once Lutheranism became an established religion of state. Others place weight on the influence of mystical spiritualists such as Jacob Böhme (1575–1624) or maverick insiders such as the Rosicrucian Johann Valentin Andreae (1586–1654) and his broad circle of Lutheran-Calvinist millenarians, pansophists, and alchemists.

Many factors combined in the movement founded by the Frankfurt pastor Philipp Jakob Spener (1635–1705). In 1670 he formed his "Collegium Pietatis"; in 1675 he published his *Pia Desideria*, the core text of the movement. Spener taught personal piety over dogma, good works over formal religious observance, study of the Bible over service to the worldly church: practical Christianity and renewal of the church by and through the spiritual rebirth of its members. The initial focus of the movement was urban rather than rural. Soon Pietist "collegia" were found in most German-speaking Lutheran cities from Bern to Hamburg and Stockholm, and by the 1690s the movement had gained such momentum that the orthodox felt seriously threatened. Two aspects of its further development are important for eighteenth-century Protestantism.

Pietism became the foundation and mainstay what has been termed the Protestant Evangelical Awakening (Ward, 1992). This was fed by a widespread fear of a "confessional Armageddon." Despite the stability afforded by the Peace of Westphalia, continuing religious conflict elsewhere fueled anxieties about a possible breakdown in Germany. Huguenots expelled from France and refugees from the bloody suppression of the Camisard rebellion of 1702–5 fueled these anxieties (Ward, 1999: 16–18). In Silesia, revival was a reaction to the Habsburg persecution of Protestants, who were ministered to by Pietist missionaries from Halle, who in turn broadcast news of their suffering and of their extraordinary religious experiences. Pietist groups also coordinated the "rescue" of the Protestants expelled from Salzburg in 1731 (Walker, 1992). Pietism formed the bedrock of the Moravian movement, which grew from modest beginnings on Nikolaus von Zinzendorf's (1700–60) estate at Herrenhut in Saxony, and which proved even more active and more successful than the original Pietists in missions to the Baltic, the United Kingdom, and the American colonies. Revival also swept through the Calvinist communities of northwest Germany and into the Dutch Republic, the key figure here being the mystic Gerhard Tersteegen (1697–1769) (Ward, 1999: 128–31). By 1800 Pietism had transformed the religious culture of much of Protestant Europe and had determined the predominantly Baptist and Methodist character of American Protestantism. If the "awakening" failed to transform society as a whole, it certainly shaped the modern world as much as the Enlightenment did.

The second key aspect of the development of Pietism was its interaction with the secular authorities. In Brandenburg-Prussia, a predominantly Lutheran territory with a Reformed Calvinist ruling house, the Pietists purposefully forged a strong alliance with the state. Early initiatives such as the foundation of the Halle orphanage in 1695 by Hermann August Francke (1663–1727) involved a range of practical and commercial enterprises, some missionary, others with wider social and Christian reforming aims. The monarchy supported them because they were useful social and economic reformers, a movement that could mobilize and discipline the laity in the service of state and society. Another attraction was that they disrupted the alliance between the established Lutheran Church and the estates.

A similar effect is apparent in England. The Hanoverians were acutely aware of the need to secure their rule. The Society for the Propagation of Christian Knowledge (1698) and the Society for the Propagation of the Gospel (1701) were originally founded to supply the needs of the American colonies. After 1715, however, they came increasingly under the influence of the German Pietists imported by the Hanoverians. Christianizing the population at home, combating Quakerism and dissent, and integrating Wales and Scotland all became part of the Anglican mission, though the colonies remained a key concern. John Wesley (1703–91), originally a xenophobic High Churchman, was changed by his encounters with the London and Herrenhut Moravians. His conversion experience at Herrenhut led to the first of his field preaching tours in England in 1739. Though it later became a separate church, Wesley's Methodist movement initially saw itself as network of loyal Anglicans seeking to renew the Church of England from within (O'Gorman, 1997: 302–9). Wesley remained loyal to the Crown throughout his life; indeed his initial antipathy to the Hanoverians turned into steadfast support for George III and opposition to the Wilkites and other radicals, both political and religious.

Elsewhere Pietism assumed a more radical political complexion. In Württemberg, for example, Pietism became linked with the resistance of the estates to the absolutist tendencies and Catholic sympathies of the ruling dynasty (Fulbrook, 1983). Despite the initial success of the orthodox authorities at the University of Tübingen in having Pietists expelled, the movement gained ground steadily. By 1743 a government decree recognized the Pietist conventicles as lawful and formally accepted them into the territorial church. Pietism thus ultimately joined the establishment in Württemberg and shaped the development of the Württemberg church into the twentieth century. Elsewhere, however, it fragmented into radical separatism, individual spiritualism, or quiet Philadelphian communitarianism lived out in domestic communities characterized by piety, humility, unostentatious good works, and a simple faith (Maurer, 1999: 28–30).

By 1700 the turn towards rationalism was also already well under way. Pietism itself predisposed many Lutheran thinkers to enlightened ideas. The attack on the dogmatic certainties of orthodox Lutheranism and the new emphasis on personal piety and practical Christianity encouraged a sense of a need to "modernize" the church. Other significant influences such as John Locke, Pierre Bayle, English deism, physico-theology, and Spinoza also persuaded many of the need for a new approach. The discussion of natural religion was central to the emergence of a new theological consensus. The discussion flourished most openly in England; elsewhere there were few open converts to its most radical forms. Most German Lutheran thinkers formulated their views in opposition to what were perceived as atheistic tendencies.

This was due primarily to the development of philosophical rationalism in the Protestant German universities from about 1680, and in the new periodical literature that emerged in the 1720s. In different ways the leading thinkers of this movement, such as Leibniz (1646–1716), Christian Thomasius (1655–1728), and Christian Wolff (1679–1754), all sought to reconcile reason with revelation and faith, and to reconcile the findings of new scientific discoveries with traditional Christianity. They did not reject the established Lutheran Church but they insisted that religion must eschew the destructive confessional polemics of the past. Like the Pietists, though opposed by them, they were concerned with practical religion. They insisted that religion must be useful to man and society (arguing from an optimistic view of the potential of human reason rather than, like the Pietists, from the need of the individual to atone for his sins). Philosophical rationalism achieved its most systematic elaboration in the 1720s in the writings of Christian Wolff, whose students and disciples set the tone until the 1780s.

German Lutheranism proved singularly susceptible to the influence of Enlightenment ideas. There was no conflict between the new philosophy and the dominant theological trends. In view of the integration of the German territorial church into the state, the symbiotic relationship of *Aufklärung* and Lutheran thinking also had important practical consequences. Protestant churchmen engaged enthusiastically in the cause of practical reform. Some argue that their strong commitment to a "Christian" reform of society under the direction of the state fostered inherently quietist and conformist traditions in German society. Yet they were by no means uncritical of authority, and their commitment to reform rather than revolution mirrored attitudes in the German lands generally.

The new direction in theology was initiated by Johann Franz Buddeus (1667–1729) and Christoph Matthäus Pfaff (1686–1760) (Saine, 1997). Both combined elements of traditional orthodoxy with new Pietist attitudes in their efforts to combat atheism. Their "rational" or "enlightened" orthodoxy was translated into a wholehearted embrace of Wolff's system by Siegmund Jakob Baumgarten (1706–57), a man praised by Voltaire as the "crown of German scholars" and by others as the "oracle of the German theologians." From 1734 he transformed Halle, formerly the center of north German Pietism, into the leading university of the Protestant *Aufklärung* or Neologism that dominated Lutheran theology for the next half-century.

The Neologians measured everything against reason. They did not reject revelation, but viewed anything that did not conform to reason as an accidental historical addition or as plain deception. In Scripture they sought by means of textual analysis to distinguish between the word of God and the historical description of human actions. They affirmed the divinity of Christ. However, they tended to view him not as the Son of God or as the savior but as a noble teacher of mankind like Socrates. Their strongly historical approach and emphasis on social ethics also generated a strong commitment to religious toleration and a renewed interest in the reunification of the Christian churches. Some later charged that the Neologians had destroyed religion and deprived theology of its meaning and content. Frequent sermons on subjects such as inoculation, eating habits, even prudent coppice management or animal husbandry, seem to justify the derision subsequently poured on them. On the other hand sermons against slavery, dueling, torture, capital punishment, or simple bad government confound any view that the enlightened clergy were merely servile conformists (Stroup, 1984).

The Neologians were finally undermined by the reaction against the news of the French Revolution. Increasingly, during the 1790s, any form of practical or rational Christianity seemed suspect as incitement to rebellion against properly constituted authority. It was several decades before enlightened Protestantism reappeared as liberal Protestantism, though now struggling to make up ground lost to conservative and traditionalist tendencies.

Coexistence and Toleration

Arguments for religious toleration, at least among Christians, had been advanced since the sixteenth century. By 1700 numerous theological, political, and economic arguments for toleration were available. Equally, however, almost all states had evolved into confessional states that equated religious conformity with political loyalty (Whaley, 2000, 2006). In practice only weak regimes or areas in which the competing confessional groups were equally balanced in political terms did toleration settlements develop, for example before 1650 in Transylvania, Hungary, or Poland. The norm was the confessional state that regarded the church as an essential partner and its institutions, down to the grassroots in the parishes, as essential agencies of government. If the century also saw the gradual decline of theories that justified kingship by divine right, coronation ceremonies everywhere generally still emphasized the proximity of the newly crowned king to the church and to God. Frederick the Great, who insisted on a relatively modest and emphatically secular ceremony, was the exception rather than the archetypical model of his age (Aston, 2002: 153–6).

In general, the eighteenth century saw the strengthening of aspirations to make the confessional state work. Enlightened reform of the churches, both Protestant and Catholic, sought to make them more useful to state and society. The reformers aimed to make Christianity a vehicle for the promotion of good citizenship. The extent to which that was successful must be open to doubt: none of the eighteenth-century church reform movements really mastered the religious beliefs of the people. Popular religion remained stubbornly superstitious. Even the educated elites were often in thrall to "scientific" beliefs that would be regarded as deeply superstitious in the early twenty-first century.

There was, however, considerable scope for minority groups, either Christians or Jews, to be specifically licensed: permitted to exist as religious communities, generally without political rights and often against payment of special tributes or taxes. This kind of concession was particularly common in the Holy Roman Empire, where mercantilist and cameralist theorists advocated the favorable treatment of economically useful minorities provided they did not threaten or disrupt the prevailing religion. An unusual feature of the Peace of Westphalia was that it guaranteed the property rights and freedom of conscience of the Lutheran, Calvinist, and Catholic subjects of the Holy Roman Empire: no ruler could oblige anyone to convert, and while, under certain circumstances, rulers could force those who did not subscribe to the official faith to leave, they were subject to elaborate rules concerning the management or sale of the individual's property. The idea that this made the Holy Roman Empire into an "exemplary multi-confessional country in the middle of Europe" is probably a little optimistic (Schindling, 1996: 59). In those places, mostly imperial cities, where a bi-confessional or tri-confessional status quo was confirmed in 1648 there is little evidence of any genuine growing together of the religious communities during the eighteenth century (François, 1991; Gantet, 2001).

Overall, arguments for toleration gathered ground steadily. Pragmatic arguments based on economic motives were probably most important. However, notable examples of persecution, such as the expulsion of the Huguenots from France in 1685 or of the Protestants from Salzburg, strengthened pleas for the humanity and reasonableness of toleration. If toleration became a Protestant cause in the first instance and if Protestant states extended toleration first, the polemics of Voltaire and Diderot were also important in generating a wider sense that toleration was a simple human duty in Christian or Western society. In the case of the Jews, especially in the north European Ashkenazi communities, that intellectual drift was mirrored by a Jewish Enlightenment that developed both indigenously and in parallel to the movement from Pietism to rationalism in northern Lutheranism (Feiner, 2002). From about 1750 religious freedom became viewed as one of a number of inalienable human rights (Whaley, 2006). This gained expression in the Virginia Bill of Rights of 1776, for example, but the development of the idea in most parts of the Old World was interrupted by the French Revolution of 1789.

Revolution and Renewal

If the French Revolution began as a political constitutional reform movement at least partly led by the clergy, it soon took a more radical turn. The Jacobins formally abolished Christianity in 1793–4 and imposed a new cult of reason, thereby creating essentially a secularized version of an extreme confessional state. A more significant development was the Directory's adoption of the doctrine of state neutrality in matters of religion in 1795, a policy also advocated by influential German commentators (Whaley, 2006) That was probably also closer to how Thomas Paine (1737–1809) understood the concept of freedom and its application to the role of the state in religious matters. "Mind thine own concerns," he admonished both those who would withhold toleration and those who would grant it; each, he said, was in reality equally despotic (Paine, 2000: 102). The main effect in France of the radical anti-Christian campaigns of the Jacobins seems to have been to intimidate many people from practicing as Christians. Only a small minority was attracted by the new deistic religious cults that sprang up; the majority internalized their religion, though Catholic clergy played a key role in the Vendée Revolt of 1793–6. Despite sometimes protracted regional resistance, the long-term result of the Jacobin phase was to shatter "the assumption that state and historic faith were mutually supportive" in France (Aston, 2002: 217).

Even before the "export" of the French Revolution brought militant anti-Christian ideology to many parts of Europe, the fear of revolution had generated a reaction against progressive reform. Everywhere the reformers were now suspect as subversive elements, and the reinforcement of traditional religion seemed the most logical way of inoculating the people against revolutionary ideas. Most governments persisted in (mis)representing the French as atheists and subverters of authority, order, and morality. Then, when resistance to French invasion and occupation became a necessity, traditional religion often formed an important unifying bond. Religion was probably more important than royalism in the counter-revolution. Indeed even in the 1790s there were signs of tension between the two. Some religious revivalists were buoyed up by precisely the same hopes for the general improvement of mankind as had inspired the revolutionaries. Consequently their visions of monarchy and society often contained "democratic" elements that made them deeply suspect to the monarchical regimes. The Prussian monarchy was not alone in fearing the "Jacobin" tendencies of some of its own supporters such as Novalis or Fichte, just as Hardenberg's diagnosis of the need for "democratic principles in a monarchical government" struck many conservative nobles as playing with fire (Whaley, 1996: 65).

Elements of the revolutionary and Napoleonic regimes survived to shape the post-1815 political-constitutional settlement. In particular the legislation granting freedom of worship to Christians who did not belong to the dominant or established church or to the Jews proved difficult to roll back completely. However, restrictions on the grant of civil and political rights to such groups frequently remained in force: the question of their removal became one of the most bitterly debated issues of the nineteenth century. The revival of both Catholic and Protestant churches after 1815 was marked by the launch of internal missions designed to reclaim the ground lost during the period before 1815. That had an obvious social dimension as the churches sought to "Christianize" the expanding urban centers. It also had an important political dimension. Germany was not the only country where the churches, along with others, fought a running battle against the "ideas of 1789" (Burleigh, 2005).

Bibliography

Aston, N., *Christianity and Revolutionary Europe c.1750–1830* (Cambridge, 2002).

Beales, D. E. D., *Prosperity and Plunder: European Catholic Monasteries in the Age of Revolution, 1650–1815* (Cambridge, 2003).

Beutel, A., *Aufklärung in Deutschland* (Göttingen, 2006).

Brown, S. J. and T. Tackett (eds.), *Cambridge History of Christianity*, vol. 7: *Enlightenment, Reawakening and Revolution 1660–1815* (Cambridge, 2006).

Burleigh, M., *Earthly Powers: The Conflict between Religion and Politics from the French Revolution to the Great War* (London, 2005).

Carroll, M. P., *Madonnas that Maim: Popular Catholicism in Italy since the Fifteenth Century* (Baltimore, 1992).

Clark, J. C. D., *English Society 1688–1832: Ideology, Social Structure and Political Practice during the Ancien Régime* (Cambridge, 1985).

Clark, J. C. D., *English Society, 1660–1832: Religion, Ideology and Politics during the Ancien Régime* (Cambridge, 2000).

Darnton, R., *Mesmerism and the End of the Enlightenment in France* (Cambridge, MA, 1968).

Evans, R. J. W., *The Making of the Habsburg Monarchy 1550–1700* (Oxford, 1979).

Feiner, S., *The Jewish Enlightenment* (Philadelphia, 2002).

François, E., *Die unsichtbare Grenze. Protestanten und Katholiken in Augsburg 1648–1806* (Sigmaringen, 1991).

Fulbrook, M., *Piety and Politics: Religion and the Rise of Absolutism in England, Württemberg and Prussia* (Cambridge, 1983).

Gantet, C., *La Paix de Westphalie (1648): Une histoire sociale, XVIIe–XVIIIe siècles* (Paris, 2001).

Gay, P., *The Party of Humanity: Essays in the French Enlightenment* (New York, 1964).

Goujard, P., *L'Europe catholique au XVIIIe siècle: Entre intégrisme et laïcisation* (Rennes, 2004).

Greyerz, K. v., *Religion und Kultur. Europa 1500–1800* (Darmstadt, 2000).

Hersche, P., *Muße und Verschwendung. Europäische Gesellschaft und Kultur im Barockzeitalter* (2 vols., Freiburg, 2006).

Hope, N., *German and Scandinavian Protestantism 1700–1918* (Oxford, 1995).
Hsia, R. P., *The World of Catholic Renewal 1540–1770* (2nd edn., Cambridge, 2005).
Israel, J. I., *Radical Enlightenment: Philosophy and the Making of Modernity 1650–1750* (Oxford, 2001).
Klueting, H., "'Zweite Reformation'" – Konfessionsbildung – Konfessionalisierung. Zwanzig Jahre Kontroversen und Ergebnisse nach zwanzig Jahren," *Historische Zeitschrift*, 277 (2003), 309–41.
McManners, J., *Church and Society in Eighteenth-Century France* (2 vols., Oxford, 1998).
Maurer, M., *Kirche, Staat und Gesellschaft im 17. und 18. Jahrhundert* (Munich, 1999).
Midelfort, H. C. E., *Exorcism and Enlightenment: Johann Joseph Gassner and the Demons of Eighteenth-Century Germany* (New Haven, 2005).
O'Gorman, F., *The Long Eighteenth Century: British Political and Social History 1688–1832* (London, 1997).
Outram, D., *The Enlightenment* (Cambridge, 1995).
Paine, T., *Political Writings* (2nd edn., Cambridge, 2000).
Pammer, M., *Glaubensabfall und wahre Andacht. Barockreligiosität, Reformkatholizismus und Laizismus in Oberösterreich 1700–1820* (Vienna and Munich, 1994).
Porter, R., *Enlightenment: Britain and the Creation of the Modern World* (London, 2000).
Saine, T. P., *The Problem of Being Modern or the German Pursuit of Enlightenment from Leibniz to the French Revolution* (Detroit, 1997).
Schindling, A., "Glaubensvielfalt als Kulturkonflikt. Europa in der Frühen Neuzeit," in Klaus J. Bade (ed.), *Die multikulturelle Herausforderung. Menschen über Grenzen – Grenzen über Menschen* (Munich, 1996), 46–66.
Schlögl, R., *Glaube und Religion in der Säkularisierung. Die katholische Stadt: Köln, Aachen, Münster 1700–1840* (Munich, 1995).
Schulze, W., *Einführung in die neuere Geschichte* (Munich, 1987).
Shaw, J., *Miracles in Enlightenment England* (New Haven, 2006).
Stroup, J., *The Struggle for Identity in the Clerical Estate: Northwest German Protestant Opposition to Absolutist Policy in the Eighteenth Century* (Leiden, 1984).
Vovelle, M., *Piété baroque et déchristianisation en Provence au XVIIIe siècle: Les Attitudes devant la mort d'après les clauses des testaments* (Paris, 1973).
Walker, M., *The Salzburg Transaction: Expulsion and Redemption in Eighteenth-Century Germany* (Ithaca, 1992).
Ward, M. R., *The Protestant Evangelical Awakening* (Cambridge, 1992).
Ward, M. R., *Christianity under the Ancien Régime 1648–1789* (Cambridge, 1999).
Whaley, J., "Thinking about Germany, 1750–1815: the birth of a nation?," *Publications of the English Goethe Society*, ns 66 (1996), 53–72.
Whaley, J., "A tolerant society? Religious toleration in the Holy Roman Empire, 1648–1806," in R. Porter and O. P. Grell (eds.), *Toleration in Enlightenment Europe* (Cambridge, 2000), pp. 175–95.
Whaley, J., "Religiöse Toleranz als allgemeines Menschenrecht in der Frühen Neuzeit?," in G. Schmidt, M. van Gelderen, and C. Snigula (eds.), *Kollektive Freiheitsvorstellungen im frühneuzeitlichen Europa (1400–1850)* (Frankfurt am Main, 2006).

Chapter Twelve

Popular Culture and Sociability

Beat Kümin

> [Our hamlet contained] only two houses. . . . My grandmother and the woman next door were sisters, devout old ladies whom other godly women from the area often visited. There were many pious people, then. . . . Their teacher was a tall man who lived off a little spinning and alms. . . . My grandmother often took me along to their meetings. I cannot remember what exactly went on, only that I got incredibly bored. I had to sit quietly or even kneel. . . . Now and then, however, my grandfather snatched me away up the mountain to where our cows were grazing. Here he showed me different kinds of birds, beetles and worms, while he cleaned the fields. . . . I cannot remember whether other boys attended, but do recall some adolescent girls playing with me. (Bräker, 1789: ch. VI)

Reminiscing about his youth in the 1740s, Ulrich Bräker – the son of a rural laborer in the Swiss Toggenburg – records a broad panorama of sociable occasions: neighborly exchange, religious assemblies, agricultural work, and children's games. His memories about them are mixed, reflecting the differentiated nature of everyday life and the ambivalence of many aspects of popular culture:

> [In 1737, a group of over 100 villagers assembled outside] the dwelling house of Charles Jones, Gent. did make an Assault upon Mary his wife and in a sporting manner did demand were the black Bull was, meaning the said Charles Jones, and in such Riotous manner did run up and down the Church Town of Aveton Gifford [Devon, England] with black and Disguised Faces carrying a large pair of Rams Horns tipt like Gold and adorned with Ribbons and Flowers with a mock child made of rags, and having an Ass whereon the said John Macey [a miller] and John Pinwell [a laborer] rid, dressed in a Ludicrous manner, back to back, with beating of Drums and winding of Hunting Horns and . . . and Reading a Scandalous Libellous paper, making loud Huzzahs Hallows and out Cries and so continuing for the space of 5 hours. (Reay, 1998: 157–8)

This notorious practice, known as "charivari" or rough music, was directed against members of the community who fell foul of accepted norms and values, here probably by fathering an illegitimate child. Combining elements from oral as well

A Companion to Eighteenth-Century Europe, First Edition. Edited by Peter H. Wilson.
© 2014 John Wiley & Sons, Ltd. Published 2014 by John Wiley & Sons, Ltd.

as written culture, it featured an idiosyncratic mixture of processions, dramatic scenes, and moral censure, with more than a hint of violence and disorder. It is this multiplicity of meanings which makes the study of popular culture such a challenging exercise.

The State of Research

Ever since the pioneering work of Antonio Gramsci, students of popular culture have faced enormous methodical obstacles due to the indirect nature of surviving source material (court records, chapbook literature, and visual depictions – to name but a few of the most prominent genres – all being "tainted" by the influence of learned elites), imprecise demarcations (with regard to the range of people, activities, and values to be scrutinized), and complicating variables such as region, gender and socio-economic setting (Scribner, 1989). Yet despite a barrage of fundamental questions the concept inspired a continuous stream of anthologies (e.g. Beauroy et al., 1976; Dülmen and Schindler, 1984; Kaplan, 1984; Harris, 1995; Reay, 1985; Yeo and Yeo, 1981), source collections (Furnari 1980; Geldern and McReynolds, 1998; Mullan and Reid, 2000) and works of synthesis, both on a national (Muchembled, 1985) and wider comparative level (Burke, 1994; Rogers, 2006). Simplifying dramatically, metanarratives have moved from Peter Burke's seminal distinction between a universally shared "little tradition" and a "great tradition" reserved to learned elites (who tended to withdraw from the former by the end of the early modern period), towards notions of a more differentiated range of overlapping and interacting "cultures" (Camporesi, 1991; Reay, 1998). In a related shift, scholars now often aim to detect how specific texts, rituals, and artifacts get "appropriated" by users in different contexts, rather than hoping to reconstruct the cultural profile of an entire group (Chartier, 1987).

Mindful of the need to avoid acknowledged problems of definition (stretching "culture" to include virtually all aspects of human experience while limiting the pool of "popular" subjects too rigidly), this brief survey adopts a pragmatic approach. In what follows, "popular culture" is taken to include all "articulations" of commonly held meanings, attitudes, and values addressed to an audience without specific qualifications of education or wealth. The emphasis thus lies on forms of communication primarily based on (but by no means restricted to) face-to-face exchange, local custom, and the vernacular. This kind of framework combines a clear focus – sociable interaction (rather than private mentalities or purely individual pursuits) – with the necessary flexibility regarding the occasions, participants, and media involved. It thus requires close scrutiny of where, when, and why people came together.

Building on foundations laid in French scholarship (Agulhon, 1966; Gutton 1979), historians have become increasingly attuned to the importance of sociability patterns for the cultural life of any group or period, not just through institutionalized bodies such as confraternities and academies, but also everyday contexts like meals and rites of passage (Otto Ulbricht in Albrecht et al., 2003: 372). The eighteenth century, of course, has long been acknowledged as the "associational age" (Clark, 2000; Im Hof, 1982). Contemporaries joined a plethora of societies dedicated to literary, musical, scientific, charitable, or simply convivial objectives. In England alone, some 12,000 emerged during the 1700s (Clark and Houston, 2000: 587).

Upmarket venues for gatherings – principally the salons and coffeehouses of major cities – allowed select elites to engage in polite reasoning informed by a proliferation of newspapers and learned periodicals (Ellis, 2005; Kale, 2005; see chapters 8 and 9 above). At the same time, traditional pastimes like carnivals, midsummer celebrations, and tavern drinking came under sustained attack, be it from belated enforcement campaigns of post-Tridentine Catholicism, societies for the reformation of manners in England, or Enlightenment critique in many parts of the continent (Burke, 1994: 270–9; Garrioch, 1986: 180; Malcolmson, 1973). In many ways, this echoed the disciplinarian zeal of sixteenth-century reformers, only this time the agenda reflected primarily secular and moral rather than theological motives. What flourished, in contrast, were commercial initiatives, i.e. more regular and increasingly professional ventures in the worlds of theatre, opera, sport, and the nascent entertainment industry, all tapping into growing spare resources among the upwardly mobile middling sort (Plumb in McKendrick et al., 1983; Rosseaux, 2006). The market thus permeated the cultural sphere, and few levels of society or groups remained immune to its lure. A desire for conspicuous consumption infected even the lowest income groups, with much investment in domestic furnishings, clothes, and "luxury" goods such as tobacco (Brewer and Porter, 1993; Mohrmann, 1993), but at times this had devastating consequences, as in the English gin epidemic of the early eighteenth century (Medick, 1983).

The following discussion tests and reviews this established picture, concentrating on the broad "middling" strata between poor and marginal people on the one hand and the gentry and nobility on the other (for social marginals, see chapter 7). Which activities characterized popular culture? How polarized was cultural life in town and country? To what extent did the eighteenth century mark a break with the past? Evidence drawn (mainly) from English-, French- and German-speaking Europe will help us to address these fundamental questions.

Activities, Media, and Venues

There has been much interest in the most spectacular aspects of popular culture, notably charivaris (subtly deciphered by Natalie Zemon Davis for early modern France), plebeian rioting (in E. P. Thompson's seminal discussion of the "moral economy" of the English crowd), and the gruesome, but invariably well-attended spectacle of public executions (investigated in the German context by Richard van Dülmen). Inspired by anthropological findings, all of these studies emphasize the ritual – often punitive or purifying – dimensions of such practices, their ambivalent relationship to the existing social order, and the manifold sources and media involved. What mattered to participants was to defend the rule of custom, patriarchal structures, notions of just government, and the right of subsistence (Schindler, 2002).

The early modern witch-hunt, probably the single most startling phenomenon, may have subsided by the eighteenth century, but fears and suspicions persisted, above all in rural communities. It should not be forgotten that prosecutions were still brought and "offenders" still executed. Anna Göldi, a Swiss domestic servant accused of harming – and then inexplicably healing – a child in her care, became one of the last victims in western Europe. Formally sentenced as a "poisoner," but widely believed to be a witch, she was decapitated at Glarus on June 13, 1782. The case sent shock waves through Enlightenment circles and the German press (Historical Dictionary of Switzerland). Many more criminal proceedings related to what authorities regarded as another corrosive aspect of popular attitudes, that of illegitimate sexual relations. Three years after Göldi's case, a London jury convicted Jane Allen for committing bigamy, i.e. marrying another man at a time when she was still the wife of butcher Robert Allen; in 1726 the same court had sentenced the brothel-keeper Margaret Clap "to stand in the Pillory in Smith field, pay a Fine of 20 Marks, and suffer two Years Imprisonment . . . for keeping a House in which she procur'd and encourag'd Persons to commit Sodomy" (Proceedings of the Old Bailey).

Rather less has been said on everyday activities, even though they affected a much larger number of people on a more regular basis. The "merry" Middle Ages (in itself a rather debatable concept) lay in the distant past, but many contemporaries felt that the 1700s ushered in an "age of pleasure" after a long period of religious austerity, military devastation, and economic stagnation – a constellation once subsumed under the broad umbrella of the "crisis of the seventeenth century." Urbanization boosted the differentiation and expansion of entertainment opportunities at a time when Enlightenment philosophers explicitly linked the concepts of virtue and pleasure (Clark and Houston, 2000: 576). No comprehensive listing can be attempted here, but brief examinations of prominent spare-time pursuits and other contexts for popular sociability may provide an impression of the phenomenon as a whole.

As in other periods, convivial drinking, board and card games, musical performances, and dancing provided a basic repertory of pastimes, particularly in association with rites of passage like weddings or seasonal festivities linked to feast-days, carnivals, fairs, and harvests. In metropolitan environments, new leisure opportunities included garden walks and weekend excursions to beauty spots and outdoor facilities beyond the city walls. An anonymous poem of 1773 emphasizes the widespread appeal of such trips in Paris:

> From every *quartier* of the city,
> on Sundays and holy-days, there a procession
> of decent folk from every trade,
> cobblers, tailors, wig-makers,
> fish-wives and patching women,
> vegetable-peelers and laundry-maids,
> serving-girls, lackeys and scrubbers,
> dandies from the harbour or porters,
> and here and there soldiers
> and their fishwives
> who, with no fear of the devil,
> turn their backs on the sermons
> and gallop off to the pleasure-gardens
> where the cheap wine is drunk . . .
> (Roche, 1981: 265)[1]

On top of Bacchanalian indulgence and an emerging taste for shopping, organized attractions ranging from cock-fighting right through to opera performances proliferated as well. Artists like the English actor David Garrick acquired celebrity status, and the same is true of the new "sports idol," the bullfighter in Spain (Burke 1994:

249; Porter and Roberts, 1996). Yet the countryside was by no means barren ground for those in search of distractions, as other examples from the field of sport may illustrate. At the upper end of the social spectrum examined here, German Romantics discovered ice-skating as a "symbol of stepping out of the city" and an opportunity to experience "free nature." In 1776 Wilhelm Heinse, an enthusiastic practitioner, wrote of the "sky-rising bliss . . . to be able to fly over the ice at the lightning speed of steel" (Carmen Götz in Albrecht et al. 2003: 191). Towards the other end of the scale we find the English village shopkeeper Thomas Turner, who enjoyed a rather different pastime. On June 20, 1757 he

> walked up to the common with an intent to see a cricket match played between an eleven of the Street quarter and an eleven of the Nursery quarter [of the Sussex village of East Hoathly], but when I came there, they not having enough to play, so that I was constrained to play for one, which I did, and we had the good fortune to beat the Nursery eleven 72 runs. I went down to Jones's [alehouse] with the rest of the gamesters and stayed till 11.15. I spent only my shilling as a gamester. (Vaisey 1984: 101–2)

Convivial gatherings like this would have been marked by much joking and carousing. Surviving ballads convey an impression of likely topics of amusement. In *John Blunt* (1785), for example, a pair of elderly alehouse keepers gets ransacked by late-night invaders who drink their beer, eat their meat, and even abuse the old woman on the bedroom floor, simply because the couple had been too lazy to lock their front door before going to sleep (text and tune in Bodleian Library Broadside Ballads). Yet the themes of popular songs ranged very widely, encompassing politics and religion as well as frivolity and coarse humor. Travelers through Swiss Protestant cantons were surprised to find peasants performing psalms and other spiritual music in the tavern (Kümin 2005: 36), while Russian folk songs – already avidly collected by eighteenth-century scholars in a quest to capture the country's "soul" – often dealt with issues of subsistence migration or outlaws roaming the land (musical samples in Geldern and McReynolds, 1998: 41–20).

Yet popular culture (as defined above) included much more than leisure pursuits. Economic relations are dealt with elsewhere in this volume, but harvesting, workshop production, the sealing of business deals, and visits to markets and fairs should at least be mentioned as typical examples of work-related gatherings (see chapter 4 above). Religion remained a key motive for popular sociability, too, in spite of a long-standing convention to associate the early modern period with processes of secularization. In "advanced" societies like England, the monopoly of the established church may have been broken, but regular assemblies continued to take place in Anglican as well as Nonconformist places of worship (not to speak of the séances of the enthusiast French Prophets: Mullan and Reid, 2000: ch. 2). On the continent, Pietist meetings reinvigorated religious fervor in many Protestant areas (including Ulrich Bräker's Toggenburg). Baroque Catholicism, however, evolved the most elaborate and ostentatious range of opportunities, ranging from Sunday Mass, public processions, confraternities, and countless specialized cults in the localities right through to lavish programs of church rebuilding and mass pilgrimages to sacred sites such as Altötting (Bavaria), Einsiedeln (Swiss Confederation), Mariazell (Austria), Santiago de Compostela (Castile), Scherpenheuvel (Brabant), and many others. The

Figure 9 Goya, *Riña en la venta nueva*, 1777. A brawl between men of different regional origin arising from a card game (played at the table on the right) outside a rural tavern near Madrid. A policeman (with a pistol) approaches from the left. *Museo Nacional del Prado*

latter was a truly astounding phenomenon, as a few quantitative indicators may illustrate: scrutiny of evidence for the south of the Holy Roman Empire suggests a density of 1 pilgrimage site per 2,000 inhabitants and an average length of "religious mobility" of up to 1.5 weeks per parishioner each year (i.e. on top of regular feast-days!). Even a "middling" destination easily attracted around 30,000 visitors per annum. At Loreto in Italy, priests celebrated 30 masses a day, but still failed to keep up with demand. Journeys to a miracle-working image or relic owed their mass appeal to an ingenious combination of inner spiritual yearning and outward display of confessional pride with elements of pleasure trips and a temporary removal from everyday constraints (hence the concern of some preachers that participants came to venerate Bacchus and Venus rather than the saints). In locations like Maria Trost near Graz, nineteenth-century Sunday excursions (and ultimately the modern holiday) directly derived from the pilgrimage movement (Hersche 2006: chs. 2.4 and 4.3).

Another neglected source of sociability is popular politics and local government. Across Europe, literally hundreds of thousands of middling men regularly met to discuss matters of common concern. This phenomenon extended far beyond exceptional cases like the Swedish Riksdag – where peasant delegates helped to decide matters of state – to regional representative assemblies such as German *Landtage*, the French *états provinciaux*, Swiss *Landsgemeinden* (the sovereign body of rural cantons comprising all male householders), Italian city councils, and even village government in the remotest provinces. Local administration and poor relief involved choosing, supervising, and supporting constables, churchwardens, and other officials.

Extraordinary demands such as repairs to the local church required particularly extensive social interaction. Records of the French parish of Mettray near Tours in the mid-1760s document the holding of "assemblies of the inhabitants and landowners" (for example on April 24, 1763, following Mass), negotiations about the need for urgent redress, election of commissaries (in this case a surgeon, merchant, roofer, and carpenter), decisions about equitable assessment levels, liaisons with the rector and central government officials, and the delicate process of extracting payment from non-resident contributors (Maillard in Follain, 2000: 353–75). Thomas Turner, too, spent much time dealing with his fellow villagers about matters of communal concern. On April 10, 1765, he "went to Mr. Joseph Burges's [alehouse], where there was a public vestry holden for to settle the yearly accounts of the overseers and choose new overseers etc., when Mr Carman and myself made up our accounts with the inhabitants, and there was due to the parish the sum of £177s. 3¼d." (Vaisey, 1984: 318). At the regional level, eighteenth-century England experienced the "commercialization" of politics. Both of the emerging parties, Tories and Whigs, endeavored to boost support through local rallies. Their ideological outlook mattered, of course, but success very much depended on the administration of lavish hospitality to prospective voters at inns. One Hertfordshire candidate spent no less than £3,000 in 31 different public houses to secure his election as an MP in 1784 (Brewer in McKendrick et al., 1983: 241).[2]

Oral exchange was the most congenial medium in nearly all of these situations. Face-to-face communication, however, invariably involved ritual and performative elements as well, most obviously in "formalized" church services, shaming practices and carnival customs (Burke, 1994: xi; Furnari, 1980: 119–36; Reay, 1998: 1). Written and print culture, too, constantly interacted with orality in this period. A classic case is the early modern almanac, which owed its widespread appeal to a tailor-made mixture of practical advice (weather forecasts), religious information (liturgical calendar), and entertainment features. Annotations and amendments preserved in surviving Portuguese copies testify to the readers' active engagement with their texts and images (Luis, 1989). Single-leaf prints such as the "Truthful Depiction and extensive Description of a terrifying, cruel and previously-unseen Animal which was spotted on 15 November 1725 near the city of Jerusalem after it had caused much damage to Humans and Cattle and only put to death with much effort," which juxtaposed a woodcut illustration of a fantastic creature with an explanatory text borrowing elements from the legend of St. George killing the dragon, also successfully tapped into Europe's hunger for sensationalist stories (Einblattdrucke der Frühen Neuzeit). The (provincial) printers-cum-entrepreneurs behind the French *bibliothèque bleue*, to take a final example, issued thousands of different books targeted at an audience below the level of the social elites. Thanks to growing literacy rates and effective distribution systems, the series reached staggering circulation figures of around 1 million copies per year during the early eighteenth century. Titles tapped freely into the learned canon, with religious topics – of a distinctly Counter-Reformation flavor – and literary classics accounting for the lion's share of publications (Andries, 1989: 19, 23, 67).

In the wake of the spatial turn in the historical and social sciences, settings for popular culture attract increasing attention. Rather than as a given physical entity, "space" is seen as a relational construct, i.e. the product of interactions between agents, objects, and locations (Crang and Thrift, 2000). Streets, churchyards, market squares, and village greens hosted a great number of activities, but – as several examples have already suggested – by far the most prominent site was the public house. Alcohol served as the "ubiquitous social lubricant" in preindustrial society and most was consumed in the inns, taverns, and beer houses which punctuated the European landscape (Martin, 2001: 2). Official registers suggest a density of one drinking outlet for fewer than 100 inhabitants in eighteenth-century England and – although the ratios elsewhere typically lay between 1:200–400 – the figure could easily drop to below 1:50 in bustling commercial or pilgrimage centers (Chartres in Kümin and Tlusty, 2002: 207; Kümin, 2005: 20). Some have argued for a withdrawal of elites from this traditional venue towards the end of the *ancien régime*, others by contrast emphasize the growing respectability, regulatory supervision, and social interchange during the 1700s (for Paris see Garrioch, 1986: 180–2; for England, Clark, 1983: ch. 10). At the very least occasional encounters remained possible everywhere. On May 1, 1764, village official Thomas Turner

> dined at *The White Hart* [in Lewes, Sussex] in company with about twenty more upon a fillet of veal roasted, a ham boiled, a fore-quarter of lamb roasted, 2 hot pigeon pasties, 2 raisin and currant puddings, greens, potatoes and green salad. The reason of my dining on so elegant a dinner was on account of my having business with Mr. Baley, steward to the devisees and heirs of the Rt. Hon. Hen. Pelham Esq. deceased, who held an audit there today. . . . (Vaisey, 1984: 292)

Entirely uncontroversial is the tavern's towering role in the cultural life of preindustrial Europe, at a time when specialized venues like theaters, sports arenas, and concert halls were as yet few and far between. Many publicans provided skittle alleys, shooting ranges, or billiard tables, staged and promoted attractions such as plays, races, or bowling competitions, all in the safe assumption that money invested in facilities, performers, or prizes would pay plentiful dividends in the form of increasing drink sales. But the good old tavern also played a leading role in the associational phenomenon normally associated with the more sober and advanced world of coffeehouses. When the physical base of societies is investigated in more detail, it appears that 90 percent of English clubs actually gathered in public houses. At Brunswick in northern Germany, too, the leading "Grand Club," founded in 1780 by the bourgeois elite for "pleasant and useful conversation, scientific instruction and convivial entertainment," maintained extensive assembly rooms in a wing of the city's flagship inn, the Hôtel d'Angleterre (Albrecht in Albrecht et al., 2003: 331; Clark, 2000: 21).

On top of local sociability, inns also facilitated long-distance communication. At either end of stage-coach journeys (and indeed at regular intervals in between), public houses brought passengers into contact with fellow travelers as well as patrons from the neighborhood. Their premises were arguably the sites where the local and wider worlds intersected most frequently, enabling friendly and less friendly encounters depending on specific circumstances. In the summer of 1782, German clergyman Carl Philip Moritz dined in the company of soldiers, servants, and "rough men" at the inn of Nettlebed near Nottingham; in September 1788 his compatriot Christoph Meiners shared a meal "with coachmen, carriers and diverse pedestrians [typically members of lower social groups]" at the public house of Soyhières in the Jura mountains, and in the same year J. W. von Reinach witnessed a delicate situation at the crowded Freienhof hostelry in the Swiss town of Thun. Due to the presence of a major fair, the largest guest lounge abounded with "crowds of country folk." "The most beautiful young girls, blossoming like roses [sat] opposite their equally attractive partners" and "enjoyed supper in the best of moods to the tune of joyful love songs." As soon as two strangers started talking to the women, however, the young men made it very clear that they had no intention of sharing their companions. Reinach thus admonished the intruders to behave "more modestly," which helped to calm the nerves of the offended rural party (Kümin in Dürr and Schwerhoff, 2005: 390–1). This was a wise move, for conflicts about personal honor – fueled by copious alcohol consumption in a very public environment – sparked a deluge of violent brawls in early modern drinking houses (for France see Muchenbled 1985: 31; for the German city of Aachen, see Hirschfelder, 2004: ch. 3.1).

This multifunctional ambivalence of public houses triggered conflicting responses from the authorities. Throughout the early modern period, central and local bodies attempted to curb the number of outlets, with at best limited success. Official pronouncements abounded with detailed regulations and moral censure (in a typical statement, the governor of the Bernese dominion of Morges on Lake Geneva in the 1780s dismissed wine taverns as "pernicious" and "conducive to the ruin of individuals as well as entire communities"[3]), while acknowledging their essential contribution to trading infrastructures and social bonding among their subjects. Around 1800 one official from the north German principality of Lippe argued that "our subjects require relaxation after six days of sour and hard work and these are the hours on Saturday and Sunday evening. In all due obedience, I therefore recommend that we continue to allow visits to inns on feast days." Even members of the clergy, usually amongst the most fervent critics of the "devil's altar," could agree that "rural folks have a great need for periodic reinvigoration" by wine.[4] Alcohol taxes, furthermore, evolved into a pillar of early modern state finance, dampening government enthusiasm for overly restrictive action. Russia provides the most extreme example. In spite of moderation rhetoric by reformers like Peter the Great, himself ironically "one of the heaviest drinking" of the country's rulers, changes in the way *kabaki* were run always aimed at maximizing tsarist revenues – "all concerns expressed about any other aspect of the drinking houses have to be seen as the sheerest hypocrisy" of central authorities (Snow in Kümin and Tlusty, 2002: 203).

Patterns and Variables

The complexity of activities and settings sketched so far prevents neat generalizations and undermines all determinist models. Analysis of variables such as participants, gender, region, and chronology, however, may help to reveal some basic patterns.

Starting with a social profile, it is obvious that not everybody shared in all aspects of popular culture. Many practices were directed against outsiders – witches, adulterers, tyrants – but others – like harvest festivals – could involve near-universal participation. Historians have advanced good reasons for postulating a "withdrawal" of elites from the more boisterous and less civil pursuits, but it is equally evident that cultural boundaries were never watertight. For a start, members of the lower orders often strove to imitate the fashions and behavior of the better-off, especially in the sphere of conspicuous consumption, which in turn forced the latter to look for new ways of distinguishing themselves. However limited direct contacts might have been, this sort of mutual observation amounted to an ongoing dialogue (Mohrmann, 1993: 78).[5] Or should we say multilateral negotiations? For one key conceptual advance is the move away from a crude popular/elite dichotomy towards more differentiated models, be it a triangle highlighting the distinct position of the middling sort or indeed the notion of dynamic interaction between a multitude of overlapping and permeable sub-cultures (Mandrou in Beauroy, 1976; Harris, 1995: 15; Scribner, 1989: 184). It is clearly inadequate to study any one group or individual in isolation. Ulrich Bräker, whose reminiscences opened this essay, could not be understood merely in the agricultural and proto-industrial context into which he was born in 1735, for subsequently he enlisted as a Prussian mercenary, traveled through foreign lands, deserted, engaged in petty trade, learned to read, joined a "moral society" (which enabled him to access – and eventually review – the entire works of Shakespeare) and even won prizes for his writings; all of this in a life punctuated by bankruptcies and repeated family dramas (Bräker, 1789; Historical Dictionary of Switzerland). At the other end of the scale, we find that the lawyer and literary scholar Johann Anton Leisewitz frequented not just Brunswick's coffeehouses, but many ordinary inns and beer gardens. On one occasion in 1778 – accompanied by no less a figure than Gotthold Ephraim Lessing – he witnessed a "miserable puppet show featuring Princess Emilia's liberation from a dragon" at a country tavern. A history of sociability during the period, therefore, "cannot ignore everyday entertainments of the people, as they provided a constant backdrop to critical-enlightened reasoning" (Andreas Herz in Albrecht, 2003: 240–1).[6]

Gender, to move to another principal variable, affected the entirety of early modern existence (see chapter 2 above). Women clearly played a conspicuous part in popular culture: within the household, they transmitted norms and values as educators of their children, in local communities they participated in a network of gossip (which made and destroyed reputations) as well as seasonal celebrations, and even in the legal system women appeared not just as passive victims, but as accusers and witnesses too. Sites like spinning bees and situations like childbirth allowed specifically "female" moments of sociability. Mothers, wives, and daughters, legitimated by their nurturing role, confronted lords in bread riots and – contrary to common perceptions – participated in tavern society as well, at least on certain approved occasions (Capp, 2003). Nevertheless, "the core values of popular culture were profoundly misogynistic." Rough music targeted husband-beaters, while the physical disciplining of wives remained acceptable. Philanderers enjoyed a certain respect in polite circles, but women were told to fight their "natural" inclination towards lust and disorder in order to fulfil the ideal of chaste obedience (Amussen in Harris, 1995).

A number of factors prompted regional differentiation. Confession had a massive impact on popular mentalities, be it the virulent anti-papalism of early modern England or the nationalist Counter-Reformation fervor permeating the Spanish empire (Carrasco, 1991: 10). Such frameworks had an obvious bearing on local cultural life, even though the chasm between festive Catholic and austere "Puritan" culture may have been exaggerated. Bavarians, it is true, observed numerous saints' days and frequented monastic breweries,[7] but their lives were by no means free from disciplinarian pressures. At Bayerbach, vicar Paul Prucker clashed with innkeeper Joseph Mayrhofer over a dance event held on Easter Tuesday in 1756. According to the latter's deposition, Prucker had entered the inn, banged his stick on a table, and asked revelers and musicians to leave the premises at once. He also branded Mayrhofer a disobedient parishioner from the pulpit. Startled but resilient, the publican's wife retorted that similar "dances were staged . . . elsewhere, that they were not Lutherans and that they still hoped to go to heaven etc." In the end, the secular court admonished the priest not to act independently, but to alert the state authorities to any future misdemeanors. Even in Protestant heartlands like Bern, clampdowns on drinking and dancing met with only limited success. As a quantitative analysis of eighteenth-century consistory court records suggests, villagers supported moral campaigns at best selectively, above all when church and state concerns like the protection of family livelihoods tallied with their own (Kümin, 2005: 27).

Other types of regional variations resulted from specific agricultural systems – "the compact, densely settled pastures of the sheep-corn regions of southern England . . . with their open-field agricultural systems, tight manorial structures and other traditions of communal action, were likely to generate a more collectivist culture than the scattered, individualistic parishes that were the rule in . . . the pasturelands of north Wiltshire or west Dorset" (Underdown in Harris, 1995: 33) – distinct climatic conditions (with Mediterranean temperatures encouraging more extensive open-air activities than those in northern Europe), and differences in topographical settings (seaside communities evidently inviting different kinds of pastime than Alpine locations). Rapid urbanization, furthermore, accentuated divisions between town and country. As noted above, cities accommodated a greater number and variety of organized leisure attractions, not to speak of more educational establishments, bookshops, stage-coach links, and religious institutions. A case could also be made for the relevance of constitutional frameworks. In his *Six Books of the Commonwealth*, a classic study of different forms of government, the French political theorist Jean Bodin acknowledged the greater significance of civic conviviality in "egalitarian" republican regimes, while monarchical court culture required less immediate interaction with the population at large.

In what ways was the eighteenth century distinctive? Historians have rightly pointed to a range of characteristics, mainly the unprecedented intensity and diversity of the associational impulse (which reached far into provincial society), the rise of a consumer society, and the inherent tension between official disciplinarian campaigns and the "unabashed hedonism" of many contemporaries (Porter in Porter and Roberts, 1996: 32–3). A less dramatic, if telling, innovation is only just starting to be recognized. The advent of regular passenger services from the late seventeenth century established the stage-coach as an increasingly common venue for casual encounters. On an ever-growing number of occasions, total strangers found themselves lumped together for hours on end in a very small space. Not all were equally enthusiastic. Persons of wealth often evaded the situation by hiring individual post-chaises; others welcomed the informal opportunity to meet new people and learn about different cultures. Johann Kaspar Riesbeck, for example, declared himself "extraordinarily fond" of public means of transport, "in view of the company (even though it consist solely of Jews, Capucins and old women)" and criticized those in personal carriages "for sealing themselves off from society out of motives of class convention," while Johann Georg Heinzmann warned readers of his German travel guidebook in 1793 that a mail journey could be "as tiring to the mind as it is harmful to the body," not least due to "the often pestilential stench of unclean traveling companions; the tobacco fumes and rough, foul language of the selfsame worthy assorted fellow passengers" (Beyrer, 2006: 381–2). Alongside long-distance mobility, the coach also served a mounting desire for polite social calls, as is evident from the correspondence of the London merchant John Verney around 1700. In contrast to his gentry father, whose networks had been based on country hospitality and hunting parties, the metropolitan son preferred visiting by coach as a more fashionable means to foster bonds of friendship (Whyman, 1999: 107). Post-1789, of course, Frenchmen and -women (and above all Parisians) experienced a host of (not necessarily lasting) novelties, most spectacularly when Catholic feasts and devotions were officially replaced by civil cults dedicated to Reason, the Supreme Being, and the Fatherland.

Longer-term comparison, however, highlights considerable continuities too. Drinking, singing, gaming, and dancing provided the timeless foundation of popular sociability. Seventeenth-century London taverns, as a quick perusal of Samuel Pepys' diary will confirm, anticipated many "innovative" characteristics of coffeehouses and restaurants, be it by hosting societies or offering flexibility and choice in terms of gastronomic provision. The transformation of the public sphere, as discussed elsewhere in this volume, may have also been less exclusively rooted in the associational and institutional structures of the emerging bourgeoisie (as in the Habermas concept), given that widespread and informed public debate can already be found in such contexts as the German Reformation in the sixteenth century and the English Revolution in the seventeenth (Zaret, 2000). In many respects, therefore, new elements enriched rather than replaced traditional cultural life in this period (Clark and Houston, 2000: 576; Rogers, 2006: 405–6).

Conclusion

A survey of popular culture and sociability in the 1700s produces a dazzling panorama of heterogeneous features. Spectacular events like charivaris and riots punctuated a multitude of everyday activities associated with work, seasons, rites of passage, religious feasts, and political responsibilities. All of them combined the use of a variety of media and reflected the high dignity of principles such as custom, subsistence, and patriarchal rule. In the history of eighteenth-century cultural exchange, polite reasoning in civil society represents only the tip of the iceberg.

This cultural world was never determined by one single factor, but significant variables included social inclusion/exclusion, gender roles, and regional peculiarities. Macrohistorical trends like secularization and the "civilizing process" left their imprint, but failed to transform the picture beyond recognition. The eighteenth century saw growing commercialization and professionalization in the emerging leisure industry, a further differentiation in sites of sociability (notably coffeehouses, salons, and stage-coaches) and an unprecedented proliferation of clubs and societies. At the same time, it remained rooted in early modern tradition: the associational movement was largely based in "old" public houses and, despite all the different ecclesiastical, political, and moral pressures it faced, "the resilience of popular culture should not be underestimated" (Burke, 1994: 242; cf. Mullan and Reid, 2000: ch. 6).

Conceptually, "popular culture" remains a valuable umbrella term for practices rooted primarily in oral exchange, local settings, and the vernacular. The word "primarily," however, needs to be emphasized, for townspeople and villagers were always interacting with the wider world, be it through their clergymen, local government assemblies, visits to regional markets, participation in mass pilgrimages, or volumes of the *bibliothèque bleue* acquired from passing peddlers.

At this moment the digital revolution opens exciting new opportunities in the field. Magnificent resources like the Old Bailey Proceedings, Bodleian Broadside Ballads, German single-leaf prints, and many others are now at the researcher's fingertips. The methodical challenges remain, of course, but the prospects for further insights into popular culture may never have looked better.

Notes

1 On suburban *guinguettes* on the outskirts of Paris see Brennan 1988: ch. 3; for pleasure trips into the country in late eighteenth-century Braunschweig see Albrecht in Albrecht et al., 2003).

2 For a more extensive engagement with participatory politics cf. David Luebke's essay in this volume.

3 State Archives of Bern, Documents associated with the register of public houses of 1789: B V 147, p. 1257.

4 Ibid., B III 207, no. 45, p. 7 (statement by Minister Zehender of Ferenbalm in Bern, 1764); the secular official quoted in Linde, 1995: 41).

5 In the 1790s Christian Garve's "Theory of Social Relations" aimed to offer aspiring middling men ways to interact with higher-placed individuals through the use of reason and refined taste: Vierhaus in Albrecht et al., 2003.

6 At the same time, members of the Parisian nobility enjoyed frivolous days out in the country, where they dressed up as "commoners" to partake in popular get-togethers (De Baecque, 2000: 61). Characters like the English poet Charles Churchill, "who becomes a vice-ridden habitué of taverns and brothels," make it difficult to tell whether he is "aping the upper-class rake or reverting to the licentiousness of the" "mob." (Bertelsen, 1986: 256). For comparable overlaps in eighteenth-century art see Paulson, 1979.

7 Johann Pezzl, an anticlerical exponent of the Enlightenment, noted how monasteries like Weihenstephan "extracted a considerable amount of money from [the people of Freising] for their indeed excellent beer. Their drinking lounges function like battlefields, where clerical *Candidati Theologiae* fight over their dogmatic and casuistic hobby horses. To boost beer sales, the monks stage a stream of processions and offer thousands of years of indulgences' (Pezzl, 1784: 71).

Bibliography

Online resources

"Bodleian Library Broadside Ballads" <http://www.bodley.ox.ac.uk/ballads/ballads.htm>.
Bräker, U., *Lebensgeschichte und natürliche Ebentheuer des armen Mannes im Tockenburg* (Zurich, 1789); e-text: <http://gutenberg.spiegel.de/braeker/tocken/tocken.htm>.
"Eighteenth Century Collections Online" <http://www.gale.com/EighteenthCentury/>.
"Einblattdrucke der Frühen Neuzeit" <http://www.bsb-muenchen.de/Einblattdrucke.178.0.html>.
"Historical Dictionary of Switzerland" <www.hls.ch>.
"Proceedings of the Old Bailey 1674–1834" <http://www.oldbaileyonline.org/>.

Printed primary sources

Furnari, M. (ed.), *'700 napoletano: cultura popolare a Napoli nel diciottesimo secolo* (Naples, 1980).
Geldern, J. van and L. McReynolds (eds.), *Entertaining Tsarist Russia: Tales, Songs, Plays, Movies, Jokes, Ads, and Images from Russian UrbanLlife, 1779–1917* (Bloomington, 1998).
Mullan, J. and C. Reid (eds.), *Eighteenth-Century Popular Culture: A Selection* (Oxford, 2000).
Pezzl, J., *Reise durch den baierschen Kreis* (1784).
Vaisey, D. (ed.), *The Diary of Thomas Turner 1754–1765* (Oxford, 1984).

Secondary literature

Agulhon, M., *La Sociabilité méridionale: Confréries et associations dans la vie collective en Provence orientale à la fin du 18e siècle* (Aix-en-Provence, 1966).
Albrecht, P., H. E. Bödeker, and E. Hinrichs (eds.), *Formen der Geselligkeit in Nordwestdeutschland 1750–1820* (Tübingen, 2003).
Andries, L., *La Bibliothèque bleue au dix-huitième siècle: Une tradition éditoriale* (Oxford, 1989).
Beauroy, J., M. Bertrand, and E. Gargan (eds.), *The Wolf and the Lamb: Popular Culture in France from the Old Regime to the Twentieth Century* (Saratoga, 1976).
Bertelsen, L., *The Nonsense Club: Literature and Popular Culture 1749–64* (Oxford, 1986).
Beyrer, K., "The mail-coach revolution: landmarks in travel in Germany between the seventeenth and nineteenth centuries," *German History*, 24 (2006), 375–86.
Brennan, T., *Public Drinking and Popular Culture in Eighteenth-Century Paris* (Princeton, 1988).
Brewer, J. and R. Porter (eds.), *Consumption and the World of Goods* (London, 1993).
Burke, P., *Popular Culture in Early Modern Europe* (1978; rev. edn., Aldershot, 1994).
Camporesi, P., *Rustici e buffoni: cultura popolare e cultura d'élite fra Medioevo ed età moderna* (Turin, 1991).
Capp, B., *When Gossips Meet: Women, Family and Neighbourhood in Early Modern England* (Oxford, 2003).
Carrasco, R. (ed.), *Solidarités et sociabilités en Espagne: XVIe–XXe siècles* (Paris, 1991).
Chartier, R., *The Cultural Uses of Print in Early Modern France* (Princeton, 1987).
Clark, P., *The English Alehouse: A Social History 1200–1830* (London, 1983).
Clark, P., *British Clubs and Societies 1580–1800: The Origins of an Associational World* (Oxford, 2000).
Clark, P. and R. A. Houston, "Culture and leisure 1700–1840," in P. Clark (ed.), *The Cambridge UrbanHistory of Britain*, vol. 2: *1540–1840* (Cambridge, 2000), pp. 575–613.

Crang, M. and N. Thrift (eds.), Thinking Space (London, 2000).
Davis, N. Z., *Society and Culture in Early Modern France: Eight Essays* (London, 1975).
De Baecque, A., *Les Eclats du rire: La Culture des rieurs au XVIIIe siècle* (Paris, 2000).
Dülmen, R. V. and N. Schindler (eds.), *Volkskultur. Zur Wiederentdeckung des vergessenen Alltags (16.–20. Jahrhundert)* (Frankfurt, 1984).
Dürr; R. and G. Schwerhoff (eds.), *Kirchen, Märkte und Tavernen. Erfahrungs- und Handlungsräume in der Frühen Neuzeit* (Frankfurt am Main, 2005).
Ellis, M., *The Coffee-House: A Cultural History* (London, 2005).
Follain, A. (ed.), *L'Argent des villages du XIIIe au XVIIIe siècle* (Rennes, 2000).
Garrioch, D., *Neighbourhood and Community in Paris 1740–1890* (Cambridge, 1986).
Gutton, J.-P., *La Sociabilité villageoise dans l'ancienne France: Solidarités et voisinages du XVIe au XVIIIe siècle* (Paris, 1979).
Harris, T. (ed.), *Popular Culture in England c.1500–1850* (Basingstoke, 1995).
Hersche, P., *Mue und Verschwendung. Europäische Gesellschaft und Kultur im Barockzeitalter* (2 vols., Freiburg, 2006).
Hirschfelder, G., *Alkoholkonsum am Beginn des Industriezeitalters (1700–1850). Vergleichende Studien zum gesellschaftlichen und kulturellen Wandel* (2 vols., Cologne, 2003, 2004).
Im Hof, U., *Das gesellige Jahrhundert. Gesellschaft und Gesellschaften im Zeitalter der Aufklärung* (Munich, 1982).
Kale, S., *French Salons: High Society and Political Sociability from the Old Regime to the Revolution of 1848* (Baltimore, 2005).
Kaplan, S. (ed.), *Understanding Pop Culture: Europe from the Middle Ages to the Nineteenth Century* (Berlin, 1984).
Kümin, B., "Sacred church and worldly tavern: reassessing an early modern divide," in W. Coster and A. Spicer (eds.), *Sacred Space in Early Modern Europe* (Cambridge, 2005), pp. 17–38.
Kümin, B. and B. A. Tlusty (eds.), *The World of the Tavern: Public Houses in Early Modern Europe* (Aldershot, 2002).
Linde, R., "Krüge: Wirtshauskultur in der Grafschaft Lippe im 18. Jahrhundert," in S. Baumeier and J. Carstensen (eds.), *Beiträge zur Volkskunde und Hausforschung* (Detmold, 1995).
Luis, J., "Popular knowledge in the eighteenth-century almanacs," *History of European Ideas*, 11 (1989), 509–13.
Malcolmson, R. W., *Popular Recreations in English Society 1700–1850* (Cambridge, 1973).
Martin, A. L., *Alcohol, Sex, and Gender in Late Medieval and Early Modern Europe* (Basingstoke, 2001).
McKendrick, N., J. Brewer, and J. H. Plumb, *The Birth of a Consumer Society: The Commercialization of Eighteenth-Century England* (London, 1983).
Medick, H., "Plebeian culture in the transition to capitalism," in R. Samuel and G. Stedman Jones (eds.), *Culture, Ideology and Politics: Essays for Eric Hobsbawn* (London, 1983), pp. 84–113.
Mohrmann, R. E., "Everyday culture in early modern times," *New Literary History*, 24 (1993), 75–86.
Muchembled, R., *Popular Culture and Elite Culture in France 1400–1750* (Baton Rouge, 1985).
Paulson, R., *Popular and Polite Art in the Age of Hogarth and Fielding* (Notre Dame, 1979).
Porter, R. and M. Roberts (eds.), *Pleasure in the Eighteenth Century* (Basingstoke, 1996).
Reay, B., (ed.), *Popular Culture in Seventeenth-Century England* (London, 1985).
Reay, B., *Popular Cultures in England 1550–1750* (Harlow, 1998).
Roche, D., *The People of Paris: An Essay in Popular Culture in the Eighteenth Century* (Leamington Spa, 1987).

Rogers, N., "Popular culture," in M. Fitzpatrick et al. (eds.), *The Enlightenment World* (London, 2006), pp. 401–17.

Rosseaux, U., *Freiräume. Unterhaltung, Vergnügen und Erholung in Dresden (1694–1830)* (Cologne, 2006).

Schindler, N., *Rebellion, Community and Custom in Early Modern Germany* (Cambridge, 2002).

Scribner, R. W., "Is a history of popular culture possible?," *History of European Ideas*, 10 (1989), 175–91.

Thompson, E. P., *Customs in Common* (Harmondsworth, 1993).

Whyman, S., *Sociability and Power in Late Stuart England: The Cultural Worlds of the Verneys, 1660–1720* (Oxford, 1999).

Yeo, E. and S. Yeo (eds.), *Popular Culture and Class Conflict 1590–1914: Explorations in the History of Labour and Leisure* (Brighton, 1981).

Zaret, D., *Origins of Democratic Culture: Printing, Petitions and the Public Sphere in Early Modern England* (Princeton, 2000).

CHAPTER THIRTEEN

The Arts

MARK BERRY

The Challenge of the Eighteenth Century

A special challenge to consideration of eighteenth-century art is that, while it stands closer chronologically to us than that of the Middle Ages or the Renaissance, its aesthetics remain in many ways distinct from those of our post-Romantic age. As dissatisfaction with Enlightenment cosmopolitanism mounted, nationalism and other ostensibly "nineteenth-century" ideologies grew, yet Romanticism's art-religion and cult of the genius would have been generally incomprehensible prior to the 1790s. Many of us find it easier to consider Wolfgang Amadeus Mozart as, and therefore want him actually to *be*, the misunderstood proto-Romantic genius: first supremely elevated, then callously buried in a pauper's grave while lesser men were lauded, mocked by the gods as the funerary blizzards they dispatched kept away all but a handful of mourners, forerunners of our more discerning selves. We are bowled over by the almost Wagnerian demonic possession of *Don Giovanni* and readily succumb to the undeniable pathos of the ailing composer unable to complete his own Requiem, the Lacrimosa, of all movements, tailing off to point to the grave. Thus, we may dismiss "occasional" sacred works as relics from an age in which the church, Voltaire notwithstanding, held all too many cards of patronage and may lazily overlook the apparently "domestic" concerns of the piano sonatas. Glenn Gould, a Romantic through and through, despite or perhaps especially on account of his anti-Romanticism, went so far as to record a good number of the latter in order to show their alleged poverty of invention. Yet Mozart's oeuvre for solo piano contains riches indeed; aside from juvenilia, there is not a single piece that fails to warrant regular performance. Rarely was his art more subtle than in the final sonata in D major, KV 576; rarely did he plumb greater emotional depths than in the B minor Adagio, KV 540; rarely was Mozart more passionately vehement than in the first movement of the A minor sonata, KV 310/300*d*. (Even in the latter case, it is difficult to resist the Romantic characterization of this "exceptional" early, or relatively early, work as being written "in the wake of his mother's death." Such characterization may not, moreover, be entirely unjustified.)

A Companion to Eighteenth-Century Europe, First Edition. Edited by Peter H. Wilson.
© 2014 John Wiley & Sons, Ltd. Published 2014 by John Wiley & Sons, Ltd.

Remaining with music, there is also the case of Joseph Haydn, ever in Mozart's shadow, at least as posterity has been concerned: Haydn "the Inaccessible," as Sir Donald Tovey memorably dubbed him. The lack of overt or even covert tragedy in Haydn's life – ought he really not to have suffered a little more? – has often led to his underestimation, despite the small matter of having invented what for many constitutes the supreme form of chamber music, the string quartet. This is rendered more tempting given Haydn's prolific yet forbidding mastery of almost every musical form, although he remains undoubtedly lesser than his "tragic" younger contemporary in opera, that most public of musical arenas. The fate of Haydn and of much eighteenth-century art has been to be *not* Mozart, or rather not the Mozart of *Don Giovanni*'s "Stone Guest" scene, to be *not* Beethoven, or at least not something closer to our horizons, broader in some ways and narrower in so many others. What this art might positively be may be difficult, perhaps impossible, ultimately to define; yet we should, in the words of an old examination question, "nevertheless make the attempt." A modern historian or reader cannot break free of temporal conditions. Nor would it be desirable for us to do so, which has not prevented a sizeable party from attempting somehow to go "back to the eighteenth century," much as Jean-Jacques Rousseau once called – with about as much justification – for his public to return to Nature. Instead, we may profitably consider the distanced proximity of the eighteenth century a spur to our imagination and a shield against heirs to the sentimentalism of some of its later literature.

A chapter such as this cannot be comprehensive; yet it can point to certain important themes and to some of the historical issues attendant to consideration thereof. If little or no explicit attention is devoted to, for instance, the rise of the novel, French Rococo painting, the Baroque concerto, or the German literary revival, it is certainly not because they are unimportant. However, the broader developments they exemplify, whether socially, politically, or stylistically, may be considered in other ways, or there may simply have been impossible choices to make. I shall focus upon two fraught and partial yet nevertheless real transformations, one more socio-political and the other more traditionally art-historical, and upon the connections between the two. Consideration of the "transformation of the public sphere" will lead us toward the stylistic transition from Baroque to classical. In this context, certain artworks will be considered in a little more detail, but this is not to claim superiority to many works that go unmentioned.

Representational Culture and the Transformation of the Public Sphere

A dominant paradigm, and rightly so, in much historical writing has been the shift from the representational culture of the old regime, epitomized by Louis XIV's Versailles, to a world in which art was received by a more critical audience, often referred to as the "public sphere," sometimes prefaced by that most loaded of terms, "bourgeois." Two key works here have been those by Jürgen Habermas (1989) and Tim Blanning (2002), the latter adding profound historical sophistication, depth, and refinement to the initial model presented by Habermas, who never claimed to be writing primarily as a historian. Let us first, then, consider what is meant by "representational culture," before turning to the question of "transformation."

Detailed discussion of the nature of the "public sphere" is more properly the concern chapter 8.

It would be perverse not to begin with Versailles, even though the eighteenth century witnessed only the last 15 years of Louis XIV's rule. The arduous emancipation of the French monarchy from the clutches of the nobility during his minority determined Louis to make his intentions quite clear at the very outset of his personal rule in 1660. The power and grandeur of Nicolas Fouquet, Louis' inherited *surintendant* of finances, was a red rag to the king's bull. It was displayed in his great palace at Vaux-le-Vicomte, patronage of a large number of artists, including Molière, Nicolas Poussin, and Jean de la Fontaine, and a large private army. Fouquet's archrival, Jean-Baptiste Colbert, accused him of treason, to which were added charges of embezzlement and, just as seriously – even if not in a legal sense – usurpation of the king's cultural role. Following an outrageously lavish entertainment at Vaux involving the premiere of Molière's *Les Fâcheux*, Louis ordered Fouquet's imprisonment; thereafter, the nobles would attend *his* court and not vice versa. The stratospheric elevation of the Sun King involved not only ridding France of private armies, but also the great representational culture of Versailles: "representational" in the sense of "representing" the power of the monarch to his people and to the world. In 1623, Louis XIII had had the first royal hunting-lodge built there, but his successor had greater plans, and there began in 1661, the year of Fouquet's arrest, a series of enlargements under Louis le Vau – previously responsible for Fouquet's palace – and Jules Hardouin Mansart, continued during the reign of Louis XV, to create the resplendent palace known to the eighteenth century and indeed to us. The greatest artists, such as Molière and, perhaps most famously, Jean-Baptiste Lully, would henceforth be the king's; they would be instruments of political and cultural power. State monopolies would often complement the status of royal artists.

Thus Voltaire, in his history, *The Age of Louis XIV*, could laud "the most enlightened age the world has ever seen." He knew very well whence the cultural paradigm for his age had sprung. *Gloire* was a constant refrain and pursuit of Louis' reign, characterized above all by the splendors of Versailles. It would be misleading to say that drama, theater, ballet, painting, sculpture, landscaping, architecture, and so forth *attended* regal ceremonial; they *were* ceremonial, just as it *was* art. Versailles was both. Here there was no nineteenth-century *l'art pour l'art*, as anyone having endured the *longueurs* of a Lully *tragédie lyrique* would assent. However, having established the basis for such cultural display and its reception, let us refrain from detailing the pleasures of Louis XIV's Versailles and consider instead their eighteenth-century successors.

The 1745 opera-ballet *Le Temple de la gloire* – that word again – is concerned with the nature and glorification of kingship. Little known today, it was long renowned for L'Envie's monologue, "Profonds abîmes du Ténare," not least in the approving citation in Denis Diderot's *Le Neveu de Rameau*. The librettist is the most celebrated of eighteenth-century French writers, Voltaire, and its composer the most celebrated of eighteenth-century France, Jean-Philippe Rameau. Upon hearing of Louis XV's victory at Fontenoy, Voltaire, his popularity at court waning, wrote to the marquis d'Argenson: "O, the beautiful and glorious peace you will create! I am preparing a celebration for your return, in which the king shall be crowned with laurels." Voltaire's poem *La Bataille de Fontenoy* was transformed into a libretto at the behest of the duc de Richelieu. The resulting opera was first performed in the Grande Ecurie of Versailles before the king, accompanied by fireworks, in a celebratory winter bursting with such entertainments. This was the third of Rameau's court compositions in that year alone, following *La Princesse de Navarre* (also with Voltaire, to celebrate the wedding of the Dauphin to the Spanish Infanta) and *Platée*. Three kings visit the Temple of Glory. Bélus the bloodthirsty power-seeking king of the Assyrians and the sybaritic Bacchus are both turned away. Trajan, for whom read Louis, displays magnanimity in quelling a revolt, receives the Voltairean crown of laurels, and transforms the temple into a Temple of Happiness. The panegyric to enlightened absolutism would appear to have been just what the doctor, or rather the duke, ordered. Yet the vagaries of royal patronage worked more in Rameau's favor than in Voltaire's. The duc de Luynes recorded in his memoirs that the king at his *grand couvert* spoke approvingly to the composer yet said not a word to his librettist, who had asked him, perhaps a little too obviously, "Is Trajan satisfied?" Voltaire's exile from court was soon to begin, while Rameau, to whom Voltaire generously ceded royalties, would compose the greater part of his subsequent oeuvre for Versailles.

The accession of a Bourbon to the Spanish throne in 1700 brought a greater willingness to imitate French forms, often to the detriment of what had been hitherto considered national style. Philip V's enthusiastic patronage of the arts encouraged numerous foreign artists to flock to Madrid in search of royal commissions. Jean Ranc, who had in 1718 painted Louis XV for Versailles, now set to work on several portraits of the Spanish and Portuguese monarchs and royal families, not least the *Family of Philip V* (1722–3). Philip's wish to emulate the *gloire* of his grandfather, Louis XIV, found an able collaborator in Ranc. Charles III's reign brought Giambattista Tiepolo, among others, to Madrid. The three ceiling frescoes (1764–6) he painted for the Palacio Real – the throne room's *Glory of Spain*, the guard room's *Apotheosis of Aeneas*, and the *saleta*'s *Glory of the Spanish Monarchy* – represent to court and visitors glory national and dynastic.

Philip V's son had invaded Austrian Naples in 1734 to become Charles III, king of the Two Sicilies. He also readily appreciated the power of artistic patronage in maintaining and strengthening his position. Giovanni Paolo Panini's *Visit of Charles III to Pope Benedict XIV* (1746) memorializes a political event crucial to the king's standing in Italy and beyond. Though not especially interested in music, Charles recognized the power of opera in Neapolitan life, and in 1737 replaced the run-down Teatro San Bartolomeo with Angelo Carasale's Teatro San Carlo (hardly a coincidental choice of patron saint). Opening nights of new productions were at least as much political as artistic events, timed to coincide with birthdays and name-days of members of the ruling dynasty.

Moving beyond Bourbon lands, the Holy Roman Empire provides plentiful representational examples. By dint of the empire's complex structure, less a state than a legal order comprising all manner of hierarchies, the courts here were engaged not so much in the Habsburgs' fabled Perpetual Compromise as perpetual competition. Cultural prowess, at least as much as diplomacy, allowed smaller states and their princes to punch above their weight and more significant players to maintain and to develop their relative position.

A prime example of eighteenth-century representational culture is the Dresden court of Frederick Augustus I, "the Strong," elector of Saxony and also, from 1697,

Augustus II, king of Poland. The court painter Louis de Silvestre's celebrated 1718 portrait shows an equestrian prince at the height of his powers, very much in the line of Louis XIV. Baron Pöllnitz described the Dresden court in his 1729 memoirs as the most dazzling of the European courts: a bold claim indeed. Augustus's Grand Tour had taken in Vienna and numerous Italian cities but also Paris and Versailles, and it showed. The king-elector's most enduring legacy – in conjunction with its architect, Matthäus Daniel Pöppelmann, and hardly less so, the sculptor, Balthasar Permoser, founder of the Dresden sculptural school – is the Zwinger (1711–20): a vast open space, almost square, surrounded by galleries and pavilions. What began as an orangery was enlarged in order to provide the arena for court festivities. Allusions to so many things Roman – theaters, thermae, fora, etc. – make one wonder whether the emperor in Vienna did not take offence. Lest one forget that this was not only the work of the Saxon elector, but of this particular elector, a Polish crown stood for all to see on top of the festive gate, the Kronentor. Behind the 1718 pavilions, there were soon constructed assembly rooms and an opera house, the largest in Germany. The very public nature of representation is made clear by Augustus and Pöppelmann transforming the castle treasury into a public museum – at the pleasure, naturally, of the monarch – to which artists would dispatch their works for display. Not least amongst these were works of china, Europe's first porcelain factory having been founded in 1710 in the nearby Meissen Albrechtsburg. Indeed, Augustus planned a porcelain castle, its interior to be decorated solely with porcelain, which remained incomplete at his death.

Würzburg presents another example. We should most likely evince little interest in this Franconian ecclesiastical state during the eighteenth century were it not for Balthasar Neumann's Residenz, a result of Prince-Bishop Johann Philipp Franz von Schörnborn's decision to move from the Marienberg castle into the city of Würzburg itself. The election in 1749 of a cousin, Karl Philipp von Greiffenklau, occasioned the commissioning from Tiepolo of frescoes for the Kaisersaal, a room fit to receive the emperor, but in practice also to represent the prince-bishop's glory to all others. Tiepolo's award of Greiffenklau's features to the Emperor Frederick Barbarossa may have inflated the prince-bishop's status, yet it could hardly fail to impress anyone kneeling before him. The ceiling fresco of the palace's stairwell, completed in 1753, is one of Tiepolo's most famous works, presenting and representing the apotheosis of the prince-bishop, escorted by Genius and granted a fanfare by Fame. It depicts more than this; indeed it can fairly be said to encapsulate in its personalized depiction of the four continents European civilization's superior attitude towards the rest of the world. This is triumphantly displayed by his exploitation of Neumann's architecture to give a progressive zigzagging view of the fresco as the visitor ascends. Starting with America, Europe and Tiepolo's patron are the culmination; Greiffenklau has been well rewarded and so has posterity. Nor were Würzburg's artistic achievements confined to the visual. Operas and ballets, generally Italian, were performed in the Residenz's Weisser Saal, itself already transformed by the extravagance of Antonio Bossi's sculptural stucco and, after 1770, in a specially built theater.

The court was an extremely theatrical world, so it should come as no surprise that theater proper was so important to it, nor that boundaries between ritual and art were at best blurred. A prince might, indeed often would, be both patron and subject of a work. Thus could the cleric, playwright, and librettist Giovanni De Gamerra write in 1790:

> Theatrical spectacle, established on the basis of wise laws and of careful reform, can be regarded as a means always available to the sovereign power to inculcate in his subjects the most useful and important beliefs. . . . Has our century not seen an emperor at a performance of *La clemenza di Tito* listening to the voices of humanity and forgiveness?

De Gamerra refers not to Mozart's *La clemenza di Tito*, whose music would be composed for the following year's coronation of Leopold II as king of Bohemia, but to earlier settings of Pietro Metastasio's text. The Caesarian court poet in Vienna, Metastasio published this in 1734; first set by Antonio Caldara, Vice-Kapellmeister in Vienna, to celebrate Charles VI's birthday, we know of no fewer than 40 subsequent settings prior to Mozart's, notably by Johann Adolf Hasse (1735), Christoph Willibald von Gluck (1752), and Josef Mysliveček (1773). A tale of sovereign power, exercised judiciously in the interests of an almost superhuman clemency – for we are dealing with ideals here rather than credible "characters" in a Romantic-modern sense – was just the thing for court performance. The Roman emperor Titus Flavius Vespasianus had been acclaimed by many eighteenth-century writers as a model, proto-enlightened absolutist ruler, Montesquieu calling him "the delight of the Romans." Titus was therefore an excellent subject choice for an *opera seria*, although tougher assignments were not uncommon.

For instance, De Gamerra's first libretto, amended by Metastasio, was written for Milan's Regio Ducal Teatro. The poem for the 16-year-old Mozart's *Lucio Silla*, it achieves the near-impossible task of redeeming Plutarch's tyrannical Lucius Sulla, transforming him into an agent of Stoic clemency. Johann Christian Bach set it shortly afterwards for the Mannheim court of Carl Theodor, Elector Palatine of the Rhine, first performed for this important musical patron's name-day in 1775. (He was responsible for the great Mannheim orchestra and school of composers, and therefore in part for the rise of the Austro-German symphony, not to mention, when elector of Bavaria, Mozart's first truly great opera, *Idomeneo*.) The eighteenth-century monarch in such works, then, is presented with the ideal of a benevolent, moral ruler, which, identified with himself, he may re-present to the audience. Metastasio claimed that he had "wasted his entire life in order to instruct mankind in a pleasing way." Taking the "waste" with a pinch of salt, the important thing to recognize is the combination of pleasure and instruction. The latter perhaps has the upper hand, but is as nothing without the former, and the former is certainly not an end in itself.

Who was the audience for court opera, besides the prince and his family? Courtiers were more or less obliged to attend, albeit without payment. Noble patrons and their guests were often regular visitors, members of the middle class – for want of a better word – much less so, although they benefited from occasional free performances, for example those in Vienna and Brunswick. They made up a greater part of the audience as the century progressed, although one should not overestimate this. For an especially notable occasion, such as the premiere of Mozart's "coronation opera," competition could be very fierce indeed, even if initial reception turned out to be lukewarm. The *Krönungsjournal für Prag* reported: "The house holds a great number of persons, and yet . . . the demand for tickets was on such an occasion so great, that the supply came to an end, because of which many natives and visitors, among them persons of quality, had to go away again."

However, we should err disastrously if we considered all art or all performances to be court-related, even earlier in the century. A case in point is the rise of concert life, which had its roots in the seventeenth century, but which became more and more pronounced in the eighteenth century. Music became, at least ideally and often in some very real sense, the focus of attention, rather than an accompaniment to other social activity, be it ritual or entertainment. Habermas and Blanning have, inter alia, brought to historians' attention the importance of such events. We see in early English concerts, Habermas writes, "for the first time an audience gathered to listen to music as such – a public of music lovers to which anyone who was propertied and educated was admitted." It is neither the case that no "serious" musical listening in a quasi-modern sense had existed before, nor that most listeners became "serious," but an important transformation is taking place here. The English writer and musician Roger North commented in the 1720s in *The Musical Grammarian*, "But how and by what steps Music shot up into such request, as to crowd out from the stage even comedy itself, and to sit down in her place and become of such mighty value and price as we now know it to be, is worth inquiring about." It is indeed.

For instance, the Lübeck *Abendmusik* series following evening service was clearly defined as an event distinct from that service. By the dawn of the eighteenth century, it boasted not only the traditional organ music, carefully nurtured by Dieterich Buxtehude, but sometimes also a chorus and orchestra. Merchants in town for the market composed a large part of the audience. As the century progressed, public concerts in Lübeck, often focused upon performances of oratorios, began to supplant liturgical music in civic importance; indeed, in 1801, the post of Kantor, formerly held by Buxtehude, lapsed. The impetus given to musical life nevertheless helped provide an audience for opera, which gained a house in 1753.

Such events were rare, however, in Italy. From 1777, the Neapolitan Accademia de' Cavalieri hosted concerts, alongside dancing and occasions for gambling, yet these were for members – mostly nobles and military officers – only. Concerts in Italy tended to take place in private houses, though there was of course also much music to be heard in opera houses, churches, public religious processions, and in the conservatories. Most famous of the latter were the female institutions of Venice, including the orphans' Pio Ospedale della Pietà at which, from 1703 to 1709, Antonio Vivaldi served as *maestro di violino*. The Ospedale's "services with music" were essentially concerts; they were keenly attended by both the Venetian nobility and foreign visitors, from whom we have numerous reports of musical excellence. We should not necessarily posit opposition between court and "public" performances. More often than not they complemented each other, as in the encouragement Leopold, grand duke of Tuscany, lent to the establishment, under the auspices of concert societies such as the Armonici and Indegnosi, of public concerts in Florentine theaters. Operatic performance, which also benefited greatly from Leopold's patronage, was prohibited during Lent and Advent, when such concerts took place. George Frederick Handel's oratorios originated similarly in London and soon eclipsed his "foreign" Italian operas in popularity.

In 1725, the *Concert spirituel* series was founded in Paris by the entrepreneurial royal musician, Anne-Danican Philidor. The intention was to mount Lenten performances in the Tuileries' Salle des Suisses of both instrumental music and sacred Latin works. Admission was by ticket rather than invitation, and advertisements were placed in the press to attract an audience. The venture's privilege was granted by the Opéra, which retained Lully's monopoly from Louis XIV for public musical performance. Expansion of its remit to include secular works in the vernacular would occur after the Opéra, sensing a going concern, assumed control in 1734. There was nothing narrowly nationalistic about the programs; Italian and, increasingly, German music also had their place in the Parisian sun, helping to influence taste and composition. For instance, performances of symphonies by the Mannheim composer Johann Stamitz encouraged expansion of the orchestra and provoked interest in symphonic composition by musicians such as François-Joseph Gossec, the "father of the French symphony," and the mulatto Joseph Boulogne de Saint-Georges.

This influence was returned with interest by the enthusiasm with which Mozart and Haydn would write their Paris symphonies for the great orchestra; indeed, Mozart explicitly relished the large body of strings at his disposal, something present-day "authentic" performers willfully elect to ignore. The swaggering upward opening tutti, known since Lully as *le premier coup d'archet*, of Mozart's "Paris" Symphony, KV 297/300*a*, announces a composer confident to be heard at the highest and most public level, no longer content with the Alpine backwater of Salzburg. He wrote to his father, the composer Leopold Mozart: "I have been careful not to neglect the *premier coup d'archet* – and that is quite enough. What a fuss the oxen here make of this trick! The devil take me if I can see any difference! They all begin together, just as they do in other places." Yet, whatever his mocking tone, Paris and his success there left their mark upon Mozart. He told Leopold that so happy was he with the performance, "as soon as the symphony was over, I went off to the Palais Royal, where I had a large ice [and] said the rosary as I had vowed to do." The eminence of the *Concert spirituel* in Parisian musical life persisted until its disbandment in 1790, although a successor would be founded 15 years later.

Violinist-composers such as Giovanni Battista Viotti and Jean-Marie Leclair also benefited from the increased importance of instrumental, chamber, and orchestral music in Paris, rendering Bernard de Fontenelle's celebrated question "Sonate, que me veux-tu?" increasingly redundant. This held for a variety of instruments, not least given the great popularity of the *symphonie concertante*, of which Paris alone produced more than 150 between 1768 and 1789. Such a form – including Mozart's concerto for flute and harp, KV 299/297*c*, written for Paris – furthered greater independence and indeed virtuosity for all orchestral instruments and their performers, leading Pierre-Louis Ginguené to write more generally of concerto form in his 1791 *Encyclopédie méthodique*:

> Instrumental performance has now reached so advanced a state of perfection that there is no instrument which cannot claim to shine in a concert. . . . The flute, the oboe, and the clarinet, have long had their concertos. Even the horn has concertos [four survive from Mozart, no less], and the sad bassoon has not forgone that advantage [again witnessed by Mozart]. I have heard the nephew of the great Stamitz play concertos for the viola; concertos for the violoncello have made the reputation of more than one famous artist, and concertos have now been composed for the double bass.

The situation is not so straightforward as to permit drawing of a straight line from the existence of the *Concert spirituel* to the composition of double-bass concertos. However, there is a definite relationship here between the growth of a public, the institution of public concerts, the esteem granted instrumental virtuosity, the greater prowess of the orchestra, and of course the importance both Baroque and classical musical esthetics attached to *concertante* form of one variety or another, which benefited from greater expressive capacity and intellectual recognition as it became influenced by the development of Austro-German sonata forms. Mozart's series of mature piano concertos stands as the apogee of eighteenth-century achievement in this respect, and it should be remembered that these works were generally intended for his own performance at subscription concerts, although this did not preclude publication.

By the end of the century, listeners to music and audiences for art in general were increasingly expected to work with their imaginations, a reflection of the increasing fortunes of idealist esthetics – and, indeed, the very idea of esthetics in a modern sense – at the expense of mimesis. This went hand in hand with imperatives towards both "popularity" and *Bildung* – a difficult word to translate, but which might be rendered as humanist "self-cultivation." They might seem contradictory, and to some extent were; yet equally, the latter impulse required some measure at least of the former. The Swiss esthetician Johann Jacob Breitinger wrote in about 1740 of *ars popularis*, art possessing a "popularity" in the sense of reaching beyond a small circle of initiates and being of practical use. The extent of the public for and its interest in the letters between Julie and Saint-Preux in Rousseau's *La Nouvelle Héloïse* had been well illustrated by the large number of letters Rousseau received asking how things turned out. This may not have been criticism at anything other than the most lowly level, but critical engagement it remained. Towards the end of the century Christian Garve, an essayist and translator into German of works ranging from Cicero to Edmund Burke and Adam Smith, praised this as the best approach for instruction of educated readers, whether in literature or his own brand of "popular philosophy." Immanuel Kant considered Garve's review of the *Critique of Pure Reason* to have vulgarized and misrepresented his intention; such was or at least could be the price of "popularity." An instructive contrast may be drawn between Metastasio, "wasting" his life that he might instruct mankind – especially courtly mankind – "in a pleasing way," and the Saxon poet, Christian Fürchtegott Gellert, whose priorities lay with the profound pedagogical responsibility he felt for his Leipzig students. Strongly influenced by the third earl of Shaftesbury's esthetics, Gellert tipped the Englishman's careful equilibrium between the truths of the good and beautiful towards exaltation of the former. Gellert's view that literature should not only or even principally entertain, but should also improve societal taste and morals, corresponds with the elderly Haydn's statement of belief – he once called Gellert his "hero" – that he had done his duty "and have been of use to the world through my works."

Yet in order to be "of use," to further the interests of *Bildung*, there had to be some sort of public and some sort of education thereof – and, moreover, a desire from some sections of the public, and its critical organs, to be educated. Thus it was of vital import to Gluck and Ranieri Calzabigi (see below) that their reform operas coincided with the birth of serious Viennese theatrical criticism, just as the latter had been assisted by having the issues raised by operatic reform as material for its development. The Parisian mid-century controversy over the relative merits of French and Italian opera, the *Quérelle des Bouffons*, fed upon both genuine esthetic differences and an audience willing to participate in a great pamphlet war. The coffers of the Paris Opéra, by now at least as much as Versailles the guardian of venerable *tragédie lyrique*, managed nevertheless to swell through staging both French and Italian works to an eager audience. Writers on the Paris salons of the 1750s would go so far as to identify themselves as dissenting voices of the "nation," speaking against the stranglehold of the French Academy. Johann Wolfgang von Goethe might argue in his essay *On Harsh Judgements* that "the true artist must ignore his public, just as the teacher disregards the whims of his children." These were harsh words from the author of so wildly popular a "hit" as *The Sorrows of Young Werther*, and Goethe was as aware as anyone that pedagogy, though not a meeting of equals, was far from a straightforward case of disregard. As representational culture ceded some ground to the marketplace, bourgeois or otherwise, artists both benefited – not least by the progress of copyright – and suffered from its whims.

Questions of Style: Baroque, Rococo, and Classicism

These socio-esthetic questions bring us more properly to the realm of esthetics, not so much in the abstract as to another paradigm of writing on eighteenth-century art. This is related to, yet not reducible to, the partial transition from a culture based upon representation into one focused upon a critical public sphere, and the tension between the two. The principal issue here is stylistic, a transition from the (courtly) Baroque to the (enlightened) classical, slightly complicated by the presence, intermediate or otherwise, of the Rococo. This approach might be termed art-historical rather than socio-political. It is not my intention to erect a wall between the two, but rather to consider the former in light of the latter.

The word "style" derives from the Latin *stilus*: a needle used to write upon wax-coated tablets. This manner of inscription gives plenty of scope for "gendered" consideration of "style"; further comment on this must be deferred. An opposition between style and idea is implicit in this straightforward understanding, yet the relationship is more complex, more dialectical, in terms of art history broadly construed. Many questions are raised, which can only really be mentioned here in passing, yet which should nevertheless be borne in mind when considering the art of any period. Do we concentrate upon those features that unite an epoch, or upon what grants specific utterances esthetic worth, what the artist is "trying to say"? Is he successful in doing so, and to what extent is this conditioned by temporal constraints? Do we consider the artist in terms of the unifying style or even conflicting styles of his time, what he has in common with other artists, or in the "difference" he makes? Does a specific artwork gain significance through or despite its general heritage? How much importance should we ascribe to the artist's intention, implicit or explicit, or even to the artwork itself, and how much to the ways in which it is received and transformed? Such methodological concerns are of importance not only in terms of more abstract esthetics, but in determining how, if at all, it might be possible for us to consider artworks historically.

But there is a specifically eighteenth-century aspect to problems of style. In the sense generally understood by modern historians of the visual arts, the idea of style

Figure 10 Jacques-Louis David, *Oath of the Horatii*, 1785. *akg-images/Erich Lessing*

has its roots in Johann Joachim Winckelmann's 1764 *History of Ancient Art*, which applies the term to ancient Greek art, characterized by "noble simplicity and calm greatness," which he compares with the art of a subsequent period, the Renaissance. Stylistic periods as conceived thereafter have in large part been understood in terms of their relationship, whether imitative or deviant, towards "classical" Greek art. Neoclassicism, as spearheaded by Winckelmann, defined itself not only in terms of the ancient world but also against its Baroque and Rococo predecessors. A return to the "classical" represented a preference for "natural" form and beauty, an elevation of eternal verities over recent deviations. Rococo has sometimes been ambiguously applied to music, but is essentially a *post facto* pejorative term appertaining to the visual arts. The French *rocaille* referred to the irregular edges of rocks and shells, often used for garden grottoes, and from the 1730s onwards was employed for a more general decorative style, the *genre pittoresque* or *rocaille*. Its metamorphosis into the stylistic usage "Rococo" seems to have arisen in the studio of Jacques-Louis David, denoting a revolutionary denigration, esthetic and moral, of *ancien régime* laxity by contrast with the rigors of classicism: Rococo signified the style of Madame de Pompadour, immortalized in François Boucher's portrait (1756; figure 7 above). The self-sacrificing heroes so characteristic of French painting from the 1770s onwards were portrayed as a "patriotic" riposte to the corrupting *oisivité* of Versailles. Thus David's *Oath of the Horatii* (1785; figure 10) could be staunchly monarchical in its portrayal of military virtue, while standing as a contrast to the sorry state to which the existing French monarchy had sunk. Virtue was no longer the preserve of the existing order, but of the sons. Esthetic and political criticism were inextricably entwined in this "unmasking" of "façades." This is closer to Pierre-Agustin Caron de Beaumarchais' *Le Mariage de Figaro* than to its less brazenly political adaptation by Lorenzo Da Ponte and Mozart.

Similar criticisms, without the actual words "Rococo" or "Baroque," may be found throughout the eighteenth century, for instance in Voltaire's 1731 *Temple de goût*. Winckelmann wrote equally pejoratively in 1755 of "Baroque taste," deriving the term from a Portuguese word denoting "pearls and teeth of unequal size." Diderot employed the term three years later to describe "bizarre" architecture, such as that of Francesco Borromini and Guarino Guarini, which displayed "the ridiculous taken to excess." Music, however, appears to have witnessed the word's first artistic usage, in an anonymous letter occasioned by the 1733 Paris première of Rameau's first opera, *Hippolyte et Aricie*. Printed in the *Mercure de France*, it presented the opera's novelty as "du barocque"; its melody was incoherent, its harmony unduly dissonant, and its meter chaotic. Charles de Brosses, in his *Lettres familières écrites d'Italie en 1739 et 1740* (actually written about 15 years later) compared architecture and music in similar terms, "Baroque" encompassing both the mock-gothic ornamentation of the Roman Palazzo Doria Pamphili, as extended in the early 1730s by Gabriele Valvassori, and the *recitativo secco* of Italian *opera seria*: "at once so Baroque and so monotonous."

The morally improving classical, then was to replace both this and the merely frivolous Rococo. For Winckelmann, "the only way for us to be great, and if at all possible, immortal," was "by imitating the ancients." Such is the context for Gluck's crystallization of plans for operatic reform, opera, which should have been the inheritor of Attic tragedy, being seen instead to have degenerated into an undramatic farrago of vocal and scenic exhibitionism. (It is hard not to sympathize in the case of, say, Vivaldi's operas.) This is witnessed in the following words from the 1769 dedication, actually penned by Gluck's librettist, Calzabigi, of *Alceste* to Leopold, grand duke of Tuscany. The preface is a landmark document in the history of musical drama:

> I have striven to restrict music to its true office of serving poetry by means of expression and by following the situations of the story, without interrupting the action or stifling it with a useless superfluity of ornaments; and I believe that it should do this in the same way as telling colors affect a correct and well-ordered drawing, by a well-assorted contrast of light and shade which serves to animate the figures without altering the contours. Thus I did not wish to arrest an actor in the greatest heat of dialogue in order to wait for a tiresome *ritornello* . . . nor to wait while the orchestra gives him time to recover his breath for a cadenza. . . . I have sought to abolish all the abuses against which good sense and reason have long cried out in vain. . . . Furthermore, I believed that my greatest labor should be devoted to seeking a beautiful simplicity . . .

Beauty, simplicity, "naturalness," reason, and above all dramatic truth are the order of the day. Style and idea are identical; or at least such is the claim. It is, moreover, largely borne out in Gluck's series of "reform operas." The first, *Orfeo ed Euridice*, still bears signs of courtly entertainment, not least in its concluding ballet. Indeed, it is debatable whether Gluck's classicism is ever quite so pure as to shake this off entirely: for his conquest of Paris in the 1770s Gluck was dependent on the patronage of Marie Antoinette, as was rendered abundantly clear in the solo and chorus, "Chantez, célébrez votre reine," from *Iphigénie en Aulide*. Yet by the time we reach his penultimate and greatest opera, *Iphigénie en Tauride*, premiered in Paris in 1779, we are in the realm of drama as understood and saluted by nineteenth-century composers such as Berlioz and Wagner. Interestingly for purists, Gluck borrowed freely from earlier operas in this, his most "dramatically truthful" work, and on one occasion from Johann Sebastian Bach, himself no stranger to self-borrowing, even in so great a "work" – assemblage almost seems more appropriate – as the Mass in B minor. Handel was most notorious of all for his "borrowings," both from himself and from others. Yet Friedrich von Schiller owned that he had never before the second *Iphigénie* opera been so moved by "such pure and beautiful music."

However, there is more than purity here; Gluck's classicism is served by the most "Romantic" music he wrote. The opening minuet ('Le Calme') is savagely interrupted by an orchestral storm, both real and representative of Iphigenia's inner demons from her dream: psychoanalysis almost beckons. Replete with orchestration born of a lavish French eighteenth-century tradition – above all that of late Rameau – yet whose innovatory qualities presage Berlioz, the tempest climaxes as Iphigenia, soon joined by her priestesses, implores the gods to aid them. The preface to *Alceste* had declared that the overture's role was to presage the impending drama. Introduction of a vocal element bound together more closely still what had previously tended to be self-sufficient movements. Gluck not only sets the scene for the drama; he plunges us into it. Louis Petit de Bachaumont wrote of the premiere in his *Mémoires secrets*: "The opera was much applauded; it is a new genre. It is really a tragedy . . . in the Greek style." Gluck, it seemed, had discovered the ever-elusive "secret of the ancients." If so, it was renewal rather than restoration.

The Baroque and Rococo were not dead, however, far from it; nor were they or had they been merely frivolous. Consider the city of Salzburg. In the person of its greatest son, Mozart, far from coincidentally, were united perhaps the century's greatest syntheses of Baroque, Rococo, classical, and proto-Romantic, of Italian, French, and German styles and traditions. Many of the city's most important surviving buildings, such as the cathedral, the Residenz, and the Schloss Mirabell, date back at least to the seventeenth century, a legacy of, amongst others, Archbishop Wolf Dietrich von Raitenau and his vision of transforming the medieval city into a German Rome. Out had gone many of the Altstadt's houses in favor of the squares that may still be seen today, but realization of this Baroque vision took time, continuing into the eighteenth century, by which time it unsurprisingly became colored by newer styles. Some architects were imported from Italy, for instance Giovanni Gaspare Zuccalli, to whom we owe the Katejanerkirche (1685–1711).

However, the most important single figure in this respect was the imperial court architect, Johann Bernhard Fischer von Erlach, influenced not only by Italian Baroque architects such as Borromini, Gianlorenzo Bernini, and Zuccalli in Salzburg itself, but also by the French-born early classicist Jean Baptiste Mathey, much of whose work had been done in Bohemia. Fischer added substantially to the realization of Baroque Salzburg with the Markuskirche (1699–1700); the Dreifaltigkeitskirche (1694–1702), the most important ecclesiastical building in the Neustadt; and the

Kollegienkirche (1696–1707). Modern Italian symmetries were thereby introduced into German architecture. Favored by Archbishop Johann Ernst von Thun-Hohenstein, Fischer found himself replaced in Salzburg on his patron's death by a rival, Johann Lukas von Hildebrandt, who rebuilt the Residenz and the Schloss Mirabell, adding to the latter the marble hall and grand staircase, decorated by Georg Michael Donner. Undeniably classical is Salzburg's lead *Mariensäule* (1766–71), work of the brothers Wolfgang and Johann Baptist Hagenauer, which stands without a hint of incongruity upon the square in front of the Baroque cathedral.

Johann Martin Schmidt's altarpieces in Salzburg's abbey church of St. Peter, are utterly Rococo in their riot of joyous celebration. It was here, most appropriately, that Mozart's great yet incomplete Mass in C minor, KV 427/417*a*, received its first performance in 1783. Mozart's sister Nannerl noted in her diary the presence of "the whole musical establishment of the court": Mozart may have been most unceremoniously expelled from that court and may have rejected its monotony in favor of marketing himself in the uncertain Viennese marketplace, yet his erstwhile milieu was not blind to his art. The Mass itself is an especially audacious and ecumenical blend of styles, epitomized by the combination of an almost sinfully beguiling operatic "Et incarnatus est" and in the "Baroque" choral homage paid to Bach and Handel. Mozart had been avidly devouring their counterpoint at the suggestion of his patron, Gottfried van Swieten (president of Joseph II's Educational Commission and subsequently librettist for Haydn's crowning masterpiece, *The Creation*).

The Bachian example of heightened harmonic intensification through contrapuntal means would inspire much of Mozart's subsequent composition, culminating in the Armored Men's chorale prelude in *Die Zauberflöte*, this final *Singspiel* being Mozart's most extraordinary synthesis of eighteenth-century styles, "popular" as well as "learned." No one else could have combined so perfectly Viennese popular theater, the Italianate coloratura of the Queen of the Night, and the mysteries of Rosicrucianism, but such an ambition is not in itself atypical. This synthetic unity in diversity, if so tired a cliché may be forgiven, is more characteristic of eighteenth-century art than stylistic purity. It is easily forgotten that Bach owed much to Italian concerto style, even in his most "Lutheran" works, the church cantatas. (Bach's great passions stand so far above the banality of classification that it seems almost blasphemous to make the attempt, proof that the present author is far from free of the Romantic world-view.)

If the *Encyclopédie* is the greatest monument to the synthetic instructive ambitions of the French Enlightenment, we see in Fischer's writing and practice similar, albeit more delimited, purpose. His 1721 *Entwurff einer historischen Architektur* was a pioneering work of comparative architecture. Since the Renaissance, the influence of Marcus Pollo Vitruvius' *De Architectura* had been incalculable; Fischer sought to correct this account, classical in almost every sense, by locating the origins of architecture in Jerusalem. Part III even went so far as to consider "a few buildings by the Arabs and Turks, and also new Persian, Siamese, Chinese and Japanese building." Fischer's masterpiece is the Vienna Karlskirche, Charles VI's votive church (figure 11). Despite the emperor's general favor towards Hildebrandt, Fischer won the architectural competition, and work commenced in 1715, completed after Fischer's death by his son, Joseph Emanuel. Fischer aimed to set in harmony those ideas he believed to underpin the most important churches of the Western world, and

Figure 11 Karlskirche, Vienna

explicitly included pagan and Jewish allusions. It stands as a real architectural equivalent to his *Entwurff*, with a "Baroque" seriousness of purpose here as genuine as that of the "classical" Gluck. The Temple of Solomon, the Pantheon, Hagia Sophia, the Roman Baroque, and St. Paul's Cathedral are amongst the inspirations. The central façade is modeled on the portico of a Greek temple, while the Trajanic columns on either side, displaying images from the life of St. Charles Borrower, allude in their structure both to the promontory Pillars of Hercules (or Straits of Gibraltar) and the twin pillars of Solomon's Temple, Boaz and Joachim. Charles VI is not forgotten. The Habsburg claim to the Spanish throne is impressed upon us by the reference to the Pillars of Hercules; moreover, to glorify Charles Borromeo was also to glorify his imperial namesake, as was recollection of his imperial predecessors, Solomon and Trajan. Only the most exalted comparisons would suffice for a Habsburg.

The eighteenth century was, then, an age rich in artistic achievement, understanding of which should not be confined to connoisseurship. Patronage and reception are also worthy of the historian's attention, and not only in narrowly "historical" terms; important in themselves, these issues can also assist us in greater understanding of artworks themselves. History and esthetics need not be suspicious of one another, let alone stand mutually opposed; indeed, we witness in the eighteenth century the birth of that idealist tradition which helps us to understand why this should be so.

To return to where we began, Mozart becomes both more and less interesting than his Romantic caricature. This need not detract from the awe we feel before his greatest works; it should enrich our appreciation. Moreover, to consider these works, greater and lesser, is a vital task for the historian, who would be as unjustified in rejecting them as irrelevant to his concerns as he would rising literacy rates or the storming of the Bastille.

Bibliography

Barnard, F. M., *Herder's Social and Political Thought: From Enlightenment to Nationalism* (Oxford, 1965).

Bennett, B., *Beyond Irony: Eighteenth-Century German Literature and the Poetics of Irony* (Cornell, 1993).

Blanning, T. C. W., *The Culture of Power and the Power of Culture: Old Regime Europe 1660–1789* (Oxford, 2002).

Boyle, N., *Goethe: the Poet and his Age* (Oxford, 1991).

Braunbehrens, V., *Mozart in Vienna* (Oxford, 1991).

Brookner, A., *Jacques-Louis David* (London, 1980).

Brooks, P., *The Novel of Worldliness: Cre'billon, Marivaux, Laclos, Stendhal* (Princeton, 1969).

Bruford, W. H., *Culture and Society in Classical Weimar* (Cambridge, 1962).

Bryson, N., *Word and Image: French Painting of the Ancient Regime* (Cambridge, 1981).

Burke, P., *The Fabrication of Louis XIV* (New Haven, 1992).

Burrows, D., *Handel* (Oxford, 1994).

Cassirer, E., *The Philosophy of the Enlightenment* (Princeton, 1951).

Chartier, R., *The Cultural Origins of the French Revolution* (Durham, NC, 1991).

Crow, T. E., *Painters and Public Life in Eighteenth-Century Paris* (New Haven and London, 1985).

Curl, J. S., *The Art and Architecture of Freemasonry* (London, 1991).

Girdlestone, C., *Jean-Philippe Rameau: His Life and Work* (London, 1957).

Habermas, J., *The Structural Transformation of the Public Sphere: An Inquiry into a Category of Bourgeois Society* (Cambridge, MA, 1989).

Harries, K., *The Bavarian Rococo Church: Between Faith and Aestheticism* (New Haven and London, 1983).

Heartz, D., *Mozart's Operas* (Berkeley, 1990).

Heartz, D., *Haydn, Mozart, and the Viennese School 1740–1780* (New York and London, 1995).

Honour, H., *Neo-Classicism* (Harmondsworth, 1977).

Irwin, D., *Neo-Classicism* (London, 1997).

Landon, H. C. R., *Haydn: Chronicle and Works* (5 vols., London, 1976–80).

Levey, M., *Painting in Eighteenth-Century Venice* (New Haven, 1994).

McVeigh, S., *Concert Life in London from Mozart to Haydn* (Cambridge, 1993).

Morrow, M. S., *Concert Life in Haydn's Vienna: Aspects of a Developing Musical and Social Institution* (New York, 1988).

Mylne, V., *The Eighteenth-Century French Novel: Techniques of Illusion* (Manchester, 1981).

Niklaus, R., *The Eighteenth Century, 1715–1789*, vol. 4 of P. E. Charvet (ed.), *A Literary History of France* (5 vols. in 6, London, 1967).

Pascal, R., *The German Sturm und Drang* (Manchester, 1953).

Price, M. B. and L. M. Price, *The Publication of English Literature in Germany in the Eighteenth Century* (Berkeley and Los Angeles, 1934).

Reed, T. J., *The Classical Centre: Goethe and Weimar 1775–1832* (London, 1980).
Rosen, C., *The Classical Style* (2nd edn., London, 1997).
Saul, N. (ed.), *Philosophy and German Literature, 1770–1990* (Cambridge, 2002).
Schroeder, D. P., *Haydn and the Enlightenment: The Late Symphonies and their Audience* (Oxford, 1990).
Sewter, A. C., *Baroque and Rococo Art* (London, 1973).
Smith, R., *Handel's Oratorios and Eighteenth-Century Thought* (Cambridge, 1995).
Smither, H. E., *A History of the Oratorio*, vols. 1–3 (Chapel Hill, NC, 1977).
Ward, A., *Book Production, Fiction and the German Reading Public 1740–1800* (Oxford, 1974).
Watkin, D., *The Architect King: George III and the Culture of Enlightenment* (London, 2004).
Wellesz, E. and F. Sternfeld, *The Age of Enlightenment 1745–1790* (Oxford, 1973).
Willey, B., *The Eighteenth-Century Background: Studies on the Idea of Nature in the Thought of the Period* (London, 1940).
Wilson, M., *Eighteenth-Century French Painting* (Oxford, 1979).
Wittkower, R., *Art and Architecture in Italy 1600–1750* (Harmondsworth, 1958).
Wolff, C., *Bach: The Learned Musician* (Oxford, 2001).
Zaslaw, N., *The Classical Era: From the 1740s to the End of the Eighteenth Century* (London, 1989).

Part III

State and Society

Chapter Fourteen

Russia

Lindsey Hughes

The story of Russia in the eighteenth century is a story of success, if one judges by contemporary yardsticks. A country that in 1700 was by far the biggest in Europe became even bigger, pushing its boundaries to the Baltic and Black seas and westwards into central Europe. Between 1750 and 1791 alone Russia acquired 8.6 million square miles of land. In 1719 the population was estimated at 15.5 million, in 1762, 23.2 million, in 1782, 28.4 million, and by 1795, 37.2 million (41 million including the Polish provinces). Figures for the 1780s estimate about 18 million Russians, 7 million Ukrainians, 5 million Belarusians, 2 million Poles, half a million or more Finns, Tatars, Latvians, Jews, Lithuanians, and Estonians, smaller numbers of Chuvash, Moldavians, Germans, Swedes, Mordvinians, Bashkirs, Urdmuts, Karelians, Komi, Mari, and others. Territorial expansion was matched by international status. A fringe nation that in 1700 found itself humiliated by Sweden and deserted by its allies by 1800 was a decisive voice in European affairs and poised, after some ups and downs, to force its will and presence into the heart of Europe (Evtuhov et al., 2004; Lieven, 2006).

Strictly speaking, what I shall refer to in this essay as Russia (Rossiia) was the Russian empire (*Rossiiskaia imperiia*), a title claimed after the Treaty of Nystad in 1721, but used earlier and informally by other sovereign states who regarded the tsar of Muscovy as the equivalent of "despotic" Eastern potentates like the emperor of China. What Russia's rulers envisaged was parity with the Habsburg emperor and echoes of ancient Rome. The eighteenth-century *imperiia* was ruled by five emperors (*imperatory*) and four empresses (*imperatritsy*), although the old Muscovite titles of "tsar" and "tsaritsa" continued to be used for various purposes, not least by the population at large. Opponents of innovation detected the number of the Beast (666) in the numerical value of the letters in *imperator* (Shmurlo, 1912: 27). In 1799, when some religious dissidents agreed to pray for Paul I in return for concessions, they insisted on calling him tsar, not emperor (Cherniavsky, 1961).

Of Russia's eighteenth-century monarchs the formative influence was the "Tsar-Reformer" Peter I Alekseevich, the Great (r. 1682–1725, until 1696 jointly with his half-brother Ivan V Alekseevich) (Anisimov, 1993; Cracraft, 2003; Hughes, 1998).

A Companion to Eighteenth-Century Europe, First Edition. Edited by Peter H. Wilson.
© 2014 John Wiley & Sons, Ltd. Published 2014 by John Wiley & Sons, Ltd.

Any account of our period is bound to begin with his watershed reign, which is unequalled by any in contemporary Europe in its impact on its country's fortunes. According to contemporary rhetoric, godlike, Peter transformed his country "from non-existence into being" (Riasanovsky, 1985). Most modern historians, following the lead of the tsarist historian Vasilii Kliuchevskii (1841–1911), regard war as the "lever" of Peter's reforms. He was at war with Sweden from 1700 to 1721, which necessitated reform of the army and stimulated the development of the Russian navy, which Peter first formed in 1696 to capture Azov from the Turks. The war economy was based on "active government entrepreneurship" in manufacture and mining, aimed at supplying the army and navy, alongside attempts to encourage private enterprise and reduce state monopolies. Protectionist tariffs defended Russian trade. Maximizing the collection of revenues and recruitment led to such measures as provincial reform (1708–9), creation of the Senate (1711), rationalized government departments (creating the colleges, 1717–18) and the poll tax (first collected 1724), while the Monastery Department (1700–1) eased the confiscation of church revenues. The Military Statute (1716) and Naval Statute (1720) spread military principles into civilian life.

Peter's experiences helped develop a broader vision of efficient government. After the conflict with Sweden ended, he issued a series of major edicts (*reglamenty*), based on the principles that administration should run like a well-oiled machine and that no state employee should err as a result of ignorance. These included the General Regulation (1720, for the internal management of the colleges), the Spiritual Regulation (1721) and the Table of Ranks (1722). The last, based on Swedish, Danish, and Prussian models, allocated elite military and administrative personnel to fourteen ranks. While it was meritocratic in the sense that no one, however high-born, could claim a post unless qualified, the Table of Ranks recognized nobles as the natural leaders of society by granting hereditary nobility to any commoner who attained the lowest rank in the army or navy or rank 8 in the civil service. The Table remained in operation until 1917, although under Peter's successors it became harder for outsiders to use it as a route to ennoblement.

Most of Peter's innovations were borrowed directly from abroad, a topic that remains a key issue in the historiography of Russia today. The debate touches on his debt to his predecessors (whose "Westernizing" reforms, for example recruiting foreigners, he freely acknowledged) and, more controversially, on questions of "backwardness" and the cost of Westernization, especially in culture. Contacts with western European military personnel in Moscow as a youth and a pioneering tour of Europe in 1697–8 persuaded Peter of the superiority of Western civilization. To become more like Europeans, for example, Russians must look like them. Therefore in 1698 Peter ordered his nobles (boyars), and later all townsmen, to shave their long beards and replace flowing robes with Western dress (Hughes, 2004a). The dress reform applied also to elite women. At the old Russian court in Moscow the sexes were strictly segregated, which foreigners saw as a distinctly "Asiatic" custom. Under Peter, noblewomen were obliged to emulate their European counterparts, abandon seclusion, and socialize with men, regardless of the shock to their modesty (Hughes, 2001). This paved the way for the feminized courts of his successors.

From 1703 the foreign lifestyle enjoyed by (imposed upon!) a tiny minority took place against the backdrop of the new port of St. Petersburg, designed by foreign architects (notably Domenico Trezzini (*c.*1670–1734) (George, 2004). Recognized as the capital from the early 1710s and a major center for trade and shipbuilding, St. Petersburg was dubbed "a great window recently opened in the north through which Russia looks on Europe" (Cross, 2004). It was a sort of "blank sheet," an anti-Moscow, on which Peter could create a model for his new empire. The city's layout was, at least on paper, planned; its spirit was rational. In 1718 it acquired its own police (public order and welfare) administration, in imitation of Paris, which Peter visited in 1717. Variously hailed as "new Amsterdam" and "new Venice," St. Petersburg developed its own inimitable combination of imperial grandeur and "Muscovite" squalor.

The establishment of St. Petersburg, achieved by forced labor and the compulsory resettlement of its new inhabitants, including nobles and merchants, relied upon the edicts of an autocratic monarch, sometimes accompanied by physical violence and oral threats. The decades before Peter's birth, especially under his father Tsar Aleksei Mikhailovich (r. 1645–76) saw the consolidation of absolutism, as rudimentary representative bodies such as the Assembly of the Land died out (the last was summoned in 1653) and the church lost ground to the state in administering its courts and lands, as well as ceding power in return for protection against the "Old Believer" schism that occurred in the 1650s and 1660s. When the last patriarch Adrian (who held office from 1690 to 1700) repudiated all "newly introduced foreign customs" and appealed to the tsar to protect the Orthodox faith from "Latin and Lutheran heretics" (Esipov, 1917: appendix, p. 72), he was clearly at odds with westward-looking developments promoted by the state, not to mention young Peter's personal inclinations. When Adrian died Peter did not appoint a successor, and in 1721 he abolished the post of patriarch, replacing church government by one man (a potential rival to the secular power) with a "Holy Governing Synod" of clergymen, structured like a government department and firmly subordinated to the emperor (Cracraft, 1971). Guidelines for its orderly administration were published in the Spiritual Regulation (1721, supplement 1722), which was co-authored by Archbishop Feofan Prokopovich (1681–1736), a Ukrainian scholar who became Peter's spokesman in ideological matters, one of several well-educated Ukrainians who served the early emperors and empresses. In 1722 the lay post of over-procurator was created to act as the tsar's "eye" in church affairs, a position that carried considerable power to the end of the tsarist era.

The "Petrine legacy" would be a key element in the decision-making and ideological trappings of his successors. It included commitment to the maintenance and expansion of empire, to Western culture and manners for the elite and, more generally, to the spread of enlightenment, and to autocratic rule. It also demanded adulation of the emperor himself, that "greatest of great men." Empress Elizabeth based her reputation on being Peter's daughter and often appeared in an adapted uniform of the tsar's own Preobrazhensky Guards, as did Catherine II, who would claim to be his "spiritual daughter," although she secretly abhorred his crude manners. Indeed, many of the more idiosyncratic aspects of Peter's personal legacy had to be quietly abandoned or retained only symbolically; these included his practice of shipbuilding, wood-turning, dentistry, and other crafts, and his creation of a "world turned upside down" in which a mock-tsar presided over Peter's promotions in the armed forces and a "Drunken Assembly" parodied traditional Muscovite piety and customs (Zitser, 2004).

Peter's legacy included a Law of Succession (1722) which required the reigning monarch to nominate his own successor, with regard to "worthiness" rather than birthright (hitherto custom had favored male primogeniture). This reform was prompted by the traumatic events surrounding the death of Peter's eldest son, Alexis (1690–1718), who was put on trial and condemned to death for plotting regicide (Bushkovitch, 2001). Rejection of St. Petersburg and the fleet and indifference to military affairs were among Alexis's alleged crimes.

The 1722 law would produce some interesting transitions of power, none of which seriously threatened Russia's stability. Peter's successor was his second wife, Catherine I (r. 1725–7), a woman of Livonian peasant origins, the first female beneficiary of a laconically worded edict that made no distinction of gender (Hughes, 2004b). Peter failed to nominate an heir, but it suited a powerful faction at court, led by his closest associate Prince Alexander Menshikov (1673–1729), to interpret Peter's coronation of Catherine as his consort in 1724 as a reflection of his plans for the succession. At Menshikov's instigation, she nominated Peter's grandson, Peter II Alekseevich (r. 1727–30), son of the ill-fated Alexis and the last Romanov of the male line, whose reign was cut short by smallpox. By the time of his accession Peter II was firmly in the clutches of the aristocratic Dolgorukii clan, who banished Menshikov. The Dolgorukiis and their allies then invited the duchess of Courland Anna Ivanovna (r. 1730–40), daughter of Tsar Ivan V, to become empress on the basis of conditions that would have significantly limited autocracy (Anisimov, 1994). Anna was persuaded by opponents of the would-be ruling clique, with backing from the guards, to reject the conditions and rule as autocrat in preference to "multiple tyranny."

The childless Anna nominated a successor early in her reign, preferring to keep the Crown with her own branch of the family. Her elder sister Ekaterina married the duke of Mecklenburg in 1716 and had a daughter Anna Leopoldovna, whose future son was her aunt's nominee. Anna obliged by marrying the duke of Brunswick in 1739, and in 1740 produced a son, Ivan, who at the age of 6 months came to the throne as Ivan VI Antonovich. His reign was short-lived. The prospect of a long regency made his protectors vulnerable. Waiting in the wings was Elizabeth (r. 1741–61), the daughter of Peter I and Catherine I, who won the guards' support to overthrow Ivan on the grounds that his German entourage threatened Russian national interests, thus "saving" Russia in the conquering spirit of her father (Anisimov, 1995).

Elizabeth's nominated successor was her nephew, Peter I's grandson, Karl Peter Ulrich of Holstein (r. December 1761–June 1762 as Peter III Alekseevich). In 1745 she married him off to the German princess Sophia-Frederika-Augusta of Anhalt-Zerbst, who took the name Ekaterina Alekseevna when she converted to Orthodoxy, but is better known to posterity as Catherine the Great (r. 1762–96). In June 1762 Catherine deposed her husband on the grounds of the threat he posed to the Russian state and church. He died under arrest, possibly by accident. Recently historians have attempted to restore Peter's reputation (Leonard, 1993), especially with respect to his role in devising major legislation, but the picture of an "inadequate" monarch presented in Catherine's memoirs is hard to erase.

Catherine II's own reputation has undergone a thorough revision over the past few decades, both in the works of Western historians (Dixon, 2001; Griffiths, 1973; Madariaga, 1981) and their Russian colleagues (Kamenskii, 1992, 1997b), who in the Soviet period were unable to devote a single monograph to her reign. Basing their assessment of Catherine on the understanding and values of her time rather than modern sensibilities, they paint a collective picture of enlightened absolutism without tyranny and genuine reform "from above," set against a background of successful foreign policy. Even so, the belief that Catherine brought only the "veneer" but not the substance of reform has proved resilient. Discussion of the apparent disparity between her pronouncements on paper and concrete achievements have centered on her Great Instruction, or *Nakaz*, for the guidance of a Legislative Commission, which she summoned in 1767 to discuss the recodification of the laws (Dukes, 1977; R. Jones, 1989). Sometimes mistakenly described as a draft law code or, equally unjustly, as a piece of propaganda to get easy publicity abroad, the *Nakaz* is best seen as a discussion paper in which the empress tried out ideas on representatives of her better-educated subjects (W. Jones, 1998).

Its main theme was the improvement of law-based monarchy, rooted in the premise that sovereigns must rule in harmony with laws and regard them as binding. Chapter 1, article 6, declared: "Russia is a European state," for which the right form of government was monarchy, not the despotism that some writers thought appropriate to vast non-European empires. At the same time, the monarch must be absolute, "for there is no other authority except that which centers on his single person that can act with a vigor proportionate to the extent of such a vast dominion" (Chapter 1, article 10). Thus Catherine set her mission squarely in the European context, but with due consideration for the special nature of her realm.

Much of the text of the *Nakaz* was lifted openly from European thinkers, notably Montesquieu's *On the Spirit of the Laws* (1748) and the Milanese jurist Cesare Beccaria's *On Crimes and Punishments* (1764). (Catherine was ahead of her time in her abhorrence of torture and cruel punishments.) Its wider context was the Enlightenment of the *philosophes*, of which Catherine had direct experience through correspondence with Voltaire and Friedrich Melchior Grimm, as well as her voluminous reading. In 1773–4 she would entertain Denis Diderot, meeting him several times each week for informal conversations. Catherine entered into the spirit of philosophy for philosophy's sake, hoping to stimulate her educated subjects in the right direction. But she soon realized that many of her ideas were too radical for Russia (she was advised to remove references to limiting serfdom from the final version of the *Nakaz*) and that the *philosophes* were happier with abstractions than reality. When Diderot expressed the view that Russia was a "blank sheet" which would be easier to reform than Western countries with their set ways, Catherine retorted "You only work on paper, which will put up with anything, whereas I, poor empress, work on human skin, which is notoriously irritable and ticklish" (Madariaga, 1981: 339).

Even judgments of Catherine's personal life have softened. That she had 12 official lover-consorts consecutively over a period of 44 years seems hardly shocking, while the manner in which consorts were "retired" was generally dignified. In office and out, they were successfully integrated into a network of kinship and intimacy that worked well as long as statesmen with actual power, non-lovers, were not threatened. The only one who rocked the boat was Prince Grigorii Potemkin (1739–91), lover-consort from 1774 to 1776, but who latterly was Catherine's virtual co-ruler, a major actor in foreign and military affairs, and probably her husband (Montefiore, 2000). Even Potemkin was distanced from real power in home affairs. His reputation once suffered as much neglect and distortion as Catherine's. Among the many myths about him, for example, is that he created fake "Potemkin villages" to impress the empress when she visited her new territories, rumors propagated by enemies prompted by the admittedly lavish preparations made for such tours.

Catherine was succeeded by her son Paul (r. 1796–1801), who discarded a number of her policies (McGrew, 1992). Their dislike was mutual: Paul had lived in fear of his mother reassigning the succession to his eldest son Alexander. Despite a genuine desire to improve Russia, especially the moral fiber of the nobility, Paul aroused hostility among the ruling elite and was murdered in his bedchamber in a palace coup. His successor Alexander I (r. 1801–25) promised to rule in the "spirit" of his grandmother. He did not repeal Paul's Law of Succession (1797), which restored primogeniture in a strict framework of law.

All these monarchs and/or their advisers faced similar challenges above and beyond Peter I's modernizing legacy, behind which Muscovite values and conditions continued to lurk. They inherited a population organized on the principle of a society of orders, in which each had his place (only males were counted in censuses) with regard to obligations to the state, and a rural economy based on subsistence agriculture, in which some 90 percent of the population were peasants, and 50 percent of those were serfs. Throughout the eighteenth century registered town dwellers (merchants and artisans) never exceeded 4 percent of the population, although urban populations were boosted by incomers such as peasant traders, foreign merchants, military personnel, and in-between categories or *raznochintsy* (Wirtschafter, 1994). Boosting urban growth, including the building of solid town centers and new towns in conquered territories, was a prime aim of Catherine II, who in 1785 issued a Charter to the Towns, which established urban councils, courts, and other elected bodies in the hope of stimulating an active third estate. The "Catherine credit system" encouraged commercial and industrial development in the provinces, with the extension of the banking system (a loan bank for nobles and merchants had been established in 1754) into a more sophisticated network of credit institutions. In 1786 the State Paper Money Bank was established.

The ruling elite or nobility comprised no more than 1 percent of the population (Madariaga, 1995). At the beginning of the century all were liable to compulsory state service. In 1762 this requirement was abolished, but the nobility, as organized in the Table of Ranks, remained the backbone of central and provincial government, as well as the officer corps of the armed forces. The eighteenth-century Russian nobility, known collectively as the *dvorianstvo*, emerged from the sixteenth- and seventeenth-century "boyar elite" and provincial nobility, the former based in and around Moscow and filling higher commands during military campaigns, the latter in the localities, where they were liable for military service as cavalrymen. Provincial servitors initially supported themselves on service estates (*pomestie*) allocated by the Crown, while most boyars inherited land (*votchiny*), but this distinction disappeared in Peter I's reign, by which time nobles treated all their estates as their hereditary property, as they did the peasants that worked them. Yet serf ownership was not a defining feature of noble status. A significant proportion owned no serfs at all, living off their service salaries or working their own land. It has been calculated that over 50 percent of nobles owned fewer than 20 male serfs, while a mere 1 percent owned more than a thousand. In 1797, 83.8 percent of landowners had fewer than 100 serfs. The richest landowners had estates scattered all over Russia, in some cases incorporating factories and mineral wealth. These magnates could deploy their serfs in imaginative ways, too, for example in theatrical troupes. The Sheremetev estate at Ostankino near Moscow boasted one of the most famous.

In Muscovy an elite within the elite served the tsar personally, carrying out ceremonial duties in addition to practical ones. A select few formed the advisory boyar council, the nearest thing to an institutional path to power, although by the end of the century the council was so big that real influence depended on gaining further distinction through kinship links, personal relations ("chemistry") with the ruler, and talent. These continued to determine the careers of a select elite even during Peter's reign. For the nobility as a whole a series of reforms, culminating in the Table of Ranks, rationalized promotion, training, and salaries and imposed specializations (young men were allocated to army, navy, or civil service at an early age), while other edicts defined cultural norms.

The Russian nobility was supposed to distinguish itself from the rest of the population, but without laying claim to freedom or political power. The perks that came with compliance, such as access to court (for an aristocratic minority), elite schools (for example the Cadet Corps, founded in 1731) and regiments, good salaries, the right to own serfs, and exemption from direct taxes and corporal punishment, apparently suppressed demands for power-sharing. Throughout the century nobles established no corporate or representative institutions on their own initiative. There was little support in 1730 for the unpredictable advantages of constitutional government. Instead, in the coming decades nobles restricted their demands to a reduction of compulsory service (to 25 years in 1735) and to having their privileges recognized in law (or laws repealed, such as the unpopular Law of Single Inheritance (1714–31). It was accepted that concessions would come "from above" and that patriotic "sons of the fatherland" would be duly grateful to their magnanimous sovereigns. In 1762 Peter III (and/or his advisers) ended compulsory service on the grounds that "coarseness in those who neglect the general good has been eradicated." The decree was not an invitation to wholesale retirement, however. All loyal subjects must "despise and scorn all those people who have never served anywhere, but spend all their time in sloth and idleness, and do not subject their children to any useful education for the benefit of the fatherland, for they are negligent of the common good, and they will not be allowed to appear at Our Court, or at public meetings or celebrations" (R. Jones, 1973).

Most nobles continued to serve for salaries and honors. In 1773–4 the rebellion led by the Don Cossack Emel′ian Pugachev, claiming to be Peter III returned to occupy his rightful throne, in which thousands of nobles perished, reminded them, too, of how they sometimes needed government armed protection. Catherine II's extensive Provincial Reform of 1775 included measures for increasing nobles' participation in local government and promoting corporate feeling through elected assemblies (Hartley, 1999). These and other privileges were consolidated in the Charter to the Nobility of 1785 (R. Jones, 1989), which codified existing laws, as part of an overall vision of a well-regulated society in which each social category knew its place. It confirmed the nobles' freedom from compulsory service, taxes, and corporal punishment, and their right to enter the service of friendly foreign powers, to purchase villages, and to exploit their lands through the sale of products, mining, and industry. Importantly, it recognized the nobles' inalienable right to their property, banning deprivation of titles or property without trial by peers. If the old historiography regarded the Charter as yet more perks for the already privileged at the expense of the "have-nots," revisionist historians see it as a first step towards civil rights, a modernizing rather than a conservative measure.

On paper, the Russian nobility seemed to have won a major victory with little effort. In reality, the model of a magnanimous monarch and a grateful nobility prevailed. As always, the monarchy called the tune. For example, elected assemblies were never allowed to operate on a national level. Events during Paul I's reign, when the emperor ignored most of the Charter's provisions, demonstrated how much the elite still relied upon the monarch's goodwill and his or her respect for the law. In the absence of institutions to push for reform, a palace elite resorted to the short, sharp remedy of assassination, in the expectation that the new emperor had their interests at heart.

One of the consequences of the 1762 emancipation was to allow the better-off nobles time and security to enjoy cultural pursuits. In the first half of the century such initiatives were firmly in the hands of the monarch to a degree seen nowhere else in Europe. Peter I did not hesitate to impose Western norms by decree. He also worked by example, importing paintings (a major acquisition was Rembrandt's *Return of the Prodigal Son*) and sculptures, and hiring foreign artists, architects, and engravers. Although some historians refer to a "print revolution" in Peter's reign, publishing remained modest by western European standards and, again, firmly in the hands of the state. Peter's practical priorities directly influenced the publication of translated manuals on such topics as shipbuilding, navigation, fortification, hydraulics, mathematics, and geography, some corrected in his own hand (Marker, 1985). Between 1708 and 1710 he introduced a new simplified alphabet, called the civil script, for secular publications. The *Honourable Mirror of Youth* (1717), a behavior book compiled from Erasmus and other sources, was a typical example of a state-sponsored work aimed at further civilizing the still crude nobility, whose education remained rudimentary and practical.

Early in his reign Peter founded specialist schools such as the Moscow School of Mathematics and Navigation (1701; from 1715 the St. Petersburg Naval Academy). A decree of 1714 established the so-called cipher or arithmetic schools, without a diploma from which nobles were not allowed to marry; but there is little evidence that penalties were imposed. Peter lacked the resources to educate even his nobility systematically, and most Russian nobles acquired the rudiments of education at home, as they had done earlier, receiving more specialized tuition once they had embarked on their service careers. The Russian Academy of Sciences (opened after Peter's death in 1725) was run almost exclusively by and for foreigners, because of the lack of suitably qualified Russian graduates. The first full Russian member was the polymath Mikhail Lomonosov (1711–65), whose secondary education was at the Moscow Academy (founded in 1687), a church-run establishment that compensated to some degree for Russia's lack of tertiary schooling. Indeed, outside the capitals, church schools remained the major source of tuition, some offering a modern curriculum.

Peter's nobles, tied as they were to lifelong service in an era when Russia was almost constantly at war, had little time for new culture, still less for becoming artists or authors themselves. The longest print runs continued to be religious in content, including the Psalter, from which Russians learned to read. Religious sensibilities still defined tastes. Sculpture in the round, disapproved of by the Orthodox Church as the art of graven images, failed to find practitioners (the first Russian sculptures were active only in the latter part of the century), while icon-painters did a brisk trade, despite the growing popularity of portrait-painting among the elite. During Peter's reign there was no permanent theater (a playhouse in Moscow run by Germans closed down), comparatively little music, and virtually no published *belles lettres*, although syllabic poetry praising the achievements of state and monarch was encouraged at court.

Under Peter's successors Western art forms put down deeper roots, always with strong imperial support. Anna and Elizabeth sponsored opera, ballet, and orchestral music, usually performed by visiting foreign troupes. Elizabeth patronized the work of the architect Bartolomeo Rastrelli (1700–71), whose rococo masterpieces (in the 1740s and 1750s) included the Catherine Palace at Tsarskoe Selo and the Winter Palace in the center of St. Petersburg, both of which formed suitably lavish backdrops for courtly entertainments, in which monarch and nobles presented Russia's positive image (Wortman, 1995). In 1757 Elizabeth founded the Imperial Academy of Fine Arts in St. Petersburg. Basing its teaching methods on those of academies in Italy, France, and Germany, it aimed to give students a firm grounding in classical art and the Old Masters. For the next century it remained virtually the only source of training for generations of Russian painters, sculptors, and architects. In 1755 Russia's first university opened in Moscow.

Under Catherine II, herself an outstanding collector, patron, and autodidact, the Russian nobility found both the incentive and the educational environment to become sponsors of culture in their own right. Catherine promoted the education of the nobility – her Smolny Institute for Noble Girls (1764), for example, provided a finishing school for generations of young ladies – but she also sought to create a "better sort of citizen" by founding schools for non-nobles. Unsuccessful experiments in the 1760s gave way to more systematic provision under the 1775 provincial reform and the 1786 Statute on National Schools, which envisaged co-educational high schools and primary schools in provincial and district towns. Tuition was free of charge; corporal punishment was banned; the curriculum was secular. If by the end of Catherine's reign only about 62,000 children were being educated in 549 state institutions, it was because most people could not see the point of educating their children, as well as because there was inadequate funding and teacher shortages. Even so, in the Russian context, the schools were an achievement.

In and around St. Petersburg Catherine's favored architects working in the classical style, such as Giacomo Quarenghi (1744–1817), Ivan Starov (1745–1808), and Charles Cameron (1746–1812). Elegant manor houses in imitation of the St. Petersburg mansions sprang up all over Russia, providing work for graduates of the Academy of Arts as well as foreigners and serf artists. Here nobles could also cultivate literary pursuits (W. Jones, 2000). An estimate puts male literacy in the empire in the 1790s at between 3 and 7 percent (cf. France, 47 percent, Britain, 68 percent, Prussia, 80 percent). At the beginning of Catherine's reign practically all the literature published in Russian was imported from abroad. The empress herself commissioned translations, sponsored literary journals on the British model (1769, the first issue of *About This and That*), and wrote plays. By the end of the century a more independent literary public, made up of women as well as men, was forming, with private individuals allowed to run printing presses from 1783. Talented Russian writers, such as Gavrila Derzhavin (1743–1816) and Nikolai Karamzin (1766–1826), won readers and headed extended literary circles which attracted many of the leading figures of their day. Russia's eighteenth century was an era of cultural apprenticeship, during which Russians mastered international forms and genres, as did their counterparts elsewhere. In the following century, with the rediscovery of national roots, the arts in Russia would develop their own distinctive face.

The mass of the population, the peasantry, had no experience of this Western culture. Some 50 percent were serfs, the rest fulfilled their obligations to the state, the Crown, and (until 1764) the church. In the non-black-earth regions in the north and northwest, where the majority lived, Russian peasant households, regardless of status, engaged in arable farming (rye and oats) based on a three-field rotation, with supplements to diet and income obtained through hunting and gathering and small crafts (Moon, 1999). Serfdom was fixed in law in Russia in 1649 and retained its basic character throughout our period, i.e. serfs and their offspring were the inalienable property in perpetuity of their owners, who could sell, bequeath, transfer, and mortgage them, marry them off, send them as conscripts, and so on. The state might intervene in its own interests – in 1721 Peter I issued an edict granting non-nobles the right to buy serfs for factories – or to curb abuses – in the same year Peter tried to ban the cruel practice of breaking up families during serf auctions. Numerous imperial decrees reminded landowners that they had a duty of care to their peasants in times of crisis. However, the state preferred to rely on the landlords to police the conscription of serfs for the army and the collection of taxes (from 1724 the poll tax). The landlord, in turn, relied on the village commune (*obshchina*) to extract dues on the basis of the peasants' collective responsibility. Work, too, was organized by various combinations of stewards and peasant self-regulation through the commune. The repartition of land by the commune to take account of changing household composition was one of the many mechanisms which perpetuated serfdom by making it tolerable.

By and large historians have discarded the old class analysis of serfdom, which viewed it purely in terms of struggle and exploitation. Recent studies have shifted from explanations based on coercion to acknowledging that to a large extent serfdom met the needs of the peasants themselves by producing an economy of sufficiency in areas on the margins of viability for agriculture. Peasants, it is argued, were not uniformly "victims," but generally retained some control over their own lives, even though in our period they handed over something like half their earnings to owners and the state. They thought not in terms of maximizing profits or "progress," still less of individual liberties, but of feeding themselves and their families. When prompted from outside, as during the revolt of Pugachev, who urged peasants to slaughter landlords, local discontent could erupt in rebellion, but this was the exception, not the rule. Peasants were more likely to murder other peasants than to kill the authorities. The image of the cruel landlord making his peasants' lives a misery was also exceptional. Rather, the landlord's absence tended to reinforce the peasants' belief that the land was theirs, because they were the ones who worked it. Being tied to the land implied entitlement to land.

There was some discussion among the elite of the "peasant question" (Bartlett, 1990; Madariaga, 1974). Catherine II believed that serfdom must and would disappear. In theory, she said in her memoirs, "the great motivator of agriculture is freedom and private property. When each peasant is assured that what belongs to him does not also belong to another, he will improve it." But this did not mean that serfs were ready for freedom now or that their owners were economically or psychologically prepared either. The politically expedient decision to safeguard the landowning rights of the nobles made it impossible to free peasants with land unless the masters voluntarily relinquished some. Catherine and her immediate successors sought sporadically to mitigate serfdom rather than abolish it, for example with bans on the enserfment of orphans and illegitimate children, prisoners of war, and state peasants ascribed to factories. Paul I's decree of 1797 specified that peasants should not work more than three days per week on their lords' land and that Sunday must be a day of rest. Neither Alexander I or Nicholas I, who both disapproved of serfdom, dared to touch it. Serfdom was ended (in 1861) only when it began to hamper Russia's status in world affairs. Until then, "autocracy and its alliance with a serf-owning nobility was an exceptionally effective (and ruthless) mechanism for mobilizing resources from a vast and pre-modern realm" (Lieven, 2006: 12).

The Orthodox Church admonished the various social categories to accept their God-given lot. Religion dominated the world-view not only of peasants but also of most nobles, making them accept the status quo. Yet religion has all too often disappeared from historians' record of Russia after the 1720s. The late Soviet cultural-historical blueprint identified a period of "transition" under the impact of increased contact with the West and a decline in the church's power, followed by the virtual imposition of a secular outlook under Peter I. Indeed, the Spiritual Regulation did limit entry into monasteries and directed priests towards educational, administrative, and welfare activities. "Superstition" was decried. The number of saints' days celebrated at court, and of holy days associated with miracle-working icons, was reduced (Hughes, 2000). These processes were consolidated in 1762 by Peter III with the transfer of church peasants to the state, a measure ratified by Catherine II in the spirit of Enlightenment in 1764, after which the former church peasants were administered in the Department of Economy.

Undoubtedly, then, the Russian Orthodox Church lost some of its independence in the eighteenth century, and one may speak of "secularization" in various senses, such as the state-sponsored propagation of secular culture; but recent research suggests that the role of religion in Russians' lives, from the peasants to the court, complemented secular developments. Even Peter I, who was denounced as "ungodly" by conservative opponents, prayed three times a day during Holy Week, assiduously commissioned churches, traveled with a miracle-working icon of the Savior, and relied on church hierarchs for ideological support. His daughter Elizabeth was well known for her piety, which verged on the superstitious, while Catherine II, an astute convert from Lutheranism, focused in her accession manifesto on the "salvation" of Orthodoxy and was meticulous in her observance of major festivals. The court records (*Iurnaly i kamer-furíerskie zhurnaly*) show that the daily lives of all the eighteenth-century emperors and empresses were replete with religious ritual (Dixon, 2007).

Visits to Moscow, Russia's religious capital, in particular, allowed rulers and court to keep in touch with Orthodoxy's roots. Coronations continued to be celebrated in the fifteenth-century Kremlin Cathedral of the Dormition, surrounded by the relics of the patriarchs. In the latter part of the century, the church was expected to spread Enlightenment values, in the form of sermons and tracts, along with the teaching that the tsarist regime was ordained by God. There was no rigid line drawn underneath pre-Petrine "Holy Russia" and a secular world of enlightened absolutism.

The Orthodox Church was the state's ally in foreign policy, from blessing icons before battles to supporting campaigns on behalf of co-religionists abroad. In the final analysis, the major commitment of all Russia's monarchs was to war. For this purpose the ability quickly to mobilize huge peasant armies and deploy them to north, south, and west under trained commanders was crucial, as was the capacity to raise revenues internally without (until Catherine II's reign) resorting to foreign loans.

When judged purely by territory gained, Peter I's acquisitions, though relatively modest, represented a significant increase in Russia's status in northeast Europe. In 1686 his sister Sophia (r. 1682–9) and her advisers committed Russia to the Holy League against the Turks. When the League folded in the late 1690s, all Russia had to show for its efforts was the port of Azov at the mouth of the Don, captured in 1696 (and relinquished by the Treaty of Adrianople in 1713). Peace with Turkey in August 1700 allowed Peter immediately to switch his focus to the Baltic and reclaim his "patrimony" in Ingria and Karelia, which were "unjustly" seized by the Swedes in the early seventeenth century. Acquiring ports was a fundamental aim. It is unlikely that Peter would voluntarily have faced the Swedish army, the best trained and equipped in Europe, alone. During his Grand Embassy in 1697–8 he discovered that his own aspirations dovetailed with those of Denmark, eager to limit Swedish power in the western Baltic, and Augustus II of Poland (r. 1697–1704, 1709–33), who, in his dual capacity as elector of Saxony, had his eyes on Swedish Livonia, where discontented nobles promised to back anti-Swedish action. However, this alliance collapsed almost immediately, with the Danes forced into surrender, a Russian army beaten by the Swedes at Narva in November 1700, and Augustus pursued back into Saxony by Sweden's young king, Charles XII (r. 1697–1718). The latter strategy allowed Peter to re-equip and pursue an independent campaign in the eastern Baltic, taking Nöteborg in 1702 and, in 1703, Nyenkans (the site of future St. Petersburg). Thereafter, inconclusive action in Poland, which saw Augustus deposed and the Swedish "puppet" Stanisław Leszczyński installed, made Peter resort to a scorched-earth policy on Russia's western borders in the face of Charles XII's march into Ukraine, where he was lured by promises of aid from Hetman Ivan Mazepa (1645–1709) and his Cossacks. Menshikov's destruction of Mazepa's base knocked out this support. Following one of the coldest winters in living memory, the Russian and Swedish main armies met in battle for the first time at the town of Poltava in June 1709. The Russian victory over the much smaller and exhausted Swedish army, whose home population was in no position to support it, was hailed as a virtual revolution in northern Europe. Russia was able to restore alliances (in 1709 with Denmark, Poland, and Prussia), capture Swedish ports on the Baltic (Riga, Reval, and Viborg in 1710), and arrange several diplomatic marriages, notably Peter's son Alexis in 1711 to Princess Charlotte-Christina-Sophia of Wolfenbüttel. Hereafter the Romanovs became entwined with the Protestant houses of northern Europe.

The Great Northern War dragged on, prolonged by intervention on Sweden's behalf by a Britain squadron in the Baltic, by successful Russian action, supported by its fleet, in Finland in 1713–14, and allied action in Pomerania, where Sweden was deprived of its remaining German possessions. By the Treaty of Nystad (September 10, 1721) Sweden ceded Livonia, Estonia, Ingria, and part of Karelia to Russia. Attempts by Sweden later in the century, in wars from 1741 to 1743 and 1788 to 1790, to win back lost territories failed, and in 1809 Finland, which Russia ceded in 1721, would join the empire.

The broad consequences were summed up by one of King George I's officials in Hanover: "Germany and the entire North have never been in such grave peril as now, because the Russians should be feared more than the Turks . . . and are gradually advancing closer and closer to our lives" (Bagger, 1993: 38–9). Russia's increased power in northeast Europe was reflected in its domination of Poland, now a virtual protectorate, which had borne the brunt of military operations for two decades. Moreover, the focus on north European affairs had not suppressed Russia's aspirations in the south and east. In 1711 Peter went to war with Turkey. The military outcome was a near-disaster when the Turks surrounded the under-supplied Russian army on the Pruth, while attempts to turn the operation into a crusade foundered when the Orthodox rulers of Moldavia and Wallachia failed to deliver promised support. In 1722–3 Russia waged a successful campaign for commercial aims along the western shore of the Caspian, capturing Derbent, Baku, and Gilan from Iran. In the 1730s Russia had to let these conquests go, but a marker had been put down. Exploratory expeditions and trade missions to central Asia and China, to the far north and to the Pacific, sponsored by Peter and his successors, all pointed to the further spread of empire.

In the decades following Peter I's death foreign policy was conducted by Andrei Ostermann (1686–1747), whom Elizabeth replaced with Aleksei Bestuzhev-Riumin (1693–1766). In general, Russia had a series of highly competent foreign ministers and an increasingly professional diplomatic service. Ostermann's Russo-Austrian treaty of 1726 underpinned Russian alliances for much of the century. Austria reckoned to limit Russian interference in Habsburg Orthodox territories, while allowing Russia a freer hand in Orthodox lands ruled by Poland and Turkey. The pact determined the outcome of the War of the Polish Succession (1733–5), in which Russia and Austria headed off the election of a French candidate for the Polish throne, the former Swedish-sponsored Stanisław Leszczyński, allowing a Polish confederation to elect the Austrian candidate Augustus III (r. 1733–63), son of Augustus II. Russia enjoyed Austrian support for war with Turkey in 1735–9. Costly victories in Crimea and Moldavia secured the restoration to Russia of Azov and some adjoining lands after France intervened to determine the terms of the Peace of Belgrade (1739). A Russian expeditionary force to the Rhine hastened the conclusion of the War of the Austrian Succession (1740–8), in which Prussia and France lined up against Austria and Britain. The next few years saw the consolidation of an anti-Prussian policy in St. Petersburg, underpinned by Empress Elizabeth's dislike of Frederick II.

In the Seven Years War (1756–63) Russia's armies, in alliance with Austria and France, enjoyed some tactical victories against Prussia and in 1760 even temporarily occupied Berlin. Patriotic Russians were justly proud of their success in battle against the highly regarded Prussians. However, internal misgivings over war aims, mounting financial pressures, and desertion rates, then Elizabeth's death at the end of 1761, led to Russia's withdrawal, at the initiative of the new Emperor Peter III, who idolized Frederick II. Excessive admiration for Prussian military trappings was to hasten Peter's downfall.

Catherine II proved to be one of the great diplomats of her era, with the expert assistance of Nikita Panin (1718–83) and, from 1781, Alexander Bezborodko (1747–99). One of the first significant acts of her new government in 1763 and a cornerstone of Panin's "Northern System" was a treaty with Prussia, which sanctioned joint intervention to place the Polish nobleman Stanisław Poniatowski (r. 1764–95) on the Polish throne. Much to Catherine's disgust, King Stanisław instituted constitutional reforms and played down the issue of the rights of non-Catholics in Poland, which Catherine claimed to champion. Russia responded with armed intervention. When Cossack rebels pursued Poles across the border into a dependency of the Crimean khanate, the Turks, encouraged by the French, demanded that Russian troops immediately evacuate Poland. Russia and Turkey were at war.

Initial Russian conquests in the First Russo-Turkish War (1768–74) were impressive, including Khotin and Bender, the key Turkish fortress on the Dniester river. In 1770 a Russian squadron won a naval victory over the Turks at Chesme in the Aegean. Crucially, a Russian army occupied Crimea, which in late 1772 accepted the offer of nominal independence in return for Russia's occupation of most of its ports. Crimea proved the biggest stumbling block to Russian and Turkish negotiations, but Russia's need to deploy troops against the Pugachev rebellion hastened a resolution in the form of the Treaty of Kuchuk Kanardji (Kűçűk Kaynarca, 21 July 1774), which gave Russia the Black Sea coast between the Dnieper and the Bug, freedom for its merchant vessels to navigate the sea and straits, and Crimean independence.

Europe's major powers viewed Russia's military and naval successes glumly. In particular, the Austrians were reluctant for Moldavia and Wallachia to fall under Russian rule. A passive Poland was brought to the rescue: the division of spoils during the first partition of Poland (1772) between Austria, Prussia, and Russia represented a way of compensating Russia, which acquired "ancestral" lands in the grand duchy of Lithuania (eastern Belarus) and southeastern Latvia, bringing some 1,800,000 new subjects into the empire (Lukowski, 1999).

Russia acted as a mediator in the Treaty of Teschen between Austria and Prussia (1779) and in the 1780s took advantage of the American War of Independence to forge the League of Armed Neutrality, allowing neutral countries to trade, which harmed British interests. Increasingly, Russian interests at home were oriented towards the south, with its promise of fertile lands and new ports. More grandiosely, Potemkin devised the Greek project, the goal of which was the creation of a new Russian Greek empire at Constantinople. In 1780 Catherine and Emperor Joseph II of Austria made a secret alliance, which allowed Russia to impose the outright annexation (1783) of Crimea. Despite protests from abroad, Catherine went ahead with a tour of her new territories in Joseph's company, visiting Crimea and Russia's new naval base at Sebastopol early in 1787. In September the Turks, irritated also at Russian attempts to interfere in Moldavia, Wallachia, and Georgia, declared war. In 1788 Russia captured the fortress city of Ochakov that controlled part of the Dnieper estuary. In 1789 Austrians and Russians, under Potemkin's command, occupied the Dniester region down to the Black Sea, then in 1790 Joseph II died and his successor Leopold II pulled out of the war. The Russian Black Sea fleet and armies pressed on, but eventually Prussia persuaded Catherine to reduce Russia's demands to the annexation of the territory between the lower Dnieper and lower Dniester. The Treaty of Jassy (January 9, 1792) confirmed the Treaty of Kuchuk Kanardji, Russia's possession of Crimea and Ochakov and an extension of its Black Sea coast.

In 1788 the Warsaw Sejm, encouraged by a defensive treaty with Prussia, began to work towards reforming the monarchy. Catherine was alarmed by the prospect of a revived Poland with a real army, allied to Prussia, and the limitation on the opportunities for Russia and other states to interfere in Polish affairs. In 1792 she engineered a confederation of dissident Polish magnates and dispatched troops. The Russians and Prussians then cheated on their Polish allies and announced a second partition, whereby Russia obtained central Belarus and the eastern three-fifths of what had been Polish Ukraine. A third partition followed in 1795, following the revolt of Tadeusz Kosciuszko. Prussia and Austria shared the remainder of ethnic Poland, and Russia obtained Lithuania, Courland, and what remained of western Belarus and Ukraine. Poland vanished from the map and the powers vowed not to use the word again.

Imperial success brought fresh permutations of the old challenge of how to cope with newly annexed populations of different races and faiths. In Catherine's reign Russia did penetrate further west, as though to underline its claim to be a European state; but at least half the empire was outside Europe and the European sections were not all Russian. By the mid-1780s the proportion of ethnic Russians in the empire was less than 50 percent, a figure that did not change much until the fall of the Soviet Union. Catherine favored as far as possible governing the multinational empire uniformly. Minorities, she believed, should "by the gentlest means be brought to the point where they Russify" (Kamenskii, 1997a: 210). For the time being, however, the speed of expansion meant as far as possible using existing institutions and customs. For example, in the many Jewish communities acquired by Russia during the partitions of Poland (up to half the world's Jews), the councils known as kahals continued to perform a number of functions and Jews could also elect members to new local bodies. However, opposition from local non-Jews ensured that restrictions remained (Klier, 1986). Catherine urged religious toleration and encouraged the use of local languages in schools. The notorious "Russification" policies that precipitated the collapse of tsarism would not bite for another century.

Catherine's expansionist policies were unpopular with many of her subjects, although there were no public outlets in Russia for expressions of dissent. Any hope of respite in foreign affairs was crushed by changes to the international order brought about by the French Revolution and, closer to home, the volatile policy of Paul I. His attempts to call general peace conferences having failed, in 1798 he joined the Second Coalition against France, then in 1800 broke with Austria and Britain and declared friendship with Napoleon. Paul's attempts to act as "restorer of Europe" had antagonized most of Russia's former allies by the time his death was announced in March 1801. A military division on its way to challenge the British in India was recalled.

Russia's eighteenth century thus ended, to use a cliché, in both triumph and tragedy, with a touch of farce. At home the foundations of autocracy and serfdom seemed as solid as ever. Abroad, no major power could ignore Russia in its foreign policy. The expansion of empire was spectacular and brought tangible benefits, too, trade out of the Baltic and Black Sea ports (Odessa, founded in 1794, soon became one of the empire's biggest cities), and new opportunities for agriculture on the fertile soils of New Russia. But the world was changing under the impact of revolutionary France, from which Europe's eastern fringes were not immune, as events in Poland showed. Catherine II shuddered along with other crowned heads at the news of Louis XVI's execution in 1793. As it turned out, the Romanovs, Paul excluded, got off lightly; there was little sign of internal protest sparked by revolutionary ideas, with the exception of the notorious case of Alexander Radishchev's privately published *Journey from St. Petersburg to Moscow* (1790), whose author Catherine denounced as a "worse rebel than Pugachev" for his attack on serfdom and autocracy. Overwhelmingly, the Russian nobility accepted the deal consolidated in its Charter of 1785, but without any compunction about doing away with a ruler who failed to keep his side of the bargain. The new emperor Alexander I seemed set to grant liberties both to individual estates and perhaps to Russia itself. Yet he would prove to be as much the prisoner of the twin pillars of autocracy and serfdom as his eighteenth-century predecessors.

Bibliography

Anisimov, E., *The Reforms of Peter the Great: Progress through Coercion in Russia* (Armonk, 1993).

Anisimov, E., "Anna Ivanovna," *Russian Studies in History*, 32 (1994), 37–72.

Anisimov, E., *Empress Elizabeth: Her Reign and her Russia* (Gulf Breeze, FL, 1995).

Bagger, H., "The role of the Baltic in Russian foreign policy 1721–1773," in H. Ragsdale (ed.), *Imperial Russian Foreign Policy* (Cambridge, 1993), pp. 36–55.

Bartlett, R., "The question of serfdom: Catherine II, the Russian debate and the view from the Baltic periphery," in R. Bartlett and J. Hartley (eds.), *Russia in the Age of the Enlightenment* (London, 1990), pp. 142–66.

Bushkovitch, P., *Peter the Great: The Struggle for Power, 1671–1725* (Cambridge, 2001).

Cherniavsky, M., *Tsar and People: Studies in Russian Myths* (New Haven, 1961).

Cracraft, J., *The Church Reform of Peter the Great* (Stanford, 1971).

Cracraft, J., *The Revolution of Peter the Great* (Cambridge, MA, and London, 2003).

Cross, A. (ed.), *St Petersburg, 1703–1825* (Basingstoke, 2004).

Dixon, S., *Catherine the Great* (Harlow, 2001).

Dixon, S., "Religious ritual at the eighteenth-century Russian court," in M. Schaich (ed.), *Monarchy and Religion: The Transformation of Royal Culture in Eighteenth-Century Europe* (Oxford, 2007), pp. 217–48.

Dukes, P. (ed.), *Russia under Catherine the Great*, vol. 2: *Catherine the Great's Instruction (Nakaz) to the Legislative Commission, 1767* (Newtonville, MA, 1977).

Esipov, G. V., *Raskol'nich'i dela*, vol. 2 (St. Petersburg, 1861).

Evtuhov, C. et al., *A History of Russia: Peoples: Legends, Events, Forces* (New York, 2004).

George, A., *St Petersburg: The First Three Centuries* (Stroud, 2004).

Griffiths, D., "Catherine II: the republican empress," *Jahrbücher für Geschichte Osteuropa*, 21 (1973), 323–44.

Hartley, J., *A Social History of the Russian Empire* (London, 1999).

Hughes, L., *Russia in the Age of Peter the Great* (New Haven, 1998).

Hughes, L., "The Petrine year: anniversaries and festivals in the reign of Peter the Great (1682–1725)," in K. Friedrich (ed.), *Festive Culture and Germany and Europe from the 16th to the 20th Century* (Lewiston, 2000), pp. 148–68.
Hughes, L., "From caftans into corsets: the sartorial transformation of women during the reign of Peter the Great," in P. Barta (ed.), *Gender and Sexuality in Russian Civilization* (London, 2001), pp. 17–32.
Hughes, L., "A beard is an unnecessary burden," in R. Bartlett and L. Hughes (eds.), *Russian Society and Culture and the Long Eighteenth Century* (Münster, 2004a), pp. 21–4.
Hughes, L., "Catherine I of Russia: consort to Peter the Great," in C. C. Orr (ed.), *Queenship in Europe, 1660–1815: The Role of the Consort* (Cambridge, 2004b), pp. 131–54.
Jones, R., *The Emancipation of the Russian Nobility, 1762–1785* (Princeton, 1973).
Jones, R., "The Charter of the Nobility: a legislative landmark?' *Canadian American Slavic Studies*, 23 (1989), 1-16.
Jones, W. G., "The spirit of the *Nakaz*: Catherine II's literary debt to Montesquieu," *Slavonic and East European Review*, 77 (1998), 658–71.
Jones, W. G., "Literature in the eighteenth century," in N. Cornwell (ed.), *The Routledge Companion to Russian Literature* (London, 2000), pp. 25–35.
Kamenskii, A., *Pod seniiu Ekateriny: Vtoraia olovina XVIII veka* (St. Petersburg, 1992).
Kamenskii, A., *The Russian Empire in the Eighteenth Century* (New York, 1997a).
Kamenskii, A., *Zhizn' i sud'ba imperatritsy Ekateriny Velikoi* (Moscow, 1997b).
Klier, J., *Russia Gathers her Jews: The Origins of the "Jewish Question" in Russia, 1772–1825* (DeKalb, ILL, 1986).
Leonard, C., *Reform and Regicide: The Reign of Peter III of Russia* (Bloomington, 1993).
Lieven, D. (ed.), *The Cambridge History of Russia*, vol. 2: *Imperial Russia, 1689–1917* (Cambridge, 2006).
Lukowski, J., *The Partitions of Poland: 1772, 1793, 1795* (Harlow, 1999).
McGrew, R., *Paul I of Russia* (Oxford, 1992).
Madariaga, I. de, "Catherine II and the serfs: a reconsideration of some problems," *Slavonic and East European Review*, 52 (1974), 34–62.
Madariaga, I. de, *Russia in the Age of Catherine the Great* (London, 1981).
Madariaga, I. de, "The Russian nobility, 1600–1800," in H. M. Scott (ed.), *The European Nobilities in the 17th and 18th Centuries* (2 vols., London, 1995), vol. 2, pp. 223–73.
Marker, G., *Publishing, Printing, and the Origins of Intellectual Life in Russia, 1700–1800* (Princeton, 1985).
Montefiore, S., *Prince of Princes: The Life of Potemkin* (London, 2000).
Moon, D., *The Russian Peasantry 1600–1930* (London, 1999).
Riasanovsky, N., *The Image of Peter the Great in Russian History and Thought* (New York, 1985).
Shmurlo, E., *Petr Velikii v otsenke sovremennikov i potomstva* (St. Petersburg, 1912).
Wirtschafter, E., *Structures of Society: Imperial Russia's "People of Various Ranks"* (DeKalb, ILL, 1994).
Wortman, R., *Scenarios of Power: Myth and Ceremony in Russian Monarchy*, vol. 1 (Princeton, 1995).
Zitser, E. A., *The Transfigured Kingdom: Sacred Parody and Charismatic Authority at the Court of Peter the Great* (Ithaca, 2004).

Chapter Fifteen

Poland-Lithuania

Jerzy Lukowski

"The Commonwealth of the Two Nations: the Polish and Lithuanian" – Rzeczpospolita Obojga Narodów, Polskiego i Litewskiego – came into being in 1569. The kingdom of Poland and the grand duchy of Lithuania had been linked through a personal union under the Jagiellonian dynasty since 1386, elective in Poland, hereditary in the grand duchy. A formal, federal union was engineered by King Sigismund II Augustus at the Lublin Sejm (parliament) of 1569, as a means of keeping together an inheritance for which he had no legitimate heirs.

The "Two Nations" label could not begin to do justice to the complex of peoples and faiths of this commonwealth (or even republic – the same word, *rzeczpospolita*, serves as both in Polish). Historians generally accept that the population, on the eve of the 1772 partition, stood at some 14,000,000 – some 19 people to the square kilometer. This was, as contemporaries bewailed, an underpopulated land (France had a population density of around 50 people to the square kilometer), with the most densely settled areas located in the west, center, and south (around the towns of Poznań, Warsaw, and Kraków), and to the north, along the corridor of the lower Vistula and its delta. Least peopled were the eastern lands of the grand duchy. Categorizing the population is difficult, not least because a readily understandable modern taxonomy is hopelessly anachronistic. In terms of "ethnicity," rather less than half the population was Polish, at least in the sense of Polish being its first language. There were something over a million Lithuanian-speakers, concentrated in an area corresponding largely to modern-day Lithuania. About a million Jews – the largest single Jewish population anywhere at the time – spoke primarily Yiddish. The great bulk of the grand duchy and the eastern half of Poland proper were inhabited by peasants speaking Belarusian or Ukrainian. The towns of the north and west contained significant German-speaking elements, especially in the relatively densely urbanized terrains of Polish or "Royal" Prussia (as opposed to "Ducal" Prussia, which belonged to the electors of Brandenburg, who, in 1701, secured a kingly title derived from their Prussian possession). Scatterings of very different nationalities could always be found: Armenians, Vlachs, Russian Old Believers, Islamic Tatars (Friedrich, 2000; Hundert, 2004; Lukowski, 1991).

A Companion to Eighteenth-Century Europe, First Edition. Edited by Peter H. Wilson.
© 2014 John Wiley & Sons, Ltd. Published 2014 by John Wiley & Sons, Ltd.

Territorially, the Commonwealth was second in size only to European Russia. In 1582 it covered some 815,000 km^2; between 1634 and 1655, it expanded to over 990,000 km^2; after the armistice of Andrussovo with Muscovy of 1667 (confirmed by the peace of Moscow of 1686), it fell back to 733,500 km^2. Modern-day metropolitan France (significantly larger than its late eighteenth-century predecessor) covers 547,030 km^2. By contrast, present-day Poland, at 312,685 km^2, occupies less than half of its 1772 extent. The first partition of 1772 marked a new and drastic contraction from which Poland never recovered: by 1795 it had been erased from the map.

A consensus has emerged among historians that the ruling noble class, the *szlachta*, accounted for some 6 or 7 percent of the population (10 percent used to be the accepted figure) – on a par with their counterparts in Hungary or Spain. For most of the eighteenth century, in their own eyes, only nobles counted as Poles proper, regardless of whoever else might speak their language. Although the petty nobles of the grand duchy might still speak Lithuanian, almost all spoke Polish as their first language, and had done so since the sixteenth century. Polish historians used to take it largely for granted that the once Lithuanian nobility had been fully Polonized *tout court*; yet although Lithuanian nobles did refer to themselves quite naturally as "Poles" and to their state as "Poland," it is quite clear that for the great majority a sense of Lithuanian identity, separateness, and local patriotism was always strongly present. The nobility formed a demographic veneer, deeper in the west but ever thinner towards the east and southeast. In economic terms, they were a massively disparate grouping: a score of great families owned huge estates, latifundia, consisting of dozens of towns and hundreds of villages. At the bottom of the scale were thousands of landless nobles, eking out what existence they could. Only slightly better off were the nobles living in *zaścianki*, villages almost exclusively inhabited by their kind, working their plots of land themselves, wretched and frequently illiterate. Even in the later eighteenth century, illiteracy may have been the lot of around half of those laying claim to noble status (Frost, 1995).

Cultural unity was reinforced by powerful intangibles. A founding myth of an ancestral Sarmatian people who once conquered the Polish lands and who resisted the incursions of ancient Rome had been elaborated during the Renaissance. A much stronger bond derived from the overwhelming Catholicism of the *szlachta*, who in the sixteenth century had counted numerous Protestants in their ranks, but a highly effective Counter-Reformation had reduced these to a marginal role. Even less important were Orthodox nobles, largely reduced to a few pockets in more isolated areas of the grand duchy. The most loudly trumpeted tie of all was the theoretical equality of all nobles. This was nonsense in fact, but the idea was paid solemn lip-service. Very poor or landless nobles might be subject to discriminatory measures of one kind or another (particular taxation, or even labor services) by the better-off, but the ideology of noble equality ignored such minor inconveniences. Non-propertied nobles attracted suspicion on the grounds that they were more likely to be dependent on or in service to richer nobles, but since there was no legal stipulation of a landowning minimum the boundary between landed and non-landed nobles was frequently difficult to ascertain. The rest of the population consisted mainly of serfs (*poddani* – literally, the *szlachta*'s "subjects"). Town-dwellers accounted for at most a fifth of Poland's inhabitants: only a minority of these could regard themselves as being free, in that they lived in royal, as opposed to private, towns. Even many of the royal towns were primarily agrarian in character, their inhabitants almost indistinguishable from peasants. The three great towns of Royal Prussia, Thorn, Elbing and especially Danzig, with their German-speaking, Protestant elites, though fully committed to belonging to the Rzeczpospolita, constituted a truly powerful urban force and could afford to treat the nobility around them with a patrician aloofness when they so chose. Warsaw, the second-largest city, had a population of under 30,000 for most of the century (around 1710, it was probably closer to 10,000), although it had more than tripled in size by the late 1780s. By then it had easily overtaken Danzig as the Commonwealth's most populous urban center.

The Polish nobility inhabited a universe of immensely potent values and dreams. At its heart lay a conviction that they alone constituted the free nation – for most of the eighteenth century, "Pole" and "citizen," *obywatel*, were synonymous with nobleman, *szlachcic*. The most potent threat came from the elective monarch, forever seeking to expand his powers, most notably through his "distributive right," *ius distributivum*, that is, his power of patronage. In a sense, the *szlachta* were right: any monarch who took his *métier* seriously was bound to try to evade the restrictions placed on him by the constitutional settlement of 1572–3 had. His first target was to try to arrange some form of succession, something emphatically forbidden by Polish law. In doing so, monarchs only compounded the mistrust which existed between them and the nobility (Lukowski and Zawadzki, 2001). In the *szlachta*'s eyes, a good monarch would abide by the constitutional restraints imposed on him, reward the deserving through his powers of patronage, and consequently be able to count on the election, by a grateful nation, of his bodily heir. Augustus III (r. 1733–63) came to be regarded as an exemplary king because he seemed to have resigned himself to this status quo.

The privileges which the nobility enjoyed had supposedly been acquired by ancestors who had laid down their lives in defense of the Rzeczpospolita and those selfsame liberties; each generation of nobles declared its readiness to do the same, in a never-ending justification of their place in the state. Their freedom, indeed, their Commonwealth itself, was the sum total of all these privileges: no taxation without their consent; exemption from all customs on articles imported for their personal use; freedom from arrest without trial (unless apprehended *in flagrante*; this meant they could not be imprisoned until after a guilty verdict had been brought against them). Since 1496, landownership had been restricted to nobles (the inhabitants of a few larger towns excepted); all prelacies, bishoprics, and most canonries were reserved to nobles. With the establishment of the so-called Tribunals between 1578 and 1581 as the supreme courts of Poland and Lithuania for the hearing of the bulk of the *szlachta*'s civil and criminal litigation, the nobility conducted most of their own judicial proceedings, independently of the monarch, through their own elected judges. A panoply of political institutions consolidated the *szlachta*'s position. Over 70 political assemblies, the *sejmiki* (55 after 1772), meeting periodically throughout the year, provided the machinery of local self-government. They elected officials, tax collectors, and local and national judges, and saw to financial and administrative needs.

The most visible activity of the *sejmiki* was the election of envoys (*posłowie*) to the central parliament, the Sejm, and furnishing them with a (notionally) mandatory instruction. Since 1573 the monarch had been constitutionally obliged to call a Sejm every two years: it would normally sit for a six-week period, though it could agree to a prolongation. In a national emergency, an extraordinary Sejm could be convened. The delegated envoys formed a Second Chamber. The royal council, or Senate, consisting of 12 Catholic bishops and 134 laymen, formed the First Chamber. It was accepted that the principal motor of legislation lay in the Chamber of Envoys, though for any measure to be enacted into law, the consent of all three "estates" (*stany*) of the Sejm was necessary – that is, of the envoys, the senators, and the monarch himself. In a full complement, there should have been some 200 envoys, but because many elections were disrupted their actual number could be half that figure or much lower. The nobles alone enjoyed representation. Although a number of leading towns, which had in the past been awarded noble status, technically enjoyed the right to return representatives, in practice these were never more than small lobbying groups, with no formal role in law-making.

This network of representative institutions and their associated mandates reinforced the nobility's sense of ownership of the Commonwealth. What, however, truly made them stakeholders in their polity was the elective nature of the monarchy. This had been consolidated during the first interregnum of 1572–3 following the demise of the Jagiellonian dynasty. All adult male nobles were entitled to vote in the royal election, the choice had to be unanimous, and no successor could be elected *vivente rege*, during the ruling king's lifetime. Each successive monarch had to swear that he would do nothing to bring about the election of a successor. This so-called "free election" was one of the great cornerstones of the nobility's "golden liberty" (*złota wolność*).

Royal election had a twofold purpose. Symbolically, it reinforced the nobility's sense of possession. Practically, it permitted the nobles to repair all that had gone awry (*exorbitantia*) in the previous incumbent's reign and impose on the new ruler a fresh set of constitutional conditions (the *pacta conventa*) designed to protect their freedoms. This was best done by preserving intact ancestral laws and institutions without change: *omnis novitas nociva est*, "every innovation is harmful," was a much-invoked saying. So much so, that even from the early seventeenth century the Sejm's most important function was not so much to pass new laws as to preserve an established liberty. The Sejm was never a powerful body in its own right, despite much rhetoric to the contrary: it was a forum for debate in a geographically sprawling polity which had never been anything like centralized, and whose political class regarded regional and local privilege as part of a wider "liberty" which had to be preserved in full. It was closer in character to the Imperial Reichstag than to Britain's Parliament or Sweden's Riksdag. Throughout the sixteenth century, the Sejm had always labored to decide by an overwhelming consensus of its members. If a substantial minority disagreed, and refused any compromise, Poland's parliament preferred to drop contentious business or even to disperse without enacting law. In 1652, its inability to assert itself as a sovereign institution led to just one envoy bringing all proceedings to a halt: the notorious *liberum veto* had arrived, whereby the opposition of a single individual could disrupt the proceedings of the entire Sejm, invalidating even legislation that might have been agreed earlier in the session. Thereafter, unsurprisingly, more and more sessions were disrupted. Even when the veto was not formally used, its influence was felt in endless filibustering which ground a session to an inconclusive dissolution at the end of the statutory six-week term. The practice of disruption spread to the *sejmiki*, leaving individual constituencies unrepresented and key judicial and administrative posts unfilled for years at a time.

The veto could be overridden by recourse to a Confederacy, a league with a stated set of particular aims to which nobles signed up, and whose rank-and-file members left the leadership to decide among themselves – in practice, by majority agreement. Potentially, confederacies could have been used to effect reforms – as indeed they were after 1764. But until then, the nobility used them above all to return to what they understood to be, or could pass off as, the arrangements of the past. Confederacies were called on only in emergencies, such as foreign invasion and interregna, when confederated parliaments might enact substantial legislation by majority acclamation.[1]

"Liberty" was reserved for the nobility. To extend it to other groups (most obviously, townsmen) would lead to an alliance of throne and commoners which would inevitably replace freedom by despotism. This was the lesson taught by the history of republican Rome and, more recently, the frequently invoked monarchical coup of 1661 in Denmark. There was no nuanced understanding (or, at least, none was openly articulated) of the cultural or even political freedoms which might exist under a monarchic umbrella elsewhere. A strong monarchy was simply equated with *absolutum dominium*. Poles were prepared to acknowledge that Britain or the United Provinces enjoyed freedom – but those countries were so different as to make their particular type of liberty quite inappropriate to Polish conditions. Most Poles were prepared to give their admiration to the Venetian republic and its seemingly unchanging institutions – but, again, Venice was a small city-state too different to serve as a model for Poland's sprawling agrarian Commonwealth. Only after the 1770s did Britain emerge as a possible model for Poland to follow (Butterwick, 1998).

What drove Polish politics was competition for central and local office, and for tenures of the so-called *królewszczyzny*, "Crown lands," immense tracts of property in the gift of the monarch (which he was legally bound to reallocate to a new tenant within six weeks of the death of the old incumbent). The Crown lands collectively accounted for about a sixth of the Commonwealth's area; their tenure could make a huge difference to the fortunes of a given family. Possession of land and office, in turn, gave their holders a degree of influence over the administration of justice (many judicial posts were in the gift of greater office-holders) and recommendations to royal favor. As a result, the royal distributive power was simultaneously courted, feared, and opposed. Reformers argued for removing it from the king's person altogether and replacing it with some form of election: but for as long as the *liberum veto* remained in place, any electoral alternative would simply break down.

In its late sixteenth- and early seventeenth-century heyday, in a Europe marked by hand-to-mouth government, the Commonwealth could hold its own in the conflicts in which it was involved. But the *szlachta*'s refusal to extend their privileges to other groups which felt they had a justified claim to them, most notably the cossacks of the Ukrainian territories, helped provoke a hugely destructive rebellion in 1648, which, in turn, sucked in other powers: Muscovy, Sweden, Transylvania, the Crimean Tartars, and the Ottoman Porte, Brandenburg. Particularly between 1655 and 1660, Poland was subject to a massive wave of invasions, known as the *Potop*, or "Deluge." With the assistance of other European powers, the Commonwealth was able to survive these travails, albeit at the cost of yielding, in 1667, extensive stretches of territory in the east to Moscow. Royal efforts to secure a reform of the state failed – the nobility saw in almost any reform a potential assault on their "golden liberty" (Frost, 1993). The signal role played by Polish forces in the relief of Vienna in 1683 seemed to confirm the state's military capabilities. But this was an illusory last hurrah. The self-governing institutions of the *szlachta*'s world had been capable of seeing them through the seventeenth century – just. But in the eighteenth, when Poland had to face modernized neighbors, kitted out with permanent bureaucracies, effectively centralized monarchic control, and truly permanent, large standing armies, the institutions in which the *szlachta* saw the very machinery of liberty proved utterly inadequate.

A cataclysm comparable to the deluge once again engulfed the Commonwealth between 1700 and 1721 – the Great Northern War. This long conflict began as an exercise between Frederick IV of Denmark, Peter I (the Great) of Russia, and Elector Friedrich Augustus I of Saxony to relieve the young Charles XII of Sweden of his country's extensive territories on the southern and eastern Baltic. In 1697 Friedrich Augustus had been elected King Augustus II of Poland. His reign had begun well. In 1699 the Commonwealth, since 1683 a member of the Holy League against Turkey, had recovered, at the general peace of Karlowitz, substantial territories lost to the Ottoman Porte in 1672. The needs of the Turkish war, and violent factional disorders in Lithuania, had enabled Augustus to bring considerable numbers of Saxon troops into his new realm. From this springboard, he hoped to conquer Sweden's possession of Livonia (which, between the 1560s and 1620s, had belonged to Poland), with a view to turning it into a hereditary possession which would ultimately enable him to convert his Wettin dynasty's position in Poland from a purely elective to a hereditary one. Although he received informal military assistance from some of the Polish-Lithuanian magnates, officially, the Rzeczpospolita was not involved in his schemes.

Charles XII upset his enemies' designs: he knocked Denmark out of the war, routed the Russians at Narva in November 1700, and forced Augustus out of Livonia and pursued him into his Polish-Lithuanian territories. He rejected Polish protestations of neutrality and offers of mediation, offering peace only if Augustus were deposed, which the Poles would not do. To reject their own elected king was an affront to the *szlachta*'s sense of sovereignty and constitutional proprietorship. True, in 1704 an intimidated rump of noblemen elected an anti-king, Stanisław Leszczyński, but he never commanded wider support. Charles XII bogged himself down for years in chasing Augustus around Poland, but only in 1706 did he strike into Augustus' electoral heartland of Saxony and forced him to abdicate his Polish throne. In 1708 he judged Saxony and Poland sufficiently pacified to turn directly against Russia – an adventure which ended with his defeat at Poltava in July 1709, although the war itself dragged on until 1721.

Historians have still not built up anything like a full picture of the material and demographic damage wreaked by the Deluge and the Great Northern War. It is clear, however, that in the space of three generations Poland-Lithuania was twice afflicted by the equivalent of Germany's Thirty Years War – which had largely passed it by. Cities and towns were devastated – most did not recover before the end of the Commonwealth. The wars had been, amongst other things, religious conflicts between

Catholics, Orthodox, and Protestants (with the Jews seen as fair game all round): a militant Catholicism was consolidated, the once flourishing Lutheran and Calvinist communities were left defensive and beleaguered, even if they still managed to retain a degree of toleration and legal protection far greater than that of most European denominational minorities, despite much black propagandizing to the contrary. The nobility's suspicions of the monarchy as the natural enemy of its liberty were confirmed, not least because, following his restoration after Poltava, Augustus II had sought to lighten the burdens on his devastated electorate of Saxony by stationing many of his troops on Polish soil. Saxon exactions provoked the Polish nobility into setting up the Confederacy of Tarnogród in 1715. The resulting conflict was terminated by the compromise Treaty of Warsaw of 1716 between Augustus and his Polish subjects. The terms were confirmed by the "Silent" Sejm of February 1, 1717, so called because, by prior agreement between the parties, it was convened for one day only, purely for the purpose of bringing, without debate, the Treaty of Warsaw into law (Frost, 2000).

The 1716–17 settlement fixed the Polish constitutional system for over the next 50 years. The strength of the army was set at 24,000 units of pay – which translated in practice to an armed force of around 12,000 men. This was about as much as the nobility could stomach in their ravaged Commonwealth, but it was to be hopelessly inadequate at a time when 100,000 was fast approaching as something of a minimum for a major power. The tiny army was provided with fixed, secured revenues. The Sejm required Protestants in most of Poland to dismantle places of worship constructed since 1632.

The real beneficiary of the settlement, and of the Great Northern War as a whole, was Russia. In 1700 Poland still had the capacity to be a potential partner; by 1717 it was well on the road to reduction to satellite status. It was courtesy of Peter the Great that Augustus was restored. In January 1719 he sought to escape his reliance on Russia by concluding the Treaty of Vienna, with Austria, Britain, and Hanover, all alarmed by Russia's recent rise to prominence. But the Sejms of 1719–20, influenced and intimidated by Russia, refused to confirm the treaty, fearing that they would be dragged into fresh conflict. Peter consciously promoted himself as the protector of Polish liberties, precisely to consolidate his influence over the weakened and hamstrung Commonwealth. Indeed, since 1667, differing combinations of Poland's neighbors had regularly agreed among themselves to permit no alterations to the Polish constitution: a weak Poland suited them all, not least Brandenburg-Prussia, whose rulers had long been keen to acquire territory on the lower Vistula which would permit a significant *arrondissement* of their dynastic possessions. Prussia and Russia made more such agreements between themselves than any other powers (Lewitter, 1970; Lukowski, 1985).

The Peace of Nystad of 1721 brought the Great Northern War to an end – but Russia ensured the exclusion of Poland, even though so much of the conflict had been fought on its territory. If further evidence of the extent of Russian influence were needed, it was forcefully supplied by the next interregnum. Following the death of Augustus II in 1733, the overwhelming mass of the nobility voted for the accession of the old Swedish-backed anti-king, Stanisław Leszczyński; thanks to Russian military intervention, Augustus II's son, Friedrich August II, was able to secure election by a rump assembly as Augustus III. Russian military backing allowed him, after the bloody conflict known as the War of the Polish Succession, to consolidate his position on the throne by 1736.

Polish politics were above all focused on parochial concerns. Although Poles were conscious of the threat of outside intervention, the main fear of the great majority of the politically engaged was of the internal, monarchic threat rather than of external dangers. Poland had been submerged during the Deluge: it had resurfaced. It had almost gone under during the Great Northern War, its territories served as a "wayside inn" for all the major combatants during the Seven Years War (1756–63), its neutrality notwithstanding; Russian arms twice determined the outcome of its interregna, in both 1733–6 and 1763–4. At least one late eighteenth-century publicist portrayed periodic foreign incursions as a necessary price to pay for the preservation of Polish liberty (Rzewuski, 1789: 11–12). It was a view bolstered by the misconceived belief that Europe needed Poland as a vital source of grain supplies, and that Poland's existing condition was a necessary part of the European balance of power. Europe would not therefore allow any lasting damage to the Commonwealth. Internally, the nobility's commitment to their Commonwealth was incalculably strengthened by the huge capital of emotion and blood invested in it: the rhetoric of readiness to sacrifice "our lives and fortunes" in defense of the Commonwealth and its liberties was no hollow outpouring. The fact is that, throughout their history, ordinary nobles (not all, but certainly significant numbers) were prepared to risk life and property in fighting off invaders: successfully during the Deluge and the Great Northern War; less successfully during the War of the Polish Succession of 1733–6 and the turbulent early years of the reign of Stanisław August Poniatowski (1764–95), but nonetheless in sufficient numbers to underpin the rhetoric with reality. The present was linked to the past by the benison of the sacrifices of generations of ancestors. This emotional incubus was no easy matter to shake off.

There were those who appreciated that all this was a fool's paradise. In 1717 one of Augustus II's closest advisers, Bishop Konstanty Szaniawski, told the Prussian envoy that the *liberum veto* was an "absurdity" and that the sooner the Commonwealth secured British-style parliamentary rule the better (Gierowski, 1971). But this was not something that Szaniawski dared proclaim publicly. The privileges of the Polish nobility were so extensive that any attempt to restrict the veto or to impose order on its political processes was bound to involve a significant degree of restriction of those privileges. As a result, any attempt at reform could easily and plausibly be presented as a march towards despotism. The all-pervading electoral processes of the Commonwealth, summed up in the phrase "noble democracy" (the expression emerged in the 1770s), involved the participation of thousands of nobles who felt their rights and privileges (even if these were often more important psychologically than practically) would be jeopardized by constitutional change. Even the most powerful, reform-inclined magnates were prisoners of noble opinion and prejudice. For most, it was simply easier to abide by the status quo. Change could only come if a critical mass among the nobility could be persuaded to support it. While it was comparatively easy to point to the shortcomings of Poland's political processes (which many preferred to ascribe to the moral failings of present generations, compared with the greater virtues of their ancestors), it was much more problematic as to how exactly "reform" (even if the principle that it should take place found support) would be conducted without endangering liberty.

The eighteenth century saw only one detailed attack on the *liberum veto* – the four volumes of *On the Means to Successful Counsels*, produced between 1761 and 1763 by a clergyman of noble birth, Stanisław Konarski (1700–73). His devastatingly painstaking analysis, which went far beyond the veto to take on a whole array of *szlachta* misconceptions and suggest a new form of government inspired by British parliamentarianism, provoked outrage and support in equal measure. Though rightly regarded as a seminal piece of Polish political literature, its impact was much reduced by the excitements of the interregnum which followed the death of Augustus III on October 5, 1763. It was a coterie around the powerful Czartoryski family, long-standing admirers of the British constitution, who gained the upper hand over their disorganized "republican" opponents. At the confederated Sejm of May 1764 they pushed through a series of major reforms and sealed their success in September by the election as king of the nephew of the Czartoryski leaders, Stanisław Poniatowski. He adopted the middle name "August," to signify his determination to renew the Polish world, just as Augustus had once renewed the Roman one (Butterwick, 1998; Zamoyski, 1997).

The flaw in the Czartoryski–Poniatowski success was that it was made possible largely by the military assistance of Catherine II of Russia. Peter the Great and his immediate successors had been content to keep Poland in a condition of ungovernability. Catherine wanted a Poland that she could manage: from the outset of her reign she appreciated that, sooner or later, Russia would come to a major settling of accounts with the Ottoman empire in the Black Sea area. A quiescent and controllable (as opposed to anarchic and unpredictable) Poland would offer valuable supply lines and convenient military transit routes. Catherine wanted to cap her hold over Poland by saddling it with a Russian guarantee of its constitution. She was prepared to accept some administrative reform, principally in bringing order to the Commonwealth's finances and greater discipline to its minuscule army. The role of the new king was to do her bidding. She felt she had the measure of Poniatowski. After all, during his diplomatic missions to St. Petersburg between 1755 and 1758, she had taken him as a lover (Zamoyski, 1997). But the empress was not prepared to tolerate any major reforms (certainly not the repeal of the veto) which might threaten to make of Poland a truly independent sovereign power. She was more than seconded in her determination by her new ally, Frederick II of Prussia, who, like his predecessors, saw in a strong Poland a major threat to his own geographically exposed Prussian territories.

There was a second strand to Catherine's plans. She hoped to restore Poland's Protestants to something like the influence they had enjoyed in the later sixteenth and early seventeenth centuries, a position in which they would be utterly dependent on Russian support. In an enlightened age, the empress would win kudos among Europe's easily impressed *philosophes*, while consolidating the geopolitical practicalities of an enhanced hegemony over eastern Europe. But these plans rapidly ran into problems. Radical reforms and the abolition of the veto was precisely what Poniatowski and the Czartoryskis wanted. As for the Protestants, their position was far weaker numerically than it had been two centuries previously. Any efforts to bolster it were bound to antagonize an overwhelmingly Catholic nobility which was otherwise comfortable with the toleration accorded to their Protestant confrères. Even Frederick the Great warned Catherine against stirring up a religious hornets' nest in Poland, pointing out that no one in Poland was actually being persecuted for their beliefs – their exclusion from office was "une vraie bagatelle."[2] Catherine and her advisers disregarded similar warnings from their own ambassador in Warsaw: the assumption in St. Petersburg was that a Poland with no real army would simply back down before Russian demands.

At the May 1764 Sejm, the Czartoryskis did indeed shackle the hitherto virtually irresponsible ministers heading the Polish-Lithuanian treasuries and armed forces with commissions answerable to the Sejm, which began to bring real order into the administration. They were even able to make a start on curbing the veto, but only by imposing tentative limitations in convoluted language all but incomprehensible to outsiders. But the attempt by them and the king to clarify this legislation at the Sejm of 1766 brought an immediate response from Russia and Prussia: unless the veto was restored in full, Warsaw would be destroyed. The helpless Poles gave way. The Russians then began to push for enlarged rights for Protestant and Orthodox nobles (though it proved almost impossible to find any Orthodox *szlachta* of any standing), and were indeed able to secure their right to places in the Sejm and Senate during the extraordinary Sejm of 1767–8. They went on to impose a guarantee of a minimally reshaped constitution, which rescinded the veto only for the most marginal legislation. Catherine achieved these objectives by deliberately concealing her ultimate intentions, and through a systematic campaign of military terrorization and deportation of opponents to the Russian interior. Outraged nobles came together at Bar, in southeast Poland, in February 1768, to proclaim a confederacy aimed both at repelling Russian intervention and rolling back what reforms (supposedly smacking of royal despotism) had been enacted.

The Confederacy of Bar unleashed some four years of guerrilla war combined with an anti-royalist Fronde. Russian troops would almost certainly have suppressed the movement, had not Turkey become involved. The Ottomans realized that, if Russia mastered Poland, it would secure a position of overwhelming strategic superiority over them. Following Russian violations of the Turko-Polish border, the Porte declared war against Russia in October 1768. The conflict proved disastrous: the Turks were to suffer one crushing defeat after another. But it prevented Russia from suppressing Bar. The extent of Russian successes alarmed the Austrians, who feared their own position in the Balkans would be weakened. With Austria allied to France and Russia to Prussia, the prospect of a new European conflagration loomed. The situation was brilliantly exploited by Frederick the Great, who was able to persuade both the Austrians and the Russians that the accumulating tensions between them could be defused if they "compensated" themselves with territory from a Poland in no position to defend itself. Furthermore, the need to preserve a balance between the protagonists, urged Frederick, required compensation for his own kingdom of Prussia. The upshot was the three conventions of St. Petersburg of August 5, 1772. Between them, Russia, Prussia, and Austria agreed to relieve the Poles of about one-third of their territory and population. The largest share went to Austria; the smallest, but strategically most valuable, went to Prussia; it was understood that Russian influence would remain paramount throughout what remained of the Commonwealth. Russia was to seal its position by the Treaty of Kuchuk Kanardji with Turkey, in July 1774, which, though conferring only relatively small territorial gains on Russia near the Black Sea, effectively turned the Ottoman dependency of the Crimea into a

Russian protectorate (which Russia was to annex outright in 1783) (Lukowski, 1999; Scott, 2001, 2006).

The shattered Poles were unable to resist. The Confederacy of Bar collapsed. An intimidated confederated Sejm, meeting from April 1773 to April 1775, ratified the partition and concluded a new constitutional settlement. The veto remained, as in 1767–8, for all but minor legislation; the king was stripped of most of his distributive powers, which were vested in the Sejm, which in turn, was to elect every two years a new central executive, known as the Permanent Council, composed of 18 senators and 18 envoys and chaired by the monarch. Its relatively feeble jurisdiction was more closely defined at the turbulent confederated Sejm of 1776, in a process which completed the constitutional settlement (guaranteed by all the partitioning powers in 1775) associated with the first partition. Russia continued to exercise a close, stifling protectorate over the still extensive (if strategically exposed) remnant of the Commonwealth. Catherine II systematically rejected Stanisław August's pleas for further confederated Sejms which might enact a real degree of reform. Russia indeed, encouraged opposition to the king in a deliberate ploy to keep his reforming instincts in check.

Almost the only positive thing to have emerged from the partition settlement was the creation, in October 1773, of a Commission for National Education. This was in effect Europe's first ministry of education. It was made possible by the dissolution by the Papacy of the Jesuit order, at the behest of France and Spain, in June 1773. Though much of the Jesuit estate disappeared into the possession of Russia's hangers-on, enough remained to provide a viable base for an extensive network of colleges. Individual teaching orders had been modernizing their curricula since the 1740s, but the dissolution allowed the Commission to put all these efforts onto a systematic basis. The king, keenly interested in education, and like-minded reformers, felt educational reform was vital if the conservatism of the *szlachta* was ever to be broken down and if they were to come to accept the need for wider change. Despite the partition, the 1770s did see a startling intellectual rebirth in Poland, especially in Warsaw (the processes involved have still to be satisfactorily explained), with its bookshops, publishers (many of them set up by foreign immigrants), coffeehouses, and salons. A law enacted by the 1773–5 Sejm specifically affirmed the right of free speech "*in politicis*," though that had always been part of a nobleman's birthright. The result was a large volume of European Enlightenment-inspired literature, energetically advocating genuine social reform, washing over a largely hostile rural nobility. Politics remained sterile: the Sejms of 1778, 1780, 1782, 1784, and 1786, unconfederated, could look only to minor matters and act as a safety-valve for vicious, if pointless, factional politics. Only the 1780 Sejm dealt with a truly major issue, that of expanding the rights of townsmen and peasants. But the envoys unequivocally rejected all efforts to improve the position of commoners within the state.

Yet in one major respect even the least productive, as well as the most brutally bullied, Sejms of Poniatowski's reign did serve to alter *szlachta* attitudes. During Augustus III's reign, only one Sejm (1736) had enacted legislation; under his successor, all did so. A generation of nobles began to appreciate that their parliaments could actually achieve something concrete (no matter how unpalatable it might be), beyond the mere defense of ancestral freedoms. The 1780s also contributed to a sense of frustration, at least among political activists. When, in the autumn of 1787, a fresh war erupted between Russia and Turkey, with Austria supporting Russia, a sense of the imminent breakdown of the international regime in eastern and central Europe was palpable. In July 1788, Russia's problems were compounded by the outbreak of war with Sweden. Prussia, under Frederick William II, actually began to encourage Polish hopes of breaking away from Russian dominance. Prussia's aim was simple: to maneuver the Poles into ceding it yet further valuable territory in the west and north. Stanisław August saw the dangers; most politicians did not.

The Sejm which met in October 1788 was to sit, much to its own surprise, until June 1792 – hence its usual label of "the Four Year Sejm" (Lord, 1915). Conscious of Russia's distractions, it confederated itself and launched a prolonged attack on some of the key institutions created since 1775 as symbols of Russian domination – most notably the Permanent Council. Simultaneously, this new parliament groped towards a workable, modernized state reconcilable with *szlachta* republicanism. All too often, it acted under the spur of emotion rather than rational calculation. It voted to set up a 100,000-strong army, and only later inched its way to discussing the means to finance it. In an emotional catharsis, its participants gloried in heaping insults, opprobrium, and provocation on Russia, with little thought for the possible consequences; Prussia was hailed as a new friend, with little real consideration as to its motives. Those who, like the king, took a more rational view of events, found they were powerless to control a torrent of patriotic fervor. This was the freest, least constrained Sejm Poland had seen for at least a century: its envoys and senators were anxious that that freedom be fully respected – with the result that it was almost impossible to impose any kind of discipline on its proceedings, which were frequently characterized by mind-numbingly vacuous exercises in garrulity. Yet for all that, the Sejm did assume responsibility for government and establish itself as a genuinely ruling body; its participants began to appreciate what genuine governance involved. By Polish standards, it achieved much: it set up a wholly new system of local and national administration, and agreed to unprecedented taxation. Its activities sparked off a veritable tidal wave of polemic and debate in which nothing was off limits. For the first time in Poland's history, a massive debate was undertaken on the merits of a hereditary versus an elective monarchy. If there was little discussion of the *liberum veto*, it was because most participants took it for granted that it would finally be abandoned – only a diehard few supported it. Over the previous generation the veto had simply died a natural death.

Yet for all the excitement *szlachta* society remained intensely conservative. A core of reformers wanted to extend greater political participation, including parliamentary representation, to townsmen. Most nobles were firmly opposed. Reformers wanted to emancipate the serfs – again, most nobles were opposed. If nobles were prepared to accept that successive interregna had been a disaster for Poland, they remained intensely suspicious of hereditary monarchy, which reformers regarded as a *sine qua non* of effective modernization. In April 1791, it is true, townsmen were given limited representation in the Sejm – but, at the same time, municipal offices were opened up to the nobility, a maneuver which could only help consolidate the noble hold on the Commonwealth. Indeed, as the Sejm itself drew on, provincial noble society began to be alarmed at what this unpredictable assembly might do. At bottom, it was not just a strong monarchy that the *szlachta* were suspicious of – it was of any kind of strong government.

Given these tensions, the slow pace of change becomes understandable. The Sejm's own envoys bewailed its cumbersome proceedings. In November 1790 a fresh contingent of envoys was elected, almost doubling the size of the assembly. A combination of interminable debate and a consciousness that the favorable international situation could not last for ever (Russia's ally, Austria, concluded a separate armistice with Turkey in July 1790; Sweden made peace with Russia in August) led a combination of the king, reformers, and sympathetic envoys and senators to stage what was in effect a constitutional coup on May 3, 1791. A new constitution, laboriously worked out behind the scenes over several months between the king and key reformers, was sprung on the assembly. A primed, enthusiastic public gallery urged change. After seven hours of debate, the constitution was overwhelmingly accepted.

The so-called "Statute of Government" (Ustawa Rz dowa) was a statement of governing principles, not a detailed blueprint – the details followed in a weighty mass of supplementary legislation enacted over the next few months. It was remarkable document which accommodated seemingly strong government to noble republicanism. It took the risk of proclaiming the monarchy hereditary in the Wettin rulers of Saxony: Stanisław August lacked a direct heir, sympathizers of Saxon rule remained strong, and the assignment of the throne to a ruling House which had strong links with Poland appeared a sensible way of evading the debilitating hazards of interregna. It specifically stated, however, that the education of future princes would be the responsibility of the Commonwealth – they would be inculcated in sound republicanism. The *liberum veto*, "subversive of government, destructive of society," was abolished. A new supreme executive, the Custodial Council of the Laws (Straż Praw) was established under royal presidency. In a truly astonishing move in Polish conditions, it would require only the king's signature, and just one ministerial countersignature, to issue legally binding decisions. It could not, of course, make legislation – that was the sole right of the Sejm, which would, from now on, have a full two-year term, instead of the six-week term which it had hitherto been so hamstrung by. The British doctrine of monarchic irresponsibility was incorporated into the constitution: only ministers were answerable to the Sejm and liable to dismissal on a two-thirds majority vote of censure. The April 1791 Law on Towns, which allowed them to return representatives who could vote on commercial matters, was reaffirmed. The toleration of all faiths was proclaimed. All the existing rights and privileges of the nobility were confirmed. So, in effect, was serfdom, although serfs were assured of "the protection of the law and the national government." More tangibly, peasant immigrants to Poland (including those who had fled abroad but chosen to return), were proclaimed free.

In fact, the constitution was far less radical than it might have appeared. Extensive machinery to safeguard against possible ministerial and monarchic despotism was built in, permitting appeals from the Custodial Council to the Sejm. The veto may have been abolished, but the enabling legislation insisted on a 75 percent majority for new taxation. Since no independent state courts existed to hear peasant grievances, "concessions" to them would mean little. The new Law on Towns opened up municipal offices to the nobility – which meant that they could consolidate their grip on the Commonwealth even further. The royal distributive power was to be almost totally abolished for Poniatowski's successors (Butterwick, 1998; Lukowski, 1994).[3]

The country was divided over the Statute of Government, but how far is impossible to say. The king and his supporters put in a massive propaganda effort to win over opinion. The overwhelming majority of the political establishment, assured of a reform which promised more effective government while leaving their position unchanged, indeed, if anything strengthened, rallied round. *Sejmiki* meeting in February 1792 overwhelmingly endorsed the new order. Serious opposition came only from a handful of great magnates, but these had the ear of the Russian government, which had no intention of enduring such a show of independence in its satellite state. Frederick Augustus III, elector of Saxony, had not been consulted about the offer of the succession and knew better than to accept if Russia objected. In January 1792 Russia and Turkey made peace. On April 27 in St. Petersburg, 13 malcontents put their signatures to an act of confederacy, denouncing the May 3 constitution as an exercise in both despotism and Parisian democracy (the French Revolution served as a catch-all pretext for Russia's subsequent actions in Poland). The act itself was postdated to May 14 and it was claimed it had been drawn up in the village of Targowica, just inside the Polish border from Russian Ukraine. It appealed to Catherine to restore Poland's ancient liberties.

On May 18, 90,000 battle-hardened Russian troops began to cross into Polish territory. Poland's armed forces had been built up to barely half the 100,000 decreed by the Sejm. The bubble of unreality in which the Four Year Sejm had existed was burst. The assembly dispersed on May 31, leaving the king to pick up the pieces. The outnumbered, inexperienced army could do little. Stanisław August acceded to the Confederacy of Targowica on July 23 in a vain effort at damage limitation. The confederacy could exercise no real authority. Its leaders were more interested in self-enrichment and score-settling than in proper government. The country threatened to collapse into anarchy. This provided a pretext for Russia and Prussia, which now washed its hands of its Polish connections, to embark on a second partition, finalized in St. Petersburg on January 23, 1793. Russia annexed a massive 250,000 km^2 in the east, Prussia 57,000 km^2 in the west, along with the much-desired port of Danzig. Austria was not involved – it was fighting against revolutionary France and (erroneously) expected to make territorial gains from the fledgling French republic. All that remained of Poland was a rump state centered on Warsaw, in effect a Russian province which clearly would not survive much longer.

The end was precipitated by a desperate insurrection in 1794, led by Tadeusz Kościuszko, who had distinguished himself fighting on the American side in the War of Independence, and in the 1792 fighting. Although Russian troops were cleared from Warsaw and the Lithuanian capital, Wilno, and although Warsaw initially held out against a siege by joint Prussian and Russian forces from July to September, the end was never in doubt. An outnumbered Kościuszko was defeated and captured by the Russians at Maciejowice on October 10. On November 4, Russian forces under General Alexander Suvorov stormed the Warsaw suburb of Praga, massacring some 16,000 people. On October 24, Russia, Prussia, and, this time, Austria, finalized agreements for a Third, tripartite partition. The lion's share went to Russia, although Prussia secured Warsaw, which sank to the status of a frontier town (Lord, 1924–5). Although during and in the wake of the Napoleonic Wars, a kind of Poland was resurrected in the shape of the quasi-states of the duchy of Warsaw and the Congress

Kingdom of Poland, they had no truly independent existence. A sovereign Polish state was restored only in November 1918.

Notes

1 Until the 1767–8 Sejm, voting as such was not used: envoys voiced their approval (or opposition) at final, block readings of the legislation.
2 Frederick II to Count Victor Solms von Sonnenwalde, December 28, 1766 (*Politische Correspondenz*, vol. 25, no. 16 418).
3 For a fine contemporary translation of the constitution by the Polish minister in London, Franciszek Bukaty (admittedly, pointedly tailored towards an English readership) see the *Annual Register* for 1791, pp. 177–200.

Bibliography

Butterwick, B., *Poland's Last King and English Culture: Stanisław August Poniatowski 1732–1798* (Oxford, 1998).

Butterwick, R. (ed.), *The Polish-Lithuanian Monarchy in European Context, c.1500–1795* (Basingstoke, 2001).

Davies, N., *God's Playground: A History of Poland* (2 vols., 2nd edn., Oxford, 2005).

Fiszman, S. (ed.), *Constitution and Reform in Eighteenth-Century Poland: The Constitution of 3 May 1791* (Bloomington, 1997).

Friedrich, K., *The other Prussia: Royal Prussia, Poland and Liberty, 1569–1772* (Cambridge, 2000).

Frost, R. I., *After the Deluge: Poland-Lithuania and the Second Northern War* (Cambridge, 1993).

Frost, R. I., "The nobility of Poland-Lithuania, 1569–1795," in H. M. Scott (ed.), *The European Nobilities in the Seventeenth and Eighteenth Centuries* (London, 1995), vol. 2, pp. 182–222.

Frost, R. I., *The Northern Wars: War, State and Society in Northern Europe, 1558–1721* (Harlow, 2000).

Gierowski, J., *W cieniu ligi północnej* (Wrocław, 1971).

Gierowski, J. and A. Kamiński, "The eclipse of Poland," in *The New Cambridge Modern History*, vol. 6 (Cambridge, 1971), pp. 681–715.

Hundert, G. D., *Jews in Poland-Lithuania in the Eighteenth Century: A Genealogy of Modernity* (Berkeley, 2004).

Kaplan, H., *The First Partition of Poland* (New York, 1962).

Levine, H., *Economic Origins of Antisemitism: Poland and its Jews in the Early Modern Period* (New Haven, 1991).

Lewitter, L. R., "Poland, Russia and the Treaty of Vienna of 5 January 1719," *Historical Journal*, 3 (1970), 3–30.

Lord, R. H., *The Second Partition of Poland* (Cambridge, MA, 1915).

Lord, R. H., "The third partition of Poland," *Slavonic Review*, 3 (1924–5), 481–98.

Lukowski, J. T., "Towards partition: Polish magnates and Russian intervention in Poland during the early reign of Stanisław August Poniatowski," *Historical Journal*, 28 (1985), 557–74.

Lukowski, J. T., *Liberty's Folly: The Polish-Lithuanian Commonwealth in the Eighteenth Century, 1697–1795* (London, 1991).

Lukowski, J. T., "Recasting Utopia: Montesquieu, Rousseau and the Polish Constitution of 3 May 1791," *Historical Journal*, 37 (1994), 65–87.

Lukowski, J. T., *The Partitions of Poland 1772, 1793, 1795* (Harlow, 1999).
Lukowski, J. T. and H. Zawadzki, *A Concise History of Poland* (2001; 2nd edn., Cambridge, 2006).
Rosman, M. J., *The Lords' Jews: Magnate–Jewish Relations in the Polish-Lithuanian Commonwealth during the Eighteenth Century* (Cambridge, MA, 1990).
Scott, H. M., *The Emergence of the Eastern Powers, 1756–1775* (Cambridge, 2001).
Scott, H. M., *The Birth of a Great Power System 1740–1815* (Harlow, 2006).
Teter, M., *Jews and Heretics in Catholic Poland: A Beleaguered Church in the Post-Reformation Era* (Cambridge, 2005).
Walicki, A., *The Age of Enlightenment and the Birth of Modern Nationhood: Polish Political Thought from Noble Republicanism to Tadeusz Kościuszko* (Notre Dame, 1989).
Zamoyski, A., *The Last King of Poland* (New York, 1997).

Chapter Sixteen

The Empire, Austria, and Prussia

Peter H. Wilson

Places, Names, and Interpretations

Anyone writing about the heart of eighteenth-century Europe is confronted by the problem of national history and identity. The political units that once encompassed central Europe have not only long disappeared, but also failed to make the transition into neat nation-states; the form of political organization commonly held to have dominated nineteenth- and early twentieth-century Europe. The principal central European political unit was the Holy Roman Empire that encompassed not only Germany, but also modern Belgium, Luxembourg, Austria, the Czech Republic, and parts of Denmark, Poland, and France. Most of northern Italy technically still fell under the emperor's feudal jurisdiction, though it was not represented in imperial institutions. While extensive, the empire had not followed the pattern of western European countries that developed as unitary monarchies with a single capital and central institutions. This makes it very difficult to write its history, because it does not appear to fit the European norm. Moreover, its two largest components, Austria and Prussia, developed their own autonomous existence by the early eighteenth century that, to many later writers, completely overshadowed the empire and rendered it largely irrelevant. Austria had long been the leading power within the empire, but from the later seventeenth century acquired extensive additional land beyond its frontiers, chiefly in Hungary, the Balkans, and southern Italy, later in also in Poland. These lands constituted a separate dynastic empire that increasingly acted as an independent force in European relations. Prussia proper never belonged to the empire, lying beyond its northeastern frontier along the Baltic shore. It had been linked to the empire by dynastic union to Brandenburg since 1618, and only become more important when raised to a kingdom in 1700. The first part of the hyphenated "Brandenburg-Prussia" was gradually dropped as the latter more than quadrupled in size through the acquisition of Polish territory after 1772. These gains, along with the conquest of Silesia at Austria's expense in 1740–2, made Prussia a second central European great power distinct from the empire to which a considerable part of its territory still formally belonged.

A Companion to Eighteenth-Century Europe, First Edition. Edited by Peter H. Wilson.
© 2014 John Wiley & Sons, Ltd. Published 2014 by John Wiley & Sons, Ltd.

Austria and Prussia both survived the empire's demise in 1806 at the hands of Napoleon. Already rivals for influence while the empire existed, both became competitors for the mastery of the "Third Germany," the mass of minor principalities into which the rest of German-speaking central Europe was divided (Simms, 1998). This competition has profoundly shaped how the history of this part of Europe has been written, not least since Leopold von Ranke and the other Germanic founders of the modern discipline of history were working as these events unfolded during the nineteenth century. The depiction of the past was central to the debate on "German" identity and the political battle between Prussia and Austria over the creation of a single German state and how such a state should be governed. Germany's role in the outbreak of the two twentieth-century world wars, as well as the harrowing experience of Hitler and the Holocaust, have cast further shadows. As a result, central European history has generally been viewed from a national perspective, imposing the frontiers of later states onto the past and writing about parts of the empire as if these were already independent countries. The German perspective has predominated, with a tendency to relate eighteenth-century (and earlier) events to the subsequent course of German history. At its most extreme, this leads to the depiction of German development following a "special path" (*Sonderweg*), allegedly deviating from the Western democratic norm down its own peculiar authoritarian route to world war and the Holocaust (Hagen, 1991).

Recent research has made the teleological special path untenable. Not only is it clear that the empire was still an important factor, but its continued existence means that we need to see Austria, Prussia, and the other German principalities like Bavaria as something more than the building blocks of later nation-states. These essentially political issues provide our entry into the considerable specialist literature on eighteenth-century central Europe. Political history helps define the geographical boundaries of research, and it assumes perhaps even greater importance in writing on central Europe because many German historians view the state as a motor for wider change and shape their analyses accordingly.

The Holy Roman Empire

The difficulty in defining the empire led Samuel von Pufendorf to describe it as a "monstrosity" in 1667, describing how it had degenerated from a "regular kingdom" into an "irregular" one (Wilson, 2006). The theme of decline was followed by subsequent writers, who argued that the Peace of Westphalia of 1648 left the empire an empty shell by effectively making its component territories independent states. Apparently reduced to little more than a loose federation, it seemed the empire could be conveniently ignored as historians concentrated on the much simpler task of tracing the development of the individual states, especially Austria and Prussia, that became so important in the eighteenth century. The strong tradition of regional history (*Landesgeschichte*) allowed the smaller principalities to find their place in this narrative of political centralization, as there was still room for separate histories of Bavaria, Hanover, Saxony, and other places. In turn, this approach allowed "German" history to be fitted into wider debates, notably that on absolutism, since centralization at territorial level appeared to fit a common European pattern.

A large number of studies published since the 1960s indicate that the imperial constitution was far from fossilized after 1648 and that its development cannot be fitted into a simple process of steady decline towards inevitable collapse (Aretin, 1993–7). These findings pose considerable methodological problems, because they require an explanatory framework to relate them to the work on the individual component territories. The process of German reunification in 1990 stimulated an existing trend towards describing the empire as a federal structure. The success of the western Federal Republic of Germany that absorbed the bankrupt communist East Germany encouraged a more positive assessment of federalism as a form of political organization. It also allowed the incorporation of much twentieth-century scholarship, whilst rebutting a central tenet of the "special path" thesis that German development was inherently deviant and undemocratic. The empire thus could appear more "modern" than centralized Prussia, because it devolved functions to its component territories that nonetheless remained within a common framework (Umbach, 2000). The major flaw with this interpretation is the difference between modern federalism and the actual structure and practice of imperial politics. Federalism implies an equality of association that was fundamentally alien to the feudal, hierarchical imperial constitution. Federalism existed as a tendency towards the accumulation of power in the hands of a few princes with larger territories that became the basis of the sovereign kingdoms and grand duchies to emerge from the empire's collapse in 1806. These were then grouped into a much more obviously federal structure when Napoleon marshaled them into the new Confederation of the Rhine. Those that survived the Napoleonic era retained their sovereignty when they combined with Austria and Prussia in the German Confederation in 1815. In other words, federalism was a force eroding the traditional imperial structure and pushing towards the political organizations that replaced it.

An alternative has been proposed by Georg Schmidt's model of a "complimentary empire-state" (Schmidt, 1999). This explains the empire's confusing structure by identifying different levels of authority within its constitution, each with distinct, but complementary functions. While these institutions remain important to Schmidt's analysis, his main emphasis is on political culture in his argument that the empire functioned because most of its inhabitants shared common values and norms. For this reason, he dubs the empire the "first German nation state," arguing that the basis of its national identity was its political culture, not notions of birth and language that became central to later German nationalism. The counterpoint to Schmidt's interpretation is offered by Peter-Claus Hartmann who borrows explicitly from the language of the European Commission to describe the empire after 1648 as a "central Europe of the regions," with the multi-layered political structure embodying the "principle of subsidiarity" whereby key functions were devolved to the territories for the common good (Hartmann, 2001). In place of Schmidt's nation-state model, Hartmann stresses cultural diversity safeguarded by the imperial constitution. Earlier interpretations regarded such diversity and devolution as a sign of weakness, arguing that the "age of absolutism" required the strong hand of a hereditary monarch to provide direction and security amidst fierce international competition. Hartmann rejects this, arguing that the close proximity of different forms of regional government in the empire stimulated cultural and economic development, assisted by the regulatory framework of the imperial constitution.

Recent interpretations such as these have been necessary to dispel the stubborn legacy of nineteenth-century historiography, which presented the empire in terminal decline. However, there is a danger that they will replace the critical continuity of the "special path" thesis with a new, positive teleology culminating in federal democracy and the European Union. The best way to understand the empire is to follow the eighteenth-century German publicist Johann Jacob Moser, who wrote that "Germany is governed in the German manner" (Moser, 1967). By this he meant that the empire was not only a distinct political system, but that each component territory had its own particular form of government that had evolved over many centuries. Its constitution was an accretion of written laws and precedents that permitted each territory to develop separately provided it did not transgress the common imperial norms.

The empire was a monarchy, but power had never been centralized and so political development cannot be described as "declining" towards greater independence of the component territories. Even after the loss of Lorraine (1738) and other regions, the empire still covered 687,000 km^2 in the eighteenth century, making it much larger than France and too extensive to be ruled directly from a single center. The imperial title was elective, but elective monarchy was not uncommon in Europe. Poland and the Papacy remained elective monarchies, as did Bohemia to 1627 and Hungary to 1687. The emperor had always governed in collaboration with his leading vassals, and imperial political history was essentially a record of the changes in how this interaction took place. The Peace of Westphalia left the emperor as sovereign whilst codifying princely powers as lesser, territorial sovereignty (*Landeshoheit*). This made the princes exclusive representatives for their subjects in all imperial institutions, enhancing their status of imperial immediacy (*Reichsunmittelbarkeit*) with no intervening lord between them and the emperor. All other nobles, clergy, and commoners were "mediate" territorial subjects governed by one or more intermediary rulers under the emperor's overall jurisdiction. Together with the magistrates governing the 51 imperial cities, the 93 principalities and 139 other immediate territorial lordships collectively constituted the "imperial estates" (*Reichsstände*) who shared in the empire's governance with the emperor in common institutions, of which the imperial diet (Reichstag) was the most important.

The principalities and lordships were either ruled by hereditary secular rulers or senior clerics elected by the local cathedral or abbey chapter. The 67 ecclesiastical territories collectively comprised the "Holy Roman" part of the empire, with their Catholic character guaranteed by the Peace of Westphalia. All territorial rulers were grouped in a complex hierarchy so that, despite their common status of immediacy, they were not equals. A senior group of princes had acquired the exclusive right to elect each emperor. These "electors" included three archbishops (Mainz, Cologne, and Trier), and a varying number of secular colleagues. Originally, there were four secular electors (Bohemia, the Palatinate, Saxony, Brandenburg), but Bavaria was raised to an electorate in 1623, followed by Hanover (1692), while the Palatine and Bavarian titles were merged when the latter dynasty died out in 1777. The electors debated in a separate "college" in the Reichstag and enjoyed other privileges setting them apart from the 61 secular and 24 ecclesiastical principalities that each had one vote in the college of princes. The 99 secular counts were obliged to share four princely votes, while the 40 abbots and priors had two. The imperial cities formed a third, subordinate college whose representation was confirmed in 1648.

However, the actual situation was more coherent than these numbers suggest, because political representation in imperial institutions was associated with the territories, not the people who ruled them. Thus, it was possible for a princely family to accumulate several territories, including combining an electorate with several principalities and counties, as in the case of the Hohenzollern dynasty ruling Brandenburg-Prussia. Of the then 60 secular princely votes in 1767, 17 were held by the five secular electors who shared a further two with other princes, while 27 families held the rest. Accumulation was also possible amongst the ecclesiastical lands where, for instance, the bishopric of Münster was often linked to the neighboring electorate of Cologne through the choice of the same ruler by the respective cathedral chapters. Secular dynasties also acquired influence within the church lands by promoting the clerical careers of younger sons. In this way, Cologne came to be held by the Bavarian Wittelsbachs continuously between 1582 and 1761.

Accumulation of political representation concentrated power at the top of the empire's feudal hierarchy. The Habsburgs enjoyed the premier position through their hereditary possession of the Austrian principalities, the kingdom-electorate of Bohemia, and various enclaves in southwest Germany, as well as (after 1700) the former Spanish Netherlands (modern Belgium and Luxembourg). Their acquisition of Spain's former Italian possessions also made them the dominant force in "imperial Italy" (*Reichsitalien*), since these lands were also imperial fiefs. Possession of so many lands made the Habsburgs the obvious choice in each imperial election and secured an unbroken hold over the imperial title between 1438 and 1740. Emperor Charles VI's death in that year exposed the dynasty's weakness, since he left no male heirs and his daughter, Maria Theresia, was ineligible to stand for election herself. The crisis triggered the War of the Austrian Succession that was both an international struggle over the Habsburg inheritance and an imperial civil war as the Bavarian Wittelsbachs temporarily acquired the imperial title in 1742 after an interregnum. Bavaria's defeat and the death of the Wittelsbach emperor Charles VII in 1745 paved the way for the election of Maria Theresia's husband Francis Stephen of Lorraine as successor. Her fecundity not only ensured an ample supply of further candidates, but left archdukes spare to pursue careers in the church lands. For instance, Max Franz was elected to both Cologne and Münster in 1784, having already acquired representation in the college of princes in 1780 by becoming grand master of the Teutonic Order.

However, it was already clear well before 1700 that the Habsburgs' imperial influence derived as much from their superior material resources as their formal constitutional powers. It was not so much that the imperial constitution lost its meaning, but rather that the increasingly uneven distribution of both formal powers and material resources gradually polarized imperial politics. The numerous territories had coalesced into four groups by the early eighteenth century, of which only the first remained a significant factor in wider European relations (Duchhardt, 1990). The first group contained Austria and Prussia as great powers. Austria was by far the largest and most powerful and remained so throughout the eighteenth century, despite the rise of its Prussian rival (Ingrao, 2000). The Habsburgs hereditary possessions encompassed 251,000 km^2 by 1714, giving them direct control of over 36 percent of the empire. The loss of Silesia to Prussia after 1740 reduced this, but still left them with over 31 percent of imperial territory by the 1790s. In the meantime they had acquired their own dynastic empire beyond the imperial frontiers. Already covering 90,000 km^2 in the later seventeenth century, this grew following conquests from the Ottoman Turks, as well as a significant share in the inheritance of their Spanish cousins in 1700. Some land was lost in unsuccessful wars against France, Spain, and the Turks in the 1730s, but far more was acquired through participation in two of the three partitions of Poland after 1772. Habsburg possessions beyond the empire grew to 494,000 km^2 by 1795, or more than double the size of their lands under imperial jurisdiction.

Prussia's expansion began during the Thirty Years War where, more by luck than design, Brandenburg profited from Sweden's rivalry with the Habsburgs to acquire considerable territory scattered across northern Germany. Further minor conquests came at Sweden's expense from 1715 to 1721, followed by the much more significant gain of Silesia, which was conquered by Frederick II during the War of the Austrian Succession. The inheritance of East Frisia (1744) and Ansbach-Bayreuth (1792) added further lands within the imperial frontiers, bringing the total to 131,800 km^2, or 19 percent of the empire. More remarkable still was the dramatic expansion of Prussia itself at Poland's expense after 1772, which increased Hohenzollern territory beyond the empire to 177,900 km^2 by 1795. Of these gains, the most significant was the seizure of Polish Royal or west Prussia in the first partition, since this secured a land bridge between Brandenburg and Hohenzollern eastern Prussia. Like the Habsburgs, the Hohenzollerns now held more land outside the empire than within it, but likewise their "German" lands were more densely populated (Dwyer, 2000).

No other German dynasty could match this. Even after the Zweibrücken branch inherited all the Wittelsbach lands, including both Bavaria and the Palatinate in 1799, they came a very poor third with only 54,000 km^2 of territory. Prussia's conquest of Silesia effectively put Saxony out of the running since it destroyed Saxon hopes of establishing contiguous territory between their electorate and the kingdom of Poland they ruled between 1697 and 1763. Hanover had even less land. Altogether, these four electorates totaled around 123,000 km^2 after 1714, or less than 18 percent of the empire. They retained some weight in European relations, chiefly because of their dynastic connections to other kingdoms, but were greatly overshadowed in imperial affairs by Prussian expansion.

The other rulers collectively held around a third of the empire, with their share declining to 217,700 km^2 (1792) as Prussia and the larger electorates acquired additional duchies and counties. They can be subdivided into two groups according to influence and material resources. The more important still played a role in imperial affairs and, thanks to dynastic connections and military potential, aspired to become more prominent internationally as well. This group included the three ecclesiastical electorates, as well as the relatively large church lands of Salzburg, Münster, and Würzburg, and around 10 secular principalities, chiefly those ruled by long-established dynasties such as Hessen-Kassel and Württemberg. The more important of these principalities survived the empire's collapse to become sovereign states after 1806. The final group contained around 60 ecclesiastical and secular princes and lords, as well as the 51 imperial cities, most of which were comparatively small, and all of which depended heavily on the empire to sustain their distinct identity. The annexations that accompanied the empire's demise between 1802 and 1806 came chiefly at their expense.

Austria and the Empire

The presence of so many distinct territories curbed monarchical centralization, but did not render the emperor impotent. The Peace of Westphalia reserved considerable formal authority for the emperor and left him with the initiative in the key institutions. It also segregated Habsburg territory as a distinct entity largely beyond imperial jurisdiction. Opinions differ over Austria's subsequent relationship to the empire (Brauneder and Höbelt, 1996). Austrian historians have tended to write the history of the Habsburg lands after 1648 as if they were already a separate country, mirroring the nineteenth-century Borussian tradition charting Prussia's rise as a distinct great power. Neither perspective has much time for the empire, focusing instead on the centralization of power within Austria or Prussia, and analyzing the development of administration, taxation, and other issues commonly associated with "state-building." The idea of Austrian distinctiveness at least captures something of the language of eighteenth-century imperial politics that spoke of the "emperor and empire" (*Kaiser und Reich*). This dualism is difficult to translate into English, which only has one word for "imperial," whereas German has *kaiserlich*, pertaining to the emperor, and *reichisch* for the empire. Certainly, the interregnum of 1740–2 represented a sea-change in thinking about Austria's place in the empire. Though the Habsburgs recovered the title in 1745 and held it to 1806, contemporaries already distinguished much more clearly between the common *Reich* institutions, and the private Habsburg imperial interests.

However, recent research stresses the continued significance of the empire to Austria, even after 1740. The imperial title was the basis of the Habsburgs' international prestige. The late medieval ideology of the "imperial translation" held that the empire was the direct continuation of the ancient Roman empire in its final, Christian form. This placed the emperor as the foremost European monarch with the duty to defend Christendom. The gradual integration of the Muslim Ottoman empire into the European states system, especially after the first formally permanent peace treaty in 1699, undermined the spiritual significance of the imperial title but did not eliminate it entirely. The Holy Roman title also lost prestige when the Habsburgs were forced to acknowledge the sultan (1606) and tsar (1721) as emperors. Napoleon's creation of a new French empire in 1804 prompted them to adopt their own hereditary Austrian title later that year, but they drew directly on the existing symbols and crown in their presentation of this. The majority of Germans still regarded the Habsburgs as the *proper* imperial dynasty well into the nineteenth century. The shrillness of Borussian claims about Prussia's "historic mission" to unite Germany is a response to this and reflects the difficulty of getting the Hohenzollerns accepted as *imperial*, even after the creation of the Second Empire in 1871.

The imperial title also gave access to political influence and material resources. The empire remained a feudal hierarchy with the princes and other rulers subordinate to the emperor as his vassals. They were obliged to seek confirmation of their possessions on their accession, and even Frederick II of Prussia still paid his feudal dues to the imperial treasury in the later eighteenth century. As sovereign, the emperor alone had full powers of ennoblement, enabling him to attract clients from across Germany, and to curry favor amongst the princes by agreeing requests to elevate their own servants. The political importance of patronage helps explain why so many princes sought royal titles during the eighteenth century; only Prussia was successful, although Hanover, Saxony, Hessen-Kassel, and other minor principalities were associated with foreign kingdoms for considerable periods.

The emperor could summon support through the empire's system of collective security established in the late fifteenth century and linked to arrangements intended to preserve peace amongst the imperial estates. All rulers had been obliged to forswear violence and submit their disputes to arbitration through the Reichskammergericht, a supreme court jointly managed by the emperor and the imperial estates. The emperor maintained his own Reichshofrat, which had partially overlapping jurisdiction and often dealt with similar cases. The development of both courts forced the territories to create their own judiciaries, since those that failed to do so were more exposed to imperial intervention. Imperial law guided territorial development since it formed the basis for most princely and civic legislation well into the eighteenth century. The two supreme courts had similar roles. They were to resolve conflicts between territories over borders, tariffs, and other matters, or within their ruling dynasties over inheritance and like matters. In addition, they acted where territorial judiciaries failed to settle problems, including disputes between rulers and their own subjects that formed between a tenth and a quarter of the annual caseload. A large body of research has now established that the courts functioned far more effectively than previously thought. The Reichshofrat was able to take over when the Reichskammergericht became overwhelmed, handling an average of 2,000 to 3,000 cases a year during the eighteenth century, compared to around 240 annually at the Reichskammergericht. The latter broke down completely from 1705 to 1709, but revived after an extended "visitation," or investigation by an imperial commission. Another visitation from 1766 to 1776 revived the court after further problems in mid-century. The system relied on the princes to enforce the verdicts, but was not entirely toothless. The rulers of Nassau-Siegen, Mecklenburg, and other smaller territories were deposed by the courts during the eighteenth century, partly in response to appeals by their own subjects.

The imperial legal system obviously failed to prevent Austria and Prussia fighting in 1740–5, 1756–63, and 1778–9. The threat of the imperial ban (the highest sanction making the target an outlaw) failed to deter Frederick II from starting the Seven Years War in 1756, but the minor princes did provide over 25,000 men to help Austria execute the court verdict against him after 1757. These conflicts were great power struggles related to wider international tensions (Showalter, 1996). It is often forgotten that the system otherwise largely eliminated violent conflict within the empire, despite the numerous competing jurisdictions, dynastic jealousies, and other potential causes. The few princes who did take the law into their own hands were firmly punished, as the heavily armed landgrave of Hessen-Kassel discovered when he tried to annex the county of Schaumburg-Lippe in 1787.

The courts also gave the emperor considerable political influence. Though he could not determine their verdicts, he could influence the outcome, for example by delaying a decision. The constant friction ensured there were numerous cases running concurrently. The emperor could favor a prince in one case while opposing him in another. Since imperial intervention was rarely overt, the princes' faith in imperial justice remained largely unshaken and they continued to look to him for favor (Haug-Moritz, 1992; Hughes, 1988; Wilson, 1995).

The same laws binding the imperial estates to keep the "public peace" obliged them to assist in collective defense against external enemies. In the sixteenth and seventeenth centuries this generally involved fighting the Turks, a duty no Christian felt able to dodge entirely. Habsburg expansion into the Balkans after 1683 removed the Turks as an immediate danger, and German assistance in Austria's wars with the Ottomans ceased after 1739 (Hochedlinger, 2003). It is a measure of the Habsburgs' recovery after the Thirty Years War that they were able to reorientate collective defense westwards to repel French aggression that mounted during the reign of Louis XIV. The lesser territories lay predominantly in the west and south, directly in the path of the French armies, and so their rulers willingly cooperated with the emperor in reforming defense obligations in 1681–2 (Wilson, 1998). The empire did not have its own permanent army, but relied on the territories to provide troops according to quotas agreed in imperial institutions. Soldiers could be mobilized for internal peacekeeping or external defense. The emperor was not formally obliged to ask the Reichstag to declare war, since an invasion automatically triggered the system, but Emperor Leopold I (r. 1658–1705) chose to do so during the wars with France in order to lend greater legitimacy to his management of the imperial war effort. Mobilization was coordinated by the *Kreise*, or imperial circles, that had been established in the sixteenth century by grouping most of the territories into one of 10 regions (Dotzauer, 1998). The Habsburg lands were segregated into the Austrian and Burgundian *Kreise*, reflecting their distinct place within the empire. The presence of Brandenburg, Saxony, and Hanover inhibited the development of the Upper and Lower Saxon *Kreis* that only existed on paper in the eighteenth century. However, the other seven regions continued to function after 1700, especially because of the necessity of coordinating defense. Those, like Swabia and Franconia, that contained large numbers of small territories performed a wider range of functions through their regional assemblies (*Kreistage*).

Assistance through imperial defense was significant, averaging 40,000 men a year during the War of the Spanish Succession, 34,000 during the War of the Polish Succession, and 25,000 to 32,000 during the Seven Years War. It enabled the Habsburgs to divert most of their own troops to pursue their dynastic goals during international conflicts. Only 15,000 troops were provided during the French Revolutionary Wars, but this was partly because many territories paid cash in lieu of their contingents. Prussia drew the equivalent of 10,000 men in money that subsidized its forces against France 1793–5, while Austria had arrangements with 60 territories for the equivalent of around 12,000 men. Many more troops were provided outside the formal framework through bilateral agreements with the emperor or his allies. Imperial law permitted alliances provided these were not directed against the emperor or empire. Apart from Prussia, few territories dared oppose the Habsburgs directly during the eighteenth century. Bavaria and Cologne collaborated with France during the War of the Spanish Succession, but their electors were both driven into exile and only recovered their lands thanks to French pressure in the peace negotiations. Bilateral arrangements meanwhile provided the Habsburgs and their allies with 33,000 men at the start of the war, rising to over 100,000 at its height. Another 25,000 were sent during the Turkish War of 1716–18, with 54,300 following in the War of the Polish Succession, and 28,500 in the conflict against the Ottomans in 1737–9. Similar arrangements sent 55,000 men to assist against Prussia at the start of the Seven Years War, in addition to those sent under formal imperial obligations. The emperor was also able to use imperial prerogatives to recruit directly into the Austrian army, consistently drawing far more men than the more infamous Prussian recruiters managed to procure in the empire throughout the eighteenth century.

Prussia and the End of the Empire

Brandenburg was the weakest electorate and played a marginal role prior to the seventeenth century. Borussian historiography greatly magnified its importance to substantiate claims it was destined to unite Germany. While jettisoning this agenda, much later research has followed the Borussian path of tracing Prussian development as a process of state-building whereby disparate and allegedly under-resourced lands were welded together by able and far-sighted rulers to make a potent, centralized, and efficient monarchy. Frederick William is dubbed the Great Elector for having laid the administrative foundations and established the standing army between 1640 and 1688. His son, Frederick, has undergone a positive reappraisal since the tricentenary of his coronation as Prussian king in 1701 as modern scholars recognize the significance of the royal title, especially in buying access into the select club of Europe's crowned heads. His successor, Frederick William I, is credited with consolidating both the army and administration between 1713 and 1740, bequeathing Frederick II the means to attack Austria when it was at its most vulnerable following Charles VI's death in 1740.

However, Prussia's rise only appears inevitable in retrospect, and its power was largely unproven before 1740 and certainly overshadowed by the more showy courts and international connections of the Bavarian, Saxon, and Hanoverian electors. Prussia's victories in 1740–5 were not only over Austria, but also indirectly over its other German rivals. Saxony lost the chance to obtain Silesia, while Bavaria's imperial ambitions left it ruined. Prussia was established as the second power in the empire, and both Britain and France followed by courting its alliance. The War of the Austrian Succession was also the first major war fought by the Habsburgs without substantial support from the empire. German abstinence reflected a widespread desire to avoid entanglement in great power politics. To Austria, however, it was little short of betrayal, and the program of internal reforms begun before the war ended was intended to enhance the monarchy's ability to fight a future conflict without imperial assistance (Blanning, 1994; Dickson, 1987). Though unintended, it reinforced Austrian distinctiveness, not least in the minds of those directing Habsburg policy. Further changes followed from the fact that the next war was directed, not against France or some other external foe, but at forcing Prussia to relinquish Silesia. Long-standing enmity towards France was dropped in the famous "reversal of alliances" completed by 1757 when France agreed to back Austria against Prussia. Despite being joined by Russia and Sweden, the new combination failed to crack Prussia during the Seven Years War, not least because its formation automatically split the "old system" of Britain and Austria, since Anglo-French rivalry drove Britain to support Frederick II.

Prussia gained no territory, but its mere survival confirmed its great power status. Austria's failure to recover Silesia signaled the impossibility of returning to the pre-1740 balance in central Europe and opened serious questions about the empire's future. Neither Austria nor Prussia wanted to destroy the empire, yet it was clear the traditional imperial structure could not accommodate two powers of their size and aspirations, raising the possibility of partition along the lines of an Austrian-dominated south and a Prussian north. The danger paradoxically heightened the empire's significance, since the other European powers recognized its utility in denying Austria and Prussia direct access to the resources of the Third Germany, while the latter sought survival in imperial renewal. The period after 1763 witnessed alternate attempts by Austria and Prussia to play the imperial constitution against the other, effectively thwarting efforts from Hanover, Saxony, and some minor princes to strengthen it. The Second and Third Partitions of Poland (1793 and 1795) radically altered the balance as Austrian and Prussian gains at Poland's expense dramatically widened the gap in resources between them and the other princes. Austria and Prussia had a combined military strength of 126,000 men in 1695, compared to 150,000 troops maintained by other German rulers. One hundred years later the two great powers commanded 692,700 men, compared to only 106,000 across the rest of the empire.

Polarization coincided with France's internal implosion following the 1789 revolution, removing one of the principal international props for the central European balance. The empire was unable to avoid being drawn into the struggle with revolutionary France, because the unexpected failure of their initial campaign prompted Austria and Prussia to collaborate in using the imperial constitution to draw on German resources from 1793. The French revolutionaries were not prepared to deal with existing structures and sought innovative ways to neutralize threats to their country. They saw no utility in preserving the empire, and signed a separate treaty with Prussia in 1795, allowing it to withdraw from the war taking all of northern Germany with it into a neutral zone that lasted until 1806. Prussia's unilateral withdrawal in the midst of an imperial war effort was unprecedented. It also is a measure of that country's much-trumpeted internal reforms and supposed efficiency, since impending bankruptcy and the difficulty of quelling revolts in the newly annexed Polish provinces forced it to make peace. France was able to concentrate on defeating Austria, achieving this by 1797 and forcing the Habsburgs to accept it four years later.

The Peace of Lunéville (1801) paved the way for the political reorganization of central Europe that was to sweep the empire away and continue throughout the Napoleonic era to the Vienna Settlement of 1815. The middling princes capitalized on their modest military potential and dynastic connections to deal directly with France, Russia, and Britain. The Reichstag was compelled to accept a settlement that had already largely taken place on the ground, and sanctioned the mediatization of over 100 smaller territories in 1803. The reorganized empire was given no time to consolidate, as Napoleon's renewed victory over Austria in 1805 allowed him to revise French relations with central Europe. The middling princes were herded into the

Confederation of the Rhine in July 1806, leaving Emperor Francis II little choice but to abdicate the following month. Napoleon was now free to turn on Prussia, which had failed to intervene. Prussia's defeat in October 1806 completed the end of the old political order in central Europe.

Social and Political Continuities

The bicentenary of these events has sparked renewed interest in their significance. It is already becoming clear that the changes only affected part of the established order. The political map was redrawn, reducing the imperial mosaic to Austria, Prussia, and 37 enlarged principalities, newly minted kingdoms and surviving urban republics like Hamburg. Nonetheless, it still remained a patchwork, and the empire featured in all the plans for a post-Napoleonic settlement since it was unthinkable to let either Austria or Prussia dominate all Germany, while partition was equally unacceptable. The new German Confederation lacked many of the features that made the empire distinctive, notably its Holy Roman aspect, since all the church lands were secularized in 1803. Nonetheless, there were deeper continuities that mean we must look beyond the level of high politics and engage more with social and other aspects.

First, these profound changes took place without a French-style revolution. There were German Jacobins, but they were a tiny minority, and popular unrest, such as it existed, was mainly directed at the burdens of war rather than demands for change. There was no mass exodus of German nobles, the major princely dynasties remained in power, and even the mediatized minor rulers retained many special rights until these were abolished in the 1848 revolution. The apparent solidity of German dynasticism raises questions about the strength and effectiveness of German princely rule during the eighteenth century and its relations to society. There is a substantial debate whether the German princes can be classed as absolute (Wilson, 2000). The standard interpretation sees the Habsburgs and Hohenzollerns as absolute monarchs, ruling largely without formal constitutional constraints, except in Hungary where the Habsburgs were obliged to consult the diet. Internal policy is also customarily discussed as progressing from conventional state-building absolutism in the first half of the century to more enlightened reforms in the second. The other princes are largely dismissed as petty despots, indulging fantasies of grandeur with their mistresses, palaces, and miniature armies (Vann, 1984). This latter aspect has undergone significant revision in recent years, with some scholars (Blanning, 1974; Ingrao, 1987) suggesting that absolutism, enlightened or otherwise, worked best in the smaller territories where there were often fewer barriers to reform.

Others doubt the appropriateness of the term "absolutism," and some suggest that all European monarchies were variations on "consultative government" (see chapter 28). Certainly, it is appropriate to investigate the limits to princely power. Many of these were practical. Administration remained patchy, inefficient, and often corrupt even by eighteenth-century criteria. Officials were supposed to serve the prince, but could be a source for covert or even open opposition, as in the case of the Württemberg privy councillors (Vann, 1984). There were also legal restrictions. Even apologists for absolutism distinguished between it and arbitrary rule, expecting princes to observe imperial and territorial laws, including agreements made with their subjects. This explains the survival of the territorial estates (*Landstände*), or formal representative bodies that existed in most principalities and many counties. The estates in Württemberg, Mecklenburg, and several other territories successfully prosecuted their princes in the imperial courts for breaches of territorial charters during the eighteenth century (Haug-Moritz, 1992; Hughes, 1988; Wilson, 1995). Nonetheless, it is clear that princely rule underwent significant changes during the seventeenth century, enhancing the ruler's authority with a shift away from consultation in formal bodies like the estates and towards more informal arena, such as the princely courts. Estates remained after 1700, even in Brandenburg-Prussia, but their competence was often circumscribed, integrating them more closely with the territorial administration under princely authority. Prolonged warfare from 1672 to 1714 made it difficult to object to taxation that not only increased greatly, but became permanent, with the estates simply discussing the means of raising it, rather than its level. They retained their own committees, archives, and even separate treasuries, but they generally remained on the periphery, while other princely institutions expanded in line with the territorial state's increased engagement in wider aspects of daily life.

There is considerable controversy over the nature, purpose, and impact of this state expansion (Dipper, 1991; Wilson, 2004). The general view sees a shift from the early seventeenth-century concern for enforcing Christian morality and confessional orthodoxy, through the late seventeenth- and early eighteenth-century preoccupation with material power, to later eighteenth-century enlightened impulses. While this paradigm has some validity, motives were always mixed, and often the content of government measures remained remarkably consistent but was repackaged in line with prevailing intellectual trends. This cannot be reduced to a cynical attempt by those in power to justify their policies, and there is certainly no sense that German rulers initiated reforms from above to avoid revolution from below. Even after 1789 most were convinced there was little immediate danger of a general uprising, because they believed their governments were already responding to popular concerns.

Official measures were influenced by religion and enlightened philosophy, but also the norms and values embedded in the imperial political culture. These in turn expressed the corporate character of central European society (Ogilvie, 1999). The basic functional division into clergy, nobles, and commons was woven into the fabric of imperial and territorial law that, essentially, was intended to regulate corporate society and resolve its problems peacefully. No legally recognized group was entirely without rights, expressed as "liberties" and linked to the communal basis of most social organization. Society, and the political structures it supported, was built around households conceived as partnerships of husband and wife with distinct, but complementary roles (Ogilvie, 1996; Wunder, 1998). Households were patriarchal in the sense that the "house father" was regarded as taking precedence, yet they were also considered incomplete without the "house mother." Other family members, and anyone else lodging there, were subordinate to parental authority, linking the household to social and political order. People belonged through their household to the wider community of the village, the town, and thence to the territory (Walker, 1971). Other communities that lacked a familial basis, such as religious foundations, journeymen's fraternities, and military units, nonetheless embodied many of the same norms. These arrangements had been greatly strengthened by the increased emphasis on marriage and morality accompanying the sixteenth-century Protestant Reformation and Catholic renewal. Despite fashionable enlightened secularism, the Christian component remained fundamental throughout the eighteenth century in the minds of householders and state administrators alike. Revisions to territorial law continued to favor householders over the unmarried and the propertyless, for example by regulating inheritance to reinforce primogeniture and prevent the uneconomic subdivision of property. Those who, by choice or misfortune, fell outside settled society were stigmatized and targeted as marginals, deviants, and potential subversives.

Such practices created substantial problems, not least in restricting the ability of state and society to adapt to change. The demographic losses of the Thirty Years War had been made up by 1714 when the empire had around 20 million inhabitants, but sustained growth from the 1730s added a further 9 million by 1800, while there were another 19 million people in the Habsburg and Hohenzollern lands beyond the imperial frontiers. Growth placed increasing pressure on the unequally distributed resources, prompting migration (especially to North America), pauperization, and underemployment. The so-called enlightened reforms were largely intended as a response to these problems, but those deciding policy found it difficult to step outside the mental world of corporate society. The widespread presentation of the prince as "father of his people" (*Landesvater*) reflected how notions of the household penetrated to the very center of power. The juridified character of social and political disputes inhibited calls for change, because corporate rights made it possible for ordinary people to oppose unwelcome innovations or adverse conditions by taking action in local, territorial, and imperial courts (Rowe, 2003). Absolutism denied people a formal voice in major decisions, but left wide scope for the management of their local and private affairs. Moreover, princely rule only functioned with the tacit consent of the governed and because official measures were bent to fit popular concerns (Wegert, 1994). The so-called German "police state" was not necessarily "well ordered," and we must question the social disciplining thesis that sees official policy as molding society from above (Raeff, 1983; Schlumbohm, 1997).

These considerations return us to our opening discussion about the "modernity" of social and political arrangements in eighteenth-century central Europe. A major reason for the empire's collapse was the reluctance of its rulers to sacrifice established patterns of dealing with their subjects in order to confront the military challenge of revolutionary France. Old Prussia suffered the same fate in 1806, while Austria only escaped thanks to its greater size and resources. Despite their application of some enlightened ideas, German rulers could not embrace the notion of individual human rights without questioning the corporate basis of the entire social and political order. Their subjects generally clung to similar beliefs. Most looked to the authorities as potential allies to regulate society, curb landlords' demands, and protect them from market forces, as well as external enemies. To the frustration of the German Jacobins and later revolutionaries, they rejected abstract concepts of equality that contradicted their own cherished special privileges (Wegert, 1992). Nonetheless, the destruction of the imperial hierarchy by 1806 removed a fundamental pillar of the old order, opening established social and political arrangements to more profound change as the underlying problems, already present in the 1790s, grew deeper towards the middle of the nineteenth century.

Bibliography

Aretin, K. O. Frhr. v., *Das alte Reich 1648–1806* (3 vols., Stuttgart, 1993–7).

Blanning, T. C. W., *Reform and Revolution in Mainz 1743–1803* (Cambridge, 1974).

Blanning, T. C. W., *Joseph II* (Harlow, 1994).

Brauneder, W. and L. Höbelt (eds.), *Sacrum Imperium. Das Reich und Österreich 996–1806* (Vienna, 1996).

Dickson, P. G. M., *Finance and Government under Maria Theresia 1740–1780* (2 vols., Oxford, 1987).

Dipper, C., *Deutsche Geschichte 1648–1789* (Frankfurt am Main, 1991).

Dotzauer, W., *Die deutsche Reichskreise (1388–1806)* (Wiesbaden, 1998).

Duchhardt, H., *Altes Reich und europäisches Staatenwelt 1648 bis 1806* (Munich, 1990).

Dwyer, P. G. (ed.), *The Rise of Prussia 1700–1830* (Harlow, 2000).

Hagen, W. W., "Descent of the Sonderweg: Hans Rosenberg's history of old-regime Prussia," *Central European History*, 24 (1991), 24–50.

Hartmann, P. C., *Kulturgeschichte des Heiligen Römischen Reiches 1648 bis 1806* (Vienna, 2001).

Haug-Moritz, G., *Württembergischer Ständekonflikt und deutscher Dualismus* (Stuttgart, 1992).

Hochedlinger, M., *Austria's Wars of Emergence: War, State and Society in the Habsburg Monarchy 1683–1797* (London, 2003).

Hughes, M., *Law and Politics in 18th Century Germany: The Imperial Aulic Council and the Reign of Charles VI* (Woodbridge, 1988).

Ingrao, C. W., *The Hessian Mercenary State: Ideas, Institutions and Reform under Frederick II 1760–85* (Cambridge, 1987).

Ingrao, C. W., *The Habsburg Monarchy 1618–1815* (2nd edn., Cambridge, 2000).

Moser, J. J., *Neues Teutsches Staats-Recht* (20 vols., Frankfurt, 1766–75; repr. Osnabrück, 1967).

Ogilvie, S. (ed.), *A New Social and Economic History of Germany*, vol. 2: *1630–1800* (London, 1996).

Ogilvie, S., "The state in Germany," in J. Brewer and E. Hellmuth (eds.), *Rethinking Leviathan* (Oxford, 1999), pp. 167–202.

Raeff, M., *The Well-Ordered Police State: Social and Institutional Change through Law in the Germanies and Russia 1600–1800* (New Haven, 1983).

Rowe, M., *From Reich to State: The Rhineland in the Revolutionary Era* (Cambridge, 2003).

Schlumbohm, J., "Gesetze, die nicht durchgesetzt werden. Ein Strukturmerkmal des frühneuzeitlichen Staates?," *Geschichte und Gesellschaft*, 23 (1997), 647–63.

Schmidt, G., *Geschichte des alten Reiches 1495–1806* (Munich, 1999).

Showalter, D. E., *The Wars of Frederick the Great* (London, 1996).

Simms, B., *The Struggle for Mastery in Germany 1779–1850* (Basingstoke, 1998).

Umbach, M., *Federalism and Enlightenment in Germany 1740–1806* (London, 2000).

Vann, J. A., *The Making of a State: Württemberg 1593–1793* (Ithaca, 1984).

Walker, M., *German Home Towns: Community, State and General Estate, 1648–1871* (Ithaca, 1971).

Wegert, K. H., *German Radicals Confront the Common People: Revolutionary Politics and Popular Unrest 1789–1849* (Mainz, 1992).

Wegert, K. H., *Popular Culture, Crime and Social Control in 18th Century Württemberg* (Wiesbaden, 1994).
Wilson, P. H., *War, State and Society in Württemberg, 1677–1793* (Cambridge, 1995).
Wilson, P. H., *German Armies: War and German Politics 1648–1806* (London, 1998).
Wilson, P. H., *Absolutism in Central Europe* (London, 2000).
Wilson, P. H., *From Reich to Revolution: German History 1558–1806* (Basingstoke, 2004).
Wilson, P. H., "Still a monstrosity? Some reflections on early modern German statehood," *Historical Journal*, 49 (2006), 566–76.
Wunder, H., *He Is the Sun, She Is the Moon: Women in Early Modern Germany* (Cambridge, MA, 1998).

Chapter Seventeen

The Scandinavian Kingdoms

Michael Bregnsbo

Three Kingdoms – Two States

Eighteenth-century Scandinavia had two states, a Danish and a Swedish one. Both were composite states, including territories other than their present-day namesakes. While Norway remained a distinct kingdom, it was ruled by the Danish king and remained politically and administratively subordinate to Denmark. The Swedish state included present-day Finland which, unlike Norway, was not a separate kingdom but an integral part of Sweden. A number of territories outside Scandinavia belonged to the two states. The Danish monarchy controlled the duchies of Schleswig and Holstein, and the counties of Oldenburg and Delmenhorst; the latter three still formally part of the Holy Roman Empire until 1806. The Danish king also ruled Norway's former Atlantic possessions of Iceland, Greenland, and the Faroe Islands, as well as small colonies in India, Africa, and the Caribbean. Sweden lost its Baltic possessions in Ingria, Estonia, and Livonia to Russia in 1719, as well as ceding Bremen and Verden to Hanover, but still retained Pomerania on the German Baltic coast, complete with the major cities of Stralsund and Greifswald. Thus, both Scandinavian kings were also German princes with rights in the empire. Sweden also acquired the small Caribbean island of St. Barthelemy in 1784.

Danish and Swedish historiography has often been written from the perspective of modern frontiers, and historians have only recently begun considering the composite character of both kingdoms by focusing on the political, social, economic, and cultural interaction of the component parts, and considering what this meant for the political decision-makers in Copenhagen and Stockholm.

Even if Scandinavia is often considered more or less a historical unit, the eighteenth-century kingdoms were nonetheless heterogeneous in many respects. Both were predominantly agrarian, but social organization and the conditions of the peasantry varied significantly. The farmers in Denmark proper were tenant farmers under landlords who exercised wide jurisdiction over their peasants (see below). By contrast, many Norwegian farmers owned their land, and tenancy, where it existed, ran on a commercial basis with no feudal elements. Furthermore, legislation ensured that

A Companion to Eighteenth-Century Europe, First Edition. Edited by Peter H. Wilson.
© 2014 John Wiley & Sons, Ltd. Published 2014 by John Wiley & Sons, Ltd.

farms could stay within the same family and pass undivided from the father to his eldest son. As for Sweden, three different kinds of farmers existed, namely peasants with "Crown land" (*kronojord*) who were tenants under the Crown, those with "nobility land" (*frälsejord*), who were tenants under an aristocratic landowner, and those with "taxation land" (*skattejord*), who owned their land themselves. Unlike Norway, but like Denmark, Sweden had large landed estates owned by aristocrats with tenant farmers. But Sweden knew nothing of the kind of feudal rights which were common in Denmark, and peasants on "taxation" and "Crown" lands were represented in the Swedish diet (Riksdag). Certainly, full serfdom did not exist in Denmark proper, but her agrarian society probably had more in common with eastern Europe than with Norway.

There were also important differences between the Scandinavian nobilities. Norway lacked a nobility of any significance during the eighteenth century, in contrast to Denmark, where noble status was primarily attached to the possession of landed estates. Such privileges could be acquired by any landowner, noble or not, while nobility was not worth much if one was a nobleman without owning land. Danish absolutism did not openly favor nobles with formal regulations granting them preferential treatment, or securing a monopoly on senior military and civil appointments. On the contrary, the king frequently appointed commoners to posts as he pleased, exercised exclusive rights to ennoble them, and often invited foreign nobles to assume important positions in the Danish military, government, and administration. This gave Danish society an element of meritocracy lacking in most other parts of eighteenth-century Europe, though social mobility remained heavily dependent on royal favor. Such opportunities were less common in Sweden, where the aristocracy, though heterogeneous, remained united by common privileges such as a monopoly of all higher military and civilian posts and exclusive rights to own "nobility land." Swedish nobles, in contrast to those in Denmark, also exercised considerable political influence through representation in their country's diet.

There were also economic differences between the Scandinavian kingdoms relating to their geography, with Sweden and Norway having more in common with each other than with Denmark, which lacked several of the sectors that were important to its two northern neighbors. Forestry played a considerable role in the Norwegian and Swedish economies, including subsidiary trades such as tar-burning and charcoal production. Fishing and hunting were likewise important, especially in Norway, as was mining, and both countries had numerous "factory towns" centered around metallurgical (iron, copper, silver) or lumber works. Yet the Swedish constitution differed fundamentally from that of Denmark-Norway (as will be discussed below), and though they fought no major wars after 1720, relations were far from cordial between the two states for the remainder of the eighteenth century. In short, apart from their shared Lutheran faith organized in state churches, the Scandinavian kingdoms appeared to have little in common.

International Relations

A basic condition for the foreign policies of both Scandinavian kingdoms was their location around the Baltic, providing access to the rest of the world and attracting the interest of Britain and other western European powers, which took grain, timber, tar, and other vital products from the region. It was in the interests of these foreign powers to ensure that neither of the Scandinavian kingdoms secured exclusive control over the Baltic, and so external intervention was directed at preserving both as viable, preferably mutually distrustful, states.

Sweden became a European great power during the Thirty Years War and remained one until the Great Northern War (1700–21), which saw a series of coalitions between Denmark, Saxony-Poland, Russia, Prussia, and Britain-Hanover all intent on ending Swedish dominance in northern Germany and the Baltic. This conflict coincided with the War of the Spanish Succession, in which some of the participants, notably Britain and Saxony, were also embroiled. The Swedish army, under the young warrior-king Charles XII, initially forced Denmark and Saxony to leave the coalition, but they rejoined his enemies later. Nonetheless, despite suffering a major defeat at Poltava on June 28, 1709, as well as Charles' 15-year absence from his kingdom, Sweden fought on against considerable odds. Manpower and fiscal resources were almost exhausted when Charles returned in 1715, yet he managed to conscript a new army and invade Norway. Hostilities with the Danish state largely ceased when Charles was shot during the siege of Fredrikshald in 1718. It remains a matter of debate whether the bullet was fired by one of the Norwegian defenders or by a Swede who saw the king as the main obstacle to peace. Either way, the king's death led to a coup and a change of foreign policy in favor of peace. Charles' sister Ulrica Eleonora was elected ruling queen; in 1719 she transferred her power to her consort, Frederick of Hessen, who now became king. Though exhausted from decades of warfare, Sweden still remained free of enemy troops and repelled a Russian amphibious invasion in 1719. The new leadership managed to play Sweden's enemies off against each other, but while this mitigated the effects of hostility, it could not prevent eventual defeat. At the peace treaties between 1719 and 1721, Sweden had to cede Bremen-Verden to Hanover, parts of Pomerania to Prussia, and Keksholm Län, Ingria, Estonia, Livonia, and parts of Finland to Russia. The reason why the consequences of defeat were not still more serious was due to the continued foreign interest in the Baltic balance that ensured that Britain and other powers did not want to weaken Sweden too much. But her status as a great power was gone. Structural explanations have been advanced for this. While the two Scandinavian powers had been fighting each other for centuries, other states emerged in the region: Prussia and Russia. The latter had now become the dominant power, squeezing out Swedish influence and presiding over the region as a whole. Others favor arguments highlighting human agency, blaming Charles XII's stubborn, reckless, and uncompromising personality for Sweden's decline, or at least arguing that he hastened a structural development which in the long run would have been unavoidable.

Even if Denmark made no territorial gains during the Great Northern War, the elimination of Sweden as a great power significantly improved Danish security. Traditionally, historians have considered the Danish state to have been a "satisfied power" without territorial ambitions from this time on. This interpretation fits smoothly with the country's self-image as a small and peaceful state during most of the twentieth century, but it is a retrospective view. Certainly, the eighteenth-century Danish state was strongly armed: measured in relation to the number of inhabitants, only Prussia had a larger army and only Britain had a larger navy. Recent research casts doubt on the previous belief that these armaments were purely defensive. While there were no attempts to reconquer the provinces of Scania, Halland, and Blekinge, which had been ceded to Sweden in 1658, the Danish government had not abandoned ambition should a suitable opportunity occur. Offensives were prepared against Sweden at various times during the 1730s and 1740s, and had the Danish state been offered the right rewards by its prospective allies it might have gone to war, but diplomatic intervention from other powers prevented it.

Denmark's main external problem after 1720 was not Sweden, but the parts of the duchies of Schleswig and Holstein which were under the control of the duke of Gottorp. This ducal family was a branch of the Danish royal family which, because of its loyalty towards the enemies of the king of Denmark during the seventeenth century, had been rewarded with full sovereignty for its small and scattered possessions. Relations were strained, and the Gottorp dukes had their own ambitions. Gottorp itself was not a military threat, but the duke's sovereignty was recognized internationally and his family had married into the Swedish and later the Russian ruling dynasties. Thus, any unilateral action against Gottorp from the Danish side would entail immediate international implications. By its peace with Denmark in 1720, Sweden, along with Britain and France, recognized Danish sovereignty over Gottorp's share of the duchy of Schleswig, but not over that of Holstein. This proved an unsatisfactory solution to Danish security concerns in general and the Gottorp problem in particular. The Danish Crown sought a powerful ally to help resolve these difficulties and potentially assist in recovering the lost provinces from Sweden. Britain was the partner from the early 1720s until 1742, when Denmark switched to France.

Meanwhile, the threat from Sweden declined thanks to internal changes in that country following the defeat in the Great Northern War. Royal absolutism had been abolished and the diet granted a greater say in political affairs, including external relations. Since important decisions now required lengthy consultation with the diet, it was impossible for Sweden to keep its plans secret and launch surprise attacks on its neighbors as it had done in the past. Moreover, other powers interfered directly in Swedish politics, including bribing members of the diet, in order to advance their own interests. While hopes of recovering the land lost in the Great Northern War were not entirely abandoned, Sweden followed a defensive policy until 1738, when it signed an alliance with France leading to an ill-prepared war against Russia in 1741–3 that, among other things, resulted in a temporary Russian occupation of Finland. Still, the defeat did not prove as disastrous as expected, because the question of succession to the throne was linked to the peace negotiations with Russia. The Swedish diet elected the Russian candidate, Duke Adolf Frederick of Holstein-Gottorp, as successor of the childless King Frederick I after an election in which the Danish Crown Prince Frederick V had also been a candidate and had not lacked support within Swedish society. Sweden nevertheless renewed its French alliance later during the 1740s and, consequently, had to declare war on Prussia in 1757 during the Seven Years War. Sweden did not distinguish itself during this campaign and concluded peace in 1762 on the pre-war territorial basis.

The election of a Gottorp to the Swedish throne in 1743 was a serious blow to Denmark's endeavors to resolve its security concerns. At least both countries shared an ally in France, which prompted King Adolf Frederick to renounce claims on the duchy of Schleswig on behalf of himself and his family and to make certain concessions regarding Holstein. Denmark remained a French ally during the Seven Years War, but did not intervene. As that conflict drew to a close around 1762, the Gottorp problem again became acute, because Grand Duke Charles Peter Ulrich succeeded to the Russian throne as Tsar Peter III. Russia had never accepted the renunciation of Gottorp rights in Schleswig or Holstein, and Peter III was determined to use all his new resources as tsar to regain his possessions and redress the wrongs that he and his family had suffered. He quickly made peace with Prussia in the Seven Years War, in order to free Russia to attack Denmark. Though France declined to give any diplomatic support, still less any military assistance, Denmark chose to fight. Fortunately, before hostilities began, Peter III was deposed by the coup that made his wife, Catherine II, Russian empress. Her perspective on the Baltic differed fundamentally from the narrow dynastic concerns of her murdered husband. She wanted to preserve Denmark as a member of a Russian-dominated Nordic system in which it would counterbalance Sweden and deter that country from renewing its efforts to recover the Baltic provinces lost by the peace settlement of 1719–21. Denmark's still relatively powerful navy increased its weight in Catherine's calculations. Furthermore, in order to avoid Sweden rebuilding its military might, the empress agreed with Denmark to preserve Sweden's post-1718 constitution which, it was thought, rendered rapid decision-making difficult. Any change in this constitution in favor of strengthening royal power was to be considered cause for war. Thus, Russia's concern for its general Baltic predominance inclined it to settle Denmark's more local problem with the Gottorps. Denmark and Russia concluded a preliminary treaty in 1767, followed by a definitive arrangement in 1773 in which the northern German possessions of Oldenburg and Delmenhorst were transferred to the Gottorps in exchange for their territories within the duchies of Schleswig and Holstein. A century-old security problem had now been solved to the Danes' satisfaction.

By then, however, another threat was emerging. King Gustavus III had staged a *coup d'état* in 1772 and reintroduced absolutism in Sweden (see below). This was cause for war under the terms of the Danish–Russian alliance, but Catherine was then involved in a war with Turkey and Denmark was in no position to fight alone. However, knowledge of Gustavus' long-term plans to conquer Norway compelled the Danish government to remain heavily armed and accept growing dependency on Russia as the price for continuing the defensive alliance.

Sweden continued her traditional policy of a French alliance. Gustavus seized the opportunity of Russia's distraction of another Turkish war to attack in 1788. Strong opposition from within the diet, as well as from separatist circles in Finland, forced Gustavus to present himself as the victim of Russian aggression. The Swedish offensive soon came to a stand-still. Under the terms of the Danish–Russian alliance, Russia demanded that Denmark declare war on Sweden. To fulfill her alliance obligations, Denmark sent a small force from Norway to attack the important Swedish port of Gothenburg, but soon stopped operations after British and Prussian objections. Following a convincing Russian naval victory, Sweden agreed peace without territorial losses in 1790. By the end of the century, Sweden was accepting the new balance of power in the Baltic by shifting from reliance on France towards friendship with Russia.

Denmark's avoidance of war for most of the period after 1720 enabled its trade to prosper under the country's neutral flag. Danish history records this era as the "flourishing trade period" and considers it a golden age of progress and reform. However, Danish commercial exploitation of neutrality incurred British hostility during the Revolutionary and Napoleonic Wars, because it was seen as a way of circumventing the blockade imposed on France and its allies. The Danish government provided naval escorts for its merchantmen and instructed them to refuse British demands for inspection. After clashes between Danish and British warships in 1800, the Danish state joined the Russian-led League of Armed Neutrality with Sweden and Prussia. Consequently, Britain attacked Denmark at the battle of Copenhagen on April 2, 1801, and forced it to leave the League. Though heavily outnumbered, the Danes had chosen to fight because the consequences of defeat by Britain appeared less serious than what would happen if they abandoned their allies: Russia was prepared to let Sweden conquer Norway and Prussia to occupy Schleswig, Holstein and Jutland. While the greed of Danish merchants may have led to the abuse of the country's neutral flag and precipitated the British attack, the general avoidance of major wars certainly favored trade and contributed towards wealth accumulation, capitalist development, and the formation of an urban middle class that together helped transform Danish society and economy. Sweden still harbored designs on Norway that the changed circumstances produced by the Napoleonic Wars allowed it to implement with annexation in 1814. Denmark, however, had given up hopes of recovering its lost provinces and concentrated on promoting trade and prosperity. Both countries had lost international influence and were open to interference from more powerful European countries concerned to preserve the balance in the Baltic.

Political Systems and Domestic Politics

Denmark proved by far the more stable of the two Scandinavian kingdoms. Royal absolutism was introduced in 1660 and given a written constitution with the Royal Law of 1665. This gave the king all legislative, judicial, and executive power, and freed him from the obligation to consult his estates or any council before levying new taxes or declaring war: in short, he was allowed to do as he pleased provided he remained Lutheran, and did not alienate any territory or change the Royal Law. There were no assemblies, parliaments, or aristocratic councils to challenge his political authority in either Denmark or Norway. While this system remained officially in force until 1848, power struggles and political changes nonetheless occurred during the eighteenth century.

Beneath the surface of absolutist rule, the Danish monarchy continued to rely heavily on the consent and goodwill of its subjects. Danish peasants were usually tenants who rented their farm from a landlord. Besides cultivating the land of their tenancy, they had to perform labor service (*hoveri*) on their lord's estate, either themselves or by hiring a substitute laborer. Landlords retained a strong position within rural society, and had been given many tasks in local administration by the Crown. The local landlord was in charge of collecting state taxes from the peasantry on his estate, and, if the peasants were unable to pay, the landlord vouched for the amount. Besides often being entitled to appoint the local vicar and judges, landlords were entrusted with conscription. Each had to select a number of young men in proportion to the size of the peasantry and, in order to ensure that sufficient able-bodied peasants were available, formal "adscription" (*stavnsbånd*), or registration of peasants, was introduced in 1733. From then on, no young man was allowed to leave his native estate without his landlord's permission. Though motivated by military reasons, this regulation also meant that young men could not move to places where they were offered better wages and working conditions and so it was also a means of securing sufficient cheap labor, both for landlords and tenant farmers in their capacity as employers of laborers and farmhands. This system has traditionally been regarded in Danish historiography as the height of the peasantry's suppression and degradation.

The practice of transferring important local administrative duties to the landlords has been interpreted by Danish historians as a farming-out of state power, and has been regarded as a sign of weakness: the Crown did not have the absolute power it claimed because it had to leave such vital administrative functions to private landowners. However, recent revisionist historiography has stressed that it should rather be seen as a sign of strength: a government that can farm out key functions like tax collection and conscription and nonetheless obtain its revenue and its soldiers in fact looks quite strong.

Certainly, the actual exercise of power varied between successive monarchs, while individuals and groups competed for influence under the surface of royal authority. King Frederick IV (r. 1699–1730) probably came closest to the ideal of the monarch handling all state affairs personally rather than leaving matters to ministers or civil servants. He strove hard to master the detail of administration and to make all decisions himself. Later kings, however, did not manage this, partly because they were not up to it personally or intellectually, and partly because the expansion of administration and its growing intrusion into daily life at local level made it physically impossible for any single individual to make decisions. Christian VI (r. 1730–46) did his best, but, for the rest of the century, none of his successors had the ability or will to succeed. Frederick V (r. 1746–66) was an alcoholic and addicted to sexual violence. That this did not produce a major crisis demonstrates the strength of Danish absolutism. Strong royal rule had by then existed for decades, entrenching patterns of behavior and administrative routines that continued to function thanks to loyal servants of the Crown, even when the king himself was unable or unwilling to exercise his formal rights directly. The lord chamberlain, in whom Frederick V had infinite trust, ran the country, together with the ministers of the royal council. They were all foreign, German-born aristocrats (the most famous of whom was the foreign minister, Count Bernstorff) who entered Danish service and acquired large landed estates in Denmark. They favored international neutrality to let trade and shipping prosper, while their cosmopolitan outlook prompted a more open cultural policy, inviting writers and artists of international renown to settle in Denmark and thus lend luster to the Danish court. Government subsidies were offered to foreign industrialists willing to seek their fortune in Denmark, while other "friends" were given posts in the administration and armed forces. Native Danes perceived this as discrimination and believed the foreign aristocrats were also favoring their own landed financial interests at the expense of other sectors of the economy. As landowners, the governing aristocrats were not against agrarian reforms so long as these remained tailored to raising productivity rather than emancipating peasants. Their economic interests also led them to oppose changes to the Danish military system, which relied on a small professional cadre backed by peasant conscripts. Reform-minded officers wanted to improve training by lengthening the period of conscription, but aristocratic ministers blocked this because it would extend the time their peasants would be unavailable for labor on their estates. Other, more radical, proposals were rejected, because it was feared they would undermine the regulatory framework of adscription upon which landlords relied to control their peasants.

Frederick V's death in 1766 removed the aristocrats' principal supporter, and the reformers hoped that the accession of Christian VII, barely 17 years old, would open the door to significant changes. Within a couple of years it became clear that the new monarch was mentally deranged and even less capable of exerting personal authority than his father. Absolutism's structural flaws also became more apparent. Whereas the aristocratic ministers under Frederick V had always been sure that the king would sign all documents they placed before him while not approving measures proposed by others, things were no longer so certain under Christian VII. Royal government grew unstable as reformers circumvented established, formal channels and tried to influence the king directly, culminating in the regime of the reform-minded, German-born doctor and royal favorite Count Johann Friedrich Struensee (1770–2). Struensee introduced a number of sweeping reforms which, however, were ill prepared, and hit many influential people in their pockets; his love-affair with Queen Caroline Matilda also caused widespread indignation, and his foreign birth discredited him among many who would otherwise have supported much of his program. Struensee was deposed by a coup in 1772 and later executed by a new government headed by the king's stepmother, dowager-queen Juliana Maria and her favorite, the commoner Ove Høegh-Guldberg. The new regime curried favor among the middle class circles alienated under Frederick V. Danish replaced German as the language of command in the army in 1773, and was placed on the grammar school curriculum two years later. Matters culminated in the Naturalization Act of 1776, which restricted government and military appointment to those born within the territories of the Danish state. It remains open whether this should be seen as Danish nationalism or as patriotism in the sense of a policy favoring the interests of the middle classes but including the large number of German-speakers in Copenhagen, as well as German-speakers from the duchies. Much research still needs to be done into the terms "Danish" and "German," which not only did not mean what they do today, but which also had different definitions according to which social group was using them at the time.

As a political ploy the policy certainly worked, for the regime enjoyed substantial support, notably when it tried to exploit the commercial opportunities offered by Danish neutrality during the American War of Independence. Freedom of the press, introduced by Struensee, was maintained with certain modifications and became especially liberal during the 1790s until it was strongly curbed in 1799. Nonetheless, the government remained fundamentally conservative, refusing to countenance peasant emancipation or economic liberalization. Juliana Maria and Guldberg were overthrown in 1784 in a bloodless coup led by Crown Prince Frederick (later Frederick VI) who took charge of government on behalf of his father, Christian VII.

The new regime initiated a policy of reforms, modernization, and dynamism. During the last two decades of the eighteenth century, the Danish government promoted land enclosure, ending the system whereby each tenant farmer worked up to 100 scattered plots by consolidating holdings into single, enclosed fields. Other legislation encouraged tenants to buy rather than rent land. The remaining feudal elements were removed from tenancy agreements, while government officials assumed the landlords' former local administrative responsibilities, culminating in the abolition of adscription in 1788. Danish historiography traditionally considers these Great Agrarian Reforms as one of the finest hours in Danish history and as an example of enlightened absolutism at its best. Without denying their significance, recent research has tended to adopt a more nuanced and less high-flown attitude. Rather than the result of government initiatives, the reforms now appear to have been the result of rising prices, because the more dynamic economy encouraged surplus sale on the free market, making the old subsistence-orientated methods obsolete. Landlords and tenants pushed for changes that would widen their chances of profiting from the new conditions. Government action also had little to do with the dramatically improved output that stemmed instead from technological improvements and introduction of new crops such as trefoil which enabled productivity to be increased. Critics have also pointed out that the role of the government tended to be fairly peripheral: initiatives for reform and change were taken locally, with the government only responding by introducing legislation to facilitate a development. Finally, while the reforms liberated peasants from the landlords' dominance, they also propelled social polarization. The number of farms was fixed, and for fiscal reasons the law strictly forbade parcellization into smaller agricultural holdings. As the population was growing rapidly, the result was the creation of a wealthy rural middle class of propertied farmers whose numbers remained relatively static, while an increasingly proletarianized and pauperized underclass of smallholders and laborers soon constituted the majority in the countryside.

Norway had a system of government and a constitution in common with Denmark. Apart from brief periods when it had its own viceroy, Norway was administered directly from Copenhagen for most of the eighteenth century with the main state departments simply managing Norwegian affairs alongside Danish business. Norway's relations with the Copenhagen government remain a matter of controversy centering especially on the so-called grain monopoly. A reciprocal arrangement was instituted in 1735 whereby Danish grain and that from the duchies was given monopoly access to Norwegian markets in return for similar concessions for Norwegian pig iron in Denmark, Schleswig, and Holstein. Some see the arrangement as a measure of solidarity between the partners of the same state at a time of severe economic crisis. But many historians regard it as Danish exploitation of Norway, causing hardship and hunger, even if the ban on foreign grain imports was temporarily lifted in times of dearth. The grain monopoly was abolished in 1788. Taxation provided a second area of controversy. Tax levels in Norway were low compared to Denmark, the duchies, and indeed to other European countries, a fact that has been used to claim that the country was treated gently by the Danish Crown. This has to be set against the fact that Norwegians were also comparatively poor and that this poverty was, some claim, due to Danish exploitation. The bulk of Norwegian revenue was remitted to Copenhagen and so spent outside the country. However, by the 1770s the Danish

Crown had become aware of Swedish designs on Norway, and treated its Norwegian subjects with the utmost caution, avoiding anything that might jeopardize their loyalty. There is certainly evidence of expressions of Norwegian identity, as well as resentment of Danish oppression, by the late seventeenth century. However, it remains unclear whether this constituted nascent Norwegian nationalism and a desire for independence or merely a demand that local interests receive more attention in Copenhagen.

Whereas the Danish-Norwegian constitution remained unchanged from the later seventeenth century, Swedish politics saw many changes. The three main political institutions of king, diet, and (until 1789) council were present throughout the century, but the balance between them underwent fundamental alterations. Sweden entered the eighteenth century as an absolute monarchy, though not one as firm and well-defined as its Danish rival, not least because the Swedish diet retained some powers. Absolutism was abolished following Charles XII's death, ushering in what is known as the Age of Liberty. The diet was now to be summoned at least every third year, and had legislative and fiscal powers as well as control over foreign policy. It consisted of four estates: nobility, clergy, burghers, and peasants (though the latter excluded those who lived on the nobles' lands). The members of the council were accountable to the diet, which could dismiss them. The king nonetheless retained some important rights, including the deciding vote in the event of deadlock amongst royal councillors, as well as a say in state appointments and power over external relations when the diet was not in session, though he could still not declare an offensive war without its consent.

The Age of Liberty was also one of faction, as tensions grew between the nobles and other social estates, attempts were made to assert greater royal power, and, above all, rival political parties emerged. The so-called Hats first gained power in 1738–9 and favored an aggressive foreign policy in alliance with France, a country to which they were also attached culturally and ideologically. Originally, they were fiercely constitutionalist and supported a strong diet and only limited power for the king, but they grew more royalist as circumstances changed during the 1760s. At that time they also became increasingly aristocratic, losing touch with their original support amongst industrialists, tradesmen, officers, civil servants, and others who might loosely be considered middle-class. The rival Cap party also underwent changes. It coalesced during the 1740s in opposition to the Hats, opposing pro-French foreign and cultural policies and instead favoring Britain, whose economy they admired. Originally they wanted to strengthen royal power as the best way to achieve their goals. During the 1750s, however, things changed, and they favored a strong diet, limited royal power, free trade, and a restrictive fiscal and monetary policy. They now captured much of their rivals' former social base among the growing middle classes and supporters of anti-aristocratic interests. They displaced the Hats in 1765–6, and introduced freedom of expression. Even though Swedes were still prohibited from criticizing religion or the royal family, they now enjoyed greater liberty in this regard than most other Europeans.

The growth of party strife opened Swedish politics to greater external interference. The Hats accepted bribes from the French, while the Caps received payments from Russia, Britain, and Denmark. Still, neither group can be dismissed as an agent for foreign powers. Indeed, both had many of the characteristics of modern political parties, including ideologies, organization, and a disciplined presence in the diet. While this has led some to claim that they were the first modern parties, recent research rather underlines their character as networks amongst individuals and groups without, however, denying the existence of different ideological aims and convictions.

The parliamentary character of Swedish politics is further illustrated by the fact that the diet remained the political center and used its powers to dismiss members of the council it did not trust. King Frederick of Hessen (r. 1720–51) remained more or less a representative monarch. His successors, however, endeavored to increase royal power. Adolphus Frederick (r. 1751–70), and especially his ambitious consort Louisa Ulrica, tried to expand royal power, but their coup failed in 1756. A less direct attempt was made in 1768 when the king abdicated in order to force new elections to the diet in the hope that this would produce a Hat majority and pave the way for constitutional changes. The Hats did acquire the majority, but the constitution remained unchanged.

The presence of organized parties and a powerful parliament should not be interpreted as modern democracy, however. The members of each estate were primarily concerned to promote their narrow interests and privileges, while the nobility's peasants and the rural and urban lower classes – together constituting a significant section of the population – remained disenfranchised. Many political actors, especially from the peasant estate, saw a strong monarch as a better safeguard against the landlords than a strong diet where the nobility held the commanding voice. Still, compared with the Danish state, a large proportion of Swedes engaged actively in the formal political process and it is especially noteworthy that the peasants were directly represented in the country's chief political institution. Yet to contemporaries this system looked old-fashioned and hopelessly inefficient. Indeed, this motivated Danish and Russian intervention in Swedish affairs, since the cumbersome parliamentary system was considered a guarantee against Sweden ever resuming a greater role in the Baltic.

Having failed to obtain the diet's approval to change the constitution after his accession in 1770, Gustavus III seized power by a coup in 1772, strengthening royal authority at the expense of both the diet and council. Only the king could now appoint councillors and civil servants, who were answerable to him alone. He assumed the exclusive right to ennoble whom he pleased, as well as responsibility for foreign policy, though he still had to seek the diet's consent to declare war. Furthermore, he now shared legislative power with the diet. The latter still had the power to grant taxes, whereas the king alone decided the use of the revenue. The coup and the new constitution appear to have enjoyed initial support from a population that had grown weary of party strife and ideological confrontations in the diet. Moreover, Gustavus appealed to the traditional well of royalist sentiment amongst the peasantry. Gustavus was a complicated, devious, enigmatic, and inscrutable personality. He was highly intelligent and charismatic, he often behaved eccentrically and theatrically, but he was certainly able to make quick and audacious decisions and was not afraid of playing for high stakes, as was demonstrated by his war with Russia in 1788–90. His personality, true motives, and relationship to European absolutism remain a matter of some controversy.

His cultural role is perhaps clearer. Swedish historiography presents the Gustavian Age as a cultural heyday, and the king was certainly personally interested in art and learning, founding a royal opera and academies of science and letters. His many reforms included the modernization and humanization of criminal law, economic liberalization, and the introduction of freedom of religion and tolerance for Jews. Thanks to these credentials, he is often numbered amongst Europe's "enlightened despots." However, opposition grew from the mid-1780s, and the war against Russia has been seen as a deliberate attempt to divert attention. When Swedish forces met with defeat, Gustavus manipulated the strong anti-aristocratic and patriotic sentiments of ordinary Swedes to push through the Union and Security Act of 1789. This abolished the council and gave the king power to declare war without the diet's consent. The diet still shared legislative power with the king and was given an increased role in the administration of the public debt. In return for their support for these changes, the peasants were given improved and exclusive opportunities to buy land. Again, it remains a matter of debate whether Gustavus was appealing to genuinely nationalist sentiment or mobilizing more traditional grievances and patriotism.

The nobility were the principal losers in the constitutional changes of 1789, and it was a group of aristocratic conspirators that was behind the assassination of Gustavus at a masked ball in 1792. The king's lingering death – he did not expire for another week and a half – thwarted plans for an aristocratic coup. The new regime, a regency under his brother for his young son, Gustavus IV Adolphus, refrained from harsh reprisals. Though the assassin was executed, the other conspirators escaped with remarkably light sentences. Nonetheless, the Gustavian constitution remained in force and was retained by Gustavus IV Adolphus when he achieved his majority and assumed personal rule in 1796. His strong sentiments against the French Revolution and, later, against Napoleon led to disastrous foreign political results for Sweden and ended with him being deposed in 1809 and replaced by a new dynasty, the Bernadottes, whose descendants still hold the Swedish throne.

This chapter opened by stressing difference, both between the two principal Scandinavian kingdoms and amongst their component lands. Their eighteenth-century experience also reveals that they had much in common. Sweden and the Danish state slipped into diplomatic and military dependency on other European powers. Both witnessed conflict and change over land ownership and utilization. Their governments attempted reforms that can be labeled enlightened and modernizing, including the introduction of freedom of speech and religious toleration. Their societies became more clearly stratified along class lines, and included a middle class that was more important politically as well as socially. Yet these broadly common developments were also fueling new ideas of distinct national identities in which differences in language and heritage played an important role.

Bibliography

Barton, H. A., *Scandinavia in the Revolutionary Era, 1760–1815* (Minneapolis, 1986)

Carlsson, S. and J. Rosén, *Svensk historia* (2 vols., Stockholm, 1961–2).

Danielsen, R., et al., *Norway: A History from the Vikings to Our Own Times* (Oslo, 1995).

Dyrvik, S., *Truede tvillingriker 1648–1720*, vol. 3 of *Danmark-Norge 1380–1814* (Oslo, 1998).
Dyrvik S. and O. Feldbæk, *Mellom brødre*, vol. 7 of *Aschehougs Norgeshistorie* (Oslo, 1995).
Feldbæk, O., *Nærhed og adskillelse 1720–1814*, vol. 4 of *Danmark-Norge 1380–1814* (Oslo 1998).
Gustafsson, H., *Political Interaction in the Old Regime: Central Power and Local Society in the Eighteenth-Century Nordic States* (Lund, 1994).
Hatton, R. M., *Charles XII of Sweden* (London, 1968).
Jespersen, K. J. V., *A History of Denmark* (Basingstoke, 2004).
Kirby, D., *Northern Europe in the Early Modern Period: The Baltic World 1492–1772* (Harlow, 1990).
Metcalf, M. F., *A History of the Swedish Parliament* (Stockholm, 1987).
Oakley, S. P., *War and Peace in the Baltic, 1560–1790* (London, 1992).
Roberts, M., *The Swedish Imperial Experience 1560–1718* (Cambridge, 1979).
Roberts, M., *The Age of Liberty: Sweden 1719–1772* (Cambridge, 1986).
Rystad, G., et al. (eds.), *In Quest of Trade and Security: The Baltic in Power Politics, 1500–1900* (2 vols., Lund, 1994–5).
Scandinavian Economic History Review, published by the Scandinavian Society for Economic and Social History and Historical Geography since 1953.
Scandinavian Journal of History, published under the Auspices of the Historical Associations of Denmark, Finland, Norway, and Sweden since 1976.
Sogner, S., *Krig og fred 1660–1780*, vol. 6 of *Aschehougs Norgeshistorie* (Oslo, 1994).

Chapter Eighteen

The Dutch Republic

J. L. Price

The eighteenth century in the Dutch Republic has conventionally been seen as a period of decline after the great achievements of the previous century – the Dutch Golden Age. Already by the later decades of the century a perception of relative failure was evident, causally linked to what was seen as a falling away form the solid burgher virtues which had been the bedrock of Dutch success. This interpretation of the century has dominated its historiography ever since, not least because this perceived failure of a decentralized republic helped to validate its replacement by the centralized Orange monarchy of the nineteenth century. Recently, however, a more nuanced picture of the period has begun to emerge. First the absolute nature of Dutch economic decline was questioned (de Vries, 1968), and then other aspects of Dutch life in the eighteenth century began to be seen in a rather more positive light.

However, no amount of revisionism can disguise the fact that in the eighteenth century the Dutch Republic did decline politically, economically, and even culturally. At the beginning of the century the Republic still appeared, at least to outsiders, to be at the height of its powers. It was about to play a major part in War of the Spanish Succession which effectively brought an end to the threat of French hegemony in Europe. It still appeared to be the dominant economic force in Europe, and its colonial possessions, especially in the East Indies, continued to be the envy of its rivals. By this time Dutch art and literature were already past their great days, but the Republic remained the center of the Republic of Letters and the leading force of the pre-Enlightenment in Europe. In harsh contrast, long before the end of the century the Republic had been transformed into a by-word for political, economic, and even cultural impotence. Not only had it ceased to be a major power, it was hardly able to sustain the military and naval forces fitting for a minor power, and was in no condition to pursue an effective independent foreign policy. Its political system had become incapable of decisive action, being crippled by internal divisions which were seemingly incapable of resolution. With regard to the economy, there was a lively and sometimes acute discussion of the problem of decline, but little or nothing was done. Culturally, not only had the Dutch lost much of their

A Companion to Eighteenth-Century Europe, First Edition. Edited by Peter H. Wilson.
© 2014 John Wiley & Sons, Ltd. Published 2014 by John Wiley & Sons, Ltd.

distinctiveness, they tended to see this as an improvement. The French invasion of 1795 can be seen as an act of euthanasia for a country which was but a pitiful shadow of its former self.

Yet, however abject the demise of the Republic can be made to appear, its vulnerability before the armies of revolutionary France was no greater than that of many other small states, and indeed the whole political system of western and central Europe was hardly more resilient than that of the Dutch. The country was still relatively prosperous, and the fiscal problems of both the province of Holland and the Republic as a whole are no more than a striking example of a pervasive problem of *ancien régime* Europe. Here as elsewhere the entrenched interests of privileged groups prevented effective reform. In other words, seen in a European perspective, much of the discussion of the peculiar failings of the Dutch state in the eighteenth century begins to look decidedly parochial. One of the problems has been the tendency to look back from the perspective of the failure of the Patriot movement and the debacle of 1795, with the consequence that the history of the whole century has been written as leading inevitably to this sorry conclusion. Change the perspective, however, and the Dutch experience for much of the eighteenth century seems far less bleak, despite the weaknesses of the political system and the uncertain economic adjustments of the time. The catastrophe of the last years of the century appears more the result of a radically changed situation in Europe than the inevitable result of internal weakness and decay.

The failings of the eighteenth century have seemed more glaring in comparison with the glories of the Golden Age, but recent research has made this contrast both less clear and less harsh. On the one hand, many of the problems which were to loom large in the eighteenth century were already evident in the later decades of the seventeenth. Indeed, economic decline – which was at the root of most if not all of the later problems – can be traced as far back as the middle of the seventeenth century. In this sense the eighteenth century was a continuation of, rather than a contrast with, the seventeenth. It can also be argued that the Golden Age in its fullest sense was only experienced by the province of Holland (and, to a lesser extent, the maritime region as a whole) while the land provinces and States Brabant shared little or nothing of its prosperity and cultural fecundity. For these areas of the Republic the eighteenth century saw improvement rather than decline in many aspects of life, from modest economic improvements to a relative freedom from the disruptions of war.

While the eighteenth century saw the definitive transformation of the Dutch Republic from a major to a minor power, it nevertheless remained one of the more prosperous countries in Europe, with a relatively tolerant society, and its cultural achievements, while modest, were nevertheless real. It experienced serious problems economically, socially, and politically but remained possibly the most civilized country in Europe.

From Major Power to Minor Role in Europe

The year 1648 marked the end of the Thirty Years War and, not coincidentally, also of the Eighty Years War between the Dutch and Spain. Helped by an alliance with France from 1635 onwards, the Dutch Republic had finally forced Philip IV of Spain to recognize Dutch independence, and emerged from this long period of conflict as a major power in Europe. To some extent, the relative power of the Dutch at mid-century was a consequence of the weakness of other states as much as of their own innate strength. From 1648 onwards France was weakened by the period of internal political strife known as the Fronde, England was preoccupied by civil war and its consequences, while Spain struggled to subdue revolts in Portugal and Catalonia while continuing a war with France. Much of the rest of Europe needed time to recover from the strains of the Thirty Years War. Indeed Sweden, though nominally one of the victors, never really recovered, and the Austrian Habsburgs, in addition to exhaustion from the war, were hamstrung by the permanent threat posed by the Ottoman presence in Hungary. However, when England and especially France resolved their internal conflicts, the balance of power in Europe was bound to change, and in the later decades of the century the consolidation of Austrian power and the rise of Brandenburg further complicated the situation.

The Dutch suffered their first major blow in a war at sea with an aggressive English Republic which exposed major deficiencies in their fleet (First Anglo-Dutch War, 1652–4), though when the restored monarchy tried to repeat this triumph a decade later the Dutch proved able to match the English in naval strength and overmatch them financially (Second Anglo-Dutch War 1664–7). However, the threat to the Dutch position which set the tone for the rest of the century came from the France of Louis XIV. The French invasion of 1672 seemed at one point likely to wipe the Republic off the map, but also brought to power the prince of Orange, William III, who spent the rest of his life opposing with greater or lesser success what he saw as French hegemonic ambitions. The Dutch, at the head of a coalition including the Austrians and an almost entirely impotent Spain, were able to clear the French from their territory and then fight them to a standstill at the Treaty of Nijmegen in 1678. Further hostilities between France and a Dutch-led coalition flared up in the Nine Years War (1688–97), but the major achievement of Dutch foreign policy in this period was the intervention in England in 1688. England had joined with the French in the attack on the Dutch Republic in 1672, but was soon forced out of the war and subsequently remained effectively neutral. The Dutch invasion and the "Glorious Revolution" of 1688 brought the prince of Orange to the English throne as William III, and England into the coalition against France – which was probably the prime reason for the intervention.

The Dutch Republic was thus a major power throughout the second half of the seventeenth century, with a fleet only matched by that of England and an army which was the equal that of any other state but France (and the Ottoman empire – but that was of no immediate concern to the Dutch). Their military effort came to a peak during the War of the Spanish Succession when the Dutch were able to deploy an army of over 100,000 in the southern Netherlands. However, this period also showed the first signs that the Dutch system was creaking under the financial strain of continued warfare: the unprecedented effort on land, together with English strength at sea, meant that the Dutch navy was neglected. Indeed, the conventional account is that the Treaty of Utrecht marked both the apogee of Dutch achievement and the end of the Dutch Republic as a major power. In this interpretation it never recovered from the enormous strain of the series of wars against France and emerged from the conflict as at best a second-rate power. For the rest of the century it was incapable of supporting both a major army and a powerful navy, and was often unable to produce either. This was partly a consequence of financial weakness but also of a persistent deadlock within the Dutch political system between Holland, which favored naval expenditure, and the land provinces, which gave priority to the army. The necessity of unanimity in the States General on important financial issues meant that without significant concessions from either or both sides no decisions could be reached. Such compromises proved increasingly difficult to achieve, with the consequence that both army and navy suffered. Thus it is argued that a combination of fiscal weakness and a fundamental failure of the political system led to military and naval impotence.

While there is a measure of truth in this picture, it can be argued both that the Dutch decline was much less rapid and that the fiscal problem was far more intractable than it suggests. It is true that within only a few years of the end of the War of the Spanish Succession the admiralties were unable to provide an adequate force for a minor campaign in the Baltic (Bruijn, 1993: 148–9), but on the other hand as late as the War of the Austrian Succession (1740–8) the Dutch state was still capable of fielding a significant military force. It is estimated that the effective strength of the Dutch army at this period reached at first 60,000 and then rose to 85,000–90,000 by the last years of the war (van Nimwegen, 2002: 103). After this the Republic was able to avoid war for over 30 years. However, when war finally came it was with England (1780–4) and was a disaster, with the navy being totally unable to defend Dutch shipping and, worse, colonies from the English fleet. So the collapse of the Dutch Republic as a major power can perhaps better be seen not as a phenomenon of the eighteenth century as a whole but only of its final decades, or at most of its second half. In contrast the fiscal legacy of the wars with France seems to have hamstrung the Republic's finances throughout the century. The Republic's wars were financed by borrowing and this debt, heavy enough in the late seventeenth century, grew to enormous proportions during the War of the Spanish Succession. Previously, war had been financed largely on the credit of the States of Holland and, although the debt of the States General increased significantly, this continued to be the case in the eighteenth century. It has been argued that Holland was never able to shake off the burden of debt it was left with after the end of the French wars (Liesker, 1985). The Dutch Republic had been born in war and lived with war for much of its century of greatness, but its economy was expanding until at least mid-century and stable for another quarter-century and so was able to bear this burden without too much strain. By the beginning of the eighteenth century at the latest, the Dutch economy was far less buoyant and consequently less able to support the growing costs of war.

There is another dimension, however, to these fiscal problems, and one that links to a structural weakness common to *ancien régime* states: fiscal reform was blocked by the entrenched interests of privileged groups (Dessert, 1985). In the course of the seventeenth century the regents – i.e. the urban oligarchs who controlled the politics of the province – tended to drift away from trade and manufacture and become more reliant on investments, and with the weakening economy of the following century this tendency became even more marked. Apart from the Dutch East India Company (VOC), by far the most reliable investment available was the provincial debt of Holland. So the regents – and the same was probably true of the nobles and oligarchs of the other provinces as well – needed Holland (and the States General) to carry a large load of debt. Quite literally those who ruled the Republic had a heavy investment in the existing fiscal system, so no significant reform proved possible.

However, the whole question of Dutch decline is perhaps to a significant extent misconceived. The Republic was an unusual state for early modern Europe in that it had no territorial claims or ambitions against its neighbors. (Its policies outside Europe were a rather different matter.) Its highest ambition was to be left alone to concentrate on the economy. International circumstances in the late sixteenth century and throughout the seventeenth had compelled them to fight for their independence from Spain, to defend their merchant fleet from England, and for their survival – as they saw it – against France. After the War of the Spanish Succession, however, the international situation changed fundamentally as far as the Dutch were concerned. Britain was now a major power, committed to keeping France in check, and the Dutch could to some extent rest easy under its protection. Moreover, France was no longer the hegemonic threat it had seemed under Louis XIV: its military strength was balanced not only by that of Britain but also by Austria and the rising power of Prussia – not to mention Russia, which became increasingly involved in European affairs in the course of the century. Circumstances no longer forced the Dutch to fight for their survival and so they could afford to keep a low profile for much of the century. From this perspective, the relatively passive role of the Dutch in eighteenth-century Europe can be seen as a success rather than a failure – at last they were free to concentrate on peaceful pursuits.

The Failings of the Political System

The republican and decentralized constitution of the Dutch Republic has been seen as both a symptom and a cause of Dutch decline. Indeed, so discredited was the republican system that when a new Dutch state was created after the Napoleonic period it was deliberately designed as a centralized monarchy – the very antithesis of the Republic. It was thought that the Republic's fundamental weakness was that provincial concerns had often prevailed over national ones and that the Dutch nation needed a strong monarchy which would recognize and pursue its interests. However, the system which was seen as having failed so signally in the eighteenth century had brought success in the seventeenth. So the question should be, "What went wrong?" The Dutch regents of the eighteenth century have had a thoroughly bad press, not perhaps entirely undeserved: for much of the century they seemed to combine self-satisfaction with a leaven of hypocrisy. Yet there was also much to be said for the relatively free and tolerant society which the political system delivered and preserved. What was lacking was the ability to reform even the most egregious faults in the republican structure despite the best efforts of a series of well-meaning and able politicians.

It is not easy to explain the Dutch political system in a few words but its essentials are not too complicated. The Republic was composed of seven provinces, of which Holland was only one, and it is typical of the ambiguities of the Dutch system that while each was regarded as sovereign, the Union binding them together was seen as indissoluble. In practice, this meant that each province formally had a veto in the States General, the representative body which was the highest political authority in the Republic. A fundamental problem was the imbalance between the provinces: Holland had around 40 percent of the population and probably well over 60 percent of the wealth of the Republic, yet it had only one vote in the States General. For politics to run effectively, Holland needed a considerably bigger say in practice than the formal system would seem to allow. The role of the princes of Orange is even less easy to explain. They were stadhouders, or governors, of a majority of the provinces (until the death of William III the office in Friesland and Groningen was held by a cadet branch of the family) and head of the army. These were appointed positions making them formally the subordinates of the provincial states in the first instance and of the States General in the second. However, their powers of political patronage were considerable, particularly in the land provinces and, after Maurits' coup in 1618, they were effective leaders of the Republic for much of the rest of the century, interrupted only by the first stadhouderless period between 1650 and 1672. After the French invasion of 1672, *regeringsreglementen* were introduced which greatly increased the political powers of William III as stadhouder in the land provinces. Nevertheless the financial power of Holland meant that even the most powerful of the princes of Orange could not push their policies through without at least its passive acquiescence.

The death of William III without issue in 1702 sparked off a backlash against what many felt had been a heavy-handed rule, and the second stadhouderless period lasted until 1747 (this is something of a misnomer as the cadet branch of the Nassau family inherited the Orange title and kept the stadhouderships of Friesland and Groningen). Although there was a certain amount of political unrest in the towns of the land provinces aimed at unseating the regents put in power by William, at best such disturbances changed the personnel but not the system of government. In response to the problems, especially the financial ones, facing the Republic in the aftermath of the War of the Spanish Succession, proposals were made to deal with what were beginning to seem major weaknesses of the republican system. The leading politician Simon van Slingelandt (secretary to the Council of State and, later *raadpensionaris* of Holland) deployed his formidable legal and historical expertise to argue for the necessity of some limitation on provincial autonomy and the power of local oligarchies in order to strengthen central government, but nothing was achieved. This failure was hardly surprising as those with most to lose had the power to prevent any change.

Change came, however, with the Orange restoration of 1747–8. As in 1672, military setbacks in the war against France led to popular movements in favor of the prince of Orange, and William IV's appointment as stadhouder in all the provinces that had avoided one since 1702 was accompanied – again as in 1672 – by purges of the urban oligarchies, particularly in Holland, to ensure loyalty to the new regime. The Republic was led for the rest of its existence by successive princes of Orange with unprecedented powers. For the first time they were stadhouders in all the provinces and their powers in the land provinces were greater than they had ever been (Gabriëls, 1990). Yet this opportunity for significant reform was not taken, partly as a result of accidents of death and personality, but also because the deep-seated characteristics of the political system made peaceful change almost inconceivable. William IV died in 1751, and there was a long regency during William V's minority. After he came of age it quickly became apparent that he was not the man to use his powers to push through radical change. He regarded his own position and that of his house as rooted in and dependent on the existing political system, and feared that change would threaten the future of both. However, it is too easy to blame his personal failings: a stronger man – a Frederik Hendrik or a William III – might have been able to use his enormous influence to make significant reforms, but it can be doubted. As it was, William V was not even able to break the impasse between the land provinces and Holland over military as opposed to naval expenditure, with the result that neither was adequate and the Republic went into the Fourth Anglo-Dutch War (1780–4) woefully unprepared. For real change, it would have been necessary to break the resistance of the oligarchy – nobles as well as regents – through unleashing democratic forces which would have been difficult if not impossible to control. In the end the princes of Orange were just as much an integral part of the existing political system as the regents, and had even more to lose.

The Patriot movement of the 1780s promised radical change but was wrecked by foreign intervention and, possibly more importantly, its own inner contradictions. Inspired in part by English radicalism and the example of the American Revolution, and spurred on by the all too evident failures of the existing regime, the Patriots aimed at a broadening of political participation, though they were divided as to how far this should go. The movement started as an attack on the overweening powers of the stadhouder in the land provinces, and was taken up initially by the regents as a weapon against the power of the prince of Orange. All too soon, however, it became evident that the movement involved an attack on the power of the oligarchy, and so forced the regents to choose between their zeal for reform and the preservation of the political system as a whole. The regents in the main fell back on the prince of Orange in order to preserve their own power and privileges as well as his. Again, it is too easy to see them as solely concerned with narrow self-interest: the regents had wanted to restore the balance between themselves and the prince, not to destroy the Republic, which they revered. The end came, however, through foreign intervention, with the citizen militias set up with such patriotic fervor by the Patriots proving unwilling to take on Prussian troops, sent in under the pretext that the Patriots had insulted the princess of Orange, who happened to be the sister of Friedrich Wilhelm II. The leading Patriots fled into exile until a further, more thoroughgoing foreign intervention in 1795 gave them the chance to return and attempt to create a new Dutch state under French tutelage.

As the eighteenth century progressed the need for reform to the creaking institutions of the state became ever more obvious, but the recourse to pure republicanism and then to an Orange restoration proved entirely inadequate to deal with problems inherent in the system itself. The inability of Holland and the land provinces to find a working solution to the impasse over military versus naval spending was proof that a political system which relied on compromise was breaking down. In the seventeenth century Dutch politicians had been prepared to put practical solutions above constitutional niceties. In the following century this was apparently no longer the case.

The Problems of the Economy

Both Dutch decline as a major power and their domestic political difficulties can be attributed very largely to the economic problems faced by the country in the eighteenth century. For much of the previous century growing prosperity had enabled the Republic to fight major wars against Spain, and then England and France, without too much strain on the political system. Only in 1672 did near-collapse against France lead directly to a major political upheaval. (The other two crises – in 1618 and 1650 – arose from the problems peace brought to a state born in and accustomed to war.) In contrast, after the end of the War of the Spanish Succession the Republic had to fight only one major war before 1780, and yet its government was in almost permanent financial difficulties. Changes in the Dutch economy were among the reasons for these fiscal problems. Yet the contrast between the seventeenth and eighteenth centuries should not be overplayed, economically at least. The period of explosive economic growth had already ended by the mid-seventeenth century, and from that point on problems had became increasingly apparent in almost all sectors of the economy. On the other hand, in the eighteenth century the Republic continued to be a prosperous country, at least in comparison with most of Europe. It was, however, no longer the economic powerhouse of Europe, and was being outstripped in both trade and manufactures by Britain.

The basic problem for the Dutch was the secular depression in European agricultural prices which set in around the middle of the seventeenth century and lasted for over a hundred years. One of the first signs of this negative conjuncture was the ending of the great drainage projects which had transformed the landscape of Holland in the late sixteenth and early seventeenth centuries. Spurred on by the promise of high agricultural profits, enormous sums had been invested in the reclamation of lakes and marshes, with the help of wind-driven water pumps of improved design. North Holland in particular had been changed from something like an archipelago to a solid land mass. Such projects came to an end quite abruptly by the 1640s – with the exception of Zeeland-Flanders, which is a special case (van Cruyningen, 2000). Although the Dutch economic boom is associated most obviously with trading and manufacturing success, a vital element in the overall growth of the economy was a dynamic, market-oriented rural sector (de Vries, 1974). In Holland in particular agricultural specialization stimulated, as well as being facilitated by, growth in other sectors of the economy. Concentration on dairy farming and the fattening of beef cattle, for example, was made possible by Dutch domination of the Baltic grain trade, which in turn was encouraged by the increased demand for imported grain as a consequence of the shift away from growing bread grains at home. Conversely, the later fall in agricultural profitability had damaging knock-on effects throughout the economy. Dairy farming in particular was heavily dependent on exports and so was vulnerable to falling prices in its market areas.

The most successful areas of Dutch manufacturing were also geared to export and proved vulnerable to foreign competition and the tariff barriers raised by governments in response to mercantilist theories. The specialist textile towns, Leiden (wool) and Haarlem (linen), were particularly hard hit and experienced dramatic falls in population by the end of the century. The decline in the textile industry as a whole, however, was not as severe as this might suggest, as production moved to rural Overijssel and other areas where a cheaper labor force could be found (Trompetter, 1997; van Zanden, 1993). The shipbuilding industry, concentrated along the Zaan by the beginning of the century, also suffered from falling orders from abroad, and its decline, though slower, was just as severe in the end. One of the few industries to flourish in the eighteenth century was distilling. The production of gin and brandy brought prosperity and demographic growth to Schiedam, the center of the industry, but the social costs of the increased consumption of spirits must have been considerable throughout the country.

The most spectacular area of Dutch success in the late sixteenth and early seventeenth centuries, however, had been trade, and here the situation is far from being a simple tale of inexorable decline. It now seems clear that the Dutch trading economy did not so much decline as fall behind its competitors in the course of the eighteenth century. The contrast between what was at best a stagnating trade system with the dynamic growth of English commerce in Europe and beyond was particularly galling to the Dutch, who had become accustomed to out-trading the English almost effortlessly in the previous century. There were fluctuations in the volume and overall profitability of Dutch trade over the eighteenth century, but in the main it held its own with only some minor blips and, indeed, was showing some resilience by its later years. What it did not do was expand significantly and, moreover, it tended to narrow its range and concentrate on those areas and sectors where the Dutch had the most advantages, such as trade within northwest Europe and the Baltic, and with their colonies. The trade with India and the Dutch East Indies became relatively more important. Internally, too, commerce tended to concentrate on Amsterdam and Rotterdam to the detriment of other towns of Holland, which lost both trade and population. Thus, although there was no absolute decline in Dutch trade, structural change meant that towns like Enkhuizen and Hoorn in Holland's Northern Quarter were hit almost as severely as Leiden and Haarlem.

Other economic sectors which had contributed significantly to the Republic's prosperity in the past, such as the fisheries and whaling, proved unable to take up the slack from the stagnation of trade and manufacturing decline. The herring fishery had provided an important export article as well as a valuable addition to the Dutch diet, and was also labor-intensive, and so had played an important part in the general growth of the Dutch economy. However, North Sea herring shoals were found off the Scottish and English coasts, and the Dutch had no particular advantages except superior organization to keep them ahead of their many competitors. In the eighteenth century this no longer seems to have been enough. The closing off of foreign markets, together with what seems to have been a significant change in European consumption patterns, also weakened the demand for Dutch herring. As a consequence the size of the herring fleet fell from around 500 busses in the mid-seventeenth century to less than 150 in the later eighteenth century. This decline meant not only a fall in export earnings, but also a significant loss of employment opportunities in Holland. The sector had employed about 6,000–7,000 seamen around 1650; after the 1750s this figure must have dropped by more than two-thirds (de Vries and van der Woude, 1997: 293–307). The consequences for Enkhuizen, which had been by far the most import center of the fishery, were severe. The sector may also have been hit by over-fishing, as the catch per boat seems to have fallen considerably in the second half of the century. This is certainly true of whaling:

already by the second half of the seventeenth century whales were beginning to retreat under the Arctic ice, necessitating the use of more expensive ships specially designed to resist pack ice. By the eighteenth century whales were beginning to be much more difficult to find, and it seems that their numbers must have fallen considerably, leading to a steep decline in Dutch whaling.

Holland was particularly hard hit by these developments, just as it had been the prime beneficiary of the Dutch economic boom. As has been noted, the textile towns Leiden and Haarlem suffered particularly badly, along with the small trading towns of North Holland. Indeed, the population of most of the towns of Holland fell in the course of the late seventeenth and the eighteenth centuries. Amsterdam more or less held its own, as did Rotterdam, but only Schiedam actually grew significantly on the basis of the boom in distilling. The process of economic contraction also brought about a transformation in the countryside of North Holland. In the middle of the seventeenth century the region had been remarkable for the variety of its economic activities: alongside market-oriented dairy farming, it also produced seamen for the fisheries and merchant fleet, and maintained a wide range of artisanal and transport services. Even villages in the very heart of the region, such as De Rijp and Graft, fitted out herring busses and showed an almost urban range of economic activities and services. Yet by the late eighteenth century North Holland had been transformed into an almost purely farming region. Holland, along with Zeeland, was also the chief victim of the attacks of the *paalworm*, a crustacean which burrowed into and weakened the wooden supports of the dikes protecting these low-lying provinces. This infestation necessitated large-scale renewal of the water defenses, and this put an enormous extra burden on rural communities which were already having to struggle with low agricultural prices and the recurrent cattle plagues which also hit the Republic in the eighteenth century.

In a sense the economic Golden Age for Zeeland was much more short-lived than in Holland. In particular its trading towns, after a brief boom at the end of the sixteenth and the first decades of the seventeenth century, could not compete with those of Holland, and so in this sector the eighteenth century saw not so much a decline as an intensification of the problems which had plagued the province for much of the previous century. The situation for agriculture in the province was both more complicated and less gloomy. In contrast to much of the Republic, agriculture in Zeeland concentrated on wheat, as the area was unsuitable for cattle, either dairy or beef, because of a shortage of fresh water. As grain prices fell in the late seventeenth century, the large-scale cultivation of madder was introduced, which went some way to bolster falling agricultural profits. From around 1740 the agrarian economy also began to benefit from a recovery in the price of wheat (Priester, 1998), and so the later eighteenth century witnessed a rise in agricultural prosperity in this province at least.

In general, the eighteenth century may well have seen the economic balance between Holland and the land provinces tip significantly in the latter's favor. Overijssel, Gelderland, Drenthe, and States Brabant had not shared in the Dutch economic boom of the Golden Age, largely because of the effects of constant warfare. Only after the coming of peace in 1648 did these provinces experience a mild economic recovery. Despite the depression in agricultural prices and the intermittent visitations of the cattle plague, they did rather better than the maritime region in the eighteenth century, particularly after prices began to pick up in the second half of the century. Also, the move of textile manufacture to Overijssel and North Brabant provided a further boost to the economy of this region at Holland's expense. The land provinces certainly did not boom, but they did not suffer the economic blows which the decline in manufactures and the herring fishery inflicted on Holland, nor did they undergo the population loss which afflicted most of the towns in that highly urbanized province. Indeed, there is some evidence for a rise in population in the land provinces, and in the Over-Betuwe region this reached around 60 percent between the middle of the seventeenth and the end of the eighteenth century (Brusse, 1999). The more peaceful nature of the eighteenth century clearly benefited this region as a whole.

Colonial trade became an increasingly important part of the Dutch trading system as it became less competitive elsewhere. After the loss of Brazil, in the Americas the Dutch were left with only Surinam and a few West Indian islands and, although the plantations established there were profitable, their great colonial achievements were in the east. The VOC had established a network of trading posts from the west coast of India to Japan, and in the course of the eighteenth century came to control most of Sri Lanka and Java. However, the costs of establishing their rule put an enormous strain on the finances of the VOC, and it proved increasingly vulnerable to competition from the English East India Company, which proved more adept at satisfying changing patterns of demand in Europe. The VOC continued to pay handsome dividends to its shareholders, ensuring continued political support, but its financial and other problems in the east continued to multiply. In the end, however, it was the Republic's inability to protect its colonies from the depredations of the English navy during the Fourth Anglo-Dutch War that demonstrated the effective bankruptcy of the Dutch colonial system.

A Conservative Enlightenment

While the problems of the economy together with the more constricted international role were perhaps the central concerns of the Dutch towards the end of the eighteenth century, later commentators have instead concentrated on the perceived cultural decline. Just as the seventeenth century was the only period when the Dutch state was able to act as a major power, so the cultural flowering of the Golden Age set standards which the Dutch have never since been able to match. Seventeenth-century Dutch painting was a major innovative influence in the history of art and, while it had no comparable international impact, Dutch literature too hit its peak of achievement at this time. In the eighteenth century, by contrast, both art and literature have been seen as mediocre at best, producing slavish imitations of foreign – especially French – models, and yet smugly convinced of their own peculiar merit. Perhaps Dutch culture in the eighteenth century was less distinctive than it had been in the century before, but it had never been the conscious aim of Dutch artists, writers, and intellectuals to distance themselves from the broader stream of European culture. On the contrary they shared a common set of ideals and aims with the rest of Europe, and wished for nothing better than to be successful in putting these into practice. In an important sense Dutch distinctiveness in the Golden Age was inadvertent rather than deliberate, and was a product of the distinctive nature of Dutch economy and society at that time. In the eighteenth century the Dutch were more successful in conforming to general European standards in art and literature, however disappointing the result may seem to posterity.

In any case such negative views of Dutch cultural achievements in the eighteenth century are steadily being replaced by a more nuanced approach willing to see the Dutch experience in its own terms, and especially in the context of broader European trends. It can be argued that, while Dutch culture in general moved closer to the European mainstream, it nevertheless maintained a certain distinctiveness, even if this was not always a good thing. This was a conservative culture, certainly in comparison with some of the more dynamic aspects of the European Enlightenment, but this was partly because Dutch society had already achieved most, if not all, of the aims of the moderate Enlightenment. This was a country where the public sphere was already well developed, religious toleration was firmly established in practice if not in theory, and arbitrary government had been defeated more than a century earlier. Prosecutions for witchcraft had ended in Holland by the beginning of the previous century and in the whole of the Republic by its second half – though the hostile response to Balthasar Bekker's *The World Bewitched* (1691–3), which questioned established beliefs and practices regarding witchcraft, is a reminder that the issue was still a sensitive one, particularly to Bekker's fellow ministers of the Reformed Church. However, in general the eighteenth century saw the triumph of rational religion with only very faint echoes of the religious disputes which had threatened to tear the Republic apart in the previous century. The spiritual descendants of the theological precisians of the Golden Age turned rather to the cultivation of an internal spirituality fostered by Pietism. On the other hand, it is true that another form of witch-hunt made its appearance in the course of the eighteenth century. The discovery of networks of homosexuals led to short-lived moral panics, waves of prosecutions, and a number of death sentences (van der Meer, 1995: esp. ch. 3). Nevertheless, what most of enlightened Europe strove for, the Dutch Republic had already achieved.

It should not be forgotten that to a considerable extent it was the Dutch – not the English or French – who were the pioneers of what became known as the Enlightenment. In particular, Dutch learned periodicals of the late seventeenth century – Pierre Bayle's *Nouvelles de la République des Lettres* and Jean Le Clerc's *Bibliothèque universelle* among others – were collectively the communications center of the Republic of Letters, and publishing was one Dutch industry that continued to flourish well into the eighteenth century. The Dutch may not have been the most important innovators in pre-Enlightenment Europe, but they were certainly indispensable intermediaries. In the main, the Dutch Enlightenment served to confirm established values rather than challenge them. The fundamental civic values cherished by the Dutch were already firmly established at the beginning of the century and, until the upsurge of Patriot ideas in the 1780s, the established political system was regarded as sacrosanct rather than as a barrier to necessary reforms. Developments in science too were understood in an essentially Christian context: the Book of Nature was regarded as a supplementary revelation rather than as a challenge to a religious interpretation of the world and man's place in it.

While it is true that the great days of Dutch art were already over by the final third of the seventeenth century, Dutch artists continued to produce very respectable work in genre and landscape on the lines laid down by the seventeenth-century masters, and Cornelis Troost introduced something new with his satirical comments on contemporary life among the wealthy. Similarly, in literature one can point to the spectatorial writings of Justus van Effen, the comedies of Pieter Langendijk, and towards the end of the century the first Dutch novel – *Sarah Burgerhart* by Betje Wolff and Aagje Deken (women no less!). Yet the influence of French classicism – and of French language and culture in general – tended to stifle innovation, and even at the end of the century literature was still being judged very largely by the degree to which it conformed to the canons derived from the Latin and Greek classics. Although not quite literature, one work of history was both a major contribution to the Dutch understanding of their past and much more readable than the chronicles and histories of the Golden Age – Jan Wagenaar's *Vaderlandsche historie* (1749–59). Although running to 20 volumes it was a bestseller, partly because its judicious tone served to vindicate a decidedly republican version of the country's past. As history was written with more than one eye on its implications for contemporary politics, so political controversy tended to be cast in historical terms. A prime example of this was the so-called *Witten-oorlog* (War over de Witt) in the 1750s in which Wagenaar played a major part. In a blizzard of pamphlets orangists and republicans disputed under the guise of commenting on the role of the great seventeenth century *raadpensionaris* Johan de Witt. Even during the Patriot period historical justifications of greater or lesser validity continued to be wheeled out to support political actions or proposals.

The liveliness of such public debate is a reminder that one of the most prominent characteristics of Dutch society was that it continued to be a "discussion culture" as it had been in the previous century (Frijhoff and Spies, 2004). Indeed, such discussion and debate over public issues was institutionalized in the later eighteenth century by the emergence of numerous societies designed to promote reform in various areas of Dutch life. The best known – or certainly the most memorable – of these had the splendid title *Tot Nut van 't Algemeen* (For the Common Good), and this gives some flavor of the spirit in which these societies operated. A favored technique was to offer a prize for the best essay on a question set by the society. This activity was perhaps more important in expressing and mobilizing middle-class and lower-middle-class opinion than for any of the specific conclusions reached, let alone reforms carried out.

The End of the Republic

The French invasion of 1795 brought the Dutch Republic to an end after over 200 years of independent existence, and ushered in a period of constitutional experiments under French tutelage. This ignominious end has been seen as the final proof of the political, economic, and even moral bankruptcy of the Republic in its final century of existence. Yet, taken in a European perspective, this defeat seems more a consequence of the peculiar circumstances of the time than of an inexorable process of decline. All the states of Europe proved vulnerable to the forces unleashed by the French Revolution, with the exception of Britain and Russia at different extremes of the continent. So the collapse of the Republic was not a sign of any particular weakness of the Dutch state, but rather of the general weakness of the state system of *ancien régime* Europe.

On a more positive note it can be tentatively suggested that in the course of the eighteenth century a new sense of national unity developed which began to transcend local and provincial loyalties. In an important sense the Dutch nation was the creation of over 200 years of living and working together under the Republic. Even at the end of the seventeenth century, it can be argued, the essential sense of identity for most of the inhabitants of the Republic came primarily from family, from town, and from province, with any sense of belonging to a Dutch state remaining much more tenuous. By the late eighteenth century such a sense of belonging to a single people was more readily expressed and, presumably, felt among the politically articulate at least. The Patriot movement in particular sought to foster the idea of working for the common good of the people of the Netherlands. It was in these years that the centralized Dutch state of the following century was envisioned. The eighteenth century may have been a period of problems and even decline, but it can at least be said to have given birth to the Dutch nation.

Bibliography

Bots, H. and W. W. Mijnhardt (ed.), *De droom van de revolutie. Nieuwe benaderingen van het patriottisme* (Amsterdam, 1988).

Brake, W. P. te, *Regents and Rebels: The Revolutionary World of an Eighteenth Century Dutch City* (Oxford, 1989).

Bruijn, J. R., *The Dutch Navy of the Seventeenth and Eighteenth Centuries* (Colombia, SC, 1993).

Brusse, P., *Overleven door ondernemen. De agrarische geschiedenis van de Over-Betuwe 1650–1850* (Wageningen, 1999).

Cruyningen, P. J. van, *Behoudend maar buigzaam. Boeren in West-Zeeuws-Vlaanderen 1650–1850* (Wageningen, 2000).

de Vries, J., *De economische achteruitgang van de Republiek in de achttiende eeuw* (Leiden, 1968).

de Vries, J., *The Dutch Rural Economy in the Golden Age* (New Haven, 1974).

de Vries, J., and A. M. van der Woude, *The First Modern Economy: Success, Failure, and Perseverance of the Dutch Economy, 1500–1815* (Cambridge, 1997).

Dessert, D., *Argent, pouvoir et société au grand siècle* (Paris, 1985).

Faber, J. A., *Drie eeuwen Friesland. Economische en sociale ontwikkelingen van 1500 tot 1800* (3 vols., Wageningen, 1972).

Frijhoff, W. and M. Spies, *1650: Hard-Won Unity* (Basingstoke, 2004).

Gabriëls, A. J. C. M., *De heren als dienaren en de dienaar als heer. Het stadhouderlijke stelsel in de tweede helft van de 18de eeuw* (The Hague, 1990).

Gijswijt-Hofstra, M. and W. Frijhoff (eds.), *Witchcraft in the Netherlands: From the Fourteenth to the Twentieth Century* (Rotterdam, 1991).

Israel, J. I., *The Dutch Republic: Its Rise, Greatness and Fall, 1477–1806* (Oxford, 1995).

Jacob, M. C. and W. W. Mijnhardt (eds.), *The Dutch Republic in the Eighteenth Century: Decline, Enlightenment and Revolution* (Ithaca, 1992).

Jong, J. J. de, *Met goed fatsoen. De elite in een Hollandse stad, Gouda 1700–80* (Dieren, 1985).

Jongste, J. A. F. de, *Onrust aan het Spaarne. Haarlem in de jaren 1747–1751* (Dieren, 1984).

Kleyn, S. R., *Patriots republikanisme. Politieke cultuur in Nederland (1766–1787)* (Amsterdam, 1995).

Kooimans, L., *Onder regenten. De elite in een Hollandse stad, Hoorn 1700–1780* (Dieren, 1985).

Leeb, I. L., *The Ideological Origins of the Batavian Revolution. History and Politics in the Dutch Republic 1747–1800* (The Hague, 1973).

Liesker, R., "Tot zinkens toe bezwaard. De schuldenlast van het Zuiderkwartier van Holland 1672–1794," in S. Groenveld et al. (eds.), *Bestuurders en geleerden* (Amsterdam and Dieren, 1985), pp. 151–60.

Meer, T. van der, *Sodoms zaad in Nederland. Het ontstaan van homoseksualiteit in de vroegmoderne tijd* (Nijmegen, 1995).

Mijnhardt, W. W., *Tot Heil van 't Menschdom. Culturele genootschappen in Nederland, 1750–1815* (Amsterdam, 1987).

Nimwegen, O. van, *De Republiek der Verenigde Nederlanden als grote mogendheid* (Amsterdam, 2002).

Prak, M., *Gezeten burgers. De elite in een Hollandse stad, Leiden 1700–1780* (Dieren, 1985).

Priester, P., *Geschiedenis van de Zeeuwse landbouw circa 1600–1910* (Wageningen, 1998).

Schama, S., *Patriots and Liberators: Revolution in the Netherlands 1780–1813* (London, 1977).

Switzer, H. L., *"De militie van den staat." Het leger van de Republiek der Verenigde Nederlanden* (Amsterdam, 1991).

Trompetter, C., *Agriculture, Proto-Industry and Mennonite Entrepreneurship: A History of the Textile Industries in Twente, 1600–1815* (Amsterdam, 1997).

Wessels, L. H. M., *Bron, waarheid en de verandering der tijden. Jan Wagenaar (1709–1773), een historiografische studie* (The Hague, 1997).

Willemsen, R., *Enkhuizen tijdens de Republiek* (Hilversum, 1988).

Woude, A. M. van der, *Het Noorderkwartier* (Wageningen, 1972).

Zanden, J. L. van, *The Rise and Decline of Holland's Economy: Merchant Capitalism and the Labour Market* (Manchester, 1993).

Chapter Nineteen

The Italian States

Gregory Hanlon

The Italian States in the Eighteenth Century

Periodization always entails some violence towards the data, especially when one slices the dough of historical continuity into neat, hundred-year packages. As far as the political evolution of the Italian peninsula is concerned, it is possible to identify two eighteenth centuries. The first, the long eighteenth century, began with the cessation of hostilities between Bourbons and Habsburgs in 1660, which restored a long period of equilibrium and stability. Although peace was violently disrupted during the Dutch War (1672–9), the wars of the League of Augsburg (1689–97), and the wars of the Spanish Succession (1701–14), the Polish Succession (1733–5), and the Austrian Succession (1740–8), Italian states were usually unwilling participants or nervous spectators with little influence on the outcome. When the great powers parceled out territories to the victors and arranged the peaceful transfer of others with a mind to the balance of power, they did not question the basic rules of the political game in Italy, nor did these transfers trigger profound political, social, or economic transformations. The second, short, eighteenth century witnessed more rapid political change, often guided by the new principles of social utility elaborated by Enlightenment philosophers. These transformations became increasingly ambitious after 1750, but came to an abrupt end in the years before 1800, when fear of the French Revolution incited princes and aristocrats to discontinue their sweeping reforms.

Italy and Europe during the Long Eighteenth Century *c.*1660–1750

Despite intermittent hostilities between Spain and France, there would be minimal territorial modifications there until the Treaty of Utrecht in 1713. The cause of this was less the resilience of Spain than the French preoccupation with borders in Germany and the Low Countries. Italy was never more than a sideshow for the Sun King and his ministers. Faced with French ascendancy, and disinclined to marshal their own forces through a series of defensive alliances, Italian states began to align

A Companion to Eighteenth-Century Europe, First Edition. Edited by Peter H. Wilson.
© 2014 John Wiley & Sons, Ltd. Published 2014 by John Wiley & Sons, Ltd.

themselves with Louis XIV via dynastic marriage. The new French power presented little danger to Italian princes, for, unlike his ancestors, Louis made no attempt to extend his kingdom over the Alps.

More in reaction to French encroachments in Germany and the Low Countries than from concern with their projects in Italy, the German Habsburgs contemplated a return in force to the peninsula. The relatively small number of territorial states makes the political map of Italy in 1690 look simple in comparison with Germany. This is a bit misleading. Italy still contained numerous imperial fiefs, around 300 territories held by about 60 great families. Most of them were situated in marginal areas, like the Langhe hills bordering Piedmont and Liguria or in the Tuscan Apennines. Some of these fiefs had been devoured by ambitious territorial princes such as the dukes of Parma and Tuscany, but were never fully incorporated into the princes' other territories. Out of weakness, Madrid allowed Austria in 1680 to restore its pretensions to supervise and submit to taxation those situated in the duchy of Milan (Aretin, 1978). Leopold I planned for the recovery of imperial control beginning in 1683, starting with the fiefs scattered throughout Italy, and then intended to exploit the ambiguous legal status of the Italian principalities themselves (Pugliese, 1932).

In 1690, in response to Louis' aggression in the Rhineland, Leopold I dispatched a large portion of his army from Hungary to northern Italy, joining forces with Spain and the duke of Savoy. Territories caught in the grip of armies were customarily expected to furnish food, money, forage, and vehicles to the soldiery, on pain of their forcible seizure. The imperial fiefs were the first to be taxed for the maintenance of the troops. Italian princes were soon summoned to provide huge "contributions" to the imperial cause, in proportion to their wealth and population (Storrs, 2005). Not having military forces of their own, they were compelled to comply. The pointed elevation of imperial plenipotentiaries above the princes themselves added to their mortification (Niccolini, 1938). Many parts of northern and central Italy recognized a kind of double suzerainty of pope and emperor. The imperial ambassador in Rome pointedly stressed his intention to curtail papal influence in Italy, even in the Papal States (Pastor, 1957: 662–9). The emperor maintained a growing standing army, and he intended to use it to his advantage.

The War of the Spanish Succession saw imperial troops return in force, with instructions to force Italian neutral territories to furnish provisions to the army. The commander Prince Eugene unilaterally declared imperial suzerainty on portions of the Papal States, while Emperor Joseph I declared that all the Italian princes were his vassals. Only Piedmont cheerfully acknowledged imperial suzerainty, but, disposing of an army of its own, it paid nothing for the maintenance of the Germans. The Gonzaga of Mantua, who recognized the Bourbon succession to Milan and who joined the French, were chased from their duchy in 1707. Italian princes protested, and pleaded their cases for exemption. The victory at Turin by Prince Eugene over the French in 1706, and the subsequent evacuation of the peninsula by Bourbon forces, led to even more imperial requisitions, with fewer diplomatic niceties. Pushed into a corner by emperor Joseph I, Pope Clement XI declared war on the empire, but then capitulated when an Austrian column marched towards Rome.

Although the grand alliance against Louis XIV failed to eject the Bourbon King Philip from the throne of Spain, the Peace of Utrecht in 1713 rewarded Austria with the Spanish Netherlands, with the duchy of Milan (adding Mantua to it), and the kingdoms of Sardinia and Naples. Imperial troops took up quarters in both northern and southern Italy, in numbers much greater than those formerly dispatched from Spain (Hanlon, 1998: 305). For his service to the allied cause, the treaty rewarded Duke Victor Amadeus II of Savoy-Piedmont with the former Gonzaga territories of the Monferrato, and a rich portion of the duchy of Milan bordering his states. Most of all, he fulfilled the age-old ambition of his house by acquiring a royal crown, that of Sicily.

Spanish military recovery under the Bourbons, marshaled by the able Italian cardinal Alberoni, soon caught everyone by surprise. In 1718 a Spanish amphibious invasion took Sardinia from the Austrians and Sicily from the Piedmontese. It required a brief European alliance of France, Britain, and Austria in order to make Philip V relinquish territories that still felt a close bond with Spain. When the dust settled, Austria extended its control from Naples to Sicily, while Victor Amadeus had to be content with the much more primitive and sparsely populated island kingdom of Sardinia. The Parman queen of Spain, Elizabeth Farnese, still intended to recover territories in the peninsula for her two sons. Italian questions figured high on the list of points of tension in European courts determined to maintain a balance of power. The Habsburg emperor Charles VI insisted on the rights of his house over all of northern Italy. In these years, more than one Habsburg subject out of three was Italian (Quazza, 1938).

The brief War of the Polish Succession, which began in 1733, was a violent check to Habsburg ambitions in the peninsula. A French and Piedmontese (now called Sardinian) army quickly ejected the Germans from Lombardy and Emilia, and a year later a seaborne army from Spain reconquered the kingdoms of Naples and Sicily. By the end of 1735 the imperials were almost entirely expelled from Italy. By the terms of peace, Emperor Charles VI recovered Milan, but lost another portion of it to the king of Sardinia, and he relinquished southern Italy entirely to the Spanish Bourbons, who created an autonomous kingdom of the Two Sicilies there under the adolescent Prince Charles. As compensation for handing his duchy to France, Duke Francis of Lorraine, the young husband of the heir to the imperial throne Maria Theresia, succeeded the Medici grand dukes in Florence in 1737. Europe then awaited the impending extinction of the male Habsburg line with bated breath. Charles VI convinced European chancelleries to consent to the smooth succession of his daughter Maria Theresia to the Austrian throne and to allow her election to the imperial dignity, through the Pragmatic Sanction. Despite these diplomatic successes, the ramshackle, decentralized Habsburg empire looked very weak.

The gratuitous invasion of Silesia by the young king of Prussia, Frederick II (the Great) opened the War of the Austrian Succession. Soon a great coalition of European states mobilized against Austria, each intending to share the spoils. German electors elevated the Bavarian elector to the imperial dignity, though he died soon after. The Spanish Bourbons, still directed by Queen Elizabeth Farnese, marched an army overland to seize Savoy, now that Sardinia had joined forces with the empress. Another Spanish force arrived by sea to operate in Emilia, hoping to eject the Austrians from northern Italy. With British financial and naval support, Austria quickly recovered, helping the Sardinians pin French and Spanish troops to the Alps, and making a bold gamble to recover by force the kingdom of Naples. The Spaniards and Neapolitans checked this advance at Velletri not far from Rome early in 1744. On the other hand, large-scale operations in the Po valley drove the "Gallispans" (Franco-Spanish) back into the Alps (Wilkinson, 1927). The war in Italy finally concluded in 1748 after a rash French assault directly against Piedmont failed on a mountain top.

Throughout these wars, most Italian princes and republics hesitated to become involved. Duke Francesco III of Modena departed from his pro-Habsburg stance in 1742, only to see his duchy quickly overrun by imperial and Sardinian forces. The cautious Venetian senators adopted a policy of armed neutrality that could not prevent the terra firma being mauled by belligerent armies, chiefly imperial. Tuscany, even under the Habsburg-Lorraine Grand Duke Francis, declared neutrality in the conflict. Pope Benedict XIV complained vigorously to Madrid and Vienna about the way in which their armies disturbed central Italy, but he could do nothing to prevent it. Only King Charles Emmanuel III of Piedmont-Sardinia welcomed this war, and actively prepared for it by beefing up his standing army to over 40,000 men. But Sardinian policy veered unpredictably from a pro-Bourbon to a pro-Habsburg stance depending upon which ally had the most to offer. Sardinia only rallied to the imperial cause in 1742 once the empress transferred yet another slice of rich territory from the duchy of Milan. The soldier-king was hoping for a resumption of war after 1748 so that he might complete his conquest of Milan and any other territories (such as Corsica, or the Genoese republic) weak enough to succumb.

Repeated wars against Bourbon France and Spain brought only disappointment to Vienna. Now Maria Theresia was consumed with the desire to recover Silesia from the upstart king of Prussia. She made her peace with the Bourbons in 1756 and multiplied marriages of her daughters and sons with princes in Paris, Madrid, Naples, Parma, and Modena. Piedmont-Sardinia had no other recourse but to accept what would become a durable peace in northern Italy until the end of the century. The Seven Years War (1756–63) pitted the Habsburgs and Bourbons against their British and Prussian enemies and so bypassed Italy almost entirely. In the aftermath of the conflict, Genoa gradually lost control of restive Corsica, and finally sold it to France in 1768. After a French army quickly overcame the insurgents there, the entire Italian area experienced over a generation of tranquility.

These wars gradually simplified the Italian geopolitical map. The dukes of Savoy and kings of Sardinia eventually extinguished the swath of mountain fiefs in the Langhe districts and in Monferrato. Parma seized the Landi states in the Apennines, and eventually absorbed Guastalla too, while Modena extended its control over neighboring Novellara and Mirandola, and eventually absorbed the Cybo statelet of Massa and Carrara in 1780. Tuscany annexed most of the Malaspina fiefs in the Lunigiana valley leading to the Po valley.

While Bourbon power collapsed following the imperial victory at Turin in 1706, Elizabeth Farnese's policy of restoring Spanish influence to Italy was largely successful. From 1734 her son Charles ruled in Naples and Sicily, and he was a docile satellite until her death. Her younger son Philip ruled in Parma after 1748, in a miniature state modeled upon France. Bourbon territories sometimes acted in a dynastic bloc, as when the Spanish, French, and Neapolitan monarchies stood behind the dukes of Parma against papal pretensions. However, the French monarchy of the last three Louis cared little for Italian questions, and relinquished the peninsula to the Spanish, and then Austrian, sphere of influence (Simeoni, 1986: 1).

The imperial couple in Vienna ruled over a much-reduced duchy of Milan, and tiny Mantua in Lombardy, in addition to the alpine Trentino valleys where Austrian archdukes had reigned since the Middle Ages. Lorraine emissaries governed the grand duchy of Tuscany in the name of the emperor, and patiently reduced its autonomy with each passing decade. Modena also returned to the Habsburg alliance, where a Habsburg prince inherited the duchy after 1803. Austrian *influence* continued to expand through the marriage of the young King Ferdinand of Naples to Maria Carolina, sister to Marie Antoinette. Once she had borne a son in 1776, her influence in the kingdom was determinant, and Naples gradually fell into the Austrian sphere as well. This Austrian hegemony beginning in 1690 would weigh heavily upon Italian history for much of the nineteenth century.

Stability and Continuity in the Italian State System

Military turbulence masks the institutional continuity of the early eighteenth century, whose roots plunged deep into the city-state traditions of the late Middle Ages. Medieval communes developed a wide array of institutions and realms of competence on their own without much outside interference. The larger entities devoured most of the smaller ones in the course of the fourteenth and fifteenth centuries until barely a dozen "territorial" states remained. But the territorial states were themselves conglomerates of city-states that accepted the tutelage of a "dominant" city in exchange for local autonomy under the direction of leading families (Mannori, 1994: 2).

The city-state legacy was exceptionally long-lived, and in some ways still flourishes today. The dukes of Milan left much power in the hands of nine subject cities. When Venice expanded into the terra firma in the fifteenth century, it recognized the autonomy of about a dozen cities in its hinterland, and left them supervision over their respective rural hinterlands. Florence's expansion culminated in the conquest of Siena in 1559, but typically, the Sienese elites retained their autonomy. The Papal States comprised 13 different provinces, several of which were headed by papal-appointed legates. Legates in Ferrara, Ravenna, and Bologna ruled alongside the traditional patrician assemblies (Chadwick, 1981; Gross, 1990; Prodi, 1987). Smaller states adopted similar principles: the duchy of Parma and Piacenza constituted two autonomous territories, with two palaces. The little Modenese state with its ducal institutions in the capital took care to dispatch an Este prince to Reggio Emilia.

The Habsburg Lands: Milan, Naples, and Sicily

Spain had ruled Milan almost at arm's length. A military governor appointed from Madrid (not always a Spaniard) was assisted by a committee of military and administrative specialists, often local personalities. Milan was a regional capital in the Spanish empire, and the governor maintained diplomatic contacts with much of Italy and Austria. Daily government remained in the hands of 60 leading patricians, who supervised justice and taxation. Their relatives held key church benefices throughout the region too, and Spain habitually requested its functionaries to avoid conflicts with the clergy and to respect their immunities (Canosa, 1993: 39, 200). Lombards of every social category remained loyal to the Spanish Crown until Austrian Habsburgs ejected the Bourbon governor in 1706. The Austrian Habsburgs hardly changed the region's administrative structure until after 1750.

Emperor Charles VI (r. 1711–40) was not more inclined to modify the structures he found in Naples (from 1707) or Sicily (from 1720). Those kingdoms were ruled by viceroys as they were in the time of Spanish dominion (Gallo, 1995). The initial imperial attempts to restrict contraband and to stimulate a more active trading and manufacturing economy bore little fruit. In Naples, the city nobility dominated both the tribunals and the grain-provisioning administration, the Annona. The legal and fiscal administration was largely in the hands of a very numerous class of professional jurists, collectively termed *togati*, whose power derived from the accumulation of offices and intermarriage with other officials. Spanish viceroys had always sought a balance between these *togati* and the feudal aristocracy in the capital city (Rao, 2000).

In both Sicily and the Mezzogiorno, much of the power outside the capital cities lay in the hands of feudal nobles, who retained most of their prerogatives until the French regime abolished fiefs outright in 1806. Monarchs relied on the feudal nobility and their officers to keep order in the countryside, as they did in Spain or central Europe (Maiorini, 2000). While they were not authorized to meddle in the levy of local taxes or in the selection of members of local government, feudal lords were prone to exercising an officious authority in defiance of the law. The power of the 1,350 feudal families was not immobile, however. In the 1680s, energetic viceroys ensured that anti-bandit laws were applied in the fiefs. The marques del Carpio browbeat lords who turned a blind eye to bandit gangs in the Abruzzo, and with Spanish troops and enough militia he succeeded in establishing a permanent peace (Sabbatini, 1995). If lords (who increasingly resided peacefully in the capital) browbeat their vassals in the fiefs thereafter, it was in more legalistic ways (Lucacs, 1981). After 1707 the Habsburg emperor could rely upon the force of a substantial German garrison to maintain order. When a Bourbon force under Prince Charles invaded Naples from the north in 1734, most of the kingdom's nobility cheered the return of the Spanish connection and hoped that Madrid would maintain the status quo (Calabria, 1981; Vittorio, 1984).

The Principalities: Tuscany, Parma, Modena, Mantua

With the exception of the Gonzaga of Mantua, the great wars left the princely dynasties intact. The Este, the Medici, and the Farnese ruled their duchies (Modena, Tuscany, and Parma respectively) uninterruptedly from the mid-sixteenth century at least, and by 1700 nobody could imagine another regime, especially since these dynasties legitimized themselves by multiplying marriages with the Bourbons and Habsburgs. The princes' duties were to maintain social stability and to distribute justice equitably to all their subjects (Nubola, 2001). They were aided by a corps of professionally trained bureaucrats from aristocratic families whose cultural outlook was very similar across northern and central Italy. Aristocrats and jurists enhanced the power of the prince over the entire state, though cities retained important privileges with respect to the countryside. The princes held sway even in remote corners of their territories with the aid of large bodies of peasant militia, kept well in hand by ducal functionaries.

Italian princes pioneered courtly culture and institutions in the late Renaissance, and made their city palaces the locus of power and preferment. There was no clear separation between the property of the state and that of the ruling house, and so dynastic events were pretexts for the massive outlay of public expenditure. Italian ducal courts numbered between 300 and 800 placeholders around 1700, exclusive of the guards and the subalternate personnel. Court ritual (influenced by Spanish and French models) established international norms for the representation of power, and it proved powerfully integrative of Italian aristocrats. Local nobles made it a point of honor to attend palace ceremonies and to splurge on the cost of appearing in them, in part out of sociability, in part out of the desire to make themselves known to princes and ministers who were always seeking new talent (Fantoni, 1994: 58–66; Sabbadini, 2001). The rock-solid foundations of Italian principalities like Tuscany, Modena, Mantua, Parma, and Piedmont lay in bargains the dynasties had struck with social elites. Princes recognized the social pre-eminence of feudal lords who frequented the court. They rewarded loyal service by city patricians and even well-born outsiders with nobility, new or vacant fiefs, and ever grander titles. Urban aristocrats not only dominated city assemblies; they also staffed the academies, the universities, and the professions, and held the best benefices of the church as well. Fiefs were still very numerous, but feudal prerogatives and revenues declined relentlessly as subjects and vassals enjoyed increasing liberty to appeal to urban tribunals and to the prince himself as a last resort (Prodi, 1987: 72). While princes made little effort to eliminate fiefs and feudataries, they ceased to create new ones as the eighteenth century progressed, and left them only limited rights of administration (Hanlon, 2007). This domestication of the nobility was contemporary to the one unfolding in the France of Louis XIV.

We should not consider the period to be one of political immobility, but rather of creeping absolutism, a gradual growth of personal rule by the dukes, who supplanted elected tribunals staffed by urban patricians with jurists and specialists trained in colleges and universities, operating at the ruler's discretion. The social peace perhaps reflected the lower tax pressure in Italy in comparison with other countries. Finances were administered through a multitude of separate offices, each with its own chests. Direct taxation relied on self-assessment and self-declaration to government officials, so landowners usually declared property and income well below their real level (Waquet, 1990: 242–50). Indirect taxation consisted in duties called *gabelles*, levied on merchandise, or on state monopolies such as salt or legal paper, on staples such as grain, and on the luxuries and vices (wigs, brandy, tobacco) of people with more disposable income. Governments preferred to multiply *gabelles* rather than increase direct taxation on family incomes, for the latter required a large and relatively honest and efficient bureaucracy, as well as a detailed cadaster, all of which were still in the future. These revenues were leased (farmed) out to consortia of businessmen who needed to collect more money than they had paid for the concession. In Tuscany alone there were more than 100 customs offices, levying an array of different taxes on goods of every description as they moved from one point to another. Privileged social groups such as the clergy and the aristocracy paid lower duties on most goods, or no duties at all. In addition to tax farming, most states borrowed heavily from bankers, aristocrats, and religious houses in order to meet urgent expenditures. This state recourse to borrowing had the effect of making social elites financial stakeholders in the political stability of their states (Rosa, 1998). Princes did little to standardize or unify the collection of taxes until well into the eighteenth century.

These duchies have looked archaic to subsequent generations for the obsequious obedience the rulers displayed towards the doctrines and hierarchies of the church. The dukes, their wives, and, still more, their mothers, strove to maintain a Counter-Reformation atmosphere at court, in stark contrast to French or north European courts. Italian princes were enthroned at the summit of a patronage system governing both the state and the church. Pious monarchs like Cosimo III of Tuscany supervised the behavior of the clergy and kept tutelage over good religion and morals (Fantoni, 1993). Sovereigns were also assiduous devotees of shrines, spending lavishly to build or decorate them, and they promoted specific saints for public veneration. The church was a pillar of princely absolutism throughout Italy, and, conversely, the princes' popular support owed something to their support for religion. Jesuits controlled secondary education for nobles and for the middle class until well into the eighteenth century. Yet even Cosimo III pressured the clergy to pay new taxes and to help shoulder the burden of fiscality in his states. And in doing so, the princes gradually peeled away some of the immunities championed in Rome (Bizocchi, 1989).

The Papal Monarchy

The papal monarchy was distinct from all the others because the monarch and the senior dignitaries who helped the pope rule were all ecclesiastics. Cardinals rose through the ranks of the church bureaucracy by passing from committee to committee (called Congregations) dealing with religious affairs or with political and administrative ones. Like urban patricians in city-states, papal bureaucrats held a wide variety of positions in succession, from war to water control. The great majority of the 70-odd cardinals were Italian, with an increasing trend towards those hailing from central and northern Italy (Ago, 1990: 15–19). Until the late seventeenth century, the popes placed the daily administration and patronage in the hands of their nephews, raised immediately to the rank of cardinal. Cardinal nephews enriched themselves and their relatives for the duration of the pope's mandate, before losing all power to a new pontiff. After 1692, the chief administrator became the secretary of state, who was not related to the pope and had less control over the papal finances. There was no preordained plan to centralize authority or make administrative structures uniform from one part of the Papal States to another. Popes and cardinals had spent colossal sums on building projects, making Rome a model modern city. Still, the level of direct taxation was quite low, about a third of the level paid in France or in Lombardy, and only a sixth of what an Englishman paid. But the small scale of their military contributions spared them the need to revamp their finances.

The Aristocratic Republic of Venice

Long a major European power, Venice's fortunes sagged slowly during the long seventeenth century despite escaping the horrors of the Thirty Years War. The Ottoman invasion of Crete in 1645 unleashed a long period of guerrilla war in the Balkans and amphibious operations in the Aegean, first centered on the siege of Candia (to 1669), then in Dalmatia and Greece (1684–99), and culminating in the anticlimactic and rapid loss of its Greek possessions in the Peloponnesis (1715–18). The state ceased to count as a European power after the Peloponnesis fiasco. In theory the 14 provinces of the republic formed a confederation, rooted in the patrician assemblies of each district capital. In practice, only patricians of Venice decided on war and peace, dominated the tribunals dealing with public security, and determined which industries could operate across the state. Venice wielded disproportionate power, but the city also paid taxes far in excess of the terra firma cities. This no doubt explains the general tranquility of the Venetian republic during the age of Tiepolo, Goldoni, and Casanova. Economic stagnation, battle, and plague reduced the number of active male nobles eligible for office from over 2,000 in the 1620s to barely 1,000 in the 1790s. Only a handful of wealthy patricians wielded real power, however, moving from one key committee to another over a long career. The republic sold nobility to new families to pay for the great wars, but it could not stanch the hemorrhage of blue blood (Davis, 1962). A "citizen" class drawn essentially from families with a legal background staffed many of the offices (Zannini, 1992).

Piedmontese Absolutism

If there was little rapid change in most of Italy in the decades following the Thirty Years War, the exception was Piedmont. It too constituted an assemblage of territories spanning both sides of the Alps: Piedmont proper, the duchy of Savoy, the traditional French-speaking seat of the ruling dynasty, the Occitanian county of Nice on the Mediterranean coast, and the mountainous Val d'Aosta bordering on the Swiss Valais. Piedmont, where most of the population lived, long remained outside the urban heartland of northern Italy. Turin only began to flourish when the dukes transferred their court there in the 1560s.

The ambitious soldier-dukes of Savoy relished the dangerous game of international politics with their powerful neighbors France, Spain, and Austria. The ultimate prize was not to unite Italy or expel foreign powers, but to acquire a royal crown for themselves. The creation of a Piedmontese standing army in 1661 was an important milestone in Italian history. Like other forces in the Holy Roman Empire, this army was maintained in peacetime by renting units of it to Venice or the king of France for service far away from home. The army allowed the duke to reward his nobles with patronage and advancement, and they acquired precious combat experience in the meantime. Denied an autonomous aggressive role by European powers, the dukes built a network of substantial fortresses throughout their state, and transformed Turin into the most powerful stronghold in Italy.

The domestic policies of Duke Victor Amadeus II (r. 1684–1730) were mirror images of those of Louis XIV. At home he repressed Vaudois Protestants in their Alpine valleys, while facilitating the persecution of Huguenots escaping from France. Most of his other measures were fiscally inspired, with the ultimate aim of hiring more soldiers. He imported from France the institution of the *intendant* (called *referendari*), trusted and experienced civilian officials holding a commission to oversee the smooth administration of a single district for several years. He sharply increased the salt *gabelles* in order to pay for his standing army, and then brutalized the Piedmontese regions that rose in rebellion against the heavier duties. He curtailed the abilities of local assemblies in Savoy and Nice to negotiate and levy the taxes assessed on them. Victor Amadeus was especially preoccupied with issues of church jurisdiction. Powerful kinship groups did their utmost to invest their wealth in church benefices for their sons, and established a host of new ones in the late seventeenth century. This placed their assets outside the tax system (Torre, 1992). After 1710 the duke moved to control charity in the state, and then established a state university designed to produce ducal functionaries. This activism soon brought him into a conflict with the papacy that was only resolved through a new concordat with Rome in 1729.

Noblemen constituted the other powerful interest group with extensive tax exemptions. Victor Amadeus, like his ancestors, forced nobles to prove the legality of their tax exemptions, interfered in the autonomy of feudal jurisdictions, and distributed new patents of nobility and new fiefs to rising families. In exchange, the Savoyard state destined the great majority of lucrative military commissions to titled aristocrats, though this prestigious servitude subjected them to the scrutiny of a new war ministry (Loriga, 1991).

After 1713 the new king enlarged his peacetime army to over 20,000 men, many of whom belonged to expensive Swiss and German mercenary units. This heavy burden forced Victor Amadeus to revamp the administrative structure of his state to provide for them. A crucial instrument in this transformation was the *perequazione* or land register, inaugurated in the 1690s but not completed until after the War of the Spanish Succession. The duke's passion for order and regulations led to an attempt to unify the various legal codes and customary law. Meanwhile, numerous mercantilist ventures were introduced to reduce reliance on foreign countries for raw materials and manufactured goods (Symcox, 1983).

The successors of Victor Amadeus II would follow in his footsteps for most of the century, making them look more cautious and conservative than they really were. Charles Emanuel III (r. 1730–74) placed great emphasis on industrial development and technological innovation, often sponsored by schools designed to train military officers (Ferraresi, 2004; Ferrone, 1984). Towards the end of his reign, in 1773, the king decided to eliminate the feudal system in Savoy proper by having peasant communities purchase those rights from their lords. All of these measures found an echo in other Italian states in the course of the eighteenth century, but none of them owe anything to the Enlightenment. This was largely the heritage of the "administrative monarchy" on the model of Louis XIV. The standing army's creation and its continual expansion drove the process.

The Short Eighteenth Century, *c.*1750–1790

The relation of the secular state to the Catholic Church, its hierarchy and its theology, was the primordial political issue in Italy throughout the entire century. All the Italian states embarked upon policies designed to curtail ecclesiastical jurisdiction (Diaz, 1979). The Catholic Church in 1700 was at the height of its influence. Never had the clergy been so numerous and disciplined. Never had clerics been so well born and erudite. Under the last Medici grand dukes, ecclesiastics in Tuscany constituted over 3 percent of the entire population, (over twice the level of France) and priests and nuns constituted perhaps over 4 percent of the population in the kingdom of Naples. There the clergy probably constituted the absolute majority of literate adults.

For well over a century, people of all social classes had voluntarily sponsored a massive shift of resources towards the church and its ministers. There was little sign that the demand for religious services was abating (Toscani, 1982). Land bequeathed to the church by the faithful, or land purchased by religious entities, was everywhere subject to mortmain – that is, it could not revert in future to secular uses. Church jurisdiction and immunities proved an increasingly thorny issue for government ministers. The Papal Congregation of Immunities pounced on rulers who arrested delinquent clerics, and excommunicated magistrates who pried criminals from churches where they enjoyed sanctuary. Religious houses complained loudly whenever states taxed them, or whenever governments contemplated limiting property transfers to the church. Monarchs like the king of France or the emperor made light of papal pretensions from the late seventeenth century onwards. In Italy, some bold writers questioned the historical basis of Rome's claims, and suffered arrest for it.

State bureaucrats, following France and then Piedmont, began to conceive of religion more in utilitarian terms of public morality than in terms of revealed truth and salvation. There is no rigid date governing these matters, but the 1720s and still more the 1730s marked a sea-change in cultural history. The ultimate libertine Medici duke, Gian Gastone, abolished the pious committees that dominated policy in his father's long reign and curtailed the state employment of clergy in the duchy (1723). This more utilitarian mindset eventually permeated the papal government itself after 1740, in the person of Pope Benedict XIV Lambertini, who reduced the number of feast-days in the calendar, removed legends from the breviary, and lightened ecclesiastical censorship, all while multiplying the concordats with Italian states. These were treaties between secular governments and the church, which governed the fiscal status of the institution, placed limitations on the recruitment of future ecclesiastics, and stipulated the mechanisms by which important benefices were assigned to subjects of the prince.

The church proved unable to uproot an insidious new current in intellectual life imported from Britain: the Freemasons. These arrived in the wake of the exiled Stuart court in Rome, and via English merchant communities in Livorno and elsewhere. Their influence was soon felt in court academies protected by princes. Soon secular writers were advocating that these princes should remove censorship from the hands of ecclesiastics appointed by Rome. Concurrently, Italian states enacted laws against mortmain, and placed increasing obstacles in the path of those who wished to leave pious bequests. After about 1750 the Italian upper classes no longer volunteered to aid the Inquisition, and it became *bon ton* to doubt the tenets of traditional religion and to mock the more zealous instruments of the church, such as Jesuits and Franciscan friars. Starting in about 1760, Italian academicians affected an anti-clerical stance that would turn the papal retreat into a rout.

Habsburg Reforms after 1740

The reforms we attribute to the Enlightenment began in earnest in Habsburg territories, where the popes had little purchase. The first impetus belongs to Tuscany, where the absentee Grand Duke Francis Stephen sent Lorrainer functionaries to rule through a collegiate regency council in Florence. Florentine and Sienese patricians no longer enjoyed easy access to a prince who wished to protect their interests. Francis

Stephen sought instead to reduce the number of Tuscan functionaries on the pretext of controlling spending (Pansini, 1968; Waquet, 1979). The absentee grand duke did not plunder Tuscany's resources for the advantage of Vienna, but the prince did not believe in maintaining the status quo. The Lorrainers strove from the outset to uproot patrician corruption in public office, beginning with a clampdown on routine contraband activities by privileged groups. Grand Duke Francis Stephen was one of the first princes to restrict the activities of the Papal Inquisition after it arrested and tortured a Freemason poet. The prince sought to reduce censorship by priests designated from Rome, although censors were usually ecclesiastics nominated by the prince. Finally, Tuscany was the first state to abolish mortmain. Foreign ideas, especially in French, or translated from the French, infiltrated the Tuscan academies, whose numbers and membership multiplied after mid-century. They embraced the secular spirit of the times (Cochrane, 1961).

The reform trend accelerated after the death of Francis Stephen, because his son and heir Leopold (Pietro Leopoldo) arrived from Vienna to take up residence in Tuscany. A gifted monarch inspired by Enlightenment currents, he did his utmost to increase administrative efficiency, mainly by abolishing the patrician committees of the past. By 1768 Tuscan tax collection was the sole responsibility of hired officials (Cochrane, 1973). The grand duke abolished all the remaining rotative and elective offices in Florence and Siena. The following year, Leopold abolished most of the existing confraternities that channeled charity without much state supervision. To forestall protests from Rome, he established the exequatur (1769) by which the papacy required state authorization to publish church decrees in Tuscany (Diaz, 1979: 581). Leopold hoped to make even more sweeping changes to popular religion by convening a synod of reform-minded bishops at Pistoia in 1787, but the unpopularity of the new mindset in the general population forced him to suspend the most radical measures. The grand duke adopted a new criminal code in 1786 inspired by the Lombard *philosophe* Cesare Beccaria, which abolished both torture and the death penalty, while instituting legal safeguards against arbitrary arrest. Leopold also trusted market forces to effect economic progress in his state, by first easing up economic regulations, and then abolishing guilds outright. Sensitive to physiocratic theory that extolled the public utility of a prosperous rural middle class, he attempted to expand the powers of local government in order to involve landowners in public affairs. Finally, he instructed his officials to prepare a proper constitution, finished in 1782, that foresaw a legislative assembly to be elected from the General Will (Cochrane, 1973: 454–83).

The Habsburg program in Tuscany served as a catalyst for the more fitful but ambitious one unfolding in Milan (Capra, 1979; Grab, 1983–4). There were very few changes to the Milanese government before 1750, but the loss of the duchy twice to Bourbon troops, and the distinct lack of overt local loyalty motivated Empress Maria Theresia to impose a centralizing program on Lombardy. From 1733 to 1763 the Habsburg monarchy was continually obsessed with preparing for war, so the principal task of her Lombard administrators was to find the money to feed the garrison and to raise more soldiers (Donati, 1982). Starting in 1756, Vienna tried to impose identical administrative structures on its Lombard provinces by doing away with the city-state autonomy enjoyed by the secondary centers. The empress and her ministers embarked on an ambitious project to map and assess every field, pasture, and house in the territory. A precise cadaster would allow the state to draw taxes more efficiently, and for this it was resolutely opposed by local elites. Maria Theresia and her chief adviser, Prince Kaunitz, overruled local resistance, however. By 1765 they had restructured government in order to give nominated officials greater control over taxes, and they multiplied the number of low-born functionaries to administer them in outlying localities (Mozzarelli, 1982). They aimed to create a more impersonal bureaucracy less reliant on aristocratic clientage, and more compliant to instructions from Vienna. This would place single functionaries in a chain of command that bypassed the old patrician committees.

Kaunitz himself was close collaborator with Lombard intellectuals like Pietro Verri and Cesare Beccaria, who belonged to a circle whose reflections were published via the "Caffè" academy. Vienna tapped into the talent pool of Lombard intellectuals to serve on high-profile government committees dealing with economic reform and urban administration. As influential functionaries, these Italians felt little sympathy with titled Milanese patricians, whose control over the local bureaucratic machinery was being continually eroded. In 1786 Joseph II finally stripped local elites of power by centralizing the administration yet again and subjecting it to a Viennese ministry. Not all reform measures taken in Vienna were applied automatically to Milan, however. Italian remained the language of administration in all the Lombard territories as in the Trentino. Measures establishing military conscription in German-speaking districts were never applied in the Italian territories (Levy, 1988: 47ff).

Emperor Joseph II proved much more doctrinaire and radical than his mother in applying reforms to Catholic devotion. These were in part inspired by creeping Jansenist thought emanating from France, which belittled and scorned traditional Catholic devotion articulated around saints and theatrical ceremonies. Social elites held collective demonstrations of devotion to be a useless distraction from "true" religion. By the 1780s the state began to shut down convents and monasteries with small numbers of inmates. One drastic measure in 1786 simply abolished the majority of Milan's confraternities and reassigned their property to other public uses. One use was the creation of state-financed elementary schools with a mandate to encourage mass literacy, an idea borrowed from Bourbon Parma (Marchesini, 1992: 93–115). The Crown decreed that all future priests would have to receive their training at the University of Pavia, where the curriculum was established by theologians working for the state. They produced a Jansenist catechism for compulsory use in the empire. Before the decade was out, other sweeping measures stripped the altars of much of their finery. Crosses and images posted all over the city were removed or destroyed on the pretext that they obstructed traffic (Garrioch, 2004). As in Florence, there was no groundswell of public opinion pushing for changes in religious practice, and many of these measures were deeply resented.

The Habsburg reforms in Tuscany and Lombardy had important repercussions in the whole peninsula. In Modena, Francesco III d'Este launched his own drive for efficiency after 1748, to supervise city magistrates more closely and to curb feudal jurisdictions. In the late 1750s he established a Bureau of Sovereign Jurisdiction, aimed at reducing Roman influence. By 1764 the state had imposed restrictions on the publications of bishops, and ignored the Inquisition, until Duke Ercole III suppressed the tribunal outright in 1785. In 1764 the duke consolidated charities under state control. In the 1770s and again in 1787 the dukes and their advisers tried to convert money left for masses to public charities instead (Montecchi, 1986; Nicassio, 1992).

Bourbon Reforms after 1734

Southern Italy was far from the city-state zone of Italy in political and cultural matters. Naples was always the undisputed capital of the Mezzogiorno, with no other center emerging as a counterbalancing focus. Under the Bourbon King Charles, Naples would acquire a whole array of political and cultural monuments that would reflect the power and prestige of the monarchy: a palace, a proper court, resident ministers and ambassadors, a royal opera theater, a manufacturer of fine porcelains. Charles also received an army (largely Spanish) as a gift from his parents. This was not merely an instrument of domination, for he tried to attract Neapolitan aristocrats into its ranks as cadres (Maiorini, 1992; Rao, 1987). The optimistic reforms designed to bulk up this force, as in Piedmont, were always disappointing. Neither nobles nor commoners shared any great desire to serve in the somnolent garrisons along the south Italian coast.

Charles III proved in every way a conscientious ruler. The king's instrument for reform was a Tuscan law professor, Bernardo Tanucci, who was keen to increase the king's jurisdiction at the expense of churchmen and aristocrats. Many of the Neapolitan judges craved this stronger royal presence, which promised to raise their own profile over that of the other privileged groups (Maiorini, 2000). The king and Tanucci quashed an incipient uprising of pro-Austrian feudataries via a special tribunal, the Giunta d'Inconfidenza. Alongside the feudataries, Tanucci created two other "classes" of nobles in 1756, recognizing the noble status of non-feudataries living in cities on the one hand, and then elevating to noble status a number of families judged worthy of it as recognition for their services to the state. Despite this dilution of blue blood, the minister and his master emphasized the social primacy of the old nobility. Across Europe, states were attempting to foist a service ethic on well-born elites, and kings used their monopoly to confer nobility in order to widen the social classes at their service. Both the army and the court multiplied lucrative offices that rewarded docile visibility around the throne. With some lag with respect to other parts of Italy and Europe, the Bourbons successfully domesticated the once turbulent nobility of Naples and southern Italy (Montroni, 2000; Rao, 2000). Tanucci had considerable success with the kingdom's finances; blessed with population growth, a durable peace and a modicum of efficiency in government departments, he doubled state revenue while decreasing the relative weight of taxation. He obtained a concordat with Rome in 1741 that finally stemmed the expansion of the priests. The minister reflected Bourbon sensitivities in his mild anti-clericalism. Tanucci followed the anti-Jesuit tendencies of the other Bourbon monarchies and hounded them out of the kingdom in 1767, and then followed precedents elsewhere in Italy to abolish ecclesiastical mortmain between 1769 and 1771. King Ferdinand and his Habsburg queen, Maria Carolina, exploited a catastrophic earthquake in Calabria in 1783 to close down monasteries wholesale, and confiscated church lands in order to finance reconstruction.

Bernardo Tanucci had an even freer hand in determining policy after 1759, because King Charles departed to succeed his half-brother Ferdinand to the throne of Spain, leaving his adolescent son Ferdinand as king of Naples in his place. Tanucci retained this grip on power until Queen Maria Carolina bore Ferdinand an heir in 1775. She then elbowed Tanucci out of the way and replaced him in 1778 with a Jacobite naval officer from Tuscany, John Acton. Acton first became the minister of finance and commerce in 1782, and eventually chief minister in 1789. The cosmopolitan royal servant created a notable navy with its dockyards and arsenals in the course of a few years. He augmented the army by adding foreign units and officers, and buttressed the kingdom's fortifications. The Habsburg queen opened wide the door to the Freemasons in order to counteract the Spanish influence, and advanced members of the lodges to important positions at court. The later reforms resembled measures elsewhere in Italy in their attempt to curtail feudal autonomy. Tanucci's solution was to extend royal jurisdiction over every fief without a direct heir, and he ceased to confer fiefs on new houses when the old dynasties extinguished. The Crown was listening to proposals to abolish the feudal system entirely in the 1780s. In the 20 years after 1770, about a third of the kingdom's population reverted directly to royal jurisdictions (Rao, 2000).

In Sicily the Bourbons began their rule with the traditional light hand that had always characterized foreign monarchs. Spanish manners, customs, and dress were still part of daily life, and Spanish survived in official documents until the 1760s. In 1770 the barons exercised feudal jurisdiction in 280 out of 360 communities. Historians have been very harsh towards Sicilians who confided much more in tight patron–client relationships than in the power of the state to promote the common good. After a brief revolt in Palermo over the high price of bread in 1773, Ferdinand and Tanucci decided to disrupt this status quo, and to target aristocrats in particular for abuse of power. In 1781 Ferdinand dispatched Domenico Caracciolo, a moderate anti-clerical and Freemason long resident in Paris, to impose the Enlightenment on Sicilians. In 1782 he simply swept away the Spanish Inquisition. Caracciolo thought that privilege should only be compensation for public service. He simultaneously pruned back the number of officials on the payroll, and subjected the others to more frequent audits. The minister adopted a leveling trend against aristocrats that led many to believe, rightly, that he was undermining the traditional constitution of the island. As in Naples, the Crown began to suppress fiefs upon a rupture in succession, which announced a gradual elimination of the institution from the Mediterranean kingdom.

Conclusion

A half-century of ambitious reforms unsettled all of Italy by the time Napoleon Bonaparte's French armies invaded the peninsula in 1795. The population had increased from 13 million to about 18 million inhabitants over the century, but there is evidence that living standards were declining. Enlightenment administrations were by now preoccupied with economic matters. For a generation they had stabilized their currencies, multiplied new highways, abolished guilds, erected commercial tribunals with more expeditious procedures, promulgated the freedom of the grain trade, and encouraged other physiocratic reforms. The French and their satellite administrations supported the spirit of this reform legislation. Despite the diffuse confidence in social and economic progress, Italy lagged behind northwest Europe in popular literacy, in the transformation of its industries, and in the autonomy of its commerce. It had not recovered its relative standing in Europe lost during the Thirty Years War. We can perceive only the faintest glimmer of Risorgimento ideals of national unity and regeneration. That development belongs entirely to the nineteenth century.

Bibliography

Ago, R., *Carriere e clientele nella Roma barocca* (Rome, 1990).

Aretin, K. O. v., "Liordinamento feudale in Italia nel XVI e XVII secolo e le aue ripercussioni sulla politica europea," *Annali dell' Instituto Storico Italo-Germanico in Trento*, 4 (1978), 51–94.

Bizocchi, "Politica fiscale e immunità ecclesiastica nella Toscana medicea fra repubblica e granducato (secoli XV–XVIII)," in H. Kellenbenz and P. Prodi (eds.), *Fisco, religione, stato nell'età confessionale* (Bologna, 1989), 355–85.

Calabria, A., "Per la storia della dominazione austriaca a Napoli, 1707–1734," *Archivio Storico Italiano*, 139 (1981), 459–78.

Canosa, R., *Milano nel seicento: grandezza e miseria nell'Italia spagnola* (Milan, 1993).

Capra, C., "Riforme finanziarie e mutamento istituzionale nello stato di Milano: gli anni sessanta del secolo XVIII," *Rivista Storica Italiana*, 91 (1979), 313–68.

Carpanetto, D. and G. Ricuperati, *Italy in the Age of Reason 1685–1789* (Harlow, 1987).

Chadwick, O., *The Popes and European Revolution* (Oxford, 1981).

Cochrane, E., *Tradition and Enlightenment in the Tuscan Academies, 1690–1800* (Chicago, 1961).

Cochrane, E., *Florence in the Forgotten Centuries, 1527–1800* (Chicago, 1973).

Davis, J. C., *The Decline of the Venetian Nobility as a Ruling Class* (Baltimore, 1962).

Diaz, F., "L'Italie des princes éclairés," *Annales de l'Histoire de la Révolution française*, 51 (1979), 581–93.

Donati, C., "Esercito e società civile nella Lombardia del secolo XVIII," *Società e Storia*, 17 (1982), 527–54.

Fantoni, M., "Il bigottismo di Cosimo III: da leggenda storiografica ad oggetto storico," in *La Toscana nell'età di Cosimo III: atti del convegno di Pisa-San Domenico Fiesole, 1990* (Florence, 1993), pp. 389–402.

Fantoni, M., *La corte del granduca: forme e simboli del potere mediceo fra Cinquecento e Seicento* (Rome, 1994).

Ferraresi, A., *Stato, scienza, amministrzione, saperi: la formazione degli ingegneri in Piemonte dall'antico regime all'inità d'Italia* (Bologna, 2004).

Ferrone, V., "Tecnocratici militari e scienziati nel Piemonte dell'antico regime: alle origini della Reale Accademia delle Scienze ei Torino," *Rivista Storica Italiano*, 96 (1984), 414–509.

Gallo, F., "La Sicilia di Carlo VI: riforma amministrativa e ricerca del consenso (1719–1734)," *Cheiron: Dilattare l'impero*, 21 (1995), 187–226.

Garrioch, D., "Lay–religious associations, urban identities and urban space in eighteenth-century Milan," *Journal of Religious History*, 28 (2004), 35–49.

Georgelin, J., *Venise au siècle des Lumières* (Paris, 1978).

Grab, A., "Enlightened despotism and state-building: the case of Austrian Lombardy," *Austrian History Yearbook*, 19/20 (1983–4), 43–72.

Gross, H., *Rome in the Age of Enlightenment: The Post-Tridentine Syndrome and the Ancien Régime* (Cambridge, 1990).
Hanlon, G., *The Twilight of a Military Tradition: Italian Aristocrats and European Conflicts, 1560–1800* (London, 1998).
Hanlon, G., "In praise of refeudalization: princes and feudatories in north-central Italy from the sixteenth to the eighteenth century," in N. Eckstein and N. Terpstra (eds.), *Social Capital in Early Modern Europe* (Turnhout, 2007).
Levy, M. J., *Governance and Grievance: Habsburg Policy and Italian Tyrol in the Eighteenth Century* (West Lafayette, 1988).
Loriga, S., *Soldats. Un laboratoire disciplinaire: l'armée piémontaise au XVIIIe siècle* (Paris, 1991).
Lucacs, A. B., "Le 'universitates' meridionali all'inizio del regno di Carlo di Borbone," *Clio*, 17 (1981), 208–26.
Maiorini, G., "Nobilità napoletana e cariche amministrative: i presidi provinciale nel Settecento," in M. A. Visceglia (ed.), *Signori, patrizi, cavalieri in Italia centro-meridonale nell'età moderna* (Rome, 1992), pp. 309–25.
Maiorini, M. G., "The capital and the provinces," in G. Imbruglia (ed.), *Naples in the 18th Century: The Birth and Death of a State* (Cambridge, 2000), pp. 4–21.
Mannori, L., *Il sovrano tutore: pluralismo istituzionale e accentramento amministrativo nel principato dei Medici, secc. XVI–XVIII* (Milan, 1994).
Marchesini, D., *Il bisogno di scrivere: usi della scrittura nell'Italia moderna* (Rome, 1992).
Montecchi, G., "La censura di stato nel ducato estense dalle origni alla fine del Settecento," in A. Biondi (ed.), *Formazione e controllo dell'opinione pubblica a Modena nel '700* (Modena, 1986), pp. 23–49.
Montroni, G., "The court: power relations and forms of social life," in G. Imbruglia (ed.), *Naples in the 18th Century: The Birth and Death of a State* (Cambridge, 2000), pp. 22–43.
Mozzarelli, C., *Sovrano, società e amministrazione locale nella Lombardia teresiana (1749–1758)* (Bologna, 1982).
Nicassio, S. V., "For the benefit of my soul: a preliminary study of the persistence of tradition in eighteenth-century Mass obligations," *Catholic History Review*, 78 (1992), 175–96.
Niccolini, F., "Cosimo III de'Medici e Antonio Carafa," *Archivo Storico Italiano*, 96 (1938), 69–91, 180–225.
Nubola, "Supplications between politics and justice: the northern and central Italian states in the early modern age," *International History Review*, supplement 9, 46 (2001), 35–56.
Pansini, G., "Les Réformes de François-Etienne de Lorraine en Toscane (1737–1765)," in *La Lorraine dans l'Europe des Lumières: Actes du Colloque de Nancy, 24–27 octobre, 1966* (Nancy, 1968), pp. 359–66.
Pastor, F. L. v., *The History of the Popes from the Close of the Middle Ages*, vol. 32 (London, 1957).
Prodi, P., *The Papal Prince: One Body and Two Souls: The Papal Monarchy in Early Modern Europe* (Cambridge, 1987).
Pugliese, S., *Le prime strette dell' Austria in Italia* (Milanand Rome, 1932).
Quazza, G., *Il problema italiano e l'equilibreo europeo 172–1738* (Turin, 1938).
Rao, A. M., "Esercito e società a Napoli nelle riforme del secondo Settecento," *Studi Storici*, 28 (1987), 623–77.
Rao, A. M., "The feudal question, judicial systems and the Enlightenment," in G. Imbruglia (ed.), *Naples in the 18th Century: The Birth and Death of a State* (Cambridge, 2000), pp. 95–117.
Rosa, L. De, "Immobility and change in public finance in the kingdom of Naples, 1694–1806," *Journal of European Economic History*, 27 (1998), 9–28.

Sabbadini, R., *La grazia e l'enore: principe, nobilità e ordine sociale nel ducati farnesiani* (Rome, 2001).
Sabbatini, G., "Fiscalità e banditismo in Abruzzo alla fine del Seicento," *Nuova Rivista Storica*, 79 (1995), 77–112.
Simeoni, L., *L'assobimento austriaco del ducato estense e la politica dei duchi Rinaldo e Francesco III* (1919; Modena, 1986).
Storrs, C. D., *War, Diplomacy and the Rise of Savoy, 1690–1720* (Cambridge, 1999).
Storrs, C. D., "Imperial authority and the levy of contributions in 'Reichsitalien' in the Nine Years War (1690–1696)," in M. Schnettger and M. Verga (eds.), *L'Impero e l'Italia nella prima età moderna* (Bologna, 2005), pp. 241–73.
Symcox, G., *Victor Amadeus II: Absolutism in the Savoyard State, 1675–1730* (Berkeley, 1983).
Torre, A., "Politics clothed in worship: state, church and local power in Piedmont, 1570–1770," *Past & Present*, 134 (1992), 42–92.
Toscani, X., "Ecclesiastici e società civile nel '700: un problema di storia sociale e religiosa," *Società e Storia*, 17 (1982), 683–716.
Vittorio, A. di, "Ancora a proposito di storia della dominazione austriaca a Napoli, 1707–1734," *Archivio Storico Italiano*, 142 (1984), 607–22.
Waquet, J.-C., "La Toscane après la paix de Vienne (1737–1765): prépondérance autrichienne ou absolutisme lorrain?," *Revue d'Histoire Diplomatique*, 93 (1979), 202–22.
Waquet, J.-C., *Le Grand Duché de Toscane sous les derniers Medicis* (Rome, 1990).
Wilkinson, S., *The Defence of Piedmont, 1742–1748* (Oxford, 1927).
Zannini, A., "Un ceto di funzionari amministrativi: i cittadini originari veneziani, 1569–1730," *Studi Veneziani*, 23 (1992), 131–45.

Chapter Twenty

Iberia: Spain and Portugal in the Eighteenth Century

Christopher Storrs

The history of eighteenth-century Spain and Portugal has largely been overshadowed by that of earlier, apparently more heroic periods in the histories of both countries, and by that of other states in the eighteenth century. Yet both were once great states which – although in some respects dependent upon other states (Portugal on Britain, Spain on France) – had overseas empires to support them and were reviving in the eighteenth century. Both also experienced modernizing reform. The history of the two states also throws important light on some key eighteenth-century themes, including the nature of political power (and the reality of absolutism), relations between center and periphery, empire, nationhood, and (cultural) renewal and its impact on what were deeply Catholic states and their populations. In this latter connection, in addition, the experience of Spain and Portugal is relevant to the debate about the national or supranational character of what we call the Enlightenment. Understanding of these subjects has not been helped by the fact that, particularly in Spain, many of these issues have been approached in a partisan manner, with an eye to contemporary concerns and debates about the character of the state and the existence and nature of nationhood (Garcia Carcel, 2002).

Late Seventeenth-Century Spain

The period from the later seventeenth century and the first half of the eighteenth century (1665–1746) has long been a sort of Dark Ages of Spanish history, its neglect sharply contrasting with the attention paid to the second half of the eighteenth century. This eclipse owes much to the greater concern with explaining the collapse of the Spanish *antiguo regimen* from 1808, but also reflects a widely held view that the reign of the last Spanish Habsburg, Charles II (r. 1665–1700), was of little interest, representing as it did the culmination of the "Decline of Spain." This decline, which was to be measured by successive military setbacks and the loss of territories such as Portugal (1668), was attributed to a combination of, on the one hand, demographic loss, economic downturn in Spain (or rather in Castile, and a failure to shift the burden to a less depressed periphery), exhaustion of the silver of the Indies,

A Companion to Eighteenth-Century Europe, First Edition. Edited by Peter H. Wilson.
© 2014 John Wiley & Sons, Ltd. Published 2014 by John Wiley & Sons, Ltd.

and domestic political difficulties, including the physical and mental weakness of the king, Charles, and on the other hand of the recovery of France under Louis XIV. What kept the Spanish empire going, it is suggested, was less Spain's intrinsic strength, and more the intervention and support of its former enemies, above all England and the Dutch Republic.

However, this somber picture increasingly appears too bleak. Historians are now more alert to the nuances of Spain's situation, and to the role of Bourbon – and later enlightened – propaganda in creating a negative image of late Habsburg Spain as "decadent," and ripe for revival from 1700 under a new, more dynamic dynasty (MacKay, 2006). Revisionist historians have instead identified signs of recovery, even reform initiatives, under Charles II, which anticipated Bourbon measures. Above all, 1680 – and the monetary reform of that year – rather than 1700 has been suggested as the real turning point in a longer-term, secular cycle of improvement and renewal (Kamen, 1980). Others have challenged specific aspects of the decline thesis, including – rather controversially – the supposed collapse of the Indies trade and of silver remittances from Spanish America to metropolitan Spain (Morineau, 1985). It has been suggested, too, that the clash between center (Castile) and periphery (Aragon), exemplified in the revolt of the Catalans (1640–52) was followed by a period of greater consensus which also promoted stability and resilience. There is a danger that revisionist historians may paint too rosy a picture of Spain's situation at the close of the seventeenth century, but the Spanish empire handed on to his successor by Charles in 1700 was – apart from the loss of Portugal and pockets of Spanish Flanders – almost identical to that he had inherited in 1665 and in better shape than has usually been acknowledged (Storrs, 2006).

The War of the Spanish Succession

Nevertheless, 1700 was an important date, and was followed by major changes in the composition of the Spanish monarchy, in the relation between the parts of that empire, and in its government. The advent of the first Bourbon king of Spain, in the person of Louis XIV's grandson, the duke of Anjou, as Philip V (r. 1700–46), brought a monarch who was undoubtedly more charismatic, more dynamic, and more capable than his predecessor. Crucial, however, was the outbreak of the War of the Spanish Succession (1701–14), in which Bourbon France and Spain were pitted against the Grand Alliance of England, the Dutch Republic, and the Austrian Habsburgs and their allies (including Portugal). Although an international struggle, this conflict brought war to the heart of Spain itself, indeed civil war: aided – and in part impelled – by Philip's foreign enemies, and also giving expression to persisting tensions between the territories of the Crown of Aragon (Aragon, Catalonia and Valencia, and the Balearic Islands) and Castile, the former declared for Philip's Austrian Habsburg rival and future Holy Roman Emperor, Charles VI, "Charles III" of Spain.

The true extent and social distribution of support for "Charles III" in the Crown of Aragon is a matter of debate. Equally, some historians believe "Charles III" represented an alternative political model – less absolutist, more respectful of the distinctive political traditions of the Crown of Aragon – to Philip V. But whether Charles was genuinely committed to a more constitutional regime must be doubted. In any event, the viability of this alternative depended upon the support of Charles's allies, above all Britain. The withdrawal of that support from 1710, ensured the collapse of his challenge to Philip V by 1713–14 (Albareda, 2002).

Philip's success owed a great deal to the military, naval, and financial support given by his grandfather, Louis XIV (Kamen, 1969), commencing a theme of French influence running through the history of eighteenth-century Spain (Kuethe and Blaisdell, 1991). French financiers, administrators, soldiers, and others played a major part in Spain's war effort and in the overhaul of Spanish institutions to 1714. However, while acknowledging the role of French individuals and ideas, historians have perhaps neglected the role of Philip's reform-minded Spanish ministers, men like Jose de Grimaldo and Melchor de Macanaz, and an atmosphere – evident in 1700 – which hoped for change (Castro, 2004). Historians, preoccupied with the impact of the War of Spanish Succession on the Crown of Aragon have also failed to acknowledge fully the contribution of Philip's Castilian subjects to his ultimate victory. But nor can we ignore that of Philip's other non-Castilian territories in Iberia, Navarre and the Basque Country, which are too often overlooked by those who see the periphery as meaning primarily, or only, the Aragonese territories, and which retained significant autonomy within the post-war Spanish state .

The reconquest of the Aragonese territories, which began in 1707 with the pivotal victory at Almansa, allowed Philip to suppress the distinctive Aragonese political system, characterized by the so-called *fueros*. This further enabled the king to integrate those territories more effectively into a more obviously Castilian state, a development encapsulated in the so-called *Nueva Planta* (New System) imposed on Catalonia in 1716 and which apparently solved the problem of Castilian–Aragonese relations which had dogged Habsburg Spain. Spain was also, arguably, on the way to becoming a nation-state. Further, the succession struggle reshaped its empire. On the one hand, the territories in Italy and Flanders, which had long been integral parts of the monarchy, had been lost (as had Gibraltar and Menorca); on the other hand, Philip retained the Americas, which now – and more obviously than before – defined Spain's overseas empire.

This "Castilianized" polity was much more "absolutist" in ethos and practice than its Habsburg forerunner, and reflected the French political model of administrative – rather than the traditional Spanish model of judicial – monarchy. Many of the councils which characterized Habsburg government, which advised the king and functioned as tribunals, disappeared with the territories for which they were responsible; even those which survived – notably the Council of Castile – found their powers and responsibilities curtailed in favor of the emerging French-style secretariats of state (Castro, 2004).

These developments had important consequences for the nobility, which approximated to perhaps 10 percent of the total population. Individual greater nobles (grandees) and *titulos* (titled nobles) fell foul of the new regime and, collectively, lost formal political power. However, they retained social pre-eminence and the grandees remained important, if informal, patrons and powerbrokers. As for the untitled nobles, the *caballeros* and *hidalgos*, they continued to find opportunities in the state structure, the rise of an administrative nobility paralleling the eclipse of the grandees. Other privileged groups continued to play a key role: much of Bourbon Spain was still under only the indirect control of the Crown. Royal authority was mediated by

– among others – ecclesiastical bodies, including (as in Portugal) the distinctive military orders, and myriad feudal lords.

Spain's Resurgence after 1713

The quarrel between Philip V and "Charles III" continued until 1725 when the latter finally recognized the former. Philip had hopes of the French throne, and resented the territorial losses and trade concessions, including the grant of the *asiento* and related privileges to Britain, forced on him in 1713. The precise focus of Spain's revanchist ambitions (which did not extend to Flanders) was also influenced by the fact that Philip's second wife, Isabel Farnese, had dynastic claims in Italy and wished to press these on behalf of her sons, Charles and Philip, because the throne of Spain would pass to Philip's sons by his first wife, Marie Louise of Savoy. Contemporaries and historians have rightly acknowledged Isabel's role in the shaping and execution of Spanish policy in these years, but more recent historians have questioned the extent of her influence.

These ambitions ensured that, for more than 30 years following the Peace of Utrecht, Spain was the single greatest threat to peace in Europe. In 1735, during the War of the Polish Succession, Philip and Isabel's eldest son Charles was installed as king of Naples and Sicily, following the Spanish conquest of those territories. These developments ensured the revival of Spain as a major power in the (western) Mediterranean, and above all in Italy, where some welcomed the return of the former imperial power. During the War of the Austrian Succession, which was preceded by the opening of hostilities with Britain in the West Indies (from 1739), Spanish forces recovered possession of the duchy of Milan, and secured the duchy of Savoy for Philip and Isabel's younger son, Philip. However, this proved to be the high tide of Spain's recovery in Europe: the war ended with Spain failing to retain either Milan or Savoy, although the young Philip received Parma and Piacenza.

This remarkable revival of power and influence within a generation of the end of the War of the Spanish Succession owed something to external factors, including the relative weakness of Spain's neighbors and enemies: both Britain and France faced succession problems. But Spain's success also rested on a remarkable domestic achievement. A succession of able ministers – including José Patiño (1670–1736), a contemporary of Walpole and Fleury who has not attracted the attention he merits – presided over a major overhaul of the army and the navy. The transformation of the former included the creation of a large standing force in Spain itself, its continued modernization, and the overhaul of the Castilian militia in 1733. The army also benefited from the development of more effective administrative and financial support, including a network of French-style provincial *intendants* (Clonard, 1851–9). As for the navy, the fleet was increased, its bases reorganized, and better provision made for recruiting crews (via the so-called *matricula de mar*, a registration scheme modeled on that of France) and for supplying the fleet (McNeill, 1985).

This transformation of Spain's armed forces also rested upon achievements in other spheres, including a remarkable growth of royal revenues. In 1739 Philip was effectively forced to declare bankruptcy, but Spain was perhaps better able to carry the burden of his ambitions in view of the apparent recovery of the population, and the fact that the economy, too, was in better shape. Nor can we ignore the continued contribution of Spanish America, which in 1738 reportedly contributed 3 million pesos to a total royal income of 16 million. No other European state – except perhaps Portugal (see below) – received so much from its overseas territories. Not entirely surprisingly, however, the continued demand for money and men for war had important domestic political consequences. Despite these remarkable successes, royal exploitation of Spain's resources in pursuit of what some subjects did not regard as essential Spanish interests provoked some resentment: a "Spanish party" expressed hostility towards Isabel and the Italians and other foreigners she favored (Egido Lopez, 1968, 1971).

The death of Philip V apparently closed those so-called "Dark Ages" mentioned earlier. In fact, however, the reign of his immediate successor, Ferdinand VI (r. 1746–59) also remains under-researched, although it was one of some significance, witnessing an important shift of focus in foreign policy away from Europe and towards the Atlantic. The reign also saw a number of important reforms, including the concordat with Rome of 1753, which further extended the authority of the Crown over the Spanish church, promoting the regalist agenda. Other measures included the first steps towards the overhaul of the complex fiscal system, and the assumption by the state of a greater role in tax collection. Both developments are associated with Ferdinand's chief minister, the marquis of Ensenada, who ordered a census – invaluable to the historian – in 1749. Ensenada was dismissed in 1754, but for some the reforms of Ferdinand VI anticipated – and were more radical in impulse and implication – than those of his half-brother and successor, Charles III (r. 1759–88).

Charles III, Enlightenment, and Reform

Charles III's reign coincides with the flowering or peak of the Enlightenment, although Spain's relationship to that movement has provoked some debate. Earlier historians, both those who took a positive view of the movement and those (Spanish historians) for whom the Enlightenment was a pernicious development, emphasized the extent to which the Spanish Enlightenment was a foreign import, drawing on and inspired by French influences. There is undoubtedly some truth in this. More recently, however, historians have noted the native sources of Enlightenment, emphasizing the importance of a group of so-called *novatores*, active before 1700, in promoting experiment-based knowledge and understanding in medicine, history, and other disciplines (Mestre Sanchis, 1998). A leading exponent of this new approach was the Benedictine monk Benito Feijoo. Typically, in his *Teatro critico universal* (1727–39) and *Cartas eruditas* (1742–60), Feijoo pitted Newtonian ideas against Aristotelian scholasticism. A separate development was the founding of new cultural institutions, some of them private initiatives which were subsequently institutionalized by the Crown, and including the Royal Academy of History (1737). The Crown also sponsored an expedition to Peru in 1735, whose findings (published in 1748) represented another Spanish contribution to contemporary scientific advances. While acknowledging the contribution of new thinking in the eighteenth century and showing greater regard for questions of gender (Smith, 2006), historians are now more sympathetic to the continued influence of older, Spanish traditions and writers (including the so-called *arbitristas* of the seventeenth century) on the Spanish

Figure 12 Goya, *El motin de Esquilache.* The rioting in Madrid against the reforms associated with the royal minister, Esquilache, mixed conservative opposition to change with popular grievances at high prices. © *Institut Amatller d'Art Hispànic, Barcelona*

Enlightenment. At the same time, and reflecting the persistence of distinctive peripheral cultures, just how uniformly "Spanish" the Enlightenment in Spain was is a matter of debate: Gregorio Mayans, who retired to his native Valencia and from there urged the improvement of historical scholarship, represented a distinctive contribution to the study of Spain's Enlightenment, one in part inspired by nostalgia for the earlier suppression of the Crown of Aragon's separate identity (Lluch, 1999).

These new currents provided the backdrop to Charles III's reforms. Charles arrived in Spain in 1759 with extensive previous experience of reform and its difficulties, as king of Naples (and Sicily) since 1735. He also brought with him some of the Neapolitan ministers who had implemented that reform program. These included Leopoldo de Gregorio, marquis of Esquilache, who was effectively Charles's chief minister in Spain for the first years of his reign. For many historians, the reforms of these years make Charles an exemplar of the distinctive approach to reform known as enlightened despotism. Spanish reforms certainly embraced many of the areas reformed by other enlightened despots, although it is arguable that there was a distinctive emphasis on measures to stimulate economic development, associated particularly with the count of Campomanes and his circle (Llombart, 1992). Typical of this concern was the attempt to liberalize or "free" trade within Spain and its empire (see below). However, the efforts to liberalize the grain trade prompted widespread anxiety about the price of bread, which precipitated serious rioting in Madrid and elsewhere in the spring of 1767. Charles III was forced to flee his capital, and to dismiss Esquilache, in what was probably the most serious threat of revolution from below faced by any monarchy in western Europe before the French Revolution (Vilar, 1972).

Whether the rioting (at least in Madrid) was really "popular" has long divided historians. A commission of inquiry identified – deliberately and probably wrongly – the Jesuits as the secret, organizing hand, and in 1767 they were expelled from Spain and the Indies, furthering another important strand of the reform program, religious reform (Andres-Gallego, 2003). Influenced by Campomanes, reform continued: in the army, education, and in popular culture and entertainment – enlightened opinion was, for example, generally hostile to bullfighting. Further efforts to stimulate the economy included the construction of new roads, new towns, created in the Sierra Morena (Andalucia), and further liberalization of imperial trade. In their efforts to stimulate reform, ministers sought to mobilize provincial elites through the so-called Economic Societies, another example of a private initiative taken up by the Crown (Shafer, 1958; Windler, 1992).

Some question Charles III's enlightened, reforming credentials, observing that his priority appeared to be the army and war (Equipo Madrid, 1988). For others, the attack on the Jesuits and other ecclesiastical powers and practices was little more than a continuation of a traditional regalism which was about royal authority rather than enlightenment. Some doubt the validity in late eighteenth-century Spain of the concept of enlightened despotism. For them, the schism between authority and the reformers was confirmed by the fact that Charles allowed the Inquisition to arrest and condemn one of the most radical of his reform-minded ministers, the Peruvian Pablo de Olavide, *intendente* of Seville. Historians also disagree about the extent to which Spain had been transformed by Charles III's death, and about the degree of alienation from the absolute monarchy of those who had expected, and wanted, further and more radical reform: some believe Charles passed on to his successor a Spain transformed, modernized, and stable; others only see the failure of reform and growing disillusionment. Those inclined to this latter view can point to the fact that Spain remained an overwhelmingly Catholic society, and to the growth of a critical periodical press in the 1780s, including *El Censor*, whose editor fell foul of the Inquisition (Sanchez Blanco, 2002).

Spanish America

Recent decades have seen a remarkable flowering of Atlantic studies. Curiously, however, much of that work ignores the fact that the Atlantic and Caribbean remained very much a Hispanic – indeed, an Iberian – space. For Spanish America, or the Indies – the term preferred by Spanish writers – the accession of Charles III meant more than that of Philip V. For some historians, the seventeenth century witnessed a shift in the balance of power within Spain's empire at the expense of the authority and real power of king and ministers in Madrid, and in favor of the creole elites in the Indies; a process of "Americanization" which ensured that much of the wealth of the Indies remained there. There is much in these arguments, but we should not be misled into thinking that the Indies were slipping away from Spain. Sums spent locally on defense ensured that the Indies remained Spanish. Nor should we think of the creole elites of Spanish America as wanting independence. Nevertheless, the Indies retained by Philip V in 1713 probably did enjoy greater autonomy than a century earlier.

After 1713, Philip sought to reinvigorate the system of controls whereby Spain monopolized trade with the Indies. In 1717 Patino removed the Casa de la Contratación, the local body which oversaw the monopoly, from Seville to Cadiz, the real seat of the trade since *c.*1680 and in 1720 his *Proyecto Real* (Royal Project) proposed reorganizing the Habsburg system of regular *flotas* and *galeones* linking Cadiz to selected ports in the Indies, though the scheme was not entirely successful (Walker, 1979). The new commercial companies were rather more successful and contributed to Spain's growing colonial trade. Mercantilist writers such as Geronimo de Uztariz and Jose Campillo y Cossio forcefully reiterated the view that the colonies existed for the benefit of Spain. It was not only commerce which attracted attention. There was also growing recognition in Spain of the need for administrative reform to ensure more effective defense in the Indies. This found expression in the creation of the viceroyalty of New Granada (in 1717 and, after that proved abortive, again – and permanently – in 1739) carved out of that of Peru.

These changes paralleled important developments within Spain's American empire, which continued to expand throughout the eighteenth century, as the king's agents pushed northwards into California and elsewhere. Among the most striking internal changes was the rise of New Spain, or Mexico, and the eclipse of Peru. The two viceroyalties increased their combined silver production from 8.3 million pesos in 1700 to 33 million in 1800, but Mexico was by then by far the most important source. Other developments followed from this. By 1790 Mexico City was one of the largest cities of the Spanish empire, and the largest in North America.

Nevertheless, the Spanish Indies remained vulnerable. This was dramatically demonstrated during the Seven Years War when Havana, linchpin of the Spanish Caribbean, fell in 1762 to the British. Havana was restored at the peace, but the episode triggered an overhaul of the imperial system, what has been called the "second conquest" or "second empire," a process closely associated with the conde de Galvez. New administrative units were created, including viceroyalties, captaincies general, and intendancies and (in the 1780s) a network of provincial *intendants* was established. Equally important, fewer offices were sold to creoles in the second half of the eighteenth century, more so-called *peninsulares* (from Spain) benefiting instead. In addition, a permanent Army of America was established, and the colonial militias developed, recruits being attracted by the grant of military privilege, although historians disagree about the impact and significance of these changes, and their contribution to the long-term militarization of Latin America and its politics. To fund these reforms, new taxes were introduced. Some trade-off was necessary, Charles and his ministers seeking to buy support for their innovations (Kuethe and Inglis, 1985). Nevertheless, the additional burden caused resentment and contributed to riots, including those which erupted at Quito (Peru) in 1765, and to the Tupac Amaru revolt (Peru) in 1780, the most serious Indian uprising since the sixteenth century. Another important target of reform in the Indies was the church, over which the Crown sought greater control.

The Indies were an integral part of the efforts to liberalize the Spanish economy. Essentially, the object was to promote freer trade, but still excluding non-Spaniards, effectively creating a Spanish imperial free-trade area. The first liberalization (allowing more Spanish and Spanish American ports to participate in the trade) occurred in 1765, the second (bringing more ports into the scheme) in 1778. These were important developments, although the impact on the volume of trade is a matter of debate. Nevertheless, it now seems clear that trade boomed, in part reflecting the general prosperity of Spanish America: between 1778 and 1796 exports from Spain to America grew by 400 percent and exports from America to Spain by more than 1,000 percent. In many respects, reflecting the persistence of traditional ideas (in Spain) about the relationship between the colonies and the metropolis, the composition of that trade was little changed. The proportion represented by precious metals fell but remained substantial, accounting for more than 75 percent of total exports to Spain from Peru *c.*1780.

The origin of these imperial reforms, and the impact, both of reform and of the Enlightenment, on Spanish America is a matter of debate. Recent historians have suggested that the reforms were less deliberate and structured than a largely eulogistic historiography implies. As for the impact, poor funding meant that corruption continued, stimulating discontent with the quality of public administration by those affected. More important, and equally contentious, is the extent to which Enlightenment and reform transformed attitudes towards Spain (Aldridge, 1971; Whitaker, 1942). Spanish America, with its nascent press, Economic Societies, and other reforming bodies, was fully connected with the Spanish Enlightenment, and through it with the broader European Enlightenment. For some historians, however, the Enlightenment stimulated a growing rejection by the local elites of inefficient, irrational Spanish rule, and the emergence of a local – even "nationalist" – loyalty, rather than one embracing the empire as a whole. This is by no means clear-cut, and the opposite may have been the case: the Peruvian and Mexican elites were essentially conservative, and remained attached to Spain. Revisionist historians also doubt whether the reforms gave the creoles greater confidence, such that they were readier to throw off the Bourbon yoke after Napoleon's ousting of the Bourbons in Spain in 1808. We should also beware of seeing the discontents around 1780 as anticipating events around 1820, and as indicating an underlying, more fundamental, inclination towards independence. Most creoles appear to have responded to the intensification of absolutism after 1763 with a sullen acceptance of the need for closer imperial control as the price of economic growth and social stability.

The French Revolution and the Origins of 1808

Just why the Bourbon monarchy collapsed in 1808 is, inevitably, a matter of debate. For some, the accession of Charles IV (r. 1788–1808) followed by the French Revolution, transformed Spain's prospects, undermining a society which had not been seriously weakened by the Enlightenment into one which was divided and critical of absolute monarchy. Others see Spain as already at odds with itself before 1789. Charles IV's reign was initially characterized by reaction, designed in part to exclude the threat from across the Pyrenees. Charles joined the First Coalition against revolutionary France, but soon reverted to the more traditional eighteenth-century pattern of alliance with France against Britain. This proved disastrous for Spanish sea power and imperial communications, cutting the revenue stream from America, undermining the absolute monarchy – and with it the entire *antiguo regimen*. The curtailment of the revenues from the Indies, just as Spain was engaged in a costly war, prompted the raiding of ecclesiastical property from 1798. This measure, superficially in accordance with the findings of the reformer Gaspar Melchor de Jovellanos's *Report on the Agrarian Law* (1795), was in fact less a measure of "enlightened" reform than part of an attempt to underpin government credit and the war effort at the expense of the church (Herr, 1989). The disruption of communications with America prompted the opening of the Indies trade to foreign neutrals in 1797.

War and its demands further undermined the stability of Spanish political life, resulting in the coup of 1808 whereby Ferdinand VII overthrew the discredited royal favorite, Godoy (and Charles IV himself). This was followed later that year by Napoleon's installation of his brother, Joseph Bonaparte, on the Spanish throne instead of Ferdinand, and the extension of the supposed benefits of the French Revolution to Spain in the form of the Constitution of Bayonne. Spain and its empire disintegrated in a series of provincial revolts, among whose long-term consequences was the near-dissolution of Spain's American imperium. The latter is, inevitably, a subject of debate, some historians emphasizing the positive aspirations of the creoles, others the failure of Spain and the Spaniards to reassert metropolitan authority in the overseas colonies. Which of these two was more important, not surprisingly, varied from one part of the vast Spanish American empire to another, and with time.

Portugal

Portugal's "long eighteenth century" stretches from 1668, when Spain finally acknowledged Portuguese independence, to 1807, when the king fled to Brazil following a French invasion, or even to the liberal revolution of 1820 and the declaration of independence by Brazil in 1825. In many respects, the history of this period reveals a similar pattern of interest and neglect to that of Spain. The period 1668–1755 has been neglected, particularly by Portuguese historians, in favor of the supposedly national war of "Restoration" before 1668, and the era after 1755 as the prelude to the collapse of the Portuguese *ancien régime* from 1807. The neglect is more pronounced, perhaps because the country has been generally regarded as of less importance even than Spain throughout the eighteenth century. And yet Portugal remained an important imperial state, and the efforts of reformers, both before and after 1755, merit greater attention than they have hitherto attracted.

The reigns of the two Braganza monarchs during and after the War of Restoration – John IV (r. 1640–56) and Afonso VI (r. 1656–68) – witnessed a remarkable process of state rebuilding, with the emphasis on security. The extensive and often impressive fortifications dating from this period still dot the Spanish–Portuguese frontier. But the restored Portuguese state remained a corporate one, in which the Crown was not all-powerful, nor sought to be such (Hespanha, 1998). More important, victory over Spain owed a great deal to the latter's commitments elsewhere, and to the aid given by Spain's other enemies, notably the United Provinces, England, and France. In return, those states demanded extensive privileges for their merchants in Portugal, privileges which in some respects hindered Portuguese efforts to maximize trade and customs revenues. One means of overcoming Portugal's difficulties was to exploit and develop its own economic resources, as was attempted by the third count of Ericeira, "the Portuguese Colbert," although the results were patchy (Hansen, 1981).

In fact, Portugal remained small and weak, not least vis-à-vis Spain, and continued to depend upon the support of more powerful foreign allies, above all England (Britain after 1707), which valued Lisbon as an anchorage for its fleet and merchant shipping en route to and from the Mediterranean. This political connection contributed to the growing English taste for "port wine" from northern Portugal. In 1703, as part of Portugal's entry into the War of the Spanish Succession against Philip V of Spain, King Pedro II (r. 1683–1706) confirmed – in the so-called Methuen Treaty – the privileges of the English merchants in Portugal in return for equally privileged access to the English market for Portugal's port wine and British help against Spain (Francis, 1966). In succeeding decades British merchants exploited their position to entrench themselves, and so gain illegal access to Portugal's monopoly trade with Brazil, and the gold needed for Britain's trade with the east.

Remarkably, during and after the War of Restoration the Portuguese had managed to retain, and recover, much of their overseas empire. This was less evident in the east, where the former "State of India" was greatly reduced, and continued to contract in the face of local (notably the Omani and Maratta challenges) into the eighteenth century. Nonetheless, Portugal retained Goa and Macão, while its African possessions supplied a profitable trade in slaves with the Americas. Most important, however, the Portuguese recovered Brazil, with its lucrative plantations, from the Dutch, underpinning a marked shift in the structure of the Portuguese overseas empire in favor of Brazil. The discovery there, at Minas Gerais, of gold in 1694, followed later by diamonds, further confirmed Brazil's enormous value (hitherto founded on sugar and tobacco), and underpinned much of the prosperity of early eighteenth-century Portugal (Russell-Wood, 2000). It also allowed the king to rule without grants from the Cortes, thus underpinning royal absolutism. Pedro II and his successor, John V (r. 1706–50), made serious efforts to ensure that this new wealth benefited Portugal and its Crown, but leakage (notably through smuggling) was inevitable. In consequence, Portugal functioned as a conduit for Brazilian gold to reach the rest of Europe, and did not itself fundamentally benefit from this new wealth.

The importance of diplomacy, and of foreign contacts, had a profound impact on some among Portugal's political, social, and cultural elite. The latter, sometimes called *estrangeirados* by those who thought them too influenced by foreign attitudes and models, included Luis da Cunha, Portugal's minister at the Utrecht peace congress (1713), and the fourth count of Ericeira. Ericeira was a leading patron of new ideas, and a member of various informal, private discussion groups, including the Academia dos Ilustrados. He was also director of the Royal Academy of History, founded in 1720 by John V, and a member of the Royal Society of London. These men and their associates contributed to the diffusion in Portugal of the ideas of Newton and other foreigners. Martinho de Mendonça de Pina Proenca, a former governor of Minas Gerais and associate member of the Royal Academy of History, wrote a treatise on education (1734), which was influenced by Locke and Fénelon. Dr. Jacob de Castro Sarmento, a Jewish doctor who fled Portugal in 1721, and who hoped to propagate more enlightened ideas there, began a translation of Bacon's *Novum Organum* as a contribution to the reform of medicine in Portugal. He also translated into Portuguese essays by Newton. Antonio Nunes Ribeiro Sanches was another Jewish doctor who fled Portugal, in 1726, to escape the Inquisition; after studying at Leiden under Boerhaave and serving as court physician in Russia he settled in France, contributing an article on venereal illnesses to Diderot's *Encyclopedia*. He, too, continued to write and publish in Portuguese. Newtonian ideas also reached Portugal through the work of Luis Antonio Vernei, a member of the Order of the Oratory, which had established itself in Portugal after 1640. The real influence and significance of the *estrangeirados*, always a small minority, remains a matter of debate (Cardozo, 1971). Like Spain, Portugal remained fundamentally Catholic, but the new ideas may have had some impact: between 1715 and 1755 trials for sorcery and witchcraft peaked, not least because, infiltrated by university-trained physicians and surgeons, the Inquisition was – in what might be thought of as a "modernizing" way – pursuing popular healers (Walker, 2005).

Perhaps the most successful of the *estrangeirados* was Sebastião Jose de Carvalho e Melo, marquis of Pombal (1699–1782), a protégé of the fourth count of Ericeira. Pombal's ascent to the position of chief minister of King Joseph I (r. 1750–77) was confirmed by his response to the devastating earthquake which struck Portugal in 1755. It killed about 15,000 people in the capital, Lisbon, alone, about 10 percent of its total population, and also destroyed thousands of dwellings as well as many of the records necessary to reconstruct the history of Portugal before 1755. Pombal played a key role in rebuilding the capital along more "modern" and rational lines following this major catastrophe.

As unrivaled chief minister thereafter, Pombal carried out wide-ranging reform which in many respects echoed "enlightened" innovation elsewhere. However, just how he fits into the Enlightenment is a matter of debate (Maxwell, 1995). It is difficult to regard him as truly "enlightened," particularly in view of his intolerance of opposition: his fall was followed by the release of about 800 "political prisoners," men who had crossed him. Subsequently, and particularly in Portugal itself, those of Pombal's reforms which reduced the authority and influence of the church – and above all his persecution of the Jesuits (see below) – ensured that he became a hero for nineteenth-century liberals who sought to reduce clerical power, and that he was demonized by, above all, the Jesuits and their supporters. In his own day Pombal's character and regime impressed themselves on a wider European public, and in some respects provided a model for reformers outside Portugal.

In part prompted by an economic downturn from the 1750s, and a slump in revenues from Brazil, where gold production fell dramatically (Russell-Wood in Bethell, 1987), Pombal sought to stimulate Portugal's commerce, and to reduce its dependence on Britain (Maxwell, 1968). He hoped to achieve this with the creation of a Board of Trade and of a number of monopoly companies to trade with and develop the Brazilian interior (1755), to control port wine production and export (1756), to handle Brazil's sugar exports (1759), to carry on the trade of Mozambique, and to revive the fishing industry of the Algarve (1773). The efforts to develop Brazil were resisted by the Jesuits, who particularly opposed government policy towards the native Indians. Armed resistance was followed by the expulsion of the Jesuits from Portugal and its empire in 1759. This helped provoke a breach with the Papacy between 1760 and 1769, during which a regalist ideology underpinned the extension of secular, state control over ecclesiastical institutions in Portugal. The censorship was transferred in 1768 from the control of the Inquisition to a new royal body, the Real Mesa Censoria. Reform also affected education: a business school was established in Lisbon in 1759 (Rodrigues et al., 2004), and a college in 1761 for the training of young nobles. The curriculum of Portugal's leading university, Coimbra, was modernized in 1772, a measure which attracted the interest of reformers abroad, including Campomanes. Steps were also taken to make government more effective, including the establishment in 1761 of a single central treasury. The army, whose shortcomings were exposed by defeat in the Seven Years War, was overhauled by the count of Schaumburg-Lippe, one of many foreigners who contributed to the process of Enlightenment and reform in Pombaline Portugal. In many respects, these reforms represented an epoch-making bid for full sovereignty by the royal state, fracturing an older political model (Hespanha, 1998). However, as with so many of the changes decreed by the enlightened despots, we still do not know enough about the real impact of Pombal's reforms.

The death of Jose I and the accession of his more conservative and orthodox daughter, Maria I (r. 1777–1816), triggered the fall of Pombal and the abandonment or reversal of some of his reforms, though by no means all, not least because of the continued political influence of key collaborators of the fallen minister, including Jose de Seabra da Silva. In 1779 the duke of Lafoes promoted the foundation of the Royal Academy of Science, whose published *Memorias economicas* sought to stimulate agricultural and other improvement (Hespanha, 1998), and in 1790 there began a process of administrative reform (Nogueira da Silva, 1998). At the same time, Portugal's foreign trade benefited from the involvement of other states in the American War of Independence and French Revolutionary Wars, which increased Portugal's value as a supplier of cotton to Britain, for example. These developments, the growth of the press and of a reading public, and the further spread of other Enlightenment institutions and values, including Freemasonry from the 1760s, all contributed, particularly following the French invasion and the flight of the royal family to Brazil (1807), to the weakening of Portugal's *ancien régime*.

The collapse of that regime included the loss of Brazil. The most effective means of governing Brazil had been under discussion for some time, exemplified by Rodrigo de Souza Coutinho's report of 1798 on this subject (Mansuy-Diniz Silva in Bethell, 1987). Brazilian independence, like that of Spanish America, owed something to the cutting of links with the metropolis from 1807, as well as the association of the Brazilian elite with the broader Enlightenment through cultural and educational links with Portugal. These influences contributed to a growing resentment of control from Portugal among some of that elite, a mood which found expression in a number of abortive plots, including the so-called Inconfidencia Mineira (1789) and Revolucão dos Alfaiates (1798) (Alden in Bethell, 1987;

Russell-Wood, 1998). The significance of these conspiracies, and the extent of their support, is debated, but they undoubtedly presaged the final break of 1825 (Alden in Bethell, 1987; Maxwell, 1973).

Bibliography

Spain

Aguilar Pinal, F., *La España del absolutismo ilustrado* (1991; Madrid, 2005).

Albareda, J., *Felipe V y el triunfo del absolutismo: Cataluña en un conflicto europeo (1700–1714)* (Generalitat de Catalunya, 2002).

Andres-Gallego, J., *El Motin de Esquilache, America y Europa* (Madrid, 2003).

Brading, D., "Bourbon Spain and its American empire," in L. Bethell (ed.), *The Cambridge History of Latin America*, vol. 1: *Colonial Latin America* (Cambridge, 1984), pp. 112–62.

Brading, D., *The First America: The Spanish Monarchy, Creole Patriots, and the Liberal State 1492–1867* (Cambridge, 1991).

Castro, C. de, *Campomanes: estado y reformismo ilustrado* (Madrid, 1996).

Castro, C. de, *A la sombra de Felipe V: Jose de Grimaldo, ministro responsible (1703–1726)* (Madrid, 2004).

Clonard, conde de, *Historia organica de las armas de infanteria y caballeria españolas* (16 vols., Madrid, 1851–9).

Colloquio Internacional Carlos III y su Siglo (2 vols., Madrid, 1998).

Cruz, J., *Gentlemen, Bourgeois and Revolutionaries: Political Change and Cultural Persistence among the Spanish Dominant Groups 1750–1850* (Cambridge, 1996).

Egido Lopez, T., *Prensa clandestina española del siglo XVIII: "El Duende Critico"* (Valladolid, 1968; 2002).

Egido Lopez, T., *Opinión publica y oposición al poder en la España del siglo XVIII (1713–1759)* (Valladolid, 1971; 2002).

Equipo Madrid, *Carlos III, Madrid y la ilustración* (Madrid, 1988).

Fernandez, R. (ed.), *España en el siglo XVIII: homenaje a Pierre Vilar* (Barcelona, 1985).

Fisher, J. R., *Bourbon Peru, 1750–1824* (Liverpool, 2003).

Garcia Carcel, R., *Felipe V y los Españoles* (Barcelona, 2002).

Herr, R., *The Eighteenth Century Revolution in Spain* (Princeton, 1958).

Herr, R., *Rural Change and Royal Finances in Spain at the End of the Old Regime* (California, 1989).

Kamen, H., *The War of Succession in Spain 1700–15* (London, 1969).

Kamen, H., *Spain in the Later Seventeenth Century 1665–1700* (London, 1980).

Kuethe, A. J. and Blaisdell, L., "French influence and the origins of the Bourbon colonial reorganisation," *Hispanic American Historical Review*, 71 (1991), 579–607.

Kuethe, A. J. and Inglis, G. D., "Absolutism and enlightened reform: Charles III, the establishment of the Alcabala, and commercial reorganization in Cuba," *Past & Present*, 109 (1985), 118–43.

Llombart, V., *Campomanes, economista y politico de Carlos III* (Madrid, 1992).

Lluch, E., *Las Españas vencidas del siglo XVIII: claroscuros de la ilustración* (Barcelona, 1999).

Lynch, J., *The Spanish American Revolutions 1808–1826* (London, 1973; 1986).

Lynch, J., The institutional framework of colonial Spanish America," *Journal of Latin American Studies*, 24 (1992), 69–81.

McNeill, J. R., *Atlantic Empires of France and Spain: Louisbourg and Havana 1700–1763* (Chapel Hill, 1985).

MacKay, R., *"Lazy, Improvident People": Myth and Reality in the Writing of Spanish History* (Ithaca and London, 2006).
Mestre Sanchis, A., *La ilustración española* (Madrid, 1998).
Morineau, M., *Incroyables gazettes et trésors merveilleux* (Cambridge, 1985).
Noel, C., "Charles III of Spain," in H. M. Scott (ed.), *Enlightened Absolutism: Reform and Reformers in Eighteenth-Century Europe* (Basingstoke, 1990), pp. 119–43.
Ringrose, D., *Madrid and the Spanish Economy 1560–1850* (Berkeley, 1983).
Rodriguez, L., "The Spanish Riots of 1766," *Past & Present*, 59 (1973), 117–46.
Rodriguez O., J. E., *The Independence of Spanish America* (Cambridge, 1998).
Sanchez Blanco, F., *El absolutismo y las luces en el reinado de Carlos III* (Madrid, 2002).
Sarrailh, J., *La España ilustrada de la segunda mitad del siglo XVIII* (Mexico, 1957).
Shafer, R. J., *The Economic Societies in the Spanish World 1763–1821* (Syracuse, 1958).
Smith, T. A., *The Emerging Female Citizen: Gender and Enlightenment in Spain* (Los Angeles, 2006).
Stein, S. J. and B. Stein, *Silver, Trade and War: Spain and America in the Making of Early Modern Europe* (Baltimore, 2000).
Stein, S. J. and B. Stein, *Apogee of Empire: Spain and New Spain in the Age of Charles III, 1759–1789* (Baltimore, 2003).
Storrs, C., *The Resilience of the Spanish Monarchy 1665–1700* (Oxford, 2006).
Velasco Moreno, Eva, *La Real Academia de la Historia: una institución de sociabilidad* (Madrid, 2000).
Vilar, P., *La Catalogne dans l'Espagne moderne* (Paris, 1962).
Vilar, P., "El 'motin de Esquilache' y las 'crisis del antiguo regimen'," *Revista de Occidente*, 107 (1972), 119–249.
Walker, G. J., *Spanish Politics and Imperial Trade 1700–1789* (London,1979).
Weber, D., *Barbaros: Spaniards and their Savages in the Age of Enlightenment* (New Haven, 2005).
Whitaker, A. P., et al., *Latin America and the Enlightenment* (New York, 1942).
Windler, C., *Lokale Eliten, seigneurialer Adel und Reformabsolutismus in Spanien (1760–1808)* (Stuttgart, 1992).

Portugal

Alden, D., *Royal Government in Colonial Brazil, with Special Reference to the Administration of the Marques of Lavradio, Viceroy 1769–79* (Berkeley, 1968).
Alden, D. *The Making of an Enterprise: The Society of Jesus in Portugal, its Empire, and Beyond, 1540–1750* (Stanford, 1996).
Aldridge, A. O. (ed.), *The Ibero-American Enlightenment* (Urbana, 1971).
Andrade Arruda, J. J. de, et al., "Decadence or crisis in the Luso-Brazilian empire: a new model of colonization in the eighteenth century," *Hispanic American Historical Review*, 80 (2000), 865–78.
Bethell, L. (ed.), *Colonial Brazil* (Cambridge, 1987).
Boxer, C., *The Golden Age of Brazil, 1695–1750* (Los Angeles, 1962).
Boxer, C., *The Portuguese Seaborne Empire, 1415–1825* (London, 1969).
Cardozo, M., "The internationalism of the Portuguese Enlightenment: the role of the *estrangeirado*, *c*.1700–*c*.1750," in A. O. Aldridge (ed.), *The Ibero-American Enlightenment* (Urbana, 1971), pp. 140–210.
Cavaliero, R., *The Independence of Brazil* (London and New York, 1993).
Ferreira Carrato, J., "The Enlightenment in Portugal and the educational reforms of the marquis of Pombal," in J. A. Leith (ed.), *Studies on Voltaire and the Eighteenth Century*, vol. 167 (Oxford, 1977), pp. 359–93.

Fisher, H. E. S., *The Portugal Trade* (London, 1971).
Franca, J.-A., *Une ville des lumières: La Lisbonne de Pombal* (Paris, 1965).
Francis, A. D., *The Methuens and Portugal (1691–1708)* (Cambridge, 1966).
Francis, A. D., *Portugal, 1715–1808: Joanine, Pombaline and Rococo Portugal as seen by British Diplomats and Traders* (London, 1985).
Godinho, M., "Portugal and her empire, 1680–1720," in J. S. Bromley (ed.), *The New Cambridge Modern History*, vol. 6: *The Rise of Great Britain and Russia 1688–1725* (Cambridge, 1971), pp. 509–40.
Hansen, C., *Economy and Society in Baroque Portugal 1668–1703* (Minneapolis, 1981).
Hespanha, M. (ed.), *O Antico Regime (1620–1807)* (Lisbon, 1998).
Maxwell, K., "Pombal and the nationalisation of the Luso-Brazilian economy," *Hispanic American Historical Review*, 48 (1968), 608–31.
Maxwell, K., "Pombal: the paradox of enlightenment and despotism," in H. M. Scott (ed.), *Enlightened Absolutism: Reform and Reformers in Later Eighteenth Century Europe* (London, 1990), pp. 75–118.
Maxwell, K., *Pombal: Paradox of the Enlightenment* (Cambridge, 1995).
Maxwell, K., *Conflicts and Conspiracies: Brazil and Portugal 1750–1808* (Cambridge, 1973; reissued London, 2004).
Nogueira da Silva, A. C., *O modelo espacial do estado moderno: reorganizacão territorial em Portugal nos finais do Antigo Regime* (Lisbon, 1998).
Oliveira Marques, *History of Portugal* (2nd edn., New York, 1976).
Rodrigues, L. L., D. Gomes, and R. Craig, "The Portuguese School of Commerce, 1759–1844: a reflection of the 'Enlightenment'," *Accounting History* (2004), 53–71.
Russell-Wood, A. J. R., *The Portuguese Empire 1415–1808: A World on the Move* (Baltimore, 1998).
Russell-Wood, A. J. R., "Holy and unholy alliances: clerical participation in the flow of bullion from Brazil to Portugal during the reign of Dom João V (1706–1750)," *Hispanic American Historical Review*, 32 (2000), 815–37.
Schwartz, S. B., *Sovereignty and Society in Colonial Brazil* (Los Angeles, 1973).
Schwartz, S. B., "Brazil: ironies of the colonial past," *Hispanic American Historical Review*, 80 (2000), 681–94.
Shaw, L. M. E., *The Anglo-Portuguese Alliance and the English Merchants in Portugal, 1654–1810* (Aldershot, 1998).
Viana Pedreira, J. M., "From growth to collapse: Portugal, Brazil and the collapse of the old colonial system (1750–1830)," *Hispanic American Historical Review*, 80 (2000), 839–64.
Walker, T. D., *Doctors, Folk Medicine and the Inquisition: The Repression of Magical Healing in Portugal during the Enlightenment* (Leiden, 2005).

Chapter Twenty-One

France

Michael Rapport

Defining "France"

During the revolutionary discussions on the reshaping of France, the comte de Mirabeau said that old regime France had been not so much a unitary state as a loose aggregation of disunited provinces. The eighteenth century had seen France acquire a shape which was closer to its recognizably modern outline. The ever-vulnerable northern frontier with the Spanish Netherlands (which, after 1713, became Austrian) remained ragged and porous as before, but the most important annexations of the eighteenth century included Lorraine, which passed over to France in 1766 on the death of Stanisław Leszczyński, the deposed king of Poland who, as father-in-law of Louis XV, had been given the duchy after the War of the Polish Succession (1733–5). A further addition came in 1768, when Genoa, honoring an old debt to France, ceded Corsica. By 1789, France had some 60 provinces of varying size, in which privilege was entrenched in varying strength. Successive monarchs tried to neutralize these rights and created administrative units called *généralités* to impose taxation directly. These never succeeded entirely in sidestepping the power of provincial institutions, nor in eliminating recent memories of provincial autonomy. Moreover, there were enclaves within the kingdom which were still controlled by foreign princes, most notably in the south, where Avignon and the Comtat Venaissin were still ruled by the pope, while in the northeast the German princes of the Holy Roman Empire had enjoyed some sovereignty and jurisdiction over their territories in Alsace since its annexation by France in 1648. Ecclesiastically, France had 135 bishoprics, while juridically the kingdom was split between the south, which lived under the Roman legacy of written law, and the north, which was split into 60 "General Customs" or varieties of customary law. There was also a broad linguistic divide, by which the north spoke the *langue d'oïl* and the south the *langue d'oc* (both named after the way local people said "yes"). Within these regions, there was a rich variety of local dialects, or *patois*, and on the peripheries, the people spoke non-French languages such as a form of German in Alsace, Flemish in the far north, Breton in lower Brittany, Basque in the furthermost southwestern corner, and Catalan in Roussillon.

A Companion to Eighteenth-Century Europe, First Edition. Edited by Peter H. Wilson.
© 2014 John Wiley & Sons, Ltd. Published 2014 by John Wiley & Sons, Ltd.

Economically, too, the kingdom was split into internal customs zones as well as different areas for the *gabelle*, the tax on salt, which offered lucrative, if dangerous, career opportunities in smuggling (Jones, 1995). While the revolutionaries of 1789 displayed little patience for this apparent morass of practices and customs, many of those who benefited from the complex map of local rights and corporate privileges protested vehemently when they were destroyed in the tumultuous session of the National Assembly on August 4, 1789.

Interpretations

Since the revolutionaries leveled the old regime so dramatically, it is scarcely surprising that in 1856 Alexis de Tocqueville could muse: "the Ancien Régime, so near to us in time, but overshadowed so completely by the Revolution" (Tocqueville, 1966). Although the term *ancien régime* was coined in 1789 to mean the "old order," it was soon used to castigate a system which needed the wrecking-ball of the revolution so that a modern, unitary France could emerge from the debris. The decades prior to 1789 can easily be seen as an era in which the *ancien régime* fumbled its way towards its inevitable demise. As historians simultaneously enjoy the benefits and navigate the difficulties presented by hindsight, there is the temptation to focus on the failures of the old order, since its fate is common knowledge. Not everyone has agreed with this approach. De Tocqueville himself was adamant that the attitudes, mentalities, and practices which characterized the modern world were less the creatures of the French Revolution than continuities from the prerevolutionary epoch, but naturally he still explores the actual *collapse* of the old order. Most modern historians, while not denying that the old regime permitted the play of economic, social, and cultural change, are finally compelled to emphasize the constraints which it imposed on them (Godechot, 1965). This is especially true of historians labeled (not always accurately) as "Marxists," who suggested that the old regime economy was dynamic enough to produce a prosperous, self-confident bourgeoisie, but that in the end the restrictions imposed by a state and a society dominated by the aristocracy prevented this burgeoning class from realizing its potential. In this view, the antagonism which thus arose between the bourgeoisie and the nobility was the primary cause of the French Revolution. Yet from the 1960s this interpretation was battered by a barrage of criticism from "revisionist" historians, who questioned the established assumptions about old regime society and politics. While the debate which raged over the next two decades or more focused on the origins of the French Revolution, the research stimulated by it has encouraged a reassessment of *ancien régime* society itself. Weighing up the strengths and weaknesses of the old order, François Furet concludes that, "far from being reactionary, or imprisoned by self-interest, the monarchic state in the eighteenth century was one of the foremost agents of change and progress – a permanent building-ground for 'enlightened' reform" (Furet, 1996). Peter Jones has gone further and, like de Tocqueville, emphasized the continuities between the reforming efforts of the *ancien régime* and the early achievements of the revolution (Jones, 1995). Yet other historians insist eighteenth-century France was more than just a prologue to the revolutionary epic, and try to see the period in its own terms. Colin Jones points out that for much of the century "politics would be conducted not at all in the anticipation of the Revolution of 1789 – as historians sometimes blithely assume – but in dialogue with Louis XIV's reign" (Jones, 2002).

The Absolute Monarchy

Louis XIV died in 1715, having ruled in person since 1661 and leaving behind a political and cultural legacy which would dominate the reigns of his two successors – Louis XV and Louis XVI – until the absolute monarchy itself crumpled in 1789. The "Sun King" had sought, with some success, to apply the theories of absolute monarchy to his kingdom. Louis' ideas of government were heavily influenced by the sixteenth-century theorist of sovereignty, Jean Bodin, and by others, including his tutor, Bishop Jacques-Bénigne Bossuet, who argued that royal authority was sacred, paternal and absolute (Baker, 1987a: 32). Yet there was also a hard, pragmatic reason to argue that the king's will was law. Louis was deeply marked by his childhood experiences during the political turmoil of the Fronde, the great aristocratic rebellion of the mid-seventeenth century. He and many of his subjects believed that there was no alternative to an overarching sovereignty which, expressed in strong, centralized government, could hold at bay the destructive forces of religious and political dissension, social unrest, and foreign invasion (Sturdy, 1998). It was for this reason, as well as his deeply held personal convictions, that led Louis to insist on religious uniformity. Some 90 percent of French people were Catholic, but to Louis, religious minorities like the Protestants (Huguenots) and Catholic dissenters like the Jansenists were dangerous because they allegedly subverted the unity of the kingdom. Under Louis XIV, the church's efforts to tighten its grip on French religious life was a way of reinforcing royal attempts to ensure domestic peace and stability. Most dramatically of all, in 1685 Louis revoked the Edict of Nantes, which had theoretically protected the rights of Protestants since 1598. The close alliance between the French church and the king was expressed in the dispute between Louis XIV and the pope over the Gallican rights, whereby the kings of France, in return for paying annates to Rome, had the right to nominate French bishops and to draw on the income from vacant benefices. When Louis tried to apply these rights to the newly annexed regions and confiscated church property to finance his wars, the pope protested. The king eventually yielded in 1693, but not before the General Assembly of the French clergy issued the Gallican Articles in 1682, which denied papal infallibility, upheld the rights of the French church, and declared that the pope had no authority over the king in secular affairs, and that in spiritual matters papal rulings were subject to the agreement of a general council. In the compromise of 1693 these articles were withdrawn, but Gallicanism remained a potent political force in the eighteenth century.

At Versailles, the king made his decisions with the advice of his councils, the most important of which was the Conseil d'en Haut, to which the king invited his most trusted advisers – ministers of state – to discuss royal policies. The royal will was enforced in the provinces by the *intendants*, officials whose recent origins dated back to the early seventeenth century, but who had much older antecedents. In the 1670s, Louis XIV began the practice of attaching one *intendant* to each *généralité*, of which there were 36 by 1789. The *intendant* was appointed by the controller general (the king's finance minister) from among the elite of the legal profession. Once in their *généralité*, an *intendant* was meant to fulfill a very wide remit, such as encouraging economic development, ensuring a fair and swift collection of taxation, overseeing local government, justice, and civil–military relations, and maintaining law and order. In this gargantuan task he was served by local assistants, or *subdélégués*; he reported directly to the king's ministers, and could, if need be, call in the army. Yet despite being vested with royal authority, the *intendants* could not function without the cooperation of the local elites, and so had to proceed with care. As an instrument of royal power, however, the *intendants* grew to rival the provincial governors, who were drawn from the great noble families, but who in 1776 saw the basis of their power – military recruitment – cut away by the reorganization of the kingdom into new military zones.

Louis XIV and his successors never became absolute monarchs in the sense that they were able to destroy all legal and political institutions which restricted their power, level the entrenched privileges of the nobility, the clergy, the provinces, and towns and suppress their subjects. Even in theory, absolutism had its limits. The king was, at least, answerable to God. Bossuet himself declared that royal authority was "subordinated to reason," meaning that it could not be the instrument of "passion or caprice," but had to work for the benefit of the nation whose care was entrusted to the monarch (Baker, 1987a). The king was also bound by the "fundamental laws," which he promised to observe on his coronation. These included the Salic law of succession (by which only the king's direct male heirs could ascend the throne) and the rule that the king must be a Catholic (dating to the coronation in 1594 of Henri IV, whose conversion from Protestantism to Catholicism helped end the Wars of Religion). In addition, the king was also meant to adhere to Christian principles, defend the Catholic Church, extirpate heresy, protect his subjects, and keep them in peace and prosperity. In other words, he was not to be a capricious tyrant (Swann, 2001). The problem was that there was no clear legal demarcation between what constituted a just, "absolute" monarchy and what was to be considered "despotic" or tyrannical: even the "fundamental laws" were never written down in any legal document. This meant that the legal limits to royal power were open to debate, an "open frontier . . . rather than an immovable defensive wall" (Sturdy, 1998).

Royal initiative was blunted by the fact that even the king's own administrators were not a professional civil service in the modern sense. Rather, in the practice of venality, the cash-hungry Crown sold life-term offices to raise money from its richest subjects, who bought positions for their personal enrichment and social advancement. Financial posts allowed their holders to make a profit from collecting royal taxes and paying them out for government purposes. These "tax farmers" behaved not as civil servants but as private businessmen, not only handling money on behalf of the Crown, but also lending money drawn from their profits to the royal treasury (Bosher, 1970). Judicial offices conferred social prestige and privileges such as tax exemptions. The highest offices for sale carried titles of nobility. The problem was, of course, that, since office-holders actually owned their positions, the Crown lost direct control of the post. Despite periodic attempts to reduce the number of venal offices, these efforts were partial, such as the abolition of the purchase of military offices on the eve of French intervention in the American War of Independence. There was never any systematic attempt to make a clean sweep of venality: it was simply too lucrative a source of royal income (Doyle, 1996). It meant, however, that no matter how prosperous France might become, the government lacked the structures to enable it to benefit from the nation's wealth.

The Crown's power was also restrained by plethora of law courts, provincial assemblies, municipalities, and local and personal privileges which remained intact even under Louis XIV, whose reign is held to be the high tide of "absolutism" in France (Cobban, 1963). Even Louis XIV recognized that to level all these would be to alienate too many vested interests and that he would struggle to control his kingdom without their acquiescence. Among the most important of these interests were the *parlements*, of which by 1789 there were 13, as well as four "sovereign councils" which enjoyed similar powers. All these bodies were supreme courts of appeal in their respective jurisdictions. By far the most prestigious and most powerful was the *parlement* of Paris, which heard appeals from no fewer than 164 lower courts extending over about a third of the French kingdom. In addition to their judicial functions, they oversaw matters relating to public order (including the all-important grain trade) and municipal government, and they heard appeals from church courts. They were also pivotal in limiting royal power since they had a legislative role, which was to ensure that no royal decree contradicted existing laws, including the "fundamental laws" and provincial privileges. Royal edicts had to be registered by the *parlements* before they became legal, since the supreme courts were held to be the depositories of the law. Prior to registration the judges had the right to issue "remonstrances," which pointed out problems with the royal decree. Louis XIV managed to nullify this right in 1673, but it was restored on his death. The king could impose his will through a ceremony called the *lit de justice* (literally, "bed of justice," after the divan upon which the king sat), in which he (or, in the provinces, the royal governor) appeared in the *parlement* and, after listening to the magistrates' objections, declared the edict registered. Yet such a display of royal power could inflame the *parlement* and (in the later eighteenth century) public opinion, so it was not to be undertaken lightly. Yet the fact that even a monarch as powerful as Louis XIV did not abolish the *parlements* altogether suggests that the Crown accepted the constructive role which they played in legislation. The registration of an edict gave the new law a legitimacy which a simple decree would not. For most of the century the *parlements* did not seek to weaken royal power, but to ensure that it acted within the framework of the laws. So while there were periods of severely disruptive political conflict between the king and the *parlements*, for most of the time they worked together in a "symbiotic relationship" (Campbell, 2006; Swann, 2001).

Besides the *parlements*, at the end of Louis XIV's reign some provinces still had estates, which were assemblies representing the three orders: the clergy, the nobility, and the "third estate," which in practice meant the towns and *communautés*, which were gatherings of villages. The provinces which retained estates (the *pays d'états*) were all on the periphery of the kingdom and were, therefore, strategically too important to be alienated by any heavy-handed centralization. The most important power they enjoyed was the right to negotiate the taxes directly with the Crown and to distribute the burden. In practice these provinces were more lightly taxed than the other two-thirds of the kingdom, the *pays d'élection*, where money was collected directly by the Crown.

France as a Great Power, 1715–1789: Continental Commitments and Global Ambition

During his personal reign, Louis XIV fought no fewer than four major wars. Apart from his own apparently unquenchable thirst for glory and his often outrageous manipulation of dynastic claims, Louis also haphazardly struggled to secure the Spanish throne for his immediate family and sought to reduce the strength of the Habsburgs in Europe. He flexed French muscle on both military and commercial fronts. For Jean-Baptiste Colbert, trade was nothing less than a "perpetual war" between rivals over who should control most of it. In mercantilist style, Colbert believed that the world's wealth was finite, so the government should seek, through strong state intervention, to encourage commerce and manufacturing. Wealth – measured above all in bullion – would be attracted into the kingdom at the expense of its foreign rivals. By enriching his subjects, the king hoped that they would support a heavier tax burden. Louis indeed imposed extraordinary taxation on his subjects, and while much of it targeted the rich, the poor suffered too. The famine of 1693–4 and the vicious winter of 1708–9, which reduced the French population respectively by 10 and 4 percent, came in the middle of Louis' two final, disastrous wars, those of the League of Augsburg (1689–97) and of the Spanish Succession (1701–14). French overseas imperialism was linked to French entanglements in Europe. Colbert hoped to wrest control of as much as possible of the lucrative colonial commerce from France's maritime rivals, especially the Dutch and the English/British. While not obvious at the time, Louis XIV had committed France to a dual "amphibious" role – global and maritime on the one hand, continental and military on the other.

When the Sun King died, his heir was his 5-year-old great-grandson, who was entrusted to the Regent, Philippe duc d'Orléans. Besides steering a short-lived experiment in consultative government, the Polysynodie, Orléans' time at the helm provided much-needed military restraint and financial retrenchment (Shennan, 1972). An unsuccessful challenge by one of Louis XIV's illegitimate sons, the duc de Maine, supported by Spain, brought France briefly into conflict with its southern neighbor in 1718–19, but otherwise the regency was a period of international peace for France. Remarkably, it was characterized by a rapprochement with Britain and the Netherlands, both of whom in 1717 sealed an alliance with France, lasting until 1731. When Orléans died in 1723, Louis XV, who reached his majority at the tender age of 13, declared that he wished to rule personally, but in 1726 the reins were taken by the aged but energetic Cardinal André Hercule de Fleury. Over the next 17 years the king's first minister worked hard to ensure that France enjoyed international peace and domestic stability. Fleury could not avoid involvement in the War of the Polish Succession, since the emergence of Russia as a great European power endangered France's eastern allies of Poland and the Ottoman empire. Yet for France this new conflict was not on the same disastrous scale as Louis XIV's conflagrations. With British and Dutch neutrality, France could concentrate all its efforts on the continent, and at the conclusion Fleury secured the promise of Lorraine on Stanisław Leszczyński's death.

The War of the Polish Succession would be the only eighteenth-century conflict in which the French managed to concentrate solely on the continent. Despite Fleury's misgivings, France entered the War of the Austrian Succession (1740–8), because other French ministers saw an opportunity to weaken the Habsburgs. Fleury died in 1743, at last signaling the true beginning of Louis XV's personal rule. That year, the renewal of the Franco-Spanish "Family Compact," first signed in 1733, brought France into direct conflict with Britain, which had been waging a maritime war against Spain since 1739. What had started for France as a continental war now became an imperial struggle. Until then, France had tacitly accepted British naval superiority, but with imperial rivalries intensifying, particularly in North America, the French had to expand their navy. The growing importance of the overseas empire to the French Crown is suggested by the fact that, at the peace signed at Aix-la-Chapelle (1748), Louis XV returned French conquests in the Low Countries in exchange for territory lost to the British in America. France and Britain were now at the forefront of a European arms race, made all the more expensive because it enveloped not only armies, but navies as well. Between 1745 and 1785, the French fleet expanded from 98 men-of-war to 268, as against the British, whose navy grew in the same period from an already impressive 235 to a truly awe-inspiring 447. It was a contest which, combined with its continental commitments, France would find hard to sustain.

The peace after Aix-la-Chapelle was no more than a truce – and fighting erupted between British and French colonists in America well before the official outbreak of the next war in Europe itself. This Seven Years War (1756–63) was preceded by the

Figure 13 Major units of the French navy in their principal Atlantic base at Brest. © *Musée de la Marine, Paris, France/Lauros/Giraudon/The Bridgeman Art Library*

"Diplomatic Revolution" with profound repercussions for the French monarchy. The French, abandoned by their erstwhile Prussian allies, now signed a defensive alliance with Austria intended to provide France with security in Europe and so permit concentration on the global struggle with Britain. The war did not work out that way. Not only were they sucked into a major war – and defeat – in Europe, but they also tried to sustain a considerable war effort overseas, with disastrous consequences. At the peace treaty in Paris, France lost virtually all of its territory in Canada and India. These shattering blows intensified public hostility toward the Austrian alliance (Blanning, 1986). This rebounded sharply on the public image of the monarchy, with public ire turning with special virulence on Maria Theresia's daughter, Marie Antoinette, who married the Dauphin (heir to throne) in 1770.

Nonetheless, the alliance did ensure peace in Europe for France while it was engaged in the next great conflict: the American War of Independence. There was an irony to absolutist France intervening on the side of the American republican rebels in 1778. Yet there were compelling motives: a war of revenge against the British would please public opinion; victory would restore a global balance between France and Britain, which might form the basis of a lasting peace; and there was hope that France would reap the commercial dividends of an alliance with an independent American republic. The war was militarily successful, but there were serious fissures beneath the polished surface. Although it was not immediately obvious, the cost of the war had brought French finances close to bankruptcy. Moreover, the French had been successful in the American war because, in an inversion of their involvement in the War of the Polish Succession, they had no campaigns to fight in Europe, and so could concentrate all their resources on the conflict overseas. The eighteenth-century wars, therefore, exposed the central problem which France faced as a global power. France had both maritime ambitions and heavy continental commitments, and while it could successfully prosecute one or the other, it could not pursue both simultaneously without running the risk of defeat on all fronts. Finally, the financial pressures exerted by the almost endemic warfare of the century and the reactions of public opinion ensured that Bourbon foreign commitments would ricochet into domestic politics. Yet there were home-grown issues as well. In the first half of the century, one of the most important of these was a controversy over Jansenism.

Politics and the Jansenist Controversy

Jansenism was named for the bishop of Ypres, Cornelius Jansen, whose propositions in *Augustinus* (1640) argued in a manner similar to that of Calvinism that man could not be saved by good deeds and religious observance, but only by God's grace, which is granted only to an elect few. Good works and piety were a means of showing that one was one of the elect, but they were not the path to salvation. Its apparent similarities to Protestantism and its preaching that political institutions were reflections of human, not divine, will alarmed Louis XIV, who pressed the pope to act. Eventually, in 1713, the Papacy issued the bull *Unigenitus*, which declared Jansenism to be heretical. This condemnation would set Louis XIV's successors on a collision course not only with a vocal minority of the French clergy, but also with the *parlement* of Paris.

In 1717 a group of French bishops and some 3,000 clerics, "appealed" against the papal bull, demanding that it be referred to a general council of the Catholic Church. The implication that papal religious authority should be subject to a temporal assembly outraged Pope Clement XI, who excommunicated the "appellants" in 1718. Yet in France the issue was not just about a conflict between Jansenists and anti-Jansenists. For many in the French clergy and in the political establishment, *Unigenitus* attacked the independence of the Gallican church – and both the alleged "heresy" and Gallicanism found staunch defenders within the *parlement* of Paris. While Jansenists were a minority amongst the clergy and magistrates, the defense of the Gallican church against an apparently overbearing Papacy broadened the appeal of their cause. There were two major disputes: one starting under Fleury in the late 1720s, the other under Louis XV in the 1750s. The Paris *parlement* took center-stage in both. There were never more than 15–20 lawyers in the court (out of a full complement of 250) who were actually Jansenist, but they shrewdly used wider jurisdictional and constitutional arguments to rally the other jurists to their cause. Attempts to defrock clerics who did not adhere to *Unigenitus* angered the *parlement*, which heard appeals from such priests and which was protective of its jurisdiction in these matters. The enforcement of the papal bull also appeared to ride roughshod over Gallican liberties – and the *parlement* pointedly reiterated the Gallican Articles during the dispute in the 1720s. Government heavy-handedness against Jansenists sometimes ignored the *parlement*'s legislative role, which aroused the magistrates' ire. The religious quarrel, in other words, spilled over into constitutional issues, in which the *parlement* expressed its opposition to the Crown in terms of its role as the depository of public authority, representing the interests of the nation, and referring to the "constitution" of the kingdom. During the crisis of the 1750s the *parlement* hurled some heavy rhetorical missiles at the king, claiming to be defending the fundamental laws of the kingdom, speaking of the "constitution," and insisting that the *parlements* were one body, a "unique and universal parlement" (Swann, 1995). The disputes also brought ordinary people into politics: Jansenism took root in Paris, reaching into artisanal households, as well as those of nobles and bourgeois. Jansenist propaganda appealed to the "people" as the incorrupt arbiters in their struggle against their persecutors – the Jesuits and the orthodox (*dévots*) (Farge, 1994).

The Jansenist and Gallican *parlementaires* scored the last victory in the sectarian dispute when, in 1762, they dissolved the Jesuit order in France. Louis XV himself belatedly ratified the measure in 1764 and at a stroke removed one of the bitterest enemies of Jansenism. The Jansenist triumph meant, however, that the debate now focused increasingly on the constitutional issues rather than the religious schism. In this process, oppositional ideas of more recent, Enlightenment, vintage emerged as great sources of inspiration, yet they inhabited the same constitutional language used by the Jansenists (Van Kley, 1996). Although more radical ideas circulated in the shape of Rousseau's *Social Contract* (1762), the most influential political writer prior to the revolution was probably Montesquieu, whose *De l'esprit des loix* (1748) was one of the most widely read books of the century. A *parlementaire* himself, he argued that the best form of monarchy was one in which royal power was restrained by acting through intermediate bodies. It was an idea which the French public would take very seriously. The new controversies were based on questions of finance, which in turn were rooted in the mounting cost of France's foreign policy commitments.

Politics and Finance

The deficit left from Louis XIV's wars, amounting to 2,000 million livres in 1715, had saddled his successors with a burden of debt which they never managed to shake off, not least because of involvement in no fewer than five international conflicts up to 1789. These fresh conflicts overburdened the royal debt and precipitated the old regime's collapse in the late 1780s. Yet there was no linear, inexorable increase in the deficit between 1715 and 1789. For one, there were finance ministers (controllers-general) whose careful management periodically succeeded in reducing the debt. For another, the eighteenth century saw impressive economic growth. Textiles expanded, and by the 1780s, leaps had been made in metallurgy. French manufacturing hit a serious crisis in that decade, not least because of the ravages of British competition brought by a free trade treaty signed in 1786. Yet overall, the eighteenth century witnessed the early emergence of a rational French choice in competing for international markets: the emphasis on high-value, luxury goods such as silks, fashions, cabinets, and coaches, as well as the perennially popular French wine and brandy. The most dynamic area of French economic activity was overseas commerce, which more than tripled between 1716 and 1787. Within that figure, French colonial trade, mostly with the slave plantations in the Caribbean, increased tenfold. Between the 1720s and 1780s, the value of French seaborne trade increased from 50 percent of that of England and Wales to 80 percent (Crouzet, 1990; Félix, 2001; Goubert, 1973; Heywood, 1992).

Despite the dynamism of important economic sectors, however, French society remained solidly agrarian. Here, too, there were areas of development, particularly in the Paris basin, where the large urban population encouraged the expansion of large-scale farms growing food for the market. French agriculture as a whole just managed to keep up with the burgeoning population (which after 1715 recovered from the disasters of the previous century and grew by a third, from 21.6 million to 28.6 million by 1789). This was achieved by an extension of the land under cultivation. Nonetheless, the price of bread alone may have consumed as much as half of a landless rural laborer's wages in a good year, while in times of harvest failure that proportion rose to close to 90 percent, leaving little money for anything else. For the majority, standards of living remained stagnant at best, and while starvation was slowly becoming a nightmare of the past, periods of poor harvests still spelled misery for much of the population. Rural poverty had important implications for tax-raising: as economic theorists after the mid-eighteenth century argued, a poor peasantry made a poor kingdom. The peasantry were saddled with paying the tithe to the church, as well as a range of dues owed to the lord of the manor (*seigneur*). In addition to these financial and material burdens, the state also reaped its share through a range of direct and indirect taxation (Jones, 1988). While it is now clear that the tax burden was no worse (and indeed may have been lighter) than that imposed on the poor in Britain, in France peasant grievances were compounded by an awareness that those most able to pay – the nobles, the bourgeois landowners, and urban corporations – had fiscal privileges which, while not exempting them from all taxation, meant that they sacrificed proportionately less (Jones, 2002; Markoff, 2006). The government was well aware of these discrepancies, and royal attempts to address them were at the root of many of the political controversies that dogged relations between the king, the nobles, and the clergy in the eighteenth century.

The first experiment involved the smooth Scottish financial shaker John Law. Reversing Colbert's ideas, Law argued that it was not the amount of precious metals amassed by the government that mattered, but rather the boost given to trade, which could just as easily be oiled by paper money as by precious metals. Between 1716 and 1719 Law opened a bank, which issued banknotes (becoming the only legal tender in the country), and a joint-stock business trading with the vast French territory of Louisiana. The state's creditors were encouraged to convert the money owed to them by the government into company shares, thus liquidating the monarchy's debt. The scheme was immensely popular at first, and Law was made controller general in 1720. Yet the system began to overheat and news of a famine in Louisiana boded ill, while those financiers who were now excluded from handling the government's money connived to shatter public confidence in it – and shatter it did. The value of the shares, which had reached dizzying heights, plummeted as the system went from boom to bust in a matter of months, and Law fled the country. Royal debts had initially been reduced, but the mess afterwards left three times the original liabilities. Fortunately, peace and the natural growth of the French economy allowed the state to recover from the fiasco, which had a contemporary British parallel in the South Sea Bubble of 1720 (Murphy, 1997). Politically, the failure of the Law system brought a deep layer of the population into direct contact with the vagaries of government finance, through financial investment, political pamphlets, cartoons, and broadsheets: it was an early exercise in the politicization of public opinion.

After the War of the Polish Succession, the careful management of skilled controllers-general, such as the hard-nosed Philibert Orry between 1730 and 1745, allowed some recovery in the state finances. Moreover, between the two great Jansenist controversies of the early 1730s and the 1750s, relations between the Crown and the *parlements* were relatively peaceful. In 1749 the Paris *parlement* registered an edict for a peacetime tax, the *vingtième*, or 5 percent levied on all incomes, even those of nobles and (initially) the clergy. The controller general who introduced this new tax, Machault d'Arnouville, also established a sinking fund to reduce the state deficit. Nonetheless, inadequate revenue failed to cover the full cost of the War of the Austrian Succession, which added some 719 million livres to the debt. Military expenditure now represented nearly half of government expenditure, compared to a third during the peaceful 1720s. In both decades, much of the rest was used simply to pay interest on the debts inherited from Louis XIV or those of more recent vintage. During the Seven Years War, Louis XV's capitulation to the *parlements* over the Jansenist controversy was due in no small part to his need for money: a second and then a third *vingtième* were imposed. Expenditure still exceeded revenue, and by 1763 the royal debt had once again reached the catastrophic levels left by Louis XIV. When the controller general, Henri-Léonard de Bertin, sought to maintain wartime levels of taxation after the peace, the *parlements* rebelled, resulting in two related political crises which permanently damaged public confidence in the monarchy.

The first was the Brittany Affair of 1763 when the *parlement* of Rennes opposed the efforts of the royal governor, the duc d'Aiguillon, to register the financial edicts. The ensuing clash culminated in the mass resignation of the *parlement*. The Crown retaliated by having six of the leading Breton magistrates arrested and charged with conspiracy against the king. When the *parlement* of Paris protested against this heavy-handed treatment, the king responded with a thundering assertion of royal absolutism in what became known as the "flagellation session" of March 3, 1766. Yet the monarchy's basic flouting of the rule of law enraged public opinion, and the magistrates sought to indict d'Aiguillon. The governor bullishly insisted on a full trial before the *parlement* itself, and the session opened in 1770. The judges used the case as a platform from which to castigate Louis XV's style of government and the king intervened, declaring the duke innocent, making a mockery of the process. All this occurred during a severe economic crisis, famine, and a sharp drop in government revenue. The current controller general, the Abbé Terray, responded with a partial bankruptcy and mooted the possibility of new taxation, all of which stoked public and judicial ire (Bosher, 1972). *Parlementaire* protests against the king's behavior led the chancellor, René de Maupeou, to exile the magistrates at the beginning of 1771. It was the start of a "revolution," in which the Crown tried to abolish the *parlements* altogether and introduce new courts with greatly reduced jurisdictions. Unsurprisingly, the reforms met with protests from the provincial *parlements*. That of Bordeaux declared that the Crown had overthrown the fundamental laws of the kingdom and that the reforms should be approved not only by the *parlement* of Paris, but also by the old representative assembly of the realm, the Estates General (which had not met since 1614) (Doyle, 1974). Ruthlessly, Maupeou silenced the opposition by exiling the magistrates. With the main legal constraints removed, the Crown could pursue the financial retrenchment which it so desperately needed. Terray managed to raise extra taxation, and by the time Louis XV died in 1774, state finances were recovering from the crisis of 1770. Yet the victory of royal authority came at a heavy political price.

Public Opinion and the Collapse of the Absolute Monarchy

Most historians are skeptical about seeing Maupeou's experiment of 1771–4 as an exercise in "enlightened absolutism," brushing aside aristocratic resistance to reform, for the wider benefit of the state and the nation. Alongside the surge of royal power and Terray's financial measures, there was no root-and-branch effort to reform finances or administration, or to release the productive capacities of the population. There was, in other words, "no reformist counter-balance" to the brute force of royal power (Furet, 1996). On the contrary, the Maupeou "revolution" suggested to public opinion that France was not so much an absolute monarchy governing through law, but a "despotism" (Doyle, 1987). Public perceptions were a serious matter because "public opinion" was emerging as a political force in two ways. First, socially, there was an expansion in literacy and access to literature of all kinds. In 1715, literacy rates stood at 29 percent for men and 14 percent for women. By 1789 (although there were still dramatic regional variations), the figures had risen respectively to 47 and 27 percent, while in Paris they may have been as high as 90 and 80 percent. Meanwhile, access to and ownership of printed material broadened. This expansion of the reading public was accompanied by an intellectual development, which defined "public opinion" as an independent, overarching arbiter of taste and, ultimately, of politics. It did not mean the collective opinion of all the people, but rather of those who were educated, literate, and engaged with the literary and political issues of the day. Jansenist literature had made an early eighteenth-century contribution to the emergence of the concept of the "public," but it was not until the mid-century political crisis that the idea gained wider acceptance and that all sides of the religious and constitutional debate began to engage seriously with the "public" and tried to win them over. The royal government itself understood that, unless it wanted to rule by naked force alone, it had to secure public support for its policies. Yet it wavered between a surprising lightness of touch and a rigid application of censorship, which made it look simultaneously capricious and inept (Blanning, 2002; Chartier, 1991; Darnton, 1982).

With the Maupeou crisis, the monarchy had won a battle against the *parlementaires*, but it began to lose the war for public opinion. While only Voltaire stuck his head above the parapet and defended the government, the rest of the writers and publicists, many of them soaked in Montesquieu's ideas on a limited monarchy, poured out a cascade of pamphlets defending the magistrates. The Crown may well have broken the *parlements*, but in the process it destroyed public confidence in the absolute monarchy itself. The opponents of royal power began to style themselves as "patriots," meaning that they put the interests of the "people" or the "nation" above the despotic interests of the Crown. Much of this new stress on "patriotism" had been given a powerful boost during the Seven Years War (Bell, 2001), yet "patriotism" came to mean more than love of one's country, to include sacrifice of one's sectional interests – even privileges – for the greater good of the nation.

Louis XVI tried to repair the damage by following the advice of his aged minister, Jean-Frédéric Maurepas, to restore the *parlements* on his accession in 1774. With hindsight, some historians see this as a terrible blunder (Cobban, 1963), but more recent writers regard it as a genuine attempt to broaden political support for the Crown (Price, 2001). Louis XVI also sincerely tried to make the deeper structural reforms of French society neglected by Maupeou in 1771–4. Louis' first controller general of finance, Anne Robert Jacques Turgot, was a "physiocrat," who believed that a kingdom's wealth lay in the land and that good government involved removing all obstacles to the exploitation of agricultural wealth. Turgot's "Six Edicts" signaled an assault on French corporate society to free the economy from restrictions. He foundered on the resistance of the guilds and the *parlements*, which defended the privileges which were under attack, while there was a rash of food riots in the "Flour War" of 1775, stemming from poor harvests coinciding with the liberalization of the grain trade (Dakin, 1939). Turgot was dismissed in 1776, and his ultimate successor was Jacques Necker, a Genevan banker who was responsible for finding the money for French intervention in the American War of Independence. To do so, Necker certainly imposed economies at home, but he funded almost 67 percent of the war effort through borrowing. To bolster public confidence (and thereby government credit), Necker was allowed to publish the first accounts of royal finances, the *Compte rendu au roi*, in 1781. These were highly misleading, because Necker classified the war costs as "extraordinary expenditure" thus implying a surplus of 10 million livres. He was dismissed when he demanded a place on the royal council, from which he was barred because of his Protestantism. Unsurprisingly, he has remained a controversial figure, but some of his biographers have defended his record as a financier and as a reformer (Harris, 1970, 1979). One of his successors, Charles-Alexandre de Calonne, appointed in 1783, eventually informed the king in August 1786 that around half of government revenue was required merely to service the debt, and that other expenditure could only be met through additional loans. Besides borrowing more, however, Calonne also proposed radical administrative and fiscal reforms. Since the nobility clung to their fiscal privileges, Calonne tried to bypass *parlementaire* opposition by summoning an Assembly of Notables, handpicked from the great and the good of the kingdom who, it was hoped, would support the Crown. The Assembly met from February to May 1787, but it insisted that only the Estates General could consent to new taxation and to reform. Calonne was dismissed and succeeded by Loménie de Brienne as the *parlements* took up the call for an Estates General. In leading the charge, the magistrates were once again locked in a bitter political struggle with the king, culminating in May 1788 with the exile of the leading *parlementaires* and remodeling the courts through a *lit de justice.* It was the last attempt of the Crown to rule as an absolute monarchy, but this merely prompted resistance from the provincial *parlements*, while a torrent of pamphlets supported the magistrates against royal "despotism." With public and judicial resistance stiffening and with financiers nervously withholding credit to the cash-starved government, Brienne gave way and promised to summon the Estates General. When the royal treasury was forced to suspend payments altogether in August 1788, Brienne fixed May 1, 1789 for the first meeting and then resigned, urging the king to appoint the popular Necker in his place. Necker, on returning to court, announced that he could do little until the Estates General met: it was an admission that the days of absolute monarchy were over.

The convoking of the Estates General was the victory of a coalition of the *parlements* and "patriotic" opinion, but this alliance blew apart at the moment of its triumph. In September 1788 the *parlement* declared that the estates should meet in such a way that would ensure that the privileged orders – the clergy and the nobility – would predominate. In response, patriots turned not only against absolutism, but also against aristocratic privilege, claiming that the third estate, elected by the commoners, represented the sovereign nation. The pamphlet war was still raging when the Estates General met in May. During the ensuing political deadlock, the third estate declared itself to be the National Assembly with the duty to draft a constitution for the kingdom. The king seems to have resolved to restore his authority by using force. In this electrified atmosphere, the food shortages due to the poor harvests of the previous year kicked in, accompanied by catastrophic unemployment, stirring up social unrest in the major cities and the "Great Fear" in the countryside. On July 14 the Parisians stormed the Bastille and the king was advised that his soldiers would not necessarily obey orders. Royal authority collapsed across France and power fell to the National Assembly, which began the task of giving France a constitution. In the countryside, peasant fear and loathing of seigneurialism boiled over into attacks on manor houses and the burning of legal deeds recording the rights of landlords. To restore something resembling peace to the countryside, the National Assembly took the dramatic step on the night of August 4 of abolishing both seigneurial rights and the complex mass of privileges enjoyed by corporations, cities, and provinces. The Gordian knot of privilege and custom which had defined French society was swept away. Henceforth, the people of the kingdom were meant to be equal citizens of one community: France. At a stroke, the old regime had ended.

Bibliography

Antoine, M., *Louis XV* (Paris, 1989).
Baker, K. M. (ed.), *The Old Régime and the French Revolution* (Chicago, 1987a).
Baker, K. M. (ed.), *The French Revolution and the Creation of Modern Political Culture*, vol. 1: *The Political Culture of the Old Régime* (Oxford, 1987b).
Bell, D. A., *The Cult of the Nation in France: Inventing Nationalism, 1680–1800* (Cambridge, MA, 2001).
Blanning, T. C. W., *The Origins of the French Revolutionary Wars* (Harlow, 1986).
Blanning, T. C. W., *The Culture of Power and the Power of Culture: Old Regime Europe 1660–1789* (Oxford, 2002).
Bosher, J. F., *French Finances 1770–1795: From Business to Bureaucracy* (Cambridge, 1970).
Bosher, J. F., "The French crisis of 1770," *History*, 57 (1972), 17–30.
Briggs, A., *Early Modern France 1560–1715* (Oxford, 1977).
Campbell, P. R. (ed.), *The Origins of the French Revolution* (Basingstoke, 2006).
Chartier, R., *The Cultural Origins of the French Revolution* (Durham, NC, 1991).
Cobban, A., *A History of Modern France*, vol. 1: *1715–1799* (3rd edn., Harmondsworth, 1963).
Crouzet, F., *Britain Ascendant: Comparative Studies in Franco-British Economic History* (Cambridge, 1990).
Dakin, D., *Turgot and the Ancien Régime in France* (London, 1939).
Darnton, R., *The Literary Underground of the Old Regime* (Cambridge, MA, 1982).
Darnton, R., *The Forbidden Bestsellers of Pre-Revolutionary France* (London, 1996).
Doyle, W., *The Parlement of Bordeaux and the End of the Old Regime, 1771–1790* (New York, 1974).
Doyle, W., *Origins of the French Revolution* (Oxford, 1980).
Doyle, W., "The parlements," in K. M. Baker (ed.), *The Old Régime and the French Revolution* (Oxford, 1987), pp. 157–67.
Doyle, W., *Venality: The Sale of Offices in Eighteenth-Century France* (Oxford, 1996).
Doyle, W., *Jansenism: Catholic Resistance to Authority from the Reformation to the French Revolution* (Basingstoke, 2000).
Doyle, W. (ed.), *Old Regime France* (Oxford, 2001).
Farge, A., *Subversive Words: Public Opinion in Eighteenth-Century France* (Cambridge, 1994).
Félix, J., "The economy," in W. Doyle (ed.), *Old Regime France* (Oxford, 2001), pp. 7–41.
Furet, F., *The French Revolution 1770–1814* (Oxford, 1996).
Godechot, *France and the Atlantic Revolution of the Eighteenth Century, 1770–1799* (New York, 1965).
Goubert, P., *Louis XIV and Twenty Million Frenchmen* (London, 1970).
Goubert, P., *The Ancien Régime: French Society 1600–1750* (London, 1973).
Hardman, J., *Louis XVI* (New Haven, 1993).
Harris, R. D., "Necker's *compte rendu* of 1781: a reconsideration," *Journal of Modern History*, 42 (1970), 161–83.

Harris, R. D., *Necker: Reform Statesman of the Ancien Régime* (Berkeley, 1979).
Heywood, C., *The Development of the French Economy, 1750–1914* (Basingstoke, 1992).
Jones, C., *The Great Nation: France from Louis XIV to Napoleon* (London, 2002).
Jones, P. M., *The Peasantry in the French Revolution* (Cambridge, 1988).
Jones, P. M., *Reform and Revolution in France: The Politics of Transition, 1774–1791* (Cambridge, 1995).
Markoff, J., "Peasants and their grievances," in P. R. Campbell (ed.), *The Origins of the French Revolution* (Basingstoke, 2006), pp. 239–67.
Murphy, A. E., *John Law: Economic Theorist and Policy-Maker* (Oxford, 1997).
Price, M., "Politics: Louis XVI," in W. Doyle (ed.), *Old Regime France* (Oxford, 2001), pp. 223–48.
Shennan, J. H., *Philippe Duke of Orleans: Regent of France 1715–1723* (London, 1979).
Sturdy, J., *Louis XIV* (Basingstoke, 1998).
Swann, J., *Politics and the Parlement of Paris under Louis XV, 1754–1774* (Cambridge, 1995).
Swann, J., "The state and political culture," in W. Doyle (ed.), *Old Regime France* (Oxford, 2001), 139–68.
Tocqueville, A. de, *The Ancien Régime and the French Revolution* (Glasgow, 1966).
Van Kley, D. K., *The Religious Origins of the French Revolution: From Calvin to the Civil Constitution, 1560–1791* (New Haven, 1996).

Chapter Twenty-Two

Britain and Hanover

Torsten Riotte

The Act of Settlement of 1701 declared Sophia, the German electress of Hanover and, in the case of her death, her Protestant descendants, heirs to the British throne. This parliamentary act secured the succession of the house of Hanover. Dynastic rights played a crucial role in the Hanoverians' claim, but their Protestant faith proved more important. Historians have identified more than 50 claimants with stronger dynastic links who were disqualified because of their Catholic faith. The Hanoverian succession was to guarantee a Protestant succession and was known to contemporaries as such. From 1714 up to 1837 Great Britain and Hanover were connected through their head of state. When Georg Ludwig, Sophia's eldest son, traveled to Great Britain in the autumn of 1714 to be crowned George I, he did not abdicate as Hanoverian elector. He ruled conjointly as king of Great Britain and elector in the Holy Roman Empire, as did his successors up to William IV. It was only because there were different laws of succession that the two Crowns (Hanover had been elevated to the status of kingdom in 1814) were separated in 1837. That a single person should rule over two sovereign states was not unusual in early modern Europe. The elector of Saxony became king of Poland in 1697, while Swedish kings ruled over parts of Pomerania between 1648 and 1814. Such connections have been described as "personal unions" or, more recently, as "composite statehood" (Elliott, 1992). Historians have argued whether two linked sovereignties represented distinct international realities. Opinions are still divided in the case of Great Britain and Hanover. Though both states signed contracts, declared war, or negotiated peace individually, the separation of other characteristics defining an autonomous international body was less clear-cut.

Historiography

How did contemporaries regard the Personal Union? The Victorians' representation of their immediate past has blurred eighteenth-century views on Great Britain's German connection. Many saw the accession of young Queen Victoria in 1837 as the dawn of a new era. Living and working conditions were undergoing dramatic

A Companion to Eighteenth-Century Europe, First Edition. Edited by Peter H. Wilson.
© 2014 John Wiley & Sons, Ltd. Published 2014 by John Wiley & Sons, Ltd.

change, while science and engineering displayed rapid progress. The Victorian world seemed far removed from Hanoverian realities, and distancing themselves from the past became a crucial element in defining the new age. The attribute "Victorian" was used as early as 1839 to emphasize the differences between the two historical periods. As the nineteenth century progressed, the expanding British empire and the small Hanoverian kingdom grew so far apart in character and size that only few could believe that the Personal Union had mattered politically, economically, or culturally in the decades before 1837. The *Spectator* wrote after the death of George V, the last king of Hanover, in 1878: "Nothing in history is more strange, though it seems to us all so natural, than the quiet, persistent, immovable refusal of the English people, a refusal continued through seven generations, to care anything about Hanover." For some time, scholarly opinion confirmed the judgment that Britain had not cared, either in the eighteenth century or later. Adolphus William Ward saw the Personal Union as little more than "an official flourish of style, indulged in on the one [the Hanoverian] side but left quite unreciprocated on the other [the British]" (Ward, 1899). There was little interest in a connection that did not match the paradigm of historical progress and political success. It is only very recently that historians have reconsidered these views. Further research into the importance of the Protestant interest, the image of monarchy under the Georges (Smith, 2006), and the role of the Holy Roman Empire (Thompson, 2006) and continental Europe in British politics (Simms and Riotte, 2007) has revealed a previously neglected Hanoverian dimension in eighteenth-century British history. Although Great Britain's rise to a colonial empire based on its maritime strength was a central feature in its eighteenth-century history, British history between 1714 and 1837 can only be fully understood if the European and Hanoverian dimensions are equally taken into account.

The Legacy of the Glorious Revolution

The Act of Settlement gives clear indication that the connection between Great Britain and Hanover needs to be understood as part of the legacy of the Glorious Revolution of 1689 and the subsequent reign of William III and his wife Mary. With William of Orange, a foreigner had been established on the British throne. British experiences under William shaped their attitudes to the German dynasty that was to rule in Britain for most of the eighteenth century. A central restriction of the Act, for example, laid down that the monarch was to leave Great Britain only with parliamentary consent. Although this clause was repealed in 1716, it illustrated the difficulties of composite statehood. Was George I more German prince than British monarch? His most authoritative biographer emphasizes that he was both king and elector (Hatton, 1978). George I traveled to Hanover six times after his accession in 1714. Each time, he took with him one secretary of state, other ministers, and numerous courtiers, leaving behind a regency in Britain. While British foreign policy had generally abstained from direct involvement in political negotiations on the continent and aimed at taking foreign political decisions independently, George I brought British politics and politicians to Europe. George II traveled to Hanover as frequently as his predecessor, visiting his electorate 12 times between 1727 and 1755, sometimes staying several months during the summer (Richter-Uhlig, 1992). The pattern only changed with the accession of George III (1760), who never set foot in his German dominions, despite considering doing so, notably during the severe political crises of the 1780s. Other aspects of the Personal Union also underwent a change around the same time, but it would be wrong to assume that the connection between the two states completely lost its significance after the Seven Years War. The period after 1760 indeed differed from that under the first two Georges, but the Personal Union retained importance until the Congress of Vienna in 1814–15 (Riotte, 2005). Thereafter, there was only one further royal visit, when George IV briefly toured Hanover after his accession in 1821.

Family Links

Other members of the royal family appeared more often on the continent. The Hanoverian dynasty acquired partial possession of the neighboring bishopric of Osnabrück through the Peace of Westphalia (1648) that stipulated alternate rule between a Catholic bishop and a Protestant duke from their family. This practice continued after the Hanoverian succession in 1714 and provided an additional important channel of information between the empire and Britain. The duke of York, for example, moved to the empire during the 1780s, and wrote frequently to his father, giving information about the German possessions. George III was also kept informed by others, not least through an extensive project to map the electorate (Schnath, 1931), but this was not the same as visiting in person and undoubtedly elements of the Personal Union suffered from the monarch's prolonged absence. Court life almost completely disappeared in Hanover after 1760 despite the presence of some of George III's sons, who were educated at the University of Göttingen or stationed in the electorate's capital as officers in the Hanoverian army.

German Personnel

Members of the royal family were not the only ones to keep the monarch informed about his German lands. In addition to the extensive, established network of British diplomats across Europe, Hanoverian representatives also reported to London. The Hanoverian envoy at the Reichstag (imperial diet) in Regensburg proved a highly valuable source of information, because British representation there was both patchy and often incapable of grasping the intricacies of German princely politics. Similarly, Hanoverian representatives at Berlin and Vienna played a crucial diplomatic role alongside their British colleagues. It has been suggested that the Hanoverian diplomatic service declined during the late eighteenth century. While this might be an indication that the British monarch relied more on the prestige and standing of his British representatives at the larger European courts, Hanover's importance in diplomacy within the empire increased and its intelligence remained valuable throughout the Personal Union. In particular, Hanoverian agents played a vital role in intercepting foreign secret correspondence and reporting the contents to London right up to the end of the Napoleonic Wars.

When George I left Hanover he laid down regulations for how the administration of politics should be conducted in the electorate. A group of privy councillors

(*Geheime Räte*) decided most domestic issues, while the more important decisions, particularly those concerning foreign policy, were still referred to the monarch. George took with him two of his councillors to handle correspondence between London and Hanover. Some of his Hanoverian entourage had already moved to the British capital to ensure a smooth transition of power. However, there were few opportunities for Hanoverians in British politics. William of Orange had installed a large number of Dutch courtiers in crucial political positions after his victory in 1689, and their presence was widely resented by the British political elite. The Act of Settlement laid down clear restrictions regarding foreigners, forbidding them or any person naturalized after 1714 from being employed in "an office or place of trust." Although this seems to imply a clash of British and Hanoverian interests, the juxtaposition of a British and a Hanoverian faction would be misleading. Particularly during the early stages of the Personal Union, British and German politicians collaborated against their domestic enemies. For example, while Stanhope certainly played a crucial role in the events that led to the resignation of the Hanoverian Bernstorff in 1719, he happily collaborated with Bernstorff's Hanoverian opponents, Johann Philip von Hattorf and Friedrich Wilhelm von Goertz, in his struggle against their German rival. The most successful collaboration was that between the secretary of state Newcastle and the Hanoverian minister Gerlach Adolph von Münchhausen, whose "partnership" (Dann, 1991) left its mark on British foreign policy particularly from the late 1740s right until the outbreak of the Seven Years War. Such collaboration between the British political elite and their Hanoverian colleagues was just as frequent as rows over a supposed preference of the monarch for his German dominions and his Hanoverian subjects.

The German Chancery

After the first tumultuous years of George I's reign, the Hanoverian representation in London obtained a more consistent character during the 1720s. The so-called "Hanoverian Junta" had largely left Britain by then. Those Hanoverians who stayed in London withdrew from active political life. Hans Casper von Bothmer, the Hanoverian envoy to Great Britain under Queen Anne and, according to Brendan Simms, for a brief moment in 1714, "the most powerful man in London" (Simms, 2007) spent the period after 1720 as a private gentleman in a property provided by George II. The house, known as Bothmer palace, was situated in the City of Westminster and would soon be extended to a larger property, its address, 10 Downing Street. The only politically active Hanoverian in London after 1720 was the electorate's official representative who had his office in St. James's Palace. This two-room space was known to British contemporaries as the German Chancery (or Chancellery). In many ways it worked like a foreign representation in London. No regular meetings between British and Hanoverian statesmen were held. The Hanoverians had to apply to the foreign secretary for an audience. The Hanoverian minister did not attend British cabinet meetings. However, the head of the Chancery possessed two political assets of crucial importance: direct access to the king, and proximity to the monarch and to the British political sphere, particularly to the court. The Chancery had great potential for a gifted politician, but only one Hanoverian succeeded in using it fully. This had less to do with British reservations than the concern of the government in Hanover that anyone sent to London would be physically closer than themselves to the monarch and could become difficult to control. The Hanoverian government never sent a potentially ambitious candidate to London until the nomination of Ernst Herbert, Count Münster as head of the Chancery in 1805. Even during the period of closest collaboration in the late 1740s and early 1750s, the Hanoverian minister Gerlach Adolph von Münchhausen remained in the German electorate, while his younger brother took up the post in London. Failure to secure the London appointment prompted the able and ambitious Karl August von Hardenberg to leave the Hanoverian ministry and enter Prussian service, where he rose to prominence as a reformer. The Hanoverian's ministry's fears were fully justified: Count Münster used his new position to secure the ministry's dissolution a few months after his arrival in London in 1805. Historians disagree whether he did this to improve government efficiency in the wake of the French occupation of the electorate that the ministry failed to prevent in 1803, or (as his critics claimed) to place some of his protégés in key positions. Either way, it is clear that Münster was well informed about events in Hanover as well as familiar with British political circles. He is a particularly good example of how the Hanoverian minister in London communicated and collaborated with his British colleagues. Münster's private papers contain correspondence with many of the prominent figures in British political life, including Pitt the Younger, Fox, Canning, and Castlereagh. Such ties and the fluidity with which figures like Münster operated in both Britain and Hanover belie the traditional juxtaposition of British and Hanoverian interests. Rather than seeing the two as inherently hostile, it is more useful to look at different factions in both states and to discuss who supported the interests of the Personal Union and who disapproved of any involvement with Hanover or Great Britain respectively.

Protestant Interest

George I gained the British Crown in 1714 thanks to his Protestantism. Arguably, the most important legacy of the Glorious Revolution was religious. Throughout the Hanoverian period, defense of the Protestant interest played a crucial role in a century that would otherwise be known for the secularism of the Enlightenment. Later historical interest in scientific advances and philosophical debates distract from the fact that the confessional divide still mattered. Andrew Thompson has shown how denomination impacted on politics. His account of the British response to the crisis between Catholics and Protestants in the German city of Heidelberg from 1719 to 1724 reveals links between diplomacy and political culture and a political public, illustrating that foreign policy "was based on ideas, not just immediate interests" (Thompson, 2006: 229). Despite the shift away from the religious strife of an earlier period, the eighteenth century and British-Hanoverian history in particular kept their religious characteristics. These shaped politics and policies as much as society and statesmen. Thompson's second example, the Thorn crisis from 1724 to 1727, examines how the execution of a disputed number of Protestants (probably fewer than 15) in this Polish town caused a European crisis. The impact of Protestantism on political decision-making can be difficult to assess, not least because British governments were prepared to deal with Catholic Austria and France while, at the same time, having no reservations about declaring war on a Protestant power like Prussia, as they did in 1806 (Simms, 1995). Still, neither commercial nor power-political concerns alone can explain eighteenth-century political decision-making, nor does focusing on such explanations help to illuminate why religious disputes still provided a source of European conflict. The core of British political culture remained the defense of the Protestant interest, and this was closely connected with the idea of British rights and liberties. Although the impact of confessional aspects is less obvious for the reign of George III and the two subsequent monarchs, George still struggled with Pitt the Younger over Catholic emancipation in 1801. As he emphasized to his opponents, the defense of the Protestant faith provided the only legitimate argument for the house of Hanover in its claim to the British throne. Catholic emancipation remained blocked in Britain until 1829. In addition to its ideological significance, the Church of England also provided a valuable arena for patronage, as all Hanoverian monarchs used their influence over ecclesiastical appointments to establish and reward a trustworthy clientele and to create a court faction.

Dynastic Policies

Religious considerations also guided the Hanoverian royal family's choice of marriage partners. Dynastic links retained political importance. When seeking a partner for himself or his children, each Hanoverian monarch preferred the leading northwest European Protestant royal houses of Orange, Prussia, or Denmark. Caroline of Ansbach, George II's wife, provides a good example, as she was closely related to the Prussian Hohenzollern dynasty. The lesser German princely families offered a less desirable alternative if no suitable Protestant royal was available. George III's Hanoverian advisers and British confidant only proposed Charlotte of Mecklenburg-Strelitz in 1761 once the other candidates had been rejected. Finally, in more difficult situations family ties were used to find partners. George III's sister Augusta persuaded her brother that her daughter Caroline would be the right choice for the notoriously indebted Prince of Wales, who was only looking for a bride to solve his financial problems. The future George IV's wife, Caroline, was the daughter of his relative, the reigning duke Charles William Ferdinand of Brunswick. The two Carolines provide a clear illustration of the importance of dynasty to the creation of a positive image of monarchy for the British public. Caroline of Ansbach-Bayreuth, the wife of George II, played a crucial role in popularizing the Georgian monarchy. Her embrace of English culture helped, it has been claimed (Smith, 2006: 83–95), to Anglicize the royal family, in contrast to her father-in-law George I, whose behavior was considered too "Germanic" by the British crowds, while her own husband, George II, lacked her charm and charisma. Caroline of Brunswick achieved very different results with her public appearances. Most notorious for her rows with her husband George IV, the latter refused her access to his coronation and divorced her in 1821. The unprecedented public row about the Queen Caroline affair damaged the reputation of both that monarch and the monarchy.

German and British Identity

George IV only had himself to blame for his poor public image, but all Hanoverian monarchs faced potential problems because of their German origins. Frederic, Prince of Wales was the first to distance himself from the German legacy. His premature death in 1751 left his son George (III) as successor. He opened his reign in 1760 with a speech in Parliament declaring that he had been born and educated in Britain and that he would pursue a policy that was best for Britain. Still, George III's wife Charlotte was frequently represented as German with German interests and qualities. The Hanoverians, no matter how hard they tried, remained a foreign dynasty in Great Britain. Particularly during political crises this led to xenophobic attacks from the opposition or from political and radical circles. George III's self-conscious "Britishness" was aimed at his grandfather, George II, whom he despised for his German preferences, including a German mistress, Amalie Sophie Marianne von Wallmoden, who was created Countess Yarmouth. The clash between (grand)father and son is a characteristic feature in Hanoverian history that recurred over several generations. George I clashed with George II (amongst others) over the arrangements for a regency during the royal tour of Hanover in 1716. The relationship between George II and Frederic, Prince of Wales, was so bad that the heir was banned from court. George III clearly stated that he would no longer tolerate the loose moral standards accepted by George II. Yet George III was locked in a struggle with the future George IV, who not only followed a very different lifestyle but also supported the political opposition to his father's government, notoriously during the regency crisis of 1788–9. Such conflicts immediately affected British politics, as divisions in the royal family sharpened the growth of faction, as well as creating two opposing courts. The future George II would be notorious for the Leicester House circle. Frederic, Prince of Wales, resided at Carlton House as did the future George IV. As such, the rows over the legitimate successor enhanced a divide originating from before the Hanoverian succession.

Party Politics

Such tensions illustrate how the Hanoverians not only filled structures left by the Glorious Revolution, but added their own unique element to British politics. The political factions of Whigs and Tories were a legacy of the earlier period. The rivalry within the royal family reinforced the idea of two opposing factions, but it quickly became clear that this did not necessarily match the divide between Whigs and Tories. The strict separation between the two factions survived less than a year when the Whigs split over the support of George I's foreign policy in the Baltic. Even under George I, court Tories could be found in the household of the monarch, although not as part of the British government. Frederic, Prince of Wales, and George III hoped to free British politics from party interest, but failed. The Whigs were bitterly disappointed in 1812 when the restrictions of the regency ended, but George IV left a Tory government in power.

The strength of the Hanoverian rule lay in adaptation and in stability. Parliamentary restrictions on royal travel abroad were lifted. Although no Hanoverians joined the government, a small group of courtiers from the electorate remained lively and influential. The German Chancery was led by a capable minister who generally found support from the monarch and his Hanoverian colleagues at home.

Cultural and Intellectual Connections

It is difficult to judge whether the Personal Union extended beyond high politics because very little research has been done on anything other than foreign policy. As far as we know today, economic exchange between the two countries remained minimal throughout the period. The Hanoverians were interested in British industrialization and took some inspiration from British agriculture, but no joint undertakings are recorded. The electorate also supported a free-trade policy throughout the period and provided a market for British goods, but it did not gain major importance in British trade policy. Other areas of Germany seem to have been just as, if not more, important, particularly the two Hansa towns of Bremen and Hamburg. Culturally, the best-known "Hanoverian" export to Britain remains Handel. Little artistic interchange beyond the work of this great musician has been uncovered, although all monarchs employed artists and intellectuals from Hanover and continental Europe at their courts. Some Hanoverians visited London, but no record survives of professional careers in Britain outside politics. The surviving source material thus makes it very difficult to evaluate whether the Personal Union encouraged mutual cultural exchange. It clearly created a widespread interest in British life among the German electorate, particularly in Hanover itself and the university town of Göttingen, a fact which British travelers, many of them undertaking the Grand Tour, observed with surprise. The best-known example for a German–British transfer of ideas remains the University of Göttingen, which was a leading scientific institution in the Holy Roman Empire. Although the number of British students there was not as significant as is sometimes suggested, Göttingen provided an important element in a European network of scholars that, amongst others, connected British and German scientists. Thomas Biskup has shown how much the two countries benefited from this scholarly exchange. Eminent figures in Britain's scientific world, such as the presidents of the Royal Society Sir John Pringle and Sir Joseph Banks, were to be found in "a pattern of cooperation" with their Hanoverian counterparts Johann David Michaelis and Johann Friedrich Blumenbach (Biskup in Simms and Riotte, 2007: 148). Further research is needed to evaluate whether Göttingen was the exception to the rule, or whether the exchange of ideas from Britain to Hanover and the continent went beyond the academic circles.

Foreign Policy

Foreign policy proved the most controversial aspect of the Personal Union at the time and has remained so in subsequent scholarly discussion. This was largely due to the monarchical prerogative in foreign political decision-making. George I did not distinguish as clearly between his British and Hanoverian interests as his critics would have wished. Although the Act of Settlement ruled against external wars not in the British interest, it was very difficult to define what that might mean in practice. Many believed the Act had been breached already when George used the British fleet to intimidate Sweden in 1715 and compel it to surrender the duchies of Bremen and Verden to Hanover during the Great Northern War. This action caused uproar in Parliament, and impeachment was mainly avoided by the cautious conduct of the actual operations by Admiral Norris. George I continued to pursue Hanoverian aggrandizement regardless of the criticism, yet in all his foreign political decisions he (arguably) addressed British concerns. The British fleet in the Baltic not only advanced Hanoverian interests but also safeguarded British trade with Russia in northern Europe, which was threatened by the Swedes. Similarly, the Triple Alliance of 1717 between Great Britain, France, and the Dutch Republic, followed by the Quadruple Alliance including Austria a year later, whose inclusion was intended both to secure the acquisition of Bremen and Verden for Hanover and to uphold the Peace of Utrecht, was very much in Britain's interest as well. These two alliances represented a fundamental shift in British policy previously based on antagonism toward France. The Anglo-French rapprochement under the first two Georges put Britain in an unprecedented position of strength on the continent that lasted until France changed tack in 1733.

Ideological Divisions

The interlude in the long rivalry between Great Britain and France after 1717 had only been possible due to the death of the French monarch Louis XIV in 1715. Not only had the Sun King been Britain's main enemy since the Glorious Revolution, he had also sheltered George I's own personal rival, the exiled James II and his brother the Old Pretender. Hanoverian designs on Sweden's Baltic provinces led Charles XII to encourage a Jacobite rebellion in 1715. The Old Pretender landed with troops in Scotland and Ireland, and though he found some support there, he was unable to persuade the English Tories to defect in large numbers. Jacobitism remained dangerous in Scotland and Ireland, but in England it posed more of an ideological than a military threat over the next three decades. By the time of the second Jacobite rebellion in 1745, English support had reached a low point. The Scots once again joined the rebellion and marched south across the border, only to find few English Tories or radicals willing to join them. The subsequent defeat of the Jacobite army at Culloden in April 1746 arguably ended Jacobitism as a military danger. Although the Jacobite challenge was more persistent than any dissident threat to other European monarchs, its failure underlines the success of Hanoverian rule in England. George III was already known for collecting Jacobite paraphernalia.

Disagreement over the best way to safeguard British interests provided a more lasting division in British politics. The two competing concepts were the "blue water" strategy stressing naval and colonial power and the "continental commitment" strategy, entailing military and diplomatic engagement within Europe. Generally speaking, the eighteenth century saw the emergence of Britain as a great power in Europe. This did not lead to permanent British involvement in European diplomacy. Britain's island position enabled her to withdraw from the continent for certain periods while being involved during others. Britain's sea power also enabled her to compete with her greatest rival, France, not by a continental strategy, but through struggles in the colonies. Naval warfare proved more cost-efficient and, in the British case, very successful. However, British politicians discovered that naval success alone rarely compelled European opponents to make peace. Accordingly, governments of the day generally remained involved in European diplomacy, while many of the (particularly Tory) opposition demanded a strictly naval strategy.

The War of the Austrian Succession

The extent of British involvement in Europe naturally concerned Hanover. Britain abstained from interventionism for some time after George II's accession in 1727. Colonial rivalry drew British attention overseas and led to war in the Caribbean with Spain after 1739. The death of Emperor Charles VI a year later precipitated a separate European war over the Austrian succession. Together with the Great Northern War (1700–21), the Seven Years War (1756–63), and the French Revolutionary and Napoleonic Wars (1792–1815), this conflict provides a key to our understanding of the Personal Union and its impact on the two states. George II was fully aware that Hanover would be exposed to a French attack, but he also appreciated that few British politicians were prepared to join a continental coalition. The divide between the blue water policy and European interventionism was only part of the story. The traditional British strategy of supporting Austria against France was threatened by George's decision to negotiate separate neutrality for Hanover. While his British government supported Austrian efforts to secure the Habsburg candidate as the next Holy Roman Emperor, George traded his vote for the French-backed Bavarian candidate in return for a suspension of the threatened French invasion of Hanover in 1742. Far from resolving matters, this contributed to the underlying tension within Europe, attracting widespread criticism from other crowned heads, notably Frederick II of Prussia. Hostile British opinion openly accused George of putting his German interests above his obligations as a British monarch. Some of the tension disappeared when, after the downfall of Walpole, British policies changed and the government of Carteret decided to back Hanoverian military support for Austria. George II was the last British monarch to lead his troops into battle when he commanded the so-called Pragmatic Army in its victory over the French at Dettingen 1743. He was celebrated in Britain and Hanover, though critics still blamed him for wearing a yellow Hanoverian ribbon rather than British insignia. Despite the joint effort, it proved impossible to reconcile the monarch's relatively free conduct of Hanover's external relations with Parliament's influence over British foreign policy.

The War of the Austrian Succession revealed a second important development. George II was unable to repeat his father's use of Britain's resources to Hanover's advantage. George I's acquisition of Bremen and Verden during the Great Northern War represents the only incident when Hanover actively gained through British military assistance. But 1715 had provided such a precedent, not least due to the public outcry it occasioned, that no British government was prepared to support Hanoverian ambitions afterwards. While not indifferent to Hanover, the most that a British government would now do was to safeguard its security and integrity. George II thus found it impossible to secure British backing for his plan to annex the north German bishoprics of Hildesheim and Osnabrück, and, without such support, other powers like Prussia refused to countenance further Hanoverian expansion.

The Seven Years War

The years following the Peace of Aix-la-Chapelle (1748) saw a reshuffle of the European alliance system leading to the diplomatic revolution of 1755–6. Paris and Vienna joined forces, while London negotiated an alliance with Berlin in the Convention of Westminster. When these moves precipitated the Seven Years War, it seemed clear to the incumbent British government that Hanoverian interests came second to its own political and strategic concerns and that Hanoverian troops would assist in this largely British strategy. George II used his status as elector to raise large numbers of Hanoverian soldiers to join a British expeditionary force. Such military assistance represented a major element in Hanover's contribution to the Personal Union. In addition to substantial numbers of auxiliaries during the Great Northern War and War of the Austrian Succession, there were Hanoverians stationed as part of the British army in British Menorca in the 1770s and in India in the 1780s. The King's German Legion fought as a foreign corps in British service during the Napoleonic Wars (Beamish, 1832–7). Military support was a key feature appreciated by British governments. At the same time "German militarism" and "German absolutism" were condemned by the British public as a threat to British liberties. Although military support was an important asset, its size and importance should not be overstated. Still, the British government and its leader, Pitt the Elder, relied heavily on Hanoverian assistance to sustain the continental dimension of its global strategy during the Seven Years War. Pitt was as outraged as George II at the Convention of Kloster Zeven, which neutralized Hanover in September 1757. This had been forced on William, duke of Cumberland, by the French Marshal d'Estrées, who had defeated the outnumbered Hanoverian and other German auxiliaries at Hastenbeck that July. George II insisted that his troops continue the unequal fight, but Hanoverian ministers were quite pleased with the prospect of neutrality and hoped to stay out of the great power conflict. The war resumed the following year after George repudiated the Convention. The situation of the previous war had been reversed. Whereas Britons accused their king in the 1740s of putting his German interests first, now Hanoverians felt their elector placed them second behind his British subjects. Münchhausen, the leading Hanoverian minister, commented later that he had hoped Kloster Zeven would lead to a general peace, and he was decidedly unimpressed with his sovereign's behavior. The estrangement between monarch and electorate intensified during and after the Seven Years War. This was partly due to the changes in Hanover's position within the empire. From being one of the most successful and promising German lands at the beginning of the century, Hanover was now falling behind, overshadowed by Prussia, whose German and international position was consolidated by its defeat of Austrian attacks during the Seven Years War.

George III and Hanover

The accession of a new monarch in 1760 contributed to the more reserved relationship between the head of the British state and Hanover. Unhappy with his grandfather's German policies, George III decided to withdraw British forces from the war on the continent. He was perfectly aware that this would have negative consequences for Hanover. This and his earlier description of Hanover as "that horrid electorate" (Blanning, 1977) have been seen as evidence that the relationship between Great Britain and Hanover ceased to be of any importance after 1760. In fact, George acted as a responsible sovereign, following a policy of restoration and economic recovery for the electorate from the Peace of Paris (1763) up until 1780s. The most important change in the British–Hanoverian relationship was George's efforts to separate the policies of the two states more clearly. As he himself phrased it, his role as monarch of Great Britain was not to be affected by his "private interests," i.e. his German dominions. In his idealistic world-view, he thought that his government could pursue a purely British policy while his Hanoverian concerns could be dealt with in a private capacity (Riotte in Simms and Riotte, 2007). This was fine as long Britain followed an isolationist foreign policy and was not involved in diplomatic negotiations on the continent. However, there were already signs during the War of the Bavarian Succession (1778–9) that this divide might prove difficult to sustain. It became much more obvious with the question of Hanoverian membership of the League of Princes (*Fürstenbund*), an alliance of minor German rulers intended to reform the imperial constitution that was manipulated by Prussia as a device to block Joseph II's proposed exchange of the Austrian Netherlands for Bavaria. While George III also opposed the exchange and joined the League, his British ministers had just contacted Vienna about a possible alliance between Britain and Austria. It is not surprising that the prime minister, Pitt the Younger, was unimpressed by the monarch's activities in connection with his "private" interests. The outbreak of the French Revolutionary Wars increased the tension between British government decisions and George III's concerns for Hanover. This followed partly from the monarch's loss of influence in British foreign policy and partly from his reluctance to accept changes in the existing order in the Holy Roman Empire. The gap widened further with the Peace of Basle of 1795, by which Prussia left the war against revolutionary France and neutralized northern Germany, including Hanover. Whereas the *Fürstenbund* had only damaged Britain's search for an alliance, the Peace of Basle meant that Hanover was quitting a war that Britain was still fighting. Finally, Hanover went even further in 1801 and offered to join Prussia in the Second League of Armed Neutrality formed the previous year to oppose British trade in the Baltic. If Prussia accepted the Hanoverian offer, George III risked being party to an alliance directed against himself! He was already unhappy about Hanoverian neutrality after 1795, though it remains unclear whether he knew what his ministers were offering the Prussians in 1801. Nonetheless, it is obvious that his efforts to keep his British and Hanoverian interests apart proved untenable.

The Restoration of Hanover

The period of the Napoleonic Wars that followed saw the occupation of Hanover by French and Prussian troops and the division of the electorate between Napoleonic France and the newly created kingdom of Westphalia. Historians generally stress that Britain did not declare war in support of Hanover. What is overlooked, however, is that throughout the Napoleonic Wars all British governments insisted on the full restoration of the king's German dominions as a condition of peace. George III's illness and incapacity made the position of the Hanoverian minister more difficult, but Hanover was not only restored in the Vienna Settlement of 1814–15, but received some of the surrounding German territory it had long coveted. Most historians stress that the foreign secretary, Castlereagh, constrained Hanoverian demands, particularly in regard to Prussian ambitions, but it is nonetheless significant that Hanover was not wiped from the map.

The Prince of Wales had already become Prince Regent by the time of the peace congress. Despite prolonged disagreements with his father, he followed a very similar policy towards Hanover. The presence of Count Münster as Hanoverian minister in London is one factor in this continuity, but so too is the Prince Regent's own interest in and understanding of Hanoverian issues. It was he who decided to elevate the electorate of Hanover to a kingdom within the new German Confederation in 1814 and to choose his younger brother Adolphus Frederic, the duke of Cambridge, as its new administrator. Nonetheless, the Congress of Vienna emerges as a turning point in British–Hanoverian relations. Domestic issues now dominated both British and Hanoverian politics, and under George IV's successor, William IV, no international event challenged the peaceful coexistence between the two states. Without a common external threat, the two partners drifted further apart and William IV increased Hanoverian autonomy by declaring Adolphus Frederic viceroy in 1816.

Why the Personal Union Lasted so Long

By then it was already likely that the Personal Union would not survive William IV, because he lacked a male heir. The race for a successor to the British Crown was won when Edward Augustus, the duke of Kent and fourth son of George III, had a daughter, Victoria, in 1819. Had George, Adolphus Frederic's son, been born a few weeks earlier the Personal Union would have continued, because he would have been acceptable under Hanoverian law as ruler, whereas Victoria, as a woman, was excluded. Few seem to have cared by the time William IV died in 1837, raising the question why the Union had not been dissolved before.

There were certainly plans to do so. George I had already specified that Britain and Hanover were not to be ruled by the same person in the will he made in 1716. George II suppressed this will and succeeded to both in 1727. One reason was that Hanover's position within the empire made it difficult for it to unilaterally change who should rule it without risking imperial protest and, quite possibly, foreign intervention. However, there was a more fundamental reason, as became clear during discussions in the 1750s when George II himself asked his Hanoverian ministers whether the Union could be dissolved. In these debates, and in those in the following years under George III, it became clear that legitimate succession represented a political act that had far-reaching consequences for Britain as well. The Act of Settlement had not only placed a German prince on a vacant throne, it had created a legitimacy that the Hanoverians had resolutely defended thereafter. Thus, Great Britain and Hanover might not have grown closer between 1714 and 1837, but the Personal Union and the composite statehood it entailed had become a political reality for the two countries that was not easily denied.

Bibliography

Baugh, D., "Great Britain's 'blue-water' policy, 1689–1815," *International History Review*, 10 (1988), 33–58.

Beamish, N. L., *History of the King's German Legion* (London, 1832–7).

Bertram, M., *Georg II. König und Kurfürst* (Göttingen, 2004).

Birke, A. M. and K. Kluxen (eds.), *England and Hanover* (Munich, 1986).

Black, J., "The Crown, Hanover and the shift in British foreign policy in the 1760s," in J. Black (ed.), *Knights Errant and True Englishmen: British Foreign Policy 1660–1800* (Edinburgh, 1989), pp. 113–34.

Black, J., *The Hanoverians: The History of a Dynasty* (London, 2004).

Black, J., *Continental Commitment: Britain, Hanover and Interventionism, 1714–1793* (Abingdon, 2005).

Black, J., *George III: America's Last King* (New Haven, 2006).

Blanning, T. C. W., "'That horrid electorate' or 'Ma patrie germanique?' George III and the Fürstenbund of 1785," *Historical Journal*, 20 (1977), 311–44.

Dann, U., *Hanover and Great Britain* (Leicester, 1991).

Elliott, J. H., "A Europe of composite monarchies," *Past & Present*, 137 (1992), 48–71.

Geyken, F., "The German language is spoken in Saxony with the greatest purity, or: English images and perceptions in the eighteenth century," in J. Canning and H. Wellenreuther (eds.), *Britain and Germany Compared: Nationality, Society and Nobility in the Eighteenth Century* (Göttingen, 2001), pp. 37–70.

Harding, N., "Sir Robert Walpole and Hanover," *Historical Research*, 76 (2003), 164–88.

Harding, N., *Hanover and the British Empire* (Woodbridge, 2007).

Harris, R., *A Patriot Press: National Politics and the London Press in the 1740s* (Oxford, 1993).

Hatton, R., *George I: Elector and King* (London, 1978).

Königs, P., *The Hanoverian Kings and their Homeland* (Lewes, 1993); rev. edn. in German translation: *Die Dynastie aus Deutschland. Die hannoverschen Könige von England und ihre Heimat* (Hanover, 1998).

Michael, W., *Englische Geschichte im Achtzehnen Jahrhundert* (Leipzig, 1896–1945).

Michael, W., "Die Personalunion von England und Hannover und das Testament Georgs I," *Archiv für Urkundenforschung*, 6 (1928), 323–40.

Reitan, E. R. (ed.), *George III: Tyrant or Constitutional Monarch?* (Boston, 1964).

Richter-Uhlig, U., *Hof und Politik unter den Bedingungen der Personalunion zwischen Hannover und England. Die Aufenthalte Georgs II. in Hannover zwischen 1729 und 1741* (Hanover, 1992).

Riotte, T., *Hannover in der britischen Politik (1792–1815). Dynastische Verbindung als Element außenpolitischer Entscheidungsfindung* (Münster, 2005).

Schnath, G., "Die Kurhannoversche Landesaufnahme, 1764–1786," *Hannoversches Magazin*, 7 (1931), 33–53.

Schnath, G., *Geschichte Hannovers im Zeitalter der neunten Kur und der englischen Sukzession, 1674–1704* (5 vols., Hildesheim, 1976–82).

Simms, B., "'An odd question enough': Charles James Fox, the Crown and British policy during the Hanoverian crisis of 1806," *Historical Journal*, 38 (1995), 567–96.

Simms, B. and T. Riotte (eds.), *The Hanoverian Dimension in British History, 1714–1837* (Cambridge, 2007).

Smith, H., *Georgian Monarchy, Politics and Culture, 1714–1760* (Cambridge, 2006).

Taylor, S. (ed.), *Hanoverian Britain and Empire: Essays in Memory of Philip Lawson* (Woodbridge, 1998).

Thompson, A., *Britain, Hanover and the Protestant Interest, 1688–1756* (Woodbridge, 2006).

Ward, A. W., *Great Britain and Hanover* (Oxford, 1899).

Part IV

International Connections

Chapter Twenty-Three

Diplomacy and the Great Powers

Andrew C. Thompson

A Century of Change?

Eighteenth-century Europe witnessed significant realignment of its territorial borders. At the beginning of the century Poland-Lithuania occupied more land than France. At its end, Poland had ceased to exist – victim of the territorial acquisitiveness of Austria, Prussia, and Russia. In other respects, it seemed little had changed. Louis XIV was widely regarded as the greatest threat to European stability at the century's outset, and fear of revolutionary France and its most successful general, Napoleon Bonaparte, dominated diplomatic thinking at its conclusion. Rivalry between different powers is a constant of international relations. Yet the tensions between European powers in the eighteenth century have often been viewed as particularly pronounced – whereas the nineteenth century witnessed long periods of peace between the major powers, conflicts between them were much more frequent in the eighteenth century. The frequency of armed conflict has led some historians (Schroeder, 1994) to suggest that it was the nature of the eighteenth-century international system that both provoked and sustained regular wars. This chapter explores the nature of the eighteenth-century system and examines the major shifts within it. A key feature of these changes was a growing differentiation between those powers who could easily claim the epithet "great" and those now strictly of the second rank. Recognition as a great power by other states was one way such status could be achieved, but it is also important to examine the infrastructure necessary to sustain great power status, in terms of both money and men.

Nomenclature presents problems in the study of international relations. The usage adopted here is pragmatic. Generally speaking, modern forms are used but it should be remembered that boundaries were different in the eighteenth century. Thus, Austria is shorthand for the possessions of the Austrian Habsburgs that included modern Austria but also extended into the Czech and Slovak republics, Hungary, and other parts of the Balkans. The use of the names of states should also not be taken to mean that there was a sense of a national interest, distinct from that of the ruler.

A Companion to Eighteenth-Century Europe, First Edition. Edited by Peter H. Wilson.
© 2014 John Wiley & Sons, Ltd. Published 2014 by John Wiley & Sons, Ltd.

The story of international relations in the sixteenth and seventeenth centuries is dominated not by a struggle between states but by the conflicts between the two largest dynasties in Europe, the Habsburgs and the Valois/Bourbons. These two power blocs invariably found themselves on opposite sides in European conflicts and did so until well into the eighteenth century. Yet the dynamics of the international system were changing in the later seventeenth century. Louis XIV of France had succeeded to the French throne as a 4-year-old in 1643. In 1661 his chief minister, Cardinal Mazarin, died and was not replaced. Louis assumed sole control of French foreign policy with the aim of securing France's borders and enhancing French power and prestige in Europe. Louis' campaigns in the Low Countries threatened the United Provinces and, when Louis invaded in 1672, William of Orange began a campaign of armed resistance to French expansion that was to last for much of the next 30 years. In the course of his struggles against France, William eventually succeeded in mobilizing nearly all of Europe against Louis. In 1688 William was invited to cross the North Sea and replace his father-in-law and uncle, James II, on the British thrones. Following his successful landing at Torbay in November 1688, William lost little time in bringing Britain into his war against Louis as part of the Grand Alliance that he had formed with the Austrian Habsburgs and a number of other German princes. Britain was transformed by involvement in war. Parliament became a regular, rather than intermittent, feature of political life, spurred by the need to approve the taxes needed to fund the war. Moreover, following the foundation of the Bank of England in 1694, a sophisticated system of debt finance emerged in Britain, backed by parliamentary guarantee (Brewer, 1989). The growth of a national debt enabled Britain to extract resources more efficiently than previously, thus providing the means for it to compete more effectively on the international stage. The net result of these changes was that Britain, a bit-part player for much of the seventeenth century, emerged as a major force in European international relations during the Nine Years War (1688–97) and the War of the Spanish Succession (1701–14). By Louis XIV's death in 1715, the older dualism of Habsburg–Bourbon rivalry had evolved into a three-way split.

The Treaty of Utrecht (1713), which brought the War of the Spanish Succession to an end, introduced into the diplomatic lexicon a term that was to have considerable importance for future analysis of the states system – the balance of power. The idea behind the balance of power was simple: to prevent one power from becoming dominant in Europe, a balance should be maintained between powers. In any given conflict, it was the task of the unaligned powers to ally with the weaker side, rather than the stronger, to preserve the balance. Such notions accorded well with the thinking of the early Enlightenment. Just as Newton talked of a balance of forces that could be described by physics, so the relations between powers could also be balanced and described. Monarchs and ministers were becoming more interested in measuring the size of their own resources (both demographic and financial) and comparing them with those of other powers (Klueting, 1986). The most famous example of this almost statistical approach was the "political algebra" employed by Wenzel Anton, prince of Kaunitz-Rietburg, who controlled Austrian foreign policy for much of the second half of the eighteenth century. Yet Kaunitz was not alone in seeking to apply scientific calculation to the practice of diplomacy, and the balance of power was part of a broader rationalist turn in diplomatic thinking. In practical

Figure 14 The public announcement of the Peace of Rastatt that concluded the set of international treaties ending the War of the Spanish Succession in 1714, copper engraving by Pieter Schenk, 1714. *Wehrgeschichtliches Museum Rastatt*

terms, British commentators often assigned a particular role to Britain in the maintenance of the balance of power in the early eighteenth century. Britain should act as the "balancer" state, preventing either the Habsburgs or the Bourbons from becoming too powerful. Thus, while Louis lived it was right to support the Grand Alliance ranged against him. However, following his death and the succession of another youngster to the French throne, France was perceived as less threatening after 1715. Instead Austria was viewed as the greater problem for European stability by George I and Charles Townshend, his secretary of state, for the next decade or so. Consequently, Britain signed an alliance with France in 1716 and remained on good terms with France for the rest of Louis XV's minority.

The period after 1715 witnessed an unusual fluidity in international relations. Previously it had usually been clear that one power was pre-eminent in Europe. Yet France's relative passivity in the first years of Louis XV's reign meant several powers were matched reasonably evenly. Although historians blithely talk of an "international system" in the eighteenth century, in reality a single system did not emerge until the Napoleonic period. Instead, what existed was a set of three systems, with partial overlaps (Scott, 2006). In the north and east of Europe, there was a system centered on the Baltic. Russia increased her importance in the Baltic during the early eighteenth century through victory over Sweden in the Great Northern War (1700–21). In southeast Europe, Austria and Russia wanted to make territorial gains at the expense of the Ottomans. Austrian gains were more extensive in the early eighteenth century, but Russian gained far more after 1750 (Hochedlinger, 2003; Madariaga, 1981). The final system comprised the rest of Europe. There was already some degree of overlap between the systems in the early eighteenth century – British use of the Baltic as a source of naval stores ensured that Britain watched developments in the Great Northern War keenly – but they became more integrated in the years after 1740. The chief motor of this integration was the growing importance of Russia for European politics and the acceptance of Russia as an integral part of the general system by the other powers.

The Culture of Diplomacy

Changing approaches to the study of international relations reflect broader historiographical trends. Leopold von Ranke, who did so much for the development of modern historical methodology, exploited the opportunities offered by the gradual opening up of governmental archives in the nineteenth century in his own work. At the time Ranke wrote, much of the business of government was concerned with foreign relations and so this was reflected in the surviving official record. Consequently, he placed considerable emphasis on the importance of international relations for the development of states in his own writings. Arguably his work on the emergence of a great power system was part of a search for the origins of nineteenth-century patterns in the eighteenth century. Ranke argued that all states had to consider the preservation of their territorial integrity and external security above all else. These basic tenets of state survival meant that the conduct of diplomacy could be bound by neither domestic pressures nor ideological concerns. After Ranke, other historians within the Borussian, or Prussian, school enlarged his account into an entire world-view: the primacy of foreign policy (Ranke, 1950; Simms, 2003). To explain the rise and development of the Prussian state, it was sufficient to consider the difficult geopolitical position in which Prussia found itself. The dominance of this particular paradigm was such that older accounts of international relations tended to take a highly strategic approach, assuming that the unchanging dictates of "reason of state" (necessity justifying an entirely self-interested mode of political action) were sufficient to explain why a certain decision was taken. However, there is, as recent work has shown, much to be gained by placing the history of diplomacy and international relations within a broader web of cultural assumption (Bély, 1998; Blanning, 2002; Duchhardt, 1997). An understanding of the political cultures in which decisions were taken provides an important context for making sense of diplomatic history.

Diplomacy in the eighteenth century remained the preserve of monarchs. Bodin had identified the power of making war and peace as one of his marks of sovereignty, and for monarchs, keen to assert their monopolization of sovereignty within their realms, the conduct of foreign policy was a useful means to display their power. Traditional concerns, such as the furtherance of dynastic power through marriage alliances, remained an important part of the foreign policy agendas of most powers.

Indeed, it is important to remember that most states in this period were held together not by a shared language or culture but by a common ruler. Some rulers, such as Frederick II of Prussia or Catherine II of Russia, enjoyed partial success in consolidating their authority domestically, but others, most notably the Austrian Habsburgs, had to live with a higher degree of regional particularity and local privilege (Scott, 1990). In both cases, foreign political considerations played their part in determining the degree of monarchical authority. The Great Elector had reached an agreement with the Prussian nobility in 1653, whereby the *Junkers* agreed to guarantee taxes to fund the army in exchange for assurances that the elector would not interfere in the relationship between the *Junkers* and the serfs who farmed their lands. Subsequent Prussian rulers had built on this agreement to create a service nobility: Prussian *Junkers* achieved status through military service and the power of the Prussian ruler was thereby enhanced, both at home and abroad (Clark, 2006). The Austrian situation was different. For much of the late seventeenth and early eighteenth centuries the emperor was involved in wars with the Ottomans, and Austria made considerable territorial gains in the process (Hochedlinger, 2003). Yet to control these new territories proved difficult and expensive, and the only means that the emperor could find to do so was to grant large estates to his nobles along the military border. The price of Habsburg security against the Turk was a much higher degree of noble independence from central authority than was the case elsewhere in Europe.

The relationship between Crown and nobles was more generally important for diplomacy. Diplomats still tended to be drawn predominantly from the upper echelons of European society. Diplomatic etiquette reflected the status of most of its practitioners. A good diplomat was expected to be cognizant of appropriate courtly behavior and adept at cultivating contacts at his court of residence. Governments very rarely provided salaries that covered the considerable costs of the social whirl in the major European capitals so a private source of income was a virtual necessity. Many aristocratic diplomats regarded their posting as a temporary apprenticeship prior to securing a more important (and lucrative) appointment at home. With the top posts reserved for nobles, for others, domestic government service offered better opportunities for social advancement. There was, therefore, little in the way of a clear career structure for diplomats.

The reign of Louis XIV had witnessed several important developments in the way in which diplomacy was conducted. Louis had established a network of permanent missions in most European capitals. Other powers followed suit and a network of embassies and representatives soon developed. The permanent presence of foreign diplomats led to a formalization and standardization of the ways in which diplomats were treated, such as a recognition of diplomatic immunity and the right of ambassadors to worship according to their conscience, regardless of the laws of the country in which they resided. The growth of French power under Louis also meant that, in much of Europe, French became the language of diplomacy. Only southeastern Europe and the Mediterranean trod a different linguistic path. Here a form of Italian, known as the *lingua franca*, held sway. France also led the way in the growth of bureaucracy to manage foreign affairs. Other European powers followed, and Britain was unusual in only establishing a separate foreign office in 1782. Sporadic attempts were made by various European powers to provide more systematic and practical education for diplomats, such as the foundation of an Académie Politique to train diplomats in France in 1712 or the endowment of the Regius Chairs of History at Oxford and Cambridge in 1724. These attempts were only partially successful. Would-be diplomats could consult manuals on the art of diplomacy, study the vast compendiums of treaties and international law that were now being published, and, occasionally, learn the languages of the court to which they were posted. French diplomatic practice and organization tended to be exemplary. Yet other states were quick to imitate French practice so the differences tended to be those of scale rather than structure. There was, however, no widespread professionalization of diplomacy until the nineteenth century (Anderson, 1993; Frey and Frey, 1999; Scott, 2006).

Sources of Diplomatic Tension

The furtherance of dynastic interest has already been mentioned as a potential cause of trouble between monarchs. Such conflicts often appeared in the form of disputes over succession – there were wars of the Spanish (1701–14), Polish (1733–5), Austrian (1740–8), and Bavarian (1778–9) succession during the course of the eighteenth century. Even when dynastic issues were not indicated by the nomenclature of conflict, they could still lurk below the surface. The extended period of conflict between Britain and France, which lasted from 1688 to 1713 with only a short interlude of peace from 1697 to 1702, was arguably a war of the British succession. Following the deposition of James II, William III and then Anne were keen to ensure recognition of the Protestant succession in Britain from other European powers. Louis XIV was a consistent supporter of the claims of the exiled Stuarts. The continued importance of dynastic disputes in international relations is a reminder that foreign policy still reflected the interests of monarchs and an elite group of ministers around them. The pursuit of *gloire* was widely seen as a legitimate aim of foreign policy, even if the onset of the Enlightenment introduced more rationalist approaches. For a monarch to fulfill his or her role, it was vital to have a successful foreign policy and, at the very least, defend the existing borders of the realm. Foreign policy failure, as Louis XVI was to discover in France, could be the trigger for domestic unrest. Most eighteenth-century attempts at territorial expansion were presented as the legitimate defense of dynastic rights. Frederick II was unusual in his view that such defenses were solely for form's sake (Black, 2002).

Religion had been a considerable source of conflict in Europe in the late sixteenth and early seventeenth centuries. Traditionally, historians of international relations argued that the Peace of Westphalia (1648) marked the point at which religious and confessional concerns ceased to be central to the foreign policies of most European powers. While there was little support for an apocalyptic struggle between the forces of light and dark (Protestantism and Catholicism, or vice versa), after 1648 this did not mean that confessional concerns disappeared entirely from the foreign policy agenda. Westphalia attempted to set the confessional boundaries of the empire in stone, but both the Counter-Reformation and Louis XIV intervened to prevent this in the later seventeenth century. Consequently, the defense of Protestant rights and representations in defense of persecuted minorities continued to play a role in diplomatic relations between Catholic and Protestant powers. There was intermittent talk of confessional leagues, although this rarely came to much. However, British ministers in the first half of the eighteenth century were confident that an alliance with the Protestant United Provinces would prove longer-lasting than more temporary associations with Catholic powers to achieve immediate ends. At the very least, the defense of religious rights remained a useful tool to governments trying to "sell" a particular policy choice to either their own people or other powers.

National sentiment was much less pervasive as a source of international conflict until very late in the eighteenth century. Generally speaking, national feeling was more common in the more unified territories of western Europe, but even here it was not decisive. The lack of unified legal and administrative systems, coupled with relatively low rates of mass education, made the popular nationalism of the nineteenth century almost impossible. States were held together by loyalty to a ruler rather than a deeper sense of cultural belonging. The workings of the international system also mitigated against the formation of national feeling to some extent. One aspect of the workings of the balance of power was that it was rare for even a defeated power to lose everything in a peace settlement. The need to ensure that no power could become dominant made the complete destruction of another power a risky strategy. Hence it was a common feature of peace agreements for territorial exchanges to take place. The victors would usually get the better deal from such arrangements but the losers would not be left with nothing. The transfer of territories from one ruler to another therefore made the development of nationalist feeling difficult. All this changed in the 1790s. Although the content of French foreign policy was not nearly as different from that of the *ancien régime* as the revolutionaries claimed, the way in which it was presented changed markedly. Instead of mobilizing the French populace on the basis of loyalty to the monarch, the revolutionary regimes used an idea – the nation – to cajole and coerce men into the revolutionary armies. It was the declared aim of the new regime to offer assistance to other oppressed peoples, keen to throw off the yoke of monarchy. The French Revolutionary Wars also prompted the growth of national feeling in another (but unintentional) way. Napoleonic domination of continental Europe and attempts to introduce French-style centralization prompted a nationalist backlash in central Europe and a desire to preserve local rights and customs.

Resolving trade disputes was an increasingly important part of diplomatic activity. The mercantile lobby was particularly extensive in both the United Provinces and Britain. The East India companies in both countries looked to ministries for help when they felt their rights and privileges were being infringed by other powers. The negotiation of commercial agreements was one task that most diplomats would be expected to perform. At a more mundane level, merchants were often given a low-ranking diplomatic position, such as agent, in major port towns as a means to ensure that the commercial interests of their royal masters were represented and important intelligence was passed back to home capitals. The eighteenth century witnessed a considerable expansion of European interests in extra-European territories, particularly in Asia and the Americas. The struggle to obtain new territories and markets frequently provoked tensions, and these tensions fed back into disputes in Europe. The problems that eighteenth-century diplomats had to deal with arose from a number of sources. The notion of a separate and independent "national" interest was only slowly being disentangled from monarchical interests. The balance-of-power system tended to encourage a flexible approach to alliances, and a variety of options were often considered as a means to achieve a particular end. The fluidity of the international system was also encouraged by a separate development: the changes in the relative importance and standing of the European powers.

The Emergence of New Great Powers

Britain had joined France and Austria as a great power by the end of the War of the Spanish Succession. It was not until after 1740 that new aspirants to great power status emerged. Prussia and Russia had both been recognized as great powers by the end of the Seven Years War in 1763. Examining the process of their emergence throws light on what it meant to be a great power in the eighteenth century and indicates the growing gap between the major players and the second rank of powers.

Of the two, Russia's rise was less surprising. Russia already had many of the prerequisites for successful participation in great power politics. Russia's territory was both extensive and also relatively easy to defend from attack by other powers. The geographical expanse of its territory provided another significant advantage: a large population. In 1740, the tsar had approximately 18 million subjects so Russia had human resources both to run an agricultural economy and to maintain an army which was the largest on the continent until the Napoleonic period. Peter the Great had worked hard to improve both its administration and leadership, and the results of his reforms were clear from Russia's defeat of Sweden in the Great Northern War. After 1740, Russia's involvement in both the War of the Austrian Succession and, more importantly, the Seven Years War (1756–63), forced the other European powers to recognize Russian pretensions to great power status. The eagerness of other great powers to ally with Russia on equal terms reflected this new status.

Despite the protestations of later generations of Borussian historians, Prussia's leap to great power status was far from inevitable. Within the empire, Brandenburg-Prussia was one of a number of important players in the early eighteenth century. The Hohenzollerns gained royal status in 1701, but arguably some of their north German rivals had done better for themselves. The Wettin rulers of Saxony had already secured a royal title in 1697, through the election of Augustus II as king of Poland. The Hohenzollerns' other near neighbors, the Hanoverian Guelphs, had been named successors to the British thrones by the Act of Settlement (1701) and this was realized in 1714 when the death of Queen Anne brought Elector Georg Ludwig to the throne as George I. Prussia's population was not large – about 2.25 million in 1740 – and the economic base was far from ideal. Much of the soil of eastern Prussia and Brandenburg was of poor quality and there was little in the way of industry. Moreover, Prussia lacked obvious "natural boundaries" and was strategically vulnerable. There were, however, underlying explanations for Prussia's strength. Stretching back into the seventeenth century, its rulers had placed a high priority on maintaining a substantial army. Frederick William I (r. 1713–40) inherited an army of 40,000. By his death, this figure had grown to 80,000. He had introduced almost universal male conscription in 1733 through the cantonal recruitment system, in which each regiment was assigned an area and the peasants served for a set period before returning to their villages, where they remained as reserves. Additionally, Frederick William left his son a considerable war chest. Sound administration meant that state revenues were in the region of 7 million thaler a year. Frederick inherited 8 million thaler of reserves when his father died and this enabled him to fund his invasion of Silesia following the death of the Holy Roman Emperor, Charles VI (Clark, 2006; Showalter, 1996).

The emergence of both Prussia and Russia as great powers was one important consequence of the conflicts that rocked Europe in the middle decades of the eighteenth century. Yet the effects of both the War of the Austrian Succession and the Seven Years War were more widely felt. The gap between the great powers and other powers in terms of both resources and power increased in this period. One definition of a great power was the ability to fight without significant support from other powers. Spain, Bavaria, Saxony, and Piedmont had made important contributions to previous conflicts, but it was now clear that they would only be able to participate in, rather than lead, an alliance. The increased number of great powers also multiplied the possibilities for alliances between themselves. Britain no longer faced a straightforward choice between supporting the weaker of Austria and France to maintain a balance. Prussia and Russia now had to be considered as well. The increased options also made it more difficult to maintain a stable system (Anderson, 1995; Scott, 2006).

Although Russia, in particular, was now more involved in European politics, the mid-century struggles also led to a partial realignment of the fault-lines within Europe. Two different struggles for domination were now clear. In the west, France and Britain's importance for European politics as a whole was reduced by the rise of the eastern powers. Yet it had become clear that both France and Britain viewed the other as the major adversary. Conflict between the two was no longer contained within Europe. The European Seven Years War was prefigured by significant skirmishing between British and French colonial forces in North America. The British colonists were worried that French advances in the Ohio valley and from Canada might lead to the eventual encirclement of the colonies. The Seven Years War also saw significant fighting in South Asia. Between 1758 and 1762, helped by the temporary neutrality of Bourbon Spain, Britain was able to make significant advances against French colonial possessions, taking islands in the West Indies and expelling the French from Canada (Peters, 1998).

The second struggle was that between Prussia and Austria in central Europe. Frederick's seizure of Silesia was not something that Maria Theresia was willing to accept and the recovery of Silesia became an *idée fixe* of Austrian policy. Britain in particular was slow to realize the importance of Silesia for Austria. British ministers hoped to broker a compromise between Prussia and Austria during the War of the Austrian Succession so that both could participate in the more important (from the British point of view) struggle against France in the west. Austria's desire to regain Silesia was one of the causes of the major realignment that preceded the Seven Years War, usually referred to as the "Diplomatic Revolution." French rivalry with Austria had been the touchstone of conflict between the European powers for nearly two centuries but, faced with Prussian ambition, Austrian statesmen (in particular Kaunitz) were prepared to think in new ways. Kaunitz did not believe that the leading British ministers, in particular the duke of Newcastle, were interested in helping Austria recover Silesia. Consequently, Kaunitz wanted to find more useful allies for his immediate aims. Russia was wary of the growth of Prussian power and so was a potential ally. However, Kaunitz was unconvinced that Russia could be won without subsidies and, as Austria was in no position to offer any, he was keen to neutralize or win over France as a first step. It was not, however, Kaunitz who precipitated the rearrangement of diplomatic forces. Newcastle was concerned by Britain's lack of continental allies to help in the struggle against France. His advances to Austria had achieved little so he turned, instead, to Russia. In September 1755 a convention was agreed with Russia providing for troops in exchange for subsidies if Britain were attacked. Newcastle wanted to deter Frederick from attacking George II's Hanoverian possessions. In this he succeeded, as Frederick quickly turned to Britain in an effort to negate the convention with Russia and secure his own position. Britain and Prussia agreed to a vague formula of neutralizing Germany and promising not to attack one another in the Convention of Westminster (January 1756). The French were angered that Frederick had abandoned them and were, therefore, keen to listen to Austrian proposals which eventually resulted in a defensive alliance in the First Treaty of Versailles (May 1756). Frederick became convinced that he would be attacked by Russia and Austria (although Kaunitz himself wanted to win France first; he still thought the financial strain would be too great without French help) in early 1757, and so took the dramatic step of getting his blow in first and invaded Saxony in August 1756, thus precipitating more general European conflict.

The consequences of the Seven Years War were manifold. On the one hand, Britain emerged as the significant victor in the struggle with France. Britain was now clearly the dominant maritime and colonial power, and both France and Spain suffered significant losses, even if the British public felt that these should have been greater. The British victory was, however, a mixed blessing. The costs of the war had been significant for Britain and the national debt had almost doubled. Consequently, London sought to recoup some of the costs. One way to do this was to ask British colonial subjects to contribute more to the cost of their defense. While the policy seemed prudent management to the Westminster Parliament, the colonists viewed matters differently. Their slogan, "No taxation without representation," encapsulated their complaints but, from a more practical viewpoint, it was unclear, given the expulsion of the French, why so much had still to be spent on their defense. Britain's victory also made it more difficult to claim that Britain held the balance of power in Europe. The power of France had been so reduced that traditional British calls to arms, based on the need to prevent French hegemony, now sounded rather hollow. If anything, Britain had achieved an unparalleled dominance in extra-European affairs. Complaints were made that talk of the balance of power was a chimera – a mask for the naked ambitions of states. Britain, partly from choice and partly from necessity, was less involved in continental politics and more isolated in the aftermath of the war.

France suffered most from defeat in the Seven Years War. The costs of the conflict, both financial and material, had been huge. The French Crown had borrowed significant sums from both its own population and on the international markets to fund the war, and debt repayment was a heavy burden. Indeed, in the longer term, the debt was to have a major destabilizing effect on the monarchy's very existence. The losses for Louis XV were not merely financial. He had also suffered a huge hemorrhage of that vital international currency, prestige (Blanning, 2002; Riley, 1980,

1987). The Peace of Hubertusburg (1763), which settled matters within the empire, was made without French participation, despite France's position as a guarantor of the imperial constitution. Worse was to follow. France found it increasingly difficult to exert any influence within eastern Europe, both because of her own financial weakness and because Austria, Prussia, and Russia were increasingly unwilling to let extra-territorial powers play any role in their regional affairs. The alliance with Austria survived the war and was strengthened further by the marriage of Louis XV's grandson to a Habsburg princess, Marie Antoinette, in 1770. The Austrian alliance was far from popular with some sections of the French elite, who associated it with the disasters of the Seven Years War. France faced an almost impossible situation: to recover international prestige, it would be necessary to achieve a significant victory against another power (probably Britain), but the cost of such a conflict would be huge and success was far from assured.

The eastern powers operated in a sphere largely separate from France and Britain in the thirty years after the Seven Years War. Like France, Austria had borrowed significantly to fund participation in the war and was crippled with debt from it. Austria had failed to achieve most of its aims: Silesia was still in Prussian hands and, far from being reduced back to second-rank status, Prussia could now justifiably sit at the table of the great powers. A long period of peace was necessary for domestic recovery, so Austria was unable to seize the diplomatic initiative. Joseph II, who became emperor in 1765, was an admirer of Prussian reforms and sought to increase Habsburg power through emulation of his Hohenzollern neighbors. One strategy close to his heart was the consolidation of the Habsburg lands in central Europe and the disposal of outlying territories. Thus, plans to swap the Austrian Netherlands for Bavaria came to be seen as almost a "magic bullet" to solve Austrian problems (Dickson, 1987; Hochedlinger, 2003).

Austrian diplomatic impotence was magnified by the position of the two other eastern powers. Prussia had fought almost to a standstill in the Seven Years War. Indeed, it was only the accession of the Prussophile Peter III in 1762 that had prevented the destruction of Frederick's armies. Unlike other powers, Prussia had not financed her war effort through borrowing, but rather through a combination of domestic taxation and foreign subsidies. This had still placed considerable strains of the Prussian economy, and the lesson that Frederick drew from the two major wars that dominated the first half of his reign was that his successes could now only be preserved through peace (Scott, 2001).

Russia also emerged from the Seven Years War without significant foreign debts, but the costs of the war had to be met from increased domestic taxation. Peter III's reign was short-lived and his wife, Catherine II, inherited a desire to steer Russia away from an overly Prussian policy. Peace was still the order of the day, and when, to secure the election to the Polish Crown, it became necessary to secure an ally, Frederick was able to persuade Catherine that cooperation with Prussia offered the best means to achieve her aims. The Russo-Prussian treaty of 1764 created the breathing space for domestic recovery in both Prussia and Russia but it also left Austria excluded and without allies.

The chief victims of the successful recovery of the eastern powers were to be the Ottoman empire and Poland. The Ottomans declared war on Russia in 1768, worried by increasing Russian influence in Poland. Russia made significant territorial gains in southeast Europe, so much so that both Austria and Prussia were increasingly worried by Russian power. To head off the risk of unchecked Russian gains, Frederick proposed switching attention from the Balkans to Poland. He suggested that Austria, Prussia, and Russia should partially partition Poland. Although the Austrians were reluctant to support an increase in either Russian or Prussian power, they could not afford to reject an offer of an increase to their territory, especially if Prussia and Russia would make gains regardless. More importantly, neither Prussia nor Austria was in a position to prevent Russian gains unilaterally, so both sought to satisfy Catherine's territorial appetites in another direction. In the long run this strategy was unsuccessful. Although a feeling of common interest developed between the powers, Frederick's policies had unfortunate consequences for Prussian security in the longer term. First, the buffer zone that Poland had offered between Prussian and Russian territory was reduced and, secondly, the chances of Austro-Russian rapprochement increased. This was unlikely to take place while Maria Theresia lived, but Kaunitz was keen to lay the groundwork for reconciliation with Russia. Polish partition also illustrated the separateness of the western and eastern systems. Britain was largely indifferent to partition. Poland had previously been a French client in the *barrière de l'ost*, but France's inability to intervene to prevent partition was a tangible sign of the decline of French power (Lukowski, 1999).

The period between the first and the final partition of Poland in 1795 demonstrated Russia's dominance of eastern Europe and, arguably, European politics as a whole. Although the Treaty of Kutchuk-Kainardji (1774) had confirmed Russian territorial gains against the Ottomans, there was still space for Catherine to push her borders through the Crimea to the Black Sea. Russian policy towards the Crimea changed from a desire to preserve it as a useful satellite to one of outright annexation (similar to the changed Russian attitude towards Poland), and by 1783 the Crimea had been absorbed. Maria Theresia's death in 1780 had paved the way for a secret Austro-Russian treaty in 1781, and the Austrians found themselves forced to support Russia in a further war against the Ottomans (1787–92). As so often, Austria failed to derive the advantage it hoped from the alliance. Russia did not support Austrian attempts to exchange Bavaria for the Austrian Netherlands. There was no brake on Russian expansion in southeast Europe and no tangible Russian attempts to contain Prussian power. Just as in Poland, Austria had to accept Russian territorial gains with the slight consolation of being able to make some gains as well. Russia was able to exploit Austro-Prussian rivalry to ensure that an ally would always be available to support Russian expansionism and play the two powers off against each other. The revolution in France in 1789 sent ripples throughout Europe. Catherine encouraged both Prussia and Austria to resist the revolution militarily but the relatively unsuccessful campaigns of 1792 increased her bargaining power. Worried by growing unrest and signs of independence in Poland, Catherine was able to persuade Prussia (keen on the idea anyway) and Austria that a further seizure of Polish territory was necessary, and by 1795, following two rounds of losses, Poland had ceased to exist.

Part of the predicament that both France and Austria faced prior to the French Revolution was that, although they were nominally allies, neither power was really prepared to become involved in the battles of the other. Austria had hoped for French backing over the Bavarian exchange scheme, but Vergennes, the French foreign minister, was unforthcoming. He claimed that, as the 1756 alliance was defensive, it was impossible for France to back a scheme that would see Austria make unilateral gains. Moreover, Vergennes was about to intervene in the conflict between Britain and the American colonists on the side of the rebels. He was anxious that the British should not be able to divert French resources from America by provoking a more general European conflict. One of his chief motives for involvement in the Americas was a restoration of French prestige. There was, after all, little in the way of a common ideological platform between France, an absolutist monarchy, and the colonists, who were keen to rid themselves of rule by the most liberal of the European monarchies. Faced with a united Bourbon naval front, Britain tried to find continental allies. Attempts met with little success both because the eastern powers were preoccupied with their own affairs and, as war had already broken out, any alliance would involve the alliance partner in immediate military engagements. Britain, unable to distract France and Spain with a continental war, was defeated in the colonies and had to recognize American independence in 1783. Yet the French victory was a pyrrhic one. To finance the war, France had borrowed heavily and thus further destabilized the monarchy's domestic position and credit. The hope had been that the grateful colonists would thank France by altering their trading habits and concentrating their exports on France rather than Britain. Unfortunately, despite the conflict, there was a rapid return to business as usual, and the bulk of the colonists' trade with Europe continued to flow through British ports.

The Impact of the French Revolution

The disturbances in France were not initially seen by the great powers as particularly threatening. Indeed, it seemed likely that, preoccupied with revolution, France would be unable to play a significant part on the international stage, leaving the other powers with greater freedom of maneuver. Initial declarations of pacific intent by the National Assembly had disappeared by early 1792. Brissot and his followers had been arguing since the autumn of the previous year that war was needed both to spread revolutionary doctrine and to save the revolution at home. The descent into conflict would act as a means of sorting the sheep from the goats and demonstrate the power of France to other European powers. French aggression was particularly directed towards Austria, homeland of the hated Marie Antoinette, and those German princes who were harboring aristocratic émigrés. The French hoped that they might find support from Prussia, given Prussia's enmity towards Austria. However, Prussia had undergone a partial reconciliation with Austria, signified by the Convention of Reichenbach (1790) and the Treaty of Pillnitz (1791). The monarchies of the east were concerned by French revolutionary doctrine. The struggles between France and the other European powers that were to run almost continuously until 1815 were marked by a sharp ideological division between the two camps. Although older concerns with the preservation of territory remained, there was a new struggle between those who proclaimed the rights of man and those who wanted to defend the old order. Much eighteenth-century war was based around the idea of maintaining a rough balance at the conflict's end, even if the victors gained more. Such an approach has often been characterized as "limited" war, although there was, of course, nothing limited about it for those caught up in the middle. The struggle against France became something more – the European powers desired not simply to defeat France militarily but to restore a monarchical system and return Europe to as it had been in 1789.

The French Revolution has sometimes been seen as inaugurating a new era in the conduct of war, although it has been convincingly shown that, from a purely tactical point of view, the innovations often associated with the revolutionaries had earlier roots (Blanning, 1996). What the revolution did bring was an increase in both the size of armies and the number of attempts to persuade men to fight for an idea, the nation, rather than a person, the king. Yet while the revolutionaries spoke in the new language of nationalism many of the foreign policy aims of the revolutionary regime were remarkably similar to those of their monarchical predecessors – the preservation of French territorial integrity and the expansion of French power around its borders. In some ways, the role of diplomacy was diminished in this period. The revolutionaries were suspicious of foreign diplomats, regarding them as spies. Revolutionary political culture was also unimpressed by the high rank and concomitant social expectations that had accompanied diplomacy under the old regime. A further problem was that of recognition. Diplomacy as the art of negotiation between parties was predicated on the assumption that both sides were the legitimate representatives of their respective governments. The great powers were slow to recognize the legitimacy of the new French regime, and this created difficulties in reaching agreements. Moreover, the importance of diplomacy was greatly reduced under the Napoleonic regime that followed on from the revolutionary regimes of the 1790s. Napoleon sought to solve all France's problems through military, rather than diplomatic, means. He had little time for protracted negotiations. Instead he aimed to win the decisive military victory over his adversaries that would enable him to dictate terms.

Two final aspects of the international system in the era of the French Revolution are worth mentioning. The first relates to the nature of the system itself. Although the idea of five great powers who dominated European diplomacy was clear by the end of the Seven Years War, the European system remained subdivided into an eastern and western sphere. The struggle against first the revolution and then Napoleon brought the two systems together. Controlling the power of France was no longer simply a concern for Britain, as Napoleon's extensive territorial conquests in continental Europe showed. The unification of the two systems laid the foundation of nineteenth-century notions of a "concert" of Europe. All the European great powers had a common interest in seeing that peace was preserved throughout the continent. Secondly, the eventual defeat of Napoleon owed much, if not everything, to Russian power. This was not simply because of Napoleon's ill-advised invasion of Russia in 1812 but because, in the aftermath of Napoleon's defeat at the gates of Moscow, Tsar Alexander I took on the role of Europe's liberator. Napoleon was not just pushed out of Russia but, in a series of battles between 1813 and 1815, forced back within France itself.

The changes in the international system in the second half of the eighteenth century had almost entirely worked to Russia's benefit. Geographically secure (like Britain), it was able to influence European politics from the periphery, and such intervention was frequently decisive. The Vienna settlement of 1815 sought to contain the power of France and prevent any further revival of French domination of the continent. Despite having played a relatively minor role until almost the end of the struggle with Napoleon, Prussia was rewarded with extensive territories in the Rhineland to prevent an expansion of French power eastwards. Alexander's military successes gave him a decisive voice in negotiating the status of much of central and eastern Europe. Although Prussia and Austria received some territories in Poland, the bulk of it was retained by Alexander. Britain made no territorial gains in Europe, although Hanover was restored to independent status, but British colonial gains from both the French and Dutch were confirmed, and Britain retained the naval supremacy that underpinned the extra-European empire. The costs of the Revolutionary Wars had been huge. It was the need to retrench, as much as the Vienna settlement itself, that led to an extended period of peace between the great powers after 1815. It was also much easier to maintain peace when new great powers were not trying to force their way to the negotiating table. Many eighteenth-century conflicts resulted from the struggle for recognition of great power status. France and Austria, the dominant powers in 1700, were slowly eclipsed by the new great powers Britain, Prussia, and Russia.

Bibliography

Anderson, M. S., *The Rise of Modern Diplomacy, 1450–1919* (London, 1993).
Anderson, M. S., *The War of the Austrian Succession, 1740–1748* (Harlow, 1995).
Bély, L., *Les Relations internationales en Europe XVIIe–XVIIIe siècles* (2nd edn., Paris, 1998).
Black, J., *European International Relations, 1648–1815* (Basingstoke, 2002).
Blanning, T. C. W., *The French Revolutionary Wars, 1787–1802* (London, 1996).
Blanning, T. C. W., *The Culture of Power and the Power of Culture: Old Regime Europe 1660–1789* (Oxford, 2002).
Brewer, J., *The Sinews of Power* (London, 1989).
Clark, C., *Iron Kingdom: The Rise and Downfall of Prussia, 1600–1947* (London, 2006).
Dickson, P. G. M., *Finance and Government under Maria Theresia, 1740–1780* (2 vols., Oxford, 1987).
Duchhardt, H., *Balance of Power und Pentarchie: Internationale Beziehungen, 1700–1785* (Paderborn, 1997).
Ertman, T., *Birth of the Leviathan* (Cambridge, 1997).
Frey, L. S. and M. L. Frey, *The History of Diplomatic Immunity* (Columbus, OH, 1999).
Hochedlinger, M., *Austria's Wars of Emergence: War, State and Society in the Habsburg Monarchy 1683–1797* (London, 2003).
Ingrao, C. W., *The Habsburg Monarchy, 1618–1815* (2nd edn., Cambridge, 2000).
International History Review, 16 (1994), issue 4 on international relations.
Klueting, H., *Die Lehre von der Macht der Staaten* (Berlin, 1986).
Lukowski, J. T., *The Partitions of Poland: 1772, 1793, 1795* (Harlow, 1999).
Madariaga, I. de, *Russia in the Age of Catherine the Great* (London, 1981).
McKay, D. and H. M. Scott, *The Rise of the Great Powers, 1648–1815* (London, 1983).
Peters, M., *The Elder Pitt* (Harlow, 1998).
Ranke, L. v., "The great powers," in T. v. Laue, *Leopold von Ranke: The Formative Years* (Princeton, NJ, 1950), pp. 181–218.
Riley, J. C., *International Government Finance and the Amsterdam Capital Market, 1740–1815* (New York and Cambridge, 1980).
Riley, J. C., "French finances, 1727–1768," *Journal of Modern* History, 59 (1987), 209–43.
Schroeder, P. W., *The Transformation of European Politics, 1763–1848* (Oxford, 1994).

Scott, H. M. (ed.), *Enlightened Absolutism: Reform and Reformers in Later Eighteenth-Century Europe* (Basingstoke, 1990).
Scott, H. M., *The Emergence of the Eastern Powers, 1756–1775* (Cambridge, 2001).
Scott, H. M., *The Birth of a Great Power System, 1740–1815* (Harlow, 2006).
Showalter, D. E., *The Wars of Frederick the Great* (London, 1996).
Simms, B., *The Struggle for Mastery in Germany, 1779–1850* (Basingstoke, 1998).
Simms, B., "The return of the primacy of foreign policy," *German History*, 21 (2003), 275–91.
Wilson, P. H., *German Armies: War and German Politics, 1648–1806* (London, 1998).

Chapter Twenty-Four

Islam and Europe

Molly Greene

The Ottoman Empire and the European International System

The Ottoman eighteenth century begins, conveniently enough, in 1699 with the signing of the Treaty of Karlowitz, which brought to an end the long war between the Ottoman empire and the Holy League (1683–97). Ottoman historians agree that this treaty was a watershed in Ottoman–European relations, for several reasons. By the terms of the agreement, the Ottomans ceded Hungary, Transylvania, and Slavonia to the Habsburgs and returned the Morea (southern Greece) to Venice. For the first time an Ottoman Sultan formally acknowledged the defeat and the permanent loss of territory conquered by his ancestors, as opposed to a temporary withdrawal. Second, by revealing the weakness of the "terrible Turk," the Ottoman defeat ushered in a long period of instability in the Balkans, a situation, it can be argued, which lasted all the way up until the gunshots in Sarajevo in 1914 began World War I. Finally, the Ottoman negotiators at Karlowitz accepted French mediation on their behalf (Quataert, 2005: 78).

A relentless focus on decline often accompanies references to the Treaty of Karlowitz, but it was also the birth of something new. A novel kind of diplomacy emerged on the Italian peninsula during the late Renaissance in response to the incessant warfare of the period. It was continuous, rather than intermittent, and it accepted the ideas of reciprocity and equality of sovereignty. From its birth in Italy, the new diplomacy spread throughout Europe.[1] With the Treaty of Karlowitz, the Ottomans also joined this path towards a new system of international relations. Although it was not until the nineteenth century that Ottoman diplomacy truly became reciprocal and continuous, Ottoman diplomats sought both mediation and defensive alliances during the course of the eighteenth century. Between 1703 and 1774 Ottomans signed 68 recorded treaties and agreements with other states (Quataert, 2005: 75). We must also remember that while the cessation of so much territory was a severe blow, the downward trajectory of the empire remained unclear. Military victories, modest but real nevertheless, still lay ahead. Just a few years after Karlowitz, Ottoman forces roundly defeated the Russian army under Peter the Great

A Companion to Eighteenth-Century Europe, First Edition. Edited by Peter H. Wilson.
© 2014 John Wiley & Sons, Ltd. Published 2014 by John Wiley & Sons, Ltd.

on the Moldavian border, obliging him to give up all of his recent conquests; several years later the Ottomans also regained the lost fortress of Azov on the Black Sea. In their final war with Venice (1714–18) all of the Morea once again came under Ottoman sovereignty. There were also victories against the Habsburgs. The important city of Belgrade, for example, went back and forth between the two empires, and at the beginning of the nineteenth century it was still in Ottoman hands.

Any consideration of the eighteenth century must include the emergence of France as the most important ally of the Sultans, although re-emergence is actually a better word. The French–Ottoman relationship had also been close in the sixteenth century. Among many other memorable moments, the French had scandalized the Christian world – and frightened Charles V in particular – by allowing the Ottoman fleet to stay at Toulon in the winter of 1543–4, at a time when naval hostilities between the Ottomans and the Habsburgs were at their height (Braudel, 1973: 906). During the difficult seventeenth century the French could not manage a coherent, or continuous, policy in the eastern Mediterranean, but Colbert's reforms ushered in a century of French pre-eminence, both commercial and political, at the Ottoman court.

The long-standing French interest in the Ottoman empire was dictated by her equally enduring antipathy towards the Habsburgs. Eighteenth-century France continued with the staunch anti-Habsburg policy that had long been the hallmark of her foreign policy. Following the old adage that the enemy of my enemy is my friend, the French monarchy cultivated a close relationship with the Ottoman sultans, who nursed their own enmity towards the Habsburgs. The French willingness to talk to the Ottomans even as the latter were attacking the Christian Habsburgs earned Louis XIV the scornful title of the "Grand Turk of Versailles." As mentioned earlier, it was French diplomats who mediated on behalf of the Ottomans at the negotiations leading up to the Treaty of Karlowitz, and they did so again in 1740, at the end of a three-year war with the Russians and the Habsburgs (Quartaert, 2005: 78). The Ottomans repaid the favor by making the Capitulations with France permanent. The Capitulations were the agreements that regulated the position of Europeans within the empire; normally they expired upon the death of a sultan and had to be negotiated all over again. When the sultan sent Yirmisekiz Mehmed Said Efendi to Europe in 1721 to "make a thorough study of the means of civilization and education, and report on those capable of application" in the empire, it was Paris that was the ambassador's destination (Lewis, 1961: 45–6).

The increasing routinization of Ottoman diplomacy, and the close Ottoman–French ties, might seem to indicate the progressive normalization of the relationship between Europe and her Muslim neighbor in the eighteenth century. It would seem that this was so for the Ottomans.[2] In addition to the evolution of Ottoman diplomacy, at least one prominent Ottoman bureaucrat and historian, Na'ima, argued that the age of the warrior was over and the time of the bureaucrat had begun. On the European side, the criticism of Louis XIV, suggests that the idea (although not the reality) of Christian solidarity still lingered. On a more substantive level, French policy in the eastern Mediterranean had always had a strong religious component and it continued to do so in the eighteenth century. Briefly put, in the sixteenth century France had managed to replace Venice as the pre-eminent Catholic power in a part of the world that was still vitally important to Christianity. This also included patronage of and protection over the small Ottoman Catholic community, which increased

French influence and visibility in the empire. One of the most enduring examples of such visibility concerned the church of St. Francis in Istanbul. Towards the end of the sixteenth century, the church was reopened, thanks to the efforts of Henry IV's ambassador to Istanbul, Savary de Brèves. The church authorities acknowledged the French role by assigning the ambassador a special seat of honor at the front of the entire congregation at Sunday Mass. This tradition remained in force until 1914 (Frazee, 1983: 78).

The basis of French patronage of the Catholic Church was, again, the special relationship between France and the empire. Under the shield of the Capitulations, Catholic clergy could be assigned to minister not only to French merchants operating in Ottoman ports, but to Catholics more generally. It was this privileged relationship that explains why, whenever Catholic bishops needed a *berat*, or letter of appointment from the sultan, they turned to the French ambassador to procure it and, often, to pay for it.

At the beginning of the eighteenth century, France's long monopoly over the empire's Catholics came to an end. The Treaty of Karlowitz had religious as well as political significance. For the first time the Habsburgs gained some rights of protection and patronage over the Catholic communities that had traditionally looked to the French ambassador for support. Among other things, the treaty empowered the Habsburg ambassador to seek redress of injuries to Catholics in Ottoman lands, especially in Palestine (Frazee, 1983: 154). Here, too, the Treaty of Karlowitz hinted at things to come. As the Ottoman empire weakened and the Eastern Question developed, the great powers competed with each other for influence and power within the empire. An essential instrument in this competition was the claim – buttressed by the Capitulations – that they were only protecting this or that Christian community. In the relatively quiet eighteenth century, Habsburg–French rivalry did not add up to much. But it is worth remembering that the Crimean War (1854–6) had its origins in Napoleon III's pressure on the Ottomans to recognize France as the sovereign authority in the Holy Land. Russia quickly responded, insisting that it was the protector of the Christian faith in the Ottoman empire. Napoleon III reacted with a show of force in the Black Sea, and the war was on. Both Orthodox Russia and Catholic France, in other words, explicitly referenced their religious identity in claiming a right to intervene in Ottoman affairs.

For our purposes, two things are important. First, Russia was responding, of course, as the leading Christian Orthodox power. The direct religious confrontation in the Ottoman empire was always between the Catholics and the Orthodox. The Catholic Church wisely directed its missionizing towards the Orthodox, not the Muslims. Both Christian churches were dependent upon the Ottomans to show them favor and to privilege them vis-à-vis the other. And the sultans did indeed play one off against another, in a three-sided game whose origins stretched all the way back to the twelfth century when Saladin regained Jerusalem from the Crusaders.

Second, it is true that in the course of the eighteenth century France's representatives in the Ottoman empire became increasingly critical of the missionary enterprise which they had long protected and championed. Jean Louis d'Usson, Louis XV's ambassador, wrote home that there were too many missionaries, that they made "the Turks" uneasy, and that they seemed to think that the Capitulations gave them free rein to do as they liked. This impulse should not be over-emphasized. Growing anti-religious sentiment back in Europe did not automatically translate into a more secular foreign policy, especially in a part of the world so laden with Christian associations. When the pope himself ordered the dissolution of the Jesuits in 1773, the French ambassador in Istanbul ignored their continuing activity (Frazee, 1983: 163). More importantly, in the nineteenth century, as French imperial interests in the eastern Mediterranean grew, the old rhetoric of France as the protector of Catholicism in the Orient came roaring back.

Further to the west, France's ambivalent relationship to the Muslim world is also in evidence. In the course of the eighteenth century, as corsairing (piracy) declined, the North Africans tried to establish themselves as shippers between their cities and Marseilles. The French proved unwelcoming. North African traders were unable to find translators or storage space for their goods in Marseilles, and were accused of still being pirates and chased out of port.

The Ottoman Empire and European Influence

By the eighteenth century the military balance had shifted in favor of the European powers. To what extent did this translate into greater European influence within the sultan's domains? This is a matter of much debate amongst historians of the empire. The answers seem clearer for other centuries. In the sixteenth century, the Ottoman empire was not only a first-rate power, but one of the most formidable states on the face of the globe. Conversely, by the nineteenth century, nationalist movements were breaking off great chunks of territory while the Europeans, through a combination of financial and military means (the latter more often threatened than realized), made serious inroads into Ottoman sovereignty. The century in between is harder to characterize, especially because the Ottomans and the Europeans enjoyed a long period of relative peace with each other, stretching from 1718 until 1774.[3] This was obviously a blessing for all concerned, but for the historian there is no war to frame the international picture.

Ottoman historians today generally agree that, in the rush to consign the empire to the dustbin of history, the traditional view seriously overestimates European power over and within the empire in the eighteenth century. Let us begin by looking at the commercial picture. In studies of European imperialism, European merchants, and the companies back home that supported them, are often viewed as the first wave of colonization. Later on, economic control turned into political control, as in the case of the East India Company in South Asia. It is tempting to apply that paradigm to the Ottoman eighteenth century. After all, as the century wore on, trade did become more "colonial." In the early decades, the traditional pattern still adhered; trade levels were low and luxury goods predominated. Commercial exchange between Europe and the Ottoman empire then changed character. Particularly after 1750, the empire began to export more of its own raw materials and to import colonial goods. The port cities which facilitated this trade with Europe grew rapidly – the city of Izmir doubled its population from 50,000 to 100,000 over the course of the eighteenth century – and have received a good deal of attention from historians (Quataert, 2005: 115).

Two important facts must be set against these developments. First, the Ottoman empire was vast and domestic trade always overwhelmingly outweighed international trade. The scope and impact of both Ottoman exports to and imports from Europe remained limited. Second, if we take the time to read accounts of the experience of European merchants trading in the Ottoman empire, their marginality is immediately apparent. It is most instructive to consider French merchants since France, in addition to being the most vital European ally, was also the empire's most important trading partner. France accounted for 60 percent of European trade with the Levant, and French merchants – unlike the Dutch or the English – were in every *echelle* or port (Eldem, 1999: 27). Despite their ubiquity, they were never able to go much beyond the port, nor to break into the resale trade, as powerful local merchants took over once the goods arrived. Local merchants were also sufficiently well organized to boycott French traders who tried to raise the price of imported cloth in the 1720s. Eventually, though, the French formed their own counter-leagues (Eldem, 1999: 36).

Outside of Istanbul, French traders had to accept barter or delayed payment in kind. They would wait around in ports in such as Izmir while Ottoman merchants disappeared into the hinterland with their goods, only to return much later with merchandise that the French had little choice but to accept. Nor did they have any way to evaluate the prices that they were being asked to pay. In the words of one Ottoman historian, "European merchants were quite clearly at the mercy of local traders who monopolized three of the most crucial components of the market: information, distribution and pricing" (Eldem, 1999: 35).

When we turn to the reception of European culture, rather than European goods, here too Ottoman historians are revising their earlier views. The Tulip Age (1718–30) in Ottoman historiography is named after the passion for tulip gardens shared by the sultan and elite families in Istanbul. The very name conjures up a romantic image of eighteenth-century Istanbul as a pleasure garden, where "[t]he glitter of gilded palaces reflecting the Bosphorus, the scent of the roses and tulips carved on the surface of fountains and the colorful spectacle of public life in the squares and gardens of the city and its suburbs captured everyone's imagination."[4] Alongside the cultivation of tulips, we see an unprecedented burst of building in Istanbul. Airy waterfront palaces, graceful pavilions, and public gardens began to grace the capital city. Perhaps the most magnificent structure was the palace known as Sa'adabad (meaning the Abode of Happiness) commissioned by the Grand Vezir Damat Ibrahim Pasha and modeled after the chateau of Fontainebleau in France. Innovation went beyond the architectural sphere. From the beginning of the eighteenth century we see Western-style reforms – mostly piecemeal – in the spheres of education, the military, and the navy. A project submitted by a French officer in 1716 for the formation of a corps of foreign engineer officers in the Ottoman army came to nothing, but four years later another Frenchman, a convert to Islam, did successfully organize Istanbul's first fire brigade. Under Ahmet III (1703–30) the Ottoman navy began to re-equip with western European three-decker ships of the line replacing the traditional Mediterranean galley (Lewis, 1961: 46).

In September 1730 news of the fall of Tabriz to Safavid forces and of the high human toll in casualties and captives triggered an uprising in the city's populous inner quarters. The grand vezir was executed and his creation, Sa'adabad, was razed to the ground, along with gardens and pavilions throughout the city. Within days, the rebels had forced Ahmet III to abdicate in favor of his nephew (Salzmann, 2000). Known as the Patrona Halil revolt after the peddler and part-time soldier who led it, these events ended the Tulip Age.

Figure 15 Early nineteenth-century engraving of the fountain of Nevsehirli Damat Ibrahim Pasha, built 1719/20, showing the influence of Western architectural style. *Copyright © The British Library Board, All Rights Reserved. 1780. c.4*

The destruction of many of the innovative new buildings appears to offer evidence to support the old, but extremely resilient, interpretation of the relationship of the Muslim world to the West. In this narrative of the Tulip Age, Westernizing Muslim elites, convinced both of their backwardness and of Western superiority, are foiled by anti-Western popular forces.[5] More recent scholarship is more skeptical of the Westernization thesis and the supposedly reactionary nature of the Patrona Halil revolt. As with the empire's commercial history, the shadow of the West has been allowed to loom too large. This trope of the Tulip Age becomes even more suspect when we consider the fact that the term was the invention of Ahmed Refik (1880–1937), who wrote at a time when the debate over Westernization was extremely fierce and proponents of reform were interested in casting their adversaries as obstructionist fanatics in the grip of tradition (Erimtan, 2006: 264). The grip of this thinking about the Muslim world is still so strong that it is only now that basic facts are being reconsidered. It was not the mob after all that destroyed so many buildings. It was the new sultan, Mahmud I, who ordered the destruction of the Sa'adabad, and gave his courtiers just three days to raze their own villas to the ground (Salzmann, 2000: 96).

When the sultan and the Ottoman court returned to Istanbul in 1703 after an absence of several decades, it was certainly not a triumphal re-entry. In the previous half-century the empire had endured military defeats and territorial concessions (Hamadeh, 2007: 3). In these circumstances, the state's most pressing concern was to repair its prestige and to preserve, or re-create, social hierarchies. The conspicuous consumption, the opulence, and the building frenzy of the Tulip Age were not motivated by admiration of the West (though certain aspects of Western culture were appreciated), but rather by the sultan's need to shore up his legitimacy. This interpretation is strengthened by the fact that monarchs and courts across the globe – in Europe, China, Japan, and India – were engaged in similarly grandiose projects.[6] Ahmet III, then, was very much an eighteenth-century monarch. Ottoman elites, who commanded a great deal of power throughout the century, sought to keep up by building palaces and creating gardens of their own.

If too much has been made of Westernization, too little attention has been paid to "Easternization." It is only now that eighteenth-century Ottoman architecture is receiving serious study, and one author argues that it was the product of a "complex aesthetic that was neither western, nor eastern, but extremely hybrid and thoroughly uncommitted" (Hamadeh, 2007: 11). Parallel to the investigation of European institutions, there was also an upsurge of interest in Turkish and Islamic history (Evin, 1980).

More broadly, the concept of the Tulip Age distorts the history of Ottoman–European relations by isolating a specific period. Western influence was not new, nor did it end in 1730. The Ottoman court was always eclectic. The conqueror of Istanbul, Fatih Mehmet, integrated both Eastern Christian and Western Renaissance forms in his architectural projects. The 1716 project for a corps of foreign engineers, mentioned earlier, looks less like a Westernization scheme when we consider the fact that an unit of foreign technicians (*taife-I efrenciyan*) was already instituted in the fifteenth century and remained operational throughout the next two centuries (Murphey, 1983). These borrowings simply appear less problematic than those of the eighteenth century because they happened when the Ottoman empire was at the height of its military power, rather than during its "decline."

Finally, as Ottoman elites were laying out the French-style gardens in Istanbul, a trend of *turqueries* swept Europe in the eighteenth century. Operas were inspired by "Turkish" themes and fashion crazes drew their inspiration from the Orient. King Augustus II of Poland (1697–1733) was so enthusiastic about the janissary bands that Sultan Ahmet III made him a present of 12 to 15 players. Subsequently the Russians and the Habsburgs went to Istanbul to procure bands of their own, and janissary instruments became the basis of the percussion section of Western orchestras. Quataert has suggested it became more acceptable for Christian Europe to borrow elements of Ottoman culture as the "Turkish menace" receded after 1683 (Quataert, 2005: 8–9).

The fascination, it seems, was mutual but no one would suggest that the Europeans were trying to modernize their society and make it more like the Ottoman empire. In the words of one scholar: "one cannot but wonder what makes a cartouche on a fountain in Istanbul an index of westernization, and a Turkish pavilion in Vienna merely an Oriental folly" (Hamadeh, 2007: 10). Rather, the cartouche and the pavilion were both the product of a "transcultural consumer culture" (Salzmann, 2000:

92) which was itself the result of a boom in worldwide trade, and the relative peace between the Ottomans and their neighbors. This peace would be shattered in the final decades of the eighteenth century.

Upheaval

The relative stability between the Ottomans and their European neighbors began to disintegrate from the 1760s. Russia declared war on the Ottoman empire in 1768, and its fleet entered the Mediterranean for the first time two years later. By the time the war was over, in 1774, the Ottomans had suffered a disastrous defeat that ended over two centuries of naval superiority in the eastern Mediterranean. Moreover, they were compelled to surrender the Crimea to Russia, thereby losing their exclusive control over the Black Sea as well. Russia became increasingly assertive, interpreting the ambiguous terms of the Treaty of Kűçűk Kaynarca (1774) to claim a protectorate over the empire's Orthodox Christians equivalent to France's position towards the Catholics. Less noticed in the literature is that the sultan demanded, and got, the right to protect the Muslims in the Russian lands in his role as the Muslim caliph. Obviously, given Ottoman military weakness, this was a purely symbolic honor. Nevertheless, we see here the beginnings of the pan-Islamic politics that would become so important in the late nineteenth century when, in the minds of many, the Muslims had to form a united front against what they saw as a new Christian invasion.

External pressure on the empire continued relentlessly until well into the nineteenth century. Yet another conflict with the Habsburgs ended with the Treaty of Sistova in 1791, whereby the sultan ceded territory in Bosnia, but recovered Belgrade. The parallel Russo-Ottoman war (1787–92) concluded with the Treaty of Jassy setting the Russian frontier along the Dniester river. This easternmost territory, today the independent Republic of Moldova, was quickly lost again to Russia, this time for good, in 1812. Meanwhile, general European war broke out in 1792. Six years later, Napoleon invaded Egypt, thus bringing to an (albeit temporary) end the close Ottoman–French alliance that had held for the better part of three centuries. Napoleon's invasion also ended the *ancien régime* in Egypt, which is why 1798 is the conventional date for the end of the eighteenth century and, even more so, for the beginning of the modern history of the Middle East. Viewed from Istanbul, however, it makes little sense to separate the late eighteenth-century wars with Russia from the upheavals of the Napoleonic era, which, for the Ottomans, lasted until 1812. Together, the tremendous cost of these conflicts made it clear to the sultans that their rather relaxed government could not continue. The story of Ottoman reform, which begins in the late eighteenth century and continues, with ever greater effort and urgency, throughout the nineteenth century, is a long and complicated one. But at bottom all the reforms were motivated by two imperatives: to build an effective military force and to increase the central state's control over both the scale and the regularity of state income (Aksan, 2002: 257).

Napoleon's brief foray into Palestine from his base in Egypt in 1799 had no lasting results, but it provides a good example of the difficulties Sultan Selim faced when confronted by the new challenge of European invasion (Doumani, 1995). He sent a *ferman* (imperial order) to the residents of the Jabal Nablus region in Palestine, ordering them to provide troops for the effort against the French invader. Their response was to temporize and negotiate. Eventually, the sultan relented and agreed they could send 1,000 men, only half the number originally demanded. Yet two years later not even one of the promised soldiers had appeared. Desperate, the sultan agreed to a cash contribution instead, but even that was never paid in full. It was not that the leaders of Jabal Nablus were indifferent to the French attack. Fighters from Nablus actually defeated French troops in a skirmish. But their concern was to protect Jabal Nablus and they were absolutely unwilling to put themselves under Ottoman command, or to go as far afield as Egypt.

Military Reforms

In 1770, the same year that the Ottoman navy was defeated by Russia, Mustafa III hired baron de Tott, an artillery officer of French nationality and Hungarian origin, to rebuild and rearm the forts along the Dardanelles. He worked on and off for the sultan for the next five years, assisting with the opening of a new school of mathematics for the navy and with the formation and training of a new corps of engineers and artillery (Aksan, 2002). He returned to France in 1775, but then came back two years later on an eighteen-month mission to inspect the French consulates in the Mediterranean and to report on the feasibility of invading Egypt.

Sultan Selim III (1789–1807) continued the reform of the artillery and military education, but also embarked on the more politically and socially delicate task of organizing troops along European lines, wearing European uniforms, following European drill, and living in separate barracks. He set up a separate treasury, created from confiscated lands and other sources, to provide secure funding for the new force. It is for this reason, plus the fact that he gave his program a name implying a comprehensive vision – the *Nizam-i Cedid* or New Order – that the era of reform is conventionally dated from 1789.[7]

In keeping with typical Ottoman practice, inspiration for the military reforms was drawn from many places. France was not the only model. Russian and Austrian weapons were adapted, while Britain and Spain provided both machinery and expertise for Selim's new foundries (Aksan, 2002: 268). Many in the Istanbul political elite resented foreign influence in an institution as important as the military. This resentment grew during Selim's reign, because it was clear that the creation of a new army would displace the existing one: the janissaries and all those who benefited from that system. The grand vezir who was discovered in 1778 to have ration tickets for more than 600 non-existent soldiers was not untypical. The sentiment at the Ottoman court was comparable to the xenophobia at the Russian court of Peter I and Catherine II as they turned to the Germans for help in modernizing the Russian military. Eventually, these issues led to Selim's violent overthrow in 1807, temporarily ending the reforms.

A Changing Europe

As anxiety over European influence grew towards the end of the eighteenth century, the tone of European writing about the Ottoman empire also changed, becoming less friendly and more condescending and quasi-colonial. French reports on the

Levantine trade began to refer to the "apathy" of the Turk, while Ambassador Choiseul-Gouffier called the Ottoman empire "one of the richest colonies of France" (Eldem, 1999: 40).

One of the most enduring voices from that time belongs to baron de Tott, the officer serving Mustafa III in the 1770s. His memoirs, which were published in French in 1784–5, English in 1785 and German in 1787–8, were an immediate bestseller throughout Europe. Tott's account of Ottoman military reform was riddled with assertions about the supposed religious prejudices of Ottoman society preventing meaningful change, and the stupidity, even the buffoonery, of the military officers he worked with. This Enlightenment narrative remains popular and persuasive today. A recent general book on Ottoman history recounts one of Tott's tales and then comments: "The sacred laws of Islam, were, by definition, incapable of improvement, and the Ottoman government, which was the political expression of those laws, was also immutable" (Wheatcroft, 1993: 69).

The most frequently reproduced anecdote from the *Memoirs* concerns a demonstration of newly trained gunners in front of the grand vezir and a crowd of spectators. To underpin his claims of religious prejudice against rational change, Tott claims the crowd protested that pigs' hair, offensive to Islam, had been used to make the rammers. However, the French consul in Crimea, Louis Charles Peysonnel, doubted the veracity of Tott's account. For example, Tott implied that the Ottomans tried to cast brass cannon in an iron foundry as evidence of their supposed inefficiency. Peysonnel pointed out that the Tophane foundry routinely produced brass pieces and remarked that "one cannot, without injustice, accuse the Ottomans of a total ignorance in the art of founding cannon" (Arksan, 2002: 262).

Many factors helped change European views of the Ottomans. The Franco-Austrian alliance of 1756 ended the anti-Habsburg sentiment previously underpinning close relations between France and the sultan. Intellectual currents proved more important. The enlightened *philosophes* greatly admired Catherine the Great, the Ottoman empire's nemesis. The first stirrings of philhellenism, growing out of the emerging field of archeology, encouraged sympathy for the Greeks – seen as the descendants of ancient Greece – and a view of Greece as the land of liberty, occupied by the barbarian from the East (Eldem, 1999: 30).

However, philhellenism could cut both ways. British travelers to the empire were often disappointed that the present inhabitants of Greece failed to live up to their expectations. John Morritt, a recent Cambridge graduate traveling in the Peloponnesus, exclaimed "Good God! If a free ancient Greek could for one moment be brought to such a scene, unless his fate was very hard in the other world I am sure he would beg to go back again" (Todorova, 1997: 92). The British were also often unimpressed by the "tawny complexion" of Christian peasants in the Balkans, but got along famously with their Ottoman hosts, who entertained them with splendid dinners and excellent hunting. One scholar of British travel writing has suggested that what we are seeing is "the unconscious recognition of a master race by one in the making" (Todorova, 1997: 94).

The Enlightenment also proved ambivalent towards the Islamic North African states. The Maghreb was already familiar to Europeans after long, continuous contact. For example, southern European rulers had negotiated treaties with their North African counterparts since the Middle Ages, making the region "an integral part of

Mediterranean civilization" (Thompson, 1987: 1). European intellectuals gradually erased the earlier familiarity as they reordered the world through their writings in the eighteenth century (Wolff, 1994). North Africa was not a savage land, but neither was it seen as an ancient civilization, such as China or India. By the time the French invaded Algeria (1830), North Africa was regarded as "the wilds of Africa" the inhabitants of which were savages and the objects of ethnographical curiosity. "What had been a familiar part of the Mediterranean world, comprised of states with which long-standing relations existed, became a primitive and frightening African wilderness peopled by wild barbarians" (Wolff, 1994: 2).

Whatever the view of the various sojourners in the Ottoman empire toward the end of the eighteenth century, the fact is that there were many more of them than there had been in the past. By this point Greece was increasingly replacing France and Italy as the destination in the Grand Tour. The word tourist, in fact, dates from this time. Ottoman–European encounters, in other words, were both multiplying and diversifying. There was also a new dimension to these encounters. To a much greater extent than before, Ottoman subjects found that, through their relationships with Europeans, they got caught up, sometimes willingly, sometimes not, in the larger political game being played between Europe and the Ottoman empire.

The Napoleonic Wars turned the world upside down, not just in Europe but in the Ottoman and Mediterranean arenas as well. Weakness at the imperial center, combined with the proximity of European armies, inspired a series of regional adventures on the periphery of the Ottoman empire, as warlords and suffering populations sought to take advantage of the unsettled conditions to improve their position. The pan-European war also meant that everyone was looking for soldiers, and some Ottoman Christians responded to the call. Greeks served as sailors with the British navy and proved particularly adept at running the continental blockade that Napoleon was attempting to enforce across Europe. The Balkan port city of Thessaloniki grew rich on smuggling. Serbian Christians joined the Habsburg Free Corps (Jelavich, 1986: 27).

Major Ottoman figures attracted European interest, particularly Ali Pasha (*c.*1750–1822), the warlord of the Ionian islands off the western Greek coast. Napoleon's armies ended centuries of Venetian rule over the islands in 1797. A joint Russo-Ottoman naval expedition ejected the French a year later, and Russia assumed control. The islands then changed hands again after the collapse of the Russo-Ottoman alliance in 1806, before they emerged as the Septinsular Republic under British "protection" from 1814. They would remain British until the 1860s when they joined the independent state of Greece. This turbulent situation encouraged European interest in Ali, and vice versa. To the European powers, the question was no longer whether the Ottoman empire was in decline, but whether they should intervene to prop it up. Ali emerged as a potential ally, who might be bought by offering control over the Greek mainland. At one point Ali hoped that Napoleon would crown him king of Dalmatia (Fleming, 1999: 12). His position remained precarious, because he would be abandoned by any European ally seeking better relations with the sultan.

To understand Ali's point of view, we have to remember the two essential goals of Ottoman reform at the end of the eighteenth century: the development of an effective military force and greater central control over both the scale and the regularity of state income. Ali, in common with other warlords of the time, was threatened by both. This is not surprising, given that the reforms were directed precisely at provincial leaders like him, those who had been instrumental in the devolution of fiscal and military power away from the center and towards the provinces. Throughout most of the eighteenth century the tension between center and periphery had been skillfully managed by Istanbul. Provincial leaders provided the sultan with troops as needed from their own private militias. In return, the sultan gave them more access to state revenue than they had enjoyed in the past (Quataert, 2005: 48).

These arrangements fell apart under the pressure of the wars of the last quarter of the eighteenth century, in other words, under the pressure of an expanding and imperializing Europe. Faced with immensely costly wars, the sultan began demanding more troops and more money. Not only did he fail in this attempt, but powerful lords like Ali Pasha exploited the chaos of the times to tighten their control over local society. By the time the French arrived in the Ionian islands, the Ottoman reform effort was under way and Ali saw his new European neighbors as a chance to loosen ties to Istanbul and, possibly, declare his independence.

The string of European visitors coming to see the Pasha of Ioannina were all fascinated by the man they saw as the quintessential Oriental despot. Both Britain and France maintained consuls at Ali's court. The French consul, F. C. H. L. Pouqueville, who took up residence in Ioannina once Ali had established independent diplomatic relations with France in 1805, published his experiences as the *Voyage en Morée.*

He emphasized the Pasha's physical appetites, atrocities, and scheming, while ignoring Ali's political accomplishments and aspirations, as well as the larger international context. Certain episodes reappeared in plays, operettas, travelogues, and other accounts focusing on Ali: the drowning of a number of "Greek beauties," whom he tied in sacks and dumped into Lake Ioannina, his rape of his own daughter-in-law, his discovery of a pot of gold when he was an impoverished youth. As a recent study points out, "by being cast in such terms, Ali was made instantly familiar, instantly known: as an individual he may have been obscure, but as an Oriental despot he became an Eastern everyman, a type" (Fleming, 1999: 22). The presentation of Ali Pasha to a European audience is strikingly similar to Enlightenment writing on North Africa. Ali's importance as a player in the politics of the Eastern Question at one of its most volatile points is erased from the record; all that remains is the Oriental.

Ali Pasha's flirtation with independence (he only broke with the sultan in 1821) was unusual amongst Ottoman warlords, even in the highly unsettled years of the Napoleonic Wars. Most local leaders were content to stay within the Ottoman framework as long as they were free to go their own way within the area that they ruled. In fact, they often sought recognition from the sultan who, at this stage, remained the sole power bestowing legitimacy. The only clear-cut bid for independence was that made, not by an individual, but the Serbs living in the Belgrade *paşalık* (administrative district). These events, known as the Serbian revolt, were the most extreme case of the fatal combination of domestic weakness and European expansionism plaguing the empire since the 1760s. The Serbs were caught between the Habsburg and Ottoman empires, and suffered accordingly from the prolonged warfare. When the latest conflict ended with the Peace of Sistova, they also bore the brunt of the peace. Unemployed soldiers and janissaries – the latter already directly threatened by

Selim's efforts at military reform – began raiding the Serbian countryside, seizing property and imposing themselves on the local population. The Serbs turned to Selim who, like them, wanted peace and tranquility in the province, which meant curbing the janissaries, if not disbanding them altogether Selim was more determined to deal with these long-standing problems than his predecessors and gave the Serbs the autonomy they sought through three imperial orders in 1793, 1794, and 1796. The Serbs could now collect their own taxes, bear arms, and form a militia (Jelavich, 1986: 28–9). New troops were sent in from Istanbul, and the janissaries were forbidden to enter the province. The policy of arming Christians, with the implicit goal of holding off Muslim soldiers, was deeply offensive to conservative opinion in Istanbul. Selim might still have achieved his goals if the Napoleonic Wars had not disrupted his reforms. The invasion of Egypt forced him to recall his soldiers from the Belgrade *paşalık* and the janissaries swarmed back in, now with a taste for vengeance. The situation had become so desperate that the Serbians, led by a man named Karageorge, rebelled in 1804. Rather than independence, the Serbs initially only wanted Selim's help to eject the janissaries and restore their autonomy. Selim did send assistance to subdue the janissaries, but was unable to do more. Unwilling to trust him further, the Serbs turned to Russia to guarantee their autonomy. Whilst not discouraging the Serbs, Russia could not intervene since it remained allied to Selim at this point. As the Russo-Ottoman alliance collapsed in 1806, Russia threw its weight behind the Serbs who, encouraged by this and their own military successes, now demanded independence from Istanbul. As other Ottoman subjects would discover, independence was difficult to secure without foreign backing. The Serbian revolt collapsed, as Russia, facing imminent French invasion, signed the Treaty of Bucharest with the Ottomans in May 1812. Free from European enemies, Ottoman forces reoccupied Serbia in the summer of 1813, inflicting severe reprisals on the population.

Selim had, meanwhile, been deposed by a janissary-led revolt in 1807 that eventually installed Mahmud II as sultan (McCarthy, 1997: 291). Mahmud was not averse to reform and he learned from Selim's mistakes. After careful preparation, he destroyed the janissaries in a single coup in 1826, thus clearing a major obstacle to more fundamental military reform.

The parallels between the beginning and the end of the eighteenth century are striking. When the Ottoman court returned to Istanbul in 1703, the defeat at Vienna (1683) and the loss of territory sealed by the Treaty of Karlowitz hung heavy over the imperial dynasty. Humiliated by these defeats, Ahmet III had to acquiesce in the rising power of the officials who made up the ruling class. Selim, too, had discovered that the established internal balance within the elite was difficult to shift. But despite the military reversals, Ahmet III enjoyed a long and peaceful reign of over a quarter of a century while Selim, who came to the throne in the year of the French Revolution, was deposed and then killed after a tumultuous 18 years as sultan. His difficult reign and violent demise symbolize that the position of the Ottoman empire was far more serious in the early nineteenth century than it had been a century earlier. European imperial ambitions were now in full swing.

Things were also worse in the sense that, while Ahmet III had been able to work out a *modus vivendi* with Ottoman elites that hung together for most of the eighteenth century, Selim would enjoy no such consensus. The reason was that European power was deeply implicated in the internal crisis of the Ottoman empire at the end of the eighteenth century, in a way that it had not been at the beginning. Everyone in Istanbul could agree that Europe was a problem. The question was, was it a solution to the problem as well? This was a question first raised during Selim's rule, as his obviously Western-inspired military aroused fear and resentment. In the immediate context, the janissaries and other military elements resented the new troops because they threatened their own existence. The larger, more existential question would remain with the sultan and his subjects until the end of the Ottoman empire itself. But in 1812, with the reforming sultan dead and buried and Napoleon on his way to defeat in Russia, the first round of Ottoman reform had come to an end.

Notes

1 Throughout this chapter "Europe" is synonymous with "Christian Europe," in accordance with the understanding of Europe that was dominant at the time. It is understood that the definition of Europe is a contested one today.

2 With the caveat, of course, that we know much more about Europe than we do about the Ottoman empire. There is as yet no study of evolving Ottoman views on international relations in the eighteenth century.

3 At least in the Mediterranean arena. Hostilities between the Habsburgs and the Ottomans in the Balkans continued throughout the century.

4 Hamadeh, 2007: 1. The manuscript is forthcoming. I thank the author for sharing it with me in advance.

5 Lewis says that the rebels were motivated by "resentment . . . against the extravagance of the court and the 'Frankish manners' of the palace circles" (Lewis, 1961: 46–7). His discussion of the Tulip Age is discussed under the heading "The First Attempts at Westernization."

6 Quataert argues that, just like Louis XIV at Versailles, the Sultan and his Grand Vezir sought to dominate the "nobility" through conspicuous consumption (Quataert, 2005: 43). Many efforts were made at this time to impose hierarchy on an increasingly fluid society. Sumptuary laws, for example, were enforced with "unusual scrutiny" (Hamadeh, 2007: 6).

7 Ironically, the term Nizam-i Cedid was used by his Grand Vezir, writing from revolutionary France, in his letters to the sultan to describe the new situation in France. It appears that Sultan Selim adopted the term for himself (Lewis, 1961: 57). J. McCarthy writes that Selim's "reforms can be viewed as an intermediary step between Ottoman traditional reform and the Europeanizing reforms that would follow" (McCarthy, 1997: 289).

Bibliography

Aksan, V., "Breaking the spell of the Baron de Tott: reframing the question of military reform in the Ottoman empire, 1760–1830," *International History Review*, 24 (2002), 253–77.

Braudel, F., *The Mediterranean and the Mediterranean World in the Age of Philip II*, vol. 2 (London, 1973).

Doumani, B., *Rediscovering Palestine: Merchants and Peasants in Jabal Nablus 1700–1900* (Berkeley, 1995).

Eldem, E., "French trade and commercial policy in the Levant in the eighteenth century," *Oriente Moderno*, 18 (1999), 27–47.

Erimtan, C., "The sources of Ahmed Refik's *Lâle Devri* and the paradigm of the 'Tulip Age': a teleological agenda," in *Essays in Honour of Ekmeleddin Ihsanoğlu* (Istanbul, 2006), pp. 259–78.

Evin, A., "The Tulip Age and definitions of 'Westernization'," in H. Inalcik and O. Okyar (eds.), *Social and Economic History of Turkey (1071–1920)* (Ankara, 1980).

Fleming, K. E., *The Muslim Bonaparte: Diplomacy and Orientalism in Ali Pasha's Greece* (Princeton, 1999).

Frazee, C., *Catholics and Sultans: The Church and the Ottoman Empire 1453–1923* (Cambridge, 1983).

Hamadeh, S., *The City's Pleasures: Istanbul in the Eighteenth Century* (Seattle, 2007).

Jelavich, C. and B. Jelavich, *The Establishment of the Balkan National States, 1804–1920* (Seattle, 1986).

Lewis, B., *The Emergence of Modern Turkey* (Oxford, 1961).

McCarthy, J., *The Ottoman Turks: An Introductory History to 1923* (New York, 1997).

Murphey, R., "The Ottoman attitude towards the adoption of foreign technology: the role of the Efrencî technicians in civil and military applications," in J.-L. Bacquét-Grammont and P. Dumont (eds.), *Contributions à l'histoire économique et sociale de l'empire ottoman* (Leuven, 1983).

Quataert, D., *The Ottoman Empire 1700–1922* (Cambridge, 2005).

Salzmann, A., "The Age of Tulips: confluence and conflict in early modern consumer culture (1500–1730)," in D. Quataert (ed.), *Consumption Studies and the History of the Ottoman Empire, 1550–1922* (Albany, 2000).

Thomson, A., *Barbary and Enlightenment: European Attitudes towards the Maghreb in the 18th Century* (New York, 1987).

Todorova, M., *Imagining the Balkans* (New York, 1997).

Wheatcroft, A., *The Ottomans* (London, 1993).

Wolff, L., *Inventing "Eastern Europe": The Map of Civilization on the Mind of the Enlightenment* (Stanford, 1994).

Chapter Twenty-Five

Europe and the World

Philippe R. Girard

The "rise of the West" was so well engaged by the eighteenth century that few non-Western countries, Qing China and Mughal India excepted, could rival Europe's technological, economic, and political achievements. The result was an increasing European presence across the globe, either through outright colonization (western hemisphere) or in the form of missionary activities, voyages of exploration, commercial outposts, and trading networks (Africa, Asia).

Until the mid-twentieth century there were few historians, particularly in the West, to lament this development. Western expansion was widely considered a positive phenomenon, one that brought salvation, civilization, and economic development to otherwise archaic peoples. With the onset of decolonization in the 1950s, the pendulum swung in the opposite direction, this reassessment coming from both liberal critics and the former colonies. European imperialists were now accused of using "civilization" – itself a relative term – as a pretext for the greedy exploitation of their colonial subjects, resulting in a variety of evils ranging from epidemics to economic decline, racism, and the slave trade.

This school remains influential, but a growing body of literature now emphasizes the many impulses behind European expansion – not just greed and a messianic creed – and displays a sophisticated understanding of the complex interplay between European expansionists and their non-Western interlocutors. Europe's interaction with the world, it increasingly seems, was far from one-sided. Europeans borrowed much from their colonial subjects, some of whom welcomed, or even contributed to, Western imperialism. Officials in London, Paris, and Madrid, often described as meticulous masters deciding on the most minute details of imperial policy, were in fact a few of the many actors shaping the destiny of the empire, along with local elites, native peoples, private commercial interests, rival powers, and the vagaries of climate.

The Imperialist Impulse

The two factors most often cited to explain the imperialist impulse are religion and greed. But whether they intended to convert natives or to profit from them, Europeans

A Companion to Eighteenth-Century Europe, First Edition. Edited by Peter H. Wilson.
© 2014 John Wiley & Sons, Ltd. Published 2014 by John Wiley & Sons, Ltd.

discovered that reality often stubbornly refused to match the best-laid plans. Christianity often spread in a syncretic fashion, and trade restrictions were widely evaded.

Missionary activities were particularly central in Spanish imperial policy from the Counter-Reformation until the Bourbon reforms gave the Spanish Crown a slightly more secular outlook. Another focus of missionary activity was China, where 920 Jesuit missionaries were sent from 1552 to 1773. On the surface, conversion was organized, rapid, and ruthless. The Papacy divided the world into Spanish and Portuguese zones of influence (Treaty of Tordesillas, 1494) and set out to coordinate conversion efforts by the creation of Propaganda Fide (1622). Spaniards excluded Protestants, Jews, and recent converts from their colonies and baptized Amerindians by the thousands. Churches rose on the ruins of temples, and native idols were shipped home as ingots. Following the demographic catastrophe caused by the Columbian Exchange, Spaniards ordered thinly settled native populations to regroup in population centers that proved easier to control and convert (*reducción*). Within a century of the conquest of the Philippines (1565), Spain boasted that all but the Muslim south of the archipelago had embraced Catholicism.

In the long term, however, Spanish religious authorities discovered that such prompt conversions had only been half-hearted. Local artists commissioned to decorate colonial churches surreptitiously incorporated pagan symbols. Catholic saints, such as Mexico's Virgin de Guadalupe, were popular when they evoked memories of pre-Columbian deities. The church eventually chose not to submit non-Spaniards to the theological standards of the Inquisition – that is, to unofficially tolerate heresy among its colonial subjects. Despite the campaign of "extirpation," which tried until the eighteenth century to root out the last vestiges of Inca religion, Quechuas incorporated Inca gods into a unique form of Andean Christianity (Mills, 1997).

The influx of African slaves also gave rise to Afro-Christian syncretism, most notably in Haiti (Vaudou), Cuba (Santería), and Brazil (Candomblé). To convert slaves was the responsibility of slave-owners and a justification for slavery itself, but slave resistance and the dearth of qualified priests led to religions that typically borrowed from European mysticism (such as numerology), Catholic dogma (saints in particular), and West African spirit and ancestor worship. Colonial authorities tried to eradicate those religions as satanic cults that often served to galvanize slave revolts, but it is a testament to the resilience of syncretism in the New World that they outlived both slavery and colonialism (Dayan, 1996).

Particular attention has been paid to the Jesuit order, in part because it played the leading role in Spanish missionary efforts until the order was expelled from the Spanish empire in 1767 (as well as French and Portuguese colonies), and in part because it embraced methods far removed from the unilateral imposition one might expect from imperial agents. In Paraguay, and to a lesser extent California, missionaries tried to convert Native Americans through persuasion rather than coercion. Jesuits also made a concerted effort to study local languages and mores. The stated goal of these early anthropological efforts was to translate passages of the Bible more accurately, but Jesuits went as far as incorporating elements of local religions into Catholic rites as long as they did not openly conflict with essential Christian dogma. In China, where veneration of ancestors and the emperor was a traditional Confucian duty,

Jesuits argued that these practices were social rather than religious in nature and thus compatible with Christianity; Dominicans and Pope Clement XI thought otherwise, and in 1715 issued a bull on the Chinese rites controversy.

In Asia, despite growing European military muscle, missionaries were occasionally checked by reluctant local authorities. Christian presence in Japan was minimal from the mid-seventeenth to the mid-nineteenth centuries after the Tokugawa shogunate chose to expel missionaries and execute local converts; trade was also limited to a handful of Protestant Dutchmen in Nagasaki. The strategy of converting the Chinese from the top down backfired with the emergence of adamantly non-Christian rulers such as Yangzheng (r. 1723–35) (Gernet, 1985). One might argue that Europeans borrowed more from Chinese culture than the Chinese did from European culture, for a craze for all things Chinese engulfed Europe in the eighteenth century. Gottfried Leibniz and Voltaire professed their admiration for Chinese institutions; British gardeners embraced the informal Chinese style of gardens; and a taste for *chinoiseries* swept the art world.

Eighteenth-century Spain was well past its golden age and increasingly desperate to obtain the American bullion that financed the peninsular budget, but the search for profit was even more pronounced in Dutch, British, and French possessions. Monarchs generally embraced a mercantilist model under which Crown and charter companies would control markets, conquer colonies, and maximize profit. Colonies, it was held, only existed to benefit metropolitan producers; commerce should be conducted on national ships to exclude foreign goods and to train able seamen for wartime. Scholars long emphasized mercantilist trade restrictions because they were highly visible in the laws. The best-known trade network was the Spanish *flota*, which from 1564 to 1765 sailed annually from Cadiz or Seville to Havana, Panama, and Mexico. The Spanish Crown also imposed various royal monopolies on tobacco and mercury. In England, the 1651 Navigation Acts held that colonial commerce could only be conducted on ships built, owned, and captained by British subjects (the Acts were repealed in 1849). In France, Jean-Baptiste Colbert designed the *exclusif* system to exclude foreign goods from French colonies.

But trade unfolded in unsuspected ways. Decades before David Ricardo's *Principles of Political Economy and Taxation* (1817) a semi-official free-trade network flourished globally in the eighteenth century. One of the costliest items to be traded – African slaves – was increasingly excluded from mercantilist rules as the century advanced. The Spanish enforced a monopoly on the slave trade (*asiento*), but it was awarded to British merchants at the Treaty of Utrecht (1713) along with limited rights to trade with Spanish colonies, which the British consistently abused through contraband. Britain's own attempts in the 1770s to tax American commerce and limit contraband led to revolt and eventual independence for the United States. The French *exclusif* was an ad hoc scheme more than a coherent system; its many loopholes allowed many non-French merchants inside French colonies, particularly in times of war (Pritchard, 2004). By the 1790s, the United States, not France, was the main trading partner of France's Caribbean colonies. The annual Manila galleon aside, trade in the Philippines was dominated by the local Chinese community with close ties to the Asian continent. Spain, notorious for closely guarding its colonial markets, eventually concluded that mercantilism only led to high defense costs, colonial resentment against high prices, foreign contraband, and occasional crises when

Spanish *guardacostas* punished British smugglers. The point was proven in 1762 when British forces overtook the once impregnable fortifications of Havana and conducted more trade in one year of occupation than was customary in one decade of Spanish rule. Hoping to raise revenue for defense and halt the empire's long downward slide, Charles III thus instituted free trade between all Spanish ports and most Latin American ports in 1765.

Trading companies testify to the difficulty of imposing monopoly rights. Some were utter financial disasters, such as John Law's infamous Mississippi Company (1720). More lasting institutions were British companies such as the East India Company (EIC; 1600–1858), the Hudson's Bay Company (1670–present), and the Royal African Company (1672–1750), the French Compagnie des Indes Orientales (1664), and Dutch companies such as the East India Company (VOC; 1602–1799) and the West India Company (1621–1791). Despite trade advantages built in to their founding charters, the companies found it hard to exclude competitors. The EIC only lost its trade monopoly in 1813, but so-called "free merchants" had been allowed to stop at EIC-controlled ports long before. The VOC lost its monopoly in 1742 and grew increasingly distressed financially; the Fourth Anglo-Dutch War (1780–4) and the French invasion of the Netherlands (1795) eventually brought about its demise.

In fact, far from being the product of antiquated economic theories, empires were often the harbingers of modern capitalist techniques. The high cost and risk of sea voyages led investors to borrow funds and to pool them in a joint-stock company, thus pioneering modern financial techniques. Sugar plantations, heavily capitalized, integrated in international trading networks, and using a large labor force, were precursors of the modern factory system; profits from the slave trade and sugar cultivation financed the burgeoning industrial revolution in Europe (Williams, 1944).

A classic debate, following Lenin's *Imperialism: The Highest Stage of Capitalism* (1916), has tried to assess whether the lure of profit underpinned European territorial expansion. No consistent link can be identified in the eighteenth century; capitalist greed was omnipresent, but it did not necessarily lead to a lust for land, nor were the vastest colonies the most profitable. Some of Spain's colonies, particularly Mexico, provided much-needed shipments of bullion; others, such as Cuba, Louisiana, and Florida, cost more in defense than they paid in taxes and were kept for their strategic, not commercial, value. In Africa, Portuguese experiments showed that conquest was prohibitively costly due to the presence of powerful local kingdoms and tropical diseases. Portugal thus limited itself to offshore settlements (Azores, Madeira, São Tomé, Cape Verde) and coastal outposts (parts of present-day Mozambique, Guinea-Bissau, Angola) and shied away from large-scale conquest. Other powers did the same in Senegal (1638, France), Sierra Leone (1787, United Kingdom), and Cape Town (1652, VOC). Outside these stations, the European presence remained limited to temporary slave-trading on the coast until the late nineteenth century. For high-cost producers who sought the protection of mercantilist trade rules, colonial expansion could bring unwelcome imperial neighbors. At the end of the Seven Years War, for example, the British West Indian lobby argued *against* the annexation of French Guadeloupe and Martinique, which would have competed with Jamaica and Barbados for the British sugar market.

For-profit companies were also reluctant imperialists, as war was a costly venture. The VOC cautiously saw Batavia (Jakarta) as a place to collect spices and prevent others from doing the same – not as a base from which to conquer all of Indonesia. The VOC founded Cape Town as a small supply station on the way to Asia, and it was to the dismay of VOC administrators that local burghers proceeded to capture slaves and expand into the interior (Thompson, 2000).

The Indian example also shows the variety of actors and motives that brought territorial expansion. The British EIC envisioned a trading empire limited to sea lanes and trading stations to keep costs down, and remained faithful to this strategy outside of India. The situation there was chaotic due to the decline of the Mughal empire and the subcontinent's tendency toward fragmentation. Aside from territories still under Mughal rule, India encompassed rival Muslim kingdoms (Mysore), large regional powers (such as the Maratha kingdom), the growing Sikh power in Punjab, and various European outposts. Internal wars threatened to disrupt existing commercial links and might allow rival powers, most notably the French Compagnie des Indes in Chandernagor and Pondicherry, to dominate the continent and exclude the British. Personality also mattered; European agents such as France's Joseph Dupleix and England's Robert Clive, Charles Cornwallis, and Richard Wellesley frequently intervened militarily against express orders to the contrary, then forced the EIC to acquiesce in the fait accompli. The British empire was not a preordained, coherent strategy to boost profits; rather, it stemmed from the competing ambitions of over-zealous agents, local kings, French rivals, and company shareholders (Robb, 2002).

Probably as a result of the vogue of postmodernism, many historians now prefer to leave aside a standard assessment of colonialists' expressed motives and instead deconstruct works of fiction in the hope of finding hidden layers of information (Garraway, 2005). Edward Said's claims in *Orientalism* (1978) – namely, that the West stereotyped the Orient as irrational, backward, and libidinous to better justify colonial expansion – has spawned many imitators. The quest of such historians occasionally leads to the conclusion that Europeans of the era used a racist discourse, a suggestion which is not altogether adapted to the still emerging eighteenth-century concept of race. More interestingly, they draw attention to the fascination for all things foreign in popular culture. Many Europeans, who otherwise lived in a distinctly parochial world, were prone to read and fantasize about the world beyond the seas, apparently not out of some vested financial or religious interest, but merely because of its allure.

A popular genre of eighteenth-century literature was the travelogue, such as William Dampier's *Voyage to New Holland* (1704), Commodore George Anson's *Voyage around the World* (1748), and Louis-Antoine de Bougainville's *Voyage autour du monde* (1771). These included some practical information on military expeditions, tropical climates, and sea currents, but their main draw was intriguing tidbits on foreign customs that piqued the reader's fancy. Bougainville's experience in Tahiti led to a French fascination with the "noble savage" evident in Denis Diderot's *Supplément au voyage de Bougainville* (1772) and Jean-Jacques Rousseau's works. The line between travelogues and pure entertainment could be blurred, as exemplified by Daniel Defoe's *Robinson Crusoe* (1719), a novel that masqueraded as an autobiography yet drew on Alexander Selkirk's real-world experience as a castaway.

Voyages of exploration were another indication that sheer curiosity occasionally drew Europeans overseas. Pierre-Louis Moreau de Maupertuis traveled to the Arctic to help measure the length of a meridian (1736), while Charles-Marie de la Condamine participated in a similar expedition in Peru and the Amazon (1735). Danish-born Vitus Bering explored Siberia and the North Pacific for Russia from 1725 until his death in 1741. For two centuries following Ferdinand Magellan's path-breaking journey (1519–22), exploration of the Pacific was limited to the annual Spanish galleon from Acapulco to Manila and the British sailors such as Drake and Anson who sought to capture it (Glyn, 1999). But from the 1760s to the 1780s, the hope for scientific discoveries and the national glory that accompanied them led Samuel Wallis, Jean-François de la Pérouse, Bougainville, Jacob Roggeveen, and James Cook to chart Pacific islands such as Tahiti, Hawaii, and New Zealand, and "discover" Easter Island (1722).

Organizing the Colonies

Europe's overseas territorial presence was substantial by the early 1700s, particularly in the western hemisphere. Aside from its holdings along the African coast, Portugal was present in Goa, India (1510), Macau, China (1553), East Timor (1596), and, most notably, Brazil (1532). Spain's holdings spanned from the American southwest and Florida to Mexico, the Caribbean (Cuba, Puerto Rico, Santo Domingo), Central America, most of South America, Ceuta, and the Philippines. The Dutch had lost most of the holdings they had acquired in the previous century, but they maintained outposts in Indonesia (Batavia) and the Caribbean (St. Eustatius) whose commercial value dwarfed their territorial footprint. England controlled the eastern seaboard of the United States and valuable Caribbean islands such as Jamaica and Barbados. Over the following century, the EIC's limited Indian holdings in Madras (Chennai), Bombay (Mumbai), and Calcutta (Kolkata) grew to include Bengal (1757), Bihar (1765), Mysore (1799), Delhi (1803), Maratha (1818), Sind (1843), and Punjab (1849). New France stretched from the St. Lawrence in Canada to New Orleans, engulfing most of the American Midwest in between. Smaller but more lucrative French holdings included the mouth of the Senegal river, Guadeloupe, Martinique, and Saint-Domingue (Haiti). Russia had expanded into Siberia and south to the Caspian Sea by the beginning of Peter the Great's reign (1682); the eighteenth century saw further expansion in Kamtchatka, the Tatar Khanate of Crimea, central Asia, the Baltic, and eastern Europe.

When analyzing the strategies used by European powers to control their far-flung overseas territories, scholars have traditionally identified two approaches. One, exemplified by Britain, gave much leeway to local governments, which enjoyed self-government within the confines of British trading rules. The other, exemplified by France and Spain, strove to create a centralized, integrated empire in which all key decisions would stem from Paris and Madrid. This dichotomy, however, is deceptive.

On paper, Spain's bureaucratic structure was impressive. Starting with the king and the Council of the Indies in Spain, power filtered down through Spanish-appointed viceroys and *audiencias* (courts and advising bodies). Officials were tightly controlled through surprise inspections (*visitas*) and a systematic review at the end of their mandate (*residencia*). Spanish-born citizens (*peninsulares*) were appointed in preference to those born in the colonies (*criollos*) to quell separatist sentiment. Rules on blood purity (*limpieza de sangre*) further reinforced a colonial hierarchy that placed Amerindian (*indios*) and mixed-blood offspring (*mestizos*) under white leadership. Revolts, such as the Tupac Amaru uprising in Peru (1780–1), were brutally repressed.

Recent scholarship, however, tends to emphasize the reciprocal nature of Spain's imperial relations. Practical matters such as slow travel in the age of sail meant that two years routinely elapsed before an official in Manila heard from his superiors in Madrid, leaving much day-to-day independence. Even within a colony, it could take months for a message sent from Peruvian provinces located east of the Andes to reach the viceregal authorities in Lima, since the fastest route was via the Amazon, the Atlantic, Cape Horn, and the South Pacific. Transportation woes thus gave city councils (*cabildos*), in which local elites predominated, some measure of self-government. Without the cooperation of its subjects overseas and in Europe, many of whom were willing collaborators of the imperial order, Spain would never have been able to hold on to its far-flung possessions as long as it did (Kamen, 2002).

In the 1760s the Bourbon reforms sought to revive the empire by raising more revenue and increasing defense spending. Increased taxation led to resentment in some sectors of the empire; but, paradoxically, Spain's assertiveness helped some clever elites obtain a more favorable colonial contract. In exchange for freer trade rules and a dominant military role for the local militia, Cubans agreed to pay a slightly greater share of the colonial budget; the bargain was so appealing that most Cubans remained loyal to Spain when the metropolis was occupied by French troops in 1808 (Kuethe, 1986).

Like that of Spain, France's imperial bureaucracy was theoretically organized from the top down; like Spain, France found that practical matters undermined its hold on distant territories. On paper, the French minister of the navy appointed key colonial administrators, including the *gouverneur* (chief military officer) and the *intendant* (financial administrator). The rights of local subjects, including white ones, were strictly circumscribed, particularly in Canada, where the *seigneurie* system transplanted feudal land rules to the New World. In the prosperous Caribbean colonies, planters returned to France as soon as their fortune was made, thus helping to maintain close ties with the mother country. In the second half of the eighteenth century, segregationist laws and local prejudices assigned a subordinate status to free-coloreds.

But metropolitan laws and colonial realities were two distinct worlds. In the Caribbean, tropical fevers decimated colonial garrisons, leaving governors few troops with which they could impose royal dictates. Intelligent governors thus learned to ignore unpopular edicts sent from France lest influential planters riot, or even kill them. France's low emigration rate also derailed its well-laid plans for colonial administration. By the late eighteenth century, a mere 100,000 Frenchmen had left for the western hemisphere, compared with 350,000 Spaniards and 400,000 Englishmen. Natural growth had led to substantial settlements along the St. Lawrence, but everywhere else white Frenchmen formed a small minority of the territories they supposedly dominated. A handful of soldiers and adventurers was all that France could muster in the vast American interior. French administrators thus had to conclude military alliances on a voluntary basis with Native American chiefs, who were courted with offers of financial help and political autonomy. French social customs and Catholicism were embraced by some Native Americans; but, in many cases, French *coureurs des bois* (frontiersmen) were the ones going native in a surprising process of acculturation of the colonial "master" (Havard and Vidal, 2003).

This process of bargaining and accommodation mirrors that found in British colonies such as India. Early historians saw a clear demarcation between impoverished, chaotic pre-colonial India and the pacification and economic growth that followed (Polanyi, 1944); later Indian critics took the opposite stance, arguing that British nabobs drained India's immense wealth, but they too view the pre-colonial world as fundamentally different from the one that emerged under EIC, and later British, rule. Such Manichaean theories are increasingly rejected in favor of others that emphasize continuities between the pre-colonial and colonial eras and exchanges between colonizer and colonized. Large empires had traditionally found it hard to unite India's multiplicity of cultures, climates, and religions, and the British were aware that they could not single-handedly craft a British society with the limited means at their disposal. They thus ruled with the collaboration of existing elites and bureaucracies and incorporated Indian traditions while transforming sectors as varied as the law, religion, education, and trade (Robb, 2002).

Mercantilist trade rules and bureaucratic frameworks as expressed in colonial agendas must thus be approached with caution. A European territory, however neatly delineated and colored on a map, was a very different institution when taking into account local realities, particularly the creole's skills at evading colonial rules, geographic realities in the age of sail, large non-European populations, and the failure to send the number of settlers and administrators commensurate with the vastness of a colony.

Imperial Rivalries

European wars, generally pitting France against England in a variety of coalitions, were a frequent occurrence in the eighteenth century. Russia and Sweden fought in the Great Northern War (1700–21). The War of the Spanish Succession (1701–14) allowed Philip V to reign as king of Spain and its overseas empire, but it also forced Spain to relinquish many of its European territories, which it failed to regain in the War of the Quadruple Alliance (1718–20); Spain also fought in the War of the Polish Succession (1733–5). The War of the Austrian Succession (1740–8) resulted in the British occupation of the French fort of Louisburg, while the British also captured the Manila galleon in the simultaneous War of Jenkins' Ear (1739–48). Britain won the Seven Years War (1756–63) so decisively that the 1763 Treaty of Paris crushed French claims in India and gave England Senegal, Dominica, Grenada, East Louisiana, Canada, and Florida while France gave West Louisiana and New Orleans to Spain. The American War of Independence (1775–83) resulted in the independence of 13 of Britain's North American colonies; Spain also regained Florida. By the time the wars of the French Revolution (1791–1802, 1803–15) had ended, France had sold West Louisiana to the United States (1803), lost Saint-Domingue (Haiti) to former slaves (1804), and ceded Tobago, St. Lucia, and Mauritius to Britain (1814). French and Spanish colonies were routinely under British occupation during these wars, only to be returned as part of the peace negotiations.

Such French–British rivalries were nothing new, but a new development was the growing importance of imperial rivalries both as a motive for going to war and as a theater of operations. In previous centuries, it was commonly accepted in Europe that incidents taking place overseas were not a *casus belli*; peace treaties frequently incorporated a clause specifying that a resumption of hostilities "beyond the line" (across the Atlantic) had no implications for European diplomacy. But many eighteenth-century conflicts began at least in part as conflicts over territorial turf, stemming from the growing sense, especially in England, that a country's maritime and commercial power depended on its access to overseas markets (Ferguson, 2002).

Foreign theaters often acquired a dynamic of their own. Overseas participants in the War of the Spanish Succession, for example, fought for their own agenda, not for Philip V's dynastic ambitions. The victims of the 1704 Deerfield massacre had settled on the Massachusetts frontier not to uphold British claims in the region, but simply because of a lack of land further east. The Abenakis and Pennacooks who attacked them in the name of France hoped to avenge British encroachments on their ancestral lands, while France's Iroquois allies wished to take captives and adopt them.

The War of Jenkins' Ear stemmed in part from Spanish attempts to prevent British sailors from selling contraband in the empire. Conflicting French and British claims in India and North America were central in ushering in the Seven Years War; this war, which officially started in 1756, raged as early as 1754 in the Ohio region (Anderson, 2000). The American War of Independence was directly related to disputes over taxes and representation within the British empire; it drew French and British armies eager to avenge colonial losses suffered at the Treaty of Paris and to protect their possessions in the Caribbean. An obscure boundary dispute over Nootka Sound near Vancouver almost led Britain and Spain to war in 1787. The wars of the French Revolution were mainly a European ideological struggle, but they served as a pretext for renewed fighting in the Caribbean as Britain, Spain, and France attacked each other's colonies in the 1790s. Napoleon Bonaparte tried to create a new French empire centered on Egypt (1798–1801), then one centered on Saint-Domingue and Louisiana (1802–3).

With a few exceptions, Britain dominated the naval theaters of eighteenth-century colonial conflict; France played the role of the gallant, but unfortunate, adversary; other powers, such as Spain, the Netherlands, Denmark, and Russia, were incapable of presenting a serious naval challenge on their own. British naval technology was at the cutting edge – for example pioneering the systematic use of copper sheathing in the fleet – but French ships were also well designed (particularly the standardized models of Jacques Noël Sané) and were routinely incorporated in the British fleet as prizes. When allied with second-rate naval powers, France could match Britain's fleet of ships of the line. When trying to explain Britain's overwhelming dominance at sea, the scholarly consensus points to the human factor: Britain drew on a large pool of able seamen and inventive, daring officers, while France, particularly at the beginning of the French Revolution, relied on raw recruits and timid officers (Herman, 2004). Strategies and tactics differed markedly. Britain chose to station its squadrons overseas, even if that meant losing ships and men to adverse climatic conditions. French fleets usually stayed in Toulon and Brest, to be deployed as needed. French tactics were conservative and emphasized the line of battle; the British were more willing to experiment with unconventional tactics and close combat, most famously at the battles of Quiberon Bay (1759), the Saintes (1782), and Trafalgar (1805).

A weakness in the existing scholarship is that it tends to over-emphasize the role of professional navies and large fleet actions, whereas piracy and privateering had much greater influence throughout the period. A concerted British campaign largely eliminated piracy from the Caribbean in the 1710s and 1720s, but piracy thrived in the Mediterranean and the South China Sea well into the nineteenth century, thus undermining the claim that European navies completely dominated the seas. For France, British successes made privateering a centerpiece of wartime strategy. The French navy was virtually absent from the Caribbean in the 1790s, but privateers operating out of Guadeloupe and Saint-Domingue conducted the bulk of operations against England and the United States. Privateering crews were typically even more cosmopolitan than those found in professional navies and included many free-coloreds (Dubois, 2004). The privatization of warfare also made it difficult for the power issuing the letter of marque to have day-to-day control over its own naval forces.

On land, colonial powers would have preferred to exercise their military strength through professional white armies sent directly from Europe, but many factors militated against a significant European presence. When wars broke out, European troops were directed as a matter of priority to European battlefields: regiments were expensive before the draft was introduced; the attrition rate among white garrisons in tropical climates was staggering; and even massive reinforcements could not obscure the fact that non-Western peoples formed the majority of the population in virtually every European colony. Colonial powers thus resorted to Native American allies (Havard and Vidal, 2003), freed slaves (Dubois, 2004), and creole militias (Kuethe, 1986). The tripartite war that raged in Saint-Domingue from 1793 to 1798, for example, can be mistaken for a colonial equivalent to the war then pitting Spain and Britain against France in Europe. But Spain's leading generals in Saint-Domingue were Jean-François, Biassou, and Toussaint L'Ouverture, former French-African slaves who fought as Spanish auxiliaries (L'Ouverture defected to the French side in 1794). The British army included, as was customary at the time, numerous German mercenaries, as well as conservative French planters (white and mulatto) and armed African slaves. The French were unable to send reinforcements and increasingly relied on freed African slaves as soldiers and officers. Independent bands of African maroons allied themselves with all three powers depending on circumstances. Such a fluid situation, in which the dividing lines were racial, political, and social as well as national, shows that colonial specificities affected military operations even more than metropolitan strategies (Geggus, 1982).

The importance of disease in shaping Europe's encounter with the world prior to modern medical discoveries has been emphasized in seminal works such as William McNeill's *Plagues and Peoples* (1976) and Jared Diamond's *Guns, Germs, and Steel* (1998), but those theoretical breakthroughs are only beginning to filter down into the historiography on imperial conflicts. Too often, the focus remains on man-made events such as siege and battle tactics even when their significance pales in comparison with nature's own work, such as the epidemics that killed the vast majority of crews and soldiers even in wartime. Also overlooked are meteorological events, such as the hurricane of 1780 that destroyed a French and a British fleet.

Figure 16 Toussaint L'Ouverture. *From Léon Vallée (ed.), Memoirs of the Empress Joséphine (2 vols., New York: Merrill & Baker, 1903). © Mary Evans Picture Library / Alamy*

Racism and Slavery

One essential dimension of Europe's worldwide forays was racial, as Europeans encountered distinct peoples (Native Americans, Africans, and Asians) and modified the racial composition of the territories they settled through miscegenation, European emigration, and the Atlantic slave trade. It would be easy to conclude that eighteenth-century Europeans had a clear definition of such racial categories because of their extensive journeys and the brutal manner with which they treated subject peoples, but this would mistakenly apply nineteenth-century concepts of "scientific" racism to a much earlier era. In the eighteenth century race was a concept that remained in flux and incorporated both modern conceptualizations and medieval ones.

Medieval views on humankind, inspired by the Bible's description of creation, held that all humans shared a common ancestor and that physical characteristics – such as a dark skin – were a product of the climate. It was commonly believed that white mothers could even bear black children if they were affected by specific emotions during pregnancy. Race was a porous concept, often applied to social classes (such as the peasantry) deemed intrinsically different from the nobility by virtue of inferior blood. Only as the eighteenth century progressed did polygenism (the belief that humans had different ancestors) begin to take root, possibly as a result of the biological sciences' advances in taxonomy under Carolus Linnaeus and Georges-Louis Buffon. Adam and Eve's biblical role as parents of humankind was increasingly overshadowed by the story of Noah's son Ham, cursed into slavery, and now held to be the ancestor of all Africans (Hannaford, 1996). A contradictory influence was the Enlightenment's focus on a universal common man, which made it difficult for French revolutionaries to uphold racial discrimination and slavery even though their bourgeois supporters held a large stake in the commerce of black flesh (Benot, 1987).

This slow, unequal shift made for multifaceted approaches to race. French nobles in the North American interior might describe Native Americans as savages, but they also viewed their warriors as their equals because they shared an ethos of courage and sacrifice – ideals that were alien to white peasants deemed racially distinct (Havard and Vidal, 2003). Spanish colonial authorities were obsessed with *limpieza de sangre*, but such "racial" prejudices applied to suspect Jewish and Muslim converts to Catholicism (*conversos*) in addition to mestizos (who were part-Indian) and mulattos (who were part-African); Spain's dire budgetary problems also made it possible to buy certificates of purity (Martínez, 2002). The Caribbean observer Moreau de Saint-Méry identified no fewer than 128 distinct possible combinations of white and African blood, but this might be interpreted either as an indication that racism was hardening or that widespread interracial sex had made such combinations common in the first place. Since this slow hardening of racial views paralleled the growth of African slave labor in European colonies – and since "modern" racial norms were most apparent in the most prosperous sugar colonies – a historiographical debate pits those who believe that Europeans' racist beliefs explain why they resorted to African labor against those who assert that slavery grew primarily in response to economic factors and that racism was merely an *ex post facto* rationalization.

Scholarly works now frequently cite racism as one of many factors shaping labor policies. Forced labor, which only partly coincided with racial lines, was common in early modern Europe and its outposts. These ranged from serfdom (resurgent in eastern Europe) to labor taxes such as the French *corvée* and the Peruvian *mita*, naval impressment, indentured servitude (common in North America until the American Revolution), and outright slavery. The latter grew considerably in North America, the Caribbean, and Brazil in the eighteenth century, but practical factors were as crucial in favoring slavery's growth as the burgeoning racial theories: the growing European demand for sugar and other tropical products, with the resulting need for laborers; the quasi-extermination of the native population in many colonial outposts, which left no local labor pool (except in Spanish colonies like Peru and Mexico, where African slavery was consequently less widespread); the realization that tropical diseases were deadly to Europeans, thus making the initial policy of importing white laborers as indentured servants impractical in warm climates; and the rise and fall of the price of African slaves (Blackburn, 1997). Similarly, the planters' treatment of their slaves varied from paternalistic to cruel based on a multiplicity of factors such as plantation type (sugar vs. coffee), slave occupation (household vs. field slave), and ownership patterns (resident planter vs. absentee owner), in addition to the vagaries of individual sadism and racism.

Patterns of slave resistance (such as suicide, flight, and revolt) are also under debate. It is not clear, for example, whether slaves ran away because of local factors like a particular master's cruelty or whether they were inspired by a more general commitment to freedom, or even Enlightenment ideals. What is certain is that the prevalence of slave resistance served to undermine imperialist plans for a pyramidal structure in which all decisions would stem from the metropolis. Maroon communities such as Jamaica's Blue Mountains maroons, those of the Bahoruco region in Hispaniola, and Adoe's followers in Suriname (Dutch Guyana) not only warded off all European attempts at conquering their mountain strongholds but also signed treaties of non-aggression that turned them into independent realms within the officially white-dominated European colonies. Even African slave women, laboring under the triple stigma of race, class, and gender, were not hapless puppets of the slave order and instead cleverly traded sexual favors for freedom and power (Gautier, 1985).

African subjects, even when they remained within the colonial system, displayed a remarkable ability to borrow elements of European thought while remaining faithful to their African roots, thus creating a "third way" that was neither European nor African. Writing from the perspective of 1960s Black nationalism, C. L. R. James portrayed Haiti's Toussaint L'Ouverture as an anti-racist African fighting for the emancipation of his people (James, 1963), but more recent scholarship has proved that L'Ouverture had been emancipated by his master, had owned slaves himself, and was largely inspired by the economic model of the sugar plantation (Pluchon, 1989). Also idealized as an African who drew his lifelong opposition to slavery from his slave ancestry, Olaudah Equiano has now been re-evaluated as an Atlantic man of multiple allegiances who exploited slave labor yet joined the abolitionist movement, who prided himself on – and possibly invented – his Ibo (Nigerian) birth, yet aspired to British values (Carretta, 2005).

Aside from early abolitionist studies, little was known of the Atlantic slave trade before a burst of modern scholarship from the 1960s on shed light on a major historical phenomenon that resulted in the displacement of 11 million Africans, 1 million of whom died during the Middle Passage (the trade lasted from the fifteenth to the nineteenth century, but the second half of the eighteenth century marked its peak). Abolitionist estimates had initially put the death rate among slaves during the Atlantic crossing as high as 50 percent, but recent studies showed that such losses would have made the trade uneconomic and settled on a more likely loss rate of 10 percent, which declined as sailing and nutritional technologies improved in the eighteenth century, and which varied immensely from one voyage to the next based on epidemic outbreaks and the length of the voyage. This might be misinterpreted as a proof of the traders' humanitarian concern for their cargo, but the revised figures remain high for a young, healthy population during a voyage rarely lasting more than two months (Klein, 1999).

More controversial has been the growing focus on African collaboration with the European trade. Slave traders rarely caught slaves themselves or established permanent outposts; instead, the slave trade was a highly decentralized institution that relied on small slaving ships collecting their cargo from local African potentates (such as Dahomey's King Tegesibu), who were eager to collaborate since they owned slaves themselves (Thomas, 1997). This dual trend – looking at the slave trade from a business perspective and studying African complicity – is backed by considerable evidence, but some historians complain that it plays down the moral repulsiveness of a trade they compare to genocide (Ribbe, 2005).

The Atlantic slave trade has gone in a few decades from being one of the least to one of the best studied fields in world history. The downside of this historiographical onslaught has been the relative lack of scholarly interest in other forms of labor exploitation beyond the Atlantic. Comparatively little work exists, for example, on the sizeable trade in African slaves across the Indian Ocean and the Sahara desert to the Muslim world or within sub-Saharan Africa itself. Far from downplaying the evils of the Atlantic slave trade by making labor abuse appear commonplace, such comparative work would illuminate the variety of labor systems prior to the Industrial Revolution and the generalization of free wage labor.

British abolitionism has been variously attributed to religious idealism or the realization that wage labor was ultimately cheaper than slave labor. But British abolition did not achieve its goals until 1807 (slave trade) and 1833 (slavery), so a discussion of Europe's eighteenth-century anti-slavery measures must focus on the earlier, more radical, and often forgotten French abolitionist movement, which to a large extent was a product of local *rapports de force* in the colonial theater, not metropolitan policy. Louis XIV tried to limit slavery's worst abuses in the 1685 Code Noir, while Louis XVI planned on deepening its provisions, but such laws were routinely ignored by planters and even colonial courts (similarly, the 1789 Spanish Código Negro was abandoned in 1794 following planter opposition). Enlightenment philosophers and their revolutionary followers were so torn between their commitment to human liberty and their investment in sugar colonies that the National Assembly told colonial assemblies in the 1790 Barnave Decree that they should settle the matter of the free-coloreds' legal rights themselves (Benot, 1987). When the Revolutionary Wars broke off most contacts between the metropolis and the colonies, slavery persisted where planters were strong enough, as in Martinique, and was abolished in areas where the slaves had revolted, as in Haiti and Guadeloupe. All the National Assembly did was to pass a 1794 law of emancipation that merely legalized what had already taken place. Similarly, when Napoleon tried to restore slavery in 1802 his effort was successful where local forces favored slavery (as in Martinique), costly but successful where a strong black opposition emerged (Guadeloupe), and unsuccessful where the African population was both large and determined (Haiti). The French minister of the navy's vaunted claims to administer the empire from Paris, then as before, sounded hollow.

Colonial Legacy

Early historians – whom one could label members of the "classical" school – frequently glorified Western imperialism for its high-minded motives and the benefits it supposedly brought to non-Western peoples, while ignoring its more unsavory aspects, such as disease, war, and slavery. By contrast, later historians from the 1960s on – whom one could label members of the "revisionist" or "liberal" school – chose to focus precisely on these painful topics as part of a general critique of Europe's encounter with the world, now described as a greedy, violent assault on innocent peoples. Both camps survive, as the controversy that surrounded the 500-year anniversary of Christopher Columbus' first voyage to the New World can attest, but increasingly a third group of historians – "post-revisionists," one might say – has chosen to shift the focus away from the policies (good or bad) of metropolitan decision-makers and toward the intricacies of the colonial encounter at the local level. The resulting research proves that imperial theaters were marked by fusion and collaboration, not just confrontation and domination, and that very often Europeans did not have the last word. Whether it be Andean Quechuas incorporating Inca rituals into Spanish Christianity, Canadian Native Americans negotiating their support for French or British patrons, or individuals like Toussaint L'Ouverture reinventing the French plantation system as a black-dominated institution, colonial subjects created a world far different from what the metropolitan masters had envisioned.

Such conclusions are not politically innocuous. Contemporary hot topics such as foreign aid, race relations, and compensation lawsuits are directly related to Europe's colonial legacy. Good historians in the Rankean mold are those whose conclusions are dictated by the evidence they review, not a pre-set ideological agenda, but their conclusions inevitably find themselves dissected by readers eager to push a particular political agenda. For example, during the 2001 Durban conference against racism, many African rulers argued that foreign aid was a payback for African manpower exported during the heyday of the Atlantic slave trade (as well as atrocities committed during the later European colonization of Africa); in this context, any suggestion that their predecessors were willing accomplices of the trade is considered anathema. Similarly, the identity of modern Indians (in both the North American and South Asian senses of the term), and their claims of victimization or demands for independence, are undermined by those who point out that their forebears often collaborated with English settlers. So political are these historical issues that the French National Assembly has recently taken the unusual step of passing laws that liken slavery to a crime against humanity (2001), then forcing historians to emphasize the positive role of colonization (2005) – thus introducing the novel concept of historiography by legislative fiat. One can only hope that such political meddling will not impede the field's fruitful foray into the complexities of the imperial encounter.

Bibliography

Anderson, F., *Crucible of War: The Seven Years' War and the Fate of Empire in British North America, 1754–1766* (New York, 2000).

Benot, Y., *La Révolution française et la fin des colonies, 1789–1794* (1987; repr. Paris, 2004).

Blackburn, R., *The Making of New World Slavery: From the Baroque to the Modern, 1492–1800* (New York, 1997).

Boxer, C. R., *The Dutch Seaborne Empire, 1600–1800* (London, 1965).

Carretta, V., *Equiano the African: Biography of a Self-Made Man* (Athens, GA, 2005).

Cushner, N., *Spain in the Philippines: From Conquest to Revolution* (Rutland, VT, 1971).

Davis, D., *The Rise and Fall of Slavery in the New World* (Oxford, 2006).

Dayan, J., *Haiti, History, and the Gods* (Berkeley, 1996).

Diamond, J., *Guns, Germs, and Steel: The Fate of Human Societies* (New York, 1998).

Dubois, L., *A Colony of Citizens: Revolution and Slave Emancipation in the French Caribbean, 1787–1804* (Chapel Hill, 2004).

Ferguson, N., *Empire: The Rise and Demise of the British World Order and the Lessons for Global Power* (New York, 2002).

Garraway, D., *The Libertine Colony: Creolization in the Early French Caribbean* (Durham, 2005).

Gautier, A., *Les Sœurs de solitude: La Condition féminine dans l'esclavage aux Antilles du XVIIe au XIXe siècle* (Paris, 1985).
Geggus, P., *Slavery, War, and Revolution: The British Occupation of Saint-Domingue, 1793–1798* (Oxford, 1982).
Gernet, J., *China and the Christian Impact: A Conflict of Cultures* (Cambridge, 1985).
Glyn, N., *The Prize of all the Oceans* (New York, 1999).
Hannaford, I., *Race: The History of an Idea in the West* (Baltimore, 1996).
Havard, G. and C. Vidal, *Histoire de l'Amérique française* (Paris, 2003).
Herman, A., *To Rule the Waves: How the British Navy Shaped the Modern World* (New York, 2004).
James, C. L. R., *Black Jacobins: Toussaint L'Ouverture and the Santo Domingo Revolution* (1938; repr. New York, 1963).
Kamen, H., *Empire: How Spain Became a World Power, 1492–1763* (New York, 2002).
Klein, H. S., *The Atlantic Slave Trade* (Cambridge, 1999).
Kuethe, A., *Cuba, 1753–1815: Crown, Military, and Society* (Knoxville, TN, 1986).
Lawson, P., *The East India Company: A History* (New York, 1993).
McNeill, W., *Plagues and Peoples* (Garden City, 1976).
Martínez, M. E., *The Spanish Concept of Limpieza de Sangre and the Emergence of the "Race/Caste" System in the Viceroyalty of New Spain* (Ph.D., University of Chicago, 2002).
Mills, K., *Idolatry and its Enemies: Colonial Andean Religion and Extirpation, 1640–1750* (Princeton, 1997).
Pluchon, P., *Toussaint Louverture* (Paris, 1989).
Polanyi, K., *The Great Transformation* (1944; repr. Boston, 1985).
Pritchard, J., *In Search of Empire: The French in the Americas, 1670–1730* (Cambridge, 2004).
Ribbe, C., *Le Crime de Napoléon* (Paris, 2005).
Robb, P., *A History of India* (New York, 2002).
Said, E., *Orientalism* (New York, 1978).
Thomas, H., *The Slave Trade: The Story of the Atlantic Slave Trade, 1440–1870* (1997; repr. New York, 1999).
Thompson, L., *A History of South Africa* (New Haven, 2000).
Williams, E., *Capitalism and Slavery* (1944; repr. New York, 1961).
Williams, G., *The Prize of all the Oceans: The Triumph and Tragedy of Anson's Voyage Round the World* (London, 1999).

Chapter Twenty-Six

Europe and the Sea

Jan Glete

The Great Peninsula

Europe is a huge peninsula on the Euro-Asian continent, with major peninsulas (Sweden–Norway, Jutland, Italy, Balkan) and large islands (the British Isles, the Mediterranean islands, and the Baltic islands). There are many navigable rivers, mainly on the northern half of the continent. Consequently, the coasts are long in relation to the territory and a large part of the population lives close to the sea. Europe's easy access to sea lines of communication has contributed to economic development, as large quantities of cargo can move easily and cheaply on water.

Europe's geography made interaction between sea power (control of the sea with armed force), maritime trade, and political control of territories important. Sea routes around Europe pass through narrows which are easy to control; the Dardanelles–Bosporus, the entrance to the Adriatic Sea, the straits around Sicily, the Straits of Gibraltar, the English Channel, and the passages between the Baltic Sea and the North Sea. The sea is a potential highway for invasions, but for a defender with sea power it is a useful bulwark against such attacks. Consequently, sea power has made it possible to protect and control both maritime trade and territories. Several European states were only able to fight or support each other across water. Political alliances were often formed with a view of how they affected control of the seas around Europe and between Europe and the rest of the world.

Europeans have had many opportunities to use the sea for shipping, trade, fishing, plunder, and war. In the early modern period Europeans increasingly exploited these opportunities, as well as mastering the threats which the sea posed. With the exception of Russia and the Ottoman empire, Europe was dependent on the sea for direct communication with other parts of the world. By the eighteenth century this had become an opportunity, not an obstacle. Western Europe became the center of global trade and the only area where information about other parts of the world was systematically gathered and used for economic and political decision-making. The seas around the continent were thus essential not only for Europeans, but also for other peoples who had increasing contacts with Europe across the oceans.

A Companion to Eighteenth-Century Europe, First Edition. Edited by Peter H. Wilson.
© 2014 John Wiley & Sons, Ltd. Published 2014 by John Wiley & Sons, Ltd.

This European ability to connect economies and project seaborne power over long distances was the most spectacular maritime aspect of eighteenth-century history. Growing seaborne trade and European expansion around the world created a network of contacts and an international economy where the flow of merchandise became essential for the dynamic development of production and consumption. However, much of European maritime trade and naval warfare still took place in waters close to Europe. Wars in Europe were often combinations of contests on land and at sea where maritime supply routes and amphibious operations were important even for land powers on the continent.

Maritime Historiography

The sea has attracted historians interested in shipping and trade, shipbuilding, fishing and whaling, privateering, technology, warfare, naval policy-making and administration, maritime culture, and social conditions on ships and in maritime communities. Historians have approached the sea from political, economic, social, technical, and cultural perspectives, and archaeologists and ethnologists have also contributed to our knowledge of maritime history. The eighteenth century has left a rich legacy of naval archives, considerable records from customs services, admiralty courts, chambers of commerce, port authorities, and coastal communities, and important material from a few large chartered companies. Of the papers produced by ordinary shipowners, masters, or merchants engaged in maritime trade only a small fraction remain, while eighteenth-century seamen wrote little and left even less for later generations to read. This has created a marked lack of balance in research where incentives and opportunities for, and threats to, private shipping and trade are only indirectly known and where the size, composition, and activities of the European mercantile marines and their crews remain largely unexplored.

Naval historiography was dominated in the nineteenth century and the first half of the twentieth by studies of major naval operations, battles, and naval heroes. The eighteenth century, or rather the period 1688–1815, was central to such studies, most of which concentrated on the large Atlantic battle fleets. They remain fundamental, but readers need to be aware that they were written when the modern state and European imperialism were seen as the self-evident outcomes of history. European navies were regarded as instruments of national policies and expressions of national character. They were evaluated as efficient according to nineteenth- and early twentieth-century ideas about operational doctrine, professional officers, and naval administration and the primacy of the gun-armed battle fleet. This perspective held the large sailing battle fleets of this period to be shining examples of what a national state might achieve through a consistent policy. Such fleets were important in major wars, they protected trade and attacked enemy shipping, and they were key instruments for spreading European power around the world. Their administrations were, however, often evaluated as inefficient, corrupt, and dependent on various vested interests.

In recent decades, naval historians have been more interested in policy, administration, and technology (Baugh, 1965; Merino Navarro, 1981; Pritchard, 1987). Eighteenth-century privateering and trade warfare has also attracted considerable interest (Bromley, 1987; Starkey, 1990; Verhees-van Mer 1986). Naval technology has been studied with sources and methods little used by earlier generations of historians (Lavery, 1983–4; Villiers, 1991). War and society themes, such as social conditions among seamen and professionalization, patronage, and careers in officer corps, have also been studied (Rodger, 1986). Policy-making and administration are now generally assessed differently, accepting that eighteenth-century navies were unusually complex and that governments had to mobilize human and material resources, not according to formally rational organizational schemes (which all navies failed to achieve), but as practical measures suited to assembling fleets and skilled crews for protracted maritime conflicts. Much remains to be done to incorporate these perspectives within the general history of warfare.

Modern broad syntheses on naval history have begun to replace the old standard works on the subject (Bruijn, 1993; Rodger, 2004), though there is a tendency still to concentrate on one navy at a time. Comparative studies of all participants remain rare, and it is important to remember that wars are struggles between states and societies, not between armies and navies. In order to understand such struggles, we need to study the mobilization and organization of resources, as well as the policies to coordinate the multitude of political, social, and economic interests behind war efforts. The most obvious subjects to combine with naval history are seafarers, maritime communities, shipowners, and merchants, but common taxpayers, fiscal organizations, public opinion, and representative institutions are also important.

Eighteenth-century maritime and shipping history is not a neglected subject (for example Davis, 1962). However, the eighteenth century looks less spectacular in comparison with the initial period of European penetration of the world's oceans, and with the nineteenth century, with its revolution in maritime transportation and global seaborne imperialism. Trade in Europe and between Europe and the rest of the world grew steadily, but the mercantile, institutional, and technological frameworks underwent no dramatic changes. Consequently, they have attracted few historians searching for causes, effects, and alternative interpretations of wider historical development. The history of shipping and trade has also usually been studied along national lines, yet the subject is obviously international. The exceptions are trade between Europe and America, the slave trade between Africa and America, the great East India companies, and the maritime causes and effects of the War of American Independence.

Protectionism and mercantile regulations were central in the maritime policy of many eighteenth-century European states, but the contexts, causes, and effects of such policy measures have seldom been studied, especially not in a comparative way. The state as promoter and protector of national shipping and trade was a cornerstone of mercantilist policy, but economic historians have often either seen the state and its regulation as an impediment to economic growth, or regarded the restrictions as inefficient and easily circumvented by merchants. Few attempts have been made to test the validity of Adam Smith's contemporary observation that the British Navigation Act was an economically justified exception to free trade because it provided the British navy with a pool of trained seamen. Meanwhile, political historians seldom examine the economic origins and effects of the maritime policies of eighteenth-century governments. The productivity of shipping has attracted interest from economic historians, but generally from a macro perspective running over long periods, rather than for the eighteenth century in particular.

International trade encouraged alliances of interest between trading communities in different countries, but it could also create conflicts between merchants in the same country, especially if state monopolies and regulations disadvantaged certain groups. Intense contacts through shipping and trade were likely to spread ideas about technology, business opportunities, entrepreneurial practices and economic policy between regions and across national borders. As shipping and maritime trade in itself is highly international, it is unusually well suited to making international comparisons about productivity, the effects of various regulations, and the ability to adopt innovations.

Maritime culture and maritime communities have attracted increased interest from historians working in fields other than warfare and trade. Local history has been a growth area and, given Europe's long coasts, is particularly helpful for maritime history generally (Cabantous, 1980). Human beings who lived close to the sea and spent long periods at sea have often had more in common with one another than with those living further inland. Fernand Braudel's vision of the Mediterranean as a unifying factor has inspired emulation by those working on the North Sea and the Baltic to produce comparative studies of how coastal populations responded to the opportunities and challenges of the sea (Holm, 1991; Kirby and Hinkkanen, 2000). Seamen, fishermen, smugglers, and families living close to the sea have been typical objects of study. The intrusion of the state into coastal communities and the decline of traditional practices, such as the pillaging of wrecks, are important themes for the eighteenth century (Cabantous, 1993). The same applies to urban history, giving the significant numbers of eighteenth-century Europeans who lived in port cities.

The Sea, Human Endurance, and Human Inventiveness

The sea is not a natural element of man, and human activities at sea are determined by climate, technology, and human endurance. In the eighteenth century the distance in time and space between the port from which a ship or a fleet sailed and where they operated reached a technical apex. Several centuries of improving ship construction, sailing technology, navigation, and the technology of food preparation, preservation, and storage made it possible to stay at sea for several months by 1700. These improvements also enabled large ships to sail during autumn and even winter with greater safety than before. This was important for relations between sea and land power. In the eighteenth century, sea power could now operate more efficiently over long distances, and major fleets could be deployed in strategically decisive parts of the sea for long periods without needing to return to port to refit or resupply. Further improvements in these fields occurred across the eighteenth century. Whereas the strategy of continuous blockade of enemy ports was hardly feasible in 1700, the British navy employed it effectively a century later. While the introduction of steam power from the 1820s improved speed, predictability, and safety, it also made ships more dependent on land for fuel.

Health and nutrition remained constraints on extended maritime operations (Buchet, 1999; Pritchard, 1995). They affected both navies and mercantile shipping, although health conditions and provisioning on merchantmen have received little attention. It is probable that comparative studies of different navies and long-distance mercantile shipping would reveal unknown connections between administrative competence, maritime experience, and efficiency. Studies of food and medicine at sea in the eighteenth century have been concentrated on scurvy and vitamin C, but there were other problems affecting efficiency. Naval history may be rewritten as campaigns against epidemics and problems with food preservation and unbalanced food supply. Epidemics spread with great speed in the cramped conditions on a warship. They were often pronounced during the initial stages of a war when newly recruited sailors arrived from different areas, and ships assembled from overseas stations, all bringing infections against which men from other regions lacked immunity. As the crews fell victim to disease, fleets had to be reduced and operational goals scaled down. The survivors became seasoned and more resistant to infection, which may explain the improvements in operational efficiency that can be detected during protracted conflicts.

The design of a gun-carrying warship or a large merchantman was a complicated process, possibly the most demanding task to be undertaken in pre-industrial Europe. Warships must be able to fight with their guns in adverse weather, survive gales and extended periods at sea even after battle damage, move in the desired direction at the best possible speed, and provide shelter for a large crew. Merchantmen had to be built to combine sailing qualities with hulls designed for economic cargo-carrying, usually with widely different cargoes in different directions. Ship technology had become fairly standardized in Europe by the eighteenth century, although small craft were still often built and rigged in accordance with regional customs.

Theoretical and mathematical methods were developed to optimize ship design, but most of the progress in wooden-hulled sailing ship technology had already been achieved by empirical methods and the practical application of experience before 1700 (Ferreiro, 2006). The beginning of the transformation in marine engineering was imminent at the end of the century and the first steamers began to operate in the first decade of the nineteenth century. The great revolution in shipping and naval warfare connected with iron and steam did not begin until the mid-nineteenth century, however.

The rapidly growing navies and mercantile marines of eighteenth-century Europe consumed considerable amounts of timber. Teak from southern Asia and mahogany from South America were at least as good as European oak for shipbuilding, and they were increasingly exploited by Europeans. Despite growing interest from environmental historians, the few major studies of timber supply are relatively dated (Albion, 1926; Bamford, 1956). The timber problems of the eighteenth century offer a good example of how societies react to a shortage of natural resources. There is no doubt that timber prices markedly rose in the later decades of the century, but it is far from certain whether this reflected a long-term crisis in supply. Major demands for timber, primarily in wartime, frequently caused acute problems, but probably because governments relied on regulations or decrees rather than the market to manage supply. The experience of the nineteenth century indicates that a combination of market forces and improved methods of construction facilitated renewed increases in shipbuilding output.

Organizations and Structures: States and Navies at Sea

European navies had developed into a major structural precondition for warfare and international relations by 1700. They were firmly established organizations under state administration and their size had become part of the international balance of power. Like the armies, European navies had become strikingly homogeneous in structure, technology, armaments, and tactical behavior. Naval strength was measured by the number of large warships suitable for the battle line during major engagements. Such ships, which now became known as ships-of-the-line, carried large numbers of heavy guns and were built as massive wooden structures to resist prolonged enemy gunfire. Ships-of-the-line had crews of several hundred men, but few had to be experienced seamen. Most fulfilled rather unskilled tasks, primarily gun-handling under the direction of officers, gunners, and experienced seamen. Division of labor, conscious development of teamwork, and good leadership were both necessary and sufficient to form useful crews out of a mixture of men with various skills and differing levels of competence.

Ships-of-the line grew markedly in size, firepower, and sailing capabilities after 1700. The number of guns in relation to the ships' displacements decreased, but heavy guns could be mounted higher in the hull, where they could fire in rougher seas. Overall effective firepower also increased as the average size of ships-of-the-line approximately doubled between 1700 and 1800. The displacement of the typical two-decked ships built around 1800 (averaging 3,000 tonnes) equaled the size of the largest three-deckers a century earlier. Consequently, the size, manpower requirements, fighting potential, and cost of European battle fleets increased far more than is reflected in the relatively stable number of ships-of-the-line and the number of guns they carried. Smaller sailing warships were built as scouts for battle fleets and for cruiser warfare, and also for protection of trade and attack against enemy commerce. The Mediterranean galley fleets were no longer important, and they were gradually reduced and finally abolished by the end of the eighteenth century. In contrast, the Baltic powers introduced large galley flotillas for archipelago and amphibious warfare in the eighteenth century, and replaced them with gunboats by 1800 (Glete, 1993).

The European battle fleets were kept ready as instruments of policy, but they were not normally at sea, except during wars or major crises. There was a clear distinction between peace conditions, when most warships were laid up in the naval bases, and war, when as many ships as possible were manned and commissioned for service at sea. In peacetime, battle fleets were fitted out for sea only as a show of force during international crises. To send a fleet to foreign waters was a demonstration of power and political determination. It was not regarded as necessary to maintain fleets in commission in peacetime in order to improve training – in marked contrast to the permanent armies, where the constant drilling of soldiers was now considered essential.

It was possible to operate on the reduced peacetime basis because professional seamen remained available in civilian society and because naval gunnery was relatively easy to learn quickly when ships were commissioned for sea. The fact that most navies entered conflicts with crews and ships that had rarely trained together, especially in large formations, contributed to the generally conservative tactics of eighteenth-century naval warfare. The British navy was the one most likely to vary the formal line of battle and adopt more aggressive tactics, particularly in the later stages of protracted conflicts during the late 1740s and 1750s, the early 1780s, and, on a large scale, from the late 1790s (Creswell, 1972). The long periods at sea conditioned

British officers and crews to work together as teams, and instilled the confidence in their superior combat efficiency necessary to employ more flexible tactics.

Eighteenth-century navies were complex, centralized, industrial, and technically advanced organizations in societies dominated by decentralized production, agriculture, and rather simple technology. By 1700, the systems of naval administration of different European states were remarkably similar, although there were variations reflecting different political, social, and economic conditions. Typically, a central administration controlled the design and construction of warships, ran major naval dockyards for the construction and maintenance of such ships, purchased naval stores, guns, and provisions in large quantities, and employed corps of commissioned and non-commissioned officers whose professional competence and loyalty to the state were preconditions for the control of violence at sea. In wartime, the administration's main task was to keep as many warships as possible at sea and to build additional vessels and acquire resources to sustain the war effort. Warfare at sea was more dependent on the centralized administration of resources than land warfare, and naval administration was less easy to improvise than army administration. Well-developed maritime economies with port infrastructures, mercantile shipbuilding, shipping, and experienced seafarers could not be created from scratch, yet all were invaluable in mobilizing for naval wars.

Institutions and Merchants at Sea

The eighteenth century was the first time in European history when seafarers could generally benefit from one major institutional change: an effective state monopoly of violence. European states had grown stronger and more centralized over the previous two centuries and no longer tolerated private violence beyond their control. Autonomous regional organizations capable of controlling long-distance trade, like the Hanseatic League, had disappeared or at least were no longer in a position to challenge state authority. Privateering was still common at sea, but was regulated by maritime courts. Violence at sea now generally resulted from formally declared wars. Seafarers and merchants suffered from warfare, but they were treated more predictably according to international customs. Piracy in European waters had been effectively suppressed before 1700, while that in American waters was largely eliminated by the 1720s. Through a mixture of coercion and bribes, European states persuaded the North African Barbary states to abandon their long tradition of violence against seafarers later in the century.

Strong naval powers provided their mercantile shipping with warships as convoy escorts in wartime. Neutral shipping relied on their home country's international standing to guarantee immunity against belligerent warships and privateers (Feldbaek, 1980; Müller, 2004). Though powerful maritime nations, such as Britain, did not always respect the rights of minor neutrals, such as the Danes, the emergence of internationally accepted maritime customs greatly reduced the dangers and expense of seaborne trade. Merchantmen could sail alone, largely unarmed and no longer had to wait for convoys. Crews could be reduced to the minimum necessary for ship-handling, and owners and merchants could find cheaper insurance.

Institutions, in the sense of rules guiding human interaction, are increasingly recognized as vital to economic change through their role in influencing transaction costs (North, 1981). Shipping is itself a transaction cost with a long history and well suited to be examined from the perspective of several important institutions. The most significant of these are organized protection against violence, the legal forms of protecting property on a national and international level, information systems, and institutions for sharing risks and minimizing uncertainty. At sea and in ports foreigners regularly encountered each other in cooperation and competition and had to develop rules for interaction. For example, it had become established by 1700 that mercantile shipping in peacetime had unconditional rights to use all European waters. It was also generally accepted that a sovereign state had the right to enforce trade restrictions in ports under its control, typically by giving favors to ships under its own flag.

Ships and commercial cargoes were protected by law when they visited foreign ports as long as they followed local laws and regulations. Shipowning could be legally shared to spread risks among co-owners, while maritime insurance was already well developed. A growing network of officially appointed consuls in foreign ports improved information about trade opportunities and liaised between owners and the local authorities (Müller, 2004). Development remained uneven across Europe, but maritime trade now worked within institutional frameworks more akin to contemporary than early modern Europe. Risk and uncertainty were no longer related to hostile human action, but primarily to wind and weather, navigational hazards, and the slow transmission of information: problems that were radically reduced by nineteenth-century technical development (steam, navigational aids, and the telegraph).

It should be possible to measure the positive impact of such institutional change by examining shipping productivity. Economic historians, especially those interested in institutions, have applied quantitative methods with varying results, though several studies suggest productivity indeed improved over the eighteenth century (Lucassen and Unger, 2000). Most studies measure productivity by the number of seamen in relation to a ship's carrying capacity. A better method is the number of men employed in relation to the quantity of cargo carried in a year. Unfortunately, we still lack substantial runs of such data across long periods. It is probable that cargo in relation to manpower increased markedly during the eighteenth century as more ships could sail individually and react more rapidly to market conditions thanks to improved protection and information. One important example of the increased integration of the European shipping market is that Danish and Swedish cargo carriers became competitive in the Mediterranean regional trade (Andersen, 2000; Müller, 2004). It has also been argued that the critical moment of transition in European economic history was not the Industrial Revolution, but a commercial revolution involving the development of the North Sea region (the Netherlands, Great Britain, northern France) as a center of modernization and continuous growth (Ormrod, 2003). That would have been impossible without an intense exchange of goods through cheap shipping.

The seventeenth century had been a period of Dutch supremacy in shipping and maritime trade in Europe otherwise unequaled in European history (Israel, 1989). It is only a moderate exaggeration to state that the Europeans mainly traded with the Dutch rather than with each other. The Dutch Republic was the hub of international trade and Dutch merchants also played an important role in many foreign ports around Europe. By 1700 this position was threatened, partly by Britain's rapid growth as a maritime power, and partly by the growth or revival of medium-sized competitors such as France, Denmark-Norway, and Sweden, as well as some major German and Mediterranean trading and shipping centers like Hamburg and Venice. In the eighteenth century the British mercantile marine was the largest in Europe, French shipping passed that of the Dutch in size, and several European countries developed mercantile marines which carried much of their own foreign trade. The British position within eighteenth-century Europe was never as dominant as the Dutch had been in the previous century, at least not until 1792–1815, when the Royal Navy swept competitors from the sea.

The lack of a real hegemonic power in eighteenth-century shipping may have been the effect of mercantilist regulations, but it may also have stemmed from the more even spread of trading and shipping competence across Europe. The Dutch had previously enjoyed a combined advantage in shipbuilding methods, shipping productivity, methods of preserving, packing and marketing goods, a well-developed market for capital and short-term credits, and a favorable geographical position for European trade. The Dutch also had superior institutions, including protection of shipping by a Europe-wide convoy system and a network of information from Dutch entrepreneurs working around Europe. Dutch methods and expertise spread across Europe, contributing to the rise of other, competitive shipping nations during the eighteenth century. Future studies should investigate the relative role of the state, private enterprise and migrant Dutch entrepreneurs, shipmasters, and other experts in this dissemination process.

The place of the state in shipping, trade, and economic development remains a matter of debate. Many economic historians either deny that the state played a significant part or ignore it altogether, while others, like Frederic C. Lane and Douglass C. North, conclude that lower protection costs and improved property rights were important for increased productivity in shipping (Lane, 1979; North, 1981). Immanuel Wallerstein has argued that world systems of trade and political influence required a strong and well-armed state at their core, and Jonathan Israel identified the seventeenth-century Dutch Republic as a particularly effective state of that type which used its navy to protect and promote Dutch trade in an age of endemic wars (Israel, 1989).

Studies focusing more narrowly on the eighteenth century pay rather less attention to such questions, because the great maritime wars between Britain, France, and Spain obviously affected trade and European empires. A power that dominated the sea might seriously interrupt enemy trade and conquer colonies. There has been a surprising lack of interest in the causes of these wars, beyond the arguments advanced by diplomatic historians. Colonies, shipping, and trade were obviously important, but it is far from clear whether states primarily saw these assets as sources of revenue and as pawns in European diplomacy, or if they were motivated by economic concerns that trade and colonies favored domestic growth. The extent to which western European states and societies profited from the opportunities offered by the sea may lie in the differing attitudes of policy-makers and elites to these questions.

There is, however, no doubt that Europeans had developed a relationship to the sea by the eighteenth century that was unique in a global context. Governments believed that they had the right and responsibility to protect their subjects at sea, they developed large-scale organizations to control the sea, and they were thinking in European or global terms when developing naval and maritime policies. The maritime parts of the European societies may not have been much different from Chinese, Indian, or Arabic shipowners and merchants in maintaining regional and interregional networks, but they were unique in their ability to rely on state structures for physical and economic protection. They were also the only societies which had the information and power to act globally. Even powers with minor colonial ambitions, such as Denmark and Sweden, had an important trade with Asia and a keen interest of exploiting markets in America. This was a uniquely European relationship to the sea and it was central to the growth of European control of large parts of the world, a development that peaked in the nineteenth century.

Warfare in Atlantic Europe

In the early eighteenth century Britain became the largest naval power in the world; a position it would retain until World War II. It achieved this partly by default, because France, which was briefly the largest naval power in the late seventeenth century, drastically reduced its navy. The third major naval power, the Dutch Republic, also reduced its navy and remained for a long time a British ally rather than a challenger after 1688. The British superiority at sea was not, however, immediately converted into hegemony or a maritime-based global power. Britain did not reach that position until the Revolutionary and Napoleonic Wars (1792–1815). The eighteenth century saw a protracted political and economic struggle in the Atlantic hemisphere between Britain, and the Bourbon monarchies of France and Spain. The latter two periodically came close to curbing British expansionism, but ultimately failed. In the case of France, this was due primarily to the state's inability to mobilize sufficient resources, while for Spain, the lack of economic growth undermined imperial policy.

European power struggles were primarily continental between 1688 and 1714, but nonetheless significantly affected trade. Thereafter, a more distinctly Atlantic struggle over trade and colonies developed alongside wars over European territory and influence (Baugh, 1998). The former had a global dimension, as trade and colonies in Asia were also involved. This became increasingly apparent as the century wore on. An Anglo-Spanish struggle in the Caribbean began separately in 1739 from an Austro-Prussian war over Silesia in 1740, and only gradually merged into a general European conflict around 1744 that ended four years later. The next major conflict, known as the Seven Years War, saw what amounted to two separate struggles, one about the Atlantic sea lines and trans-oceanic colonies after 1754 and one about power in central Europe from 1756 (Dull, 2005). The American War of Independence (1775–83) was not at all connected with conflicts over European territories except Britain's two Spanish enclaves, Minorca and Gibraltar.

The France of Louis XIV is often seen as an early contender for sea power, defeated by the allied British and Dutch navies in 1688–1714. However, it is doubtful if Louis' naval ambitions stretched much beyond French home waters, and they may primarily have been related to his goal of weakening the European position of the Spanish Habsburg dynasty. The Spanish navy was small in that period, but Spain was allied with the Dutch from the late 1660s and also the British after 1689. These powers fought for control of the seas connecting Spain's European possessions. This interpretation is consistent with French naval policy after 1700, when the Bourbon dynasty inherited the Spanish monarchy and became a French ally. Under the strains of war the French navy was radically reduced, to the point that, by Louis' death (1715), it could no longer be rated a first-class force. This reflected a significant shift in priorities in favor of the army, as well as the absence of a Spanish threat, rather than inevitable decline.

Britain, France, and Spain were the main contenders for colonies and trade in America and Asia after the western European peace of 1713–14. Portugal and the Dutch Republic still defended their existing positions around the world, but either as neutrals or British allies rather than independent players. The differing ambitions were reflected in varied naval strength. France, Spain, and the Dutch Republic had navies of approximately the same size between the 1720s and 1740s, but they were far behind Britain's Royal Navy, which almost equaled their combined strength. Large French and Spanish naval rearmament programs after the peace of 1748 radically changed the Atlantic balance of power. The two Bourbon navies rapidly expanded and, in spite of severe French losses in the Seven Years War, they continued to grow and reached quantitative superiority over the British navy in the late 1760s. They retained that position until the late 1790s when their relative power declined, due first to repeated defeats between 1793 and 1805, and then to marked British superiority in shipbuilding. The British were normally better able to finance an active fleet at sea, but superior Franco-Spanish numbers severely restricted the Royal Navy's freedom of operations during the American War of Independence (Glete, 1993).

France was more populous than Britain, its economy was fairly expansive, and it had the potential to both dominate western Europe and to exploit the opportunities of the sea on a large scale. France developed into a major shipping nation in the eighteenth century, but colonial ambitions in North America and India were decisively defeated by the British, primarily in the Seven Years War, when financial crisis forced France to cut its naval strength drastically after 1759 (Dull, 2005; Pritchard, 1987). France refused to turn its back on the sea, and resumed a maritime policy after 1763. The avoidance of continental commitments combined with renewed naval construction contributed to France's partial success against Britain in the American War of Independence. Despite deteriorating state finances, French naval expansion continued after 1783, and the sailing navy reached its largest size ever around 1790. Thus, on the eve of revolution, France also seemed well prepared to contest control of the sea with Britain.

The Bourbon regime in Spain initially tried to restore the country's position in Italy, but turned towards the Atlantic after the new Spanish navy was defeated by the British in 1717–20. Spanish power, wealth, and status depended on keeping the sea lanes open to its American colonies. British distractions in the 1730s enabled Spain to recover part of its Italian possessions, but this made little difference to the European balance of power. By contrast, Spain still possessed the world's largest colonial empire, and it developed a navy that for most of the eighteenth century competed with France as the second largest in the world. The Spanish navy generally succeeded in defending the colonies, though British amphibious successes in the Caribbean around 1740 and in 1762 indicated that superior sea power was a threat to Spain's power in America. Shipping and trade proved even more effective means for western European penetration of the Spanish and Portuguese empires, and helped undermine the willingness of colonial elites to remain subordinate to Madrid and Lisbon by 1800.

If France profited economically from the sea while Spain utilized it successfully for imperial defense, Britain eventually outclassed both in all areas. The Royal Navy was generally sufficiently strong to intervene in at least one part of Europe outside the Channel and the North Sea, and in some wars it intervened in both the Baltic and the Mediterranean simultaneously. The period 1792–1815 has entered history as the Revolutionary and Napoleonic Wars that are generally regarded as a great struggle for and against French hegemony in Europe. They are never called the "British and Russian wars for world power status," although these two powers clearly followed long-term expansive policy goals and emerged as the two great victors by 1815. Britain's great imperial conquests in India during this period are rarely regarded as part of the same conflict, yet British power in India depended on control of the sea, and the outcome on the subcontinent might have been different if Britain had lost that control in Europe. In retrospect, the wars between 1792 and 1815 represent the culmination of a protracted struggle over control of the sea throughout the eighteenth century from which Britain emerged as the single victor, while the fighting in continental Europe largely concluded with a restoration of the pre-war balance of power between France, Austria, Prussia, and Russia. The oceans and the power to use them in wartime have henceforth remained in Anglo-Saxon hands, despite repeated challenges from France, Germany, Japan, and the Soviet Union, while in the nineteenth century Britain was the only great power with a global reach.

The Sea and Continental Power Struggles

Geography naturally concentrated trade and warfare in the Baltic, Mediterranean, and Black Sea on maritime lines of communication. Trade was mainly seaborne and could be controlled relatively easily by sea power in these rather narrow seas. It was often difficult for large armies to meet in combat without naval assistance to transport them, so that naval operations were frequently dictated by the end to create opportunities that could be exploited by soldiers on land. Roads were underdeveloped in this period, and the carrying capacity of ships easily surpassed that of land transport. This not only favored shipping as a means of trade, but made navies important for the power struggles on the European continent. It also gave the naval powers in western Europe the ability to intervene in wars elsewhere on the continent from the later seventeenth century. Britain's position as a European great power became increasingly dependent on itsability to subsidize continental allies and use its navy to intervene on the continent. The historiography of Baltic and eastern Mediterranean naval warfare, especially from a broader strategic and economic perspective, is rather dated, but the older standard works are still essential for those who do not read the languages of these regions (Anderson, 1910, 1952).

From economic and strategic points of view, the Baltic Sea connects eastern, northern, and central Europe with one another and with western Europe. The great expansion of maritime trade and permanent navies in western Europe made the Baltic region an important supplier for naval stores: timber for shipbuilding, masts and spars, hemp, flax, tar, guns, and high-quality iron for hull fastenings. It also made the region important for the western maritime powers that frequently intervened after the mid-seventeenth century, usually to influence the balance of power, and always to protect their trading interests (Rystad, 1994). The Mediterranean was primarily a sea for regional trade, but there was also an important trade between western Europe and the Levant which made the Dutch and the British interested in the regional balance of power.

The Baltic and Levant navies were tailored for regional warfare. They were more integrated than western navies with other means of defense, such as armies and fortresses. Arguably, wars here – especially the Baltic – were not won by the side with the best army or navy, but by the one able to coordinate the two, both in strategic planning and actual operations. The later phase of the Great Northern War (1700–21) was determined primarily by the control of the various sea lanes, yet the general history of the conflict is overshadowed by concentration on the more extensive land operations prior to 1709. The two primary Baltic protagonists were Denmark-Norway and Sweden, while Venice and the Ottoman empire faced each other across the eastern Mediterranean. These traditional opponents still fought over control of their respective regions into the 1710s, but later conflicts were determined by the intrusion of Russia into both seas. Naval operations determined warfare, especially in the northern Baltic, where roads were few and border regions were dominated by forests. The Russian galley fleet's ability to control the archipelago facilitated the attack on Finland in 1713–14. The Russo-Swedish war of 1788–90 saw few land operations, while both sides expended considerable resources in failed attempts to achieve a decision through amphibious operations and naval attacks on bases and cities (Glete, 2004).

Russian intrusion in both regions began around 1700. A serious land defeat in 1711 set back Russian ambitions in the Sea of Azov and the Black Sea for several decades, while Russian naval policy in the Baltic was far from consistent, with the force there fluctuating considerably in strength. Nonetheless, the development of Russian naval power was remarkable in the longer term. A squadron from the Baltic fleet was redeployed to the Mediterranean during the war against the Ottomans in 1768–74. Thereafter, naval ambitions expanded in line with Catherine II's plans to increase Russian territory and influence, and in the 1790s the country was able to send battle fleets to both the Black Sea and Mediterranean to support its armies (Saul, 1970). Neither Austria nor Prussia developed significant navies in the eighteenth century, despite possessing considerable coasts and mercantile marines. Russia, which began the century shut off from both the Baltic and Black Seas, and with few merchant ships, had gained a significant coastal presence and created a fleet that, by the early nineteenth century, was the third largest in Europe.

Bibliography

Albion, R. G., *Forests and Sea Power: The Timber Problem of the Royal Navy, 1652–1862* (1926; Cambridge, MA, 1965).

Andersen, D. H., *The Danish Flag in the Mediterranean: Shipping and Trade, 1747–1807* (2 vols., Copenhagen, 2000).

Anderson, R. C., *Naval Wars in the Baltic, 1522–1850* (1910; London, 1969).

Anderson, R. C., *Naval Wars in the Levant, 1559–1853* (Liverpool, 1952).

Bamford, P. W., *Forests and French Sea Power, 1660–1789* (Toronto, 1956).
Baugh, D. A., *British Naval Administration in the Age of Walpole* (Princeton, 1965).
Baugh, D. A., "Withdrawing from Europe: Anglo-French maritime geopolitics, 1750–1800," *International History Review*, 20 (1998), 1–32.
Bromley, J. S., *Corsairs and Navies, 1660–1760* (London, 1987).
Bruijn, J. R., *The Dutch Navy of the Seventeenth and Eighteenth Centuries* (Columbia, 1993).
Buchet, C., *Marine, économie et société, un example d'interaction: L'Avitaillement de la Royal Navy durant la guerre de sept ans* (Paris, 1999).
Butel, P., *The Atlantic* (London, 1999).
Cabantous, A., *La Mer et les hommes: Pêcheurs et matelots de Louis XV à la Révolution* (Dunkirk, 1980).
Cabantous, A., *Les Côtes barbares: Pilleurs d'épaves et sociétés littorales en France, 1680–1830* (Paris, 1993).
Creswell, J., *British Admirals of the Eighteenth Century: Tactics in Battle* (London, 1972).
Davis, R., *The Rise of the English Shipping Industry in the Seventeenth and Eighteenth Century* (London, 1962).
Dull, J. R., *The French Navy and the Seven Years' War* (Lincoln, 2005).
Feldbaek, O., *Denmark and the Armed Neutrality, 1800–1801: Small Power Policy in a World War* (Copenhagen, 1980).
Feldbaek, O., *Dansk söfarts historie*, vol. 3: *1720–1814: Storhandelens tid* (Copenhagen, 1997).
Ferreiro, L. D., *Ships and Science: The Birth of Naval Architecture in the Scientific Revolution* (Cambridge, MA, 2006).
Glete, J., *Navies and Nations: Warships, Navies and State Building in Europe and America, 1500–1860* (2 vols., Stockholm, 1993).
Glete, J., "Navies and power struggle in northern and eastern Europe, 1721–1814," in R. Hobson and T. Kristiansen (eds.), *Navies in Northern Waters, 1721–2000* (London, 2004), pp. 66–93.
Harding, R., *Seapower and Naval Warfare, 1650–1830* (London, 1999).
Holm, P., *Kystfolk: Kontakter og sammenhaenge over Kattegat og Skagerrrak, ca 1550–1914* (Esbjerg, 1991).
Israel, J., *Dutch Primacy in World Trade, 1585–1740* (Oxford, 1989).
Kirby, D. and M.-L. Hinkkanen, *The Baltic and the North Seas* (London, 2000).
Lane, F. C., *Profits from Power: Readings in Protection Rent and Violence-Controlling Enterprises* (Albany, 1979).
Lavery, B., *The Ship of the Line* (2 vols., London, 1983–4).
Lucassen, J. and R. W. Unger, "Labour productivity in ocean shipping, 1450–1875," *International Journal of Maritime History*, 12 (2000), 127–41.
Merino Navarro, J. P., *La armada española en el siglo XVIII* (Madrid, 1981).
Müller, L., *Consuls, Corsairs, and Commerce: The Swedish Consular Service and Long-Distance Shipping, 1720–1815* (Uppsala, 2004).
North, D. C., *Structure and Change in Economic History* (New York, 1981).
Ormrod, D., *The Rise of Commercial Empires: England and the Netherlands in the Age of Mercantilism, 1650–1770* (Cambridge, 2003).
Padfield, P., *Maritime Supremacy and the Opening of the Western Mind, 1588–1782* (London, 1999).
Padfield, P., *Maritime Power and the Struggle for Freedom, 1788–1851* (London, 2003).
Pritchard, J., *Louis XV's Navy: A Study of Organization and Administration, 1748–1762* (Kingston, 1987).
Pritchard, J., *Anatomy of a Naval Disaster: The 1746 French Naval Expedition to North America* (Montreal, 1995).

Rodger, N. A. M., *The Wooden World: An Anatomy of the Georgian Navy* (London, 1986).
Rodger, N. A. M., *Command of the Ocean: A Naval History of Britain, 1649–1815* (London, 2004).
Rystad, G., et al., *In Quest of Trade and Security: The Baltic in Power Politics, 1500–1990*, vol. 1: *1500–1890* (Lund, 1994).
Saul, N., *Russia and the Mediterranean, 1797–1807* (Chicago, 1970).
Starkey, D. J., *British Privateering Enterprise in the Eighteenth Century* (Exeter, 1990).
Verhees-van Mer, J. T. H., *De Zeeuwse kaapvaart tijdens de Spaanse successieoorlog, 1702–1713* (Middelburg, 1986).
Villiers, P., *Marine royale, corsaires et trafic dans l'Atlantique de Louis XIV à Louis XVI* (2 vols., Dunkirk, 1991).

Part V

Politics and the State

Chapter Twenty-Seven

Dynasticism and the World of the Court

Clarissa Campbell Orr

Definitions

The imperatives of dynasticism, and the world of the court, go to the heart of how the eighteenth-century state is defined and understood, yet both these aspects have been relatively neglected in post-war discussion. The received narrative concerning royal courts is the story of their evolution from the personal entourage of a peripatetic medieval prince to the settled royal household and its departments, which grew into the early modern institutions of state. The strong personal monarchies, such as England, France, and Spain, evolved into the absolute monarchies of the seventeenth century, though taking divergent paths between Catholicism and Protestantism at the Reformation. The seventeenth century was the heyday of the court as a setting for representational, Baroque monarchy, with throne and altar in close conjunction in the confessional state, while, in parallel, bureaucratic institutions were developing to manage affairs of state more professionally. Similarly, armies evolved from the aristocratic companies of a great lord acknowledging a feudal or royal superior to professional standing forces based on systematic procedures, staffed by noble officers and conscripted peasants. At the behavioral level, the court provided a "civilizing" function (Duindam, 1995; Elias, 1983).

The eighteenth century has been seen as an era when the Baroque magnificence of representational monarchy with its dramatization of power declined, and Rococo frivolity, together with enlightened secularism, succeeded it, while the main historical analysis has shifted from the monarch's court to the idea of the state as the locus of power. The pre-history of powerful nation-states after Napoleon, such as Prussia and Russia, takes center-stage in studies of international relations, often imbued by concepts regarding the state and the balance of power more appropriate to the nineteenth or twentieth centuries than the eighteenth, despite the frequency of wars turning on succession disputes between competing dynasties. The theme of Enlightenment is discussed increasingly in relation to the public sphere, a cultural space or process that criticizes the irrationality of hereditary right and flourishes best in coffeehouses, reading clubs, salons, and Masonic lodges, many of which can be conceptualized as

A Companion to Eighteenth-Century Europe, First Edition. Edited by Peter H. Wilson.
© 2014 John Wiley & Sons, Ltd. Published 2014 by John Wiley & Sons, Ltd.

oppositional to the court, as well as in literary or scientific societies, some of which are court-sponsored. At the same time, though, the Enlightenment can be seen as not so much a court critique as a movement spearheaded by enlightened rulers and favorites such as Frederick II of Prussia, or Pombal in Portugal (Blanning, 1974; Scott, 1990). Later eighteenth-century monarchy is alleged to incline toward bourgeois mores, until it was reinvented in national guise in the post-Waterloo settlement. It is clear that the court and dynasticism were still important around 1700, but how they fit in after 1815, and what changes there were along the way, remain imperfectly mapped.

The growth of court studies applied to this period, as well as redefinitions of absolutism (see chapter 28) have challenged this, albeit simplified, account of the role of the court as declining both in display and in relation to the state. The principal problem is the Whiggish attempt to read backwards from the nineteenth- or twentieth-century state. The nineteenth-century nation-state does not map well onto a world of composite states, such as the Austrian monarchy, or federations, such as the Holy Roman Empire. The English court rarely figures in these accounts, given a Whiggish emphasis on parliamentary development and the growth of commercial society, while the court allegedly declines; dynastic study has attracted more attention to the exiled Jacobites than to the later Stuarts or the Hanoverians (Corp, 2004).

Instead of working backwards from the modern state, it is crucial to view the state as contemporaries would have seen it: as a legal, dynastic, and nearly always composite entity. There are some helpful comparative anthologies (Adamson, 1999; Campbell Orr, 2002, 2004; Dickens, 1977; Gibbs et al., 1997), but more work, synthetic, analytical, and comparative, is needed on the eighteenth-century court.

The Dynastic Principle

We need to understand a political world where rulers' legitimacy rested on dynastic titles accumulated over centuries through inheritance, marriage, conquest, diplomacy, and international treaties. Consequently, the court was the most important institution for rulers, as the revised understanding of absolutism helps to make clear. The court was where the Crown managed its relationship with the elites, exploiting its role as the fount of honors; in turn elites often managed the regions or component parts of composite structures. Networks of clientage and patronage intersected with the growth of formal bureaucracies and were conduits of significant if informal power (see chapter 6). The court had an indispensable integrative function in multilingual, multi-ethnic, and sometimes religiously diverse entities, such as the Austrian and Prussian monarchies. Its courtiers were recruited from a cosmopolitan nobility, most obviously in Germany, Scandinavia, central Europe and Russia; but even in Britain, the court integrated English, Scottish, and Irish peers more effectively than did Parliament. The cosmopolitan character of this world is well illustrated in life of the Prince de Ligne (Mansel, 2003).

Courtly dynasticism was congruent with a social world still based, in most of Europe, on orders and corporations, where family inheritance was the principal means of transmitting wealth, status, and privilege. Dynasticism permeated not only the ruling princes and nobilities, including the nobility of Rome (who controlled one of the remaining elective monarchies of Europe, the Papacy), the ministerial nobilities of old-regime France, and the political families of parliamentary Britain; but also military and naval families, professionals in the church, law, bureaucracy, and academia, merchants and artisans in guilds, and talented artistic families, such as the Dietzenhofer (architects), or the Bachs (musicians). Family links remained paramount in the new financial institutions of the Netherlands or Britain; hereditary oligarchies dominated the republics and city-states. Loyalty to ruling dynasties, which often projected an image of paternalism, or of the reconciling adjudicator, needs to be understood within this pervasive mindset. Courts could often provide employment for generations of servants progressing from menial to more educated levels; royal families were expected to help the talented children of their servants or wet-nurses. Courtier families of higher status were eager to perpetuate their service; conversely, pleasing important families and avoiding alienating others, through the judicious exercise of patronage, was an important royal art. French families zealously guarded their "survivance" and might give the king little room for maneuver in appointments. Prosopographic studies are vital for the historian in mapping these dynastic continuities (Bucholz and Sainty, 1997; Duindam, 2003).

Dynastic Strategies and Biological Luck

Pursuing dynastic claims was a major means of royal aggrandizement, backed if necessary by military force, but sometimes achieved through diplomatic negotiations designed to balance power. But such ambitions were beyond human planning, as they rested on biological luck: the successful conception and survival of children, especially males. Many ephemeral pageants and displays at court revolved around royal births, marriages, and deaths, as well as the fortunes of war. A large family facilitated a wide dynastic "spread" and/or double marriages of sibling pairs; a second fertile generation could consolidate family links through the marriage of cousins. For Catholic and some Protestant dynasties, useful secundigenitures could be deployed in the church, including the female abbesses of the Holy Roman Empire, like the Prusso-Swedish preserve of Quedlinburg.

Failure to produce a male heir could be catastrophic for a powerful dynasty. Few Crowns permitted female inheritance, and in Britain in 1689, Sweden in 1718, and Portugal in 1777 the female heir shared power with her male consort. But the failure of powerful dynasties could enable lesser families to rise. The imminent extinction of the Spanish Habsburgs nearly resulted in the award of their vast holdings to the Bavarian electoral prince: better to aggrandize a third, related party than allow either French Bourbons or Austrian Habsburgs to increase their territorial reach. This was thwarted when smallpox carried off the candidate in 1699. When the Joseph I of Austria also died in 1711, his allies dropped support for his brother Charles' claims since death had made him the Austrian heir as well as the Spanish claimant. It was always preferable to adjust inheritance rights through diplomacy. The inheritance of the grand duchy of Tuscany after the demise of its last Medici duke was subject to protracted negotiations after the Peace of Utrecht and was resolved in conjunction with the Polish succession. The Habsburgs were awarded Tuscany, and Charles, its first Bourbon duke after the failure of the Florentine line, was awarded the kingdom of the Two Sicilies. The Bourbons now had the Spanish and French Crowns, together with secundigenitures in Parma and Piacenza (chapter 19).

Although France had won the dynastic struggle to have a Bourbon on the Spanish throne, the most powerful, geographically extensive, and well-populated nation in Europe had appalling dynastic luck. Louis XIV outlived his son and eldest grandson, bequeathing the throne to a young great-grandson who required a regent – always a difficult phase for a dynastic state until the heir reached maturity. Louis also caused offense to a nobility claiming unbroken lineage to the Middle Ages by legitimating his illegitimate children in case his all official children died. There were abortive attempts to create French–Spanish Bourbon marriages. Louis XVI's marriage to Marie Antoinette symbolized the Diplomatic Revolution, but it was never popular: the queen was always "L'Autrichienne" (Kaiser, 2000). Louis' brothers married sisters from the house of Savoy, resuming older patterns. The status of the French and Spanish Crowns made their princes attractive marriage "catches" for lesser-ranking and ambitious Catholic dynasties, assisting further in their elevation, such as the houses of Braganza, Savoy and Parma – which also supplied consorts to the Austrian Habsburgs.

Like the French Bourbons, the Austrian Habsburgs were biologically unlucky, losing rulers and heirs to smallpox and failing to produce sons, but such was the attraction of marrying into the imperial dynasty that some brides were willing to convert to Catholicism. Deprived of Spanish cousins, Leopold's son Joseph turned to the daughter of a Catholic convert, Johann Ludwig of Brunswick-Lüneburg (Hanover), but produced only daughters, who married respectively into the Bavarian and Saxon electoral houses. This would stimulate Bavarian ambition to the imperial throne, and also lay the ground for Habsburg claims to the Bavarian succession through the Bavarian second wife of Joseph II in 1778. Several plans to gain this territory and then exchange it for the Austrian Netherlands, neatly consolidating Habsburg power in central Germany, never came to fruition. Leopold's younger son, Charles VI, married a Brunswick niece of his sister-in-law, who consented to Catholic conversion – but she produced only daughters, including Maria Theresia. Her marriage to Francis of Lorraine, whose family already had Habsburg ties, restored the Habsburg's biological fortunes with 11 children surviving to adulthood. Two sons became emperors, and one, elector of Cologne (usually a Bavarian secundigeniture); Maria Carolina and Maria Antoinetta became queens of Naples and France; Maria Christina and Albert, her cousin and husband, ruled the Austrian Netherlands. Equally prolific was Maria Theresia's cousin Maria Josepha, wife of Elector Frederick August II of Saxony (also Augustus III of Poland). With this Habsburg–Bavarian marriage, the electoral Saxons could now "marry up" to kingdoms. The Saxons failed to keep the Saxon–Polish personal union because their third candidate was not of age in 1766, but the never-implemented Polish constitution of May 1791 awarded them a hereditary Polish Crown.

For many German dynasties, marriage was thus an element in rising from princely to electoral or even royal status, thanks to a determined family strategy and the careful exploitation of opportunities. To grasp the full picture, historians need to consider the candidates for marriage who were rejected or married elsewhere, as well as the final choice of brides or grooms. It might take a century for dynastic links between separate family branches to mature into a single heir or heiress through failure of one of the lines, as in the case of the Prussian and Brandenburg Hohenzollern branches in 1618, but possible claims were never abandoned as this would weaken dynastic capital. The decision of four Hanoverian ducal brothers to institute primogeniture in 1682–4 enabled them to unite several duchies and was one prong – along with financial and military assistance to the emperor against the Turks – in attaining the electoral title in 1697. Yet luck was also with them. Electress Sophia's descent from James I of England and VI of Scotland led to personal union with Britain once the Glorious Revolution ruled out Catholic Stuart succession (Hatton, 1978). The continuing marriages with German, Danish, and Dutch brides underline the extent to which they remained a continental dynasty after this union (Campbell Orr in Simms and Riotte, 2007). Similar examples of patient dynastic aggrandizement during the eighteenth century could be adduced from the houses of Württemberg, Hessen, and Mecklenburg-Schwerin, who all married daughters into the Romanov dynasty, thereby easing its western orientation and integration within the European dynastic system (Wilson in Campbell Orr, 2004). But the Pfalz-Neuberg, second in rank after the Habsburgs, ruling in two electorates (the Palatinate and Bavaria), repeatedly failed to maintain their succession in the main line, or capitalize on royal marriages.

Russian inheritance patterns were the least stable of all eighteenth-century dynasties, since Peter the Great had asserted the right of the tsar to nominate the heir – but then failed to name his own successor. Consequently, the throne went four times to women, two of whom gained it by a palace coup: Peter's daughter, Elizabeth, and then Catherine, wife and cousin of Elizabeth's nominated heir, Peter of Holstein-Gottorp. Catherine was exceptional in her ambition and ruthlessness in seizing the opportunity to rule for herself instead of exercising influence as a consort; but marriages like hers illustrate the contingencies of dynastic rule, and the hierarchies of opportunity linking tiny principalities like hers of Anhalt-Zerbst upwards to monarchies. Her husband, too, had other dynastic options, through Holstein intermarriages with the Swedish and Danish Crowns. His grandmother was the elder sister of the childless Charles XII of Sweden. Her claims to inherit from her brother had been deftly supplanted by another ambitious woman, her younger sister Ulrika Eleonora, (who then surrendered rule to her husband, Frederick of Hessen-Kassel). The Swedes nominated a Lübeck cousin of Peter's, Adolf Frederick (also Catherine the Great's cousin) when Peter became the Russian Crown Prince, but the Holstein-Gottorp claims to the Danish throne were not resolved until 1768 (see chapter 17).

Retracing these genealogical and dynastic links today may seem like an antiquarian pastime, but all ruling dynasties in the eighteenth century were steeped in genealogical history. It was an essential form of information for those exercising or seeking to increase their power, or for correct diplomacy with "brother" princes. Scholars, including Leibniz, wrote dynastic histories for them, and once the *Almanach de Gotha* began in 1766 it became an invaluable vade mecum for all courtiers.

The elective character of the Polish–Lithuanian union inhibited royal dynasticism, although Jan Sobieski's ambitious wife, Maria, had hopes for her son Jacob, while his daughter Clementina married the exiled Stuart Old Pretender James Stuart, gaining a slender chance to become the British queen. Stanisław Poniatowski never married, although the shadow of his love-affair with Catherine the Great (while she was grand duchess) assisted his election to the Polish throne. The aristocratic household of Polish and Lithuanian magnates such as the Czatoryski and Radziwill, with far greater disposable income than the Crown, also acted as rival centers of power, patronage, and glamor. Officially, Poland's consort was the Virgin Mary, Queen of Heaven. She was also the spouse of the oligarchic republic of Genoa, while Venice's aristocratic dogaressas took second place to their spouse's symbolic marriage with the sea.

The Role of the Consort

Most consorts were female because so few ruling houses permitted female rule. Prince George of Denmark, consort to Queen Anne, contrasts with Francis of Lorraine. The former was officially Lord High Admiral, but had little effective military role; he pioneered the style of modern constitutional queens' husbands, keeping them cheerful domestically while maintaining an unobtrusive public profile, and facilitating access to male circles of sociability (Beem, 2006). Francis of Lorraine took the military role of commander-in-chief and, as a man, was able to be elected Holy Roman Emperor in 1745, thus restoring Habsburg possession of the imperial title: he was a true co-ruler (Beales in Gibbs et al., 1997). Catherine II of Russia never remarried officially, though her minister and favorite Potemkin may have been unofficially her husband (Montefiore, 2000). She was projected symbolically as the wise legislator Minerva, but the paradox of female power meant that her sequence of male favorites made her the subject of lubricious cartoons, especially abroad, whereas a male ruler with a succession of mistresses – such as Augustus the Strong of Saxony – was celebrated for his potency.

Plainly, the main role of a queen consort was to produce an heir, and to represent symbolically and actually the balance of male and female at court. Sometimes arranged marriages became genuinely affectionate partnerships, such as Maria Josepha's with Augustus III of Saxony-Poland. The delayed consummation of Louis XVI's marriage to Marie Antoinette, or Gustavus III's to Sophia Magdalena of Denmark, provoked ridicule or disquiet. The homosocial if not homosexual Fredrick II of Prussia repudiated Elizabeth Christine after his accession, but still relied on her to sustain the court routines in Berlin. Elizabeth Farnese and Barbara Braganza coped admirably with depressive husbands, but Caroline Matilda's marriage to the schizophrenic Christian VII of Denmark precipitated her affair with the court physician Struensee. She was saved from execution only by the intervention of her brother George III (Campbell Orr, 2004).

In an age of enlightened, educational experiment, consorts often influenced their children's education, not always with good results. They might have the flair and connections to broker dynastic marriages, as in the case of Catherine the Great's mother, but more often had to yield to their husband's wishes, as Sophia Dorothea of Prussia found to her chagrin. Their family influence might increase with seniority and dowagerhood: dowager queen Hedwig of Sweden was an important patron and patriotic focus when her grandson Charles XII was on campaign. But George III and Gustavus III both sidelined their strong-minded mothers after their accession.

A consort was not necessarily the first choice as regent during an heir's minority, because of the rulers' military role; if chosen she was normally given a regency council to advise, or rather constrain, her. Nonetheless, Anne of Orange, regent for William V of the Netherlands, and Maria Augusta of Württemberg, regent for Carl Eugen, proved exceptionally able. A more acceptable form of female regency was to stand in during an adult ruler's absence, as in the case of the politically adroit Caroline of Ansbach and George II (Baker-Smith, 1995; Campbell Orr, 2002, 2004). There was a pervasive fear that an able queen would foment a court faction, as did Louisa Ulrica of Sweden, and as might an official mistress. But a royal woman could help lend legitimacy to a palace coup, as did Christian VII's stepmother Juliane-Christine, when Struensee was deposed. A safer avenue for a consort's talents was in cultural matters, as a patroness or agent of cultural transfer, or as the embodiment of religious observance and moral virtue in an era which tolerated a double standard of sexual morality.

The role of the consort, both real and imagined, often became a focal point of tension and blame in the revolutionary era. Marie Antoinette attracted hatred for her overt "Austrianness," which she never seemed to discard, and both her extravagance *and* her artificial informality – her shepherdess dresses were considered insufficiently regal (Goodman, 2004). Her sister, Maria Carolina of Naples, earned equal opprobrium for her alleged political meddling, and took a leading role in the counter-revolution against Napoleonic interference. By contrast the sisters' counterpart in Britain, Queen Charlotte, assisted in the redefinition of George III as a family man and focus of patriotism after his early uncertain political start, but she was not immune from the satirical prints of an unregulated commercial press.

The Iberian peninsula presented some particularly clear examples of politicized queens. Charles IV of Spain's consort, Maria Amalia of Parma, had ruled her compliant husband through her lover, the minister Godoy. Maria Joaquinta in Portugal was incompatible with her husband and avenged her frustrations politically. She led a pro-French court faction in Portugal in exile in Brazil, she became the claimant to the Iberian throne and its empire; when her granddaughter Isabella inherited the restored Portuguese throne she intrigued in favor of her younger son Miguel, initiating the nineteenth-century wars between the absolutists and the liberals (chapter 20).

The Court and the Confessional State

An important aspect of the court was its relationship to the post-1648 confessional state in an age of increasing religious toleration and changes in religious tone. At one end of the spectrum, the Lisbon court combined intensive Catholic piety with Rococo extravagance as John V used his Brazilian revenue to build the palace-monastery complex of La Mafra. Court routines were dominated by the daily, weekly, and annual liturgical calendar, though this was tempered briefly by Pombal's reforms. This Tridentine piety was revived by Maria I, who lapsed into melancholy and religious mania after her husband and first son died. John VI became regent and continued the religious rituals, the superb music, the hunting traditions, and the medieval customs when the court was removed to Rio (Wilcken, 2004).

Imperial consorts in Vienna maintained *pietas austriaca* even when they were converts (Ingrao in Campbell Orr, 2004), until the era of Maria Theresia and Joseph encouraged the church to concentrate on parochial work. The Savoyard court also remained a bastion of the Counter-Reformation. A wave of Catholic conversions in the Holy Roman Empire had repercussions on dynastic options, but Caroline of

Figure 17 Margravine Sybilla Augusta of Baden (1675–1733), copper engraving from the Paris publisher Antoine Trouvaine, *c.*1700. The cosmopolitan world of the princely court is illustrated by the margravine's French-inspired clothes and hairstyle. *Wehrgeschtliches Museum Rastatt*

Ansbach was to gain kudos in Britain as a Protestant princess who refused to convert and marry Emperor Charles VI (Hanham in Campbell Orr, 2002). In Saxony, Christina Eberhardine of Brandenburg-Bayreuth became a figurehead for Protestantism when Augustus the Strong converted in order to become king of Poland in 1697, refusing to be crowned queen of Poland or even set foot in the kingdom. Maria Josepha, on the other hand, brought Habsburg piety to the electorate and kingdom, though – tactfully for Dresden's Protestant population – the court church she commissioned had a covered arcade around which Catholic processions could ambulate without causing offense on the streets (Watanabe-O'Kelly in Campbell Orr, 2004). German Protestant princesses marrying into the Romanovs had to convert to Orthodoxy; Catholic brides were never chosen. The Calvinist Hohenzollern married Lutherans without requiring conversion, and Frederick William III's affection for his Lutheran Mecklenburg bride Luise prompted his ecclesiastical policy.

Several late Baroque courts were affected by the more inward religiosity affecting both Catholicism and Protestantism around 1700. Pietism in northern Europe could be inimical to the integral extravagance of court life, as Frederick William I of Prussia and Frederick Francis of Mecklenburg-Schwerin exemplify. Marie Leszczynska, her musically talented daughters, and the pious Dauphin represented the *dévot* counterbalance to the hedonism of Louis XV.

As heterodoxy and skepticism gained ground in the later third of the century, most courts retained an official support for religion, notably George III and Queen Charlotte at Windsor. Frederick the Great's Deist and Masonic inclinations in his Potsdam retreat were counterbalanced by his queen's interest in contemporary Christian sentimentalism. Some courts came under the influence of the new post-Enlightenment mysticism as the Enlightenment waned, notably Gustavus III in Stockholm and Frederick William II in Berlin, who both dabbled in Swedenborgianism and Rosicrucianism. In their private sociability, some of the Hohenzollerns frequented the Jewish salons that momentarily coalesced with high society in the 1790s. Regardless of rulers' personal inclinations, throne and altar throughout Europe remained officially linked (Schaich, 2007).

From Baroque to Enlightenment

The later seventeenth-century Baroque courts had been outstanding centers of royal display through secular and ecclesiastical ceremony, architecture, painting, sculpture, gardens, music, and the performing arts (Blanning, 2002). The world of the court changed during the long eighteenth century, but this was an uneven process, chronologically and geographically. Court style was based on continuity, on self-referentiality to tradition, real, reinstated, and invented; overt change was often avoided, and different court styles might coexist. But determined reformers could signal change and modernization overtly through founding new institutions or, less directly, through their court practices and patronage. In general courts moved from being centers of representational monarchy (the Baroque model), to cultural and political centers coexisting in some way with the Enlightenment. Instead of enacting power before the subject, the court aimed to educate the people. The ethos of public service laid the groundwork for the transformation of courts into national monarchies after the Napoleonic Wars, where royal collections were often donated to the state and opened to greater public access, and a fresh phase of beautifying capital cities and establishing national cultural institutions began.

Eighteenth-century courts had to accept the existence of new, often uncontrollable, elements within the public sphere: the world of literary, philosophical, antiquarian, and scientific societies, reading clubs and subscription libraries, coffeehouses and Masonic lodges, and forms of commercial entertainment – operas, theaters, concerts, assemblies, pleasure gardens – arranged by entrepreneurs and public subscription. This was most visible in Britain, where the commercialization of leisure and print culture was most advanced, where a court theater had been discontinued in favor of London venues since the reign of Charles II, and where Parliament had grown in importance since the Glorious Revolution. Nevertheless, George III and Queen Charlotte gave court life fresh continuity and purpose. Though not *the* center of fashion, nor the only significant venue of sociability and display, it was still central to national symbolic power in a composite kingdom, to Crown-elite functioning, diplomatic representation, and patriotic loyalty (Roberts, 2004). Both George III and Queen Charlotte had cultural interests congruent with a moderate, Christian Enlightenment, and the court identified itself increasingly with the philanthropy of responsibly minded, Evangelical aristocrats and middling folk (Campbell Orr in Schaich, 2007).

In contrast, the French and Spanish Bourbon courts and their Lisbon counterpart identified with the Enlightenment only later in the century. The depressive Louis XV, Philip V, and Ferdinand VI were all unsuited temperamentally to the Baroque style of representational monarchy. Louis XV's unpopularity grew when he spent more time on private pleasures than public display, orchestrated by his talented mistress Madame de Pompadour (Kaiser, 1996). Historians have consequently focused on the growth of a French public sphere during the eighteenth century as *oppositional* to court culture. The development of art criticism saw esthetic and moral questions emerge in the Parisian salons and an enlightened print culture. Revisionists now increasingly see France as a dynastic state, and pre-revolutionary political culture as a court culture, but it had relatively weak links with the public sphere (Campbell, 2005).

The court of the first two Bourbon Spanish kings similarly saw a retreat into a lavish Rococo privacy. Both men were so psychologically dependent on their wives that Charles Noel has described the early Spanish monarchy as feminized (Noel in Campbell Orr, 2004). By the reign of Charles III there had been an expansion of private aristocratic patronage, which began to coexist alongside court and ministerial initiatives, including the extensive re-planning of Madrid. The court ethos became both more serious, more financially prudent, and more enlightened, fostering a new age of native Spanish artistic achievement. Danish court culture saw a similar movement from a royal-sponsored Rococo efflorescence, to the development of a public sphere alongside the role of the court, a culture of discussion and publication of pamphlets, moral weeklies, and books, closely linked to Protestant German developments in Leipzig and Hamburg. This was helped by Fredrik V's relaxation of censorship and positively encouraged by enlightened ministers such as the Bernstorffs, uncle and nephew.

In the Holy Roman Empire courts were also successful in sponsoring the Enlightenment, instead of being the target of enlightened criticism. There was a constant flow of personnel between officialdom and academia (Blanning, 1974) and a parallel merging of service nobility and ennobled officials in the *Beamtentum*. The small principalities could often be successful patrons of the Enlightenment, giving them a significance disproportionate to their size. The role of the consort was frequently crucial, as many male rulers remained preoccupied with military matters and might serve, along with their younger male relatives, in the imperial, Russian, and Prussian armies (Wilson, 1998). Louise Dorothea of Saxe-Gotha, friend and correspondent of Voltaire and Frederick the Great, helped to make the tiny duchy's court come second after the wealthier Saxon court at Dresden; Anna Amalia of Saxe-Weimar and her son Carl August made Weimar a lasting byword for cultural achievements. The interest taken by these women in educating their sons and daughters was one element of their cultural and dynastic power. Male rulers such as Leopold of Anhalt-Dessau and Carl of Brunswick-Wolfenbüttel also fostered educational institutions; the former's Enlightenment garden at Wörlitz was designed to educate his subjects equally in historical landmarks of civilization, universal religion, German patriotism, and model agricultural methods (Umbach 2000).

Medium-sized German states also developed their cultural infrastructure, notably Duke Carl Eugen of Württemberg, who transformed Stuttgart, and Frederick II of Hessen-Kassel, who transformed Kassel, founded a gymnasium, and opened Germany's first public museum. What can seem like a link between court culture and Enlightenment modernization was often also an adaptation of German traditions of princely paternalism and cameralism; but in Charles Ingrao's analysis, the eighteenth century saw a shift in many of these smaller states, from simply glorifying the dynasty and ensuing the well-being of taxpayers to an ethos of serving the state as a whole (Ingrao, 1987).

Frederick II of Prussia, Catherine II of Russia, and Joseph II of Austria were later in developing a truly public sphere, but Frederick II tolerated public discussion, and Berlin became an important European center of print culture. These three monarchs, along with Gustavus III of Sweden, are well known as rulers consciously identifying themselves with the Enlightenment, within an absolutist framework. Joseph and Gustavus both helped to create a public sphere respectively in Vienna and Stockholm by sponsoring theater in the vernacular; both believed in the morally uplifting role of drama. Gustavus (like his cousin Catherine) wrote plays and founded the Swedish Academy of Literature. In the last third of the eighteenth century, Austria opened itself to the culture of sensibility, associated with the middling sort, and critical of the Francophile and Italianate character of court culture. Joseph met this half-way with his creation of the German National Theater, his gift of the Augarten and Prater to the city, and his opening of the art collection in the Belvedere, deliberately extending the court's role into a wider public sphere, which now included new cultural institutions – the salons, cafés, and subscription concerts. The musical patronage of court, church, and city combined to make Vienna the premier musical center of Europe (Wangermann, 1973).

Courts positioned themselves in varied ways in relation to the new forms of sociability and domesticity, as well as the areas of intellectual concern that characterize the Enlightenment. Freemasonry was an aristocratic fashion, not necessarily linked to radicalism and freethinking, and while brothers met "on the level," Grand Masters were often royal princes. Lesser members of dynastic families were free to mix in drawing rooms, salons, and assemblies. The widowed Joseph II frequented a small circle of Viennese hostesses who provided conversation and relaxed company. The childless Max Emmanuel of Bavaria and his wife held "apartements" modeled on French exclusive socializing, where the invited few played cards, within the palace, or in the Nymphenburg gardens in the summer (Babel in Adamson, 1999). Enlightened royal style is sometimes described as "bourgeois," but it would be more accurate to see a taste for informality and domesticity when monarchs were "off duty" as a royal version of the expansion of private life, evident in aristocratic patterns too.

At Kew and Windsor, informal appearances made this privacy visible and accessible; George III hoped the Prince of Wales would prove an exemplar of domestic happiness, but his arranged marriage to his cousin Caroline of Brunswick was one of the most unfortunate of the century, generating scandal and feminist critique. Large families could create a domestic flavor. At Schönbrunn, Maria Theresia's consort and family lived modestly in their private apartments,. while entertaining publicly in suitable splendor. In Tuscany, after the decadent court of the last grand duke, Gian Giannone, Peter Leopold set the official tone of court life as plain, accessible, and – with his Spanish Bourbon consort, Maria Luisa, and his 16 children – domestic, notwithstanding his several mistresses.

Residential Patterns

The need to accommodate larger families and new cultural tastes meant that courts also evolved and differed in their residential patterns. Since the seventeenth century most courts had stopped being peripatetic, and a single capital had emerged (such as Vienna for the composite Habsburg monarchy). Where courts were established in cities with their own traditions of government, town councils often lost power to the court's own economic and legal privileges. The city of Vienna declined in relation to the court, but Paris was always a rival magnet to Versailles, and the City of London a political power base independent of St. James's and the king's ministers in the Palace of Westminster. Towns always benefited economically where there was a court, because of the demands for goods, services, and accommodation. Capitals themselves were often improved. Whereas Joseph I had made only piecemeal – albeit architecturally outstanding – additions to the Hofburg, Joseph II built a hospital and academy of military surgery instead of creating or altering palaces.

Royal residences were kept in more remote provinces where governors, who were sometimes relatives, deputized for the monarch. Courts all possessed a number of residences, some of which were used seasonally, for summer pleasures and/or the hunt. Hermitages and summer pavilions proliferated. At Peterhof, the official residence proclaimed rivalry with Versailles, but to live in, Peter the Great preferred his own modest villa on the shore below. In their electorate, the Hanoverians had a city palace beside the Leine, a summer palace a few miles away at Herrenhausen, with its outstanding Baroque garden and several family buildings, and a hunting lodge at Göhrde, as well as palaces in Lüneburg and Celle representing duchies that had now been incorporated into the ruling family since adopting primogeniture. When the elector was absent in Britain, court functions were held in front of an empty throne with the ruler represented by his portrait. Gustavus III of Sweden restored the old palace at Gripsolm to stress the Holstein-Gottorp continuity with the founding Vasa dynasty and Sweden's seventeenth-century age of greatness, and held court there in the summer and autumn. The Green Salon, the queen's apartment, became the center of court sociability, while the courtiers' wing illustrates the extreme simplicity of French-influenced Swedish style. Extensive building programs could be justified as a means of providing employment. Even the Pietist Christian VI of Denmark, who had inherited a new palace, commissioned his own with this excuse, while William, duke of Cumberland landscaped Virginia Water to give employment to his soldiers after the '45 Jacobite rebellion.

Courts were intensely competitive because they were their dynasty's showcase and public face in diplomacy, not merely a reflection of the ruler's personal taste. Talented artists and decorators could be wooed from one court to another. Librarians, chaplains, and historians from the international Huguenot diaspora served in Protestant courts; Genevan and Swiss educators were to be found in London, St. Petersburg, Copenhagen, and Berlin. Courts might imitate each other or borrow eclectically from different cultural models, often, but not necessarily those where there was dynastic intermarriage or an alliance. French fashion could often be absorbed where a state was in *political* opposition to France, as at Carlton House and Brighton, owned by the intensely Francophile Prince of Wales. England exported the taste for the landscape garden throughout Europe. New buildings, such as the observatories of George

III and his Saxe-Gotha cousin Ernest, and ever more beautiful court theaters, reflected new interests. Older dynasties often embellished the traditional residence, mindful of historic continuities, but fire, such as the one destroying Madrid's Alcazar in 1734, could provide the opportunity to start afresh. The Danes were inveterate builders. Fire gave Fredrik IV the excuse to commission Fredriksberg; his son Christian VI commissioned Christiansborg; Fredrik V created the new Fredriksstaden district in Copenhagen, including the Amalienborg complex of four mansions for high court officials, one of which became Christian VII's palace when Christiansborg palace was burnt down in 1794.

Naturally there were huge variations in scale, from the few dozens comprising the court society of small German states to the thousands dependent on the courts of Versailles, Madrid, Vienna, and St. Petersburg. But these were differences of degree rather than kind. Courts at any one time might be maintaining multiple households for dowagers, siblings, adult heirs – sometimes also their wives and children – and younger children, depending on the health, fertility, and longevity of families. Gustavus III's siblings Carl, Frederick Adolf (who was governor of Ostrobothnia), and Sophia Albertina, abbess of Quedlinburg, also acted as important royal patrons of the arts, and diffused court culture and noble service in royal households across several centers. Official mistresses had their own apartments or even palaces. The French court just before the revolution numbered 12 separate households (Mansel, 1988). Courts were thus major employers for the nobility, middling sorts (who might be librarians, chaplains, physicians, tutors, or governesses), and every level downwards to the humblest kitchen scullion, as well as temporary "stars" such as musicians, singers, and decorators, who might migrate from one court to another, lured by higher salaries or new commissions.

The Rise and Decline of Courts

The Viennese court was of paramount importance within and beyond the Holy Roman Empire, because of its dual role as the headquarters of the Habsburg dynasty and the center of imperial politics. It was in theory the sole imperial court in Christian Europe until Peter the Great's western orientation included a diplomatic offensive to demand recognition of his imperial title. Lesser members of princely families served in Vienna, especially militarily. The emperor's court regulated the dynastic business of other dynasties, such as conferring titles, deciding on morganatic marriages and regencies, as well as ruling on constitutional conflicts. As territorial princes in their own lands, the Habsburgs exemplify clearly the role of courts as the milieu for the management of Crown–elite relationships (Evans, 1979). This was a delicate matter in the period 1660–1740, when great magnates were also the Crown's creditors (Asch, 2003). As with the Polish and Lithuanian nobility, Hungarian magnate households, with their multiple seats, extensive entourages, and patronage of the arts, functioned like the royal household, and often with more disposable income. Maria Theresia, however, was able to make magnates also accept courtier positions in her household. Vienna became a marriage market fostering links between the elites of the different duchies and kingdoms ruled by the dynasty.

Court etiquette and ceremony, organized by the highest court officials according to published regulations, could hark back to late medieval models. Burgundian etiquette was the basis of the Austrian, Spanish, and Bavarian courts, although the rigidity of the Spanish royal household was tempered after the Bourbon accession by French and Italian influences. But the court was also an arena for invented tradition. When two successive Wettin electors of Saxony became kings of Poland, new ceremonial buildings, ornamented with the Polish crown, projected this personal union. Neo-chivalric tournaments suggested dynastic continuity since the age of Renaissance splendor. The first king in Prussia, Frederick I, and his wife Sophie Charlotte of Hanover performed an invaluable task in setting a royal tone to Berlin court life and establishing an embryonic cultural infrastructure, which Frederick II continued.

On the Italian peninsula the papal and Tuscan courts were in decline in the first half of the century. But if papal ceremonies seemed perfunctory to visitors, Rome was still the artistic capital of Europe, and artists and architects working for many regimes sought inspiration and training there, as did Grand Tourists from all over Europe. In Tuscany, visits by connoisseurs, dealers, and artists studying in the Uffizi meant that Florentine style and workmanship informed the taste of many European courts. The court revived after 1765 with the energetic, micro-managing Duke Peter Leopold, who also founded and revivified cultural institutions (Adamson, 1999).

Peter the Great had the greatest task in creating a secular and Westernized Russian court, but he also suggested links with the previous, first century of Romanov power with his invented Order of St. Andrew (modeled on the Garter), and the reverence for the thirteenth-century king and saint Alexander Nevsky. His new capital on the Neva started in 1703 and celebrated access to the Baltic, and naval rather than military symbolism. Borrowing eclectically from classical, Swedish, Dutch, English, and French models, his household was also unusual in the degree to which it contained elements of parody. Empresses Anna and Elizabeth made the court more polite, lavish, and Francophone; Catherine the Great believed emphatically in the court as a theater of power, but her tastes in gardens, technology, and porcelain were Anglophile. Paul I abruptly reversed court style to an ascetic militarism, showing that newly empowered dynasties could vary the court ethos to personal taste more easily than those hidebound by centuries-old protocol (Dixon, 2001; Schaich, 2007).

Courts in parliamentary or elective monarchies could be paradoxically more, not less, important than those of rulers claiming absolute power, as they remained the symbolic and social center of power, had prestigious patronage and land to dispense, and ideally provided a unifying focus. Thus, the British court was an important side of a triangle which included Parliament and a commercialized sphere of print, consumption, and entertainment. Court culture in Sweden's parliamentary monarchy after 1720 was initially weaker than in its seventeenth-century heyday; but its party-political culture could facilitate a "royal" party. Under the childless Ulrica Eleonora and Friedrich of Hesse-Cassel the court was dominated by a few long-serving families. But although Adolf Friedrich's consort Louisa Ulrica failed to restore royal authority, in cultural policy she successfully raised Stockholm's profile as a center of culture in northern Europe.

Stanisław Poniatowski in Poland's elective monarchy pursued an energetic policy of reanimating the Crown as patron in parallel with constitutional reform; making the Crown hereditary in the house of Wettin was an important component of a reformed, parliamentary monarchy (Zamoyski, 1992). The house of Orange-Nassau had a fluctuating relationship with the seven republics of the United Provinces, but the dynasty's popularity among ordinary people counterbalanced the role of urban patriciates. Anne of Great Britain and Wilhelmina of Prussia, the formidable consorts respectively of William IV and V, revived the court in the Hague: William V was an important Dutch patron, making the royal art collection to public in 1774, and laying the foundation for hereditary monarchy after 1815. (Israel in Adamson, 1999).

Finally, the centrality of courts to successful rule is exemplified in the career of the newest dynasty, the Bonapartes. Napoleon created a French empire, married a Habsburg princess as his second wife, and founded a string of satellite kingdoms ruled by his family. German dynasties cooperating with him at last found themselves elevated to kingdoms or grand duchies. The revival of court culture within France was central to merging old and new elites. But equally, it was important to the Bourbon and other exiled courts to maintain some semblance of court routines – such as the appointment of officers and the reception of ambassadors – to signal they had not surrendered their legitimist claims. (Mansel, 1981, 1988). The story of dynasties and courts after 1815 is of their successful restoration and reinvention until 1914, despite the rise of constitutional monarchies and democratic politics.

Bibliography

Adamson, J. (ed.), *The Princely Courts of Europe, 1500–1750* (London, 1999).

Asch, R. G., *Nobilities in Transition 1500–1700* (London, 2003).

Asch, R. G. and A. M. Birke, *Princes, Patronage, and the Nobility: The Court at the Beginning of the Modern Age* (London, 1991).

Baker-Smith, V., *A Life of Anne of Hanover, Princess Royal* (Leiden, 1995).

Beales, D., *Joseph II*, vol. 1: *In the Shadow of Maria Theresa, 1741–1780* (Cambridge, 1987).

Beem, C., *The Lioness Roared: The Problems of Female Rule in English History* (Basingstoke, 2006).

Blanning, T. C. W., *Reform and Revolution in Mainz 1743–1803* (Cambridge, 1974).

Blanning, T. C. W., *The Culture of Power and the Power of Culture: Old Regime Europe, 1660–1789* (Oxford, 2002).

Bucholz, R. O. and J. C. Sainty, *Officials of the Royal Household 1660–1837* (2 vols., London, 1997).

Campbell, P. R. (ed.), *The Origins of the French Revolution* (Basingstoke, 2006).

Campbell Orr, C. (ed.), *Queenship in Britain 1660–1837: Royal Patronage, Court Culture and Dynastic Politics* (Manchester, 2002).

Campbell Orr, C. (ed.), *Queenship in Europe 1660–1815: The Role of the Consort* (Cambridge, 2004).

Corp, E., et al., *Court in Exile: The Stuarts in France 1689–1718* (Cambridge, 2004).

Dickens, A. G. *The Courts of Europe: Politics, Patronage and Royalty 1400–1800* (London, 1977).

Dixon, S., *Catherine the Great* (Harlow, 2001).

Duindam, J., *Myths of Power: Norbert Elias and the Early Modern European Court* (Amsterdam, 1995).

Duindam, J., *Vienna and Versailles: The Courts of Europe's Major Dynastic Rivals c.1550–1750* (Cambridge, 2003).

Elias, N., *The Court Society* (New York, 1983).

Evans, R. J. W., *The Making of the Habsburg Monarchy, 1550–1700* (Oxford, 1979).

Gibbs, G. C., R. Oresko, and H. M. Scott (eds.), *Royal and Republican Sovereignty* (Cambridge, 1997).

Goodman, D. (ed.), *Marie Antoinette: Writings on the Body of a Queen* (London 2004).
Hatton, R., *George I: Elector and King* (London, 1978).
Ingrao, C. W., *The Hessian Mercenary State: Ideas, Institutions and Reform under Frederick II 1760–85* (Cambridge, 1987).
Kaiser, T., "Madame de Pompadour and the theatres of power," *French Historical Studies,* 19 (1996), 1025–44.
Kaiser, T., "Who's afraid of Marie Antoinette? Diplomacy, Austrophobia and the queen," *French History,* 14 (2000), 241–71.
Mansel, P., *Louis XVIII* (London, 1981).
Mansel, P., *The Court of France, 1789–1830* (Cambridge, 1988).
Mansel, P., *Prince of Europe: The Life of Charles-Joseph de Ligne* (London, 2003).
Montefiore, S., *Prince of Princes: The Life of Potemkin* (London, 2000).
Olausson, M. (ed.), *Catherine the Great and Gustavus III* (Stockholm and St. Petersburg, 1999).
Roberts, J. (ed.), *George III and Queen Charlotte: Patronage, Collecting and Court Taste* (London, 2004).
Schaich, M. (ed.), *Monarchy and Religion* (Oxford, 2007).
Scott, H. M. (ed.), *Enlightened Absolutism: Reform and Reformers in Later Eighteenth-Century Europe* (Basingstoke, 1990).
Simms, B. and T. Riotte (eds.), *The Hanoverian Dimension in British History, 1714–1837* (Cambridge 2007).
Umbach, M., *Federalism and Enlightenment in Germany 1740–1806* (London, 2000).
Wangermann, E., *The Austrian Achievement* (London, 1973).
Wilcken, P., *Empire Adrift, The Portuguese Court in Rio de Janeiro, 1808–1821* (London, 2004).
Wilson, P. H., *German Armies: War and German Politics 1648–1806* (London, 1998).
Zamoyski, A., *The Last King of Poland* (London, 1992).

CHAPTER TWENTY-EIGHT

Absolutism and Royal Government

RONALD G. ASCH

Government, Administration, and the Myth of Absolutism

Until a few decades ago, the later seventeenth and the eighteenth centuries were widely seen as the heyday of absolutism. Monarchs all over Europe and their ministers drastically reduced or abolished the rights and liberties of estates and corporations, created – or so it seemed – new efficient bureaucratic institutions, attacked vested interests and traditional privileges, and transformed the established noble elites into a service nobility, or even replaced the feudal lords and squires with reform-minded officeholders who might lack even titular noble status in positions of political significance. It is certainly true that government policies became more ambitious in our period. Rulers and their ministers were no longer content to raise – preferably ever higher – taxes, to wage war, and to grant privileges and dispense justice as their forebears had done. Now they tried to implement wide-ranging projects of social and economic reform and to impose their more or less enlightened ideas on their often reluctant and less than enthusiastic subjects. As a recent study of rural society in Prussia has argued once more, the eighteenth-century state "entered as a revolutionary force, disciplining and constraining, but also enlightening and liberating" both in the villages and in the manor halls of the local nobility (Hagen, 2002: 592). On the other hand, the effects of official policies were by no means always those which had originally been envisaged, and as far as traditional social and political structures were indeed reshaped or even undermined in our period by such policies, this was often the unintentional and unforeseen consequence of more limited political projects. Moreover, beyond the spheres of war, foreign policy, and high politics in general, that is in particular on the local level, government remained much weaker than it claimed or aspired to be. In fact, to the extent that research focuses now less on political ideas, royal or princely statutes and edicts, or mere political projects and more on the daily interaction between the state and local communities, the limits of all efforts to achieve structural change – or the sort of change which would have been in accordance with the objectives and ideals which officially guided government policies – have often become all too visible. The failure of many attempts to improve the

A Companion to Eighteenth-Century Europe, First Edition. Edited by Peter H. Wilson.
© 2014 John Wiley & Sons, Ltd. Published 2014 by John Wiley & Sons, Ltd.

lot of the rural peasant population against the resistance of the landowning classes illustrates this sufficiently. Even in areas where noble power posed no major obstacle to reform, princely officeholders were often neither able to suppress the autonomy of the village community nor to win the peasants' active support for the reform policy (Zimmermann, 1983). Thus, many edicts enacted to improve the living conditions of the rural population had no real impact at all.

Kings and princes remained in most cases dependent on the cooperation of the established elites – or at least of significant sections of these elites. Even ordinary men and women could put up resistance on a small scale by withholding information or by secretly sabotaging measures enforced from above, not to mention peasant rebellions, urban riots, and similar acts of open resistance which at least in some parts of Europe such as Bohemia or Spain were by no means a thing of the past in the eighteenth century, even before 1789. In Madrid, for example, a major riot was caused in 1766 by the enlightened policies pursued by Charles III's leading minister, the marques de Esquilache. Led by the clergy, who resented Esquilache's attempts to impose higher taxes on the church, and secretly abetted by members of the ancient nobility, who feared for their privileges, the mob attacked Esquilache as a devious foreigner responsible for high food prices. Moreover, the *Madrileños* wanted to retain the traditional Spanish national costume, the long cape and the sombrero which the Italian minister had tried to suppress as incompatible with the enlightened manners he wanted to promote and as an easy disguise for thieves and thugs (see figure 12). The riot in Madrid forced Charles III to modify his policies and to dismiss Esquilache (Armillas Vicente and Corona Baratech, 1990: 402–16), and caused him to reinforce the garrisons guarding the capital.

Not just in Spain but in other countries as well, many reforms were doomed to failure without the at least passive consent, however grudgingly it may have been granted, of the local notables, right down to the wealthier peasants in the villages. Monarchs certainly could not afford an all-out confrontation with both the elites and the population at large for more than a limited period at best. Moreover, the officeholders who were to implement government policies were either closely connected to the traditional elites or guided as much by their loyalty to the patronage networks to which they owed their careers as by the publicly vaunted devotion to the public good and the abstract authority of the state.

Thus in many ways the eighteenth-century state was much weaker than older accounts of this period assumed. Prussia, for instance, often seen as an example of strong government, had a relatively small civil service. Only 100 to 150 officeholders and clerks worked in the most important central ministry, the *Generaldirektorium*, which was responsible for the public revenues but also for most areas of domestic policy in the later eighteenth century. Altogether, there were hardly more than 300 or 350 officeholders with the rank of *Kriegs- und Domänenrat* (war and demesne councillor) or its equivalent in the entire monarchy. Including clerks and similar inferior staff who lacked an academic qualification, there may have been up to 3,000 men working in the civil administration, if one does not count the officials of the *Regie*, the semi-private administration of indirect taxes (Demel, 2005: 227 n. 25; cf. Straubel, 1998), admittedly several thousand. This comparatively tiny administrative staff was responsible for a country which had slightly fewer than 6 million inhabitants in 1786. The situation was not much different in the Habsburg monarchy. As late as 1762, after the first reforms strengthening the central government, Austria and Bohemia together (excluding Hungary) were governed by only about 7,500 imperial officeholders of whom over 5,000 resided in the capital or neighboring Lower Austria. By contrast, almost 12,000 officials were employed by landowners, towns, and ecclesiastical corporations, and a further 1,700 by the regional estates (Demel, 2005: 248 n. 86).

There were of course states such as France which could rely on a much higher number of officials to collect taxes, dispense justice, and collect information. France already had a virtual army of officeholders in the mid-seventeenth century, probably as many of 45,000 (for a population of around 17 million). Immediately before the revolution, there may have been up to 80,000 venal offices (Doyle, 1996). However, these officials had either bought or inherited their offices, which they considered their personal property. They could not easily be dismissed by the king, and were all too prone to drag their feet or put up resistance when the Crown tried to enact reforms which threatened their numerous privileges. Matters were different to some extent with the royal *commissaires* (men holding a special commission which was either only temporary or could easily be revoked), such as the *intendants* sent into the provinces to supervise and control the raising of taxes, as well as to exercise responsibility for domestic and economic policies in general. But even these agents of a centralizing state belonged mostly to the same social class as the *officiers*, and in fact often held venal or hereditary offices alongside their commission. Moreover, the *intendants* and other royal agents worked largely alone with few staff to help them. Altogether, there were no more than 300 or 400 *commis* in the provinces in the 1750s. These secretaries, clerks, and technical experts were appointed by *intendants* and other officeholders as their personal assistants, but lacked clear legal status even if they sometimes held a special royal commission themselves. About the same number served in the ministries of state in Versailles (Drévillon, 2000: 313). Admittedly, the number of *commis* continued to increase during the last decades before the revolution and the various companies of tax farmers employed several thousand agents and functionaries, possibly as many as 30,000 (Bély, 1996: 38–40). However, not counting these more or less private agents, the number of *commissaires* and *commis* remained small, and from a purely administrative point of view the king's authority, extolled by theologians such as Bossuet in the preceding century as absolute and godlike, proved in practice often to be rather limited, outside the court and, perhaps, the army.

Some historians have therefore argued that absolutism itself was no more than a myth created by royal propaganda in the seventeenth and eighteenth centuries, and by the writings of historians and liberal politicians early in the next (Henshall, 1992). Recently Fanny Cosandey and Robert Descimon have summed up matters by stating, "if absolutism did not exist, it is for the very reason that it did exist," and "The stronger absolutism becomes, the weaker it becomes at the same time," two deliberately paradoxical statements which sound rather more elegant in the original French ("si l'absolutimse n'existe pas, c'est précisement parce qu'il existe"; "Plus l'absolutisme se renforce, plus il s'affaiblit": Cosandey and Descimon 2002: 233). The two French historians point out that the very growth of an administrative machinery serving the Crown also created new patronage networks and irregular procedures which we would today call corruption. The administrative system which Louis XIV and his ministers built after 1660 left an ambivalent legacy which the eighteenth century found difficult to digest, and which was clearly an obstacle to efficient government. Moreover, while calling into question and reducing older privileges, the absolute monarchy continually created new privileges, which later proved to be a serious problem when attempts were made to increase the yield of taxes.

Finances, Fiscal Reform, and the Rule of Law

The deficiencies of the so-called absolute monarchies of our period are perhaps nowhere as evident as in the sphere of fiscal administration, and in fact, one may say that public finances are a crucial key for understanding the workings of eighteenth-century government. In the eighteenth century, countries such as France and the Habsburg monarchy often found it difficult to make ends meet, and expenditure frequently exceeded available revenues. This occurred not only in wartime – understandable enough – but often for decades after the end of a major military conflict, when the debts contracted in wartime had to be paid off. This was not due to any deep economic crisis. The eighteenth century, in particular its later decades, was generally a time of protracted economic growth, but the taxation systems of the greater European monarchies rarely managed to direct the new wealth sufficiently into the royal treasury.

This is particularly obvious in the case of France. Despite the poverty of many peasants, France was not just the most populous but one of the most prosperous countries in Europe which experienced a considerable economic growth in our period. But the Crown and its agents never really managed to tax the new wealth generated by trade and commerce on a large enough scale, relying instead on traditional taxes which hit the peasant population hardest (Goldstone, 1991: 196–222). Moreover, the wealthier classes of the population, not just the court nobility and the higher clergy but the urban elites as well, failed to contribute an adequate share to the overall tax load, although repeated attempts were undertaken to curtail their fiscal privileges, especially from the 1770s (Kwass, 2000: 313–15). These attempts were not thorough enough to solve France's fiscal problems, but they did go far enough to create a great deal of resentment and a feeling of insecurity among the privileged, contributing to the crisis of the *ancien régime* during the last two or three decades before 1789.

Absolute monarchs faced a dilemma: they could proclaim their power to impose whatever laws they wished to enact and whatever taxes they deemed necessary without obtaining anybody's consent, but to do so in practice risked undermining their own rule. Louis XV expounded absolute power in the so-called "séance de la flagellation," a famous speech castigating the Paris *parlement* in March 1766. The *parlements* were supreme law courts staffed by the *noblesse de robe*, a class of mostly hereditary office-holders and judges whom the king condemned for having long obstructed royal policy. Some observers even applauded him (Antoine, 1987: 5–6). But for the elites as well as for the population at large, absolute power was only acceptable as long as it remained a largely theoretical proposition which was not actually invoked, save in exceptional circumstances, or at least not used to reduce well-established property rights. All European monarchies were, according to official political theory, systems of government based on firm legal principles as much as on the monarch's power. The rule of law and the monarch's absolute authority were seen – officially – as entirely compatible; otherwise, government would have been despotic. And no European monarch could really afford to appear to be a despot in the long run. Only if he respected his subjects' property rights, more than anything else, could he avoid giving that impression. Thus, Louis XV risked undermining his own legitimacy when he actually used the absolute power he and his predecessors had claimed ever since the late sixteenth century and dissolved the recalcitrant *parlements*, replacing them in 1771 with new courts intended to be more amenable to his will. Although the *parlements* were reinstated in 1774, it was difficult to undo the damage to the legitimacy of kingship. Maupeou, the king's minister who had broken the power of the *parlements*, had torn away the veil "which hid the monarchy's despotic face. At a stroke, he dispelled the illusions which had sustained the political system and showed that the king's power was not only theoretically limitless (which nobody ever denied) but beyond restraint in practice, too" (Doyle, 1987: 164; cf. Swann, 1995).

Generally, consent was pivotal for obtaining the information required for effective administration, policy implementation, and, above all, revenue collection. This explains the revival of older corporate bodies such as the estates, and the appearance of more modern equivalents of such institutions. This is not to deny that some estates and diets continued to decline, as for example in the Habsburg monarchy where Maria Theresia overhauled the antiquated tax system after 1748, pushing aside the estates and their officeholders and commissioners.

Nevertheless, it has been argued that the memory of the traditional diets and estates survived even where they had ceased to meet in full sessions, and remained an important element of the political culture shaping relations between rulers and their subjects. This was certainly true for many of the smaller German states and even to some extent for Prussia, where the full *Landtage* (the regional diets) in most provinces had already largely disappeared by 1720, if not earlier. Noble corporations and similar bodies continued to play an important part in local or regional administration here as elsewhere and preserved the collective memory of ancient privileges and liberties. Therefore, some historians have spoken of a phase in which the influence and sometimes the very existence of estates became concealed or "latent" (*Latenzphase*) in the eighteenth century, without, however, ever entirely disappearing (Neugebauer, 1992: 261–92). This would explain the renaissance of diets and estates that, according to recent research, marked the very end of the eighteenth century, even though others have pointed out that the lively discussion in parts of late eighteenth-century Germany about the role of the estates and how they might be modernized remained just that, a theoretical debate without any impact on real politics (Stollberg-Rilinger, 1999).

However, as most monarchs and their ministers were to realize, fiscal reform without the support of representative institutions of some kind was often difficult to achieve. A typical first step for such a reform was to create a land register, a *cadastre* or *Kataster*, because the enlightened thinkers, particularly the physiocrats, believed that a unified land tax would be the most equitable form of taxation and least detrimental to economic growth. The Italian states, which had a long tradition of local land registers, were the first to undertake efforts inspired by such ideas. The duchy of Milan, part of the Austrian Habsburg dominions after 1700, led the way with attempts to compile a land register (the *castasto*) as early as 1718, but took until 1755 to complete. The unified land tax imposed on all landed property after 1760 was based on this register (Anderson, 1990: 61–3; Reinalter, 2005: 49). Whereas the Milanese *castasto* was by and large a success, similar policies pursued in Spain at the same time encountered strong resistance among the privileged classes. To solve the recurrent financial problems of the monarchy, the marques of Enseñada, who as royal prime minister was familiar with the Italian reform debates from his time in office in Naples, decided to introduce a land register for the entire kingdom of Castile in 1749. Simultaneously, he revived the office of *intendente*, first introduced in 1714 on the French model as a royal commissioner responsible for supervising revenue collection and the administration of justice at regional and local level. The *intendentes* were to exercise vast powers extending to economic policy as well as to matters relating to security and public order (Armillas Vicente and Corona Baratech, 1990: 126–9). They were to help supervise the introduction of the *catastro* to follow the one imposed on Catalonia after the reconquest of that recalcitrant province, which supported the losing Habsburg side during the War of the Spanish Succession. The experiment failed in Castile, however. Though a register was compiled, resistance from the privileged classes frustrated all efforts to introduce planned *unica contribución* (unified tax) it was intended to support (Armillas Vicente and Corona Baratech, 1990: 207–8, 373–4; Gómez Urdánze, 1996).

An even more radical project of fiscal and agrarian reform was planned by Joseph II of Austria, the most famous of the eighteenth-century enlightened rulers. It had already become clear in the 1740s that Austria could only survive if the monarchy managed to raise new revenues. In order to do so, land owned by noble landlords had to be taxed, not just the peasant farms. A first *cadastre* completed in the 1750s facilitated this task, although noble property continued to be taxed at a much lower rate than other land. Not surprisingly, direct taxes failed to keep pace with growing expenditure and the rise in net revenue (impressive enough from around 22 million florins in the 1740s to 55 million florins in 1782), was primarily due to greater indirect tax returns (Hochedlinger, 2003: 283–4). Joseph II tried to reverse this trend. A new land register was to provide detailed information not only about property rights, but also about the rents and other services owed to each landowner. On the basis of this information, the income landowners could derive from estates let out to peasant farmers was to be limited to 17 percent of all revenues, whereas 12 percent was to go to the state. The result was a universal outcry and general unrest among the population. The privileged classes, supported by many of the emperor's own civil servants, feared a drastic reduction of their income, whereas the peasants saw such a reform as the first step to the total abolition of all feudal dues (Demel, 2005: 250–1; Reinalter 2005: 108–11) and were no longer prepared to pay even the moderate rents specified by the legislation. Joseph II's reform was a total failure; he left the monarchy saddled with even greater debts.

Frederick the Great of Prussia was prudent enough never to undertake a similar reform project. On the contrary, the legal code which he ordered his legal experts to compile during the last years of his reign, the *Allgemeine Landrecht*, enacted in 1794, eight years after his death, was a very conservative document in this respect, and clearly confirmed the privileges of the landowning nobility. Tax reform concentrated mostly on indirect taxation, which, though unpopular enough, could not be depicted as a direct infringement of well-established property rights (Koselleck, 1981).

If one looks for the limits of monarchical government in the eighteenth century, they are most apparent in the area of fiscal policy and tax reform, as the French example demonstrates. The most important French direct tax continued to be the *taille*, a sort of poll tax going back to the late Middle Ages, that took often little account of the taxpayers' real wealth and income, relying instead on antiquated data and methods of repartition. The financial administration tried to introduce a so-called *taille tarifiée* after 1760, to be based on more adequate information about taxable income. Again, this necessitated the creation of a land register, a measure which was fiercely resisted in most places by the *parlements* and similar corporate bodies whose members feared that it would be impossible in future to challenge tax demands in the law courts (Drévillon, 2000: 311–16; Touzery, 1994).

In the end it became clear that adequate information about wealth and income could only be obtained if taxpayers cooperated. To this end, Turgot, the reform-minded controller general of royal finances from 1774 to 1776, considered various projects for new municipal or provincial assemblies of local landowners. His principal adviser, Dupont de Nemours, proposed basing the franchise on the electorate's willingness to declare their own wealth. This suggestion from 1775 was revived three years later in slightly different and more ambitious form when the banker Necker was minister of finance. Although Necker fell from power in 1781, provincial assemblies for tax assessments were adopted in a modified form in most parts of France in 1787 and 1788 since they seemed to be a solution to France's financial problems (Kwass, 2000: 258–9, 360–6). These reforms came too late to avert the fall of the monarchy and may in fact have hastened it by the way in which they were implemented. All the same, they prove that in France, as elsewhere, kings and princes might proclaim their absolute power, but they had to rely on some measure of consent just to get information from their subjects. When tacit or informal consent could no longer be taken for granted, institutions had to be created in the last resort to generate and to organize explicit consent.

Reforming taxation was a difficult task in eighteenth-century Europe, not just in France. The problems the absolute monarchies encountered in raising credit were perhaps even more serious. Rulers claiming absolute authority found it harder to raise money than those controlled to a greater or lesser extent by estates and other corporate bodies that could hold them to account: another instance of absolutism as a potentially self-defeating form of government. Financial experiments, such as the colonial company founded by the Scotsman John Law in France in 1719 to administer the royal debts, were hardly designed to inspire confidence in the Crown's creditworthiness. Law admittedly managed to wipe off most of the debts accumulated under Louis XIV, but his company failed, and the state creditors who had become its shareholders lost their money (Bonney, 1995: 325, 470). Consequently, Louis XV and Louis XVI had to pay a higher rate of interest on their debts than, for example, "constitutional monarchs" such as George II and George III of Britain. In raising credit, the British state could rely on a financial institution, the Bank of England, which enjoyed the confidence of wealthy investors in Britain and in Europe, having been established by parliamentary statute and royal charter in 1694. Neither France nor Austria – which relied on the Vienna City Bank instead – ever had a similar institution. In fact, the king of France would have found it harder still without the support of corporate bodies such as numerous corporations of officeholders who were prepared to underwrite debts contracted by the Crown (Bien, 1987), but who, not surprisingly, expected political favors in return.

Of course, there were alternatives. Prussia's public finances were for most of the eighteenth century in a healthy state despite the – in proportion to the country's population – enormous size of its army and its frequent engagement in protracted warfare after 1740. Yet Prussian methods were either rather old-fashioned or decidedly unorthodox. A disproportionately high percentage of royal revenues in Prussia was generated by the rents paid for the royal domains, which were let to wealthy tenant farmers and agricultural entrepreneurs of non-noble origin. In many ways, Prussia remained a domain state as much as a tax state as late as the mid-eighteenth century, accumulating financial reserves *in specie* during peace and relying on these savings and on foreign subsidies when at war. Moreover, in wartime the king did not hesitate to debase the Prussian currency and to counterfeit coins minted by neighboring princes. By reverting to the original value of its coinage immediately after the end of the Seven Years War (1763), Prussia soon recovered solvency and paid off most of its debts. However, this could only be achieved at the cost of a severe economic crisis, caused by the ensuing sudden drop in prices and the shortage of credit, which lasted for almost a decade (Kunisch, 2004: 356–8). The country faced imminent financial collapse during the Revolutionary Wars of the 1790s when such measures were no longer adequate or feasible.

The Later Eighteenth Century: A Transformation of the *Ancien Régime*?

We have stressed the weakness of eighteenth-century monarchical government and stated that the ruler's absolute power was often more a rhetorical assertion than a political reality; prudent rulers were normally well advised to leave it at that. Nevertheless, one has to admit that after about 1740/50 a phase of more ambitious reforms set in, often seen by historians as part of a more systematic approach to politics, inspired to some extent by the ideas of the Enlightenment and implemented in Prussia, Spain, Portugal, Denmark, Russia, the Habsburg monarchy, and other countries. However, the notion of enlightened absolutism is in many ways as problematic as that of absolutism itself. The real driving force behind the later eighteenth-century reforms was often the fiscal problems we have just discussed or, at least in the case of the greater states, the desire to strengthen one's own position in the great game of European power politics, not – whatever the rhetoric of reform may have claimed – the wish to create an ideal society based on the principles of contemporary philosophy where universal happiness was the ultimate objective. Nevertheless, many countries experienced energetic policies intended to create a higher level of economic prosperity, to increase public revenues, and generally to improve public institutions such as schools, universities, workhouses, prisons, and hospitals and to fight ignorance and superstition. The changes in the traditional social structure attributed by historians to these reforms were often more the unintended consequences of measures initially directed at sustaining the established order. One of the clearest examples can be found the attempts by governments even prior to the mid-eighteenth century to impose stricter controls on local corporations, autonomous bodies, and families when dealing with social and personal conflicts, misdemeanors, and crimes.

France was one of the first countries to create a professional police force, establishing one in 1667, albeit initially only in Paris, under the command of the *lieutenant général de police.* At first, the new royal police tried to enforce the same laws, regulations, and moral norms that municipal bodies and the urban notables had always tried to defend in the past, but gradually it became more prone to interfere on its own. Increasingly from the 1690s onwards, the informal mechanisms of social control, which had maintained order and stability in the city in the past, were seen as obstacles to efficient policing. The time-honored structures of informal social control gradually collapsed, undermined by the intervention of the royal police and the possibility of appealing to the king and his agents against the judgments of municipal bodies. The police, originally intended simply to supplement local institutions and notables, became indispensable for maintaining order (Sälter, 2004: 142–3, 413–15), and the number of guardsmen acting as policemen in Paris grew accordingly to 1,000 before the revolution (Collins, 1995: 186). Admittedly, even in the later eighteenth century, individual parties and families often manipulated the authority of the police and other royal agents for their own private purposes, particularly outside Paris (Quetel, 1981: 123–37). Here France remained to a considerable extent a self-policed country, as there were only 3,000 mounted constables supplementing an assortment of municipal guards to cover the rest of the country.

The impetus for police intervention and other areas like poor relief outside Paris often came from the king's subjects. Government and administration were in this sense more a "bottom-up" than a "top-down" affair, as James Collins has remarked (Collins 1995: 185; cf. Meumann and Pröve, 2004). For example, fathers of sufficient social standing in the provinces asked the king to issue a *lettre de cachet* (a special warrant sending subjects to prison without trial) to imprison their rebellious sons, or send their wayward daughters to a monastery for some time. This enabled them to avoid the public scandal of formal legal proceedings that might damage their family's reputation. However, a recent study has shown that the king's *lieutenants de police* and their agents or *intendants* often forced fathers or parents to take such action in the later eighteenth century, even in cases when the family itself would have preferred to ignore such problems (Sälter, 2004: 414–15).

The French state tried to strengthen patriarchal authority, as defined by its servants' understanding of traditional social norms, but in doing so it undermined the ability of families to resolve problems themselves and so left them more dependent on state institutions. Some of the late eighteenth-century enlightened reformers tried to complete this process by issuing laws and regulations for every conceivable aspect of life: hygiene, funeral pomp, prostitution and illicit sex, agriculture, commerce, and of course problems of education which assumed an increasingly central place in official policy in many countries. Joseph II's policies were particularly thorough in this respect, as in so many others. The emperor also recruited a considerable police force, including a well-organized secret police to gather information about his subjects and, especially, his own officials. Joseph II thus came close to creating a perfect "police state" in the 1780s, but many of his measures failed nonetheless and the social elites probably only accepted the new control mechanisms – or what remained of them after his death – because of the threat of revolution in the 1790s and the following decades (Beales, 1987).

A similar tendency for state interference to replace communal self-regulation can be detected in the relations between the monarch and noble elites. Most eighteenth-century monarchs tried to avoid open conflicts with the nobility as such – though not necessarily with individual magnates and families. Some, like Frederick the Great, even did their utmost to preserve the status and social position of the ancient noble families. Joseph II was largely unique in his outright opposition to noble privileges. The French aristocracy and court nobility increased, rather than lost, influence over political decisions and ministerial appointments during the century. But French aristocrats could no longer exercise real political power on the national level in their own right as magnates. Rather, they acted as royal patronage brokers, or wielded influence through royal favor, and because they had enough allies and clients at court and in the administrative councils and law courts to keep their rivals and enemies at bay.

Moreover, the future increasingly belonged to a nobility created by the king and owing its status to the monarch, who in the last resort could define the nobility's identity as he wished. In France, like Spain, more utilitarian ideas of nobility gained ground. Nobility had to be justified by merits, talents, and services rendered to the state and society. Such a meritocratic rhetoric had always existed to some extent, but in the Age of Enlightenment it gained a new edge (Smith, 2005: 104–42; cf. Blaufarb, 2002). There was little room left for the mere country squire quietly enjoying his modest landed income in his castle, ruling his village, protecting his peasants against the royal or private tax collectors and participating in the rural pastimes of the village community. Moreover, although the state rarely abolished nobles' rights of local jurisdiction outright, peasants, when they had a choice, preferred to take their cases to the royal law courts, which were more efficient than those of the *seigneur*, or appealed against the judgment of their lord to these courts (Collins, 1995: 138–9, 147). Even in Prussia, where the king tended to defend the *Junkers*' position, some village communities ruined their lord by protracted legislation in the royal law courts (Hagen, 2002: 546–92).

Despite the shortcomings of the administrative structure, the tax collector, the *intendant*, and other new officeholders were agents of a centralizing power interfering in local affairs; they may not always have achieved what their royal masters had asked them to do, but their mere presence changed the day-to-day business of local and regional politics. The presence of the recruiting sergeant loomed perhaps larger still. Sweden had anticipated later developments by creating an extensive system for the recruitment of soldiers on the local level in the late seventeenth century when it dominated northern Europe as a military power. After Sweden's decline, Prussia imitated the Swedish example by assigning each regiment from the 1730s a "canton," or district from which it drew recruits from the rural and, to a lesser extent, urban population (many urban crafts and professions were exempt except in emergencies). All able-bodied men over a certain age were enrolled as potential recruits, provided they were not too short. Some were drafted, while the others remained a pool of potential future recruits. It has often been argued that Prussian system reinforced the hierarchical structure of landed society and strengthened nobles' authority over the peasant population by giving the nobility a privileged position in the officer corps. While this may initially have been the case, in the long run the opposite could occur, because soldiers and potential recruits partially escaped nobles' jurisdiction, while military service prompted them to question the seemingly God-given order of rural society. Soldiers, though subject to a harsh discipline, could be more self-assured than mere peasants, and their military service may have had an emancipatory effect (Kloosterhuis, 1996; cf. Hagen, 2002: 466–73 and Wilson, 2002).

Prussian recruitment methods were copied in the Habsburg monarchy in the 1770s where they had an even greater impact on local administration that had until then only superficially controlled the countryside. The new draft (*Konskription*), however, "intensified the sovereign's control over his subjects on a massive, even revolutionary scale" (Hochedlinger, 2003: 295), not least by providing the first adequate information about the population's size, structure, and mobility, as well as about the health individual subjects. The findings revealed the peasants' often deplorable health and miserable living conditions, which made it almost impossible to recruit enough able-bodied soldiers in many districts. The *Konskription* thus became part of a process triggering new agrarian reforms, which culminated in the 1780s. Although these reforms proved abortive in many respects, they were part of an overall attempt to modernize the monarchy, which found its parallel in many other countries including the smaller and medium-sized German principalities at the time (Wilson, 2000).

Catholic countries developed particularly radical schemes for reform in the later eighteenth century. There was a general feeling that Protestant powers like Prussia were more progressive, better developed economically, and more competitive internationally. Leading politicians in Catholic monarchies, such as Portugal, Spain, many Italian states, and the Habsburg monarchy, blamed the Catholic Church for the backwardness of their countries. In particular, they condemned the (alleged) idleness of the regular clergy, the enormous sums squandered on pious endowments, the overweening economic power and cultural authority of the church, and, above all, the supposedly pernicious influence of the Jesuits and other orders on education. Spain expelled the Jesuits from both Castile and Aragon in April 1767, and a few months later also from its colonies (Noel, 1990: 135). In 1772 the pope officially dissolved the Society of Jesus under pressure from Catholic monarchs. With the Jesuits gone, education could be reformed and modernized. Secular ideals became influential, though many of the reformers were not opponents of Catholicism, let alone Christianity as such, but only of the particular form of Baroque piety which had triumphed in the seventeenth century (Hersche, 2006: vol. 2, pp. 960–1013). Nevertheless, the attack on the power of the church was fierce. Hundreds of monasteries were dissolved in Austria during the 1780s. This process was completed in other German Catholic states after 1802–3 when the bishoprics and abbeys previously under the emperor's immediate jurisdiction were incorporated into the neighboring secular principalities. Moreover, clergymen were increasingly transformed into agents of the state, into mere civil servants, just like tax collectors. This had already been true for Protestant clergy to some extent before 1700, although noble and urban patrons continued to exert considerable influence on appointments at parish level in Protestant as well as Catholic areas.

Attacks on the church and similar enlightened measures were less controversial and often less radical in Protestant Europe, but they likewise changed the character of monarchy itself. The sacredness and mystery of royal power had gone; royal government had become "disenchanted." There may have been kings, like Frederick the

Great, whose personal charisma as military heroes could compensate for this loss of legitimacy. However, Frederick's immediate successors on the Prussian throne possessed at best the distinctly unregal aura of minor officials in the board of excise and inland revenue. Bureaucracy was replacing monarchy. The monarch was still necessary as a symbol of authority and as a focus of patriotic loyalty, but the age when monarchs had personally governed their states was past, apart from a few exceptions. The statement "the king rules but he does not govern" was now true not only for countries such as Britain with its strong Parliament, but also for states in which, at first glance, the tradition of absolutism remained alive. In this sense absolutism had indeed become self-defeating at the end of the eighteenth century.

Bibliography

Anderson, M. S., "The Italian reformers," in H. M. Scott (ed.), *Enlightened Absolutism* (Basingstoke, 1990), pp. 55–74.

Antoine, M., "La Monarchie absolue," in K. M. Baker (ed.), *The Political Culture of the Old Regime* (Oxford, 1987), pp. 3–24.

Armillas Vicente, J. A. and C. E. Corona Baratech (eds.), *La España des las reformas hasta el final del reinado de Carlos IV*, Historia General de España y América, vol. X/2 (2nd edn., Madrid, 1990).

Asch, R. G. and H. Duchhardt (eds.), *Der Absolutismus. Ein Mythos?* (Cologne, 1996).

Beales, D., *Joseph II* (Cambridge, 1987).

Bély, L. (ed.), *Dictionnaire de l'Ancien Régime* (Paris, 1996).

Bien, D. D., "Offices, corps and a system of state credit: the uses of privilege under the *ancien régime*," in K. M. Baker (ed.), *The Political Culture of the Old Regime* (Oxford, 1987), pp. 89–114.

Blaufarb, R., *The French Army 1750–1820: Careers, Talent, Merit* (Manchester, 2002).

Bonney, R. (ed.), *Economic Systems and State Finance* (Oxford, 1995).

Collins, J. B., *Classes, Estates and Order in Early Modern Brittany* (Cambridge, 1994).

Collins, J. B., *The State in Early Modern France* (Cambridge, 1995).

Cosandey, F. and R. Descimon, *L'Absolutisme en France: Histoire et historiographie* (Paris, 2002).

Demel, W., *Gebhardt Handbuch der deutschen Geschichte*, vol. 12: *Reich, Reformen und sozialer Wandel, 1763–1806* (10th edn., Stuttgart, 2005).

Dickson, P. G. M., *Finance and Government under Maria Theresia* (2 vols., Oxford 1987).

Doyle, W., "The parlements," in K. M.Baker (ed.), *The Political Culture of the Old Regime* (Oxford, 1987), pp. 157–67.

Doyle, W., *The Sale of Offices in Eighteenth-Century France* (Oxford, 1996).

Drévillon, H., "La Monarchie des Lumiéres : réforme ou utopie? 1715–1774' in J. Cornette and L. Bourquin (eds.), *La monarchie entre Renaissance et Révolution 1515–1792* (Paris, 2000), pp. 284–354.

Dwyer, P. G. (ed.), *The Rise of Prussia 1700–1830* (Harlow, 2000).

Goldstone, J. A., *Revolution and Rebellion in the Early Modern World* (Berkeley, 1991).

Gómez Urdánez, J. L., *El proyecto reformista de Ensenada* (Lleida, 1996).

Hagen, W. W., *Ordinary Prussians: Brandenburg Junkers and Villagers, 1500–1840* (Cambridge, 2002).

Henshall, N., *The Myth of Absolutism: Change and Continuity in Early Modern European Monarchy* (London, 1992).

Hersche, P., *Muße und Verschwendung. Europäische Gesellschaft und Kultur im Barockzeitalter* (2 vols., Freiburg, 2006).

Hochedlinger, M., *Austria's Wars of Emergence: War, State and Society in the Habsburg Monarchy 1683–1797* (London, 2003).

Kloosterhuis, J., "Zwischen Aufruhr und Akzeptanz. Zur Ausformung und Einbettung des Kantonssystems in die Wirtschafts- und Sozialstrukturen des preußischen Westfalen," in B. R. Kroener and R. Proeve (eds.), *Krieg und Frieden. Militär und Gesellschaft in der Frühen Neuzeit* (Paderborn, 1996), pp. 167–90.

Koselleck, R., *Preußen zwischen Reform und Revolution: Allgemeines Landrecht, Verwaltung und soziale Bewegung von 1791–1848* (3rd edn., Stuttgart, 1981).

Kunisch, J., *Friedrich der Große. Der König und seine Zeit* (Munich, 2004).

Kwass, M., *Privilege and the Politics of Taxation in Eighteenth-Century France: Liberté, égalité, fiscalité* (Cambridge, 2000).

Mat'a, P. and T. Winkelbauer (eds.), *Die Habsburgermonarchie 1620 bis 1740. Leistungen und Grenzen des Absolutismusparadigmas* (Stuttgart, 2006).

Meumann, M. and R. Pröve (eds.), *Herrschaft in der Frühen Neuzeit. Umrisse eines dynamisch-kommunikativen Prozesses* (Münster, 2004).

Neugebauer, W., *Politischer Wandel im Osten. Ost- und Westpreußen von den alten Ständen zum Konstitutionalismus* (Stuttgart, 1992).

Noel, C. C., "Charles III of Spain," in H. M. Scott (ed.), *Enlightened Absolutism* (Basingstoke, 1990), pp. 119–44.

Quetel, C., *De par le Roy: Essais sur les lettres de cachet* (Toulouse, 1981).

Reinalter, H. (ed.), *Lexikon zum Aufgeklärten Absolutismus in Europa* (Cologne, 2005).

Sälter, G., *Polizei und soziale Ordnung in Paris* (Frankfurt a. M., 2004).

Smith, J. M., *Nobility Reimagined: The Patriotic Nation in Eighteenth-Century France* (Ithaca, 2005).

Stollberg-Rilinger, B., *Vormünder des Volkes? Konzepte landständischer Repräsentation in der Spätphase des Alten Reiches* (Berlin 1999).

Straubel, R., *Beamte und Personalpolitik im altpreußischen Staat. Soziale Rekrutierung, Karriereverläufe, Entscheidungsprozesse (1763/86–1806)* (Berlin, 1998).

Swann, J., *Politics and the Parlement of Paris under Louis XV, 1754–1774* (Cambridge, 1995).

Szabo, F. A. J., *Kaunitz and Enlightened Absolutism, 1753–1780* (Cambridge, 1994).

Touzery, M., *L'invention de l'impôt sur le revenu: La taille tarifiée 1715–1789* (Paris, 1994).

Wilson, P. H., *Absolutism in Central Europe* (London, 2000).

Wilson, P. H., "The politics of military recruitment in eighteenth-century Germany," *English Historical Review*, 117 (2002), 536–68.

Zimmermann, C., *Reformen in der bäuerlichen Gesellschaft. Studien zum aufgeklärten Absolutismus in der Markgrafschaft Baden 1750–1790* (Ostfildern, 1983).

CHAPTER TWENTY-NINE

War, 1688–1812

CIRO PAOLETTI

Current General Ideas and Prejudices

The cultural heritage of the Enlightenment and the French Revolution has left an imbalance in the writing on eighteenth-century warfare, concentrating on the second half of the century and the apparently all-important topics of Frederick the Great, the Seven Years War, and the American and French Revolutionary Wars. One reason for this is the Enlightenment's long legacy – something still shaping historical writing today – that implies that those working prior to its benign influence were somehow still in the grip of Counter-Reformation darkness and unequal to the peaks reached by those who had seen the light. A second reason is the common experience of the generation of military men growing up during the later eighteenth-century wars who in turn helped shape the outlook and collective memory of those serving during the Napoleonic period. Following Napoleon and the writings of Clausewitz, the preeminent interpreter of Napoleonic warfare, few deemed it worthy to look much further into the past. After all, the victories of the French revolutionary armies, and those of Napoleon himself, seemingly demonstrated the irrelevance of earlier eighteenth-century military experience, vanquishing armies that tactically, strategically, as well as socially, appeared to be products of an earlier, vanished "old regime."

This post-Napoleonic view has implanted a lasting impression of eighteenth-century warfare as some kind of genteel minuet. Generals in powdered wigs and elegant clothes ponderously maneuvered their only slightly less finely attired soldiers in a slow, graceful military dance, which only by chance might include a battle. Casualties seemed almost accidental, the Age of Reason dictating supposedly "limited" operations designed to achieve modest goals at minimal risk. A succession of factors conspired to perpetuate these misconceptions. Given the general lack of interest in eighteenth-century warfare, few bothered to do new research, content simply to repeat earlier works, mistakes and all. Second, what little attention was given concentrated on the second half of the century to the detriment of the first. Only in Britain did a lingering remembrance of this earlier period remain, but, as time passed, this was reduced to celebrations of the duke of Marlborough as England's greatest

A Companion to Eighteenth-Century Europe, First Edition. Edited by Peter H. Wilson.
© 2014 John Wiley & Sons, Ltd. Published 2014 by John Wiley & Sons, Ltd.

general before Wellington, and to the more parochial experience of the Jacobite rebellions. This simply added to the overall distortion. Thanks to the preponderance of books in English and to their diffusion, Anglo-Saxon interpretations came to speak for the century as a whole. Declining linguistic competence compounded nineteenth-century imperial pride in Britain's achievements to discourage the use of sources in other languages, thus narrowing the available views still further.

The View from Eighteenth-Century Memoirs and Writings

To begin with, it should be stressed that military science as it developed after Napoleon was unknown in the eighteenth century. To be sure, there were common ideas, discussed by soldiers, but each commander developed his own methods according to his personality and experience. Contemporary books on warfare were primarily practical handbooks, detailing drill, maneuvers, and the like, quite different from the twentieth- and twenty-first-century professional literature. Young men and noble volunteers acquired training on campaign, as in the previous two centuries, in the wars against the Ottomans in eastern Europe. Volunteers from across Europe joined the Venetian and Habsburg forces in Hungary or the Balkans, meeting others, developing friendships, and acquiring first-hand knowledge of weapons and tactics. This largely common experience was transmitted back to other countries when the men returned. Their own training was completed in the European wars, usually involving, on the opposing side, men who were former comrades-in-arms against the Turks. They quickly mastered the local, particular details of their sovereign's army: the use of infantry and cavalry, how to march and make camp, lay siege to a fortress, organize supplies, and make reconnaissance. Such things had to be handled slightly differently than they were against the Turks, because the foe they now faced was Christian Europeans fighting in a different physical and social environment. After years of such practical schooling, encompassing perhaps a dozen campaigns and half a dozen wounds – and possibly some plunder – those who survived were ready to lead an army.

Those with a smattering of Latin might try a comparison between their own experience and that of Caesar and Hannibal. But the uncultured (and often unlettered) majority simply applied what they had learnt on the ground, remembering that time when they lost ten men in a skirmish, or the occasion when they captured a supply convoy and made their regiment happy for a week. A commander was often a teacher too. One of the most remarkable examples was Prince Eugene of Savoy, who made a lasting impact on Prussia, despite being renowned as an imperial commander. It was while serving under Eugene in 1704 that the young prince of Anhalt-Dessau, later known as the Old Dessauer, received the practical instruction he later applied drilling the Prussian infantry and turning it into the well-oiled machine with which Frederick the Great won his first spectacular victories after 1740. Frederick himself had served on Eugene's staff during the War of the Polish Succession.

Technological and Environmental Constraints on Warfare

While Frederick achieved fame combining the positions of king and commander, most eighteenth-century generals operated under the political authority of their sovereign. However, the principal constraints on their actions were practical rather than political. Primary among these were the logistical difficulties posed by the need to feed the army and its cavalry and transport animals. Early seventeenth-century armies ate what they found where they were, and this often meant very little at all. Supply services were organized in the later seventeenth century to alleviate this problem by finding, storing, and distributing food, clothing, and ordnance. The service gathered all the supplies from a wide net of minor civil producers. All was stored and, later, forwarded by water or by land to magazines closer to the actual operations, enabling forces to remain longer in the field. The army's radius of action was dictated by how much food it could carry with it, or find where it was stationed. Such a radius could be quite short, as indicated by Frederick's "five marches system." Prussian soldiers carried nine days' rations, three days' worth in packs and the rest on wagons, enabling them to advance for three days, fight, and return to camp to consume their last supplies in their original camp. The logic of such conditions encouraged commanders to attack magazines and lines of communications rather than enemy forces directly. Moreover, battles carried a high price in men and equipment, far more costly than raids on supply lines, and there was no guarantee that victory in the field would necessarily force the enemy to withdraw, whereas interdicting supplies generally achieved this end. This helps explain why successful generals were not necessarily fighting generals, and why eighteenth-century operations proceeded slowly compared to those of Napoleon and subsequent periods.

Logistics and environmental factors imposed a common timetable on all armies. Operations began in early spring, from the end of March to the end of May, depending on when the snow melted and how much mud it left. Commanders then had until the early autumn, generally late October, to achieve an advantage. Once November came they started to think of entering "winter quarters" before bad weather and mud made the already poor roads impassable, especially to larger supply wagons. The onset of winter, bringing not just snow and inclement weather but also a shortage of fodder, effectively prevented large-scale operations until the following spring. Only small-scale raiding to achieve local advantage or probe enemy defenses remained possible. Winter battles remained exceptional, at least prior to the War of the Austrian Succession.

The variety and capacity of weaponry and munitions imposed other constraints. Artillery was more affected than the infantry, who used no more than two or three types of firearms. The limited stage of technological development and manufacturing problems inhibited the standardization of firearms and calibers. However, infantry firearms were designed with relatively generous windage, allowing soldiers to pick up and use balls intended for weapons of other calibers. Matters were completely different for the artillery, where the consequences of ammunition jamming in the gun barrel could be lethal. Guns varied widely both between and within armies. For instance, the imperial (Austrian) army officially used 22 different types in 1713, while Piedmont had a dozen and France no more than eight at the same time. Technical improvements during the seventeenth century had reduced the weight of gun carriages, which consequently required fewer animals to pull them. Nonetheless, on the eve of the eighteenth century, a gun firing a 32-pound shot still required a dozen horses, while a 24-pounder needed eight, a 12-pounder six, and so on. The artillery "train" was further encumbered with munition wagons, since no fewer than six wagons or carts were required to transport the powder and shot needed to sustain just one day's shooting by a heavy gun. Sieges thus became major logistical tasks, with just 20 mortars requiring 100 to 150 wagons a day to bring up their ammunition. The Allied army besieging Mons in August 1708 used a train of 3,000 ammunition wagons and 16,000 horses.

This logistical and ordinance train was lengthened by the "camp followers" that still clung to all armies: soldiers' families, servants, sutlers, prostitutes, actors, and merchants buying pillaged goods. Reliable figures from the imperial army in northern Italy in 1701–6 suggest such non-combatants equaled the number of military personnel. If the opposing side is factored into the equation, it was not uncommon for the population in the area of operations to be outnumbered 3 to 1 by the belligerent forces. Few parts of rural Europe could feed more than twice its inhabitants, while most armies compounded the problem through waste and wanton destruction – the Prussian invasion of Bohemia in 1756 being a rare exception where the intruders paid promptly in cash. Understandably, it was difficult to concentrate substantial forces in one area for more than a short time, and strategic concentrations that look obvious to modern-day armchair generals were rarely achievable in eighteenth-century practice.

Rapid movement was all but impossible for such a mass of humanity and animals. Troops had to carry their weapons, supplies, and personal belongings together with those of their families. Consequently, most marches were short, made only in daylight, and along wide routes reconnoitered and secured in advance. Light cavalry were sent on ahead, to scout and to guard officers charged with selecting a camp site and locating supplies. Once such a site had been secured, the light cavalry rode on far ahead, while the military commissioners collected food, drink, hay, and firewood, promising to pay, though rarely doing so in full. The soldiers would start to arrive, normally a few hours later, and begin preparing their tents or shelters and cooking their dinner. The camp would then have to be dismantled the next morning and the whole process begun afresh. Under these conditions, it is scarcely surprising that operations proceeded slowly and that it was common prior to the Napoleonic Wars for armies to move no more than seven miles a day. This should not mislead us into thinking that more rapid movement was entirely impossible. For instance, Prince Eugene's advance to Toulon in the summer of 1707, or Marlborough's famous march to the Danube three years earlier (Chandler, 2004; Paoletti, 2004, 2006). However, such relatively rapid movement entailed heavy losses through straggling, fatigue, and desertion – as indeed did the comparatively more rapid maneuvers associated with Napoleonic warfare.

The hardest obstacle for an eighteenth-century army was a fortified city. If it was not taken by assault it had to be besieged, and this entailed a time-consuming process of surrounding it with heavily garrisoned entrenchments. The logistical constraints outlined above soon kicked in, rendering it difficult to sustain the forces concentrated for the attack. Sieges could certainly be planned in detail, but regular supply was generally the key to success. It was easier to besiege towns in Flanders and the Rhineland where fertile plains and good waterways ensured regular and plentiful supplies. As a result, towns there tended to be the most heavily fortified in Europe. Elsewhere, the natural environment assisted defenders. Sieges were already more difficult in central Europe and generally grew harder and less predictable the further one moved east. The Alps made Italy the most difficult theater, where invaders either met with immediate success or failed disastrously as their supply lines collapsed. Given the practical difficulties, as well as the improvements in fortification techniques since the late fifteenth century, besiegers resorted to psychological warfare to induce defenders to capitulate quickly: heavy bombardment, mining operations, and starvation were combined with positive inducements to surrender, such as safe conduct out of the fortress and even bribes to the garrison and its commander. Sieges were thus lengthy, costly, and unpredictable affairs that few generals undertook with relish. The French marshal Maurice of Saxony was one of the few with a successful track record of swift conquests.

Weaponry and Tactics

By contrast, battles, while not actively desired, were accepted with greater readiness. Contrary to the stock images of genteel "limited" war, eighteenth-century armies clashed with remarkable violence and ferocity. Prevailing organization and weaponry encouraged killing at close quarters. Pikes had been used to protect infantry armed with handguns from swifter-moving cavalry, but were discontinued in the later seventeenth century as the invention of the bayonet enabled musketeers to defend themselves even when their weapons were unloaded. Lighter, modestly improved firearms also encouraged a greater emphasis on musketry, but the absence of rifling and other technical deficiencies still inhibited long-range precision firing. Instead, infantry relied on the speed and weight of firing, standing close together for mutual protection and to deliver continuous fire at relatively short range. The principal tactical question of the eighteenth century involved the relative merits of firepower delivered by long, relatively thin lines (linear order), over the shock value of deeper, faster-moving columns. Both systems had their champions and critics. Columns maneuvered more quickly, but reduced the available frontage and hence firepower. The consequences were dramatically demonstrated by Frederick the Great at the battle of Rossbach (1757) when a few Prussian infantry battalions deployed in a firing line halted the Franco-imperial army advancing in column of march. A charge by the Prussian heavy cavalry then sent the wavering enemy racing away. Later battles, especially Wellington's victories over the French in the Iberian peninsula (1808–14) appeared to confirm the line's superiority over the column. Soldiers were drilled to fire by ranks or sections (platoons or "divisions"), so that one or more section fired while the others reloaded. However, the desire to maximize firepower stretched infantry formations to between two and four ranks, leaving them vulnerable at the point of impact to deeper columns, as well as to charging cavalry or artillery fire.

The French army was the one most associated with the use of the column, but it only officially adopted this after Folard published his theories following the War of the Polish Succession. The absence of coherent doctrine, as well as of regular exercise in large formations, prevented either system from being used uniformly. For most of the century, regimental commanders were left in most armies to employ whatever methods they thought best. Generals also tailored tactics to suit the terrain. The Piedmontese deployed in linear order throughout the century, but used columns when operating in the mountains. The Spanish followed the French practice of preferring the column, while the Prussians maneuvered in lines.

Figure 18 French arms drill *c*.1755. Plate III of Recueil de Planches, sur les sciences, les arts libéraux et les arts méchaniques: Arts militaries. *Mary Evans Picture Library*

Tactics were further complicated by the fact that infantry regiments contained different types of soldier. Most were "fusiliers," named after the flintlock fusil that replaced the matchlock musket as the standard infantry weapon around 1700, and trained to deliver steady continuous fire. Around a tenth were called "grenadiers": these were used as assault troops and for special operations, often supported by sappers. Bandsmen served not just to play military music (also developing during this century), but also to carry the wounded and bury the dead. The regimental provost and his assistants saw to discipline, while many regiments had small artillery detachments to serve one or two light "battalion" guns. Infantry regiments also acquired "light" companies during the eighteenth century, intended for reconnaissance and long-range patrols. Additional, specialist light infantry were recruited with each country employing the particular subject peoples considered best suited for these tasks. The Austrians had the Warasdiners, Pandours, and other "borderers" from the frontier with the Ottoman empire. Spain and France employed Catalan Michelets, while Piedmont recruited Waldensians. These units gradually disappeared during the eighteenth century, or were integrated into the regular line army or replaced entirely by *chasseurs*, *Jäger*, and other specially trained light infantrymen. Light infantry deployed in more extended order, while grenadiers acted in column, opening their way into enemy formations with their hand-grenades. The exact combination of the different types of infantry depended heavily on the opinions of the current commander.

Cavalry were still subdivided into the types that had evolved over the seventeenth century. Heavy cavalry, often still wearing some body armor, were deployed as shock troops. Light cavalry wore no armor and rode smaller horses, but still carried the same weapons: pistols, a sword, and a carbine. They included growing numbers of hussars, modeled on the mounted border troops employed by the Habsburgs against the Turks and wearing Hungarian-style uniforms. Dragoons had developed from mounted infantry in the seventeenth century, but increasingly became a less well armored version of heavy cavalry. Most cavalry regiments contained specialist companies like their infantry counterparts, including sharpshooters, called Carabineers, as well as elite mounted grenadiers that were often grouped together in battle for specialist tasks.

While offering protection, the bayonet was nonetheless less daunting than the pike for a charging horseman. Its adoption around the late seventeenth century encouraged a resumption of cavalry tactics based on speed and shock rather than firepower. Shock tactics were used both to drive the enemy horse from the field and to smash infantry units, especially those already softened up by musketry and artillery fire. Cavalry were also used for reconnaissance, patrols, and security. They escorted convoys, attacked by surprise, protected retreating troops, or attacked an advancing or retreating enemy. Nonetheless, their main task remained the destruction of enemy infantry formations, since artillery was still insufficiently developed to enable it to assume this task alone.

Artillery remained limited in range around 1700. The same gun would be used against all targets, simply increasing the powder charge to enable it to hit those further away. Little effort was made to concentrate fire, and individual pieces often became overheated, necessitating pails of water to cool them to a safer operational temperature. One of the most common methods of fire, used for example by the French, derived from the sixteenth-century Portuguese navy. Guns fired solid shot to strike the ground at a relatively short distance and then bounce several times before crashing through the target. The Piedmontese discovered an alternative method by chance during the siege of Turin in 1706. As powder was running short, they concentrated all available guns on the same target simultaneously. This "mass fire" proved effective against the French and Spaniards, and was soon copied by the imperial and other armies. Meanwhile, artillery experienced considerable technical improvement. The French copied the Anglo-Dutch howitzer during the later seventeenth century and disseminated this weapon to other armies. The Piedmontese developed a mountain gun that could be disassembled into three parts for transport, as well as a disposable light leather gun that could be discarded after a few shots. Breech-loading cannon had already appeared before 1700, but were not adopted widely before the mid-nineteenth century because of the difficulty of producing large numbers of reliable weapons of this type.

The artillery included other technical support services that had yet to develop their own institutional structure, though they did emerge separately in many armies during the eighteenth century. One example is the military engineers who drew maps, directed bridging and road works, and planned sieges and fortifications. Others include sappers and miners who dug trenches and mines, especially during sieges, and pontooneers in charge of portable boat bridges.

Eighteenth-century weapons were only fully effective when used en masse, necessitating the deployment of soldiers in large formations at relatively close ranges. All troops needed continuous drilling to keep formation in battle. Harsh discipline underpinned such training, relying on hard, often cruel penalties (or the threat thereof) to subordinate uneducated, superstitious, and violent men, including former criminals, and those pressed from the poor or recruited abroad. Drilling was intended to instill a mechanical perfection that would continue to operate despite the sounds, smells, and noise of battle, the presence of the enemy, and the fear of death. Desertion was rife, but offered few prospects beyond brigandage or re-enlistment. It was easiest to abscond during a march or immediately after a battle.

The first volleys created a deep and persistent smoke curtain that quickly obscured the enemy and encouraged generals to order their troops to close directly for hand-to-hand combat. Close-quarter fighting was generally deadly for those hit, and few men were wounded this way. Medical services were still rudimentary, improvised anew with each conflict, and consisting of little more than a field hospital for immediate treatment. Men who were wounded by firearms or artillery generally succumbed within a few hours from infection or loss of blood. Even infantry weapons fired such large-caliber balls that wounds were devastating, often necessitating the amputation of injured limbs. Prisoners were robbed of their clothes, as were the dead, who were generally left naked on the ground for the local inhabitants to bury. Such pillage remained a sure way to quick money, not least given the numerous sutlers accompanying the armies ready to buy stolen goods.

In addition to poor visibility, it was also difficult to transmit orders and information during battle. Mounted messengers generally needed at least a quarter of an hour to reach a wing of the army from a centrally placed commander. Even if the officer on the wing responded immediately, it would take a further 15 minutes to reply, all assuming that the messenger's horse was not shot from under him, or that he did not lose his way, or get captured. Accordingly, commanders preferred to station themselves at the center, preferably on a hill with a clear view, delegating responsibility to each section of the army to subordinates. Given that armies usually deployed in two lines, each subdivided into a center and two wings (flanks), at least six subordinate commanders were required. Their experience and ability usually made a significant impact on the outcome of the battle, given the likelihood that the overall commander would soon lose oversight of his forces once firing commenced. This made careful pre-battle planning all the more important. The chief conferred with his subordinates in a "council of war," taking advice and agreeing an overall plan in which each element of the army was assigned a specific task. The nineteenth-century fascination with charismatic supreme commanders led to much ridicule of this "war by committee," but it was not necessarily inferior, and eighteenth-century generals who did assume more exclusive control, such as Frederick the Great and Charles XII of Sweden, also suffered crushing defeats (at Kunnersdorf in 1759 and Poltava in 1709, respectively).

Strategy

Political and physical geography greatly influenced strategy, which remained largely in the mold formed in the later seventeenth century. Western, southern, and central European warfare hinged around efforts to contain potential French expansion; that in the north involved a struggle to dominate the Baltic, while eastern European conflict centered on Russian intrusion into the regions occupied by Poland-Lithuania and the Ottoman empire – two states that lost the military superiority they had enjoyed prior to the mid-seventeenth century. These developments are examined in greater detail in other chapters in this volume, which also explore the growing global dimension to European conflict, especially the consequences of Anglo-French rivalry. It is more appropriate here to examine strategy at an operational level. No permanent formations larger than a regiment existed prior to the later eighteenth century when regiments began to be brigaded together in peace as well as war, with two or more brigades forming a division. The corps system of the Napoleonic era represented a further development of these later eighteenth-century trends, by grouping several divisions, plus support troops, to create balanced formations containing sufficient infantry, cavalry, and artillery to operate alone, or in conjunction with other corps. Such flexible subdivisions did not yet exist and eighteenth-century generals simply commanded armies composed of as many regiments as the sovereign or supreme commander thought appropriate, or was able to provide. These armies detached troops as necessary, either to occupy places of importance or to form raiding or scouting parties. Large armies, especially those of the forces ranged against France, or Sweden during its last period of expansion under Charles XII, were generally composed of regiments supplied by several different states under their own subordinate generals. This aspect of coalition warfare added further command problems, and generals such as Marlborough or Eugene of Savoy spent much of each winter negotiating with alliance partners to supply the necessary troops and agree objectives for the coming spring campaign season.

The precise political configuration imparted specific features to each major war, yet it is possible to detect common patterns. This is clear in the case of France, which employed the same basic strategy from the Nine Years War (1688–97) through to the revolutionary and Napoleonic era. Since France usually faced opponents to the north and east, it had to deploy separate armies on these frontiers. One was generally larger and intended for that year's primary effort, while the other was given only a local objective, or simply instructed to defend existing positions. Forces operating in the north generally became enmeshed in lengthy siege operations because the Netherlands were studded with major fortified towns that could not be skirted without risk to supply lines. Forces in the east were usually split into two armies. One had to cross the Rhine and advance across the Bavarian plateau to attack Austria, France's principal opponent except for the era of the Franco-Austrian alliance (1756–89). The second had to cross the Alps, march through northern Italy to Trentino, and thence across the Alps into southern Austria. While alliances with Bavaria in the Wars of the Spanish and Austrian Succession twice enabled French forces to reach the Austrian frontier, forces operating in Italy generally failed, often because political considerations diverted troops to subsidiary operations against Habsburg possessions in southern Italy.

Naval Warfare

Warfare at sea is also covered elsewhere (chapter 26), but it is important to make some comparisons with land warfare here. Naval technology experienced few major changes from the end of the sixteenth century to the induction of steam propulsion in the first quarter of the nineteenth. Improvements in artillery were similar to those on land, while the main developments in sailing were those in navigation, with the ability to determine longitude accurately in the later eighteenth century, and the improved capacity for ships to remain at sea for longer periods. Otherwise, fleets shared many of the problems facing armies. They were expensive (if anything even more so), they lacked sufficient skilled, motivated recruits, and suffered a high number of casualties due to close-quarter fighting, inadequate medical care, and supply problems. Battles were likewise constrained by poor visibility and the difficulties in relaying information. Weather conditions imposed a natural lull in operations during winter, and could also affect battles directly, because a heavy swell made it difficult to fire guns on the lower deck without risk of taking in water. For this reason, many actions still took place within sight of land, rather than on the open ocean. Fighting on water also increased the consequences of mistakes, since the tightly packed crews were at risk if their ship's magazine exploded, or the ship sank.

Warfare in the Mediterranean and Baltic, as enclosed seas, still relied on oared galleys whose basic design went back to the ancient world. These could operate when the winds failed and, due to their shallow draught, could provide close support for troops on the coast. Tactics relied on gaining the advantage of the wind and using it to bring more guns to bear than could be brought by the enemy: the most famous action was to "cross the T," that is, to sail perpendicular to the enemy fleet, thereby giving it little opportunity to reply to broadside fire. This coup was difficult to achieve, and major fleet actions frequently dissolved into engagements between one or two ships from each side, just as they had done in the sixteenth century. This represented the maritime equivalent of the land clash between two long lines of infantry, with each regiment fighting it out with its immediate opponent. Such fights were also often decided with the same weapons as crews tried to board the opposing ship, and defeat its crew in hand-to-hand fighting. There were also important strategic parallels, with blockades representing the naval equivalent of sieges, and operations to command sea routes having a similar impact as those on land to dominate key bridges or passes. Privateers provided the seaborne equivalent of light troops on land, used for commerce raiding and interdicting supplies. Likewise, they gradually disappeared as such functions were undertaken by regular warships, generally specially designed for the purpose.

A Long or Short Eighteenth Century?

Writing on eighteenth-century warfare reflects the broader preoccupation with the questions of timespan, and how this is determined according to technological, political, or other "turning points." The prevailing view sees an important shift from the end of the Dutch War (1672–9) and the start of the War of the Spanish Succession. This period saw a change in weaponry, as the pike was replaced by the bayonet, while artillery experienced modest improvements in accuracy and mobility. As the tactical emphasis shifted towards firepower, logistical problems increased through the need to transport greater quantities of ammunition. The Piedmontese army had already dispensed with the pike in 1685, but the imperial army was the first first-rate force to do so. This decision, taken in 1688, is another example of the significance of the wars against the Ottomans for general European military change. The imperial commander, Margrave Ludwig of Baden, known as "Turkish Louis" from his long service in Hungary, decided that pikes were useless against the light irregular forces that formed the bulk of Ottoman armies and ordered the entire imperial infantry to adopt the bayonet and rely on firepower instead. This ended reliance on combined pike and shot, developed by Gustavus Adolphus in the Thirty Years War and perfected by Turenne and Montecuccoli during the Dutch War (Mugnai, 1998).

Another consequence of the Turkish Wars was the Habsburgs' greater use of light troops for guerrilla tactics. The latter term derives from the Spanish for "little war," a military phenomenon that spawned its own theoretical writings and practitioners during the eighteenth century. Unlike the nineteenth-century imperial idea of a "little war" involving a European punitive expedition against a more primitively armed non-European foe, the eighteenth-century concept encompassed a war of skirmishes, outposts, and raids considered necessary, but subsidiary to the "major" operations of the main armies composed of regular troops. Though the word is Spanish, much of the practice derived from conflict in the east, particularly the Great Turkish War of 1683–99, which involved a Holy League of the emperor, pope, tsar, king of Poland, Venetian senate, and many Italian princes. Ottoman troops were completely defeated on land and sea, especially at Zenta in 1697 by Eugene of Savoy, who learnt this new warfare here, rising rapidly to high command from his first campaign as a volunteer in 1683. Eugene and, on the French side, Villars, who fought with Eugene against the Turks in the imperial army, used these systems in the west during the Nine Years War. However, practices from the east only became fully integrated with western European war when Villars and Eugene rose as the supreme commanders of their respective armies in the War of the Spanish Succession. The new system was redeployed against the Ottomans by Eugene when Austria intervened in the Veneto-Turkish war of 1714–18 in 1716, scoring dramatic victories that forced the sultan to relinquish Serbia, including Belgrade. While the Ottomans have generally been considered in terminal decline, militarily as well as other respects, they in fact quickly redressed the balance, borrowing Western practice through experts such as the French general Bonneval, and defeating the Austrians in the next conflict in 1737–9.

Light troops and their tactics acquired greater importance through the growing reliance on supply trains to sustain operations. Not only could they move more swiftly than regular forces, being unencumbered by wagons or artillery, they were also ideal to raid enemy magazines and convoys. Habsburg light troops forced the French and Bavarian army to abandon Bohemia in 1742 by cutting off their supplies, and repeated their success two years later when the Prussians had invaded. The integration of such troops as a permanent element in European armies is a distinctively eighteenth-century feature. Long-serving professionals continued to provide the backbone of all major armies, however. Since it took two years to train an infantryman to be fully effective in the firing line, it was important to retain an experienced cadre around which units could be increased in wartime. Though soldiers were paid miserable wages, they collectively represented a major drain on state resources, placing a ceiling on how many could be maintained in peacetime. Overall strengths during the Seven Years War did not exceed those already mobilized during the War of the Spanish Succession. In any case, as we have seen with the problems of battlefield command, the advantage did not necessarily lie with the larger side, as Frederick's victories against superior numbers at the battles of Rossbach and Leuthen clearly demonstrate.

If these eighteenth-century characteristics were established by 1701–2, how long did they last? The eighteenth-century-style professional army disappeared with the French Revolution. Valmy (1792), ironically celebrated as the first victory for the revolutionary forces, in fact represented the last triumph of the old professional French artillery, whose firepower persuaded the invading Prussians to retreat. The next campaign, with its victory at Jemappes (November 1792), was a genuine triumph of the popular army composed of conscripts mobilized under the "Levée en Masse" ordered by the National Convention. Their poor training forced French generals to attack deployed in deep columns, exploiting mass rather than firepower. Consequently, they lost each time they encountered a well-drilled, old-style army in good defensive positions, such as the British in the peninsula after 1808. But there is another milestone. The Napoleonic period saw the last successful application of eighteenth-century logistical warfare in Kutuzov's defeat of Napoleon's invasion of Russia in 1812. By a combination of scorched earth as he retreated with skillful use of Cossacks and other light troops, Kutuzov not only forced the invaders to retreat, but almost completely destroyed them in the process. Cossacks were employed in the following 1813 and 1814 campaigns, but that of 1812 was the last time a general won by adhering strictly to eighteenth-century rules. So, in military terms the eighteenth century was definitely a long one, beginning around 1688, reaching maturity between 1701 and 1793, and coming to a close around 1812.

The Current State of Research

We have already noted the lasting impact of nineteenth-century prejudice on the historiography of eighteenth-century warfare. It remains to be seen how far this is still true today. Unfortunately, little has changed. The Seven Years War and American and French Revolutionary Wars continue to dominate writing in English. For instance, little else appeared in the last quarter of the twentieth century beyond a couple of good books on the War of the Austrian Succession (Anderson, 1995; Browning, 1993), and a useful account of the peninsular dimension to the War of the Spanish Succession left incomplete by its author's death (Hugill, 1991). The latter conflict is otherwise reduced to biographies of Marlborough and Eugene of Savoy and to accounts of the battle of Blenheim, regardless of what happened before, or in the ten years following Blenheim (whose real name, incidentally, was and still is Blindheim). Conflicts like the Great Northern War, the Turkish Wars, and those of the Polish Succession and the Quadruple Alliance are, at least in the English-speaking world, almost completely forgotten (Frost, 2000; Sutton, 1980). The later seventeenth century is better served, with recent major studies of military organization, training, and tactics (Lynn, 1997; Manning, 2006), as well as operations (Childs, 1991). Apart from coverage in general surveys (Black, 1994; Ferguson, 2003; Harding, 1999; Kennedy, 1988), the best current English writing approaches war only indirectly through social studies of military organizations (Rodger, 1986; something that the French also do well: Chagniot, 1985), or the relationship between conflict and political development. As for operations, coverage of these topics is patchy across Europe and the century generally (Storrs, 1999).

The recent tercentenary of the War of the Spanish Succession revived interest in the early eighteenth century in Britain, Germany, and Italy, prompting not just studies of Blenheim (some of doubtful value), but also new research on that conflict in Italy. Biographies have appeared, not just of key figures such as Eugene or Philip V, but also of the first Lord Cadogan, who served as Marlborough's subordinate (Jones, 1993; Kamen, 2001; Paoletti, 2001b; Watson, 2003). As a result, some authors are now looking more critically at the lazy assumptions of the past. For instance, the new interest in operational aspects raises serious doubts about the accuracy of widely accepted marching rates that were first calculated by the Hungarian historian Perjés in 1970, but which remain in print and are still cited today (Perjés, 2005). Another example is the supposed preference for siege warfare over decisive battles that is mistakenly thought to have persisted until Napoleon. Sieges had greatly varying results, while the relative significance of battles and other engagements can only be assessed when we know more about operations in general, rather than celebrated actions like Blenheim. While the work of Jeremy Black is helpful in reassessing the century as a whole, more focused work, such as that by Peter Wilson (1998) on German armies, confirms that much remains to be done to clarify our understanding of war in this period. The topic can only be explored in the necessary depth when the perspective is widened beyond those aspects of more immediate concern to the history of English-speaking countries to study the continent as a whole.

Bibliography

Åberg, A. and G. Göransson, *Karoliner* (Stockholm, 1998).

Ales, S., *Le regie truppe sarde 1750–1773* (Milan, 1989).

Ales, S., *Le regie truppe sarde 1773–1814* (Rome, 1989).

Anderson, M. S., *The War of the Austrian Succession 1740–1748* (Harlow, 1995).

Arcon Dominguez, J. L., "La guarnicìon de Barcelona en 1705," *Dragona*, 2(4) (1994), 44–9.

Aué, M. and M. Parent, *Vauban* (Vic-en-Bigorre, 1998).

Badolato, A. et al., *La battaglia di Guastalla* (Guastalla, 1984).

Barone, Enrico, *I grandi capitani dell'età moderna* (Rome, 1982).

Belhamissi, M., "Marine d'Alger et contrôle maritime à l'époque ottomane," in P. Alberini (ed.), *Aspetti ed attualità del potere marittimo in Mediterraneo nei secoli XII–XVII* (Rome, 1999), pp. 49–66.

Bérengér, J. (ed.) *La Révolution militaire en Europe (XV–XVIII siècles)* (Paris, 1997).

Black, J., *European Warfare 1660–1815* (London, 1994).

Black, J., *Britain as a Military Power 1688–1815* (London, 1999).

Brousse, Y., "Les réseaux d'information de Louvois dans les Provinces-Unies et aux Pays Bas catholiques, 1671–1691: guerre et reinsegnement à la fin du XVIIe siècle," *Révue internationale d'Histoire Militaire*, 82 (2002), 57–77.

Browning, R., *The War of the Austrian Succession* (New York, 1993).

Bruijn, J. R., "William III and his two navies," *Notes and Records of the Royal Society of London*, 43 (1989), 117–32.

Canosa, R., *Storia del Mediterraneo nel Seicento* (Rome, 1997).

Cerino Badone, G., F. Campagnolo, and M. Lucini, *Bandiere nel fango* (Turin, 2004).
Chagniot, J., *Paris et l'armée au XVIIIe siècle: Etude politique et sociale* (Paris, 1985).
Chandler, D. G., *Art of Warfare in the Age of Marlborough* (New York, 1994).
Chandler, D. G. (ed.), *Military Memoirs of Marlborough's Campaigns 1702–1712* (London, 1998).
Chandler, D. G., *Blenheim Preparation – the English Army on the March to the Danube* (Staplehurst, 2004).
Childs, J., *The Nine Years' War and the British Army, 1688–1697: The Operations in the Low Countries* (Manchester, 1991).
Cortelazzo, M., *Venezia, il Levante e il mare* (Pisa, 1989).
Corvisier, A., *La Bataille de Malplaquet 1709: L'Effondrement de la France évité* (Paris, 1997).
Coulet, H. (ed.), *L'Armée au XVIIIe siècle (1715–1789)* (Aix-en-Provence, 1999).
Delmas, J. (ed.), *De 1715 a 1871*, vol. 2 of A. Corvisier (ed.), *Histoire militaire de la France* (4 vols., Paris, 1992–4).
Duffy, C., *The Military Experience in the Age of Reason* (Ware, 1998).
Englund, P., *The Battle of Poltava: The Birth of the Russian Empire* (London, 1992).
Erichsen, J. and K. Heinemann, *Die Sclacht von Höchstädt. Brennpunkt Europas 1704* (Ostfildern, 2004).
Ferguson, N., *Empire: The Rise and Demise of the British World Order and the Lessons for Global Power* (New York, 2003).
Frost, R. I., *The Northern Wars: War, State and Society in Northern Europe, 1558–1721* (Harlow, 2000).
Gariglio D., *Le sentinelle di pietra: fortezze e cittadelle del Piemonte sabaudo* (Cuneo, 1997).
Gariglio, D., *Battaglie alpine del Piemonte sabaudo* (Collegno, 1999).
Giacomone Piana, P. and R. Dellepiane, *Militarium: fonti archivistiche e bibliografia per la storia militare della Repubblica di Genova (1528–1797), della Repubblica Ligure (1797–1805) e della Liguria napoleonica (1805–1814)* (Genoa, 2004).
Hanlon, G., *The Twilight of a Military Tradition: Italian Aristocrats and European Conflicts, 1560–1800* (London, 1998).
Harding, R., *Seapower and Naval Warfare 1650–1830* (London, 1999).
Hattendorf, J., *England in War of Spanish Succession: A Study of English View and Conduct of Grand Strategy* (New York, 1987).
Hohrath, D. and K. Gerteis (eds.), *Die Kriegskunst im Lichte der Vernunft* (2 vols., Hamburg, 1999–2000).
Houlding, *Fit for Service: The Training of the British Army 1715–1795* (Oxford, 1981).
Hugill, J. A. C., *No Peace Without Spain* (Oxford, 1991).
Ilari, V., G. Boeri, and C. Paoletti, *Tra i Borboni e gli Asburgo: le armate terrestri e navali italiane nelle guerre del primo Settecento (1701–1732)* (Ancona, 1996).
Ilari, V., G. Boeri, and C. Paoletti, *La corona di Lombardia: guerre ed eserciti nell'Italia del medio Settecento (1733 – 1763)* (Ancona, 1997).
Ilari, V., P. Crociani, and C. Paoletti, *Bell'Italia militar* (Rome, 2001).
Jones, J. R., *Marlborough* (Cambridge, 1993).
Kamen, H., *Philip V of Spain* (New York, 2001).
Kennedy, P., *The Rise and Fall of the Great Powers: Economic Change and Military Conflict from 1500 to 2000* (New York, 1988).
Kroll, S. and M. Kaiser (eds.), *Militär und ländliche Gesellschaft in der Frühen Neuzeit* (Hamburg, 2000).
Lenman, B., *Britain's Colonial Wars 1688–1783* (Harlow, 2001).
Lo Basso, L., *Uomini da remo: galee e galeotti nel Mediterraneo in età moderna* (Milan, 2004).

Lopes Pires Nunes, A., "Les guerres hollandaises au Brésil du XVIIe siècle: confrontation de deux écoles militaires," in *Acta of the XVIII Annual Conference of the International Commission for Military History*, held in Turin 1992 (Gaeta, 1993), pp. 457–62.
Lynn, J. A. (ed.), *Feeding Mars: Logistics in Western Warfare from the Middle Age to the Present* (Boulder, 1993).
Lynn, J. A., *Giant of the Grande Siècle: The French Army 1610–1715* (Cambridge, 1997).
Mandelli, M., E. Sala, and F. Testa, *La battaglia di Cassano: protagonisti, storia e vicende umane della battaglia del 16 agosto 1705 e della Guerra di Successione Spagnola in Lombardia* (Cassano d'Adda, 2005).
Manning, R. B., *An Apprenticeship in Arms: The Origins of the British Army 1585–1702* (Oxford, 2006).
Mugnai, B., *L'esercito ottomano da Candia a Passarowitz (1645–1718)* (2 vols., Venice, 1998).
Mugnai, B., "Confinari e Temerari: il militärgrenze in Croazia, Ungheria e Transilvania fra Seicento e Settecento," in *Frontiere e fortificazioni di frontiera* (Florence, 2001).
Nosworthy, B., *The Anatomy of Victory: Battle Tactics 1689–1763* (New York, 1990).
Paoletti C., "Logistica e assedi delle guerre del settecento," *Panoplia*, 27–8 (1996), 28–34.
Paoletti, C., *Gli Italiani in armi: cinque secoli di storia militare nazionale 1494–2000* (Rome, 2001a).
Paoletti, C., *Il principe Eugenio di Savoia* (Rome, 2001b).
Paoletti, C., "Errori d'impostazione storiografica e nuova valutazione dell'assedio di Tolone e della campagna sabauda in Provenza del 1707," in *Studi storico-militari 2001* (Rome, 2004), pp. 259–76.
Paoletti, C., "Prince Eugene of Savoy, the Toulon expedition of 1707 and the English historians: a dissenting view," *Journal of Military History*, 70 (2006), 939–62.
Perini, S., *La difesa militare della Terraferma veneta nel Settecento* (Sottomarina, 1998).
Perjés, G., "Army provisioning, logistics and strategy in the second half of the 17th century," repr. in J. Black (ed.), *Warfare in Europe 1650–1792* (Aldershot, 2005), pp. 109–60.
Preto, P., "Un aspetto sconosciuto del conflitto veneto-turco in Dalmazia e in Levante: la guerra chimica e batteriologica," *Atti e memorie della Società Dalmata di Storia patria*, ns 3, 14 (1989–91), 13–29.
Rodger, N. A. M., *The Wooden World: An Anatomy of the Georgian Navy* (London, 1986).
Sterrantino, F., et al., *La guerra della Lega di Augusta fino alla battaglia di Orbassano* (Turin, 1993).
Storrs, C. D., *War, Diplomacy and the Rise of Savoy, 1690–1720* (Cambridge, 1999).
Sutton, J. L., *The King's Honor and the King's Cardinal: The War of the Polish Succession* (Lexington, 1980).
Vergé-Franceschi, M., *La Marine française au XVIIIe siècle* (Condé-sur-Noireau, 1996).
Watson, J. N. P., *Marlborough's Shadow: The Life of the First Earl Cadogan* (Barnsley, 2003).
Wheeler, J. S., *The Making of a World Power: War and the Military Revolution in Seventeenth-Century England* (Stroud, 1999).
Wilson, P. H., *German Armies: War and German Politics 1648–1806* (London, 1998).

Chapter Thirty

Participatory Politics

David M. Luebke

On February 14, 1798, several thousand Swiss peasants gathered at the village of Gossau, where they cast off the authority of their lord and ruler, the abbot of St. Gallen, and declared themselves *citoyens* of a free "republic." It would be sovereign and "purely democratic": henceforth, a citizen-assembly would elect all executive officers and justices, make laws, and declare war and peace. Their self-conscious use of the French term for "citizen" echoed slogans of the revolution, and one could be forgiven for thinking that the peasants had also embraced the revolutionary ideal of universal and equal rights for all. But an analysis of the short-lived "Republic of the Territory of St. Gallen" shows that what the citizens gathered at Gossau wanted most were local autonomy and the kind of peasant-householder democracy that had existed for centuries in cantons nearby (Suter, 2004). The political model they wished to emulate, in other words, was home-grown, not revolutionary but medieval in origin. When the French introduced to Switzerland a centralized system of national, republican representation based on popular sovereignty and equality before the law, the peasants resisted with arms and violence. By the end of 1798, the new constitution had, for them, come to mean the loss of democracy and self-rule.

These events confront us with the paradoxes, continuities, and transformations of popular politics in eighteenth-century Europe. They show the ease with which ordinary people appropriated new political concepts and used them for their own purposes; they also hint at the variety of political models that were available to ordinary people, even within a corporatist framework of norms and expectations. On the other hand, they expose the constraints that law and custom typically imposed on formal involvement by ordinary people in decision-making – even in Switzerland, where the majority of inhabitants had little more say in politics than did subjects of the king of France.

Perhaps most importantly, the incident at Gossau and many others like it demolish the old stereotype of Europe's laboring classes as politically incapacitated or able to act only impulsively, in response to immediate stimuli. With few exceptions, that verdict was shared by historians across the ideological spectrum of nineteenth- and early twentieth-century Europe. Since the 1950s, however, an outpouring of research on the forms and themes of popular politics has rendered the stereotype untenable.

A Companion to Eighteenth-Century Europe, First Edition. Edited by Peter H. Wilson.
© 2014 John Wiley & Sons, Ltd. Published 2014 by John Wiley & Sons, Ltd.

Building on the pioneering work of George Rudé and E. P. Thompson, historians of eighteenth-century European society and politics have become more attuned to the strategies that common folk deployed to achieve their ends (Rudé, 1959, 1981; Thompson, 1963, 1971). As a result, historians are inclined to interpret the dynamics of power as a many-sided and multi-layered communication in which ordinary people were active participants, sometimes in confrontation with the state and the privileged orders, sometimes as donors of legitimacy, and always as arbiters of effective governance in everyday life. Inevitably, the ability of villagers and townsfolk to set the terms of these interactions was modest. Still, popular notions about justice and the common good exerted a subtle but pervasive pressure from below, one that the powerful could ill afford to ignore.

Rudé and Thompson also framed subsequent debates over the role of ordinary people in the historical processes that led to the upheavals of the century's final decade. While Rudé looked for evidence of proto-revolutionary sentiments among ordinary people, Thompson stressed the ongoing captivity of popular politics to paternalist models of social order. This essay charts a course between these viewpoints, stressing both the enduring power of corporatist norms and expectations, while also suggesting the ways in which ordinary people used these norms to challenge authority and effect change. It begins with an assessment of corporatist institutions of representation and analyzes the effects of both stratification and village sociability on their inclusiveness. It then discusses the informal means that ordinary people used to get their concerns heard, followed by an analysis of unsanctioned forms of popular political action and their relationship both to litigation and the guiding norms of popular political culture. Finally, it addresses the relationship between popular contention and two, relatively new, forces in eighteenth-century political life, the press and public opinion.

Bodies of Representation

During the eighteenth century, most European states, no matter how absolutist, retained some ceremonial vestige of the idea that legitimate rule required the consent of "the people." Even in France, the coronation liturgy asked the people to approve the royal anointee – an endorsement that was assumed to be given tacitly. A more direct sort of approbation was conferred at public homage ceremonies for newly crowned monarchs, in which subject populations gave binding oaths of obedience in exchange for promises to protect and defend. Such occasions were still quite common: in September 1786, for example, the newly crowned king Friedrich Wilhelm II of Prussia toured his realm to receive the homage of his subjects in person. In more quotidian settings too, the people were invited to endorse public acts of state power, such as criminal executions or royal proclamations (Lucas, 1988). But these occasions also exemplified another broad tendency, to squeeze the people out of formal participation in the generation of authority. The homage ceremony, once an occasion for hard-knuckled bargaining between lord and subject, had by the mid-eighteenth century lost constitutional function. To enlightened observers, these rituals had degenerated into empty charades, devoid of any power-conferring function. In 1775 Louis XVI drew the appropriate conclusions and expunged the ritual of popular acclamation from his own coronation.

What about bodies of political representation? To what extent did provincial or national assemblies – called diets or estates – enable ordinary people to engage in public life? Since the thirteenth century, these institutions had been shaped by the Roman legal maxim "that which concerns all must be approved by all" and by an assumption that the "sounder part" (*sanior pars*) of any social order should represent the whole. Underlying these precepts, from the standpoint of subjects, was a powerful and implicitly contractual expectation of reciprocity – the idea that legitimate power depended on the provision of protection and justice in return for dues, services, and tax payments. These concepts did not rule out the possibility that commoners might be represented directly as a corporate member of the social whole. Under the tricameral system that prevailed in most of continental Europe, "the people" were typically represented in one of three chambers or *curiae*, each possessing a single vote, alongside the nobility and representatives of the clergy. In the Estates General of France, for example, the third estate was composed of delegates chosen through a layered system of balloting that was broadly inclusive at the bottom, communal rung. But of course that body was not summoned between 1614 and 1789. Until the revolution, therefore, bodies of representation in France were confined to *pays d'états* located on the frontiers of the realm, where commoners were usually represented by delegates from a handful of privileged towns. Typical of these was the diet of Burgundy, in which 25 towns had full membership (Swann, 2003). Across the Pyrenees in Spain, King Philip V effectively abolished representation in Spain by consolidating the Catalan and Castilian Cortes into a single body and then depriving it of any fiscal or legislative function. The Cortes met only three times in the eighteenth century, and then only to swear loyalty to the king or to ratify matters of succession (Lynch, 1989).

In central and eastern Europe representative bodies were more plentiful, although not especially inviting toward commoners. In 1769 the German jurist Johann Jacob Moser surveyed 136 territories of the Holy Roman Empire and found that fully two-thirds of them contained territorial diets, or vestiges of them. In most cases, however, the third estate was composed of delegates from a few privileged cities. The diets' business, moreover, was increasingly conducted by standing commissions, not by the assemblies in plenum (Krüger, 2003). Several southern German territories that had no landed nobility were important exceptions to this pattern – most notably the duchy of Württemberg, where the estates were composed of commoners and clergymen. Like their colleagues in France and Spain, however, eighteenth-century German princes were increasingly disinclined to summon their estates – the Bavarian estates last met, for example, in 1669. The Polish-Lithuanian Sejm, by contrast, enjoyed a legislative monopoly and continued to exercise it until the final partition in 1795. But it also stood out for its social exclusivity: only nobles could stand for election or participate in the choice of a delegate (see chapter 15).

More inclusive were the representative bodies in an arc of states and provinces across northern Europe, from Cornwall to the frontiers of Russia. In Britain, members of Parliament were elected by 203 boroughs, two universities, and 40 counties, plus 24 Welsh and 45 Scottish constituencies; each English county elected two members, and anyone in possession of property valued at 40 shillings could cast a vote. This corresponded to roughly 24 percent of adult males in 1715. The North Sea coast of continental Europe was another zone in which rural corporations participated directly in territorial assemblies. The Dutch province of Friesland, for example, was composed of 30 rural districts (*grietenijen*), each of which elected its own magistrates (*grietmannen*) and chose delegates to the territorial estates; electoral rights extended to any adult male who met certain modest property qualifications. In neighboring East Frisia, the male freeholders in each village were entitled to elect a single, communal delegate to the third chamber of the territorial estates (Luebke, 2004). Similar arrangements were found in polities along the North Frisian coast in Ditmarschen, Schleswig, and Holstein. Unique among the national assemblies, the four-chambered Swedish Riksdag reserved two *curiae* for commoners, the third estate for burghers, and the fourth for representatives of the peasantry. Its electoral franchise was arguably the broadest in Europe: all freeholders and tenants with leases on Crown farms could vote in the election of delegates to the fourth estate – about two-thirds of all peasant householders (Roberts, 1986). The most inclusive assemblies of all were found in the Alpine peasant republics of Switzerland, where since the fourteenth century sovereign lawmaking authority had rested with an annual gathering (*Landsgemeinde*) of all adult male householders.

Stratification and Sociability

This brief overview invites two qualifications. The first concerns the effects of socioeconomic stratification on political participation. Whatever its cause – the commercialization of agriculture, say, or the stagnation of artisan production – stratification tended to diminish the number of individuals entitled to participate in elections and local decision-making generally. In Britain, the concentration of wealth had by 1800 reduced the electorate to around 17 percent of adult males. It also trimmed the circle of participation in Europe's city-states and peasant republics. The ruling patriciate of Bern, for example, shrank between 1630 and 1745 from 139 to only 77 families. Other Swiss city-states, such as Zurich, had more inclusive guild-based regimes, yet even there the number of artisans with a seat on the city council dwindled from 107 in 1599 to only 34 in 1790 (Braun, 1984). In the Dutch Republic, too, "regent" families kept a tight grip on civic and provincial government. Holland, for example, was ruled by the 36-member Senate of Amsterdam, which elected its own members to lifetime terms. Even Europe's peasant republics were becoming more oligarchic. In East Frisia, farm consolidation had by 1725 reduced the number of enfranchised householders to one adult male in ten. In the canton of Schwyz, similarly, a system of fees for candidacy to public office promoted the formation of a semi-hereditary ruling elite (Braun, 1984). Indeed, everywhere one turns in eighteenth-century Europe, the same oligarchic trend recurs with numbing regularity: the consolidation of wealth concentrated local power in ever fewer hands.

A second qualification tempers the first by considering political *sociability* – the din of local chatter and deal-making that enveloped the choice of a delegate or elected official. Consider the political culture of Georgian Britain: until the 1960s this field was dominated by Lewis Namier and his students, who argued that Britain's relatively open franchise masked a reality of aristocratic coercion in which few could vote freely. Patronage, rotten boroughs, and a dose of venality, they argued, anesthetized the electorate and kept Parliament immune to democratizing reform. All this reinforced their Whiggish narrative of progress toward democratic modernity, but at the price of writing ordinary people, and most electors along with them, out of the story. Critics of this analysis argue that it rests on anachronistic assumptions about the nature of patronage and the purpose of elections. Their studies of electioneering have exposed the enormous costs of patronage in outlays for canvassing agents, electoral treating, processions, pamphlets, and so on (O'Gorman, 1989). A new consensus has emerged around this research, which recognizes patronage as the dominant fact of political life but also understands it as a reciprocal relationship that required constant upkeep. This newer research also shows that elections were communal events – highly participatory occasions in which patronage was exposed to public scrutiny, and in which loyalties were renewed or revised and enmities resolved or left to fester. What once looked like mere vote-buying turns out to have been an elaborate ritual of local power (Dickinson, 1995).

The same criticism has been applied to politicking in the oligarchic Dutch provinces and Swiss cantons (Suter, 2004). It could also be extended to Namierite treatments of the Polish-Lithuanian Sejm. Because so many Poles held noble status – one recent estimate puts the figure at 6.5 percent of the total population in 1772 – these elections were almost as inclusive as their English counterparts. In some provinces, such as Mazovia, the nobility comprised as much as 20 percent of the total population. Delegates to the Polish-Lithuanian Sejm were chosen at provincial assemblies, or *sejmiki*, where the theatrics of patronage played out among magnates, middling nobles, and the "barefoot" gentry, many of whom were landless; as in Britain, decisions were reached by simple majority, electors demanded plenty of cajoling, and elections were often contested (Lukowski, 1991). The *sejmiki*, in short, were a good deal more inclusive in practice than they appeared on paper.

These emphases on social process and communication converge with analyses that situate representative assemblies within a much broader, multipolar process of bargaining between claimants to national or sovereign power, local elites, and common folk (Brake, 1998; Schulze, 1980; Tilly, 2004). In this matrix any combination of alliances was possible, and the eighteenth century yields many examples of them all. Ordinary subjects might align their values and interests with privileged corporations, such as the sovereign *parlements* of France, against the fiscal demands of money-grubbing monarchs, as in that kingdom's constitutional and fiscal crises of the 1770s and 1780s. Or they might ally with a prince against other orders – as in 1762, when Duke Carl Eugen of Württemberg tried to circumvent the territorial estates by building up consultative assemblies of village representatives in each of the duchy's administrative districts, or in 1772, when peasant delegates to the Swedish Riksdag acquiesced in Gustav III's coup against the estates' sovereignty and the officeholders who dominated its privileged chambers. Or finally they might try to topple an alliance between national and local elites – as in 1787, when Dutch Patriots overthrew, if only temporarily, a system of patronage that bound Orangist "regent" families throughout the republic to the hereditary *Stadhouder*, William V.

Pressure "From Below"

This approach also shifts attention toward the informal channels of political communication that ordinary subjects used to articulate their values and to press their interests. Chief among these were petitions, arguably the most broadly privileged form of political communication that existed under the *ancien régime*. In France, the Estates General of Blois codified the right to petition in 1576; in England, it had roots in the thirteenth century and was codified in the 1689 Bill of Rights. This universality was matched in the volume of petitions flowing toward authorities of every kind. While on his 1773 tour through Galicia and Transylvania, for example, the future emperor Joseph II was deluged with upwards of 15,000 petitions. So great was the tide of petitions that governments throughout Europe struggled to stem or channel it. In England, the Tumultuous Petitioning Act of 1661 prohibited groups of 10 or more petitioners from approaching the king or Parliament; in the Habsburg lands, the Imperial Court Ordinance of 1720 likewise forbade personal approaches to the emperor. But monarchs and their ministers also recognized that limits on the right to petition might undermine the legitimacy of royal authority. As one eighteenth-century Italian observer put it, "those who think to do away with petitions would overthrow the entire system of state" (quoted in Nubola, 2001).

It should come as no surprise, then, that petitions could have a profound effect on legislation. A study of the Landgraviate of Hessen-Kassel in Germany, for example, shows that its territorial estates functioned as a kind of clearing-house for popular demands, many of which found their way into ordinances on everything from tithes and brewing to taxation, fire insurance, hunting, and schools. Even though the rural population had no formal representation in these deliberations, the impact of their petitions was considerable. Beginning in the 1760s, for example, a steady stream of communal petitions prompted the estates to call for a reorganization of rural administration, which the Landgrave finally enacted in 1798 (Würgler, 1998). Recent research indicates that Hessen-Kassel was not unusual in this. In patrician Bern, popular demand for alms was the driving force behind the formation of a cantonal system of poor-relief. And in Prussia a series of petitions provoked Frederick II in 1779 to set in motion reforms that led, eventually, to the General Law Code in 1792 (Luebke, 1999).

The case of Hessen-Kassel is also exposes the readiness of elites to use petitions and signature-gathering to mobilize pressure against competitors in the game of power. In 1731 the Landgrave solicited *desideria* from communities throughout the territory and then summoned the estates to collate them into laws "for the general good of the fatherland." Here, petitions were exploited to strengthen a monarch's exclusive right to receive them, but this by no means exhausted their full range of uses. In October 1782, self-styled Dutch "Patriots" garnered signatures from all ranks of urban society in support of more inclusive government. This potential was realized most fully in Britain, where between the Restoration and the Septennial Act of 1715, mass petitions to Parliament and addresses to the king numbered in excess of 5,000 (Knights, 2005). After an early-Georgian ebb, their numbers surged again in the 1760s (Phillips, 1982). Often these campaigns worked to strengthen a monarch's position. But just as often they mobilized opposition: in 1706—7, 79 addresses from 116 localities in Scotland registered opposition to the Act of Union; in 1774–6, signatories to petitions concerning the government's American policy numbered over 50,000 (Dickinson, 1995).

It is not credible to portray these campaigns as cynical manipulations of gullible subjects. The very act of organizing a mass petition presupposed an ideological readiness on the part of British elites to embrace popular involvement in political discourse

(Knights, 2005). A vivid illustration of this willingness was the Gordon Riots of May and June 1780, when parliamentary elites mobilized London workingmen in a mass petition for repeal of the 1778 Catholic Relief Act (Rogers, 1998). That the campaign turned violent only shows how difficult it was to contain popular politics. As for gullibility, the social pattern of subscribing in mass petitions reveals that Britons who considered themselves entitled to a voice in politics far outnumbered those who actually had one. In the boroughs, the proportion of non-enfranchised signatories ranged as high as 87.6 percent (Phillips, 1989). The political nation, in short, was much larger than the electorate. The same sort of evidence from East Frisia in 1725–7 shows that there, too, electoral franchise was no barrier to a sense of political entitlement (Luebke, 2004).

The contrast with France is revealing: France lacked institutions of national representation and therefore the informal practices that nourished the growth of a political nation in Britain and the Low Countries could not arise there. Campaigns to solicit expressions of popular sentiment were seen as seditious and treated accordingly – unless initiated by the monarch, of course, as the *cahiers de doléances* were in 1789. By the same token, studies of the French provincial estates suggest that their responsiveness to petitions fell short as well. An analysis of the estates of Artois shows petitions from non-noble corporations generated only one-sixth of the assembly's business; it also shows that number of petitions received dropped precipitously after the regency and remained low for the rest of the century (Legay, 2001). Neither were the estates of Burgundy especially receptive to pressures "from below" – after all, the town mayors who populated the Burgundian third estate were beholden to the royal governors who appointed them to municipal office. But these barriers no more demonstrate the political incapacity of French subjects than do the unreformed electoral customs of Hanoverian England: throughout the eighteenth century, many towns struggled to gain a seat at the Burgundian table, though mostly without success until the 1780s (Swann, 2003). These provincial obstacles directed popular attention on the sovereign courts, especially the *parlement* of Paris, which could take the people's concerns "to the foot of the throne in ways that nobody else could" (Doyle, 1987).

These comparisons also suggest some of the ways in which structures of power and political communication shaped one another. In Britain, the massive concentration of power in a national Parliament within a restricted electoral system placed a premium on mobilizing patronage in the competition for votes. Similarly, the concentration of sovereign law-making authority in the Riksdag during Sweden's "Age of Liberty" (1720–72) drew local concerns into deliberation at the highest levels. In France, by contrast, the relative paucity of what Charles Tilly calls "protected consultation" – institutional frameworks for binding negotiation between ordinary people and governmental agents that were shielded from the arbitrary use of coercive force – combined with a mutually beneficial alliance between the Crown and provincial estates to encapsulate popular politics locally (Tilly, 2004). This arrangement improved the efficiency of royal taxation, at least until the mid-eighteenth century, and re-entrenched the privilege of local elites: in return for secure and regular tax payments, provincial notables got patronage, public works contracts, and prestige (Beik, 1985; Legay, 2001). This convergence of interest between the Crown and the provincial estates was not without conflict, of course (Swann, 2003). Still, the fact remains that, in France, no representative institution enabled common folk to counteract the alliance of royal power with local privilege.

Rebellion or Litigation?

So far this survey has examined legally sanctioned channels of political engagement, formal as well as informal. The topic of forbidden political action – demonstrations, riots, and rebellions – raises an important shift in the pattern of eighteenth-century popular politics: the near-disappearance from western Europe of large-scale rebellions between 1705 and 1775. For 70 years after the revolts of the millenarian Camisards in the Cévennes (1705) and the Tard-avisés in Quercy-Périgord (1707), no uprising in France achieved the scale, duration, or violence that had characterized countless upheavals in the two preceding centuries. The empire experienced plenty of small-scale rebellions, but none of them burst the confines of small states or provinces, as many earlier revolts had done (Luebke, 1997). Large-scale tax rebellions were virtually unknown in eighteenth-century Britain, despite spectacular increases in the overall burden. The same shift characterized cities all over Europe: with few exceptions, urban citizenries were unwilling or unable to rise in arms against municipal authorities.

To explain the peace in France, Emmanuel Le Roy Ladurie cited the improved economic climate of the eighteenth century; more predictable methods of tax collection; greater solicitude on the part of royal *intendants*; and the tutelage of an increasingly royalist Catholic clergy (Le Roy Ladurie, 1974). Others invoke the emerging alliance between royal power and provincial elites: after the Fronde, the latter rarely heeded the appeals of peasant communes for concerted resistance against royal taxmen, abandoning them instead to the horrors of louisquatorzian repression (Brown, 1999). On the few occasions when noble or urban elites *did* ally with the lower orders against a king, foreign invasion or the founding of a new dynasty was usually the spark. The most explosive of these took place in Hungary, where in 1703 peasants led by a fugitive serf, Tamás Esze, joined with Magyar nobles, led by the magnate Ferenc II Rákóczi, in an attempt to cast off Habsburg rule. Similarly in 1705, Catalan peasants, nobles, and townsfolk united to oppose invading Bourbon forces and the threat they posed to traditional Aragonese *fueros*; that same year, Bavarian peasants and townsfolk united against an Austrian army of occupation, only to be massacred on Christmas Eve. Likewise the Jacobite risings of 1715 and 1745 drew recruits from all ranks of society in Scotland and the counties of northern England.

The dates of these upheavals are telling: except for the Jacobite risings, all occurred under the sign of war in the century's first decade. But it would be mistaken to read some new political quiescence into the dearth of large-scale rebellions after 1705. One reason, arguably, is that the tactical sophistication of ordinary people evolved in tandem with the elaboration of judicial tribunals and state power generally. French rural communities had a long history of contesting the rights of seigneurs in sovereign courts – the *parlements* – but if Hilton Root's analysis is correct, both the volume and ambitions of anti-seigneurial litigation were increasing in eighteenth-century France. Moreover, because royal *intendants* had by mid-century taken over most of the political and judicial functions that had once justified the collection of seigneurial dues, French peasants were less willing to accept without question the legal bases of a lord's claim (Root 1987). Though not without misgivings, French artisans and journeymen likewise turned to the courts to impose order on the highly conflictual world of trades (Sonenscher, 1989). All this litigation reinforced the Parisian *parlement*'s widely popular claim to represent, in the absence of Estates General, the nation to the king.

In Germany, the resort to law is often described as the "judicialization" (*Verrechtlichung*) of social conflict – the deliberate channeling of social conflicts into legal disputes among subjects, lords, and princes, often before tribunals of imperial justice, as a means to prevent local conflicts from escalating into regional conflagrations (Schulze, 1980). In effect, judicialization formalized the same three-way negotiations between sovereign power-holders, local elites, and subject populations that were governed elsewhere by the balance of power. Subject populations took full advantage of these tribunals: in any given year, lords and princes of the empire comprised 30–40 percent of defendants appearing before the Imperial Chamber Court in Wetzlar. As in the royal courts of France, moreover, the objects of litigation expanded well beyond seigneurial dues and services to include the preservation of forests and commons against enclosure, their exploitation by princely monopolists, and the ravages of the noble hunt. In the process of all this litigation, German peasants acquired far more legal security in landholdings than their French neighbors. They also became habituated to the metaphors, fictions, and rhetorical styles of judicial transaction.

Did litigation also blunt the militancy of common folk? Favorable interim rulings often convinced litigants to dispense with force. But as many studies now show, litigation did not preclude more belligerent forms of pressure and might even encourage them. A study of uprisings in the Wetterau region of Germany reveals that when an imperial court agreed to hear their case, litigants withheld the disputed seigneurial dues and services pending a judicial decision (Trossbach, 1987). Moreover, the final ruling in one case might generate new conflicts elsewhere – as in 1774, when a decision of the Paris *parlement* to abolish fixed price schedules for hats alarmed the silk-weavers of Lyons (Sonenscher, 1989). Litigation, moreover, was a two-way street: while it helped prevent the outbreak of large-scale rebellion, it also constrained arbitrary rule and exposed judicial institutions to appropriation and manipulation. As a recent study of the Papal States shows, the cumulative effect of communal litigation was to cultivate "adversarial literacy" among rural folk – a manner of using the written word that exhibited keen sensitivity to the nuances of official language and, in making its legal claims stick, confounded the textual monopoly of ruling elites (Castiglione, 2005).

Bread and Community

Rebellion, in short, did not so much disappear as change shape. For 40 years, historians of Britain and France have studied the high incidence of local riots, demonstrations, and sabotage and tracked their fluctuations in response to economic crises and political events (Thompson, 1971; Stevenson, 1979; Bohstedt, 1983; Rogers, 1998; Nicolas, 2002). Their researches have exposed a symbolically rich repertoire of contentious performances, ranging from theatrical parody, verbal taunts, *charivari*, and "rough music" to the burning-in-effigy of excise men or the demolition of turnpikes, to say nothing of attacks on property, such as the maiming of hunting dogs, or the breaking of machine looms. Like "adversarial literacy," these performances often appropriated symbols of community and justice to legitimate protest. Riots against high prices for grain – far and away the most common type of protest in eighteenth-century England – often began with public processions, replete with fifes and flag-waving, that associated their demand for "just prices" with communal norms of solidarity and the equitable provision of life's necessities. In France too, tactics such as the interdiction of grain exports (*entrave*) and the sale of confiscated grain at just prices (*taxation populaire*) were crafted to define grain riots as morally imperative communal correctives against selfish hoarding and illegal exports. In both countries, women were often at the forefront of grain riots because of their prominence among purveyors of food in the marketplace and their emblematic status as caregivers to family and community (Bouton, 1993).

The causes of rioting varied greatly from place to place, of course. Ecological disasters, such as the catastrophic harvest failure of 1709–10 in France, explain some of the variability across time and space. Yet certain long-term trends cannot be reduced to environmental or narrowly economic factors. In England, grain riots became more numerous as the century wore on and increasingly were tied to political developments that were related only tangentially to the price of wheat or rye. Protests during the famine of 1740–1, for example, had been centered in East Anglia and directed solely against grain exports. The grain riots of 1794–5, by contrast, spread throughout the kingdom and were fused to protests over the costs of war (Rogers, 1998; Stevenson, 1979). In France, too, the entire century was punctuated by thousands of small-scale protests – over 8,000 distinct events between 1700 and 1793. The targets of French riots differed from those of their British counterparts: a plurality of protests – some 40 percent – were aimed at the system of royal taxation, whereas grain riots made up only 17 percent of the total (Markoff, 1996; Nicolas, 2002). As in Britain, however, the frequency and severity of French protests also rose steadily from 1760 on. In Spain, grain riots were far less frequent than in either Britain or France, but politicization was a denominator common to all three realms: everywhere, rioters responded to the expansion and liberalization of grain markets and the commercialization of agriculture (Le Roy Ladurie, 1974). They did not always grasp this connection fully. But just as often they made it explicit – most famously in March 1766, when townsfolk all across Castile rioted against Charles III's sweeping abolition of price controls on grain; and in the "Flour War" of 1775, when malnourished peasants throughout the Paris Basin rioted against the physiocratic grain market reforms of Controller General Turgot (Bouton, 1993; Rodriguez, 1973). In all these cases, grain riots amounted to assertions of communal control over vital goods in the political vacuum left by governments in slow retreat from the regulation of food and labor.

It is one thing to assert solidarity, quite another to enforce it. Grain riots were not only aimed at market liberalization; they were also orchestrated to test the communal loyalties of fence-sitters, defectors, and liminal figures such as priests, millers, mercers, and village headmen (Bohstedt, 1983; Kaplan, 1976). Thus, while rioters spoke of mutuality and solidarity in pursuit of the common good, their actions revealed the vulnerability of communal bonds to the corrosive forces of stratification and the commercialization of agriculture. There is small wonder in this, for the material bases of communal solidarity were under assault as never before. In England, the first great wave of private enclosure Acts between 1755 and 1780 eroded the already weakened common right, driving deeper the gap between prosperous tenant farmers and the mass of the rural poor. In parts of England, France, and Germany, well-to-do farmers accomplished a kind of enclosure "from below," first by monopolizing access to commons and then by partitioning them outright (Gutton, 1979; Root, 1987). In rural Europe, the eighteenth century was the age of the *coq du village* and *Bauernfürst*.

Contention and the Public Sphere

Communal values, then, still governed popular politics. And yet there is also no denying the presence of new and potentially transforming elements in eighteenth-century political culture. For Jürgen Habermas, a crucial innovation was the formation of a "bourgeois public sphere" – an urbane, socially inclusive, and autonomous field of debate that took shape in new forms of sociability (cafés, salons, reading societies) and new modes of communication (weekly newspapers, critical journals, novels). Its ethos was rational and universalizing – in a word, enlightened – and its politics ultimately ran at odds with the "representative public sphere," by which Habermas means the rituals and ceremonies that displayed royal power before a segmented society, permitted only to applaud its glories (Habermas, 1991). But as Habermas acknowledges, his scheme excludes a broad spectrum of "plebeian" communications that includes many of the forms discussed so far – demonstrations, petitioning, tavern sociability, and so on. Setting bourgeois sociability to one side, then, did new media affect the political culture of ordinary people? If so, when and how did they appropriate these tools?

At first blush, a link between "protected communication" and print culture seems obvious. Press freedom arrived first wherever the political nation was largest, and in this sense Britain was less exceptional than emblematic of a larger European correlation: censorship lapsed there *first*, when Parliament allowed the long ineffective Licensing Act to expire in 1694, giving rise to chatty "moral weeklies" such as the *Tatler* and the *Spectator*. But press freedom eventually spread throughout the northern arc of politically inclusive states. In 1766, for example, the Swedish Riksdag codified a de facto press freedom that had been emerging since 1750; in the Dutch Republic, provincial "regents" loosened their grip in the 1770s. The number of journals and the size of reading publics grew accordingly. Press freedom in Sweden led to the formation its first dailies, the rivals *Dagligt allehanda* and the *Almänna tidingar*, in 1769 and 1770 respectively; by 1780 every Dutch province had at least one regularly appearing newspaper. The evidence of stamp duties in Britain indicates that, by 1775, the "epidemic Frenzy of reading News-papers" had infected upwards of 12 million (Brewer, 1976; Harris, 1996). To be sure, censorship also eased in France during the 1750s, under the auspices of the progressive-minded *Directeur de la Librairie*, Lamoignon de Malesherbes (1751–63). But his reasons were tactical, not altruistic; and controls stiffened after the Maupeou coup of 1771 before easing again in 1775. In any case, the pre-revolutionary newspaper-reading public was only a small fraction in size of its counterpart across the Channel (Censer, 1994).

The contrast must not be overdrawn. On one hand, the suppression in 1763 of John Wilkes' *North Briton* no. 45 exposed the limits of press freedom in Britain. On the other, press freedom was possible without "protected consultation": in Denmark, for example, censorship was abolished by the autocratic minister Count Johann Friedrich von Struensee – who in so doing released a torrent of pamphlets against his own regime. In the Habsburg lands, too, censorship was abolished at the hand of an enlightened monarch, Joseph II (1781). In heavily policed France, finally, the claim of monarchs to a monopoly over legitimate opinion was never uncontested – whether by clandestine manuscript weeklies such as the *Nouvelles ecclésiastiques* or by French-language journals published outside the realm, such as the *Courrier du Bas-Rhin* or the *Gazette de Leyde* (Censer, 1994). Contentious journalism was not absent, but customarily took the form of non-periodical pamphlets and manuscript newsletters, such as Friedrich Melchior Grimm's *Correspondance littéraire.* Even so, the storm of protest that erupted over Wilkes and the *North Briton* also exposed what France and most continental monarchies lacked: a "plebeian" sphere large, literate, and vital enough to make press freedom the object of demonstrations and protest.

In one sphere, however, ordinary people took up the instruments of print culture and used them eagerly. Already in the seventeenth century, as Craig Harline has shown, common Dutch men and women began publishing petitions and grievances on the assumption that they were more likely to get a hearing if they were first carried before a reading public (Harline, 1987). Such efforts on the part of common folk to manipulate public opinion in their favor are best documented in the empire, where soon after 1700 the publication of grievances, legal briefs, and manifestos became routine in the prosecution of countless disputes, large and small. Between 1705 and 1732, for example, lawsuits involving the council and citizenry of Frankfurt generated a veritable flood of printed court briefs, pasquils, and polemical tracts, despite the council's best efforts to stop the tide. The explicit purpose of these publications was to connect courtroom transactions with a periodical-reading audience – to appeal cases, quite literally, to the *jugement de l'univers entier*, as one Swiss tract put it (Würgler, 1995). Likewise in France, barristers derived enormous popularity from their willingness to articulate their clients' grievances and carry them in print before the court of public opinion. Widely read journals, such as August Ludwig Schlözer's *Stats-Anzeigen*, reinforced the bridge between the courtroom and the public sphere by reporting on disputes or even excerpting the briefs and tracts they generated. News of popular politics, as a result, entered political discourse with a speed and regularity that would have been unthinkable a century earlier. As Franco Venturi showed, a well-read Florentine could learn in great detail about popular upheavals as far away as America, Sweden, and Russia (Venturi, 1989).

Toward Revolution?

Did these convergences signal a crisis of the old regime? The great historian of "Atlantic Revolution," R. R. Palmer, tended to interpret pre-revolutionary demands for greater liberty and transparency in government as so many rivulets in a gathering, pan-European stream of agitation against all the entrenched and self-perpetuating "constituted bodies" that claimed to represent society as a corporate whole (Palmer,

1959). But as the *citoyens* of St. Gallen showed, popular concepts of democracy could be contained within a corporatist frame of reference. Similarly, the French grain rioters' appeals to age-old communal norms raised basic questions about the legitimacy of royal authority, for as Steven Kaplan writes, "being a king meant assuming the traditional responsibilities of kingship, notably the obligation to honor the social contract of subsistence" (Kaplan, 1976). In so doing, rioters enacted the pre-absolutist, corporatist premise that the legitimate power rested on the continuity of binding reciprocities between ruler and subject (Bercé, 1974). What Palmer did not appreciate fully is that the *topoi* of early modern political culture both endorsed existing structures of power and equipped subjects with the ideological tools they needed to hold it accountable. The majority of Europeans, arguably, would not breach corporatist horizons of expectation until after 1800.

But the question remains whether a broad, popular consensus still upheld the existing social order in the closing decades of old-regime Europe. The emergence of Wilkesite radicalism in Britain and the rise of patriotic opposition to oligarchies in the Netherlands and Switzerland; conflicts over the liberalization of the grain trade during the 1760s and, beginning in the 1770s, a sharp increase in riots against the price of bread; the boom in petitioning and signature-gathering in Britain in the 1770s and 1780s; a dizzying crescendo of anti-seigneurial insurrections and urban unrest in France in the late 1780s; the explosion of labor disputes in Britain during the 1790s; all these trends indicate that European governments were finding popular politics more and more difficult to control.

Answers to the question of consensus divide British historians sharply: some, such as John Brewer, perceive in the Wilkes affair the leading edge of a great fissure within the political nation, splitting advocates of parliamentary reform from defenders of the Whig establishment (Brewer, 1976). Others argue that Wilkesite radicalism weighed little against a far more widespread loyalism and monarchism, nourished by the benefits of free commerce and informed by proto-nationalist hostility to a French Catholic "other" (Colley, 1992). At issue is the matter of legitimacy, whether the old order in Europe was still capable of satisfying popular expectations of justice and equity. German historians are largely agreed that the empire's elaborate system of adjudication and appeal diffused social tensions effectively, and that the flurry of urban and rural rebellions in the 1790s resulted in large measure from the collapse of imperial institutions before invading armies of the revolution (Blanning, 1983). French scholarship is nearly unanimous, too, but in a very different conclusion: beginning with the attempted assassination of Louis XV in 1757 (van Kley, 1984), perhaps earlier (Farge, 1994), the king of France ceased to command the quasi-religious veneration he once had enjoyed; his promoting of confessional toleration alienated the defenders of Gallican supremacy (Merrick, 1990); performances meant to highlight the monarchy's sacral character, such as curing scrofula by the "King's Touch," went into decline. His person no longer considered sacred, the king became the butt of pornographic satire, along with his wife, lovers, and courtiers (Maza, 1993).

There are solid reasons to doubt whether monarchy became "desacralized" in the minds of ordinary French peasants and artisans – had they not always possessed a language for holding authority to account, such as the "myth of the king deceived"? Did not the scrofula ceremony arouse popular indignation because Louis XV *stopped* it? Fortunately, there is little need to speculate. When in the spring of 1789 they were finally invited to present their grievances in *cahiers de doléances*, the common folk of France expressed in no uncertain terms their dissatisfaction with the existing state of affairs. In his definitive study of the *cahiers*, John Markoff shows how French villagers measured institutions of the *ancien régime* according to their utility within a broader, normative context of reciprocities between lord and subject: institutions and burdens that served a useful function might still be reformed, but those for which there was no reciprocal benefit should be abolished. The vast majority of rural *cahiers* demanded the abolition of indirect state taxes that compromised the security of life's necessities, such as the salt tax. But they also recommended the reform, not the abolition, of direct imposts such as the *taille* that supported valuable state functions. With respect to the seigneurial regime, the peasants' verdict was more damning: some 35 percent called for the elimination of seigneurial rights without compensation, and fully 18 percent demanded outright abolition of the seigneurial regime. Running through all these demands was a deep concern with social equity and "an insistence on getting the public goods for which the villagers paid." On the whole, French villagers exhibited "a thoughtful and nuanced capacity to differentiate among their burdens" (Markoff, 1996). When French peasants began attacking chateaux and destroying seigneurial archives in the summer of 1789 – the so-called "Great Fear" – it was largely because the nobles had surrendered any real military, political, or judicial function on which corporatist reciprocities might be based. There was no inconsistency between the peasants' rejection of useless exactions and the words of love and gratitude toward Louis XVI that filled their *cahiers*. Even so, the monarchy's experiment with transparency had empowered ordinary people to challenge the seigneurial regime on its own merits. Ultimately, it was the monarchy's undoing.

Bibliography

Beik, W., *Absolutism and Society in Seventeenth-Century France* (Cambridge, 1985).

Bercé, Y.-M., *Croquants et nu-pieds: Les Soulèvements paysans en France du XVIe au XIXe siècle* (Paris, 1974).

Blanning, T. C. W., *The French Revolution in Germany: Occupation and Resistance in the Rhineland, 1792–1802* (Oxford, 1983).

Blickle, P. (ed.), *Resistance, Representation, and Community* (Oxford, 1997).

Bohstedt, J., *Riots and Community Politics in England and Wales, 1790–1810* (Cambridge, 1983).

Bouton, C. A., *The Flour War: Gender, Class, and Community in Late Ancien Régime French Society* (University Park, PA, 1993).

Brake, W. P. te, *Regents and Rebels: The Revolutionary World of an Eighteenth-Century Dutch City* (Oxford, 1989).

Brake, W. P. te, *Shaping History: Ordinary People in European Politics, 1500–1700* (Berkeley, 1998).

Braun, R., *Das ausgehende Ancien Régime in der Schweiz* (Göttingen, 1984).

Brewer, J., *Party Ideology and Popular Politics at the Accession of George III* (Cambridge, 1976).

Brown, H. G., "Domestic state violence: repression from the Croquants to the Commune," *Historical Journal*, 42 (1999), 597–622.

Castiglione, C., *Patrons and Adversaries: Nobles and Villagers in Italian Politics, 1640–1760* (Oxford, 2005).

Censer, J., *The French Press in the Age of Enlightenment* (London, 1994).
Colley, L., *Britons: Forging the Nation, 1707–1837* (New Haven, 1992).
Dickinson, H. T., *The Politics of the People in Eighteenth-Century Britain* (New York, 1995).
Doyle, W., "The parlements," in K. M. Baker (ed.), *The Political Culture of the Old Regime* (Oxford, 1987), pp.157–67.
Farge, A., *Subversive Words: Public Opinion in Eighteenth-Century France* (Cambridge, 1994).
Gutton, J.-P., *La Sociabilité villageoise dans l'ancienne France: Solidarités et voisinages du XVIe au XVIIIe siècle* (Paris, 1979).
Habermas, J., *The Structural Transformation of the Public Sphere: An Inquiry into a Category of Bourgeois Society* (Cambridge, 1991).
Harline, C. E., *Pamphlets, Printing, and Political Culture in the Early Dutch Republic* (Dordrecht, 1987).
Harris, B., *Politics and the Rise of the Press: Britain and France, 1620–1800* (London, 1996).
Kaplan, S. L., *Bread, Politics and Political Economy in the Reign of Louis XV* (The Hague, 1976).
Knights, M., *Representation and Misrepresentation in Later Stuart Britain* (Oxford, 2005).
Krüger, K., *Die Landständische Verfassung* (Munich, 2003).
Le Roy Ladurie, E., "Revoltes et contestations rurales en France de 1675 à 1789," *Annales: Économies, Sociétés, Civilisations*, 29 (1974), 6–22.
Legay, M.-L., *Les États provinciaux dans la construction de l'état moderne, aux XVIIe et XVIIIe siècles* (Geneva, 2001).
Lemarchand, G., *La Fin du féodalisme dans le pays de Caux* (Paris, 1989).
Lucas, C., "The crowd and politics between *ancien régime* and revolution in France," *Journal of Modern History*, 60 (1988), 421–57.
Luebke, D. M., *His Majesty's Rebels: Communities, Factions and Rural Revolt in the Black Forest, 1725–1745* (Ithaca, 1997).
Luebke, D. M., "Frederick the Great and the celebrated case of the Millers Arnold (1770–1779): a reappraisal," *Central European History*, 32 (1999), 379–408.
Luebke, D. M., "Signatures and political culture in eighteenth-century Germany," *Journal of Modern History* ,76 (2004), 497–530.
Lukowski, J., *Liberty's Folly: The Polish-Lithuanian Commonwealth in the Eighteenth Century, 1697–1795* (London, 1991).
Lynch, J., *Bourbon Spain, 1700–1808* (Oxford, 1989).
Markoff, J., *The Abolition of Feudalism: Peasants, Lords, and Legislators in the French Revolution* (Philadelphia, 1996).
Maza, S., *Private Lives and Public Affairs: The Causes Célèbres of Prerevolutionary France* (Berkeley, 1993).
Merrick, J. W., *The Descralization of the French Monarchy in the Eighteenth Century* (Baton Rouge, 1990).
Nicolas, J., *La Rébellion française: Mouvements populaires et conscience sociale, 1661–1789* (Paris, 2002).
Nubola, C., "Supplications between politics and justice: the northern and central Italian states in the early modern age," *International Review of Social History*, 46 (2001), 35–56.
O'Gorman, F., *Voters, Patrons, and Parties: The Unreformed Electoral System of Hanoverian England, 1734–1832* (Oxford, 1989).
Palmer, R. R., *The Age of Democratic Revolution: A Political History of Europe and America 1760–1800* (Princeton, 1959).
Phillips, J. A., *Electoral Behavior in Unreformed England* (Princeton, 1982).

Roberts, M., *The Age of Liberty: Sweden, 1719–1772* (Cambridge, 1986).
Rodriguez, L., "The Spanish riots of 1766," *Past & Present*, 59 (1973), 117–49.
Rogers, N., *Crowds, Culture, and Politics in Georgian Britain* (Oxford, 1998).
Root, H. L., *Peasants and King in Burgundy: Agrarian Foundations of French Absolutism* (Berkeley, 1987).
Rudé, G., *The Crowd in the French Revolution* (Oxford, 1959).
Rudé, G., *The Crowd in History* (London, 1981).
Schulze, W., *Bäuerlicher Widerstand und feudale Herrschaft* (Bad Cannstadt, 1980).
Sonenscher, M., *Work and Wages: Natural Law, Politics and the Eighteenth-Century French Trades* (Cambridge, 1989).
Stevenson, J., *Popular Disturbances in England, 1700–1870* (London, 1979).
Suter, A., "Vormoderne und moderne Demokratie in der Schweiz," *Zeitschrift für historische Forschung*, 31 (2004), 231–54.
Swann, J., *Provincial Power and Absolute Monarchy: The Estates General of Burgundy, 1661–1790* (Cambridge, 2003).
Thompson, E. P., *The Making of the English Working Class* (New York, 1963).
Thompson, E. P., "The moral economy of the English crowd in the eighteenth century," *Past & Present*, 50 (1971), 76–136.
Tilly, C., *Contention and Democracy in Europe, 1650–2000* (Cambridge, 2004).
Trossbach, W., *Soziale Bewegung und politische Erfahrung. Bäuerlicher Protest in hessischen Territorien 1648–1806* (Weingarten, 1987).
van Kley, D., *The Damiens Affair and the Unraveling of the Ancien Régime* (Princeton, 1984).
Venturi, F., *The End of the Old Regime in Europe*, vol. 1: *The First Crisis, 1768–1776* (Princeton, 1989).
Würgler, A., *Unruhen und Öffentlichkeit. Städtische und ländliche Protestbewegungen im 18. Jahrhundert* (Tübingen, 1995).
Würgler, A., "Desideria und Landesordnungen. Kommunaler und landständischer Einfluß auf die fürstliche Gesetzgebung in Hessen-Kassel, 1650–1800," in P. Blickle (ed.), *Gemeinde und Staat im Alten Europa* (Munich, 1998), pp. 149–207.

Chapter Thirty-One

The French and European Revolutions

Alan Forrest

Few eighteenth-century political observers talked of revolution; still fewer would have predicted the wave of revolutions that had engulfed so much of Europe by 1800 and which would spread during the first half of the nineteenth century to large swathes of the extra-European world. It was a term properly applied in the natural sciences, plucked from the world of astronomy. But it featured little in the world of politics. Nor did the writers of the Enlightenment advocate the kind of violent political upheaval that was implied by the term "revolution." They did, it is true, counsel rulers to adopt enlightened social policies and give constitutional rights to their peoples. They proposed education programs that would raise levels of literacy and encourage inquiry and self-discovery. And they threw down a challenge to privilege that could not be justified in terms of public utility. In so doing they doubtless raised political awareness among their readers and helped to create a future political class within the social elite of European monarchies. But they did not advocate revolution. Indeed, the most political of them believed that only by adopting enlightened principles could the rulers of *ancien régime* Europe avoid the damaging consequences of social upheaval and satisfy public demands through reform from above.

That does not mean, of course, that there was no link between the ideas of the French Enlightenment and the revolutionary climacteric of the last decade of the century. The very act of questioning the assumptions on which secular and spiritual authority rested corroded the dual pillars of authority that were the church and the state. A humanist vision that placed man at the center of the universe and made human happiness one of the prime goals of political society could not but alter men's perceptions of the church and of their duty to God, while the idea that education could improve human understanding and contribute to man's perfectibility was viewed with horror by a clerical establishment committed to the dogma of original sin. The French state, based as it was on privilege and venal office-holding, was vulnerable both to the sniping attacks of the *philosophes* and to attacks from those who praised individualism and advocated careers open to talent. As cultural historians have emphasized, the second half of the century was a period characterized by a burgeoning public sphere, a world of salons and provincial academies, café society and print

A Companion to Eighteenth-Century Europe, First Edition. Edited by Peter H. Wilson.
© 2014 John Wiley & Sons, Ltd. Published 2014 by John Wiley & Sons, Ltd.

culture, Freemasonry and mesmerism (Chartier, 1991). Opportunities were considerable for those who wanted to socialize, to talk about public affairs, or to meet with like-minded men and women. Nor was such sociability limited to the capital. The larger provincial cities boasted bookshops and lending libraries, bringing books, newspapers, and pamphlets to the notice of a more educated clientele, while popular audiences eagerly consumed the illustrated tracts and pornographic writings of the day. But we must be careful not to exaggerate the impact of enlightened writers. The books with the largest circulation, even in the 1780s, were more likely to be works of biblical exegesis – the preferred reading of the clergy while preparing their Sunday sermons – than works of humanist philosophy, and it would be the very eve of the revolution before even Rousseau went through multiple editions (Darnton, 1982). And if there was a humanist discourse on the political left, there was also a strongly anti-philosophic discourse which underscored the essential role of the Catholic faith in supporting the social and political order (McMahon, 2001).

If historians are generally agreed that the new ideas of the eighteenth century helped to destroy confidence in the institutions of European monarchy, there is less agreement about their role in creating the revolutions that displaced them. Ideas were not nationally specific or limited by state boundaries. There was a refreshing cosmopolitanism about Europe in the second half of the eighteenth century, and especially about its elite culture. Philosophy crossed national frontiers, and the Enlightenment, when viewed from Prussia or Denmark or Scotland, was not quintessentially French. Nor were the philosophers, who in France were typically liberal nobles or independent scholars, men of leisure and often the privileged beneficiaries of royal patronage, but who in Berlin or Edinburgh were more likely to enjoy the security of solid professional success (Munck, 2000). In Holland, Scandinavia, and throughout the German-speaking lands, Kant and Spinoza would prove at least as enduring an influence as Voltaire (Israel, 2001). There were religious differences, too. In Protestant countries, where there was no Papacy to attract the ire of anti-clericals, the spirit of inquiry which the Enlightenment fostered was less concerned with deism and natural law, and less antipathetic to the vested interests of the church. In the American colonies, indeed, religion was integral to the spirit of inquiry; these were, after all, men who had – or whose ancestors had – fled from Europe precisely in order to exercise their religious beliefs without risk of persecution. Yet it is the French who were most clearly identified with enlightenment, largely because it was the French eighteenth century that ended in the turmoil of revolution.

The French Revolution not only dwarfed the other European revolutions that had gone before; it went on to dominate the entire era in European memory. Earlier revolutionary movements should not, however, be passed over in silence: they were not just precursors of the French, dry runs for the ideas that would finally come to fruition in Paris. They were significant political and social movements in their own right, a cycle of violent upheavals which had overthrown longstanding elites and given commercial and professional men a hand on the reins of government. This was true in the 1760s in the city-state of Geneva, where native-born artisans had grouped together to demand the right to vote and where constitutional rights were already being discussed 20 years before the Estates General was called to Versailles. Voltaire, significantly, lent his support to the people's cause, while one of the city's most famous sons, Jean-Jacques Rousseau, wrote pamphlets in defense of its revolution and advised on the future form of its constitution. In 1787 Holland staged its own version of a bourgeois revolution, again rehearsing many of the arguments that would be used by the French. In the following year in Brussels and Liège Belgian patriotic sentiment was mobilized against the rule of the Austrian empire, leading Joseph II to suppress the estates of Brabant – ironically on the day after the French proclaimed their National Assembly at Versailles. Even in Poland, where most western enlightened authors were available in translation, a patriotic movement was constituted by the 1780s, ready to take advantage of Russia's international entanglement in 1788 and support a reforming agenda when the Four Year Diet met in Warsaw. Here, as in Belgium, radicals would take huge encouragement from the French example after 1789 (Brake, 1989; Schama, 1977).

Britain is often presented as the one country immune to the temptations of revolution in the late eighteenth century, and solidly committed to seeking change through reform. Yet even here there were intermittent outbursts of rioting. John Wilkes had advocated popular insurgency in pursuit of civil rights, and there were instances of crowd violence, as in the Gordon Riots of 1780, when the government was blamed for having failed to meet the aspirations of the people (Dickinson, 1995). A majority of Britons might convince themselves that they had achieved the perfect equilibrium, by peaceable means, in the Glorious Revolution of 1688, but there were substantial sections of their own population who disagreed. Few had the vote: even the commercial classes on whom so much of England's prosperity was dependent had no real say in the political process; while public order was maintained by a battery of savage laws and the draconian use of the death penalty (Gatrell, 1994). The 1760s and 1770s were scarred by popular dissent and by a dramatic rise in opposition tracts advocating root-and-branch change. By the1790s there were sizeable groups of radicals in London and the major provincial cities who saw the French Revolution not as a threat but as the promise of release from despotism, while in Ireland the prospect of a French alliance gave encouragement to the United Irishmen and the movement for independence from the British Crown (Elliott, 1982).

It is perhaps curious that the British model of constitutional development, based on the separation of powers and an independent judiciary, found such muted support on the continent. The American Revolution, on the other hand, was steeped in the traditions of the British constitution, the philosophy of John Locke, and the law treatises of Blackstone. Hence the powers that were ascribed by the new government of the United States to its president, Congress, and Supreme Court were carefully differentiated, with states' rights inscribed in the constitution so as to defend the liberties of the citizen against possible abuse of power by the president and federal administration. In 1776 they used a language of liberalism and individualism, civic rights and responsibilities, to justify their call for political independence from the British Crown. They had, in the course of the eighteenth century, also distanced themselves emotionally from Britain and its empire and had given themselves a new, American, identity. Long before 1776 they had developed a culture separate from that of the mother-country, a national culture that showed itself in patterns of thought, in distinctive expression, and in material objects (Bailyn, 1992). They responded to British demands for legality by appealing to a higher, natural law, and, like John Adams, held that "liberty can no more exist without virtue and independence than the body can live and move without a soul" (Merriman, 2004).

Whereas the French also appealed to natural law, they were less concerned than the Americans to insist on a strict separation of powers. They laid down that sovereignty should no longer be enshrined in the person of the king and should in future be placed in the nation, in the people, a language that was itself suggestive of unity and intolerant of division. For how could the polity be divided or opposition tolerated, if that opposition were to the will of the nation itself (Furet, 1981)? Under the constitutional monarchy, there was of necessity a constitutional division of responsibilities, if only to limit the powers of the king, but once the monarchy was abolished, all authority was vested in a single body, the National Convention. French republicans made little reference to English precedent or to English representative traditions; Montesquieu had been replaced by Rousseau as their intellectual mentor. They did, of course, know about the seventeenth-century English Revolution, since David Hume's history of the period was a much-favored text in the final decades of the *ancien régime*; even Louis XVI is known to have read from it in January 1793 while awaiting execution in the Conciergerie. But French writers did not share Britain's optimistic reading of the Glorious Revolution of 1688. They refused to see it as a bloodless passage to representative government, preferring to regard the seventeenth century as an unbroken whole, with 1688 merely the belated outcome of a movement that had started with the Long Parliament, civil war, and the execution of Charles I. This was not a model for political change that they wished to follow, since the execution of the monarch had led to a military coup and to the puritanical excesses of Cromwell's Commonwealth. Indeed, they made repeated reference to the dangers of a putsch, and they warned of the need to exercise vigilance to protect the people from the ambitions of "un nouveau Cromwell" (Bongie, 1965).

The American Revolution, on the other hand, fired the European imagination, as the first instance where a colonized people rose against their colonial masters in the name of civil rights. For those Europeans still living under autocratic regimes, with no experience of political participation or representative institutions, this was an intoxicating message, and one that had resonances for them as well. The revolutionary movement in America could appear to have had small beginnings, as a protest against Grenville's attempts to extract additional revenue for the British Crown, which had led to angry demands that new taxes were not legal unless the colonists had direct representation in the House of Commons. But in the course of their struggle against British rule the colonists quickly adopted a discourse of political rights, using the language of nationalism and portraying themselves as a people apart from Great Britain, identified not by their European roots but by the common experience they had accumulated in the New World. The American Declaration of Independence, in its appeal to individual liberty and its proclamation of the universal rights of man, sent a strong message to those of every country who felt themselves oppressed by the arbitrary power of monarchs or the corporate structures of *ancien régime* Europe. The words were intoxicating: "We hold these truths to be self-evident, that all men are created equal, that they are endowed by their Creator with certain inalienable rights, that among these are Life, Liberty and the pursuit of Happiness." They found an echo in the columns of the French press and sympathetic listeners in salons and provincial academies, in café society and in Masonic lodges. And they would inform the French revolutionaries' Declaration of the Rights of Man and the Citizen, which was adopted in August 1789 and would be accorded the status of constitutional law under the revolution (Venturi, 1991).

That the message from America received such wide diffusion in France is due in large measure to Louis XVI's foreign policy, and to the government's decision in 1778 to send troops across the Atlantic to support the colonists' cause. To many it seemed a perverse decision, since France, too, retained the remnants of a colonial empire in the Americas and might seem to have had little interest in arousing colonial expectations to this degree. It was perverse, too, in that the royal treasury had already been drained by the cost of the recurrent wars of the eighteenth century, and most recently the disastrous military gamble of the Seven Years War, which had led to the loss of Quebec and the emasculation of the old French empire at the Peace of Paris in 1763. But French intervention in America had nothing to do with the principles of self-government which the colonists proclaimed. It was a war entered into in a spirit of revenge, and stemmed from the desire of Vergennes and other ministers to restore something of France's colonial prestige. Vergennes argued that British attention was temporarily distracted from Europe to the colonies, that the conflict offered the opportunity to avenge past injuries, and that France could hope to gain a larger slice of American trade and regain the Newfoundland fisheries (Dull, 2005) The French certainly did gain a slice of revenge, and at Yorktown the French navy inflicted a rare victory over its British rival. But there were other effects, too, and these had a more lasting impact on the polity. Those French soldiers who were sent to America and who returned to their French provinces in the 1780s had been exposed to a new and exciting discourse of liberty. And – most importantly – the costs of France's intervention pushed the monarchy towards bankruptcy and hastened the onset of revolution (Campbell, 2006). It is an instance where foreign policy had a disastrous impact on the regime's capacity to survive, and it has led historians to seek the genesis of the French Revolution in the wider geopolitics of the eighteenth century (Stone, 1994).

The American Revolution had a profound influence on France, both in spreading a new ideology of liberty and in helping to undermine the authority of the monarchy. The two revolutions shared a dislike of aristocratic privilege and preached individualism and careers open to talent. But the vogue for talking of a single revolutionary movement that swept the Atlantic world, incorporating both the American and French revolutions in a single western or Atlantic revolution of far wider geographical import, has largely passed (Godechot, 1965; Palmer, 1959), It is a view that enjoyed greatest popularity in the 1950s and 1960s, and which presented a powerful challenge to those republican historians, especially in France, who argued that the French Revolution was a social as well as a political movement that could be understood only in the context of France. The argument, as they saw it, was about twentieth-century politics as much as about eighteenth-century history. They denied the very existence of an "age of democratic revolution" that did not have France at its core. It abandoned all concessions to French exceptionalism, attacked Marxist ideas of revolution, and redefined the essence of eighteenth-century revolutions as liberal and capitalist. It also, they believed, implied a political judgment by raising the American Revolution to an international prominence which its moderation and social conservatism did not justify (Jourdan, 2004).

For nineteenth-century thinkers the central importance of the French Revolution was not in doubt, even if they disagreed about what it meant. Alexis de Tocqueville thought its primary achievement lay in the construction of a powerful centralized state bureaucracy. Edgar Quinet pointed instead to its role in developing a liberal ideology that would be a key element in nineteenth-century political change. And Karl Marx defined it as a key moment in the social development from feudalism to capitalism. Many of the leading French historians of the revolution during the twentieth century remained loyal to this republican, Marxist vision. They argued that the originality of the French Revolution lay in its intensity and its root-and-branch approach to change. They saw it not only as a revolution in political structures, overthrowing the Bourbon monarchy and instituting a republican tradition that has been an aspect of French political life for the greater part of the last two centuries. It was also a social revolution, destroying the notion of privilege and replacing the old elite of nobles and clergy with a more open society, one where men of talent could flourish and where trade and the professions could exercise power in government. And in the tradition of Marx, they argued that the importance of the revolution should be understood as its contribution to a longer historical process. Along with the revolutions in Holland and England in the seventeenth century, the French Revolution formed "the culmination of a long economic and social evolution which has made the bourgeoisie the master of the world" (Soboul, 1974).

With the decline of communism in the second half of the twentieth century this view of the French Revolution has become increasingly marginalized. A key moment was the publication in London in 1964 of Alfred Cobban's *Social Interpretation of the French Revolution*, which, while it did not challenge the assumption that the revolution should be explained in primarily social terms, raised a series of uncomfortable questions about the relevance of Marxist class descriptors, and even of the idea of class itself. Supposed distinctions between nobles and bourgeois did not work in practice, he argued, and he showed that, in their occupations, their levels of wealth, and their approach to investment, privileged and unprivileged were often hard to tell apart. The sons of noblemen and rich bourgeois followed the same law courses to qualify as officeholders under the Crown or in the service of the Paris *parlement*, and their subsequent career trajectories were often indistinguishable (Cobban, 1964).

It was left to others to go further and to reject the argument that 1789 was essentially a social revolution. Historians have increasingly reverted to a political explanation of events in France, looking particularly to the failings of royal autocracy and to political conflicts within the *ancien régime* (Doyle, 1989). They have reinterpreted the principal divisions in the France of the 1780s in political and cultural terms. The differences that counted, they believe, were differences of political outlook, between those who clung to privilege and those who embraced new ideas of constitutional reform and representative government. The schism, in other words, was not between nobles and bourgeois, but between liberals and conservatives, those who were natural advocates of change and those who preferred the security of the status quo (Blanning, 1998). And the culture they adopted was shaped less by social class than by political experience, whether their experience of salons and academies was in provincial towns or gained in the hugely intense debates of the first weeks of the revolutionary assemblies at Versailles. The new deputies may have left their provinces with competing agendas in mind; it took only a few weeks in the hothouse atmosphere of Versailles for them to be transformed into revolutionaries (Tackett, 1996).

The politics of the French Revolution have been the subject of considerable reappraisal. The Estates General assembled at Versailles on May 5, meeting, as the king instructed, in three separate estates, following a precedent last used in 1614. But even as they met, discernible differences distinguished this Estates General from its predecessors. The king's orders no longer commanded unanimous support, and in the campaigns that had been held to elect the deputies – most especially those of the third estate – they had been made aware of the wishes of their future constituents, many of them deeply influenced by the humanist ideas of the time. The king had already made one important concession, that the third estate should enjoy double the representation of the other two orders to reflect its members' numerical importance in society. Public expectation ran high, as every local community, from towns and urban corporations to the smallest villages, was invited to list its grievances in a *cahier de doléances*, and suggest to the king the reforms that were required to solve the ills of the nation. The months before the Estates General convened were given over to campaigning and pamphleteering, some of it of unparalleled venom. "What is the third estate?" thundered the Abbé Sieyes in the most famous pamphlet of the pre-revolution, to which he gave the rhetorical answer, "Everything." "What has it been till now in the political order? Nothing. What does it ask? To be something" (Sewell, 1994). The complexity of the third estate and the wide range of its demands have recently been re-examined through a content analysis of a huge corpus of these *cahiers*; from these it is clear that local experience and local culture counted more than any emerging notion of social class in the formulation of people's demands and the construction of their identities (Shapiro and Markoff, 1998).

Few deputies of the third estate would be content to abide by the king's wish that they agree to vote new taxes and disperse. They had come to Versailles determined to seize what they correctly assumed to be a once-in-a-lifetime chance to establish their permanent place in the political process, and once it became clear that the two privileged orders were in no position to offer any united resistance, they seized the initiative that was offered them and reconstituted themselves as a National Assembly. It was an open act of rebellion, taken in defiance of Louis' express wishes, and sealed by the Tennis Court Oath, whereby they each individually swore that they would not allow themselves to be dispersed or sent back to their separate orders. The king rather weakly agreed, in the process recognizing the legitimacy of the National Assembly, and the political revolution became irreversible. It was now apparent that Louis could no longer impose his will arbitrarily. The Assembly rapidly set up a constitutional committee with the task of drawing up a new constitution for France, one that would lay down exactly which powers were vested in the monarch and which in the assembly. When the constitution was finally passed, in 1791, the king had to accept that he was no longer absolute, and that he was answerable to the people for his stewardship. The third estate had achieved its ambition, and the assembly now had a permanent place in the polity (Fitzsimmons, 1994).

The French Revolution was not, however, the work of the deputies alone. From the first months the course of the revolution was affected by popular agitation, by expressions of direct democracy and the collective action of radical crowds. Fear and rumor played a major role in politics in the spring and summer of 1789, as panic spread from town to town in the Ile de France and across Paris's granary belt

(Lefebvre, 1973). Villagers expressed fears of a famine plot, turned their hatred on strangers, and listened credulously to reports of conspiracies to deny them their new-won rights. Even the king, some believed, was involved in this skein of conspiracy, as tales of aristocratic plots drove bands of angry peasants to attack chateaux, threaten estate managers, and burn feudal documents in front of their owners. Rumors spread readily, even reaching Versailles, where they helped persuade fearful nobles to make desperate concessions to the commons. Meanwhile, the radical areas of Paris produced their own form of popular politics, as crowds roamed the city seeking out guns and ammunition, before attacking the royal fortress at the Bastille on July 14. By October, their numbers swollen by marketwomen and members of the newly formed citizen's militia, the National Guard, a large crowd marched to Versailles demanding bread. When the day ended, the king and his family had accepted that they, too, should return to Paris, and exchange the safety and luxury of Louis XIV's palace for the more vulnerable surroundings of the Tuileries. Popular politics and popular violence had become central to the revolution, as had the forces of fear and paranoia (Farge, 1994). As for the Paris crowd, it had established its right to be involved in the political process, its reputation enhanced both by the act of storming the Bastille and by the heroic sacrifice of Parisians which accompanied it. In the years that followed the Bastille became a symbol of the new-found liberty of ordinary people, a symbol reproduced in scores of etchings and popular prints (Lüsebrink and Reichardt, 1997).

The years of constitutional monarchy were rich in administrative and judicial reforms that gave new meaning to the language of rights and citizenship by ensuring that all had equal access to administration and justice. The map of local government was transformed, trial by jury was guaranteed for all, and justices of the peace were introduced at local level to settle disputes in the community, without the need to drag them through the courts. At a stroke of the pen many of the injustices that had been complained of for centuries were resolved. But in the process other wounds were opened up which threatened the early harmony of the revolution. The Civil Constitution of the Clergy, implemented in 1791 with the aim of rationalizing the administration of the Catholic Church and bringing it into line with state administration and the system of justice, outraged the devout and antagonized the Vatican, while the attempt to impose an oath of loyalty on the clergy led to a damaging schism within the Catholic community (Tackett, 1985). Jurors and non-jurors competed for the souls of the faithful, with many refractory priests defying the law and staying on in their parishes. Thousands of nobles and non-juring clergy chose to emigrate, passing into neighboring countries rather than ignore their vows or renege on their religious or political principles. And Louis' own devout faith put the constitution at risk as he resisted anticlerical laws, even continuing to hear Mass from a refractory chaplain. In 1791 he tried to flee the country under cover of darkness, only to be recognized and turned back by national guards at Varennes in the east, 24 hours that undermined his credibility and lost him such public trust as he still enjoyed (Tackett, 2003). A year later, after his Swiss guards fired on a crowd at the Tuileries, killing over 200 demonstrators, the deputies concluded that he was making no effort to govern constitutionally. He was suspended, the republic declared, and new elections held. On September 20, 1792, the Convention met, and the First Republic came into existence.

The emphasis during the three years of constitutional monarchy was on political reform and the creation of a new civic order (Woloch, 1994). That is not to say, however, that the revolution was wholly unconcerned with social issues, or that these years did not also bring a wealth of social changes. The deputies were acutely conscious of the goals of their constituents, many of which had been clearly articulated in the *cahiers*. There were demands for free trade, and for the end of monopolies and commercial concessions made by the Crown to particular companies or interest groups. Townsmen complained of the high price of bread and other essential foodstuffs, or demanded more severe penalties against hoarders and speculators. And those excluded from the guilds which controlled so much of trade in the eighteenth century demanded access to the world of work and the abolition of what they saw as a damaging and exclusive privilege. Similarly, rural communities listed the exactions that rained down on peasants. Some of these were financial: the burden of taxation in a society where many of the taxes were paid only by commoners; the feudal dues that had to be paid to nobles and other landed *seigneurs*; and the tithes due to the church, which in some parts of the country were levied at rates well above the supposed tenth of a peasant's income, and which were rarely spent on the stipend of the parish priest or the social needs of the village poor. Others were burdens in kind: peasants complained of the labor service demanded by local landowners, the manual work they had to perform on the roads or in the fields, and the profitable monopolies which landowners imposed over flour-mills and wine-presses. There were honorific privileges, too, such as the right to hunt game or shoot rabbits, which the peasantry particularly resented, especially when the doves kept by nobles as a symbol of privilege wreaked havoc on the peasants' corn (Jones, 1988).

These and other privileges would be abolished during the revolution, most memorably, perhaps, in the declarations of self-denial by the nobility on the night of August 4, 1789 (Fitzsimmons, 2003). Guilds and other forms of trade association were dismantled as part of a concerted attack on the corporate structures of *ancien régime* society. These reforms did not, however, satisfy everyone. Peasants discovered that not all the debts they owed were abolished overnight. Seigneurial dues were retained in cases where they constituted property, and had to be redeemed by purchase, something which many poorer peasants were unable to afford. And if the guilds were abolished, the free labor market which the revolutionaries created did not work to the benefit of artisans and workers, especially when, under the Le Chapelier law, they were denied the right to collective negotiations on wages and working practices. It was soon apparent that the revolutionary leadership had a narrowly legalistic view of equality. Little was done to improve income levels for the poor or to guarantee a living wage, while inflation risked eroding many of the benefits which peasants and workers had obtained from the abolition of privilege. Equality was understood to mean equality before the law, equality in rights and duties, equality as citizens. It was the legal transformation that was critical here, as opposed to economic redistribution. The revolutionaries effectively destroyed the corporatism that lay at the very root of eighteenth-century French society. More than any social measure, this undermined the privileged society of orders and promoted individualism (Sonenscher, 1989).

With the abolition of the monarchy the revolutionaries' attention was again focused on creating political institutions that truly reflected the interests of the sovereign people. There was no longer any nod towards the separation of powers: for the first time in the revolution, all power – executive, legislative, and judicial – was vested in the Convention, a single chamber of 749 elected deputies (Patrick, 1972). But how was the new republic to be governed? Once again, during its early months there was no constitution, since the 1791 constitution over which so much sweat had flowed had died with the monarchy it had established. Nor were there any political parties: deputies were returned, as they had in the earlier elections, as individuals, though once in Paris they often found themselves embraced by political organizations like the Jacobin Club or the Cercle Social (Kennedy, 2000). Paris itself was, as ever, awash with alarmist rumor. The declaration of war with Austria and Prussia had raised levels of panic, until word spread that enemy forces were at the gates of the city, prepared to restore the king to the throne and wreak revenge on those who had caused his humiliation. Within a week of the Convention's meeting, popular paranoia, mingled with a lust for vengeance against their enemies, created new excesses of bloodletting as Parisian radicals burst into the prisons, pulling out suspected royalists, counter-revolutionaries, and aristocrats. Hundreds were dragged into the streets and butchered to death, a chilling reminder to the politicians of the power and simmering violence of radical politics in the capital (Andress, 2005).

Fear of renewed violence would be a constant backdrop to the new republic. As a response to the demands of war and the threat of counter-revolution in the provinces, but also to pressure from Paris, the government would introduce exceptional laws to guarantee public safety and repress all forms of political opposition. By the summer of 1794 those appearing before the special revolutionary tribunals and military commissions that had been instituted to try suspects would have no right to defense counsel, and for some categories of political crime there was no penalty other than death. Terror had become the order of the day, a terror that was to last until the war was over. Over 16,000 men and women were executed in 13 months – most famously, of course, the king and his Austrian queen, Marie Antoinette, but also nobles and clerics, émigrés unwise enough to return from exile, and thousands of ordinary people, caught up in events they often did not fully understand. The Jacobin caucus who surrounded Robespierre produced a cult of terror, drawing on the symbolism of the guillotine as well as the idealization of virtue and the tyranny of words (Arasse, 1989; Weber, 2003).

Historians' interest in the phenomenon of Terror has equaled that of contemporaries, and there has been an increasing reluctance to accept at face value the Jacobins' claim that it was justified by national emergency. Some question the idea that this was violence born of political crisis, and they emphasize that a cult of violence pervaded the revolution at the outset in 1789 (Baker, 1990; Furet, 1981; Gueniffey, 2000). And those who seek historical explanation by building models of revolution, comparing the French Revolution to those in England or in twentieth-century Russia or China, have turned terror into an essential stage of a complex historical process (Moore, 1984).

Terror is, of course, part of a much greater whole. The French republic was responsible for creating a new political culture in France and in those of France's neighbors which her armies invaded. Its central message was about popular sovereignty and the exercise of that sovereignty: everywhere they went the French laid great store by constitutional government, imposing on their satellite states constitutions that imitated their own. They emphasized the importance of elections as a means of legitimating public authority, not just for national government but at every level of administration from departments and districts to courts and tribunals (Crook, 1996). They stressed the right of every citizen to have access to administration and justice, with the division of the territory into manageable units of local government and with tribunals at departmental and district level. They believed that political participation was a public duty: indifference to the revolution was no longer an acceptable option (Lucas, 1988).

Their concern could be expressed in a host of ways that had not been available to the subjects of the Bourbon monarchy, and much recent scholarship has been concerned to unravel the various forms that revolutionary political culture could take. Commitment was not confined to the expression of one's preference in elections. Revolutionary France had a diverse and polemical print culture, producing an unprecedented effusion of political tracts, many of them circulating in bars and cafés or reproduced as wall posters for passers-by to read. There was a lively political press, both in Paris and in the majority of provincial towns, which enabled both radical and conservative views to circulate among like-minded people (Gough, 1988; Popkin, 1990). From 1789 men were urged to show their patriotism and concern for the public good by joining their local battalion of the National Guard, armed and ready to defend life and property in the event of attack or disorder (Carrot, 2001). They had a duty to ensure that their sons of military age volunteered for the army. They were encouraged to join clubs and popular societies, which built on the earlier traditions of the *cercles*, reading circles, and Masonic lodges, until by 1794 the Jacobins boasted a club network that had spread not only to every significant provincial town and city, but to many villages, too, particularly in the southeast and southwest of the country (Kennedy, 1982–2000). And whereas club membership implied a deliberate choice, an act of inscription and – at least in the early stages of the revolution – a small payment, in Paris and the larger cities everyone could go along to his section where, once again, he could play his part in the political process (Slavin, 1984; Soboul, 1964). It is no accident that when, during the Jacobin republic, suspects were interrogated about the degree of their revolutionary commitment, this should be measured by their attendance at political meetings or their membership of the National Guard. These were sacrifices that the good revolutionary was expected to make, a modest price for the benefits of citizenship.

Citizenship was an ideal that inspired admirers of the revolution, both in France itself and across Europe, an ideal which bestowed rights which rulers had no authority to deny. For many people the revolution was equated with civic rights and personal freedom, most memorably expressed in the revolutionary discourse of liberty, equality, and fraternity, and in every European country there were small bands of republicans and Francophiles who lamented their own lack of freedom and looked to France to liberate them from tyranny (Blanning, 1983). Citizenship was not expressed only in words; it was reflected in a rich variety of gestures, customs, and political symbols which could be imitated elsewhere, even in semi-educated or barely literate societies. Liberty trees, Phrygian caps, and busts of Marianne communicated the republican message even to those who could not read. The same message was driven home in everyday social habits, both through egalitarian forms of address (the use of the more familiar *tu* in place of the formal *vous*; the abolition of deferential *monsieur* or *monseigneur* in favor of the more democratic *citoyen*), and through the constant repetition of a new vocabulary of nation and people, regeneration and virtue. Ordinary transactions were carried out with the revolution's new decimal weights and measures, and for 14 years Frenchmen were reminded by their new calendar that their era began not with the birth of Christ but with that of the Republic. The revolutionary message was conveyed in the wording of laws and decrees, but also through a host of art forms – painting and caricature, songs and theater, flags, symbols, and festivals. The use by the revolutionaries of such a wide range of visual images could only help popularize these ideals by depicting them in memorable forms and in vivid colors (Hunt, 1984).

Nothing was sacrosanct. The revolutionaries did not stop at regulating the Catholic Church or imposing a clerical oath; by 1793 they had launched a program of wholesale de-Christianization, closing church buildings and denying access to religious worship, before deciding, with Robespierre, that atheism was the enemy of the sovereign people and instituting a new form of deism with the Festival of the Supreme Being (Vovelle, 1991). Kings and emperors were denounced as tyrants, and warned that they risked the wrath of their peoples. France declared war on most of Europe, fighting it with a citizen-army and purporting to carry the message of liberty to the peoples of a continent; but it was never easy to persuade others at the point of a bayonet, however ideologically they defined the aims and aspirations of their soldiers, and a war launched in defense of the motherland soon turned into one of conquest and imperial expansion (Bertaud, 1988; Forrest, 1990). The universal ideals of 1789 had been turned to the service of a new, aggressive nationalism.

With the passage of time, the last vestiges of idealism began to fade, as the Directory repressed popular agitation in the interests of order and state security, surrounding France with a buffer of malleable allies and using the army to suppress dissent. Finally, by means of a *coup d'état* on 18 Brumaire (November 1799), Barras, Sieyès, and their allies turned to the army to overthrow the elected government and impose order on the country. Many republicans believed that with the Consulate and the coming to power of Napoleon Bonaparte the revolution was effectively over, civil government having been stubbed out by the army. Others soldiered on, but refused to transfer their loyalty to the empire in 1804. Many, of course, accepted the change of regime, and continued in Napoleon's service until 1815. It is a question that has continued to divide historians – just when can the revolution be said to have ended? Was it at Thermidor, with the overthrow of Robespierre? Relatively few now subscribe to that view, pointing out how difficult it was to eradicate a revolutionary, even a terrorist, mentality after 1794 (Baczko, 1994). Others would opt for Brumaire on the grounds that it rudely emasculated the authority of the legislature which was at the heart of the revolutionary project (Crook, 1998). Others again suggest that this authority had long been trampled underfoot – by the Jacobins' resort to executive committees, or by the Directory's annulment of elections in Vendémiaire when the results went against them. These suggest that government was already placing the needs of order above the wishes of the people in pursuit of its goal of a "security state" (Brown and Miller, 2002).

It is fitting that, with so many symbolic meanings, the revolution should have become a battleground for cultural historians, intent on deconstructing revolutionary discourse and offering new, often highly gendered, explanations of their actions. For some the French Revolution is a powerful example of the autonomy of language: they point to the choice of images and metaphors preferred by contemporaries to give a cultural interpretation of the period (Guilhaumou, 1998), or examine the use of words by the Jacobins to suggest links between political ideology and the exercise of power (Jaume, 1989). Others offer feminist readings of what they see as a male public sphere that excluded women from citizenship and treated their attempts at political association with contempt (Godineau, 1998). They discuss the representation of power rather than its exercise, as is shown by the renewed interest in art and caricature, symbols and festivals (Ozouf, 1988). In particular, historians have turned to the imagery of the body politic, which was repeatedly taken up in both prints and prose throughout the revolutionary decade (Baecque, 1997). They apply methodologies borrowed from other disciplines, such as anthropology or psychology, to explain the central thrust of the revolution. Lynn Hunt, for instance, finds in the imagery of the period Freudian images of what she calls a "family romance," where the people expressed an oedipal hatred of the father-figure, the king, and the revolutionaries bonded as a band of brothers intent on seizing political power (Hunt, 1992). All have this in common, that they see the politics of the revolution in allegorical or metaphorical terms rather than taking them at their face value.

There have been other changes, too. With a decline in the concern for people as classes, there has been greater interest in their experience as individuals, whether as deputies, merchants, soldiers, or marketwomen. There has been a more systematic attempt to understand their faith and beliefs, not least their religious beliefs at a time when the revolutionaries were set on closing churches and denying ordinary men and women the solace of prayer and confession (Aston, 2000; Desan, 1990). Paris has always enjoyed pride of place in revolutionary historiography, as the city where violence and popular anger could have national impact, and it is fitting that the organization and policing of the city, graphically discussed by Richard Cobb (1970), has attracted a new generation of researchers (Andress, 2004; Garrioch, 2002; Shapiro, 1993). With the multiplication of local studies on counter-revolution and federalism, there has been greater concern to distinguish the experience of Parisians from that of provincial Frenchmen, and to give provincial history a more distinct role in the national story (Forrest, 2004; Hanson, 2003). As a consequence the revolution is now seen less as a single block, dominated by central government and ruled intransigently from Paris. For some, indeed, its main driving force was the tension between revolution and counter-revolution, which drove Paris to ever greater radicalism and intolerance (Sutherland, 2003).

Few doubt the central importance of France's revolution in the political history of the late eighteenth century. It dominated the European world of the 1790s, spreading panic among kings and princes and making that *fin de siècle* even more significant and heavy with menace than most. The message of "liberty, equality, and fraternity" which it proclaimed to the other peoples of Europe went on to reverberate around the world. In every state along the Rhine, in every country across Europe, there were small cells of patriots, often calling themselves Jacobins, to whom the message emanating from France brought hope and the promise of a better future. The ideology of the revolution was taken up by republicans in Belgium, the United Provinces, Switzerland, Poland, and the duchies and kingdoms that made up what is now Germany. It made converts amongst radicals in the London Corresponding

Society and in the northern industrial cities of England. The German poet Goethe was not alone in believing that 1789 represented the dawn of a new era in history, and when, in 1792, he witnessed the victory of the French army at Valmy, he was left in no doubt as to the importance of what unfolded before him. "From this time and place," he wrote, "a new epoch is beginning." Few during the 1790s would have disagreed (Godechot, 1983).

The impact of the Revolution was not, however, confined to Europe. It was a world event that spread its message to sugar islands in the Caribbean and to Réunion in the Indian Ocean and, in the decades that followed, to the colonies of Spain and Portugal in Central and Latin America (Sperber, 2000). In the process of being transferred to the non-white world, the central message of the revolution was altered, its emphasis turning to race and negritude. If in France it brought equality of rights to Protestants and Jews, nobles and commoners, in Saint-Domingue it gave rights to mulattos and men of color, before being engulfed in a bloody slave rebellion that resulted in the world's first black republic (Dubois, 2004). And though the subsequent history of Haiti would prove to be deeply troubled, the fact that slaves were freed – however temporarily – and that black Africans chanted the slogans of the First French Republic could not fail to inspire other colonial peoples thirsting for liberty. Independence movements in nineteenth-century Mexico, Ecuador, and Bolivia, among others, would acknowledge their debt to France (Bayly, 2004), while in the twentieth century the message of 1789 and the example of Haiti would be paraded before the peoples of colonial Africa as a source of inspiration, a model for others to follow. Negative images of Terror and guillotines were set aside as the revolution became a source of inspiration for popular movements across five continents, and an event of abiding significance in the world-wide movement for human rights.

Bibliography

Andress, D., *The French Revolution and the People* (London, 2004).

Andress, D., *The Terror: Civil War in the French Revolution* (London, 2005).

Arasse, D., *The Guillotine and the Terror* (London, 1989).

Aston, N., *Religion and Revolution in France, 1780–1804* (Basingstoke, 2000).

Baczko, B., *Ending the Terror: The French Revolution after Robespierre* (Cambridge, 1994).

Baecque, A. de, *The Body Politic: Corporeal Metaphor in Revolutionary France, 1770–1800* (Stanford, 1997).

Bailyn, B., *The Ideological Origins of the American Revolution* (New York, 1992).

Baker, K. M., *Inventing the French Revolution: Essays on French Political Culture in the Eighteenth Century* (Cambridge, 1990).

Bayly, C. A., *The Birth of the Modern World, 1780–1914* (Oxford, 2004).

Bertaud, J.-P., *The Army of the French Revolution: From Citizen-Soldiers to Instrument of Power* (Princeton, 1988).

Blanning, T. C. W., *The French Revolution in Germany: Occupation and Resistance in the Rhineland, 1792–1802* (Oxford, 1983).

Blanning, T. C. W., *The French Revolution: Class War or Culture Clash?* (Basingstoke, 1998).

Bongie, L. L., *David Hume: Prophet of the Counter-Revolution* (Oxford, 1965).

Brake, W. P. te, *Regents and Rebels: The Revolutionary World of an Eighteenth-Century Dutch City* (Oxford, 1989).

Brown, H. G., *War, Revolution and the Bureaucratic State: Politics and Army Administration in France, 1791–1799* (Oxford, 1995).

Brown, H. G. and J. A. Miller (eds.), *Taking Liberties: Problems of a New Order from the French Revolution to Napoleon* (Manchester, 2002).

Campbell, P. R. (ed.), *The Origins of the French Revolution* (Basingstoke, 2006).

Carrot, G., *La Garde Nationale, 1789–1871: Une force publique ambiguë* (Paris, 2001).

Chartier, R., *The Cultural Origins of the French Revolution* (Durham, NC, 1991).

Cobb, R. C., *The Police and the People: French Popular Protest, 1789–1820* (Oxford, 1970).

Cobban, A., *The Social Interpretation of the French Revolution* (Cambridge, 1964).

Crook, M., *Elections in the French Revolution: An Apprenticeship in Democracy, 1789–1799* (Cambridge, 1996).

Crook, M., *Napoleon Comes to Power: Democracy and Dictatorship in Revolutionary France, 1795–1804* (Cardiff, 1998).

Darnton, R., *The Literary Underground of the Old Regime* (Cambridge, MA, 1982).

Desan, S., *Reclaiming the Sacred: Lay Religion and Popular Politics in Revolutionary France* (Ithaca, 1990).

Dickinson, H. T., *The Politics of the People in Eighteenth-Century Britain* (New York, 1995).

Doyle, W., *The Oxford History of the French Revolution* (Oxford, 1989).

Dubois, L., *Avengers of the New World: The Story of the Haitian Revolution* (Cambridge, MA, 2004).

Dull, J. R., *The French Navy and the Seven Years' War* (Lincoln, 2005).

Elliott, M., *Partners in Revolution: The United Irishmen and France* (New Haven, 1982).

Farge, A., *Subversive Words: Public Opinion in Eighteenth-Century France* (Cambridge, 1994).

Fitzsimmons, M. P., *The Remaking of France: The National Assembly and the Constitution of 1791* (Cambridge, 1994).

Fitzsimmons, M. P., *The Night the Old Regime Ended: August 4 1789 and the French Revolution* (University Park, PA, 2003).

Forrest, A., *The Soldiers of the French Revolution* (Durham, NC, 1990).

Forrest, A., *Paris, the Provinces and the French Revolution* (London, 2004).

Furet, F., *Interpreting the French Revolution* (Cambridge, 1981).

Garrioch, D., *The Making of Revolutionary Paris* (Berkeley, 2002).

Gatrell, V, *The Hanging Tree: Execution and the English People, 1770–1868* (Oxford, 1994).

Godechot, J., *France and the Atlantic Revolution of the Eighteenth Century 1770–1799* (New York, 1965).

Godechot, J., *La Grande Nation: L'Expansion révolutionnaire de la France dans le monde de 1789 à 1799* (Paris, 1983).

Godineau, D., *The Women of Paris and their French Revolution* (Berkeley, 1998).

Gough, H., *The Newspaper Press in the French Revolution* (London, 1988).

Gueniffey, P., *La Politique de la Terreur: Essai sur la violence révolutionnaire, 1789–1794* (Paris, 2000).

Guilhaumou, J., *L'Avènement des porte-parole de la République, 1789–1792: Essai de synthèse sur les langages de la Révolution française* (Villeneuve-d'Ascq, 1998).

Hampson, N., *Will and Circumstance: Montesquieu, Rousseau and the French Revolution* (London, 1983).

Hanson, P. R., *The Jacobin Republic Under Fire: The Federalist Revolt in the French Revolution* (University Park, PA, 2003).

Higonnet, P., *Goodness beyond Virtue: Jacobins during the French Revolution* (Cambridge, MA, 1998).

Hunt, L., *Politics, Culture and Class in the French Revolution* (Berkeley, 1984).

Hunt, L., *The Family Romance of the French Revolution* (London, 1992).
Israel, J. I., *Radical Enlightenment: Philosophy and the Making of Modernity, 1650–1750* (Oxford, 2001).
Jaume, L., *Le Discours jacobin et la démocratie* (Paris, 1989).
Jones, P. M., *The Peasantry in the French Revolution* (Cambridge, 1988).
Jourdan, A., *La Révolution, une exception française?* (Paris, 2004).
Kates, G., *The Cercle Social, the Girondins and the French Revolution* (Princeton, 1985).
Kennedy, M. L., *The Jacobin Clubs in the French Revolution* (vols. 1 and 2, Princeton, 1982, 1988; vol. 3, New York, 2000).
Lefebvre, G., *The Great Fear of 1789* (New York, 1973).
Lewis, G. and C. Lucas (eds.), *Beyond the Terror: Essays in French Regional and Social History, 1794–1815* (Cambridge, 1983).
Lucas, C. (ed.), *The Political Culture of the French Revolution* (Oxford, 1988).
Lüsebrink, H.-J. and R. Reichardt, *The Bastille: A History of a Symbol of Despotism and Freedom* (Durham, NC, 1997).
McMahon, D. M., *Enemies of the Enlightenment: The French Counter-Enlightenment and the Making of Modernity* (New York, 2001).
Merriman, J. M., *A History of Modern Europe from the Renaissance to the Present* (New York, 2004)
Moore, Jr., B., *Social Origins of Dictatorship and Democracy: Lord and Peasant in the Making of the Modern World* (London, 1984).
Munck, T., *The Enlightenment: A Comparative Social History, 1721–1794* (London, 2000).
Ozouf, M., *Festivals and the French Revolution* (Cambridge, MA, 1988).
Palmer, R. R., *The Age of the Democratic Revolution: A Political History of Europe and America, 1760–1800* (2 vols., Princeton, 1959).
Patrick, A., *The Men of the First French Republic: Political Alignments in the National Convention of 1792* (Baltimore, 1972).
Popkin, J. D., *Revolutionary News: The Press in France, 1789–1799* (Durham, NC, 1990).
Schama, S., *Patriots and Liberators: Revolution in the Netherlands, 1780–1813* (London, 1977).
Sewell, W. H., *Work and Revolution in France: The Language of Labor from the Old Regime to 1848* (Cambridge, 1980).
Sewell, W. H., *A Rhetoric of Bourgeois Revolution: The Abbé Sieyes and What Is the Third Estate?* (Durham, NC, 1994).
Shapiro, B. M., *Revolutionary Justice in Paris, 1789–1790* (Cambridge, 1993).
Shapiro, G. and J. Markoff, *Revolutionary Demands: A Content Analysis of the Cahiers de Doléances of 1789* (Stanford, 1998).
Slavin, M., *The French Revolution in Miniature: Section Droits de l'Homme, 1789–1795* (Princeton, 1984).
Soboul, A., *The Parisian Sans-Culottes and the French Revolution, 1793–1794* (Oxford, 1964).
Soboul, A., *The French Revolution from the Storming of the Bastille to Napoleon, 1787–1799* (London, 1974).
Sonenscher, M., *Work and Wages: Natural Law, Politics and the Eighteenth-Century French Trades* (Cambridge, 1989).
Sperber, J., *Revolutionary Europe, 1780–1850* (London, 2000).
Stone, B., *The Genesis of the French Revolution: A Global-Historical Interpretation* (Cambridge, 1994).
Sutherland, D. M. G., *The French Revolution and Empire: The Quest for a Civic Order* (Oxford, 2003).

Tackett, T., *Religion, Revolution and Regional Culture in Eighteenth-Century France: The Ecclesiastical Oath of 1791* (Princeton, 1985).

Tackett, T., *Becoming a Revolutionary: The Deputies of the French National Assembly and the Emergence of a Revolutionary Culture, 1789–1790* (Princeton, 1996).

Tackett, T., *When the King Took Flight* (Cambridge, MA, 2003).

Venturi, F., *The End of the Old Regime in Europe, 1768–1789* (2 vols., Princeton, 1991).

Vovelle, M., *The Revolution against the Church: From Reason to the Supreme Being* (Cambridge, 1991).

Weber, C., *Terror and its Discontents: Suspect Words in Revolutionary France* (Minneapolis, 2003).

Woloch, I., *The New Regime: Transformations of the French Civic Order, 1789–1820s* (New York, 1994).

Bibliography

Abensour, L., *La Femme et la féminisme en France avant la Révolution* (Geneva, 1923; repr. 1966).
Åberg, A. and G. Göransson, *Karoliner* (Stockholm, 1998).
Achilles, W., *Landwirtschaft in der Frühen Neuzeit* (Munich, 1991).
Adamson, J. (ed.), *The Princely Courts of Europe, 1500–1750* (London, 1999).
Ago, R., *Carriere e clientele nella Roma barocca* (Rome, 1990).
Aguilar Pinal, F., *La España del absolutismo ilustrado* (1991; Madrid, 2005).
Agulhon, M., *La Sociabilité méridionale: Confréries et associations dans la vie collective en Provence orientale à la fin du 18e siècle* (Aix-en-Provence, 1966).
Aksan, V., "Breaking the spell of the Baron de Tott: reframing the question of military reform in the Ottoman empire, 1760–1830," *International History Review*, 24 (2002), 253–77.
Albareda, J., *Felipe V y el triunfo del absolutismo: Cataluña en un conflicto europeo (1700–1714)* (Generalitat de Catalunya, 2002).
Albion, R. G., *Forests and Sea Power: The Timber Problem of the Royal Navy, 1652–1862* (1926; Cambridge, MA, 1965).
Albistur, M. and D. Armogathe (eds.), *Le Grief des femmes: Anthologie du texts féministes du IIe empire à nos jours* (Poitiers, 1978).
Albrecht, P., "Kaffeetrinken. Dem Bürger zur Ehr – dem Armen zur Schand," in R. Vierhaus (ed.), *Das Volk als Objekt obrigkeitlichen Handelns* (Tübingen, 1992), pp. 57–100.
Albrecht, P., H. E. Bödeker, and E. Hinrichs (eds.), *Formen der Geselligkeit in Nordwestdeutschland 1750–1820* (Tübingen, 2003).
Alden, D., *Royal Government in Colonial Brazil, with Special Reference to the Administration of the Marques of Lavradio, Viceroy 1769–79* (Berkeley, 1968).
Alden, D., *The Making of an Enterprise: The Society of Jesus in Portugal, its Empire, and Beyond, 1540–1750* (Stanford, 1996).
Aldridge, A. O. (ed.), *The Ibero-American Enlightenment* (Urbana, 1971).
Ales, S., *Le regie truppe sarde 1750–1773* (Milan, 1989).
Ales, S., *Le regie truppe sarde 1773–1814* (Rome, 1989).
Alexander, J. T., *Bubonic Plague in Early Modern Russia: Public Health and Urban Disaster* (new edn., New York, 2002).
Alexander, S. and B. Taylor, "In defence of patriarchy," repr. in R. Samuel (ed.), *People's History and Socialist Theory* (London, 1981).

A Companion to Eighteenth-Century Europe, First Edition. Edited by Peter H. Wilson.
© 2014 John Wiley & Sons, Ltd. Published 2014 by John Wiley & Sons, Ltd.

Allen, R. C., *Enclosure and the Yeoman* (Oxford, 1992).
Allen, R. C., "Economic structure and agricultural productivity in Europe, 1300–1800," *European Review of Economic History*, 3 (2000), 1–25.
Allen, R. C., "The great divergence in European wages and prices," *Explorations in Economic History*, 38 (2001), 411–43.
Andersen, D. H., *The Danish Flag in the Mediterranean: Shipping and Trade, 1747–1807* (2 vols., Copenhagen, 2000).
Anderson, F., *Crucible of War: The Seven Years' War and the Fate of Empire in British North America, 1754–1766* (New York, 2000).
Anderson, R. C., *Naval Wars in the Baltic, 1522–1850* (1910; London, 1969).
Anderson, R. C., *Naval Wars in the Levant, 1559–1853* (Liverpool, 1952).
Anderson, M. S., *Europe in the Eighteenth Century 1713–1783* (3rd edn., London, 1987).
Anderson, M. S., "The Italian reformers," in H. M. Scott (ed.), *Enlightened Absolutism* (Basingstoke, 1990), pp. 55–74.
Anderson, M. S., *The Rise of Modern Diplomacy, 1450–1919* (London, 1993).
Anderson, M. S., *The War of the Austrian Succession 1740–1748* (Harlow, 1995).
Andrade Arruda, J. J. de, et al., "Decadence or crisis in the Luso-Brazilian empire: a new model of colonization in the eighteenth century," *Hispanic American Historical Review*, 80 (2000), 865–78.
Andres-Gallego, J., *El Motin de Esquilache, America y Europa* (Madrid, 2003).
Andress, D., *The French Revolution and the People* (London, 2004).
Andress, D., *The Terror: Civil War in the French Revolution* (London, 2005).
Andries, L., *La Bibliothèque bleue au dix-huitième siècle: Une tradition éditoriale* (Oxford, 1989).
Angot, A., *Etude sur les Vendanges en France* (Paris, 1885).
Anisimov, E., *The Reforms of Peter the Great: Progress through Coercion in Russia* (Armonk, 1993).
Anisimov, E., "Anna Ivanovna," *Russian Studies in History*, 32 (1994), 37–72.
Anisimov, E., *Empress Elizabeth: Her Reign and her Russia* (Gulf Breeze, FL, 1995).
Antoine, M., "La Monarchie absolue," in K. M. Baker (ed.), *The Political Culture of the Old Regime* (Oxford, 1987), pp. 3–24.
Antoine, M., *Louis XV* (Paris, 1989).
Arasse, D., *The Guillotine and the Terror* (London, 1989).
Arcon Dominguez, J. L., "La guarniciòn de Barcelona en 1705," *Dragona*, 2(4) (1994), 44–9.
Aretin, K. O. v., "Liordinamento feudale in Italia nel XVI e XVII secolo e le aue ripercussioni sulla politica europea," *Annali dell' Instituto Storico Italo-Germanico in Trento*, 4 (1978), 51–94.
Aretin, K. O. Frhr. v., *Das alte Reich 1648–1806* (3 vols., Stuttgart, 1993–7).
Armillas Vicente, J. A. and C. E. Corona Baratech (eds.), *La España des las reformas hasta el final del reinado de Carlos IV*, Historia General de España y América, vol. X/2 (2nd edn., Madrid, 1990).
Asch, R. G., *Nobilities in Transition 1500–1700* (London, 2003).
Asch, R. G. and A. M. Birke, *Princes, Patronage, and the Nobility: The Court at the Beginning of the Modern Age* (London, 1991).
Asch, R. G. and H. Duchhardt (eds.), *Der Absolutismus. Ein Mythos?* (Cologne, 1996).
Astarita, T., *The Continuity of Feudal Power: The Caracciolo di Brienza in Spanish Naples* (Cambridge, 1992).
Aston, N., *Religion and Revolution in France, 1780–1804* (Basingstoke, 2000).
Aston, N., *Christianity and Revolutionary Europe c.1750–1830* (Cambridge, 2002).
Aué, M. and M. Parent, *Vauban* (Vic-en-Bigorre, 1998).

Augustine, W. R., "Notes towards a portrait of the eighteenth-century Russian nobility," *Canadian-American Slavic Studies*, 4 (1970), 373–425.

Baczko, B., *Ending the Terror: The French Revolution after Robespierre* (Cambridge, 1994).

Badolato, A. et al., *La battaglia di Guastalla* (Guastalla, 1984).

Baecque, A. de, *The Body Politic: Corporeal Metaphor in Revolutionary France, 1770–1800* (Stanford, 1997).

Bagger, H., "The role of the Baltic in Russian foreign policy 1721–1773," in H. Ragsdale (ed.), *Imperial Russian Foreign Policy* (Cambridge, 1993), pp. 36–55.

Bailyn, B., *The Ideological Origins of the American Revolution* (New York, 1992).

Bairoch, P., J. Batou, and P. Chèvre, *La Population des villes européennes de 800 à 1850* (Geneva, 1988).

Baker, K. M. (ed.), *The French Revolution and the Creation of Modern Political Culture*, vol. 1: *The Political Culture of the Old Régime* (Oxford, 1987).

Baker, K. M. (ed.), *The Old Régime and the French Revolution* (Chicago, 1987).

Baker, K. M., *Inventing the French Revolution: Essays on French Political Culture in the Eighteenth Century* (Cambridge, 1990).

Baker, K. M., "Politics and public opinion under the old regime," in J. R. Censer and J. D. Popkin (eds.), *Press and Politics in Pre-Revolutionary France* (Berkeley, 1987), pp. 204–16; repr. in revised form as "Public opinion as political invention," in K. M. Baker, *Inventing the French Revolution* (Cambridge, 1990), pp. 167–99.

Baker-Smith, V., *A Life of Anne of Hanover, Princess Royal* (Leiden, 1995).

Bamford, P. W., *Forests and French Sea Power, 1660–1789* (Toronto, 1956).

Barker, H. and S. Burrows (eds.), *Press, Politics and the Public Sphere in Europe and North America, 1760–1820* (Cambridge, 2002).

Barnard, F. M., *Herder's Social and Political Thought: From Enlightenment to Nationalism* (Oxford, 1965).

Barnett, S. J., *The Enlightenment and Religion: The Myths of Modernity* (Manchester, 2003).

Barone, Enrico, *I grandi capitani dell'età moderna* (Rome, 1982).

Barriendos Vallve, M. and M. Martín-Vide, "Secular climatic oscillations as indicated by catastrophic floods in the Spanish Mediterranean coastal area (14th–19th centuries)." *Climatic Change*, 38 (1998), 473–91.

Bartlett, R., "The question of serfdom: Catherine II, the Russian debate and the view from the Baltic periphery," in R. Bartlett and J. Hartley (eds.), *Russia in the Age of the Enlightenment* (London, 1990), pp. 142–66.

Barton, H. A., *Scandinavia in the Revolutionary Era, 1760–1815* (Minneapolis, 1986).

Baugh, D. A., *British Naval Administration in the Age of Walpole* (Princeton, 1965).

Baugh, D. A., "Great Britain's 'blue-water' policy, 1689–1815," *International History Review*, 10 (1988), 33–58.

Baugh, D. A., "Withdrawing from Europe: Anglo-French maritime geopolitics, 1750–1800," *International History Review*, 20 (1998), 1–32.

Bavel, B. J. P. van and E. Thoen (eds.), *Land Productivity and Agro-Systems in the North Sea Area* (Turnhout, 1999).

Bayly, C. A., *The Birth of the Modern World, 1780–1914* (Oxford, 2004).

Beales, D., *Joseph II* (Cambridge, 1987).

Beales, D. E. D., *Prosperity and Plunder: European Catholic Monasteries in the Age of Revolution, 1650–1815* (Cambridge, 2003).

Beamish, N. L., *History of the King's German Legion* (London, 1832–7).

Béaur, G., *Histoire agraire de la France au XVIIIe siècle* (Paris, 2000).

Beauroy, J., M. Bertrand, and E. Gargan (eds.), *The Wolf and the Lamb: Popular Culture in France from the Old Regime to the Twentieth Century* (Saratoga, 1976).

Beck, R., *Unterfinning. Ländliche Welt vor Anbruch der Moderne* (Munich, 1993).

Beckman, J. E. and T. J. Mahoney, "The Maunder Minimum and climate change: have historical records aided current research?," *Library and Information Services in Astronomy III, ASP Conference Series*, 153 (1998), 212–17.

Beem, C., *The Lioness Roared: The Problems of Female Rule in English History* (Basingstoke, 2006).

Behrens, K., (ed.), *Frauenbriefe der Romantik* (Frankfurt am Main, 1982).

Behringer, W., *Im Zeichen des Merkur. Reichspost und Kommunikationsrevolution in der Frühen Neuzeit* (Göttingen, 2003).

Behringer, W., "Communications revolutions: a historiographical concept," *German History*, 24 (2006), 333–74.

Beik, W., *Absolutism and Society in Seventeenth-Century France* (Cambridge, 1985).

Belhamissi, M., "Marine d'Alger et contrôle maritime à l'époque ottomane," in P. Alberini (ed.), *Aspetti ed attualità del potere marittimo in Mediterraneo nei secoli XII–XVII* (Rome, 1999), pp. 49–66.

Bell, D. A., *The Cult of the Nation in France: Inventing Nationalism, 1680–1800* (Cambridge, MA, 2001).

Bély, L. (ed.), *Dictionnaire de l'Ancien Régime* (Paris, 1996).

Bély, L., *Les Relations internationales en Europe XVIIe–XVIIIe siècles* (2nd edn., Paris, 1998).

Bennett, B., *Beyond Irony: Eighteenth-Century German Literature and the Poetics of Irony* (Cornell, 1993).

Benot, Y., *La Révolution française et la fin des colonies, 1789–1794* (1987; repr. Paris, 2004).

Bercé, Y.-M., *Croquants et nu-pieds: Les Soulèvements paysans en France du XVIe au XIXe siècle* (Paris, 1974).

Bérengér, J. (ed.) *La Révolution militaire en Europe (XV–XVIII siècles)* (Paris, 1997).

Berg, M. (ed.), *Markets and Manufactures in Early Industrial Europe* (London, 1991).

Berg, M., *Luxury and Pleasure in Eighteenth-Century Britain* (Oxford, 2005).

Bermingham, A. and J. Brewer (eds.), *The Consumption of Culture, 1600–1800: Image, Object, Text* (London, 1997).

Bertaud, J.-P., *The Army of the French Revolution: From Citizen-Soldiers to Instrument of Power* (Princeton, 1988).

Bertelsen, l., *The Nonsense Club: Literature and Popular Culture 1749–64* (Oxford, 1986).

Bertram, M., *Georg II. König und Kurfürst* (Göttingen, 2004).

Bethell, L. (ed.), *Colonial Brazil* (Cambridge, 1987).

Beutel, A., *Aufklärung in Deutschland* (Göttingen, 2006).

Beyrer, K., "The mail-coach revolution: landmarks in travel in Germany between the seventeenth and nineteenth centuries," *German History*, 24 (2006), 375–86.

Bien, D. D., "The army in the French Enlightenment: reform, reaction and revolution," *Past and Present*, 85 (1979), 68–98.

Bien, D. D., "Offices, corps and a system of state credit: the uses of privilege under the *ancien régime*," in K. M. Baker (ed.), *The Political Culture of the Old Regime* (Oxford, 1987), pp. 89–114.

Bien, D. D., "Aristocracy," in F. Furet and M. Ozouf (eds.), *A Critical Dictionary of the French Revolution* (1988; English translation, Cambridge, MA, 1989), pp. 616–28.

Birke A. M. and K. Kluxen (eds.), *England and Hanover* (Munich, 1986).

Birn, R., *Book Censorship in Eighteenth-Century France and Rousseau's Response*, Studies on Voltaire and the Eighteenth Century, NS 1 (Oxford, 2005), 223–45.

Bizocchi, "Politica fiscale e immunità ecclesiastica nella Toscana medicea fra repubblica e granducato (secoli XV–XVIII)," in H. Kellenbenz and P. Prodi (eds.), *Fisco, religione, stato nell'età confessionale* (Bologna, 1989), 355–85.

Black, J., "The Crown, Hanover and the shift in British foreign policy in the 1760s," in J. Black (ed.), *Knights Errant and True Englishmen: British Foreign Policy 1660–1800* (Edinburgh, 1989), pp. 113–34.

Black, J., *European Warfare 1660–1815* (London, 1994).

Black, J., *Britain as a Military Power 1688–1815* (London, 1999).

Black, J., *Eighteenth-Century Europe* (2nd edn., Basingstoke, 1999).

Black, J., *European International Relations, 1648–1815* (Basingstoke, 2002).

Black, J., *The Hanoverians: The History of a Dynasty* (London, 2004).

Black, J., *Continental Commitment: Britain, Hanover and Interventionism, 1714–1793* (Abingdon, 2005).

Black, J., *George III: America's Last King* (New Haven, 2006).

Blackburn, R., *The Making of New World Slavery: From the Baroque to the Modern, 1492–1800* (New York, 1997).

Blackstone, W., *Commentaries on the Laws of England*, ed. E. Christian (13th edn., 4 vols., London, 1800).

Blanning, T. C. W., *Reform and Revolution in Mainz 1743–1803* (Cambridge, 1974).

Blanning, T. C. W., "'That horrid electorate' or 'Ma patrie germanique?' George III and the Fürstenbund of 1785," *Historical Journal*, 20 (1977), 311–44.

Blanning, T. C. W., *The French Revolution in Germany: Occupation and Resistance in the Rhineland, 1792–1802* (Oxford, 1983).

Blanning, T. C. W., *The Origins of the French Revolutionary Wars* (Harlow, 1986).

Blanning, T. C. W., *Joseph II* (Harlow, 1994).

Blanning, T. C. W., *The French Revolutionary Wars, 1787–1802* (London, 1996).

Blanning, T. C. W., *The French Revolution: Class War or Culture Clash?* (Basingstoke, 1998).

Blanning, T. C. W., *The Culture of Power and the Power of Culture: Old Regime Europe 1660–1789* (Oxford, 2002).

Blaufarb, R., *The French Army 1750–1820: Careers, Talent, Merit* (Manchester, 2002).

Blickle, P., "Untertanen in der Frühneuzeit. Zur Rekonstruktion der politischen Kultur und der Sozialen Wirklichkeit Deutschlands im 17. Jahrhundert," *Vierteljahresschrift für Sozial- und Wirtschaftsgeschichte*, 70 (1983), 483–522.

Blickle, P. (ed.), *Resistance, Representation, and Community* (Oxford, 1997).

Blondé, B., et al. (eds.), *Buyers, Sellers and Salesmanship in Medieval and Early Modern Europe* (Turnhout, 2006).

Blum, J., *The End of the Old Order in Rural Europe* (Princeton, 1978).

Bock, G., "Women's history and gender history: aspects of an international debate," *Gender & History*, 1 (1989), 7–30.

"Bodleian Library Broadside Ballads" <http://www.bodley.ox.ac.uk/ballads/ballads.htm>.

Bohstedt, J., *Riots and Community Politics in England and Wales, 1790–1810* (Cambridge, 1983).

Bongie, L. L., *David Hume: Prophet of the Counter-Revolution* (Oxford, 1965).

Bonney, R. (ed.), *Economic Systems and State Finance* (Oxford, 1995).

Borsay, P., *The English Urban Renaissance: Culture and Society in the Provincial Town, 1660–1770* (Oxford, 1989).

Bosher, J. F., *French Finances 1770–1795: From Business to Bureaucracy* (Cambridge, 1970).

Bosher, J. F., "The French crisis of 1770," *History*, 57 (1972), 17–30.

Bots, H. and W. W. Mijnhardt (ed.), *De droom van de revolutie. Nieuwe benaderingen van het patriottisme* (Amsterdam, 1988).

Bouton, C. A., *The Flour War: Gender, Class, and Community in Late Ancien Régime French Society* (University Park, PA, 1993).

Boxer, C., *The Golden Age of Brazil, 1695–1750* (Los Angeles, 1962).

Boxer, C. R., *The Dutch Seaborne Empire, 1600–1800* (London, 1965).
Boxer, C., *The Portuguese Seaborne Empire, 1415–1825* (London, 1969).
Boyle, N., *Goethe: the Poet and his Age* (Oxford, 1991).
Brading, D., "Bourbon Spain and its American empire," in L. Bethell (ed.), *The Cambridge History of Latin America*, vol. 1: *Colonial Latin America* (Cambridge, 1984), pp. 112–62.
Brading, D., *The First America: The Spanish Monarchy, Creole Patriots, and the Liberal State 1492–1867* (Cambridge, 1991).
Brake, W. P. te, *Regents and Rebels: The Revolutionary World of an Eighteenth-Century Dutch City* (Oxford, 1989).
Brake, W. P. te, *Shaping History: Ordinary People in European Politics, 1500–1700* (Berkeley, 1998).
Bräker, U., *Lebensgeschichte und natürliche Ebentheuer des armen Mannes im Tockenburg* (Zurich, 1789); e-text: <http://gutenberg.spiegel.de/braeker/tocken/tocken.htm>.
Braudel, F., *The Mediterranean and the Mediterranean World in the Age of Philip II*, vol. 2 (London, 1973).
Braun, R., *Das ausgehende Ancien Régime in der Schweiz* (Göttingen, 1984).
Braunbehrens, V., *Mozart in Vienna* (Oxford, 1991).
Brauneder, W. and L. Höbelt (eds.), *Sacrum Imperium. Das Reich und Österreich 996–1806* (Vienna, 1996).
Brayne, M., *The Greatest Storm: Britain's Night of Destruction, November 1703* (Stroud, 2002).
Brázdil, R., "Reconstructions of past climates from historical sources in the Czech lands," in P. Jones et al. (eds.), *Climatic Variations and Forcing Mechanisms of the Last 2000 years* (Berlin, 1996).
Brázdil, R., C. Pfister, H. Wanner, H. von Storch, and J. Luterbacher, "Historical climatology in Europe – the state of the art," *Climatic Change*, 70 (2005), 363–430.
Brázdil, R., H. Valášek, and J. Macková, "Climate of the Czech lands during the 1780s in light of the daily weather records of Parson Karel Bernard Hein of Hodonice (southwestern Moravia): comparison of documentary and instrumental data," *Climatic Change*, 60 (2003), 297–327.
Brázdil, R., H. Valášek, Z. Sviták, and J. Macková, *History of Weather and Climate in the Czech Lands*, vol. 5 (Brno, 2002).
Brennan, T., *Public Drinking and Popular Culture in Eighteenth-Century Paris* (Princeton, 1988).
Brewer, J., *Party Ideology and Popular Politics at the Accession of George III* (Cambridge, 1976).
Brewer, J., *The Sinews of Power* (London, 1989).
Brewer, J. and R. Porter (eds.), *Consumption and the World of Goods* (London, 1993).
Briggs, A., *Early Modern France 1560–1715* (Oxford, 1977).
Brockliss, L. and C. Jones, *The Medical World of Early Modern France* (Oxford, 1997).
Broman, T. H., "The medical sciences," in D. C. Lindberg and R. L. Numbers (eds.), *The Cambridge History of Science*, vol. 4: *The Eighteenth Century*, ed. R. Porter (Cambridge, 2003).
Bromley, J. S., *Corsairs and Navies, 1660–1760* (London, 1987).
Brookner, A., *Jacques-Louis David* (London, 1980).
Brooks, P., *The Novel of Worldliness: Cre'billon, Marivaux, Laclos, Stendhal* (Princeton, 1969).
Brousse, Y., "Les réseaux d'information de Louvois dans les Provinces-Unies et aux Pays Bas catholiques, 1671–1691: guerre et reinsegnement à la fin du XVIIe siècle," *Révue internationale d'Histoire Militaire*, 82 (2002), 57–77.

Brown, H. G., *War, Revolution and the Bureaucratic State: Politics and Army Administration in France, 1791–1799* (Oxford, 1995).

Brown, H. G., "Domestic state violence: repression from the Croquants to the Commune," *Historical Journal*, 42 (1999), 597–622.

Brown, H. G. and J. A. Miller (eds.), *Taking Liberties: Problems of a New Order from the French Revolution to Napoleon* (Manchester, 2002).

Brown, J., *An Estimate on the Manners and Principles of the Times* (London, 1757).

Brown, J., *On the Female Character and Education* (London, 1765).

Brown, S. J. and T. Tackett (eds.), *Cambridge History of Christianity*, vol. 7: *Enlightenment, Reawakening and Revolution 1660–1815* (Cambridge, 2006).

Browning, R., *The War of the Austrian Succession* (New York, 1993).

Bruford, W. H., *Culture and Society in Classical Weimar* (Cambridge, 1962).

Bruijn, J. R., "William III and his two navies," *Notes and Records of the Royal Society of London*, 43 (1989), 117–32.

Bruijn, J. R., *The Dutch Navy of the Seventeenth and Eighteenth Centuries* (Colombia, SC, 1993).

Brunner, O., W. Conze, and R. Koselleck (eds.), *Geschichtliche Grundbegriffe* (8 vols., Stuttgart, 1972–97).

Brusse, P., *Overleven door ondernemen. De agrarische geschiedenis van de Over-Betuwe 1650–1850* (Wageningen, 1999).

Bryson, N., *Word and Image: French Painting of the Ancient Regime* (Cambridge, 1981).

B.S. (Bréf til Stiftamtmanns úr Húnavatnssýsla 1736–1792) (National Library, Reykjavík).

Buchet, C., *Marine, économie et société, un example d'interaction: L'Avitaillement de la Royal Navy durant la guerre de sept ans* (Paris, 1999).

Bucholz, R. O. and J. C. Sainty, *Officials of the Royal Household 1660–1837* (2 vols., London, 1997).

Burke, P., *Popular Culture in Early Modern Europe* (1978; rev. edn., Aldershot, 1994).

Burke, P., *The Fabrication of Louis XIV* (New Haven, 1992).

Burke, P., *Languages and Communities in Early Modern Europe* (Cambridge, 2004).

Burleigh, M., *Earthly Powers: The Conflict between Religion and Politics from the French Revolution to the Great War* (London, 2005).

Burrows, D., *Handel* (Oxford, 1994).

Bush, M. L., "Peasant right and the peasantries of Europe under the old regime," in M. L. Bush (ed.), *Social Orders and Social Classes in Europe since 1500* (London, 1992), pp. 136–57.

Bushkovitch, P., *Peter the Great: The Struggle for Power, 1671–1725* (Cambridge, 2001).

Butel, P., *The Atlantic* (London, 1999).

Butterwick, B., *Poland's Last King and English Culture: Stanisław August Poniatowski 1732–1798* (Oxford, 1998).

Butterwick, R. (ed.), *The Polish-Lithuanian Monarchy in European Context, c.1500–1795* (Basingstoke, 2001).

Bynum, W. F. and R. Porter (eds.), *Medical Fringe and Medical Orthodoxy, 1750–1850* (London, 1987).

Cabantous, A., *La Mer et les hommes: Pêcheurs et matelots de Louis XV à la Révolution* (Dunkirk, 1980).

Cabantous, A., *Les Côtes barbares: Pilleurs d'épaves et sociétés littorales en France, 1680–1830* (Paris, 1993).

Caine, B. and G. Sluga, *Gendering European History, 1780–1920* (London and New York, 2000).

Calabria, A., "Per la storia della dominazione austriaca a Napoli, 1707–1734," *Archivio Storico Italiano*, 139 (1981), 459–78.

Cameron, E. (ed.), *Early Modern Europe* (Oxford, 2001).
Cameron, I. A., *Crime and Repression in the Auvergne and the Guyenne 1720–1790* (Cambridge, 1981).
Campbell, P. R. (ed.), *The Origins of the French Revolution* (Basingstoke, 2006).
Campbell Orr, C. (ed.), *Queenship in Britain 1660–1837: Royal Patronage, Court Culture and Dynastic Politics* (Manchester, 2002).
Campbell Orr, C. (ed.), *Queenship in Europe 1660–1815: The Role of the Consort* (Cambridge, 2004).
Campe, J. H., *Väterliche Rath für meine Tochter* (Brunswick, 1789), extract in U. Gerhard, *Verhältnisse und Verhinderungen. Frauenarbeit, Familie und Rechte der Frauen im 19. Jahrhundert* (Frankfurt am Main, 1978).
Camporesi, P., *Rustici e buffoni: cultura popolare e cultura d'élite fra Medioevo ed età moderna* (Turin, 1991).
Camuffo, D., "History of the long series of daily air temperature in Padova (1725–1998), in D. Camuffo and P. D. Jones (eds.), *Improved Understanding of Past Climatic Variability from Early Daily European Instrumental Sources* (Dordrecht, 2002).
Canning, K. and S. O. Rose, *Gender, Citizenship, Subjectivities*, special issue of *Gender & History*, 13, 3 (Nov. 2001).
Cannon, J. A., *Aristocratic Century: The Peerage of Eighteenth-Century England* (Cambridge, 1984).
Canosa, R., *Milano nel seicento: grandezza e miseria nell'Italia spagnola* (Milan, 1993).
Canosa, R., *Storia del Mediterraneo nel Seicento* (Rome, 1997).
Capp, B., *When Gossips Meet: Women, Family and Neighbourhood in Early Modern England* (Oxford, 2003).
Capra, C., "Riforme finanziarie e mutamento istituzionale nello stato di Milano: gli anni sessanta del secolo XVIII," *Rivista Storica Italiana*, 91 (1979), 313–68.
Cardozo, M., "The internationalism of the Portuguese Enlightenment: the role of the *estrangeirado*, *c.*1700–*c.*1750," in A. O. Aldridge (ed.), *The Ibero-American Enlightenment* (Urbana, 1971), pp. 140–210.
Carlsson, S. and J. Rosén, *Svensk historia* (2 vols., Stockholm, 1961–2).
Carpanetto, D. and G. Ricuperati, *Italy in the Age of Reason 1685–1789* (Harlow, 1987).
Carrasco, R. (ed.), *Solidarités et sociabilités en Espagne: XVIe–XXe siècles* (Paris, 1991).
Carretta, V., *Equiano the African: Biography of a Self-Made Man* (Athens, GA, 2005).
Carroll, M. P., *Madonnas that Maim: Popular Catholicism in Italy since the Fifteenth Century* (Baltimore, 1992).
Carrot, G., *La Garde Nationale, 1789–1871: Une force publique ambiguë* (Paris, 2001).
Carter, P., "Men about town: representations of foppery and masculinity in early eighteenth-century urban society," in H. Barker and E. Chalus (eds.), *Gender in Eighteenth-Century England: Roles, Representations and Responsibilities* (London, 1997), pp. 31–57.
Cassirer, E., *The Philosophy of the Enlightenment* (Princeton, 1951).
Castiglione, C., *Patrons and Adversaries: Nobles and Villagers in Italian Politics, 1640–1760* (Oxford, 2005).
Castro, C. de, *Campomanes: estado y reformismo ilustrado* (Madrid, 1996).
Castro, C. de, *A la sombra de Felipe V: Jose de Grimaldo, ministro responsible (1703–1726)* (Madrid, 2004).
Cavaciocchi, S. (ed.), *Il mercato della terra secc. XIII–XVIII* (Florence, 2003).
Cavaliero, R., *The Independence of Brazil* (London and New York, 1993).
Cavallo, S., "What did women transmit? The boundaries of domestic and personal property in seventeenth- and eighteenth-century Italy," in M. Donald and L. Hurcombe (eds.), *Gender and Material Culture in Historical Perspectives* (London, 2000), pp. 38–53.

Cavallo, S., *Charity and Power in Early Modern Italy: Benefactors and their Motives in Turin, 1541–1789* (Cambridge, 1995).
Censer, J., *The French Press in the Age of Enlightenment* (London, 1994).
Cerino Badone, G., F. Campagnolo, and M. Lucini, *Bandiere nel fango* (Turin, 2004).
Cerman, M. and H. Zeitlhofer (eds.), *Soziale Strukturen in Böhmen. Ein regionaler Vergleich von Wirtschaft und Gesellschaft in Gutsherrschaften, 16.–19. Jahrhundert* (Vienna and Munich, 2002).
Chadwick, O., *The Popes and European Revolution* (Oxford, 1981).
Chagniot, J., *Paris et l'armée au XVIIIe siècle: Etude politique et sociale* (Paris, 1985).
Chalus, E., "Elite women, social politics and the political world of late eighteenth-century England," *Historical Journal*, 43 (2000), 669–97.
Chalus, E., *Elite Women in English Political Life c.1754–1790* (Oxford, 2005).
Chandler, D. G., *Art of Warfare in the Age of Marlborough* (New York, 1994).
Chandler, D. G. (ed.), *Military Memoirs of Marlborough's Campaigns 1702–1712* (London, 1998).
Chandler, D. G., *Blenheim Preparation – the English Army on the March to the Danube* (Staplehurst, 2004).
Chandler, T. and G. Fox, *3000 Years of Urban Growth* (New York, 1974).
Charlesworth, A., *An Atlas of Rural Protests in Britain 1548–1900* (London, 1983).
Chartier, R., *The Cultural Uses of Print in Early Modern France* (Princeton, 1987).
Chartier, R., *The Cultural Origins of the French Revolution* (Durham, NC, 1991).
Chartier, R., G. Chaussinaud-Nogaret, H. Neveux, and E. Le Roy Ladurie, *La Ville des temps modernes: De la Renaissance aux révolutions* (Paris, 1988).
Chaussinand-Nogaret, G., *The French Nobility in the Eighteenth Century* (1976; English translation, Cambridge, 1985).
Cherniavsky, M., *Tsar and People: Studies in Russian Myths* (New Haven, 1961).
Childs, J., *The Nine Years' War and the British Army, 1688–1697: The Operations in the Low Countries* (Manchester, 1991).
Chisick, H., "Public opinion and political culture in France during the second half of the eighteenth century," *English Historical Review*, 117 (2002), 48–77.
Cipolla, C. M., *The Fontana Economic History of Europe*, vols. 2 and 3 (London, 1973, 1974).
Clark, A., *Working Life of Women in the 17th Century* (1919; London, 1982).
Clark, A., *The Struggle for the Breeches: Gender and the Making of the British Working Class* (Berkeley, 1995).
Clark, C., *Iron Kingdom: The Rise and Downfall of Prussia, 1600–1947* (London, 2006).
Clark, J. C. D., *English Society 1688–1832: Ideology, Social Structure and Political Practice during the Ancien Régime* (Cambridge, 1985).
Clark, J. C. D., *English Society, 1660–1832: Religion, Ideology and Politics during the Ancien Régime* (Cambridge, 2000).
Clark, P., *The English Alehouse: A Social History 1200–1830* (London, 1983).
Clark, P. (ed.), *Small Towns in Early Modern Europe* (Cambridge, 1995).
Clark, P., *British Clubs and Societies 1580–1800: The Origins of an Associational World* (Oxford, 2000).
Clark, P. (ed.), *The Cambridge Urban History of Britain*, vol. 2: *1540–1840* (Cambridge, 2000).
Clark, P. and R. A. Houston, "Culture and leisure 1700–1840," in P. Clark (ed.), *The Cambridge UrbanHistory of Britain*, vol. 2: *1540–1840* (Cambridge, 2000), pp. 575–613.
Clark, P. and B. Lepetit (eds.), *Capital Cities and their Hinterlands in Early Modern Europe* (Aldershot, 1996).

Clonard, conde de, *Historia organica de las armas de infanteria y caballeria españolas* (16 vols., Madrid, 1851–9).
Cobb, R. C., *The Police and the People: French Popular Protest, 1789–1820* (Oxford, 1970).
Cobban, A., *A History of Modern France*, vol. 1: *1715–1799* (3rd edn., Harmondsworth, 1963).
Cobban, A., *The Social Interpretation of the French Revolution* (Cambridge, 1964).
Cochrane, E., *Tradition and Enlightenment in the Tuscan Academies, 1690–1800* (Chicago, 1961).
Cochrane, E., *Florence in the Forgotten Centuries, 1527–1800* (Chicago, 1973).
Coleman, D., "Proto-industrialization: a concept too many," in D. C. Coleman (ed.), *Myth, History and the Industrial Revolution* (London, 1992), pp. 107–22.
Colley, L., *Britons: Forging the Nation, 1707–1837* (London, 1992).
Collins, J. B., *Classes, Estates and Order in Early Modern Brittany* (Cambridge, 1994).
Collins, J. B., *The State in Early Modern France* (Cambridge, 1995).
Colloquio Internacional Carlos III y su Siglo (2 vols., Madrid, 1998).
Conrad, L. I., et al., *The Western Medical Tradition: 800 BC to AD 1800* (Cambridge, 1995).
Cook, H. J., *The Decline of the Old Medical Regime in Stuart London* (Ithaca, NY, 1986).
Cooper, J. P., "Patterns of inheritance and settlement by great landowners," in J. Goody, J. Thirsk, and E. P. Thompson (eds.), *Family and Inheritance* (Cambridge, 1976), pp. 192–327.
Coquery, N., *L'Hôtel aristocratique: Le Marché du luxe à Paris au XVIII siècle* (Paris, 1998).
Coquery, N. (ed.), *La Boutique et la ville: Commerces, commerçants, espaces et clientèles XVIe–XXe siècle* (Tours, 2000).
Coquery, N., "The language of success: marketing and distribution of semi-lux goods in eighteenth-century France," *Journal of Design History*, 17 (2004), 71–89.
Corp, E., et al., *Court in Exile: The Stuarts in France 1689–1718* (Cambridge, 2004).
Cortelazzo, M., *Venezia, il Levante e il mare* (Pisa, 1989).
Corvisier, A., *La Bataille de Malplaquet 1709: L'Effondrement de la France évité* (Paris, 1997).
Cosandey, F. and R. Descimon, *L'Absolutisme en France: Histoire et historiographie* (Paris, 2002).
Coulet, H. (ed.), *L'Armée au XVIIIe siècle (1715–1789)* (Aix-en-Provence, 1999).
Cowan, B., "What was masculine about the public sphere? Gender and the coffeehouse milieu in post-Restoration England," *History Workshop Journal*, 51 (2001), 127–57.
Cowan, B., *The Social Life of Coffee: The Emergence of the British Coffeehouse* (New Haven, 2005).
Cracraft, J., *The Church Reform of Peter the Great* (Stanford, 1971).
Cracraft, J., *The Revolution of Peter the Great* (Cambridge, MA, and London, 2003).
Craig, M., *Dublin, 1660–1860* (London, 1992).
Crampe-Casnabet, M., "A sampling of eighteenth-century philosophy," in N. Z. Davis and A. Farge (eds.), *A History of Women in the West*, vol. 3: *Renaissance and Enlightenment Paradoxes* (Cambridge, 1993), pp. 315–47.
Crang, M. and N. Thrift (eds.), Thinking Space (London, 2000).
Creswell, J., *British Admirals of the Eighteenth Century: Tactics in Battle* (London, 1972).
Crook, M., *Elections in the French Revolution: An Apprenticeship in Democracy, 1789–1799* (Cambridge, 1996).
Crook, M., *Napoleon Comes to Power: Democracy and Dictatorship in Revolutionary France, 1795–1804* (Cardiff, 1998).
Cross, A. (ed.), *St Petersburg, 1703–1825* (Basingstoke, 2004).

Crossick, G. (ed.), *The Artisan and the European Town, 1500–1900* (Aldershot, 1997).
Crouzet, F., *Britain Ascendant: Comparative Studies in Franco-British Economic History* (Cambridge, 1990).
Crow, T. E., *Painters and Public Life in Eighteenth-Century Paris* (New Haven and London, 1985).
Crowston, C. H., *Fabricating Women: The Seamstresses of Old Regime France, 1675–1791* (Durham, NC, 2001).
Cruyningen, P. J. van, *Behoudend maar buigzaam. Boeren in West-Zeeuws-Vlaanderen 1650–1850* (Wageningen, 2000).
Cruz, J., *Gentlemen, Bourgeois and Revolutionaries: Political Change and Cultural Persistence among the Spanish Dominant Groups 1750–1850* (Cambridge, 1996).
Csendes, P. and F. Opll (eds.), *Wien. Geschichte einer Stadt*, vol. 2: *Die frühneuzeitliche Residenz (16.–18. Jahrhundert)* (Vienna, 2003).
Cunningham, A. and R. French (eds.), *The Medical Enlightenment of the Eighteenth Century* (Cambridge, 1990).
Cunningham, H., *Children and Childhood in Western Society since 1500* (London, 1995).
Curl, J. S., *The Art and Architecture of Freemasonry* (London, 1991).
Cushner, N., *Spain in the Philippines: From Conquest to Revolution* (Rutland, VT, 1971).
Dakin, D., *Turgot and the Ancien Régime in France* (London, 1939).
Danielsen, R., et al., *Norway: A History from the Vikings to Our Own Times* (Oslo, 1995).
Danker, U., *Räuberbanden im Alten Reich um 1700* (Frankfurt am Main, 1988).
Dann, U., *Hanover and Great Britain* (Leicester, 1991).
Darnton, R., *Mesmerism and the End of the Enlightenment in France* (Cambridge, MA, 1968).
Darnton, R., "The high Enlightenment and the low-life of literature in pre-revolutionary France," *Past & Present*, 51 (1971), 81–115.
Darnton, R., *The Business of Enlightenment: A Publishing History of the* Encyclopédie *1775–1800* (Cambridge, MA, 1979).
Darnton, R.,*The Literary Underground of the Old Regime* (Cambridge, MA, 1982).
Darnton, R., *The Great Cat Massacre and other Episodes in French Cultural History* (London, 1991).
Darnton, R., "The forbidden books of pre-revolutionary France," in C. Lucas (ed.), *Rewriting the French Revolution* (Oxford, 1991), pp. 1–32.
Darnton, R., *The Forbidden Bestsellers of Pre-Revolutionary France* (London, 1996).
Darrow, M., *Revolution in the House: Family, Class and Inheritance in Southern France, 1775–1825* (Princeton, 1989).
Davidoff, L., M. Doolittle, J. Fink and K. Holden, *The Family Story: Blood, Contract and Intimacy, 1830–1960* (London, 1999).
Davies, N., *God's Playground: A History of Poland* (2 vols., 2nd edn., Oxford, 2005).
Davis, D., *The Rise and Fall of Slavery in the New World* (Oxford, 2006).
Davis, J. C., *The Decline of the Venetian Nobility as a Ruling Class* (Baltimore, 1962).
Davis, N. Z., *Society and Culture in Early Modern France: Eight Essays* (London, 1975).
Davis, N. Z., *Remaking Impostors: From Martin Guerre to Sommersby*, Hayes Robinson Lecture Series, No. 1 (London, 1997).
Davis, N. Z., "'Women's History' in Transition: The European Case" (1976), repr. in J. W. Scott (ed.), *Feminism and History* (Oxford, 1997), pp. 79–104.
Davis, R., *The Rise of the English Shipping Industry in the Seventeenth and Eighteenth Century* (London, 1962).
Dayan, J., *Haiti, History, and the Gods* (Berkeley, 1996).
De Baecque, A., *Les Eclats du rire: La Culture des rieurs au XVIIIe siècle* (Paris, 2000).

de Vries, J., *De economische achteruitgang van de Republiek in de achttiende eeuw* (Leiden, 1968).

de Vries, J., *The Dutch Rural Economy in the Golden Age* (New Haven, 1974).

de Vries, J., *European Urbanization, 1500–1800* (Cambridge, MA, 1984).

de Vries, J., "Between purchasing power and the world of goods: understanding the household economy in early modern Europe," in J. Brewer and R. Porter (eds.), *Consumption and the World of Goods* (London, 1993), pp. 85–132.

de Vries, J. and A.van der Woude, *The First Modern Economy: Success, Failure, and Perseverance of the Dutch Economy, 1500–1815* (Cambridge, 1997).

Deane, P. and W. A. Cole, *British Economic Growth 1688–1959* (Cambridge, 1962).

Deceulaer, H., "Urban artisans and their countryside customers: different interactions between town and hinterland in Antwerp, Brussels and Ghent (18th century)," in B. Blondé, E. Hanhaut, M. Galland (eds.), *Labour and Labour Markets between Town and Countryside (Middle Ages–19th Century)* (Turnhout, 2001), pp. 218–35.

Defoe, D., *The Storm: or, a collection of the most Remarkable casualties and Disasters which happe'd in the late Dreadful Tempest by both Sea and Land* (London, 1704).

Defoe, D., *The Complete English Tradesman* (London, 1724), <http://www.gutenberg.org/files/14444/14444-h/14444-h.htm#CHAPTER_XXV>, accessed 23 October 2006.

Defoe, D., *A Plan for English Commerce* (2nd edn., London, 1730; repr. New York, 1967).

Dekker, R. M., "Women in revolt: popular protest and its social basis in Holland in the seventeenth and eighteenth centuries," *Theory and Society*, 15 (1987), 337–62.

Delmas, J. (ed.), *De 1715 a 1871*, vol. 2 of A. Corvisier (ed.), *Histoire militaire de la France* (4 vols., Paris, 1992–4).

Demel, W., *Gebhardt Handbuch der deutschen Geschichte*, vol. 12: *Reich, Reformen und sozialer Wandel, 1763–1806* (10th edn., Stuttgart, 2005).

Desan, S., *Reclaiming the Sacred: Lay Religion and Popular Politics in Revolutionary France* (Ithaca, 1990).

Dessert, D., *Argent, pouvoir et société au grand siècle* (Paris, 1985).

Dewald, J. (ed.), *Europe 1450–1789: An Encyclopedia of the Early Modern World* (6 vols., New York, 2003).

Diamond, J., *Guns, Germs, and Steel: The Fate of Human Societies* (New York, 1998).

Diaz, F., "L'Italie des princes éclairés," *Annales de l'Histoire de la Révolution française*, 51 (1979), 581–93.

Dickens, A. G. *The Courts of Europe: Politics, Patronage and Royalty 1400–1800* (London, 1977).

Dickinson, H. T., *The Politics of the People in Eighteenth-Century Britain* (New York, 1995).

Dickinson, H. T. (ed.), *A Companion to Eighteenth-Century Britain* (Oxford, 2002).

Dickson, P. G. M., *Finance and Government under Maria Theresia 1740–1780* (2 vols., Oxford, 1987).

Diederiks, H., "Punishment during the ancien régime: the case of the eighteenth-century Dutch Republic," in L. A. Knafla (ed.), *Crime and Criminal Justice in Europe* (Waterloo, 1982), pp. 273–96.

Dipper, C., *Deutsche Geschichte 1648–1789* (Frankfurt am Main, 1991).

Dixon, S., *Catherine the Great* (Harlow, 2001).

Dixon, S., "Religious ritual at the eighteenth-century Russian court," in M. Schaich (ed.), *Monarchy and Religion: The Transformation of Royal Culture in Eighteenth-Century Europe* (Oxford, 2007), pp. 217–48.

Donati, C., "Esercito e società civile nella Lombardia del secolo XVIII," *Società e Storia*, 17 (1982), 527–54.

Dotzauer, W., *Die deutsche Reichskreise (1388–1806)* (Wiesbaden, 1998).

Doumani, B., *Rediscovering Palestine: Merchants and Peasants in Jabal Nablus 1700–1900* (Berkeley, 1995).

Downs, L. L., *Writing Gender History* (London, 2004).

Doyle, W., *The Parlement of Bordeaux and the End of the Old Regime, 1771–1790* (New York, 1974).

Doyle, W., *Origins of the French Revolution* (Oxford, 1980).

Doyle, W., "The parlements," in K. M.Baker (ed.), *The Political Culture of the Old Regime* (Oxford, 1987), pp. 157–67.

Doyle, W., *The Oxford History of the French Revolution* (Oxford, 1989).

Doyle, W., *The Old European Order 1660–1800* (2nd edn., Oxford, 1992).

Doyle, W., *The Sale of Offices in Eighteenth-Century France* (Oxford, 1996).

Doyle, W., *Venality: The Sale of Offices in Eighteenth-Century France* (Oxford, 1996).

Doyle, W., *Jansenism: Catholic Resistance to Authority from the Reformation to the French Revolution* (Basingstoke, 2000).

Doyle, W. (ed.), *Old Regime France* (Oxford, 2001).

Drévillon, H., "La Monarchie des Lumiéres: réforme ou utopie? 1715–1774' in J. Cornette and L. Bourquin (eds.), *La monarchie entre Renaissance et Révolution 1515–1792* (Paris, 2000), pp. 284–354.

Dubois, L., *Avengers of the New World: The Story of the Haitian Revolution* (Cambridge, MA, 2004).

Dubois, L., *A Colony of Citizens: Revolution and Slave Emancipation in the French Caribbean, 1787–1804* (Chapel Hill, 2004).

Duchhardt, H., *Altes Reich und europäisches Staatenwelt 1648 bis 1806* (Munich, 1990).

Duchhardt, H., *Balance of Power und Pentarchie: Internationale Beziehungen, 1700–1785* (Paderborn, 1997).

Duden, B., *The Woman Beneath the Skin: A Doctor's Patients in Eighteenth-Century Germany* (Cambridge, MA, 1991).

Duffy, C., *The Military Experience in the Age of Reason* (Ware, 1998).

Dufour, M. L., "Problème de la variation de climat," *Bulletin de Société Vaudoise des Sciences naturelles*, 10 (1870), 359–556.

Duhamelle, C. and J. Schlumbohm (eds.), *Eheschließungen im Europa des 18. und 19. Jahrhunderts* (Göttingen, 2003).

Duindnam, J., *Myths of Power: Norbert Elias and the Early Modern European Court* (Amsterdam, 1995).

Duindam, J., *Vienna and Versailles: The Courts of Europe's Major Dynastic Rivals c.1550–1750* (Cambridge, 2003).

Dukes, P. (ed.), *Russia under Catherine the Great*, vol. 2: *Catherine the Great's Instruction (Nakaz) to the Legislative Commission, 1767* (Newtonville, MA, 1977).

Dull, J. R., *The French Navy and the Seven Years' War* (Lincoln, 2005).

Dülmen, R. v. and N. Schindler (eds.), *Volkskultur. Zur Wiederentdeckung des vergessenen Alltags (16.–20. Jahrhundert)* (Frankfurt, 1984).

Dülmen, R. van, *Theatre of Horror: Crime and Punishment in Early Modern Germany* (Cambridge, 1990).

Durkheim, E., *The Rules of Sociological Method; and Selected Texts on Sociology and its Method* (1882; London, 2002).

Dürr, R. and G. Schwerhoff (eds.), *Kirchen, Märkte und Tavernen. Erfahrungs- und Handlungsräume in der Frühen Neuzeit* (Frankfurt am Main, 2005).

Dwyer, P. G. (ed.), *The Rise of Prussia 1700–1830* (Harlow, 2000).

Dyrvik, S., *Truede tvillingriker 1648–1720*, vol. 3 of *Danmark-Norge 1380–1814* (Oslo, 1998).

Dyrvik, S. and O. Feldbæk, *Mellom brødre*, vol. 7 of *Aschehougs Norgeshistorie* (Oslo, 1995).

Eddy, J., "The Maunder Minimum," *Science*, 192 (1976), 1189–1202.
Egido Lopez, T., *Prensa clandestina española del siglo XVIII: "El Duende Critico"* (Valladolid, 1968; 2002).
Egido Lopez, T., *Opinión publica y oposición al poder en la España del siglo XVIII (1713–1759)* (Valladolid, 1971; 2002).
Ehmer, J., T. K. Hareven, R. Wall, and M. Cerman (eds.), *Family History Revisited: Comparative Perspectives* (Newark, 2001).
Eibach, J., "Städtische Gewaltkriminalität im Ancien Régime. Frankfurt am Main im europäischen Kontext," *Zeitschrift für historische Forschung*, 25 (1998), 359–82.
"Eighteenth Century Collections Online" <http://www.gale.com/EighteenthCentury/>.
"Einblattdrucke der Frühen Neuzeit" <http://www.bsb-muenchen.de/Einblattdrucke.178.0.html>.
Eldem, E., "French trade and commercial policy in the Levant in the eighteenth century," *Oriente Moderno*, 18 (1999), 27–47.
Elias, N., *The Court Society* (New York, 1983).
Elliott, J. H., "A Europe of composite monarchies," *Past & Present*, 137 (1992), 48–71.
Elliott, M., *Partners in Revolution: The United Irishmen and France* (New Haven, 1982).
Ellis, F., *Peasant Economics: Farm Households and Agrarian Development* (Cambridge, 1993).
Ellis, M., *The Coffee-House: A Cultural History* (London, 2005).
Elshtain, J. B., *Public Man, Private Woman: Women in Social and Political Thought* (Oxford, 1981).
Englund, P., *The Battle of Poltava: The Birth of the Russian Empire* (London, 1992).
Epstein, S. R., *Freedom and Growth: The Rise of States and Markets in Europe, 1300–1750* (London, 2000).
Epstein, S. R. (ed.), *Town and Country in Europe, 1300–1800* (Cambridge, 2001).
Equipo Madrid, *Carlos III, Madrid y la ilustración* (Madrid, 1988).
Erichsen, J. and K. Heinemann, *Die Sclacht von Höchstädt. Brennpunkt Europas 1704* (Ostfildern, 2004).
Erimtan, C., "The sources of Ahmed Refik's *Lâle Devri* and the paradigm of the 'Tulip Age': a teleological agenda," in *Essays in Honour of Ekmeleddin Ihsanoğlu* (Istanbul, 2006), pp. 259–78.
Ertman, T., *Birth of the Leviathan* (Cambridge, 1997).
Esipov, G. V., *Raskol'nich'i dela*, vol. 2 (St. Petersburg, 1861).
Evans, R. J. W., *The Making of the Habsburg Monarchy 1550–1700* (Oxford, 1979).
Evans, R. J. W. (ed.), *The German Underworld: Deviants and Outcasts in German History* (London, 1988).
Evin, A., "The Tulip Age and definitions of 'Westernization'," in H. Inalcik and O. Okyar (eds.), *Social and Economic History of Turkey (1071–1920)* (Ankara, 1980).
Evtuhov, C. et al., *A History of Russia: Peoples: Legends, Events, Forces* (New York, 2004).
Faber, J. A., *Drie eeuwen Friesland. Economische en sociale ontwikkelingen van 1500 tot 1800* (3 vols., Wageningen, 1972).
Fagan, B., *The Little Ice Age: How Climate Made History 1300–1850* (New York, 2000).
Fairchilds, C., "The production and marketing of populuxe goods in eighteenth-century Paris," in J. Brewer and R. Porter (eds.), *Consumption and the World of Goods* (London, 1993), pp. 228–48.
Fantoni, M., "Il bigottismo di Cosimo III: da leggenda storiografica ad oggetto storico," in *La Toscana nell'età di Cosimo III: atti del convegno di Pisa-San Domenico Fiesole, 1990* (Florence, 1993), pp. 389–402.
Fantoni, M., *La corte del granduca: forme e simboli del potere mediceo fra Cinquecento e Seicento* (Rome, 1994).

Farge, A., *Fragile Lives: Violence, Power and Solidarity in Eighteenth-Century Paris* (London, 1993).

Farge, A., *Subversive Words: Public Opinion in Eighteenth-Century France* (Cambridge, 1994).

Federico, G. and P. Malanima, "Progress, decline, growth: product and productivity in Italian agriculture, 1000–2000," *Economic History Review*, 57 (2004), 437–64.

Feiner, S., *The Jewish Enlightenment* (Philadelphia, 2002).

Feldbaek, O., *Dansk söfarts historie*, vol. 3: *1720–1814: Storhandelens tid* (Copenhagen, 1997).

Feldbaek, O., *Denmark and the Armed Neutrality, 1800–1801: Small Power Policy in a World War* (Copenhagen, 1980).

Feldbæk, O., *Nærhed og adskillelse 1720–1814*, vol. 4 of *Danmark-Norge 1380–1814* (Oslo 1998).

Félix, J., "The economy," in W. Doyle (ed.), *Old Regime France* (Oxford, 2001), pp. 7–41.

Ferguson, N., *Empire: The Rise and Demise of the British World Order and the Lessons for Global Power* (New York, 2002).

Fernandez, R. (ed.), *España en el siglo XVIII: homenaje a Pierre Vilar* (Barcelona, 1985).

Ferraresi, A., *Stato, scienza, amministrzione, saperi: la formazione degli ingegneri in Piemonte dall'antico regime all'inità d'Italia* (Bologna, 2004).

Ferreira Carrato, J., "The Enlightenment in Portugal and the educational reforms of the marquis of Pombal," in J. A. Leith (ed.), *Studies on Voltaire and the Eighteenth Century*, vol. 167 (Oxford, 1977), pp. 359–93.

Ferreiro, L. D., *Ships and Science: The Birth of Naval Architecture in the Scientific Revolution* (Cambridge, MA, 2006).

Ferrone, V., "Tecnocratici militari e scienziati nel Piemonte dell'antico regime: alle origini della Reale Accademia delle Scienze ei Torino," *Rivista Storica Italiano*, 96 (1984), 414–509.

Fisher, H. E. S., *The Portugal Trade* (London, 1971).

Fisher, J. R., *Bourbon Peru, 1750–1824* (Liverpool, 2003).

Fissell, M. E., *Patients, Power, and the Poor in Eighteenth-Century Bristol* (Cambridge, 1991).

Fiszman, S. (ed.), *Constitution and Reform in Eighteenth-Century Poland: The Constitution of 3 May 1791* (Bloomington, 1997).

Fitzsimmons, M. P., *The Remaking of France: The National Assembly and the Constitution of 1791* (Cambridge, 1994).

Fitzsimmons, M. P., *The Night the Old Regime Ended: August 4 1789 and the French Revolution* (University Park, PA, 2003).

Fleming, K. E., *The Muslim Bonaparte: Diplomacy and Orientalism in Ali Pasha's Greece* (Princeton, 1999).

Fogel, R. W., "Second thoughts on the European escape from hunger, famines, chronic malnutrition and mortality rates," in S. Osmani (ed.), *Nutrition and Poverty* (Oxford, 1992).

Follain, A. (ed.), *L'Argent des villages du XIIIe au XVIIIe siècle* (Rennes, 2000).

Font Tullot, I., *Historia del clima de España: cambios climaticos y sus causas* (Madrid, 1988).

Fontaine, L., *History of Pedlars in Europe* (Cambridge, 1996).

Fontaine, L., "Women's economic spheres and credit in pre-industrial Europe," in B. Lemire, R. Pearson, and G. Campbell (eds.), *Women and Credit: Researching the Past, Refiguring the Future* (Oxford, 2002), pp. 15–32.

Forrest, A., *The Soldiers of the French Revolution* (Durham, NC, 1990).

Forrest, A., *Paris, the Provinces and the French Revolution* (London, 2004).

Forster, R., *Merchants, Landlords, Magistrates: The Depont Family in Eighteenth-Century France* (Baltimore, 1980).

Foucault, M., *The Birth of the Clinic* (London, 1973).

Foucault, M., *Discipline and Punish: The Birth of the Prison* (Harmondsworth, 1979).

Fox, R. and A. Turner (eds.), *Luxury Trades and Consumerism in Ancien Régime Paris* (Aldershot, 1998).

Frader, L. and S. O. Rose (eds.), *Gender and Class in Modern Europe* (London, 1996).

Franca, J.-A., *Une ville des lumières: La Lisbonne de Pombal* (Paris, 1965).

Francis, A. D., *The Methuens and Portugal (1691–1708)* (Cambridge, 1966).

Francis, A. D., *Portugal, 1715–1808: Joanine, Pombaline and Rococo Portugal as seen by British Diplomats and Traders* (London, 1985).

François, E., *Koblenz im 18. Jahrhundert. Zur Sozial- und Bevölkerungsstruktur einer deutschen Residenzstadt* (Göttingen, 1982).

François, E., *Die unsichtbare Grenze. Protestanten und Katholiken in Augsburg 1648–1806* (Sigmaringen, 1991).

Franklin, B., *Poor Richard, 1733. An Almanack for the Year of Christ 1733* (Philadelphia, 1733). <http://usinfo.state.gov/usa/infousa/facts/loa/bf1733.htm>, <http://usinfo.state.gov/usa/infousa/facts/loa/bf1737.htm>, <http://usinfo.state.gov/usa/infousa/facts/loa/bf1758.htm>, accessed 23 October 2006.

Frazee, C., *Catholics and Sultans: The Church and the Ottoman Empire 1453–1923* (Cambridge, 1983).

Frederician Code (1750), in S. G. Bell and K. Offen (eds.), *Women, the Family and Freedom*, vol. 1: *1750–1880* (Stanford, 1983).

Freist, D., "Wirtshäuser als Zentren frühneuzeitlicher Öffentlichkeit. London im 17. Jahrhundert," in J. Burkhardt and C. Werkstetter (eds.), *Kommunikation und Medien in der Frühen Neuzeit* (Munich, 2005), pp. 201–24.

Frey, L. S. and M. L. Frey, *The History of Diplomatic Immunity* (Columbus, OH, 1999).

Friedrich, K., *The other Prussia: Royal Prussia, Poland and Liberty, 1569–1772* (Cambridge, 2000).

Friedrichs, C. R., *The Early Modern City 1450–1750* (London, 1995).

Friedrichs, C. R., "But are we any closer to home? Early modern German urban history since *German Home Towns*," *Central European History*, 30 (1997), 163–86.

Frijhoff, W. and M. Spies, *1650: Hard-Won Unity* (Basingstoke, 2004).

Frost, R. I., *After the Deluge: Poland-Lithuania and the Second Northern War* (Cambridge, 1993).

Frost, R. I., "The nobility of Poland-Lithuania, 1569–1795," in H. M. Scott (ed.), *The European Nobilities in the Seventeenth and Eighteenth Centuries* (London, 1995), vol. 2, pp. 182–222.

Frost, R. I., *The Northern Wars: War, State and Society in Northern Europe, 1558–1721* (Harlow, 2000).

Fulbrook, M., *Piety and Politics: Religion and the Rise of Absolutism in England, Württemberg and Prussia* (Cambridge, 1983).

Furet, F., *Interpreting the French Revolution* (Cambridge, 1981).

Furet, F., "Book licensing and book production in the kingdom of France in the eighteenth century," in id., *In the Workshop of History* (Chicago, 1984), pp. 99–124.

Furet, F., *The French Revolution 1770–1814* (Oxford, 1996).

Furnari, M. (ed.), *'700 napoletano: cultura popolare a Napoli nel diciottesimo secolo* (Naples, 1980).

Gabriëls, A. J. C. M., *De heren als dienaren en de dienaar als heer. Het stadhouderlijke stelsel in de tweede helft van de 18de eeuw* (The Hague, 1990).

Gagliardo, G., *From Pariah to Patriot: The Changing Image of the German Peasant 1770–1840* (Lexington, KY, 1969).
Gall, L., *Von der ständischen zur bürgerlichen Gesellschaft* (Munich, 1993).
Gallo, F., "La Sicilia di Carlo VI: riforma amministrativa e ricerca del consenso (1719–1734)," *Cheiron: Dilattare l'impero*, 21 (1995), 187–226.
Gantet, C., *La Paix de Westphalie (1648): Une histoire sociale, XVIIe–XVIIIe siècles* (Paris, 2001).
Garcia Carcel, R., *Felipe V y los Españoles* (Barcelona, 2002).
Garden, M., *Lyon et les Lyonnais au XVIIIe siècle* (Paris, 1975).
Gariglio D., *Le sentinelle di pietra: fortezze e cittadelle del Piemonte sabaudo* (Cuneo, 1997).
Gariglio, D., *Battaglie alpine del Piemonte sabaudo* (Collegno, 1999).
Garraway, D., *The Libertine Colony: Creolization in the Early French Caribbean* (Durham, 2005).
Garrioch, D., *Neighbourhood and Community in Paris, 1740–1890* (Cambridge, 1986).
Garrioch, D., *The Making of Revolutionary Paris* (Berkeley, 2002).
Garrioch, D., "Sounds of the city: the soundscape of early modern European towns," *Urban History*, 30 (2003), 5–25.
Garrioch, D., "Lay–religious associations, urban identities and urban space in eighteenth-century Milan," *Journal of Religious History*, 28 (2004), 35–49.
Gates-Coon, R., *The Landed Estates of the Esterházy Princes* (Baltimore, 1994).
Gatrell, V., *The Hanging Tree: Execution and the English People, 1770–1868* (Oxford, 1994).
Gautier, A., *Les Sœurs de solitude: La Condition féminine dans l'esclavage aux Antilles du XVIIe au XIXe siècle* (Paris, 1985).
Gay, P., *The Party of Humanity: Essays in the French Enlightenment* (New York, 1964).
Geggus, P., *Slavery, War, and Revolution: The British Occupation of Saint-Domingue, 1793–1798* (Oxford, 1982).
Gelbart, N. R., *The King's Midwife: A History and Mystery of Madame du Coudray* (Berkeley, 1998).
Geldern, J. van and L. McReynolds (eds.), *Entertaining Tsarist Russia: Tales, Songs, Plays, Movies, Jokes, Ads, and Images from Russian Urban Llife, 1779–1917* (Bloomington, 1998).
Gelfand, T., *Professionalizing Modern Medicine: Paris Surgeons and Medical Science and Institutions in the 18th Century* (New York, 1980).
Gentilcore, D., *Healers and Healing in Early Modern Europe* (Manchester, 1998).
Gentilcore, D., *Medical Charlatanism in Early Modern Italy* (New York, 2006).
George, A., *St Petersburg: The First Three Centuries* (Stroud, 2004).
Georgelin, J., *Venise au siècle des Lumières* (Paris, 1978).
Geremek, B., *Geschichte der Armut. Elend und Barmherzigkeit in Europa* (Frankfurt am Main, 1988).
Gernet, J., *China and the Christian Impact: A Conflict of Cultures* (Cambridge, 1985).
Gestrich, A., *Absolutismus und Öffentlichkeit. Politische Kommunikation in Deutschland zu Beginn des 18. Jahrhunderts* (Göttingen, 1994).
Gestrich, Andreas, "After dark: girls' leisure, work and sexuality in 18th and 19th century rural southwest Germany," in C. Benninghaus et al. (eds.), *Secret Gardens, Satanic Mills: Placing Girls in Modern European History* (Bloomington, 2005), pp. 54–68.
Gestrich, A., "The public sphere and the Habermas debate," *German History*, 24 (2006), 413–30.
Geyken, F., "The German language is spoken in Saxony with the greatest purity, or: English images and perceptions in the eighteenth century," in J. Canning and H. Wellenreuther

(eds.), *Britain and Germany Compared: Nationality, Society and Nobility in the Eighteenth Century* (Göttingen, 2001), pp. 37–70.

Giacomone Piana, P. and R. Dellepiane, *Militarium: fonti archivistiche e bibliografia per la storia militare della Repubblica di Genova (1528–1797), della Repubblica Ligure (1797–1805) e della Liguria napoleonica (1805–1814)* (Genoa, 2004).

Gibbs, G. C., "Government and the English press, 1695 to the middle of the eighteenth century," in A. C. Duke and C. A. Tamse (eds.), *Too Mighty to be Free: Censorship and the Press in Britain and the Netherlands* (Zutphen, 1987).

Gibbs, G. C., R. Oresko, and H. M. Scott (eds.), *Royal and Republican Sovereignty* (Cambridge, 1997).

Gierowski, J., *W cieniu ligi północnej* (Wrocław, 1971).

Gierowski, J. and A. Kamiński, "The eclipse of Poland," in *The New Cambridge Modern History*, vol. 6 (Cambridge, 1971), pp. 681–715.

Gijswijt-Hofstra, M. and W. Frijhoff (eds.), *Witchcraft in the Netherlands: From the Fourteenth to the Twentieth Century* (Rotterdam, 1991).

Gillis, J., *A World of Their Own Making: A History of Myth and Ritual in Family Life* (Oxford, 1997).

Ginzburg, C., *The Cheese and the Worms: The Cosmos of a Sixteenth-Century Miller* (London, 1992).

Girdlestone, C., *Jean-Philippe Rameau: His Life and Work* (London, 1957).

Girouard, M., *Cities and People: A Social and Architectural History* (New Haven, 1985).

Glaser, R., *Klimageschichte Mitteleuropas. 1000 Jahre Wetter, Klima, Katastrophen* (Darmstadt, 2001).

Glete, J., *Navies and Nations: Warships, Navies and State Building in Europe and America, 1500–1860* (2 vols., Stockholm, 1993).

Glete, J., "Navies and power struggle in northern and eastern Europe, 1721–1814," in R. Hobson and T. Kristiansen (eds.), *Navies in Northern Waters, 1721–2000* (London, 2004), pp. 66–93.

Glick, T. F., *Irrigation and Society in Medieval Valencia* (Cambridge, MA, 1970).

Glyn, N., *The Prize of all the Oceans* (New York, 1999).

Godechot, *France and the Atlantic Revolution of the Eighteenth Century, 1770–1799* (New York, 1965).

Godechot, J., *La Grande Nation: L'Expansion révolutionnaire de la France dans le monde de 1789 à 1799* (Paris, 1983).

Godineau, D., *The Women of Paris and their French Revolution* (Berkeley, 1998).

Godinho, M., "Portugal and her empire, 1680–1720," in J. S. Bromley (ed.), *The New Cambridge Modern History*, vol. 6: *The Rise of Great Britain and Russia 1688–1725* (Cambridge, 1971), pp. 509–40.

Goldenbaum, U. (ed.), *Appell an das Publikum. Die öffentliche Debatte in der deutschen Aufklärung 1678–1796* (2 vols., Berlin, 2004).

Goldstone, J. A., *Revolution and Rebellion in the Early Modern World* (Berkeley, 1991).

Gómez Urdánez, J. L., *El proyecto reformista de Ensenada* (Lleida, 1996).

Goodman, D., *The Republic of Letters: A Cultural History of the French Enlightenment* (Ithaca, 1994).

Goodman, D., "Women and the Enlightenment," in R. Bridenthal, S. M. Stuard, and M. E. Wiesner (eds.), *Becoming Visible, Women in European History* (3rd edn., Boston and New York, 1998).

Goodman, D. (ed.), *Marie Antoinette: Writings on the Body of a Queen* (London 2004).

Gordon, D. (ed.), *Postmodernism and the Enlightenment: New Perspectives in Eighteenth-Century French Intellectual History* (New York, 2001).

Goubert, P., *Louis XIV and Twenty Million Frenchmen* (London, 1970).

Goubert, P., *The Ancien Régime: French Society 1600–1750* (London, 1973).

Gough, H., *The Newspaper Press in the French Revolution* (London, 1988).

Goujard, P., *L'Europe catholique au XVIIIe siècle: Entre intégrisme et laïcisation* (Rennes, 2004).

Grab, A., "Enlightened despotism and state-building: the case of Austrian Lombardy," *Austrian History Yearbook*, 19/20 (1983–4), 43–72.

Gräf, H. T. (ed.), *Kleine Städte im neuzeitlichen Europa* (Berlin, 1997).

Grantham, G., "The growth of labour productivity in the production of wheat in the Cinq Grosses Fermes of France, 1750–1929," in B. M. S. Campbell and M. Overton (eds.), *Land, Labour and Livestock. Historical Studies in European Agricultural Productivity* (Manchester, 1991), pp. 340–63.

Gratton, J., R. Rabartin, S. Self, and T. Thordarson, "Volcanic air pollution and mortality in France 1783–1784, *Comptes rendus Geosciences*, 337 (2005), 641–51.

Gray, M. W., *Productive Men, Reproductive Women: The Agrarian Household and the Emergence of Separate Spheres during the Enlightenment* (Oxford, 2000).

Grazia, V. de (ed.), *The Sex of Things: Gender and Consumption in Historical Perspective* (Berkeley, 1996).

Greyerz, K. v., *Religion und Kultur. Europa 1500–1800* (Darmstadt, 2000).

Griffiths, D., "Catherine II: the republican empress," *Jahrbücher für Geschichte Osteuropa*, 21 (1973), 323–44.

Gross, H., *Rome in the Age of Enlightenment: The Post-Tridentine Syndrome and the Ancien Régime* (Cambridge, 1990).

Grove, J. and A. Battagel, "Tax records as an index of Little Ice Age environmental and economic deterioration, from Sunnfjord Fogderi, western Norway 1667–1815," in C. D. Smith and M. Parry (eds.), *Consequences of Climatic Change* (Nottingham, 1980).

Grove, J., *The Little Ice Age* (London, 1988).

Gueniffey, P., *La Politique de la Terreur: Essai sur la violence révolutionnaire, 1789–1794* (Paris, 2000).

Guilhaumou, J., *L'Avènement des porte-parole de la République, 1789–1792: Essai de synthèse sur les langages de la Révolution française* (Villeneuve-d'Ascq, 1998).

Gunst, P. and T. Hoffmann (eds.), *Large Estates and Small Holdings in the Middle Ages and Modern Times* (Budapest, 1982).

Gustafsson, H., *Political Interaction in the Old Regime: Central Power and Local Society in the Eighteenth-Century Nordic States* (Lund, 1994).

Gutton, J.-P., *La Sociabilité villageoise dans l'ancienne France: Solidarités et voisinages du XVIe au XVIIIe siècle* (Paris, 1979).

Gutton, J.-P., *Bruits et sons dans notre histoire: Essai sur la reconstitution du paysage sonore* (Paris, 2000).

Haakonssen, K. (ed.), *Enlightenment and Religion: Rational Dissent in Eighteenth-Century Britain* (Cambridge, 1996).

Habermas, J., *The Structural Transformation of the Public Sphere: An Inquiry into a Category of Bourgeois Society* (Cambridge, 1989).

Hagen, W. W., "Descent of the Sonderweg: Hans Rosenberg's history of old-regime Prussia," *Central European History*, 24 (1991), 24–50.

Hagen, W. W., *Ordinary Prussians: Brandenburg Junkers and Villagers, 1500–1840* (Cambridge, 2002).

Hamadeh, S., *The City's Pleasures: Istanbul in the Eighteenth Century* (Seattle, 2007).

Hampson, N., *Will and Circumstance: Montesquieu, Rousseau and the French Revolution* (London, 1983).

Hanlon, G., *The Twilight of a Military Tradition: Italian Aristocrats and European Conflicts, 1560–1800* (London, 1998).

Hanlon, G., "In praise of refeudalization: princes and feudatories in north-central Italy from the sixteenth to the eighteenth century," in N. Eckstein and N. Terpstra (eds.), *Social Capital in Early Modern Europe* (Turnhout, 2007).
Hannaford, I., *Race: The History of an Idea in the West* (Baltimore, 1996).
Hans, N., *New Trends in Education in the Eighteenth Century* (London, 1951).
Hansen, C., *Economy and Society in Baroque Portugal 1668–1703* (Minneapolis, 1981).
Hanson, P. R., *The Jacobin Republic Under Fire: The Federalist Revolt in the French Revolution* (University Park, PA, 2003).
Harding, N., "Sir Robert Walpole and Hanover," *Historical Research*, 76 (2003),164–88.
Harding, N., *Hanover and the British Empire* (Woodbridge, 2007).
Harding, R., *Seapower and Naval Warfare 1650–1830* (London, 1999).
Hardman, J., *Louis XVI* (New Haven, 1993).
Harline, C. E., *Pamphlets, Printing, and Political Culture in the Early Dutch Republic* (Dordrecht, 1987).
Harries, K., *The Bavarian Rococo Church: Between Faith and Aestheticism* (New Haven and London, 1983).
Harris, B., *Politics and the Rise of the Press: Britain and France, 1620–1800* (London, 1996).
Harris, R., *A Patriot Press: National Politics and the London Press in the 1740s* (Oxford, 1993).
Harris, R. D., "Necker's *compte rendu* of 1781: a reconsideration," *Journal of Modern History*, 42 (1970), 161–83.
Harris, R. D., *Necker: Reform Statesman of the Ancien Régime* (Berkeley, 1979).
Harris, T. (ed.), *Popular Culture in England c.1500–1850* (Basingstoke, 1995).
Härter, K., "Sozial Disziplinierung durch Strafe? Intentionen frühneuzeitlicher Policeyordnungen und staatliche Sanktionspraxis," *Zeitschrift für historische Forschung*, 26 (1999), 365–79.
Hartley, J., *A Social History of the Russian Empire* (London, 1999).
Hartmann, P. C., *Kulturgeschichte des Heiligen Römischen Reiches 1648 bis 1806* (Vienna, 2001).
Hattendorf, J., *England in War of Spanish Succession: A Study of English View and Conduct of Grand Strategy* (New York, 1987).
Hatton, R. M., *George I: Elector and King* (London, 1978).
Hatton, R. M., *Charles XII of Sweden* (London, 1968).
Haug-Moritz, G., *Württembergischer Ständekonflikt und deutscher Dualismus* (Stuttgart, 1992).
Havard, G. and C. Vidal, *Histoire de l'Amérique française* (Paris, 2003).
Hayley, W., *A Philosophical, Historical, and Moral Essay on Old Maids* (3 vols., London, 1785).
Heartz, D., *Mozart's Operas* (Berkeley, 1990).
Heartz, D., *Haydn, Mozart, and the Viennese School 1740–1780* (New York and London, 1995).
Hellmuth, E. (ed.), *The Transformation of Political Culture: England and Germany in the Late Eighteenth Century* (Oxford, 1990).
Hellmuth, E., "Enlightenment and freedom of the press: the debate in the Berlin Mittwochsgesellschaft, 1783–1784," *History*, 83 (1998), 420–44.
Hembry, P., *The English Spa, 1560–1815: A Social History* (London, 1990).
Henshall, N., *The Myth of Absolutism: Change and Continuity in Early Modern European Monarchy* (London, 1992).
Herman, A., *To Rule the Waves: How the British Navy Shaped the Modern World* (New York, 2004).
Herr, R., *The Eighteenth Century Revolution in Spain* (Princeton, 1958).

Herr, R., *Rural Change and Royal Finances in Spain at the End of the Old Regime* (California, 1989).

Hersche, P., *Muße und Verschwendung. Europäische Gesellschaft und Kultur im Barockzeitalter* (2 vols., Freiburg, 2006).

Hespanha, M. (ed.), *O Antico Regime (1620–1807)* (Lisbon, 1998).

Hesse, C., *The Other Enlightenment: How French Women Became Modern* (Princeton, 2001).

Heywood, C., *The Development of the French Economy, 1750–1914* (Basingstoke, 1992).

Higonnet, P., *Goodness beyond Virtue: Jacobins during the French Revolution* (Cambridge, MA, 1998).

Hippel, W. v., *Armut, Unterschichten, Randgruppen in der Frühen Neuzeit* (Munich, 1995).

Hirschfelder, G., *Alkoholkonsum am Beginn des Industriezeitalters (1700–1850). Vergleichende Studien zum gesellschaftlichen und kulturellen Wandel* (2 vols., Cologne, 2003, 2004).

"Historical Dictionary of Switzerland" <www.hls.ch>.

Hitchcock, T. and M. Cohen (eds.), *English Masculinities, 1660–1800* (London, 1999).

Hobsbawm, E., *Bandits* (London, 1969).

Hochedlinger, M., *Austria's Wars of Emergence: War, State and Society in the Habsburg Monarchy 1683–1797* (London, 2003).

Hoffman, P. T., *Growth in a Traditional Society: The French Countryside, 1450–1815* (Princeton, 1996).

Hohenberg, P. M. and L. H. Lees (eds.), *The Making of Urban Europe 1000–1994* (Cambridge, MA, 1995).

Hohrath, D. and K. Gerteis (eds.), *Die Kriegskunst im Lichte der Vernunft* (2 vols., Hamburg, 1999–2000).

Holm, P., *Kystfolk: Kontakter og sammenhaenge over Kattegat og Skagerrrak, ca 1550–1914* (Esbjerg, 1991).

Honour, H., *Neo-Classicism* (Harmondsworth, 1977).

Hope, N., *German and Scandinavian Protestantism 1700–1918* (Oxford, 1995).

Hopkins, D. R., *The Greatest Killer: Smallpox and History* (Chicago, 2002).

Hoppenbrouwers, P. and J. L. van Zanden (eds.), *Peasants into Farmers? The Transformation of the Rural Economy and Society in the Low Countries* (Turnhout, 2001).

Hoskins, W. G., "Harvest fluctuations and English economic history," *Agricultural History*, 12 (1968), 28–46.

Houlding, *Fit for Service: The Training of the British Army 1715–1795* (Oxford, 1981).

Hsia, R. P., *The World of Catholic Renewal 1540–1770* (2nd edn., Cambridge, 2005).

Hufton, O., *The Poor of 18th Century France, 1750–1789* (Oxford, 1974).

Hughes, L., *Russia in the Age of Peter the Great* (New Haven, 1998).

Hughes, L., "The Petrine year: anniversaries and festivals in the reign of Peter the Great (1682–1725)," in K. Friedrich (ed.), *Festive Culture and Germany and Europe from the 16th to the 20th Century* (Lewiston, 2000), pp. 148–68.

Hughes, L., "From caftans into corsets: the sartorial transformation of women during the reign of Peter the Great," in P. Barta (ed.), *Gender and Sexuality in Russian Civilization* (London, 2001), pp. 17–32.

Hughes, L., "A beard is an unnecessary burden," in R. Bartlett and L. Hughes (eds.), *Russian Society and Culture and the Long Eighteenth Century* (Münster, 2004), pp. 21–4.

Hughes, L., "Catherine I of Russia: consort to Peter the Great," in C. C. Orr (ed.), *Queenship in Europe, 1660–1815: The Role of the Consort* (Cambridge, 2004), pp. 131–54.

Hughes, M., *Law and Politics in 18th Century Germany: The Imperial Aulic Council and the Reign of Charles VI* (Woodbridge, 1988).

Hugill, J. A. C., *No Peace Without Spain* (Oxford, 1991).

Hume, D., "Of the rise and progress of the arts and sciences" (1742), in E. F. Miller (ed.), *Essays, Moral, Political, and Literary* (Indianapolis, 1987).
Hundert, G. D., *Jews in Poland-Lithuania in the Eighteenth Century: A Genealogy of Modernity* (Berkeley, 2004).
Hunt, L., *Politics, Culture and Class in the French Revolution* (Berkeley, 1984).
Hunt, L., *The Family Romance of the French Revolution* (Berkeley, 1992).
Hunt, M., *Commerce, Gender and the Family in England, 1680–1780* (Berkeley, 1996).
Ilari, V., G. Boeri, and C. Paoletti, *Tra i Borboni e gli Asburgo: le armate terrestri e navali italiane nelle guerre del primo Settecento (1701–1732)* (Ancona, 1996).
Ilari, V., G. Boeri, and C. Paoletti, *La corona di Lombardia: guerre ed eserciti nell'Italia del medio Settecento (1733 – 1763)* (Ancona, 1997).
Ilari, V., P. Crociani, and C. Paoletti, *Bell'Italia militar* (Rome, 2001).
Im Hof, U., *Das gesellige Jahrhundert. Gesellschaft und Gesellschaften im Zeitalter der Aufklärung* (Munich, 1982).
Imhof, A. E., *Aspekte der Bevölkerungsentwicklung in den nordischen Ländern 1720–1750* (2 vols., Bern, 1976).
Ingold, T., "Culture and the perception of the environment," in D. Parkin and E. Croll (eds.), *Bush Base, Forest Farm: Culture, Environment and Development* (London, 1992).
Ingrao, C. W., *The Hessian Mercenary State: Ideas, Institutions and Reform under Frederick II 1760–85* (Cambridge, 1987).
Ingrao, C. W., *The Habsburg Monarchy 1618–1815* (2nd edn., Cambridge, 2000).
International History Review, 16 (1994), issue 4 on international relations.
Irwin, D., *Neo-Classicism* (London, 1997).
Israel, J. I., *Dutch Primacy in World Trade, 1585–1740* (Oxford, 1989).
Israel, J. I., *The Dutch Republic: Its Rise, Greatness and Fall, 1477–1806* (Oxford, 1995).
Israel, J. I., *Radical Enlightenment: Philosophy and the Making of Modernity 1650–1750* (Oxford, 2001).
Jacob, M. C., *Living the Enlightenment: Freemasonry and Politics in Eighteenth-Century Europe* (New York, 1991).
Jacob, M. C. and W. W. Mijnhardt (eds.), *The Dutch Republic in the Eighteenth Century: Decline, Enlightenment and Revolution* (Ithaca, 1992).
James, C. L. R., *Black Jacobins: Toussaint L'Ouverture and the Santo Domingo Revolution* (1938; repr. New York, 1963).
Janssens, P. and B. Yun-Casalilla (eds.), *European Aristocracies and Colonial Elites: Patrimonial Management Strategies and Economic Development, 15th–18th Centuries* (Aldershot, 2006).
Jardine, L., *Worldly Goods: A New History of the Renaissance* (London, 1996).
Jaume, L., *Le Discours jacobin et la démocratie* (Paris, 1989).
Jelavich, C. and B. Jelavich, *The Establishment of the Balkan National States, 1804–1920* (Seattle, 1986).
Jersch-Wenzel, S., *Juden und "Franzosen" in der Wirtschaft des Raumes Berlin-Brandenburg zur Zeit des Merkantilismus* (Berlin, 1978).
Jespersen, K. J. V., *A History of Denmark* (Basingstoke, 2004).
Johns, A., *The Nature of the Book: Print and Knowledge in the Making* (Chicago, 1998).
Jones, C., *The Great Nation: France from Louis XIV to Napoleon* (London, 2002).
Jones, C. and R. Spang, "*San-culottes,* san café, san tabac: shifting realms of necessity and luxury in eighteenth-century France," in M. Berg and H. Clifford (eds.), *Consumers and Luxury: Consumer Culture in Europe 1650–1850* (Manchester, 1999), pp. 37–62.
Jones, J. R., *Marlborough* (Cambridge, 1993).
Jones, M. G., *Hannah More* (Cambridge, 1952).
Jones, P. M., *The Peasantry in the French Revolution* (Cambridge, 1988).

Jones, P. M., *Reform and Revolution in France: The Politics of Transition, 1774–1791* (Cambridge, 1995).

Jones, R., *The Emancipation of the Russian Nobility, 1762–1785* (Princeton, 1973).

Jones, R., "The Charter of the Nobility: a legislative landmark?' *Canadian American Slavic Studies*, 23 (1989), 1–16.

Jones, W. G., "The spirit of the *Nakaz*: Catherine II's literary debt to Montesquieu," *Slavonic and East European Review*, 77 (1998), 658–71.

Jones, W. G., "Literature in the eighteenth century," in N. Cornwell (ed.), *The Routledge Companion to Russian Literature* (London, 2000), pp. 25–35.

Jong, J. J. de, *Met goed fatsoen. De elite in een Hollandse stad, Gouda 1700–80* (Dieren, 1985).

Jongste, J. A. F. de, *Onrust aan het Spaarne. Haarlem in de jaren 1747–1751* (Dieren, 1984).

Jordanova, L., *Sexual Visions: Images of Gender in Science and Medicine between the Eighteenth and Twentieth Centuries* (New York and London, 1989).

Jourdan, A., *La Révolution, une exception française?* (Paris, 2004).

Jütte, R., *Poverty and Deviance in Early Modern Europe* (Cambridge, 1994).

Kaak, H., *Die Gutsherrschaft. Theoriegeschichtliche Untersuchungen zum Agrarwesen im ostelbischen Raum* (Berlin, 1991).

Kaak, H. and M. Schattkowsky (eds.), *Herrschaft. Machtentfaltung über adligen und fürstlichen Grundbesitz in der Frühen Neuzeit* (Cologne, 2003).

Kaiser, T., "Madame de Pompadour and the theatres of power," *French Historical Studies*, 19 (1996), 1025–44.

Kaiser, T., "Who's afraid of Marie Antoinette? Diplomacy, Austrophobia and the queen," *French History*, 14 (2000), 241–71.

Kale, S., *French Salons: High Society and Political Sociability from the Old Regime to the Revolution of 1848* (Baltimore, 2005).

Kamen, H., *The War of Succession in Spain 1700–15* (London, 1969).

Kamen, H., *Spain in the Later Seventeenth Century 1665–1700* (London, 1980).

Kamen, H., *Philip V of Spain* (New York, 2001).

Kamen, H., *Empire: How Spain Became a World Power, 1492–1763* (New York, 2002).

Kamenskii, A., *Pod seniiu Ekateriny: Vtoraia olovina XVIII veka* (St. Petersburg, 1992).

Kamenskii, A., *The Russian Empire in the Eighteenth Century* (New York, 1997).

Kamenskii, A., *Zhizn' i sud'ba imperatritsy Ekateriny Velikoi* (Moscow, 1997).

Kaplan, H., *The First Partition of Poland* (New York, 1962).

Kaplan, S. (ed.), *Understanding Pop Culture: Europe from the Middle Ages to the Nineteenth Century* (Berlin, 1984).

Kaplan, S. L., *Bread, Politics and Political Economy in the Reign of Louis XV* (The Hague, 1976).

Kates, G., *The Cercle Social, the Girondins and the French Revolution* (Princeton, 1985).

Keller, K., *Kleinstädte in Kursachsen. Wandlungen einer Städtelandschaft zwischen Dreißigjährigem Krieg und Industrialisierung* (Cologne, 2001).

Kennedy, M. L., *The Jacobin Clubs in the French Revolution* (vols. 1 and 2, Princeton, 1982, 1988; vol. 3, New York, 2000).

Kennedy, P., *The Rise and Fall of the Great Powers: Economic Change and Military Conflict from 1500 to 2000* (New York, 1988).

Kenrick, W., *The Whole Duty of Woman* (1753; 13th edn., Windsor, VT, 1792).

Kent, S. K., *Gender and Power in Britain, 1640–1990* (London, 1999).

Kertzer, D. and M. Barbagli (eds.), *The History of the European Family*, vol. 1: *Family Life in Early Modern Times* (New Haven, 2001).

King, L., *The Medical World of the Eighteenth Century* (Chicago, 1958).

King, L., *The Philosophy of Medicine: The Early Eighteenth Century* (Cambridge, MA, 1978).

King, S. and A. Tomkins (eds.), *The Poor in England 1700–1850: An Economy of Makeshifts* (Manchester, 2003).

Kington, J., *The Weather Journals of a Rutland Squire* (Oakham, 1988).

Kington, J., *The Weather of the 1780s over Europe* (Cambridge, 1988).

Kiple, K. F. (ed.), *The Cambridge World History of Human Disease* (Cambridge, 1993).

Kiple, K. F., *The Cambridge Historical Dictionary of Disease* (Cambridge, 2003).

Király, B. K., "Neo-serfdom in Hungary," *Slavic Review*, 34 (1975), 269–78.

Kirby, D., *Northern Europe in the Early Modern Period: The Baltic World 1492–1772* (Harlow, 1990).

Kirby, D. and M.-L. Hinkkanen, *The Baltic and the North Seas* (London, 2000).

Klein, H. S., *The Atlantic Slave Trade* (Cambridge, 1999).

Kleyn, S. R., *Patriots republikanisme. Politieke cultuur in Nederland (1766–1787)* (Amsterdam, 1995).

Klier, J., *Russia Gathers her Jews: The Origins of the "Jewish Question" in Russia, 1772–1825* (DeKalb, ILL, 1986).

Kloosterhuis, J., "Zwischen Aufruhr und Akzeptanz. Zur Ausformung und Einbettung des Kantonssystems in die Wirtschafts- und Sozialstrukturen des preußischen Westfalen," in B. R. Kroener and R. Proeve (eds.), *Krieg und Frieden. Militär und Gesellschaft in der Frühen Neuzeit* (Paderborn, 1996), pp. 167–90.

Klueting, H., *Die Lehre von der Macht der Staaten* (Berlin, 1986).

Klueting, H., "'Zweite Reformation' – Konfessionsbildung – Konfessionalisierung. Zwanzig Jahre Kontroversen und Ergebnisse nach zwanzig Jahren," *Historische Zeitschrift*, 277 (2003), 309–41.

Klußmann, J. (ed.), *Leibeigenschaft. Bäuerliche Unfreiheit in der frühen Neuzeit* (Cologne, 2003).

Knights, M., *Representation and Misrepresentation in Later Stuart Britain* (Oxford, 2005).

Knittler, H., *Die europäische Stadt in der frühen Neuzeit. Institutionen, Strukturen, Entwicklungen* (Vienna, 2000).

Knott, S. and B. Taylor (eds.), *Women, Gender and the Enlightenment* (Basingstoke, 2005).

Königs, P., *The Hanoverian Kings and their Homeland* (Lewes, 1993); rev. edn. in German translation: *Die Dynastie aus Deutschland. Die hannoverschen Könige von England und ihre Heimat* (Hanover, 1998).

Kooimans, L., *Onder regenten. De elite in een Hollandse stad, Hoorn 1700–1780* (Dieren, 1985).

Kopsidis, M., *Agrarentwicklung. Historische Agrarrevolutionen und Entwicklungsökonomie* (Stuttgart, 2006).

Koselleck, R., *Preußen zwischen Reform und Revolution: Allgemeines Landrecht, Verwaltung und soziale Bewegung von 1791–1848* (3rd edn., Stuttgart, 1981).

Kriedte, P., *Peasants, Landlords and Merchant Capitalists: Europe and the World Economy, 1500–1800* (Leamington Spa, 1983).

Kriedte, P., H. Medick, and J. Schlumbohm, *Industrialization before Industrialization* (Cambridge, 1981).

Kroll, S. and M. Kaiser (eds.), *Militär und ländliche Gesellschaft in der Frühen Neuzeit* (Hamburg, 2000).

Krüger, K., *Die Landständische Verfassung* (Munich, 2003).

Kuethe, A., *Cuba, 1753–1815: Crown, Military, and Society* (Knoxville, TN, 1986).

Kuethe, A. J. and Blaisdell, L., "French influence and the origins of the Bourbon colonial reorganisation," *Hispanic American Historical Review*, 71 (1991), 579–607.

Kuethe, A. J. and Inglis, G. D., "Absolutism and enlightened reform: Charles III, the establishment of the Alcabala, and commercial reorganization in Cuba," *Past & Present*, 109 (1985), 118–43.

Kümin, B., "Sacred church and worldly tavern: reassessing an early modern divide," in W. Coster and A. Spicer (eds.), *Sacred Space in Early Modern Europe* (Cambridge, 2005), pp. 17–38.

Kümin, B. and B. A. Tlusty (eds.), *The World of the Tavern: Public Houses in Early Modern Europe* (Aldershot, 2002).

Kunisch, J., *Friedrich der Große. Der König und seine Zeit* (Munich, 2004).

Küther, C., *Räuber und Gauner in Deutschland* (2nd edn., Göttingen, 1987).

Kwass, M., *Privilege and the Politics of Taxation in Eighteenth-Century France: Liberté, égalité, fiscalité* (Cambridge, 2000).

Lake, P. and S. Pincus, "Rethinking the public sphere in early modern England," *Journal of British Studies*, 45 (2006), 270–92.

Lamb, H. H., "Volcanic dust in the atmosphere: with a chronology and assessment of its meteorological significance," *Phil. Trans. Royal Society of London*, series A, 266 (1970), 425–533.

Lamb, H. H., *Climate, History and the Modern World* (London, 1982).

Lamb, H. H., *Weather, Climate and Human Affairs* (London, 1988).

Lamb, H. H., *Historic Storms of the North Sea, British Isles and North West Europe* (Cambridge, 1991).

Landes, J. B. *Visualizing the Nation: Gender, Representation and Revolution in Eighteenth-Century France* (Ithaca, 2001).

Landes, J. B., *Women and the Public Sphere in the Age of the French Revolution* (Ithaca, 1988).

Landon, H. C. R., *Haydn: Chronicle and Works* (5 vols., London, 1976–80).

Lane, F. C., *Profits from Power: Readings in Protection Rent and Violence-Controlling Enterprises* (Albany, 1979).

Laqueur, T. W., *Making Sex: Body and Gender from the Greeks to Freud* (Cambridge, MA, 1990).

Lavery, B., *The Ship of the Line* (2 vols., London, 1983–4).

Lawrence, S. C., *Charitable Knowledge: Hospital Pupils and Practitioners in Eighteenth-Century London* (Cambridge, 1995).

Lawson, P., *The East India Company: A History* (New York, 1993).

Le Roy Ladurie, E., *Times of Feast, Times of Famine: A History of Climate since the Year 1000* (London, 1972).

Le Roy Ladurie, E., "Revoltes et contestations rurales en France de 1675 à 1789," *Annales: Économies, Sociétés, Civilisations*, 29 (1974), 6–22.

Le Roy Ladurie, E., *The Mind and the Method of the Historian* (1974; Chicago, 1981).

Lee, W. R. "Women's work and the family: some demographic implications of gender-specific rural work patterns in nineteenth-century Germany," in P. Hudson and W. R. Lee (eds.), *Women's Work and the Family Economy in Historical Perspective* (Manchester, 1990), pp. 50–75.

Leeb, I. L., *The Ideological Origins of the Batavian Revolution. History and Politics in the Dutch Republic 1747–1800* (The Hague, 1973).

Lefebvre, G., *The Great Fear of 1789* (New York, 1973).

Legay, M.-L., *Les États provinciaux dans la construction de l'état moderne, aux XVIIe et XVIIIe siècles* (Geneva, 2001).

Lemarchand, G., *La Fin du féodalisme dans le pays de Caux* (Paris, 1989).

Lemire, B., *Fashion's Favourite: The Cotton Trade and the Consumer in Britain, 1660–1800* (Oxford, 1991).

Lemire, B., *Dress, Culture and Commerce: The English Clothing Trade before the Factory, 1660–1800* (Basingstoke, 1997).

Lemire, B., *The Business of Everyday Life: Gender, Practice and Social Politics in England 1600–1900* (Manchester, 2005).

Lenman, B., *Britain's Colonial Wars 1688–1783* (Harlow, 2001).

Leonard, C., *Reform and Regicide: The Reign of Peter III of Russia* (Bloomington, 1993).

Levey, M., *Painting in Eighteenth-Century Venice* (New Haven, 1994).

Levi, G., *Inheriting Power* (Chicago, 1988).

Levine, H., *Economic Origins of Antisemitism: Poland and its Jews in the Early Modern Period* (New Haven, 1991).

Levy, M. J., *Governance and Grievance: Habsburg Policy and Italian Tyrol in the Eighteenth Century* (West Lafayette, 1988).

Lewis, B., *The Emergence of Modern Turkey* (Oxford, 1961).

Lewis, G. and C. Lucas (eds.), *Beyond the Terror: Essays in French Regional and Social History, 1794–1815* (Cambridge, 1983).

Lewitter, L. R., "Poland, Russia and the Treaty of Vienna of 5 January 1719," *Historical Journal*, 3 (1970), 3–30.

Liesker, R., "Tot zinkens toe bezwaard. De schuldenlast van het Zuiderkwartier van Holland 1672–1794," in S. Groenveld et al. (eds.), *Bestuurders en geleerden* (Amsterdam and Dieren, 1985), pp. 151–60.

Lieven, D. (ed.), *The Cambridge History of Russia*, vol. 2: *Imperial Russia, 1689–1917* (Cambridge, 2006).

Lilti, A., *Le Monde des salons: Sociabilité et mondanité à Paris au XVIIIe siècle* (Paris, 2005).

Linde, R., "Krüge: Wirtshauskultur in der Grafschaft Lippe im 18. Jahrhundert," in S. Baumeier and J. Carstensen (eds.), *Beiträge zur Volkskunde und Hausforschung* (Detmold, 1995).

Lindemann, M., *Health and Healing in Eighteenth-Century Germany* (Baltimore, 1996).

Lindemann, M., *Medicine and Society in Early Modern Europe* (Cambridge, 1999).

Llombart, V., *Campomanes, economista y politico de Carlos III* (Madrid, 1992).

Lluch, E., *Las Españas vencidas del siglo XVIII: claroscuros de la ilustración* (Barcelona, 1999).

Lo Basso, L., *Uomini da remo: galee e galeotti nel Mediterraneo in età moderna* (Milan, 2004).

Locke, John, *Some Thoughts Concerning Education*, vol. 37, pt. 1 (New York, 1909–14).

Lopes Pires Nunes, A., "Les guerres hollandaises au Brésil du XVIIe siècle: confrontation de deux écoles militaires," in *Acta of the XVIII Annual Conference of the International Commission for Military History*, held in Turin 1992 (Gaeta, 1993), pp. 457–62.

Lord, R. H., *The Second Partition of Poland* (Cambridge, MA, 1915).

Lord, R. H., "The third partition of Poland," *Slavonic Review*, 3 (1924–5), 481–98.

Loriga, S., *Soldats. Un laboratoire disciplinaire: l'armée piémontaise au XVIIIe siècle* (Paris, 1991).

Lucacs, A. B., "Le 'universitates' meridionali all'inizio del regno di Carlo di Borbone," *Clio*, 17 (1981), 208–26.

Lucas, C., "The crowd and politics between *ancien régime* and revolution in France," *Journal of Modern History*, 60 (1988), 421–57.

Lucas, C. (ed.), *The Political Culture of the French Revolution* (Oxford, 1988).

Lucassen, J. and R. W. Unger, "Labour productivity in ocean shipping, 1450–1875," *International Journal of Maritime History*, 12 (2000), 127–41.

Luebke, D. M., *His Majesty's Rebels: Communities, Factions and Rural Revolt in the Black Forest, 1725–1745* (Ithaca, 1997).

Luebke, D. M., "Frederick the Great and the celebrated case of the Millers Arnold (1770–1779): a reappraisal," *Central European History*, 32 (1999), 379–408.

Luebke, D. M., "Signatures and political culture in eighteenth-century Germany," *Journal of Modern History*, 76 (2004), 497–530.

Luis, J., "Popular knowledge in the eighteenth-century almanacs," *History of European Ideas*, 11 (1989), 509–13.

Lukowski, J. T., "Towards partition: Polish magnates and Russian intervention in Poland during the early reign of Stanisław August Poniatowski," *Historical Journal*, 28 (1985), 557–74.

Lukowski, J. T., *Liberty's Folly: The Polish-Lithuanian Commonwealth in the Eighteenth Century, 1697–1795* (London, 1991).

Lukowski, J. T., "Recasting Utopia: Montesquieu, Rousseau and the Polish Constitution of 3 May 1791," *Historical Journal*, 37 (1994), 65–87.

Lukowski, J. T., *The Partitions of Poland: 1772, 1793, 1795* (Harlow, 1999).

Lukowski, J. T., *The European Nobility in the Eighteenth Century* (Basingstoke, 2003).

Lukowski, J. T. and H. Zawadzki, *A Concise History of Poland* (2001; 2nd edn., Cambridge, 2006).

Lüsebrink, H.-J. and R. Reichardt, *The Bastille: A History of a Symbol of Despotism and Freedom* (Durham, NC, 1997).

Luu, L. B., *Immigrants and the Industries of London, 1500–1700* (Aldershot, 2005).

Lynch, J., *The Spanish American Revolutions 1808–1826* (London, 1973; 1986).

Lynch, J., *Bourbon Spain 1700–1800* (Oxford, 1989).

Lynch, J., The institutional framework of colonial Spanish America," *Journal of Latin American Studies*, 24 (1992), 69–81.

Lynn, J. A. (ed.), *Feeding Mars: Logistics in Western Warfare from the Middle Age to the Present* (Boulder, 1993).

Lynn, J. A., *Giant of the Grande Siècle: The French Army 1610–1715* (Cambridge, 1997).

MacKay, R., *"Lazy, Improvident People": Myth and Reality in the Writing of Spanish History* (Ithaca and London, 2006).

Madariaga, I. de, "Catherine II and the serfs: a reconsideration of some problems," *Slavonic and East European Review*, 52 (1974), 34–62.

Madariaga, I. de, *Russia in the Age of Catherine the Great* (London, 1981).

Madariaga, I. de, "The Russian nobility, 1600–1800," in H. M. Scott (ed.), *The European Nobilities in the 17th and 18th Centuries* (2 vols., London, 1995), vol. 2, pp. 223–73.

Magnusson, L., *An Economic History of Sweden* (London, 2000).

Maiorini, G., "Nobilità napoletana e cariche amministrative: i presidi provinciale nel Settecento," in M. A. Visceglia (ed.), *Signori, patrizi, cavalieri in Italia centro-meridonale nell'età moderna* (Rome, 1992), pp. 309–25.

Maiorini, M. G., "The capital and the provinces," in G. Imbruglia (ed.), *Naples in the 18th Century: The Birth and Death of a State* (Cambridge, 2000), pp. 4–21.

Malcolmson, R. W., *Popular Recreations in English Society 1700–1850* (Cambridge, 1973).

Mandelli, M., E. Sala, and F. Testa, *La battaglia di Cassano: protagonisti, storia e vicende umane della battaglia del 16 agosto 1705 e della Guerra di Successione Spagnola in Lombardia* (Cassano d'Adda, 2005).

Manley, G., "Snowfall in Britain over the past 300 years," *Weather*, 24 (1969), 428–37.

Manley, G., "Central England temperatures: monthly means 1659 to 1973," *Quarterly Journal of the Royal Meteorological Society*, 100 (1974), 389–405.

Manning, R. B., *An Apprenticeship in Arms: The Origins of the British Army 1585–1702* (Oxford, 2006).

Mannori, L., *Il sovrano tutore: pluralismo istituzionale e accentramento amministrativo nel principato dei Medici, secc. XVI–XVIII* (Milan, 1994).

Mansel, P., *Louis XVIII* (London, 1981).

Mansel, P., *The Court of France, 1789–1830* (Cambridge, 1988).

Mansel, P., *Prince of Europe: The Life of Charles-Joseph de Ligne* (London, 2003).
Marchesini, D., *Il bisogno di scrivere: usi della scrittura nell'Italia moderna* (Rome, 1992).
Marker, G., *Publishing, Printing, and the Origins of Intellectual Life in Russia, 1700–1800* (Princeton, 1985).
Markoff, J., *The Abolition of Feudalism: Peasants, Lords, and Legislators in the French Revolution* (Philadelphia, 1996).
Markoff, J. "Peasants and their grievances," in P. R. Campbell (ed.), *The Origins of the French Revolution* (Basingstoke, 2006), pp. 239–67.
Marland (ed.), H., *The Art of Midwifery: Early Modern Midwives in Europe* (London, 1993).
Martin, A. L., *Alcohol, Sex, and Gender in Late Medieval and Early Modern Europe* (Basingstoke, 2001).
Martínez, M. E., *The Spanish Concept of Limpieza de Sangre and the Emergence of the "Race/Caste" System in the Viceroyalty of New Spain* (Ph.D., University of Chicago, 2002).
Mason, H. T., *The Darnton Debate: Books and Revolution in the Eighteenth Century*, Studies on Voltaire and the Eighteenth Century, 359 (Oxford, 1998).
Mat'a, P. and T. Winkelbauer (eds.), *Die Habsburgermonarchie 1620 bis 1740. Leistungen und Grenzen des Absolutismusparadigmas* (Stuttgart, 2006).
Maurer, M., *Kirche, Staat und Gesellschaft im 17. und 18. Jahrhundert* (Munich, 1999).
Maxwell, K., "Pombal and the nationalisation of the Luso-Brazilian economy," *Hispanic American Historical Review*, 48 (1968), 608–31.
Maxwell, K., *Conflicts and Conspiracies: Brazil and Portugal 1750–1808* (Cambridge, 1973; reissued London, 2004).
Maxwell, K., "Pombal: the paradox of enlightenment and despotism," in H. M. Scott (ed.), *Enlightened Absolutism: Reform and Reformers in Later Eighteenth Century Europe* (London, 1990), pp. 75–118.
Maxwell, K., *Pombal: Paradox of the Enlightenment* (Cambridge, 1995).
Maynes, M. J., *Schooling in Western Europe: A Social History* (Albany, NY, 1985).
Maza, S., *Private Lives and Public Affairs: The Causes Célèbres of Prerevolutionary France* (Berkeley, 1993).
McCarthy, J., *The Ottoman Turks: An Introductory History to 1923* (New York, 1997).
McGowan, B., "The age of the *ayans*," in H. Inalcik and D. Quataert (eds.), *An Economic and Social History of the Ottoman Empire, 1300–1914* (Cambridge, 1994), pp. 637–758.
McGrew, R., *Paul I of Russia* (Oxford, 1992).
McGrew, R., *Encyclopedia of Medical History* (New York, 1995).
McKay, D. and H. M. Scott, *The Rise of the Great Powers, 1648–1815* (London, 1983).
McKendrick, N., J. Brewer, and J. H. Plumb, *The Birth of Consumer Society: The Commercialization of Eighteenth-Century England* (London, 1983).
McMahon, D. M., *Enemies of the Enlightenment: The French Counter-Enlightenment and the Making of Modernity* (New York, 2001).
McManners, J., *Church and Society in Eighteenth-Century France* (2 vols., Oxford, 1998).
McNeill, J. R., *Atlantic Empires of France and Spain: Louisbourg and Havana 1700–1763* (Chapel Hill, 1985).
McNeill, W., *Plagues and Peoples* (Garden City, 1976; rev. edn., New York, 1997).
McVeigh, S., *Concert Life in London from Mozart to Haydn* (Cambridge, 1993).
Medick, H., "Plebeian culture in the transition to capitalism," in R. Samuel and G. Stedman Jones (eds.), *Culture, Ideology and Politics: Essays for Eric Hobsbawn* (London, 1983), pp. 84–113.
Medick, H., *Weben und Überleben in Laichingen 1650–1900. Lokalgeschichte als Allgemeine Geschichte* (Göttingen, 1996).

Meer, T. van der, *Sodoms zaad in Nederland. Het ontstaan van homoseksualiteit in de vroegmoderne tijd* (Nijmegen, 1995).

Melton, E., "Gutsherrschaft in East Elbian Germany and in Livonia, 1500–1800: a critique of the model," *Central European History*, 21 (1988), 315–49.

Mendels, F., "Proto-industrialization: the first phase of the industrialization process," *Journal of Economic History*, 32 (1972), 241–62.

Merino Navarro, J. P., *La armada española en el siglo XVIII* (Madrid, 1981).

Merrick, J., *The Desacralization of the French Monarchy in the Eighteenth Century* (Baton Rouge, 1990).

Merriman, J. M., *A History of Modern Europe from the Renaissance to the Present* (New York, 2004).

Mestre Sanchis, A., *La ilustración española* (Madrid, 1998).

Metcalf, M. F., *A History of the Swedish Parliament* (Stockholm, 1987).

Metz, K. H., "Staatsraison und Menschenfreundlichkeit. Formen und Wandlungen der Armenpflege im Ancien Régime Frankreich, Deutschlands und Großbritanniens," *Vierteljahrschrift für Sozial- und Wirtschaftsgeschichte*, 72 (1985), 1–26.

Meumann, M. and R. Pröve (eds.), *Herrschaft in der Frühen Neuzeit. Umrisse eines dynamisch-kommunikativen Prozesses* (Münster, 2004).

Meyer, J. and J.-P. Poussou, *Études sur les villes françaises: Milieu du XVIIe siècle à la veille de la Révolution française* (2nd edn., Paris, 1995).

Michael, W., *Englische Geschichte im Achtzehnen Jahrhundert* (Leipzig, 1896–1945).

Michael, W., "Die Personalunion von England und Hannover und das Testament Georgs I," *Archiv für Urkundenforschung*, 6 (1928), 323–40.

Michaelowa, A., "The impact of short-term climate change on British and French agriculture and population in the first half of the 18th century," in P. D. Jones et al. (eds.) *History and Climate: Memories of the Future* (Dordrecht, 2000).

Midelfort, H. C. E., *Exorcism and Enlightenment: Johann Joseph Gassner and the Demons of Eighteenth-Century Germany* (New Haven, 2005).

Mieck, I. (ed.), *Handbuch der europäischen Wirtschafts- und Sozialgeschichte*, vol. 4 (Stuttgart, 1993).

Mijnhardt, W. W., *Tot Heil van't Menschdom. Culturele genootschappen in Nederland, 1750–1815* (Amsterdam, 1987).

Mills, K., *Idolatry and its Enemies: Colonial Andean Religion and Extirpation, 1640–1750* (Princeton, 1997).

Mintz, S. W., *Sweetness and Power* (New York, 1985).

Mironov, B. N., *The Social History of Imperial Russia, 1700–1917*, vol. 2 (Boulder, 2000).

Mitchell, B. R., *European Historical Statistics 1750–1975* (2nd edn., London, 1981).

Mohrmann, R. E., "Everyday culture in early modern times," *New Literary History*, 24 (1993), 75–86.

Montecchi, G., "La censura di stato nel ducato estense dalle origni alla fine del Settecento," in A. Biondi (ed.), *Formazione e controllo dell'opinione pubblica a Modena nel '700* (Modena, 1986), pp. 23–49.

Montefiore, S., *Prince of Princes: The Life of Potemkin* (London, 2000).

Montroni, G., "The court: power relations and forms of social life," in G. Imbruglia (ed.), *Naples in the 18th Century: The Birth and Death of a State* (Cambridge, 2000), pp. 22–43.

Moon, D., *The Russian Peasantry 1600–1930* (London, 1999).

Moor, M., L. Shaw-Taylor, and P. Warde (eds.), *The Management of Common Land in North West Europe, c.1500–1850* (Turnhout, 2002).

Moore, Jr., B., *Social Origins of Dictatorship and Democracy: Lord and Peasant in the Making of the Modern World* (London, 1984).

More, H., *Essays on Various Subjects, Principally Designed for Young Ladies* (London, 1777).

Moreno Claverías, B., "Révolution de la consommation paysanne? Modes de consommation et différenciation sociale de la paysannerie catalane, 1670–1790," *Histoire & Mesure*, 21 (2006), 141–83.

Moriceau, J.-M., *Les Fermiers de l'Île de France: L'Ascension d'un patronat agricole (Xve–XVIIIe siècles)* (Paris, 1994).

Morineau, M., *Incroyables gazettes et trésors merveilleux* (Cambridge, 1985).

Morrow, M. S., *Concert Life in Haydn's Vienna: Aspects of a Developing Musical and Social Institution* (New York, 1988).

Moser, J. J., *Neues Teutsches Staats-Recht* (20 vols., Frankfurt, 1766–75; repr. Osnabrück, 1967).

Mosse, G. L. *The Image of Man: The Creation of Modern Masculinity* (Oxford, 1998).

Mozzarelli, C., *Sovrano, società e amministrazione locale nella Lombardia teresiana (1749–1758)* (Bologna, 1982).

Muchembled, R., *Popular Culture and Elite Culture in France 1400–1750* (Baton Rouge, 1985).

Mugnai, B., *L'esercito ottomano da Candia a Passarowitz (1645–1718)* (2 vols., Venice, 1998).

Mugnai, B., "Confinari e Temerari: il militärgrenze in Croazia, Ungheria e Transilvania fra Seicento e Settecento," in *Frontiere e fortificazioni di frontiera* (Florence, 2001).

Mullan, J. and C. Reid (eds.), *Eighteenth-Century Popular Culture: A Selection* (Oxford, 2000).

Müller, H.-H., *Märkische Landwirtschaft vor den Agrarreformen von 1807* (Potsdam, 1967).

Müller, L., *Consuls, Corsairs, and Commerce: The Swedish Consular Service and Long-Distance Shipping, 1720–1815* (Uppsala, 2004).

Munck, T., "Absolute monarchy in later eighteenth-century Denmark: centralized reform, public expectations, and the Copenhagen press," *Historical Journal*, 41 (1998), 201–24.

Munck, T., *The Enlightenment: A Comparative Social History, 1721–1794* (London, 2000).

Murphey, R., "The Ottoman attitude towards the adoption of foreign technology: the role of the Efrencî technicians in civil and military applications," in J.-L. Bacquét-Grammont and P. Dumont (eds.), *Contributions à l'histoire économique et sociale de l'empire ottoman* (Leuven, 1983).

Murphy, A. E., *John Law: Economic Theorist and Policy-Maker* (Oxford, 1997).

Musgrave, E., "Women and the craft guilds in eighteenth-century Nantes," in G. Crossick (ed.), *The Artisan and the European Town, 1500–1900* (Brookfield, VT, 1997), pp. 151–71.

Mylne, V., *The Eighteenth-Century French Novel: Techniques of Illusion* (Manchester, 1981).

Neugebauer, W., *Politischer Wandel im Osten. Ost- und Westpreußen von den alten Ständen zum Konstitutionalismus* (Stuttgart, 1992).

Nicassio, S. V., "For the benefit of my soul: a preliminary study of the persistence of tradition in eighteenth-century Mass obligations," *Catholic History Review*, 78 (1992), 175–96.

Niccolini, F., "Cosimo III de'Medici e Antonio Carafa," *Archivo Storico Italiano*, 96 (1938), 69–91, 180–225.

Nicolas, J., *La Rébellion française: Mouvements populaires et conscience sociale, 1661–1789* (Paris, 2002).

Niklaus, R., *The Eighteenth Century, 1715–1789*, vol. 4 of P. E. Charvet (ed.), *A Literary History of France* (5 vols. in 6, London, 1967).

Nimwegen, O. van, *De Republiek der Verenigde Nederlanden als grote mogendheid* (Amsterdam, 2002).

Noel, C., "Charles III of Spain," in H. M. Scott (ed.), *Enlightened Absolutism: Reform and Reformers in Eighteenth-Century Europe* (Basingstoke, 1990), pp. 119–43.

Noel, C. C., "Charles III of Spain," in H. M. Scott (ed.), *Enlightened Absolutism* (Basingstoke, 1990), pp. 119–44.

Nogueira da Silva, A. C., *O modelo espacial do estado moderno: reorganizacao territorial em Portugal nos finais do Antigo Regime* (Lisbon, 1998).

Norberg, K., *Rich and Poor in Grenoble, 1600–1814* (Berkeley, 1985).

North, D. C., *Structure and Change in Economic History* (New York, 1981).

Nosworthy, B., *The Anatomy of Victory: Battle Tactics 1689–1763* (New York, 1990).

Nubola, "Supplications between politics and justice: the northern and central Italian states in the early modern age," *International History Review*, supplement 9, 46 (2001), 35–56.

Nye, R., *A., Masculinity and Male Codes of Honor in Modern France* (Oxford, 1993).

Oakley, S. P., *War and Peace in the Baltic, 1560–1790* (London, 1992).

Offen, K., *European Feminisms, 1700–1950; A Political History* (Stanford, 2000).

Ogilvie, A. E. J., "Climate and economy in eighteenth century Iceland," in C. D. Smith and M. Parry (eds.), *Consequences of Climatic Change* (Nottingham, 1980).

Ogilvie, A. E. J., "Documentary evidence for changes in the climate of Iceland. A.D. 1500 to 1800," in R. S. Bradley and P. D. Jones (eds.), *Climate Since A.D. 1500* (London, 1992).

Ogilvie, S., "Women and proto-industrialisation in a corporate society: Württemberg woollen weaving, 1590–1760," in P. Hudson and W. R. Lee (eds.), *Women's Work and the Family Economy in Historical Perspective* (Manchester, 1990), pp. 76–103.

Ogilvie, S. (ed.), *A New Social and Economic History of Germany*, vol. 2: *1630–1800* (London, 1996).

Ogilvie, S., "The state in Germany," in J. Brewer and E. Hellmuth (eds.), *Rethinking Leviathan* (Oxford, 1999), pp. 167–202.

Ogilvie, S. and M. Cerman (eds.), *European Proto-Industrialization* (Cambridge, 1996).

O'Gorman, F., *Voters, Patrons, and Parties: The Unreformed Electoral System of Hanoverian England, 1734–1832* (Oxford, 1989).

O'Gorman, F., *The Long Eighteenth Century: British Political and Social History 1688–1832* (London, 1997).

Olausson, M. (ed.), *Catherine the Great and Gustavus III* (Stockholm and St. Petersburg, 1999).

Oliveira Marques, *History of Portugal* (2nd edn., New York, 1976).

Oliver-Smith, A., "Theorizing vulnerability in a globalized world: a political ecological perspective," in G. Bankoff, G. Frerks, and D. Hilhorst (eds.), *Mapping Vulnerability: Disasters, Developments and People* (London 2004).

Ormrod, D., *The Rise of Commercial Empires: England and the Netherlands in the Age of Mercantilism, 1650–1770* (Cambridge, 2003).

Outram, D., *The Enlightenment*, (Cambridge, 1995).

Overton, M., *Agricultural Revolution in England. The Transformation of the Agrarian Economy 1500–1850* (Cambridge, 1996).

Özmucur, S. and S. Pamuk, "Real wages and standards of living in the Ottoman empire, 1489–1914," *Journal of Economic History*, 62 (2002), 293–321.

Ozouf, M., *Festivals and the French Revolution* (Cambridge, MA, 1988).

Ozouf, M., "'Public opinion' at the end of the old regime," *Journal of Modern History*, 60 (supplement, 1988), S1–21.

Padfield, P., *Maritime Supremacy and the Opening of the Western Mind, 1588–1782* (London, 1999).

Padfield, P., *Maritime Power and the Struggle for Freedom, 1788–1851* (London, 2003).

Paine, T., *Political Writings* (2nd edn., Cambridge, 2000).

Palmer, R. R., *The Age of the Democratic Revolution: A Political History of Europe and America 1760–1800* (Princeton, 1959).
Pammer, M., *Glaubensabfall und wahre Andacht. Barockreligiosität, Reformkatholizismus und Laizismus in Oberösterreich 1700–1820* (Vienna and Munich, 1994).
Pansini, G., "Les Réformes de François-Etienne de Lorraine en Toscane (1737–1765)," in *La Lorraine dans l'Europe des Lumières: Actes du Colloque de Nancy, 24–27 octobre, 1966* (Nancy, 1968), pp. 359–66.
Paoletti C., "Logistica e assedi delle guerre del settecento," *Panoplia*, 27–8 (1996), 28–34.
Paoletti, C., *Gli Italiani in armi: cinque secoli di storia militare nazionale 1494–2000* (Rome, 2001).
Paoletti, C., *Il principe Eugenio di Savoia* (Rome, 2001).
Paoletti, C., "Errori d'impostazione storiografica e nuova valutazione dell'assedio di Tolone e della campagna sabauda in Provenza del 1707," in *Studi storico-militari 2001* (Rome, 2004), pp. 259–76.
Paoletti, C., "Prince Eugene of Savoy, the Toulon expedition of 1707 and the English historians: a dissenting view," *Journal of Military History*, 70 (2006), 939–62.
Parry, M. L., "Climatic change and the agricultural frontier: a research strategy," in T. M. L. Wigley et al. (eds.), *Climate and History: Studies in Past Climates and their Impact on Man* (Cambridge, 1981).
Parry, M. L., and T. R. Carter, "The effects of climatic variation on agricultural risk," *Climatic Change*, 7 (1985), 95–110.
Pascal, R., *The German Sturm und Drang* (Manchester, 1953).
Pastor, F. L. v., *The History of the Popes from the Close of the Middle Ages*, vol. 32 (London, 1957).
Patrick, A., *The Men of the First French Republic: Political Alignments in the National Convention of 1792* (Baltimore, 1972).
Paulson, R., *Popular and Polite Art in the Age of Hogarth and Fielding* (Notre Dame, 1979).
Peacey, J., *Politicians and Pamphleteers: Propaganda during the English Civil Wars and Interregnum* (Aldershot, 2004).
Pennant, T., *A Tour in Scotland 1769* (repr. Edinburgh, 2000).
Perini, S., *La difesa militare della Terraferma veneta nel Settecento* (Sottomarina, 1998).
Perjés, G., "Army provisioning, logistics and strategy in the second half of the 17th century," repr. in J. Black (ed.), *Warfare in Europe 1650–1792* (Aldershot, 2005), pp. 109–60.
Peters, J., *Gutsherrschaftsgesellschaften im europäischen Vergleich* (Berlin, 1997).
Peters, M., *The Elder Pitt* (Harlow, 1998).
Petráň, J., "Die mitteleuropäische Landwirtschaft und der Handel im 16. und am Anfang des 17. Jahrhunderts," *Historica*, 18 (1973), 105–38.
Pezzl, J., *Reise durch den baierschen Kreis* (1784).
Pfister, C., *Das Klima der Schweiz von 1525–1860 und seine Bedeutung in der Geschichte von Bevölkerung und Landwirtschaft* (2 vols., Bern, 1984).
Pfister, C., *Klimageschichte der Schweiz 1525–1860. Das Klima der Schweiz von 1525–1860 und seine Bedeutung in der Geschichte von Bevölkerung und Landwirtschaft* (Stuttgart, 1988).
Pfister, C. and R. Brázdil, "Social vulnerability to climate in the Little Ice Age: an example from central Europe in the early 1770s," *Climate of the Past*, 2 (2006), 115–29.
Phillips, J. A., *Electoral Behavior in Unreformed England* (Princeton, 1982).
Pinchbeck, I., *Women Workers and the Industrial Revolution, 1750–1850* (London, 1930; repr. 1981).
Písek, J., and R. Brázdil, "Responses of large volcanic eruptions in the instrumental and documentary climatic data over central Europe," *International Journal of Climatology*, 26 (2006), 439–59.

Pluchon, P., *Toussaint Louverture* (Paris, 1989).
Plumb, J. H., "The new world of children in eighteenth-century England," *Past and Present*, 67 (1975), 64–93.
Polanyi, K., *The Great Transformation* (1944; repr. Boston, 1985).
Popkin, J. D., "The *Gazette de Leyde* and French politics under Louis XVI," in J. R. Censer and J. D. Popkin (eds.), *Press and Politics in Pre-Revolutionary France* (Berkeley, 1987), pp. 75–132.
Popkin, J. D., *Revolutionary News: The Press in France, 1789–1799* (Durham, NC, 1990).
Porter, D. and R. Porter, *Patient's Progress Doctors and Doctoring in Eighteenth-Century England* (Stanford, 1989).
Porter, R. (ed.), *Patients and Practitioners: Lay Perceptions of Medicine in Pre-Industrial Society* (Cambridge, 1985).
Porter, R., *Health for Sale: Quackery in England, 1660–1850* (Manchester and New York, 1989).
Porter, R., *The Greatest Benefit to Mankind: A Medical History of Humanity* (New York, 1997).
Porter, R., *Enlightenment: Britain and the Creation of the Modern World* (London, 2000).
Porter, R. and M. Roberts (eds.), *Pleasure in the Eighteenth Century* (Basingstoke, 1996).
Porter, R. and M. Teich (eds.), *The Enlightenment in National Context* (Cambridge, 1981).
Post, J. D., "Nutritional status and mortality in eighteenth century Europe," in L. F. Newman (ed.) *Hunger in History* (Oxford, 1990).
Prak, M., *Gezeten burgers. De elite in een Hollandse stad, Leiden 1700–1780* (Dieren, 1985).
Prass, R., G. Béaur, C. Duhamelle, and J. Schlumbohm (eds.), *Les Sociétés rurales en Allemagne et en France (XVIIIe–XIXe siècles)* (Rennes, 2004).
Preto, P., "Un aspetto sconosciuto del conflitto veneto-turco in Dalmazia e in Levante: la guerra chimica e batteriologica," *Atti e memorie della Società Dalmata di Storia patria*, NS 3, 14 (1989–91), 13–29.
Price, M., "Politics: Louis XVI," in W. Doyle (ed.), *Old Regime France* (Oxford, 2001), pp. 223–48.
Price, M. B. and L. M. Price, *The Publication of English Literature in Germany in the Eighteenth Century* (Berkeley and Los Angeles, 1934).
Priester, P., *Geschiedenis van de Zeeuwse landbouw circa 1600–1910* (Wageningen, 1998).
Pritchard, J., *Louis XV's Navy: A Study of Organization and Administration, 1748–1762* (Kingston, 1987).
Pritchard, J., *Anatomy of a Naval Disaster: The 1746 French Naval Expedition to North America* (Montreal, 1995).
Pritchard, J., *In Search of Empire: The French in the Americas, 1670–1730* (Cambridge, 2004).
"Proceedings of the Old Bailey 1674–1834" <http://www.oldbaileyonline.org/>.
Prodi, P., *The Papal Prince: One Body and Two Souls: The Papal Monarchy in Early Modern Europe* (Cambridge, 1987).
Prudhomme, L. M., *Révolutions de Paris, dédiées a la nation* (Paris, 1789–94).
Pugliese, S., *Le prime strette dell' Austria in Italia* (Milanand Rome, 1932).
Quataert, D., *The Ottoman Empire 1700–1922* (Cambridge, 2005).
Quataert, J., "The shaping of women's work in manufacturing guilds, households and the state in central Europe, 1648–1870," *American Historical Review*, 90 (1985), 1122–48.
Quataert, J., "Women's history at the crossroads," in D. Simonton (ed.), *The Routledge History of Women in Europe since 1700* (London, 2007), pp. x–xv.
Quazza, G., *Il problema italiano e l'equilibreo europeo 172–1738* (Turin, 1938).
Quetel, C., *De par le Roy: Essais sur les lettres de cachet* (Toulouse, 1981).

Radcliffe, W., *Origin of the New System of Manufacture, commonly called "Power-Loom Weaving" and the Purposes for which this System was invented and brought into use, fully explained . . .* (Stockport, 1828).

Raeff, M., *Origins of the Russian Intelligentsia: The Eighteenth-Century Nobility* (New York, 1966).

Raeff, M., *The Well-Ordered Police State: Social and Institutional Change through Law in the Germanies and Russia 1600–1800* (New Haven, 1983).

Ramsey, M., *Professional and Popular Medicine in France, 1770–1830: The Social World of Medical Practice* (Cambridge, 1988).

Ranke, L. v., "The great powers," in T. v. Laue, *Leopold von Ranke: The Formative Years* (Princeton, NJ, 1950), pp. 181–218.

Rao, A. M., "Esercito e società a Napoli nelle riforme del secondo Settecento," *Studi Storici*, 28 (1987), 623–77.

Rao, A. M., "The feudal question, judicial systems and the Enlightenment," in G. Imbruglia (ed.), *Naples in the 18th Century: The Birth and Death of a State* (Cambridge, 2000), pp. 95–117.

Rasmussen, S. E., *London: The Unique City* (3rd edn., Cambridge, MA, 1988).

Rau, S. and G. Schwerhoff (eds.), *Zwischen Gotteshaus und Taverne. Öffentliche Räume in Spätmittelalter und Früher Neuzeit* (Cologne, 2004).

Rausch, W. (ed.), *Die Städte Mitteleuropas im 17. und 18. Jahrhundert* (Linz, 1981).

Raymond, J. (ed.), *News, Newspapers, and Society in Early Modern Britain* (London, 1999).

Raymond, J., *Pamphlets and Pamphleteering in Early Modern Britain* (Cambridge, 2003).

Razell, P., *The Conquest of Smallpox: The Impact of Inoculation on Smallpox Mortality in Eighteenth-Century Britain* (Southampton, 1977).

Reay, B., (ed.), *Popular Culture in Seventeenth-Century England* (London, 1985).

Reay, B., *Popular Cultures in England 1550–1750* (Harlow, 1998).

Rebel, H., "Reimagining the *oikos*: Austrian cameralism in its social formation," in J. O'Brien and W. Roseberry (eds.), *Golden Ages, Dark Ages* (Berkeley, 1991), pp. 48–80.

Reed, T. J., *The Classical Centre: Goethe and Weimar 1775–1832* (London, 1980).

Reinalter, H. (ed.), *Lexikon zum Aufgeklärten Absolutismus in Europa* (Cologne, 2005).

Reinhardt, S. G., *Justice in the Sarladais 1770–1790* (Baton Rouge, 1991).

Reitan, E. R.(ed.), *George III: Tyrant or Constitutional Monarch?* (Boston, 1964).

Rendall, J., "Women and the Enlightenment in Britain, *c*.1690–1800," in H. Barker and E. Chalus (eds.), *Women's History: Britain, 1700–1850* (London, 2005), pp. 9–32.

Rendall, J. and S. Innes, "Women, gender and politics," in L. Abrams et al. (eds.), *Gender and Scottish History, 1700 to the Present* (Edinburgh, 2006), pp. 43–83.

Ribbe, C., *Le Crime de Napoléon* (Paris, 2005).

Ribhegge, W., *Stadt und Nation in Deutschland vom Mittelalter bis zur Gegenwart. Die Entstehung der Ziviligesellschaft aus der Tradition der Städte* (Münster, 2002).

Richter-Uhlig, U., *Hof und Politik unter den Bedingungen der Personalunion zwischen Hannover und England. Die Aufenthalte Georgs II. in Hannover zwischen 1729 und 1741* (Hanover, 1992).

Rico Sinobas, M., *Memoria sobre las causas meteorológicofisicas que producen las constants sequías de Murcia y Almeria* (Madrid, 1854).

Riello, G., *A Foot in the Past: Consumers, Producers and Footwear in the Long Eighteenth Century* (Oxford, 2006).

Riley, J. C., *International Government Finance and the Amsterdam Capital Market, 1740–1815* (New York and Cambridge, 1980).

Riley, J. C., *The Eighteenth-Century Campaign to Avoid Disease* (New York, 1987).

Riley, J. C., "French finances, 1727–1768," *Journal of Modern* History, 59 (1987), 209–43.

Riley, J. C., *Sickness, Recovery, and Death* (Iowa City, 1989).

Ringrose, D., *Madrid and the Spanish Economy 1560–1850* (Berkeley, 1983).

Riotte, T., *Hannover in der britischen Politik (1792–1815). Dynastische Verbindung als Element außenpolitischer Entscheidungsfindung* (Münster, 2005).

Riasanovsky, N., *The Image of Peter the Great in Russian History and Thought* (New York, 1985).

Risse, G., *Hospital Life in Enlightenment Scotland: Care and Teaching at the Royal Infirmary of Edinburgh* (Cambridge, 1987).

Robb, P., *A History of India* (New York, 2002).

Roberts, J. (ed.), *George III and Queen Charlotte: Patronage, Collecting and Court Taste* (London, 2004).

Roberts, M., *The Swedish Imperial Experience 1560–1718* (Cambridge, 1979).

Roberts, M., *The Age of Liberty: Sweden 1719–1772* (Cambridge, 1986).

Robertson, J., *The Case for the Enlightenment: Scotland and Naples 1680–1760* (Cambridge, 2005).

Roche, D., *The People of Paris: An Essay in Popular Culture in the Eighteenth Century* (Leamington Spa, 1987).

Roche, D., *The Culture of Clothing: Dress and Fashion in the Ancien Régime* (Cambridge, 1994).

Roche, D., *Le Peuple de Paris: Essai sur la culture populaire au XVIIIe siècle* (Paris, 1998).

Roche, D., *A History of Everyday Things: The Birth of Consumption in France, 1600–1800*, trans. B. Pearce (Cambridge, 2000).

Roche, D. and G. Chabaud (eds.), *La Ville promise: Mobilité et accueil à Paris (fin XVIIe–début XIXe siècle)* (Paris, 2000).

Rodger, N. A. M., *Command of the Ocean: A Naval History of Britain, 1649–1815* (London, 2004).

Rodger, N. A. M., *The Wooden World: An Anatomy of the Georgian Navy* (London, 1986).

Rodrigo, F. S., M. J. Esteban-Parra, D. Pozo-Vázquez, and Y. Castro-Díez, "A 500-year precipitation record in southern Spain," *International Journal of Climatology*, 19 (1999), 1233–53.

Rodrigues, L. L., D. Gomes, and R. Craig, "The Portuguese School of Commerce, 1759–1844: a reflection of the 'Enlightenment'," *Accounting History* (2004), 53–71.

Rodriguez, L., "The Spanish Riots of 1766," *Past & Present*, 59 (1973), 117–46.

Rodriguez O. J. E., *The Independence of Spanish America* (Cambridge, 1998).

Roeck, B., *Lebenswelt und Kultur des Bürgertums in der Frühen Neuzeit* (Munich, 1991); expanded English translation, Leiden, 2006.

Rogers, N., *Crowds, Culture, and Politics in Georgian Britain* (Oxford, 1998).

Rogers, N., "Popular culture," in M. Fitzpatrick et al. (eds.), *The Enlightenment World* (London, 2006), pp. 401–17.

Root, H. L., *Peasants and King in Burgundy: Agrarian Foundations of French Absolutism* (Berkeley, 1987).

Roper, M. and J. Tosh (eds.), *Manful Assertions: Masculinities in Britain since 1800* (London, 1999).

Rosa, L. De, "Immobility and change in public finance in the kingdom of Naples, 1694–1806," *Journal of European Economic History*, 27 (1998), 9–28.

Rose, S. O., *Limited Livelihoods: Gender and Class in Nineteenth-Century England* (Berkeley, 1992).

Rosen, C., *The Classical Style* (2nd edn., London, 1997).

Rosenberg, C., *Explaining Epidemics and Other Studies in the History of Medicine* (Cambridge, 1992).

Rosman, M. J., *The Lords' Jews: Magnate-Jewish Relations in the Polish-Lithuanian Commonwealth during the Eighteenth Century* (Cambridge, MA, 1990).

Rosner, L., *Medical Education in the Age of Improvement: Edinburgh Students and Apprentices, 1760–1820* (Edinburgh, 1991).

Rosseaux, U., *Freiräume. Unterhaltung, Vergnügen und Erholung in Dresden (1694–1830)* (Cologne, 2006).

Rosseaux, U., *Städte in der frühen Neuzeit* (Darmstadt, 2006).

Rousseau, J.-J., *Emile* (London, 1974).

Rowbotham, S., "The trouble with patriarchy," in R. Samuel (ed.), *People's History and Socialist Theory* (London, 1981).

Rowe, M., *From Reich to State: The Rhineland in the Revolutionary Era* (Cambridge, 2003).

Rudé, G., *The Crowd in the French Revolution* (Oxford, 1959).

Rudé, G., *Hanoverian London, 1714–1808* (Berkeley, 1971).

Rudé, G., *The Crowd in History* (London, 1981).

Russell-Wood, A. J. R., *The Portuguese Empire 1415–1808: A World on the Move* (Baltimore, 1998).

Russell-Wood, A. J. R., "Holy and unholy alliances: clerical participation in the flow of bullion from Brazil to Portugal during the reign of Dom Joao V (1706–1750)," *Hispanic American Historical Review*, 32 (2000), 815–37.

Rystad, G., et al. (eds.), *In Quest of Trade and Security: The Baltic in Power Politics, 1500–1900* (2 vols., Lund, 1994–5).

Saalfeld, D., "Die ständische Gliederung der Gesellschaft Deutschlands im Zeitalter des Absolutismus. Ein Quantifizierungsversuch," *Vierteljahrschrift für Sozial- und Wirtschaftsgeschichte*, 67 (1980), 457–83.

Sabbadini, R., *La grazia e l'enore: principe, nobilità e ordine sociale nel ducati farnesiani* (Rome, 2001).

Sabbatini, G., "Fiscalità e banditismo in Abruzzo alla fine del Seicento," *Nuova Rivista Storica*, 79 (1995), 77–112.

Sabean, D., *Property, Production and Family in Neckarhausen 1700–1870* (Cambridge, 1990).

Sachße, C. and T. Tennstedt, *Geschichte der Armenfürsorge in Deutschland* (Stuttgart, 1980).

Said, E., *Orientalism* (New York, 1978).

Saine, T. P., *The Problem of Being Modern or the German Pursuit of Enlightenment from Leibniz to the French Revolution* (Detroit, 1997).

Sälter, G., *Polizei und soziale Ordnung in Paris* (Frankfurt a. M., 2004).

Salzmann, A., "The Age of Tulips: confluence and conflict in early modern consumer culture (1500–1730)," in D. Quataert (ed.), *Consumption Studies and the History of the Ottoman Empire, 1550–1922* (Albany, 2000).

Sanchez Blanco, F., *El absolutismo y las luces en el reinado de Carlos III* (Madrid, 2002).

Sarrailh, J., *La España ilustrada de la segunda mitad del siglo XVIII* (Mexico, 1957).

Saul, N., *Russia and the Mediterranean, 1797–1807* (Chicago, 1970).

Saul, N. (ed.), *Philosophy and German Literature, 1770–1990* (Cambridge, 2002).

Sauter, M. J., "Preaching, a ponytail, and an enthusiast: rethinking the public sphere's subversiveness in eighteenth-century Prussia," *Central European History*, 37 (2004), 544–67.

Scandinavian Economic History Review, published by the Scandinavian Society for Economic and Social History and Historical Geography since 1953.

Scandinavian Journal of History, published under the Auspices of the Historical Associations of Denmark, Finland, Norway, and Sweden since 1976.

Schaich, M. (ed.), *Monarchy and Religion* (Oxford, 2007).

Schama, S., *Patriots and Liberators: Revolution in the Netherlands, 1780–1813* (London, 1977).

Schama, S., *The Embarrassment of Riches: An Interpretation of Dutch Culture in the Golden Age* (London, 1991).

Schilling, H., *Die Stadt in der frühen Neuzeit* (Munich, 1993).

Schindler, N., *Rebellion, Community and Custom in Early Modern Germany* (Cambridge, 2002).

Schindling, A., "Glaubensvielfalt als Kulturkonflikt. Europa in der Frühen Neuzeit," in Klaus J. Bade (ed.), *Die multikulturelle Herausforderung. Menschen über Grenzen – Grenzen über Menschen* (Munich, 1996), 46–66.

Schlögl, R., *Glaube und Religion in der Säkularisierung. Die katholische Stadt: Köln, Aachen, Münster 1700–1840* (Munich, 1995).

Schlumbohm, J., *Lebensläufe, Familien, Höfe. Die Bauern und Heuerleute des Osnabrückischen Kirchspiels Belm in proto-industrieller Zeit, 1650–1860* (Göttingen, 1994).

Schlumbohm, J., "Gesetze, die nicht durchgesetzt werden. Ein Strukturmerkmal des frühneuzeitlichen Staates?," *Geschichte und Gesellschaft*, 23 (1997), 647–63.

Schmidt, G., *Geschichte des alten Reiches 1495–1806* (Munich, 1999).

Schmidt, J., "Inventing the Enlightenment: anti-Jacobins, British Hegelians and the *Oxford English Dictionary*," *Journal of the History of Ideas*, 64 (2003), 421–43.

Schnath, G., "Die Kurhannoversche Landesaufnahme, 1764–1786," *Hannoversches Magazin*, 7 (1931), 33–53.

Schnath, G., *Geschichte Hannovers im Zeitalter der neunten Kur und der englischen Sukzession, 1674–1704* (5 vols., Hildesheim, 1976–82).

Schneider, R. A., *Public Life in Toulouse, 1463–1789: From Municipal Republic to Cosmopolitan City* (Ithaca, 1989).

Schroeder, D. P., *Haydn and the Enlightenment: The Late Symphonies and their Audience* (Oxford, 1990).

Schroeder, P. W., *The Transformation of European Politics, 1763–1848* (Oxford, 1994).

Schultz, H., *Berlin 1650–1800. Sozialgeschichte einer Residenz* (Berlin, 1992).

Schulze, W., *Bäuerlicher Widerstand und feudale Herrschaft* (Bad Cannstadt, 1980).

Schulze, W., *Einführung in die neuere Geschichte* (Munich, 1987).

Schulze, W., "Gerhard Oestreichs Begriff 'Sozialdisziplinierung in der Frühen Neuzeit'," *Zeitschrift für historische Forschung*, 14 (1987), 265–302.

Schuurman, A. J., "Probate inventory research: opportunities and drawbacks," in M. Baulant, A. J. Schuurman, and P. Servais (eds.), *Inventaires après-décès et ventes de meubles: Apports à une histoire de la vie économique et quotidienne XIVe–XIXe siècle* (Louvain, 1988), pp. 19–57.

Schwartz, R., *Policing the Poor in Eighteenth-Century France* (Chapel Hill, 1988).

Schwartz, S. B., *Sovereignty and Society in Colonial Brazil* (Los Angeles, 1973).

Schwartz, S. B., "Brazil: ironies of the colonial past," *Hispanic American Historical Review*, 80 (2000), 681–94.

Scott, H. M. (ed.), *Enlightened Absolutism: Reform and Reformers in Later Eighteenth-Century Europe* (Basingstoke, 1990).

Scott, H. M., *The Emergence of the Eastern Powers, 1756–1775* (Cambridge, 2001).

Scott, H. M., *The Birth of a Great Power System 1740–1815* (Harlow, 2006).

Scott, H. M. (ed.), *The European Nobilities in the Seventeenth and Eighteenth Centuries* (2 vols., 2nd, expanded, edn., Basingstoke, 2007).

Scott, J., *Gender and the Politics of History* (New York, 1988; rev. edn., 1999).

Scott, J., "Gender: a useful category of historical analysis," repr. in J. W. Scott (ed.), *Feminism and History* (Oxford, 1997), pp. 152–80.

Scott, T. (ed.), *The Peasantries of Europe* (London, 1998).
Scribner, R. W., "Is a history of popular culture possible?," *History of European Ideas*, 10 (1989), 175–91.
Segal, L. *Slow Motion: Changing Masculinities, Changing Men* (rev. edn., Basingstoke, 2006).
Serna, P., "The noble," in M. Vovelle (ed.), *Enlightenment Portraits* (1992; English translation, Chicago, 1997), pp. 30–84.
Sewell, W. H., *Work and Revolution in France: The Language of Labor from the Old Regime to 1848* (Cambridge, 1980).
Sewell, W. H., *A Rhetoric of Bourgeois Revolution: The Abbé Sieyes and What Is the Third Estate?* (Durham, NC, 1994).
Sewter, A. C., *Baroque and Rococo Art* (London, 1973).
Shafer, R. J., *The Economic Societies in the Spanish World 1763–1821* (Syracuse, 1958).
Shapiro, B. M., *Revolutionary Justice in Paris, 1789–1790* (Cambridge, 1993).
Shapiro, G. and J. Markoff, *Revolutionary Demands: A Content Analysis of the Cahiers de Doléances of 1789* (Stanford, 1998).
Shaw, J., *Miracles in Enlightenment England* (New Haven, 2006).
Shaw, L. M. E. *The Anglo-Portuguese Alliance and the English Merchants in Portugal, 1654–1810* (Aldershot, 1998).
Shennan, J. H., *Philippe Duke of Orleans: Regent of France 1715–1723* (London, 1979).
Shmurlo, E., *Petr Velikii v otsenke sovremennikov i potomstva* (St. Petersburg, 1912).
Showalter, D. E., *The Wars of Frederick the Great* (London, 1996).
Simeoni, L., *L'assobimento austriaco del ducato estense e la politica dei duchi Rinaldo e Francesco III* (1919; Modena, 1986).
Simms, B., "'An odd question enough': Charles James Fox, the Crown and British policy during the Hanoverian crisis of 1806," *Historical Journal*, 38 (1995), 567–96.
Simms, B., *The Struggle for Mastery in Germany 1779–1850* (Basingstoke, 1998).
Simms, B., "The return of the primacy of foreign policy," *German History*, 21 (2003), 275–91.
Simms, B. and T. Riotte (eds.), *The Hanoverian Dimension in British History, 1714–1837* (Cambridge, 2007).
Simonton, D., *A History of European Women's Work, 1700 to the Present* (London, 1998).
Simonton, D., "Women and education," in H. Barker and E. Chalus (eds.), *Women's History: Britain, 1700–1850* (London, 2005), pp. 33–56.
Simonton, D. (ed.), *The Routledge History of Women in Europe since 1700* (London, 2006).
Slavin, M., *The French Revolution in Miniature: Section Droits de l'Homme, 1789–1795* (Princeton, 1984).
Smith, B. R., *The Acoustic World of Early Modern England: Attending the O-Factor* (Chicago, 1999).
Smith, H., *Georgian Monarchy, Politics and Culture, 1714–1760* (Cambridge, 2006).
Smith, J. M., *Nobility Reimagined: The Patriotic Nation in Eighteenth-Century France* (Ithaca, 2005).
Smith, R., *Handel's Oratorios and Eighteenth-Century Thought* (Cambridge, 1995).
Smith, T. A., *The Emerging Female Citizen: Gender and Enlightenment in Spain* (Los Angeles, 2006).
Smither, H. E., *A History of the Oratorio*, vols. 1–3 (Chapel Hill, NC, 1977).
Soboul, A., *The Parisian Sans-Culottes and the French Revolution, 1793–1794* (Oxford, 1964).
Soboul, A., *The French Revolution from the Storming of the Bastille to Napoleon, 1787–1799* (London, 1974).

Sogner, S., *Krig og fred 1660–1780*, vol. 6 of *Aschehougs Norgeshistorie* (Oslo, 1994).

Sonenscher, M., "Mythical work: workshop production and the compagnonnages of eighteenth-century France," in P. Joyce (ed.), *The Historical Meanings of Work* (Cambridge, 1989), pp. 31–63.

Sonenscher, M., *Work and Wages: Natural Law, Politics and the Eighteenth-Century French Trades* (Cambridge, 1989).

Sonnet, M., "A daughter to educate," in N. Z. Davis and A. Farge (eds.), *A History of Women in the West*, vol. 3 (Cambridge, 1993), pp. 129–37.

Sperber, J., *Revolutionary Europe, 1780–1850* (London, 2000).

Spielman, J. P., *The City and the Crown: Vienna and the Imperial Court, 1600–1740* (West Lafayette, 1993).

Starkey, D. J., *British Privateering Enterprise in the Eighteenth Century* (Exeter, 1990).

Starr, Paul, *The Social Transformation of American Medicine: The Rise of a Sovereign Profession and the Making of a Vast Industry* (New York, 1982).

Stein, R. L., *The French Sugar Business in the Eighteenth Century* (London, 1988).

Stein, S. J. and B. Stein, *Silver, Trade and War: Spain and America in the Making of Early Modern Europe* (Baltimore, 2000).

Stein, S. J. and B. Stein, *Apogee of Empire: Spain and New Spain in the Age of Charles III, 1759–1789* (Baltimore, 2003).

Sterrantino, F., et al., *La guerra della Lega di Augusta fino alla battaglia di Orbassano* (Turin, 1993).

Stevenson, J., *Popular Disturbances in England, 1700–1870* (London, 1979).

Stewart, W. A. C. and W. P. McCann, *The Educational Innovators, 1750–1880* (London, 1967).

Stollberg-Rilinger, B., *Vormünder des Volkes? Konzepte landständischer Repräsentation in der Spätphase des Alten Reiches* (Berlin 1999).

Stolleis, M. (ed.), *Policey im Europa der Frühen Neuzeit* (Frankfurt am Main, 1996).

Stone, B., *The Genesis of the French Revolution: A Global-Historical Interpretation* (Cambridge, 1994).

Storrs, C. D., *War, Diplomacy and the Rise of Savoy, 1690–1720* (Cambridge, 1999).

Storrs, C. D., "Imperial authority and the levy of contributions in 'Reichsitalien' in the Nine Years War (1690–1696)," in M. Schnettger and M. Verga (eds.), *L'Impero e l'Italia nella prima età moderna* (Bologna, 2005), pp. 241–73.

Storrs, C. D., *The Resilience of the Spanish Monarchy 1665–1700* (Oxford, 2006).

Storrs, C. D. and H. M. Scott, "The military revolution and the European nobility, *c.*1600–1800," *War in History*, 3 (1996), 1–41; repr. in J. Black (ed.), *Warfare in Europe, 1650–1792* (Aldershot, 2005), pp. 3–43.

Stothers, R. B., "The great dry fog of 1783," *Climatic Change*, 32 (1996), 79–89.

Straubel, R., *Beamte und Personalpolitik im altpreußischen Staat. Soziale Rekrutierung, Karriereverläufe, Entscheidungsprozesse (1763/86–1806)* (Berlin, 1998).

Stroup, J., *The Struggle for Identity in the Clerical Estate: Northwest German Protestant Opposition to Absolutist Policy in the Eighteenth Century* (Leiden, 1984).

Sturdy, J., *Louis XIV* (Basingstoke, 1998).

Styles, J., "Embezzlement, industry and the law in England, 1500–1800," in M. Berg (ed.), *Markets and Manufacture in Early Industrial Europe* (London, 1983), pp. 173–210.

Suter, A., "Vormoderne und moderne Demokratie in der Schweiz," *Zeitschrift für historische Forschung*, 31 (2004), 231–54.

Sutherland, D. M. G., *The French Revolution and Empire: The Quest for a Civic Order* (Oxford, 2003).

Sutton, J. L., *The King's Honor and the King's Cardinal: The War of the Polish Succession* (Lexington, 1980).

Swann, J., *Politics and the Parlement of Paris under Louis XV, 1754–1774* (Cambridge, 1995).
Swann, J., "The state and political culture," in W. Doyle (ed.), *Old Regime France* (Oxford, 2001), 139–68.
Swann, J., *Provincial Power and Absolute Monarchy: The Estates General of Burgundy, 1661–1790* (Cambridge, 2003).
Sweet, R., *The Writing of Urban Histories in Eighteenth-Century England* (Oxford, 1997).
Sweet, R., *The English Town, 1680–1840: Government, Society and Culture* (Harlow, 1999).
Switzer, H. L., *"De militie van den staat." Het leger van de Republiek der Verenigde Nederlanden* (Amsterdam, 1991).
Symcox, G., *Victor Amadeus II: Absolutism in the Savoyard State, 1675–1730* (Berkeley, 1983).
Szabo, F. A. J., *Kaunitz and Enlightened Absolutism, 1753–1780* (Cambridge, 1994).
Tackett, T., *Religion, Revolution and Regional Culture in Eighteenth-Century France: The Ecclesiastical Oath of 1791* (Princeton, 1985).
Tackett, T., *Becoming a Revolutionary: The Deputies of the French National Assembly and the Emergence of a Revolutionary Culture, 1789–1790* (Princeton, 1996).
Tackett, T., *When the King Took Flight* (Cambridge, MA, 2003).
Tantner, A., *Ordnung der Häuser, Beschreibung der Seelen. Hausnummerierung und Seelenkonskription in der Habsburgermonarchie* (Innsbruck, 2006).
Taylor, S. (ed.), *Hanoverian Britain and Empire: Essays in Memory of Philip Lawson* (Woodbridge, 1998).
Teter, M., *Jews and Heretics in Catholic Poland: A Beleaguered Church in the Post-Reformation Era* (Cambridge, 2005).
Thirsk, T., "Industries in the countryside," in F. J. Fisher (ed.), *Essays in Economic and Social History of Tudor and Stuart England* (Cambridge, 1961), pp. 217–33.
Thirsk, T., *Economic Policy and Projects: The Development of a Consumer Society in Early Modern England* (Oxford, 1978).
Thomas, H., *The Slave Trade: The Story of the Atlantic Slave Trade, 1440–1870* (1997; repr. New York, 1999).
Thompson, A., *Britain, Hanover and the Protestant Interest, 1688–1756* (Woodbridge, 2006).
Thompson, E. P., *The Making of the English Working Class* (New York, 1963).
Thompson, E. P., "The moral economy of the English crowd in the eighteenth century," *Past & Present*, 50 (1971), 76–136.
Thompson, E. P., *Customs in Common* (Harmondsworth, 1993).
Thompson, L., *A History of South Africa* (New Haven, 2000).
Thomson, A., *Barbary and Enlightenment: European Attitudes towards the Maghreb in the 18th Century* (New York, 1987).
Thomson, J. K. F., "Transferring the spinning jenny to Barcelona: an apprenticeship in the technology of the Industrial Revolution," *Textile History*, 34 (2003), 21–46.
Tilly, C., *As Sociology Meets History* (Orlando, 1981).
Tilly, C., *Contention and Democracy in Europe, 1650–2000* (Cambridge, 2004).
Tocqueville, A. de, *The Ancien Régime and the French Revolution* (Glasgow, 1966).
Todorova, M., *Imagining the Balkans* (New York, 1997).
Tomaselli, S., "The Enlightenment debate on women," *History Workshop*, 20 (1985), 101–24.
Torre, A., "Politics clothed in worship: state, church and local power in Piedmont, 1570–1770," *Past & Present*, 134 (1992), 42–92.
Toscani, X., "Ecclesiastici e società civile nel '700: un problema di storia sociale e religiosa," *Società e Storia*, 17 (1982), 683–716.

Tosh, J., *A Man's Place: Masculinity and the Middle-Class Home in Victorian England* (New Haven, 1999).
Touzery, M., *L'invention de l'impôt sur le revenu: La taille tarifiée 1715–1789* (Paris, 1994).
Treasure, G., *The Making of Modern Europe 1648–1780* (London, 1985).
Trompetter, C., *Agriculture, Proto-Industry and Mennonite Entrepreneurship: A History of the Textile Industries in Twente, 1600–1815* (Amsterdam, 1997).
Trossbach, W., *Soziale Bewegung und politische Erfahrung. Bäuerlicher Protest in hessischen Territorien 1648–1806* (Weingarten, 1987).
Turner, M. E., J. V. Beckett and B. Afton, *Agricultural Rent in England, 1690–1914* (Cambridge, 1997).
Ulbricht, O., "The world of a beggar around 1775: Johann Gottfried Kästner," *Central European History*, 27 (1994), 153–84.
Umbach, M., *Federalism and Enlightenment in Germany 1740–1806* (London, 2000).
Upton, A. F., *Europe 1600–1800* (London, 2000).
Vaisey, D. (ed.), *The Diary of Thomas Turner 1754–1765* (Oxford, 1984) .
van Horn Melton, J., *The Rise of the Public in Enlightenment Europe* (Cambridge, 2001).
van Kley, D., *The Damiens Affair and the Unraveling of the Ancien Régime* (Princeton, 1984).
van Kley, D. K., *The Religious Origins of the French Revolution: From Calvin to the Civil Constitution of the Clergy, 1560–1791* (New Haven, 1996).
Vann, J. A., *The Making of a State: Württemberg 1593–1793* (Ithaca, 1984).
Velasco Moreno, Eva, *La Real Academia de la Historia: una institución de sociabilidad* (Madrid, 2000).
Venturi, F., *Italy and the Enlightenment: Studies in a Cosmopolitan Century* (London, 1972).
Venturi, F., *The End of the Old Regime in Europe, 1768–1789* (2 vols., Princeton, 1991).
Vergé-Franceschi, M., *La Marine française au XVIIIe siècle* (Condé-sur-Noireau, 1996).
Verhees-van Mer, J. T. H., *De Zeeuwse kaapvaart tijdens de Spaanse successieoorlog, 1702–1713* (Middelburg, 1986).
Viana Pedreira, J. M., "From growth to collapse: Portugal, Brazil and the collapse of the old colonial system (1750–1830)," *Hispanic American Historical Review*, 80 (2000), 839–64.
Vicens Vives, J., *An Economic History of Spain* (Princeton, 1969).
Vickery, A., "Golden age to separate spheres? A Review of the categories and chronology of English women's history," repr. in P. Sharpe (ed.), *Women's Work: The English Experience, 1650–1914* (London, 1998).
Vilar, P., *La Catalogne dans l'Espagne moderne* (Paris, 1962).
Vilar, P., "El 'motin de Esquilache' y las 'crisis del antiguo regimen'," *Revista de Occidente*, 107 (1972), 119–249.
Villiers, P., *Marine royale, corsaires et trafic dans l'Atlantique de Louis XIV à Louis XVI* (2 vols., Dunkirk, 1991).
Vittorio, A. di, "Ancora a proposito di storia della dominazione austriaca a Napoli, 1707–1734," *Archivio Storico Italiano*, 142 (1984), 607–22.
Vovelle, M., *Piété baroque et déchristianisation en Provence au XVIIIe siècle: Les Attitudes devant la mort d'après les clauses des testaments* (Paris, 1973).
Vovelle, M., *The Revolution against the Church: From Reason to the Supreme Being* (Cambridge, 1991).
Wakefield, P., *Reflections on the Present Condition of the Female Sex with Suggestions for its Improvement* (London, 1798).
Walicki, A., *The Age of Enlightenment and the Birth of Modern Nationhood: Polish Political Thought from Noble Republicanism to Tadeusz Kościuszko* (Notre Dame, 1989).

Walker, G. J., *Spanish Politics and Imperial Trade 1700–1789* (London, 1979).

Walker, M., *German Home Towns: Community, State and General Estate, 1648–1871* (Ithaca, 1971).

Walker, M., *The Salzburg Transaction: Expulsion and Redemption in Eighteenth-Century Germany* (Ithaca, 1992).

Walker, T. D., *Doctors, Folk Medicine and the Inquisition: The Repression of Magical Healing in Portugal during the Enlightenment* (Leiden, 2005).

Wangermann, E., *The Austrian Achievement* (London, 1973).

Waquet, J.-C., "La Toscane après la paix de Vienne (1737–1765): prépondérance autrichienne ou absolutisme lorrain?," *Revue d'Histoire Diplomatique*, 93 (1979), 202–22.

Waquet, J.-C., *Le Grand Duché de Toscane sous les derniers Medicis* (Rome, 1990).

Ward, A., *Book Production, Fiction and the German Reading Public 1740–1800* (Oxford, 1974).

Ward, A. W., *Great Britain and Hanover* (Oxford, 1899).

Ward, M. R., *The Protestant Evangelical Awakening* (Cambridge, 1992).

Ward, M. R., *Christianity under the Ancien Régime 1648–1789* (Cambridge, 1999).

Watkin, D., *The Architect King: George III and the Culture of Enlightenment* (London, 2004).

Watson, J. N. P., *Marlborough's Shadow: The Life of the First Earl Cadogan* (Barnsley, 2003).

Weatherill, l., *Consumer Behaviour and Material Culture in Britain, 1660–1760* (London, 1988).

Weber, C., *Terror and its Discontents: Suspect Words in Revolutionary France* (Minneapolis, 2003).

Weber, D., *Barbaros: Spaniards and their Savages in the Age of Enlightenment* (New Haven, 2005).

Wegert, K. H., *German Radicals Confront the Common People: Revolutionary Politics and Popular Unrest 1789–1849* (Mainz, 1992).

Wegert, K. H., *Popular Culture, Crime and Social Control in 18th Century Württemberg* (Wiesbaden, 1994).

Wehler, H.-U., *Deutsche Gesellschaftsgeschichte 1700–1815*, vol. 1 (Munich, 1989).

Weiner, D., *The Citizen-Patient in Revolutionary and Imperial Paris* (Baltimore, 1993).

Wellesz, E. and F. Sternfeld, *The Age of Enlightenment 1745–1790* (Oxford, 1973).

Wellman, K., *La Mettrie: Medicine, Philosophy, and Enlightenment* (Durham, NC, 1992).

Wessels, L. H. M., *Bron, waarheid en de verandering der tijden. Jan Wagenaar (1709–1773), een historiografische studie* (The Hague, 1997).

Whaley, J., *Religious Toleration and Social Change in Hamburg, 1529–1819* (Cambridge, 1985).

Whaley, J., "Thinking about Germany, 1750–1815: the birth of a nation?," *Publications of the English Goethe Society*, NS 66 (1996), 53–72.

Whaley, J., "A tolerant society? Religious toleration in the Holy Roman Empire, 1648–1806," in R. Porter and O. P. Grell (eds.), *Toleration in Enlightenment Europe* (Cambridge, 2000), pp. 175–95.

Whaley, J., "Religiöse Toleranz als allgemeines Menschenrecht in der Frühen Neuzeit?," in G. Schmidt, M. van Gelderen, and C. Snigula (eds.), *Kollektive Freiheitsvorstellungen im frühneuzeitlichen Europa (1400–1850)* (Frankfurt am Main, 2006).

Wheatcroft, A., *The Ottomans* (London, 1993).

Wheeler, D., "The Great Storm of November 1703:a new look at the seamen's records." *Weather*, 58 (2003), 419–27.

Wheeler, D. and J. Mayes, *Regional Climates of the British Isles* (London, 1997).

Wheeler, J. S., *The Making of a World Power: War and the Military Revolution in Seventeenth-Century England* (Stroud, 1999).
Wheelwright, J., *Amazons and Military Maids: Women who Dressed as Men in Pursuit of Life, Liberty and Happiness* (London, 1989).
Whitaker, A. P., et al., *Latin America and the Enlightenment* (New York, 1942).
Whyman, S., *Sociability and Power in Late Stuart England: The Cultural Worlds of the Verneys, 1660–1720* (Oxford, 1999).
Wiesner. M., "Women's work in the changing city economy, 1500–1650," in M. Boxer and J. H. Quataert (eds.), *Connecting Spheres* (Oxford, 1987), pp. 64–74.
Wiesner. M., "Guilds, male bonding and women's work in early modern Germany," *Gender & History*, 1 (1989), 125–37.
Wiesner, M., *Women and Gender in Early Modern Europe* (2nd edn., New York, 2000).
Wiesner-Hanks, M. E., *Early Modern Europe, 1450–1789* (Cambridge, 2006).
Wilcken P., *Empire Adrift, The Portuguese Court in Rio de Janeiro, 1808–1821* (London, 2004).
Wilkinson, S., *The Defence of Piedmont, 1742–1748* (Oxford, 1927).
Willemsen, R., *Enkhuizen tijdens de Republiek* (Hilversum, 1988).
Willey, B., *The Eighteenth-Century Background: Studies on the Idea of Nature in the Thought of the Period* (London, 1940).
Williams, E., *Capitalism and Slavery* (1944; repr. New York, 1961).
Williams, G., *The Prize of all the Oceans: The Triumph and Tragedy of Anson's Voyage Round the World* (London, 1999).
Wilson, A., *The Making of the Man-Midwife: Childbirth in England, 1660–1770* (London, 1995).
Wilson, M., *Eighteenth-Century French Painting* (Oxford, 1979).
Wilson, P. H., *War, State and Society in Württemberg, 1677–1793* (Cambridge, 1995).
Wilson, P. H., *German Armies: War and German Politics 1648–1806* (London, 1998).
Wilson, P. H., *Absolutism in Central Europe* (London, 2000).
Wilson, P. H., "The politics of military recruitment in eighteenth-century Germany," *English Historical Review*, 117 (2002), 536–68.
Wilson, P. H., *From Reich to Revolution: German History 1558–1806* (Basingstoke, 2004).
Wilson, P. H., "Still a monstrosity? Some reflections on early modern German statehood," *Historical Journal*, 49 (2006), 566–76.
Windler, C., *Lokale Eliten, seigneurialer Adel und Reformabsolutismus in Spanien (1760–1808)* (Stuttgart, 1992).
Winks, R. W., and T. E. Kaiser, *Europe from the Old Regime to the Age of Revolution 1648–1815* (Oxford, 2004).
Wirtschafter, E., *Structures of Society: Imperial Russia's "People of Various Ranks"* (DeKalb, ILL, 1994).
Witham, C. S. and C. Oppenheimer, "Mortality in England during the 1783–4 Laki Craters eruption," *Bulletin of Volcanology*, 67 (2005), 15–26.
Wittkower, R., *Art and Architecture in Italy 1600–1750* (Harmondsworth, 1958).
Wolff, C., *Bach: The Learned Musician* (Oxford, 2001).
Wolff, L., *Inventing "Eastern Europe": The Map of Civilisation in the Mind of the Enlightenment* (Stanford, 1994).
Wollstonecraft, M., *An Historical and Moral View of the Origin and Progress of the French Revolution* (1794), in M. Butler and J. Todd (eds.), *The Works of Mary Wollstonecraft* (London, 1989), vol. 6.
Woloch, I., *Eighteenth-Century Europe: Transition and Progress, 1715–1789* (New York, 1982).

Woloch, I., *The New Regime: Transformations of the French Civic Order, 1789–1820s* (New York, 1994).
Woodhead, P. M. J. and A. D. Woodhead, "The effects of low temperatures on the physiology and distribution of cod *Gadus morhua* L. in the Barents Sea," *Proceedings of the Zoological Society of London*, 133 (1959), 181–99.
Woolf, S., *History of Italy 1700–1860* (London, 1986).
Woolf, S., *The Poor in Western Europe in the Eighteenth and Nineteenth Centuries* (London, 1986).
Woolf, S., "Order, class and the urban poor," in M. L. Bush (ed.), *Social Order and Social Classes in Europe since 1500* (London, 1992).
Wortman, R., *Scenarios of Power: Myth and Ceremony in Russian Monarchy*, vol. 1 (Princeton, 1995).
Woude, A. M. van der, *Het Noorderkwartier* (Wageningen, 1972).
Wrigley, E. A. and R. S. Schofield, *The Population History of England, 1541–1871: A Reconstruction* (Cambridge, MA, 1981).
Wunder, H., *He Is the Sun, She Is the Moon: Women in Early Modern Germany* (Cambridge, MA, 1998).
Würgler, A., *Unruhen und Öffentlichkeit. Städtische und ländliche Protestbewegungen im 18. Jahrhundert* (Tübingen, 1995).
Würgler, A., "Desideria und Landesordnungen. Kommunaler und landständischer Einfluß auf die fürstliche Gesetzgebung in Hessen-Kassel, 1650–1800," in P. Blickle (ed.), *Gemeinde und Staat im Alten Europa* (Munich, 1998), pp. 149–207.
Yeo, E. and S. Yeo (eds.), *Popular Culture and Class Conflict 1590–1914: Explorations in the History of Labour and Leisure* (Brighton, 1981).
Zamoyski, A., *The Last King of Poland* (New York, 1997).
Zanden, J. L. van, *The Rise and Decline of Holland's Economy: Merchant Capitalism and the Labour Market* (Manchester, 1993).
Zanden, J. L. van, "Early modern economic growth," in M. Prak (ed.), *Early Modern Capitalism* (London, 2001), pp. 69–87.
Zannini, A., "Un ceto di funzionari amministrativi: i cittadini originari veneziani, 1569–1730," *Studi Veneziani*, 23 (1992), 131–45.
Zaret, D., *Origins of Democratic Culture: Printing, Petitions and the Public Sphere in Early Modern England* (Princeton, 2000).
Zaslaw, N., *The Classical Era: From the 1740s to the End of the Eighteenth Century* (London, 1989).
Zaunstöck, H. and M. Meumann (eds.), *Sozietäten, Netzwerke, Kommunikation. Neue Forschungen zur Vergesellschaftung im Jahrhundert der Aufklärung* (Tübingen, 2003).
Zimmermann, C., *Reformen in der bäuerlichen Gesellschaft. Studien zum aufgeklärten Absolutismus in der Markgrafschaft Baden 1750–1790* (Ostfildern, 1983).
Zitser, E. A., *The Transfigured Kingdom: Sacred Parody and Charismatic Authority at the Court of Peter the Great* (Ithaca, 2004).
Żytkowicz, L., "Grain yields in Poland, Bohemia, Hungary and Slovakia in the 16th to 18th centuries," *Acta Poloniae Historica*, 24 (1971), 51–72.

Index

Monarchs and ruling princes are listed alphabetically by their first name; all other individuals are listed by surname.

A Companion to Eighteenth-Century Europe, First Edition. Edited by Peter H. Wilson.
© 2014 John Wiley & Sons, Ltd. Published 2014 by John Wiley & Sons, Ltd.